CHINESE ROMANCE
FROM A JAPANESE BRUSH

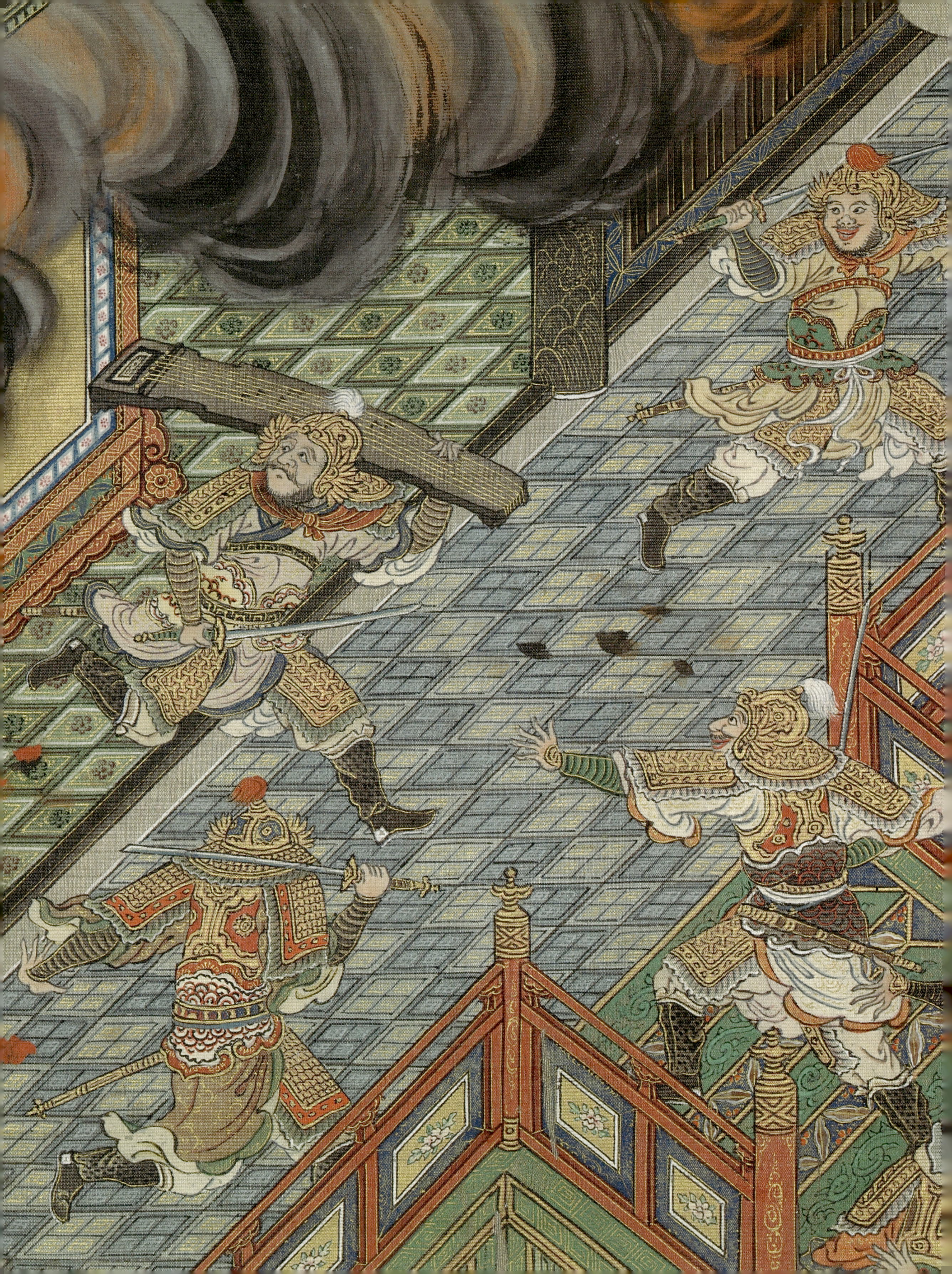

CHINESE ROMANCE
FROM A JAPANESE BRUSH

Kano Sansetsu's Chōgonka Scrolls in the Chester Beatty Library

SHANE MCCAUSLAND AND MATTHEW P. MCKELWAY

SCALA

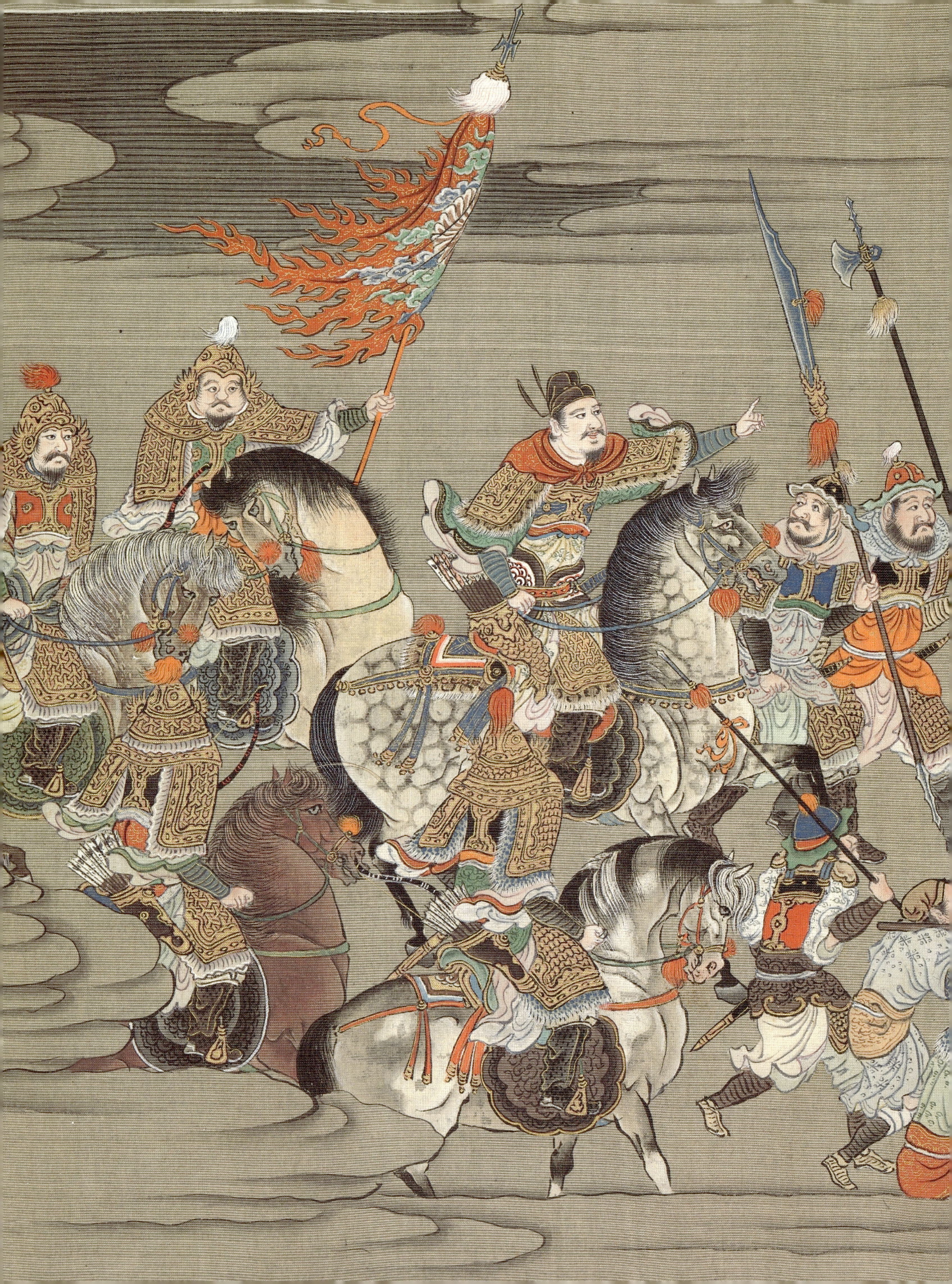

CONTENTS

Preface   7
Michael Ryan

Introduction   8
Shane McCausland

1   **Yang Guifei's story in Chinese art and literature:
a perspective**   18
Shane McCausland

2   **The Dublin *Chōgonka* scrolls by Kano Sansetsu**   34
Shane McCausland

3   **Coda: the Kuki version**   92
Shane McCausland and Matthew P. McKelway

4   **Kano Sansetsu and Kano workshop paintings
of 'The Song of Lasting Sorrow'**   106
Matthew P. McKelway

5   **Ming paintings and prints:
possible sources for Kano Sansetsu's *Chōgonka* scrolls**   150
Li-chiang Lin

6   **The *Chōgonka* scrolls: their rediscovery and conservation**   164
Yoshiko Ushioda with Jessica Baldwin

Appendix
Bai Juyi, 'Song of Lasting Sorrow'   172
Chen Hong, 'An Account to Go with the "Song of Lasting Sorrow"'   176

Notes   180
Select bibliography   186
Index   188

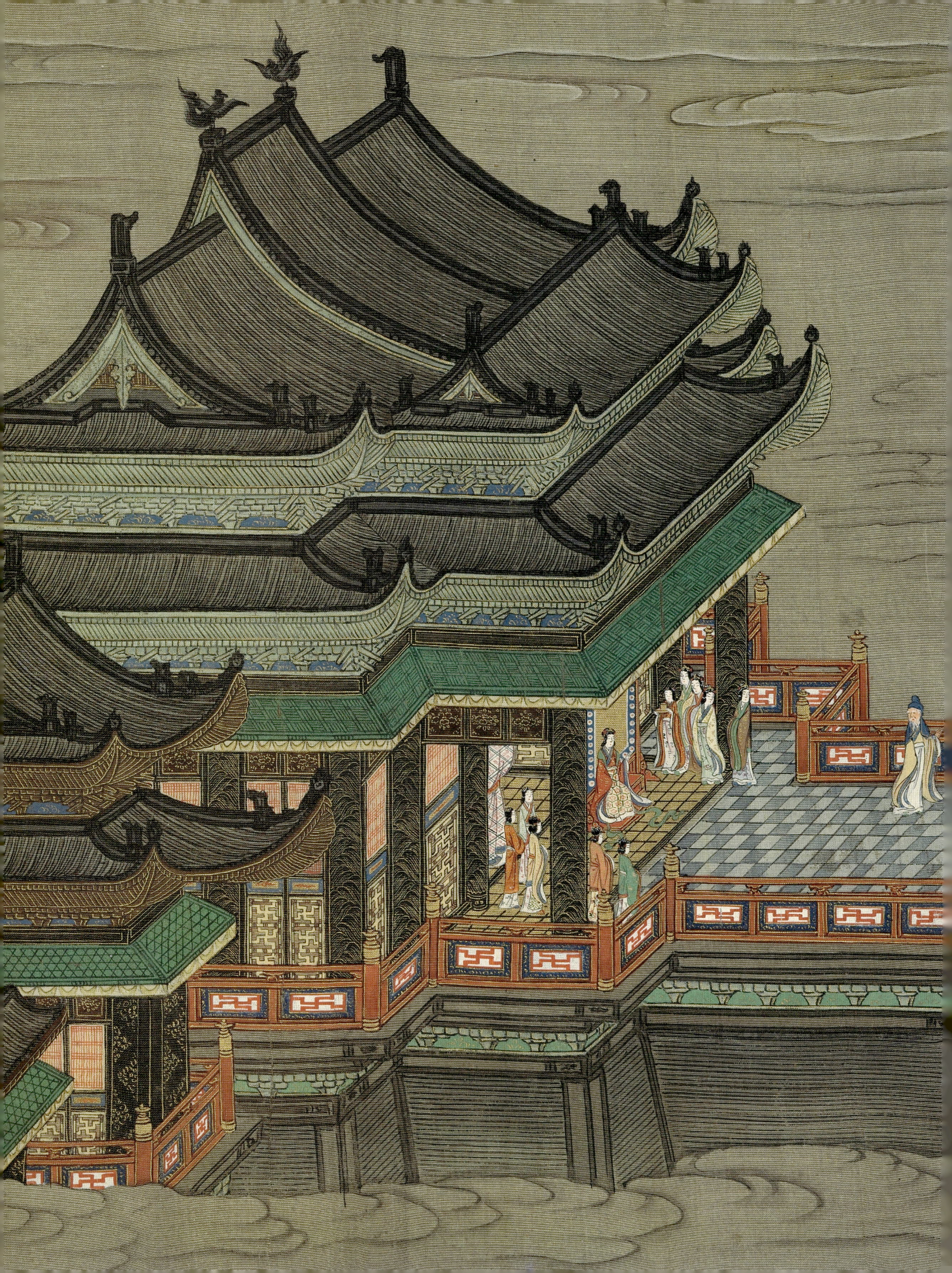

PREFACE

The two scrolls containing a pictorial version of *Chōgonka* were acquired by Chester Beatty at the sale of the Louis Gonse Collection in Paris in April 1926. Beatty's collection, which had been developing during the early part of his career in the United States, contained a number of Japanese decorative arts pieces including *inro* and *netsuke* but it was not until his visit to China and Japan in 1917–18 that his interest in East Asian art really intensified (he spent about six months in Japan and was clearly especially attracted to its culture and art). A number of important acquisitions, particularly of *Nara ehon,* date from the time of this visit and the following few years. Thereafter there was a lull in his collecting until he began in the 1950s, with expert help, to assemble his fine collection of *ukiyo-e* and *surimono.*

The *Chōgonka* scrolls were mistakenly included in the Chinese collection for many years but it was not until they were identified by Mrs Yoshiko Ushioda that their true significance began to emerge – the story of that process is told in Mrs Ushioda's account which is included here. In the early 1990s, the distinguished conservator, Mr Handa, visited the Library under the auspices of the Japan Foundation to demonstrate traditional Japanese conservation of works of art on paper and silk. During the following year the celebrated artist, Professor Ikuo Hirayama, President both of the Tokyo University of the Arts and of the Japan Art Research Foundation, visited the Library and the conservation of the *Chōgonka*, together with a number of other important works, was arranged. On completion of the conservation, which had taken place in the Handa Studio at the National Museum in Ueno, Tokyo, the *Chōgonka* scrolls formed the centrepiece of an exhibition of recently conserved works of Japanese art at the National Museum, which was viewed by Their Imperial Majesties, the Emperor and Empress, on the opening day. On the following day, Mrs Ushioda and I attended a meeting, chaired by Professor Hirayama, at which the conservation of further Chester Beatty material was planned. The Library benefited greatly from the support of the Japan Art Research Foundation and the personal interest of Professor Hirayama, and I would like to pay tribute to their generosity here.

On their return to the Library the *Chōgonka* scrolls were the subject of what was then a novel and sophisticated computer-based interactive, scripted by Mrs Ushioda and coordinated by Don Bagley, then of the Library, and they have been a focus of continuing public appreciation in our exhibitions since the Library moved to its present home in 2000.

One of the great treasures of the Library, the scrolls have been frequently studied and commented on in print. New research on the work and its background requires a new publication. It gives me great pleasure to introduce this work by my colleague, Dr Shane McCausland, Head of Collections at the Chester Beatty Library and his co-author, Dr Matthew McKelway, of Columbia University.

Michael Ryan
Director and Librarian, the Chester Beatty Library, Dublin

INTRODUCTION

AT THE HEART OF THIS BOOK is a study of an intriguing pair of Japanese picture-scrolls entitled *Song of Lasting Sorrow (Chōgonka gakan)* in the Chester Beatty Library in Dublin. The two long handscrolls that make up the painting present a full-length narrative illustration of a famous Chinese ballad about one of the great romances of Chinese history – a tragic love affair between an emperor and his concubine. The protagonists are the sixth Tang emperor, Xuanzong (685–762; r. 712–56), also known as Minghuang, and his beautiful favourite, the *femme fatale* Yang Guifei (719–56) or 'Precious Consort' Yang. For his early reign, at least, Emperor Minghuang is often seen as a paragon of a sagely Chinese ruler, while Yang Guifei has been identified as the last of the Four Beauties of ancient China. Yet, their relationship is usually cited as the cause of, or the pretext for, the An Lushan Rebellion in 755–56, which almost toppled the Tang dynasty at the height of its power. The 'Song of Lasting Sorrow' ballad was composed by the great Tang-dynasty poet Bai Juyi (772–846) in the winter of 806–07, half a century after the epic historical events on which it is based. Although the ballad was written by a Chinese poet, it was very soon transmitted to Japan and has long been celebrated in China and Japan as an exemplary romance, but also as a grave admonition.

The Dublin *Chōgonka* scrolls were composed and executed in early Edo-period Kyoto, in the late 1640s, by Kano Sansetsu (1590–1651), leader of the Kano School of painters in Kyoto. They remained in Japan, where they must have been remounted one or more times, until acquired by the French collector Louis Gonse (1846–1921), apparently in the late nineteenth century. Later, in 1926, they entered the collection of A. Chester Beatty, ending up in his Library in Dublin.[1] On Chester Beatty's death in 1968, the Chester Beatty Library became a charity maintained by the Irish state and the painting became part of this National Cultural Institution. The *Chōgonka* scrolls passed much of the mid-twentieth century unremarked. They were 'rediscovered' by chance in the Chinese collection of the Library in around 1978, but their condition was so poor that, at first, they were dismissed as inferior workshop paintings. Following the success of their remounting in Tokyo in the 1990s, they were finally re-established as one of the great early Edo works of narrative painting. The story of the scrolls' rediscovery and their later restoration is recounted in chapter six. Illustrations of the scene of Yang Guifei's execution before and after restoration show the dramatic transformation (see figs 118, 119).[2] The arguments in the pages of this book also take the study of these scrolls further, delving deeply for the first time into the extraordinary choices – as regards images, media and story-telling techniques – that the artist made in recreating a Chinese romance for a Japanese audience.

With regard to issues of connoisseurship and provenance, we noted above that the scroll set was once owned by the French writer, critic and collector Louis Gonse, but it is remarkable that this information had been lost during the twentieth century and only came to light during the remounting in the Handa Kyuseido Studio in Tokyo National Museum in the 1990s, which happened through the generosity of the Art Research Foundation under the painter and doyen of the modern Japanese art world, Hirayama Ikuō.

Because of the sorry condition of the scrolls and also possibly because the quality of the painting is not uniformly excellent throughout, questions had arisen about its authenticity in publications of the late 1970s and 1980s. Writing in the Chester Beatty Library's own catalogue of the Japanese collection in 1979, Shigeo Sorimachi described it as '… one of many fine copies of original Chinese scrolls. But the signature and seals of the artist Kano Sansetsu at the end of the second scroll are apparently added later.'[3] *(Continues on p. 14)*

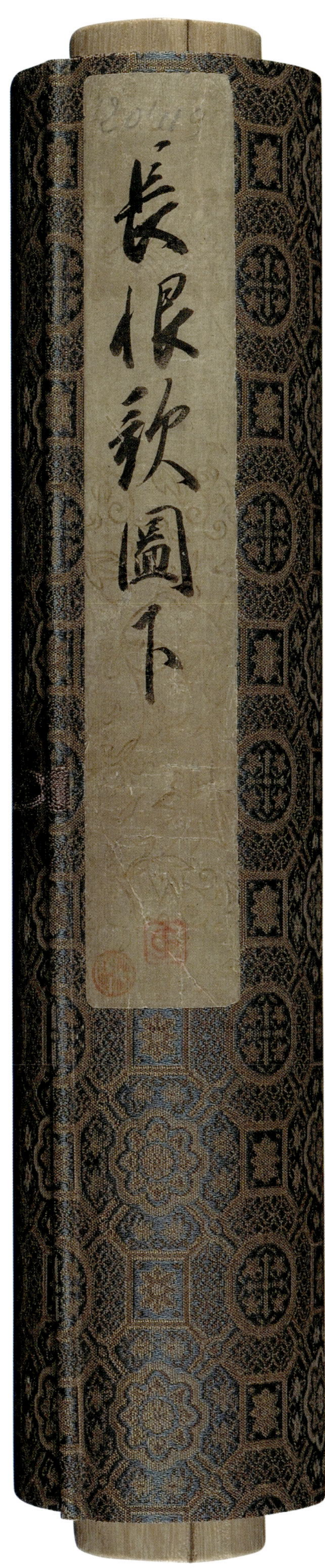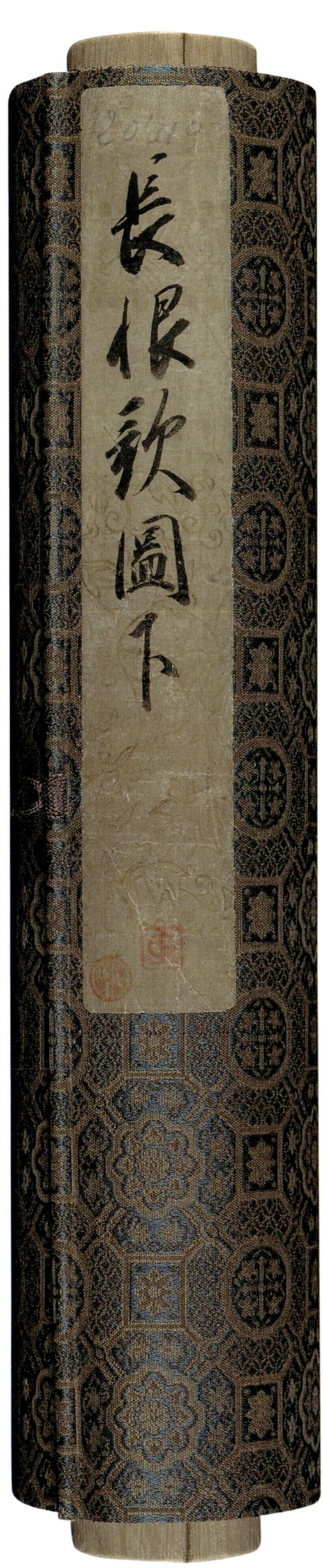

The *Chōgonka* scroll 1 (right) and scroll 2 (left). The scrolls are traditionally viewed from right to left.

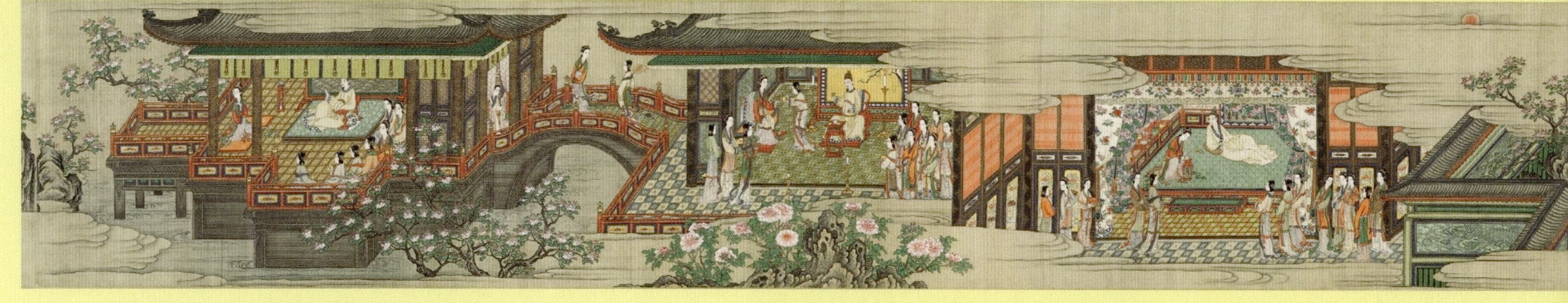

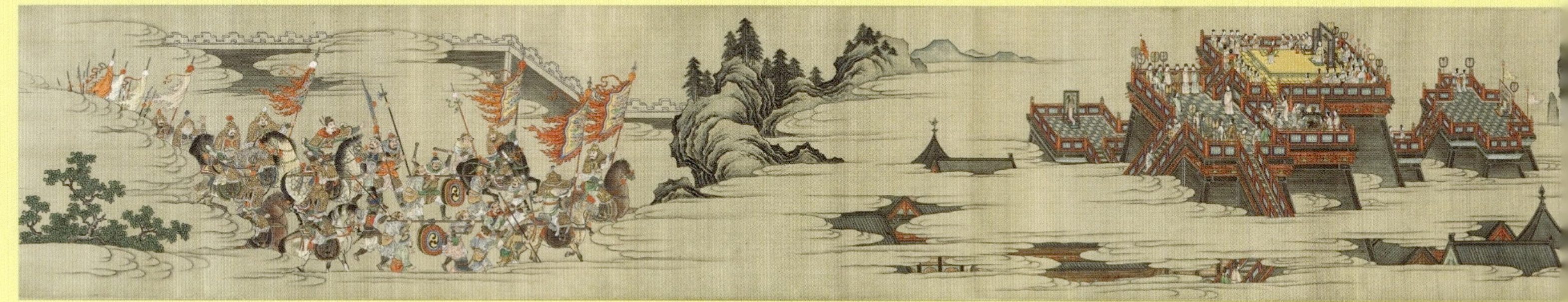

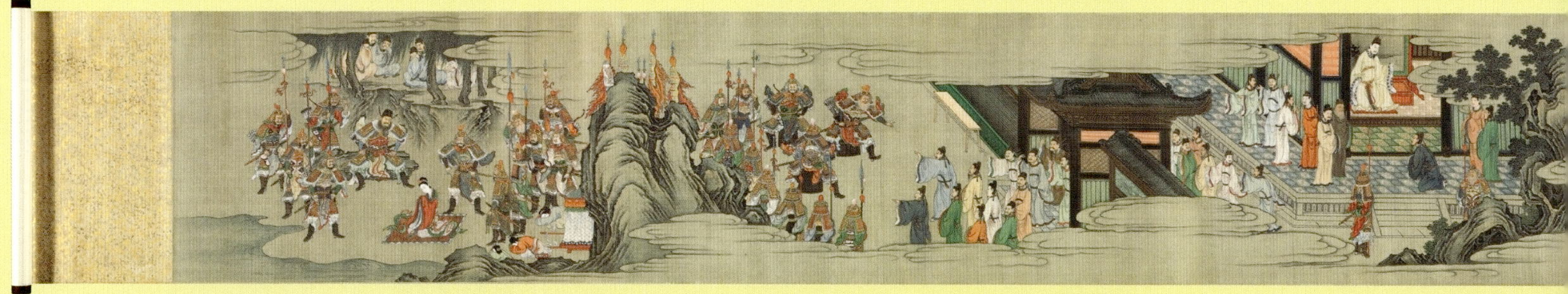

Song of Lasting Sorrow

SCROLL 1

ACT 1: Late in his reign, the emperor tires of holding the reins of government. Yearning for the kind of lady who could bring about the downfall of a dynasty, Minghuang sends scouts throughout the empire to bring beauties into the imperial harem (scenes 1–2). One day, when the emperor sees one of these new arrivals, a lady of the Yang clan, stepping frailly out of the hot springs in his palace retreat at Huaqing, he is smitten (scene 3).

ACT 2: The emperor has eyes for none among his several thousand concubines but the Yang lady, who is promoted to the rank of Precious Consort.

ACT 3: Over the next decade and a half to 756, she uses her power and influence to advance members of her own clan.

ACT 4: The emperor, consumed by a grand passion for his lady, increasingly neglects the important business of government.

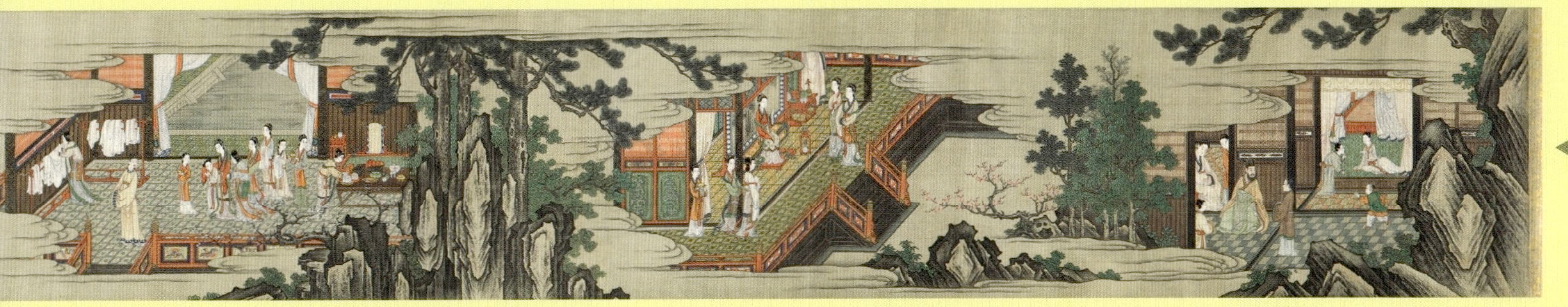

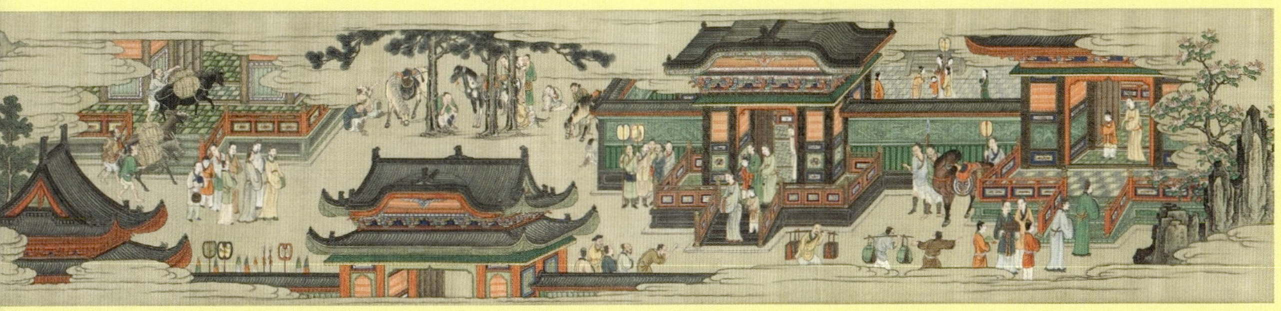

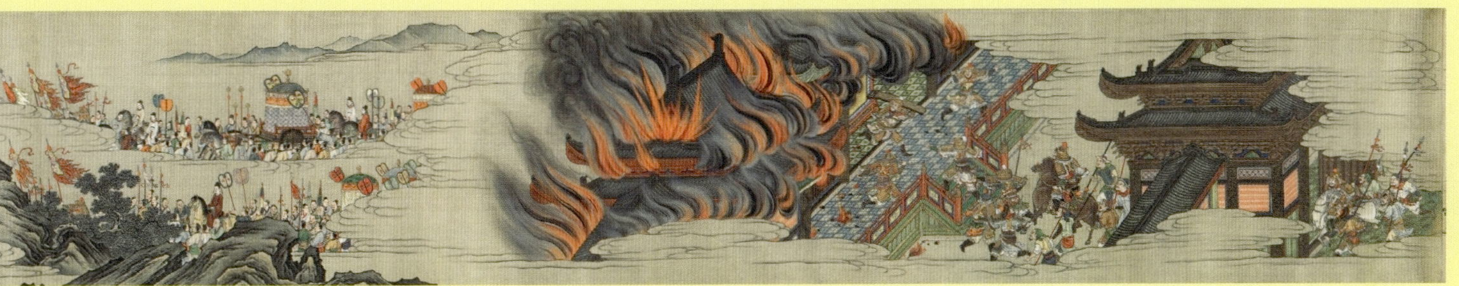

Act 5: In 756 rebellion breaks out, led by General An Lushan, Yang Guifei's adoptive son and lover, and also the emperor's favourite, who wishes to have Yang for himself and believes he can re-unite the empire. The emperor, Yang Guifei and their inner circle flee in the night, as the rebel armies approach the Tang capital Chang'an (modern Xi'an) from the east.

Act 6: The intent is to escape along the 'plank roads', the wooden bridge-like paths affixed to sides of cliffs and gulleys through the mountains of southern Shaanxi, across the Jian'ge Pass and down to Shu, the Sichuan region in the southwest, where the Yang clan has its power base. The imperial party begins its journey west from the capital along the Wei River, but is held up after just 50 km at Mawei, where the imperial bodyguard mutinies, demanding the deaths of the most powerful members of the Yang clique, including Yang Guifei. With the rebels approaching the capital not far behind, the emperor, for the sake of the dynasty, has no choice but to accede to this demand. The emperor sends a trusted eunuch to supervise the execution of his beloved.

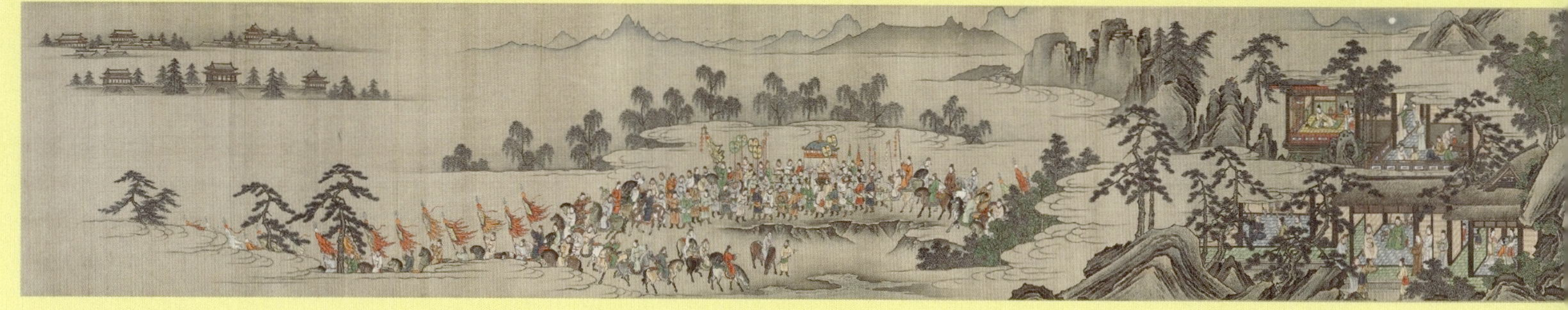

ACT 4 MINGHUANG ENGAGES A DAOIST WIZARD

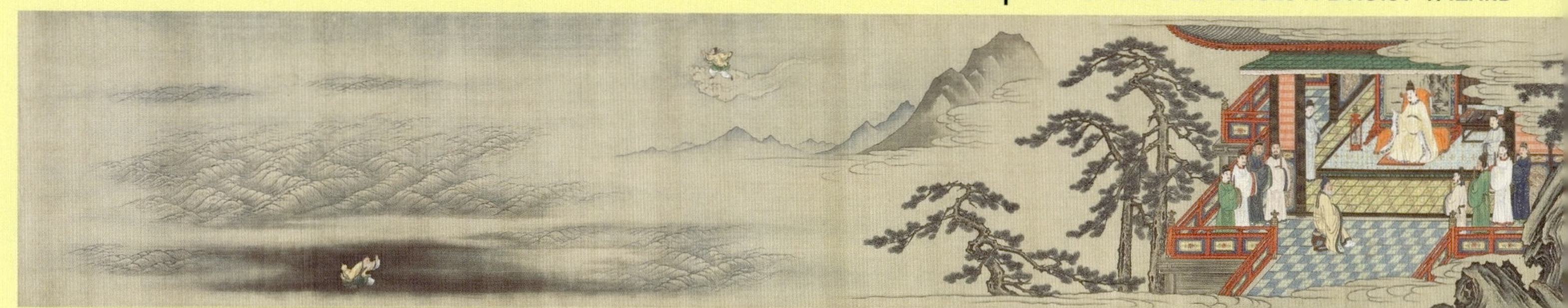

ACT 6 THE DAOIST'S INTERVIEW WITH THE SOUL OF YANG GUIFEI

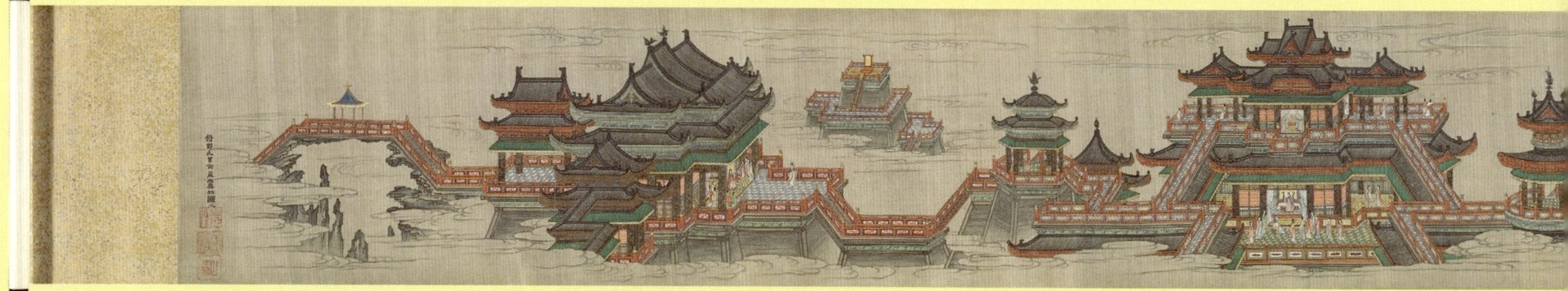

SCROLL 2

ACT 1: Following her death, the emperor is inconsolable with grief (scene 1). The imperial party must keep moving, but the emperor is unable to look upon the spot at Mawei where Yang Guifei was killed, and her body thrown in a ditch (scene 2). The fugitives travel first along the cliff-side plank roads and then in the near darkness under the towering cliffs of the Emei Mountains (scenes 3–4).

ACT 2: After arriving in exile in Shu, the grieving Minghuang hands over government of the state to his advisors (scene 1). When news arrives that the Heir Apparent has usurped the throne, Minghuang has no choice but to accede to this by abdicating. After a year's exile in Shu, and once order has been restored throughout the empire, Minghuang is permitted to return to the capital as 'retired emperor' (scenes 2–3).

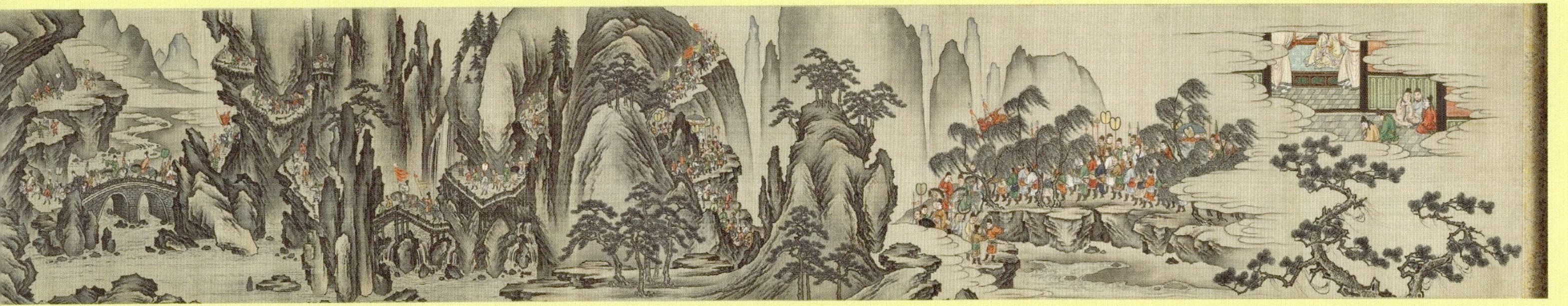

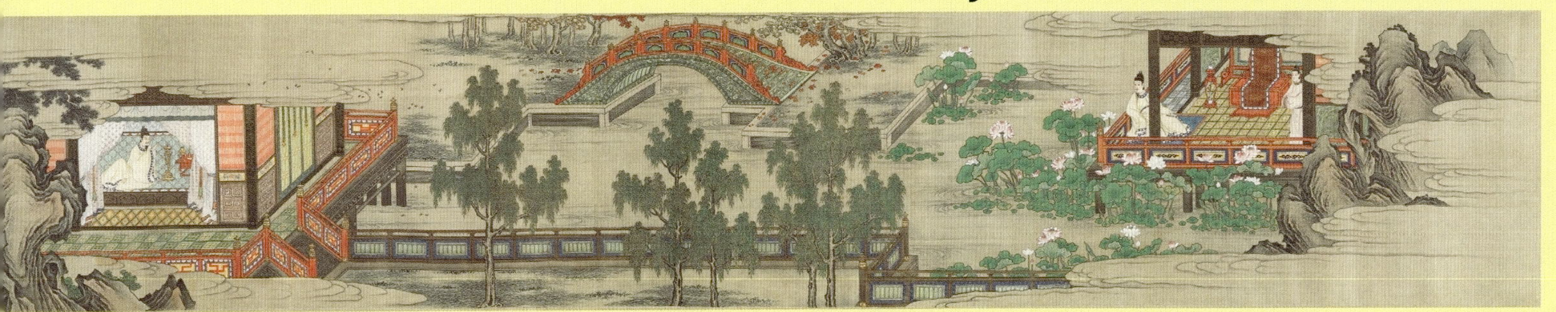

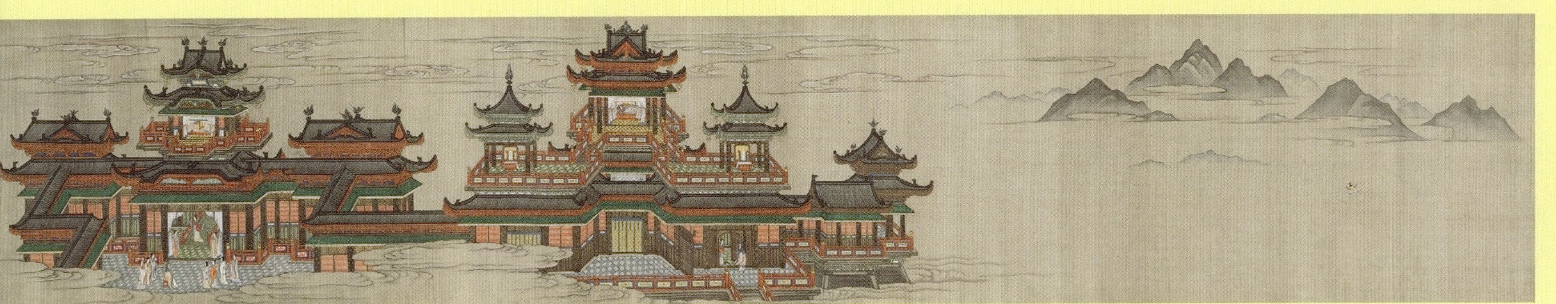

ACT 3: Back in the imperial palace, he is reminded at every turn of his past life with Yang Guifei, by the lotuses and willows with which people compared her.

ACT 4: Tormented by grief for his lost love, Minghuang hears of a Daoist wizard who has the ability to find and speak with the spirits of the deceased, summons him and sends him to find the soul of Yang Guifei (scene 1). The wizard searches the heavens and the depths of the ocean (scenes 2–3) for her.

ACT 5: The wizard then hears tell of a great lady living in the isles of the immortals across the sea, and flies there. He asks for her at the door of the palaces of the immortals and is granted an interview with the soul of Yang Guifei.

ACT 6: The ballad ends with him preparing to return to the world, taking with him love tokens for Minghuang.

In this book the authors argue from distinct perspectives that the painting was designed and largely executed by Sansetsu with the help of his studio assistants. For the most part, the quality of the assistants' work is very fine, but there are 'wrinkles' – pieces of evidence about the division of labour in this Kano School studio.

The *Chōgonka* scroll set was published in several book volumes following its remounting in the 1990s and was the subject of a multi-lingual CD-ROM documenting its restoration, made in 1996–97 by two former curators at the Chester Beatty Library, Yoshiko Ushioda (from 1970 to 1996)[4] and Clare Pollard (from 1997 to 2003). In 2006, the *Chōgonka* scrolls were again published in a handsome facsimile volume by Bensey Publishing of Tokyo.[5]

This book, it is hoped, is an opportunity to investigate the painting to a greater depth than has been accomplished up to now. We find that to study these paintings is also to explore wide-ranging themes and topics in art history and literature across cultures, from medieval China to early modern Japan to modern Ireland. Based on the collaborative work of several researchers, this book presents one such broad study of this intriguing painting, incorporating essays about its recent provenance and remounting, as well as new studies on its history and sources, and its place in East Asian visual culture.

The various approaches adopted within this investigation of the *Chōgonka* scrolls are called for, we believe, by the diverse nature of the artwork itself, which seems to have no regard for the familiar art-historical boundaries of the modern discipline. In this volume, therefore, these scrolls are the subject of new research and analysis by several art historians, who approach them from distinctive backgrounds, including Chinese painting and woodblock printing, and Japanese Kano School painting. Some of these writers are more concerned with the material object, such

as the date and context of its production and its provenance. Others are more concerned with aspects of style, including the narrative technique, the literary and visual sources in China and Japan, the lineament and colouring technique, and the production in a studio practice. The juxtaposition of these different points of view, it is hoped, will throw new light on the ways this unique painting melds China and Japan, literature and painting.

Despite his canonical status as a Kano artist, there remain many questions to be asked about Sansetsu himself and about his painting practice, his circle of patronage, and his range of sources in both Japan and China. On this last point, until a few decades ago, it was assumed that the *Chōgonka* painting may have been a copy of a Chinese original, or of Chinese sources; but it now seems clear that no such precedent existed. Indeed, the history in China of images related to this narrative is sketchy and diverse, complicating the picture we might form of even those related pictures that would have been available to Sansetsu. Additionally, narrative picture-scrolls of the *Chōgonka* type had reached a historical highpoint in the late Heian and Kamakura periods in Japan, but by the early Edo period this format was rarely adopted by the distinguished painting schools such as the one Sansetsu headed. For this reason, it is easy to overlook the scale and complexity of the *Chōgonka* scrolls as an artistic undertaking in the early Edo period. Perhaps this lack of precedent goes some way towards explaining why Sansetsu's inscription at the end of the painting states that he did it 'for the first time'. What were the particular circumstances, such as his patrons' appreciation of the text and their image of China through pictures, that enabled this painting master to create such a work 'for the first time'? Beyond this, there are questions to be asked, for example, about the originality of the pictorial narrative technique and its relation to Chinese narrative art.

Kano Sansetsu, 'The Yang lady arrives at the palace' (from **The Yang lady is discovered**), *Song of Lasting Sorrow*; scroll 1, the first length of silk.

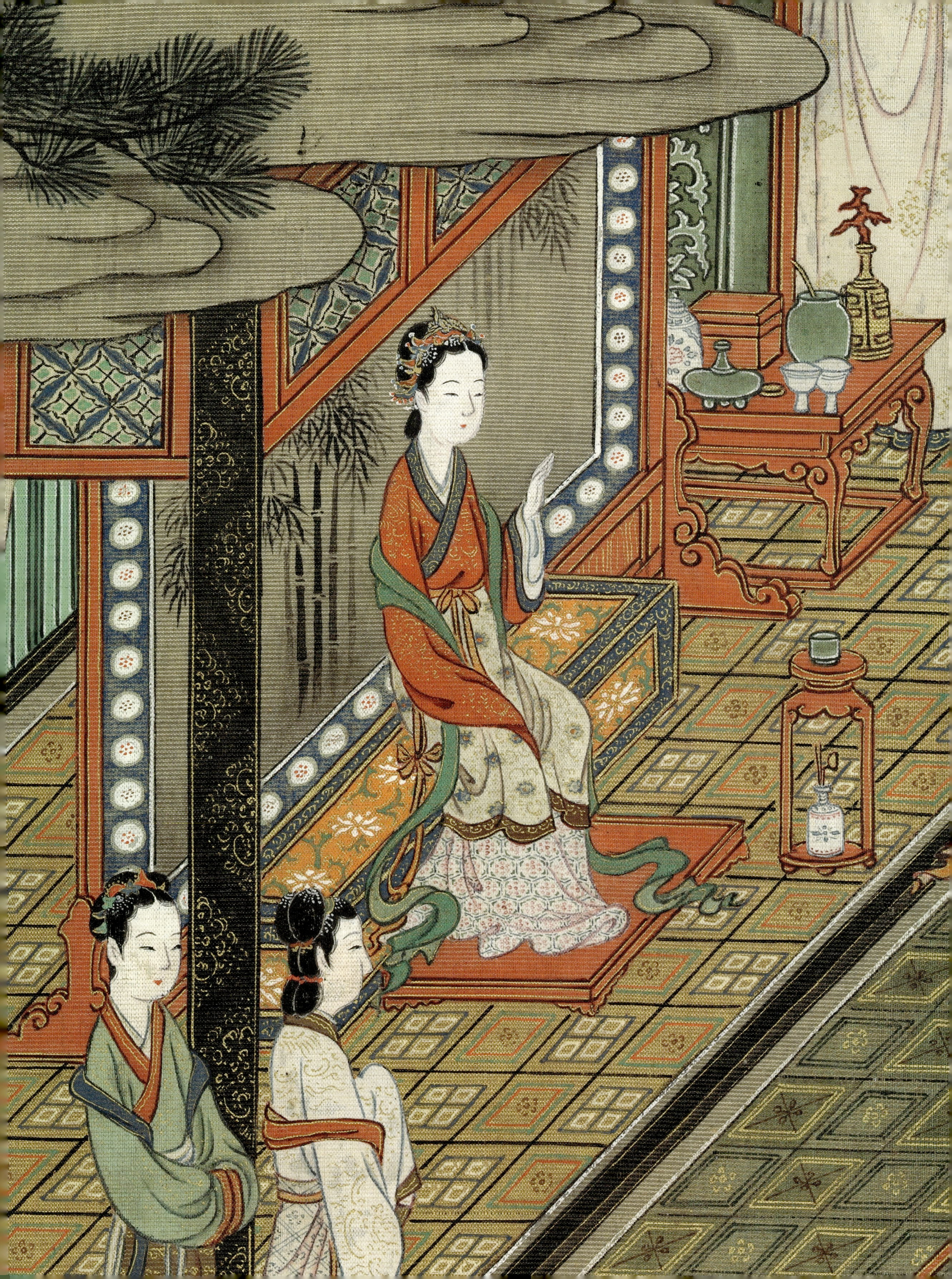

The full text of the inscription and signature at the end of the second scroll (see fig. 83) reads: 'Kano, of many generations, Sansetsu, painted this for the first time.' But just what lies behind the curious and seemingly contradictory words 'of many generations' and 'for the first time' has long intrigued viewers of the painting. The 'of many generations' implies that the artist was deeply aware of his Kano lineage. Sansetsu's formative model was his teacher, the Kano School master Sanraku (1559–1635), who may have illustrated the *Chōgonka* ballad. Additionally, there are a number of images relating to this subject by Kano School masters from the late Momoyama period (1573–1615) and early Edo Japan, upon which he could have drawn. Housed in the Freer Gallery in Washington DC, for instance, is a six-panel folding screen, *The Chinese Emperor Minghuang and his Concubine Yang Guifei, with Attendants on a Terrace* (see fig. 65), traditionally attributed to the eminent Kano Eitoku (1543–90), who was the teacher and adoptive father of Sansetu's father-in-law and teacher, Sanraku. Other paintings in the Freer include a pair of six-panel folding screens attributed to Kano Mitsunobu (1565–1608), *Scenes from the Life of the Minghuang Emperor and Yang Guifei* (see fig. 68), and a Kano School two-panel screen depicting the couple, dating to the early Edo period. These screens are in the main highly decorative, making lavish use of gold, but are less 'narrative paintings' than genre-type scenes or 'scenes from the life of' Minghuang and Yang Guifei, and as such, are almost closer to the contemporary Chinese tradition. Popular *Nara ehon* (picture-books from Nara) versions dating to the sixteenth and early-seventeenth centuries are also known, as Matthew McKelway observes (see chapter four).

In considering the creation of the *Chōgonka* scrolls, it might seem that the enduring popularity of the 'Song of Lasting Sorrow' and its illustrations over the centuries in Japan, and in early Edo-period (1603–1868) Kyoto specifically, would provide both context and precedent for the Chester Beatty Library scroll set. And yet, the specific context of its creation in mid-seventeenth-century Kyoto has long been something of a puzzle. Regarding the patronage of the Chester Beatty scrolls, Matthew McKelway offers new research.

Another set of questions raised in this study concerns a recurring theme – the complex relationship in the *Chōgonka* scrolls between the painting and Bai Juyi's text. The ballad's title, 'Song of Lasting Sorrow', is inscribed on the title slips and is indeed the narrative depicted over the course of the two long handscrolls. One of the issues this book sets out to examine, therefore, is the work's overarching narrative structure within its physical form. Each of the two handscrolls measures about 33 cm high (the silk medium is 31.8 cm high) by 11 m in length; each comprises six sheets of silk, painted in ink and bright colours, measuring about 180 cm in length. This physical form has an important connection with the division and visual plotting of the text into 'acts' and 'scenes'.

We may say the painting illustrates the text, but the latter is not actually inscribed on the painting, so how are they linked? We must argue out the reasons for linking them by examining the close adherence of the painting to the narrative of the ballad, by describing the broad learning in relation to Chinese poetry in Edo Japan, and also by introducing what we believe to be an earlier version of the work belonging to a private collection in Japan, which is inscribed with excerpts of the ballad.

There are also questions of emphasis and balance to consider. Written at the height of Japan's fascination with Chinese culture, Bai Juyi's ballad glosses over or romanticises facts of history for dramatic ends (the role of Yang Guifei is closer to victim than villain, for example).[6] Is it this outlook or some later historical interpretation of the ballad that is incorporated into the overall dramatisation of the tale in the painting? And, the ballad itself, which comprises sixty couplets written in the style of 'seven-character ancient verse', recounts events that took place between about the early 740s, when Minghuang and Yang Guifei first met, and Minghuang's death in 762. As time passes in the poem, the description of events becomes more detailed: certain early events are only briefly outlined, while the final episode – the interview between a Daoist wizard and the soul of Yang Guifei – commands almost the entire final third of the ballad. How is this weighting of events translated into images?

The first chapter of this book presents a perspective on the Minghuang–Yang Guifei story in medieval and early modern art in China. It introduces Bai Juyi's ballad itself and the more historical prose 'Account' that Bai Juyi asked his friend Chen Hong to write as a companion piece. It notes the transmission of the ballad to Japan, and its immediate popularity there in courtly literature, and identifies some of the early illustrations of Minghuang and Yang Guifei, which contributed to an evolving visual tradition. This broad approach introduces the reader to pictorial and stylistic sources of the story that go beyond the usual comparisons, such as those made between the mountain scenes (see fig. 33) and the anonymous Song-dynasty (960–1279) painting *Minghuang's Flight to Shu* in Taipei (see fig. 3) which was not a direct source, although its tradition could have been. One of the aims of this is to discover which Chinese artists, paintings and traditions might have been regarded as sources by the time of Kano Sansetsu's period of activity, and how visual depictions of them could have added to the 'authenticity' of the *Chōgonka* painting as a portrayal of a Tang-dynasty romance.

The second chapter presents, in two parts, an act-by-act and scene-by-scene study of each of the *Chōgonka* scrolls. Relevant lines of Bai Juyi's ballad head the twelve sections of this chapter.

Chapter three, a kind of coda to the previous chapter, explores an apparent preliminary version of the *Chōgonka* painting, part of a private collection in Japan.

Chapter four, by Matthew McKelway, traces the *Chōgonka* tale and other scenes of Minghuang and Yang Guifei as painting subjects by artists of the Kano workshop up to the time of Sansetsu, and discusses the position of the *Chōgonka* scroll-painting itself within Sansetsu's oeuvre. It also investigates how Sansetsu's art was understood during his lifetime and the years after; and how this can illuminate the artistic innovation and originality we find in the *Chōgonka* scrolls, particularly in light of the altogether different approach he took compared with his predecessors in the Kano painting lineage. The chapter proposes a 'reading' of the scrolls' original format based on compositional devices that achieve particular dramatic ends, and offers a hypothesis regarding the patronage and reception of the work.

In chapter five, Li-chiang Lin explores images of Minghuang and Yang Guifei in paintings and woodblock-print illustrations of Ming-dynasty (1369–1644) China, and explores which sources were transmitted to Japan and what relevance they might have had for Sansetsu's project.

In the final chapter, Yoshiko Ushioda contributes an essay reflecting on the rediscovery of the scrolls in the late 1970s and their subsequent publication, and Jessica Baldwin, current Head of Conservation at Chester Beatty, adds further remarks on their restoration and publication in the 1980s and 1990s. An Appendix contains English translations of Bai Juyi's 'Song of Lasting Sorrow' and of Chen Hong's companion 'Account'.

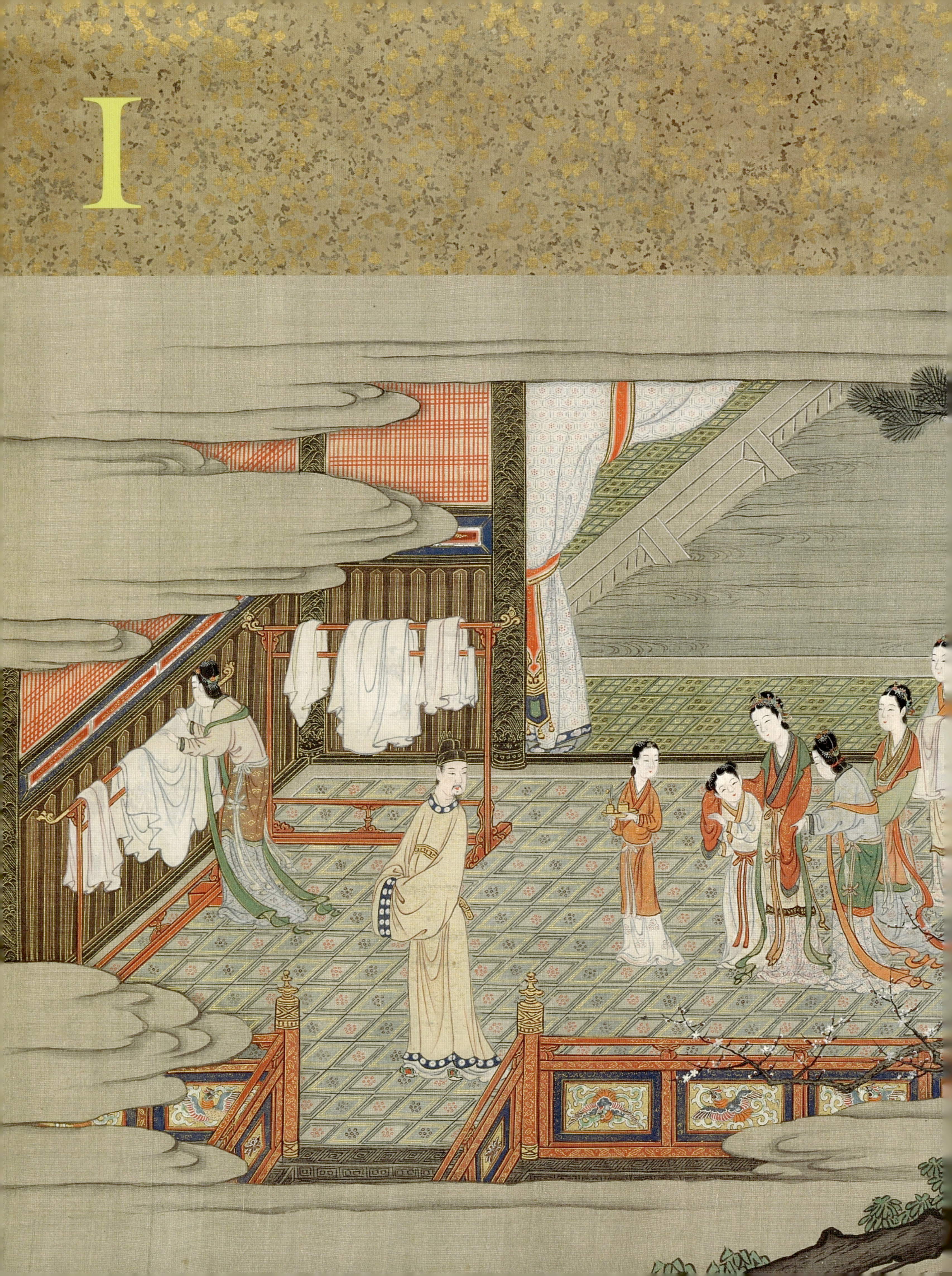
I

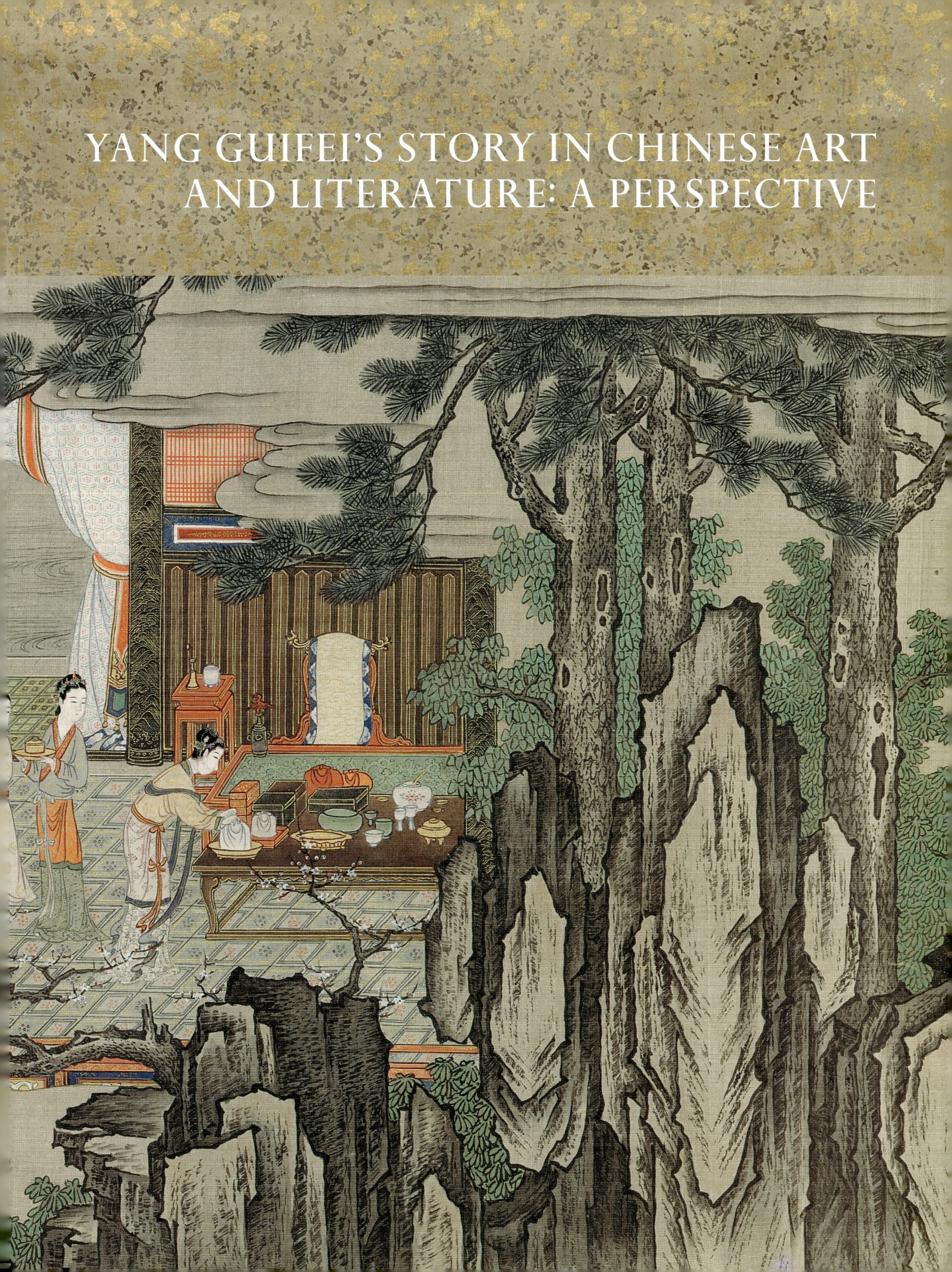

YANG GUIFEI'S STORY IN CHINESE ART AND LITERATURE: A PERSPECTIVE

THE TRAGIC ROMANCE between Tang emperor Minghuang (685–762) and his beloved Yang Guifei (719–56) had many qualities that gave it resonance in society, politics, literature and painting throughout China and Japan's history. Many poets and painters have retold – and embellished – the story, to the point where the original 'facts' have become inseparable from the romantic fictions that have sprung from them. The most famous of all these retellings, and one of the most famous Chinese poems in the history of Chinese poetry, is the romantic ballad by Bai Juyi (772–846) entitled 'Song of Lasting Sorrow' (*Chang hen ge*), which is illustrated in Kano Sansetsu's (1590–1651) picture-scrolls of the same title.

Central to the story is the figure of Yang Guifei, the virtual archetype of a *femme fatale* and one of the most remarkable beauties in Chinese history. With Xi Shi, Diao Chan and Wang Zhaojun, she is known as one of the Four Beauties of ancient China, but it is with another beautiful consort, the Han-dynasty (206 BC–AD 220) empress Zhao Feiyan or 'Flying Swallow' Zhao that she is most often compared. Both were said to be exemplary dancers, although Zhao was slender and petite whereas Yang was plump, and they were celebrated across the land for their extraordinary charms. Both rose from apparent obscurity to capture the heart of the emperor, and it may be said that both were the root cause of the near downfall of China's most powerful dynasties. In Zhao Feiyan's case, her scheming, her rivalry with her sister and their failure to produce a son meant that the emperor Chengdi of Han (r. 33–7 BC) died without an heir, which led directly to the usurpation of the throne by Wang Mang (r. AD 9–25).[7] Yang Guifei, who also competed with her sisters for the emperor's affections, is often held responsible for An Lushan's great rebellion in

755–56, which nearly toppled the Tang dynasty (618–907) at the apex of its power.[8] Part of the fascination with Yang Guifei's story is, on one hand, the sense of *déjà vu*: in light of Zhao Feiyan's story, this was history repeating itself, like a tragic romance. On the other hand, the story, already having had a precedent in history, also held the sense that it could happen again in the future.

The two reign periods of the tale's other main character, Emperor Minghuang – Kaiyuan (712–41) and Tianbao (742–56) – were celebrated as an era of flowering culture and stable government until An Lushan's rebellion shook the empire. The companion piece to Bai Juyi's ballad, Chen Hong's prose 'Account to Go with the "Song of Lasting Sorrow"', provides a fig-leaf for the end of the reign with the words, 'Afterward [that is, after Yang Guifei's execution], Xuanzong came to Chengdu [Sichuan] on his Imperial Tour, and [his son] Suzong accepted the succession at Lingwu.' The 'Imperial Tour' was a gloss on Minghuang's flight to Sichuan and, rather than having abdicated, he seems to have been deposed by his son, who was rallying troops to counter the rebellion hundreds of miles to the north in Lingwu.

The ballad focuses on romance and passion, rebellion and violence, mutiny and the tragic execution. It edits out details of Yang Guifei's illicit liaison with An Lushan as a possible cause of the rebellion, dwelling instead on Minghuang's perilous escape from the Tang capital Chang'an (modern Xi'an) through mountain passes and along plank roads to the Sichuan Basin in the southwest, an area romantically known by its ancient name of Shu. The tale concludes with scenes of mourning and longing, strong in Japanese appeal, and the consolation of the supernatural and Daoist beliefs in immortality.

This romance has nestled deep in the artistic imagination of China since some of the premier poets of the

Kano Sansetsu, 'Yang Guifei dances before Minghuang' (from **General An Lushan rebels**), *Song of Lasting Sorrow*; scroll 1, the fourth length of silk.

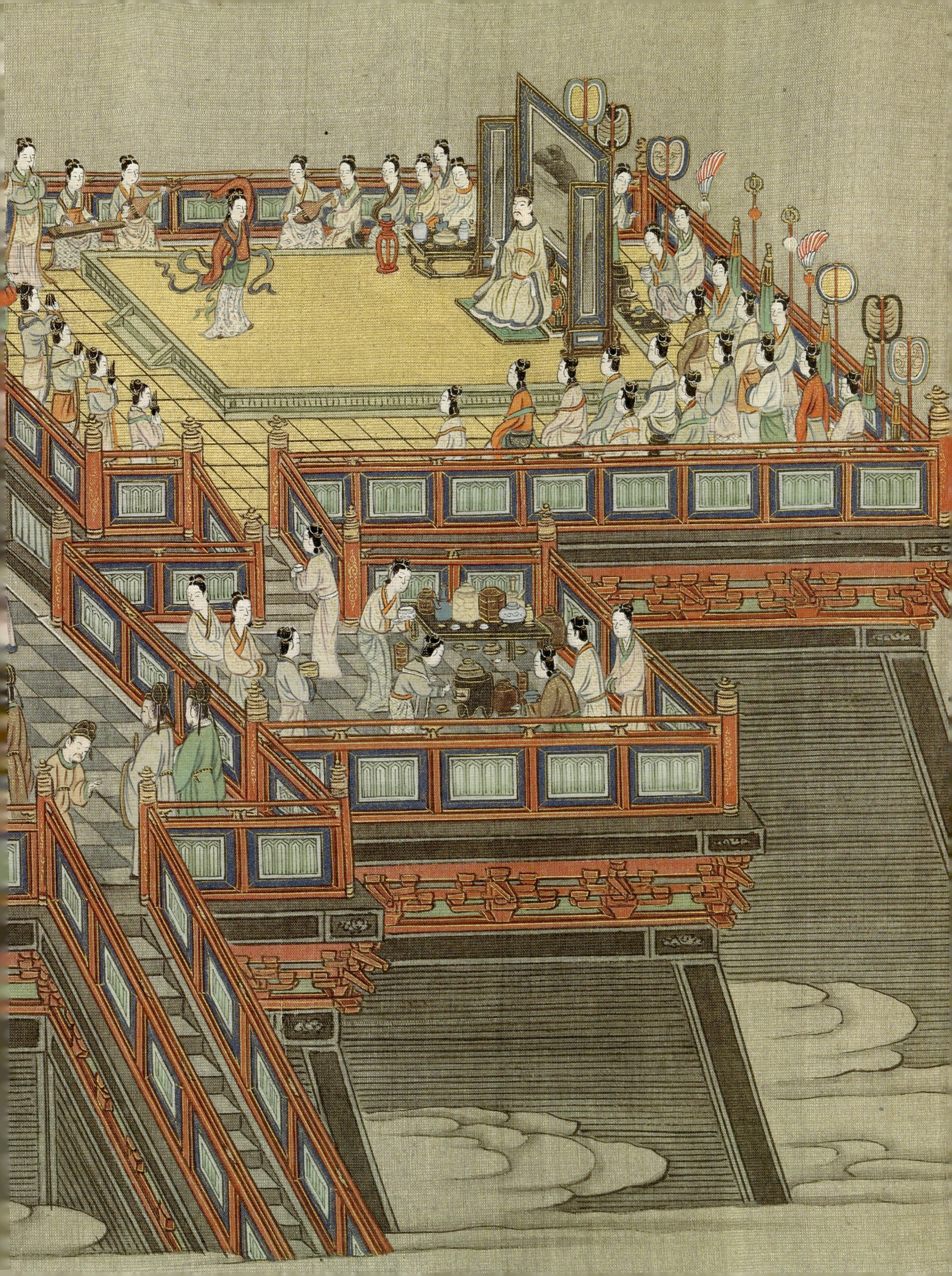

age wrote about it either directly or obliquely, among them household names like Li Bai (or Li Bo, 701–62) and Du Fu (712–70), who lived through the tumultuous times of the An Lushan rebellion. In one well-known poem, Li Bai, who was born in Sichuan, described the 'Hardships of the Road to Shu' (*Shu dao nan*), which Minghuang would have experienced in his flight from the capital to Sichuan. After the An Lushan rebellion and Yang Guifei's death, Du Fu contrasted her own beautiful life with the gruesome demise of Yang Guifei in a poem called 'Lament by the River':[9]

> *That woman, who was first of all*
> *in the Zhaoyang Galleries,*
> *went with her lord in the same palanquin*
> *and attended by his side.*
> …
> *Those bright eyes and sparkling teeth –*
> *where are they today?*
> *blood had stained her roaming soul,*
> *and she cannot get to return.*

It is noteworthy how the first couplet both magnifies and concentrates the figure of Yang Guifei. In the same way as the word 'Han', after the great early empire, was often used in later history to refer to China, the Zhaoyang Galleries here refers to the Chinese emperor's harem. It was in the magnificently decorated Zhaoyang Galleries that Han emperor Chengdi famously installed Empress Zhao Feiyan's younger sister Hede, or Bright Consort Zhao, after he transferred his favour from one to the other. The riches spent on these apartments are almost gleefully described in 'unauthorised' biographies and would have been called to mind by the mere use of the name.[10]

The notion of accompanying the emperor in his palanquin and attending by his side also has strong resonances with this period of Han history. The arrival of the teenage Zhao Feiyan in Chengdi's harem ousted from his favour another famous beauty, Consort Ban (Ban *Jieyu*). The upright Consort Ban is well known in history for having declined to ride in the imperial palanquin, a scene portrayed in the celebrated *Admonitions of the Court Instructress* scroll attributed to the early figural master Gu Kaizhi (*c*.344–*c*.406) in the British Museum. These scenes illustrate a didactic text composed by the Western Jin polymath and statesman Zhang Hua (232–300), about how court ladies should behave. The scene of 'Lady Ban declining to ride in the imperial palanquin' (fig. 1) is a narrative illustration of the text inscribed to the right of it, which outlines her reason: she had no wish to make her husband Chengdi appear like one of the frivolous rulers in history who were commonly pictured with beauties rather than wise statesmen by their sides. The text does not mention the role of Zhao Feiyan in Lady Ban's loss of favour; that appears to stem from the emperor's discomfort at her implied rebuke. However, the painter of the *Admonitions* scroll seems to have had a different idea. His depiction of a slender and pretty girl innocently playing with a puppy by the emperor's side in the palanquin seems to imply, brilliantly, that this is the pivotal moment when Lady Ban loses imperial favour and Zhao Feiyan gains it. Tang poets may well have taken for granted various powerful historical resonances, such as likening Yang Guifei to Zhao Feiyan, in their imaging of Yang Guifei in verse.

Among the eminent later Tang poets to explore the Yang Guifei story were Li Shangyin (*c*.813– *c*.58), Yuan Zhen (779–831), and, of course, Bai Juyi (772–846). Li Shangyin composed a quatrain entitled 'Dragon Pool' which evokes a banquet attended by Yang Guifei, the emperor and at least two of his sons. Historically, when Minghuang first discovered Lady Yang, she was the concubine of one of these

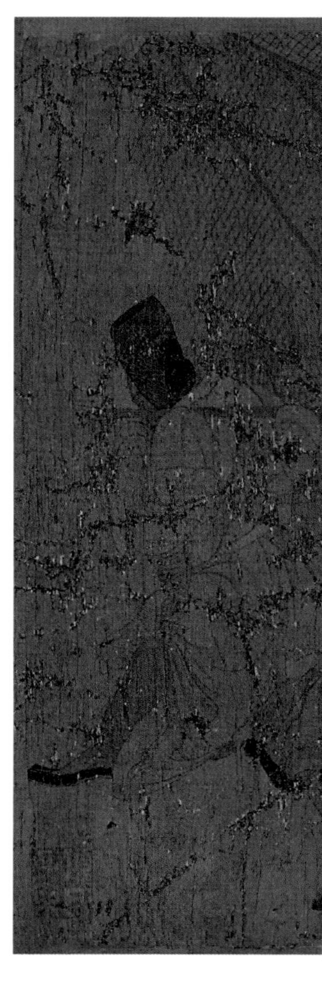

Fig 1 'Lady Ban declining to ride in the imperial palanquin', *Admonitions of the Court Instructress*, attributed to Gu Kaizhi (*c*.344–*c*.406; a 5th–6th century version after). Detail of a handscroll, now mounted as a panel; ink and colours on silk, 25 x 348.5 cm. © Trustees of the British Museum.

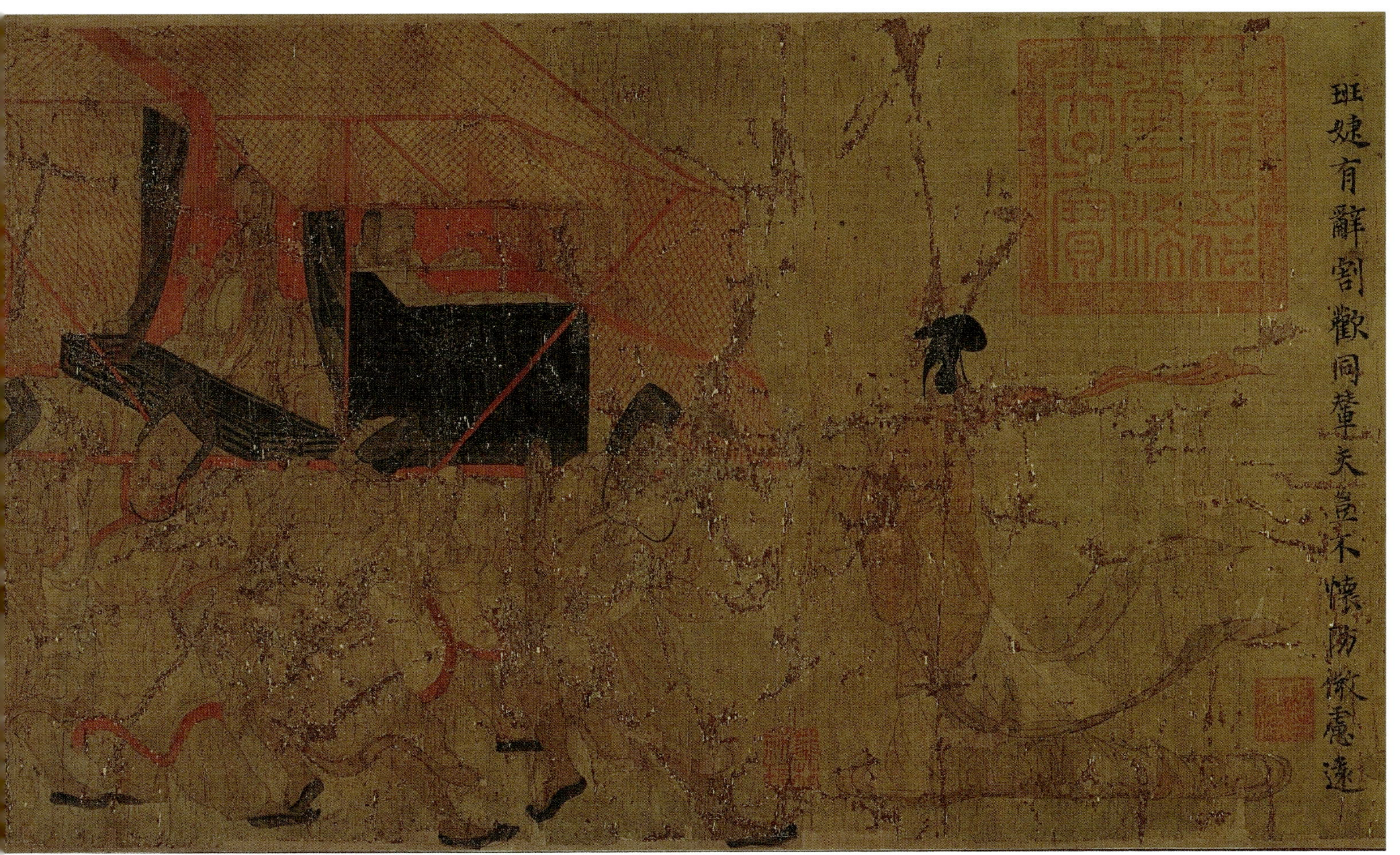

princes of the blood, the Prince of Shou, whose coldness on seeing his former concubine with his father is evoked in the final line:

At Dragon Pool he offers wine,
  and mica screens are spread,
the rams-hide drums play loudly,
  all other musicians cease.[11]

At midnight they come back from feasting,
  the water-clock drips on –
the Prince of Xue is reeling drunk,
  the Prince of Shou is sober.

Close friends and fellow poets, Bai Juyi and Yuan Zhen also both wrote poems entitled 'The Girl Who Danced the Whirl', about a popular musical dance from the Central Asian kingdom of Sogdiana. Two of the best-known dancers of this piece were in fact An Lushan, who was of Sogdian descent, and Yang Guifei. In Bai Juyi's poem, Yang Guifei, as an immortal, is referred to as Lady Taizhen, a name she took

when she became a Daoist nun for two years after Minghuang had her separate from his son:

In the final years of the Tianbao Reign,
  when the times were about to change,
everyone, lady and courtier alike,
  was learning to turn in circles.[12]

Within the court was Lady Taizhen,
  outside was An Lushan,
and these two were known most of all for
  ability to whirl.

In the Garden of the Pear Blossoms one
  gained a Consort's rank;
and beneath the Screen of the Golden Cock
  the other was raised a son.

When An Lushan did the Whirl,
  he bewildered the ruler's eyes;
even when troops crossed the Yellow River,
  it was doubted that he had rebelled.

When Yang the Prized Consort did the Whirl,
  she befuddled the ruler's heart;
when she was left dead at Mawei Station,
  he yearned for her evermore.

The place names, which would have been familiar to readers in dynastic China, give these verses an epic quality. The romance implied by the Garden of the Pear Blossoms, a place also mentioned by Bai Juyi, conveys the depth of Minghuang's affection for Yang Guifei. The mention of troops crossing the Yellow River refers to the defeat of an imperial army after it emerged from the impregnable defences at Tongguan pass, which allowed the rebels to advance on the capital. Finally, we hear of the postal station at Mawei, the site of Yang Guifei's hurried execution during the emperor's flight from the capital.

However, Bai Juyi's best-known poem on the subject of Yang Guifei and Minghuang's love affair is the 'Song of Lasting Sorrow'. The context of its composition is a matter of record. Having passed the *jinshi* ('presented scholar') civil service exam, Bai Juyi sat a further 'palace examination' on the merit of which he received a post as a county official. Although a minor post, it kept him strategically close to the court, just west of the capital Chang'an, not far from the site of Yang Guifei's execution at Mawei. From here, events are described in the closing passage of Chen Hong's 'Account to Go with the Song of Lasting Sorrow'.[13]

In winter of the first year of the Yuanhe Reign, the twelfth month (February 807), Bai Juyi of Taiyuan left his position as Diarist in the Imperial Library to be sheriff of Chou County. I, Chen Hong, and Wang Zhifu of Langya had our homes in this town; and on our days off we would go together visiting sites of the Undying and Buddhist Temples. Our discussion touched on this story, and we were all moved to sighs. Zhifu lifted his winecup to Bai Juyi and said, 'Unless such an event finds an extraordinary talent who can adorn it with colours, even something so rare will fade away with time and no longer be known in the world. Bai Juyi is deeply familiar with poetry and has strong sentiments. Why doesn't he write a song on the topic.' At this Bai Juyi made the 'Song of Lasting Sorrow'. It is my supposition that he was not only moved by the event, but he also wanted to offer warning about such creatures that can so enthral a man, to block the phases by which troubles come, and to leave this for the future. When the song was finished, he had me write a prose account for it. Of those things not known to the general public, I, not being a survivor of the Kaiyuan, have no way to know. For those things known to the general public, the *Annals of the Reign of Xuanzong* are extant. This is merely an account for the 'Song of Lasting Sorrow'.

Thus, it is believed that on a visit to the well-known Immortal Travel Temple (Xianyousi), the discussion turned to the events that had happened in this area exactly half a century before – the execution of Yang Guifei at Mawei, not far from the temple, and the onward flight of Minghuang to Shu – and that this triggered Bai Juyi's retelling of the tale in his sixty-couplet ballad, 'Song of Lasting Sorrow'.

In the later Tang poetic imagination the treament of this subject seems to have wavered between romantic escapism and grave admonition. These

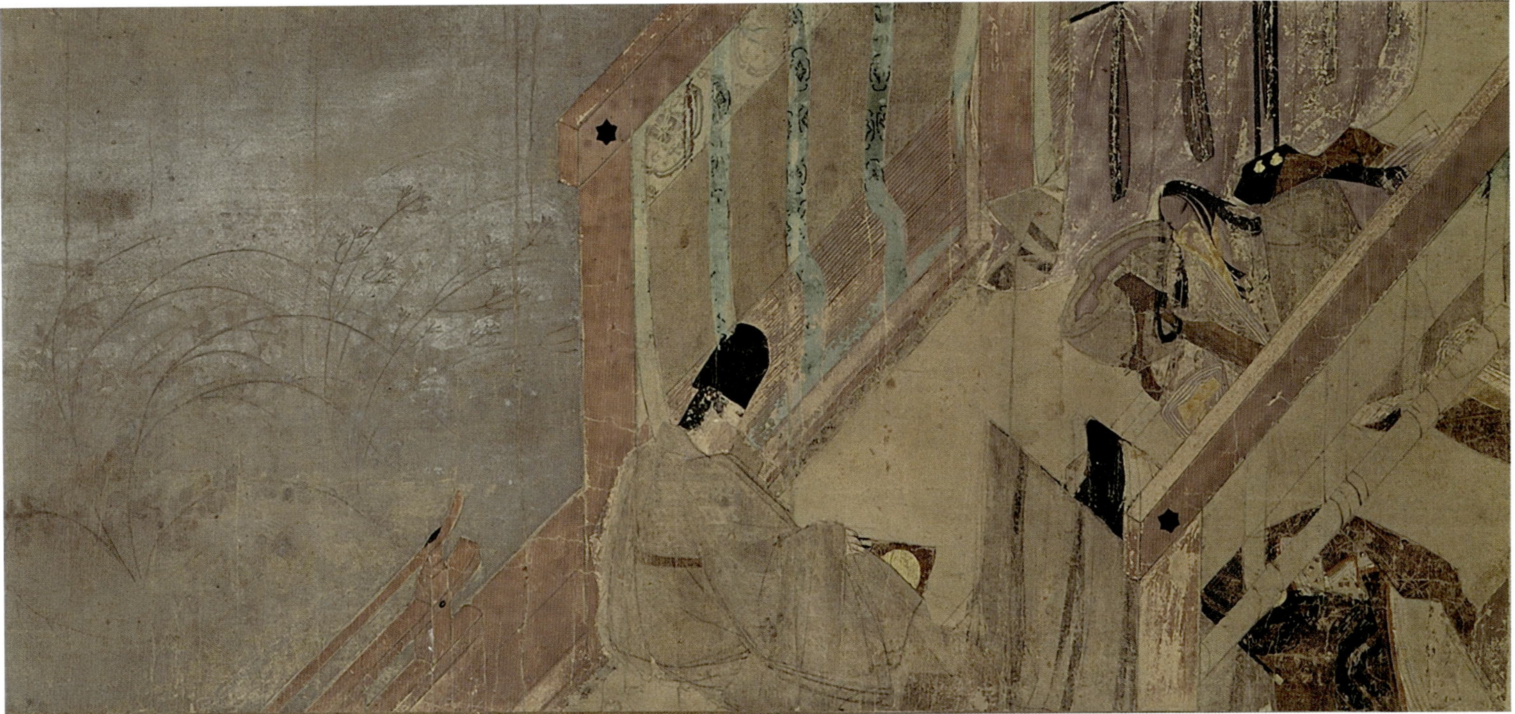

writers were, perhaps, already nostalgically aware of the passing of Chinese power and majesty – of what came to be known as the 'High Tang' (Sheng Tang), a period of cultural richness, cosmopolitan society and elegant court culture. They may already have been looking back wistfully on the time when Tang China was revered by foreign states – as inscribed in court paintings of visiting rulers seeking audiences with the Tang emperor, and of the great poets, painters and calligraphers of Minghuang's reign. One might even argue that this event marked the beginning of a transition that by the eleventh century had produced a new social class in China – the literati or scholar-official class – who aspired to guard China's tradition of principled statecraft from the partiality and pragmatism of hereditary ruling houses.

Beyond China, the tale has lain deep in the artistic imagination in Japan since the Heian period (794–1185); and it has been well known in English only since it was translated by the great early twentieth-century sinologist Arthur Waley (1889–1966) as 'Song of Eternal Remorse'.[14] The writings of Bai Juyi and other Chinese writers were quickly transmitted to the Heian court of Japan, where at that time there was a deep admiration for all things Chinese, and especially for the poetry of Bai Juyi. His style name (*zi*) is Letian, hence he is known as Hakurakuten in Japan – in fact, the title of a Nō play by Zeami

(1363–1443) about Bai Juyi's influence on poetry in Japan.

Among his many poems, this tale of love and death struck a particular chord in Japan, where a version of the myth exists in which Yang Guifei escapes to Japan. An allusion to the Yang Guifei story appears in the opening paragraphs of the early eleventh-century novel the *Tale of Genji* (*Genji Monogatari*), which is itself one of the founding topics of Japanese narrative painting (fig. 2).[15] In chapter one, The Paulownia Court, the unnamed Japanese emperor's favourite is likened by snobbish courtiers to Yang Guifei (or Yōkihi in Japanese) as a negative example – to imply that the emperor's dallying with such a low-born beauty is bound to lead to the neglect of state affairs and ultimately to rebellion and chaos. However, in a wonderfully ironic insight on the part of the story's author – the court lady Murasaki Shikibu (b. 978?) – there is the sense that the emperor is not at all disapproving of this comparison, which sees his favourite likened to one of the most beautiful Chinese women of all time. As the narrative unfolds, it emerges that prince Genji is the product of this tragic union.

By the middle of chapter one, when the emperor's favoured lady is finally hounded to death by jealous courtiers, the historical parallel becomes even more obvious. The Tang emperor Minghuang

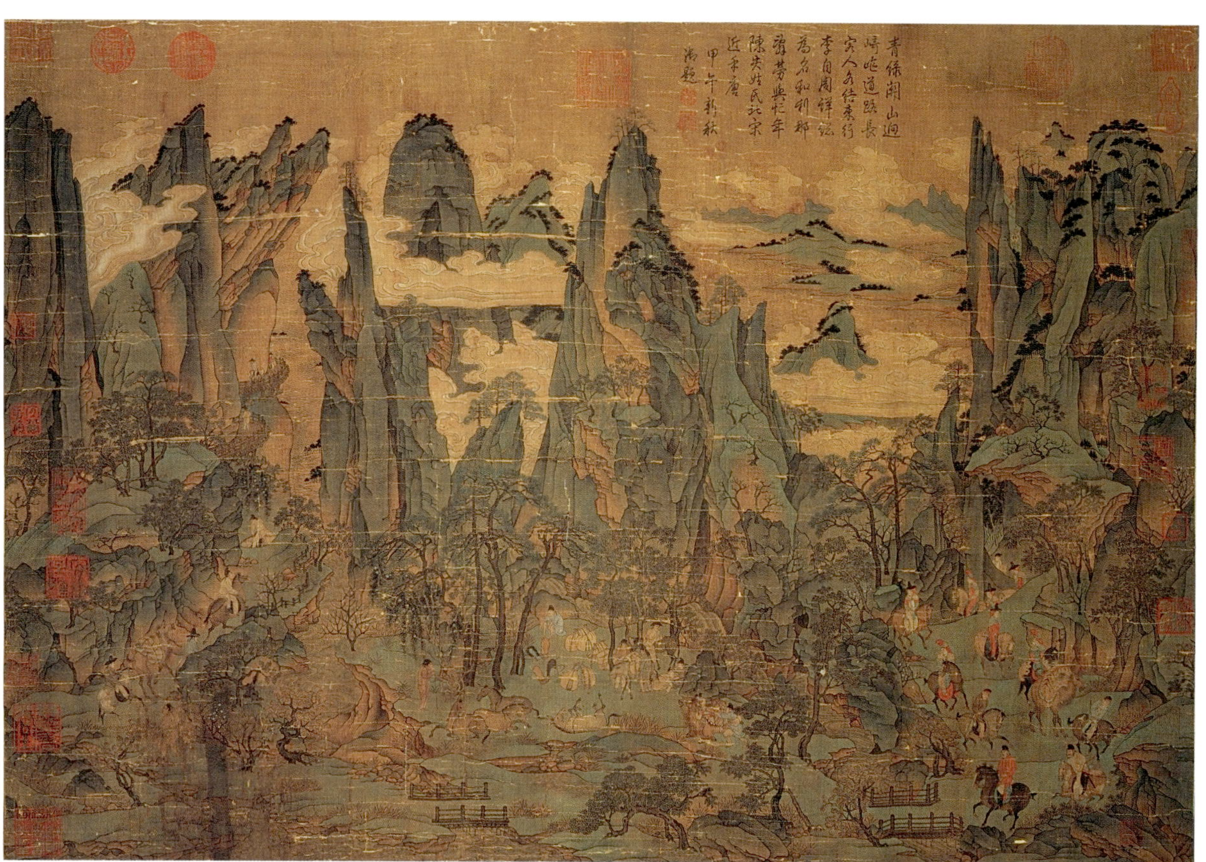

becomes the self-image for the bereaved emperor in the story. The latter is said to become 'addicted' to illustrations of *Chōgonka* made for the ninth-century Japanese emperor Uda and recites verses on the subject by Japanese and Chinese poets. In a brilliant paradox, the emperor keeps on revealing his blindspot with regard to the the moral–political lesson of the story.

If the ninth-century Japanese emperor Uda was viewing pictures of the *Chōgonka* story in the *Tale of Genji*, it seems likely that this romance between emperor and concubine, or elements of it, was a painting subject in China during the latter half of the Tang dynasty (ninth–early tenth century). It was certainly painted in the succeeding Song (960–1279) and Yuan (1271–1368) periods, as indicated by the existence of various paintings of mountain scenes in an archaistic Tang blue-and-green style. The transmission of this Tang mode or iconography suggests that the subject might have first been painted within half a century of the An Lushan Rebellion period – from about 800. Although it must have been a sensitive subject in China, Bai Juyi was writing a romance about it, so perhaps painters were at liberty to paint it also.

In the titles of paintings related to the subject, however, euphemisms are often used – as in *Minghuang's Journey to Shu* (rather than his *flight*) and *Minghuang Escaping the Summer Heat*. The depiction of melons being picked is another case in point: Minghuang's concubines are said to have picked melons by the roadside during the flight to Shu and although early critics identified 'picking melons' as a euphemism,[16] what makes positive identification of these scenes difficult are some of the ascriptions of the paintings to the early Tang landscapists Li Sixun (651–716) and his son Li Zhaodao (active *c*.670–730), who were both dead long before the flight to Shu.[17] Early mountain scenes that appear to depict this subject may be found in a number of collections. The best known are a probable Song (twelfth century?) version of a late Tang original in the National Palace Museum in Taipei (fig. 3), which has been identified with this narrative in modern scholarship,[18] and another of probable twelfth-century date in the Metropolitan Museum of Art in New York (fig. 4).[19]

The Taipei *Minghuang's Journey to Shu* is a small horizontal painting measuring 55.9 x 81 cm, now mounted as a hanging scroll. The narrative within

Fig 4 Anon. (Southern Song, mid-12th century). *Emperor Xuanzong's Flight to Shu (Minghuang xing Shu tu).* Hanging scroll; ink, colour and gold on silk, 82.8 x 113.6 cm. The Metropolitan Museum of Art, Rogers Fund, 1941 (41.138).

unfolds in three scenes from right to left. This movement and the painting's shape suggest that it might once have been part of a longer handscroll narrative. The first of these three scenes shows a party of men and women riding down from a high mountain pass, accompanied by a pack-camel. In the foreground, about to cross a bridge, is the red-robed leader. The mane of this man's horse is distinctively bunched in three plumes and he leads a party of elegant ladies through this rather unlikely scenery, which are all clues to his identity as the fleeing Emperor Minghuang. The scene in the middle shows grooms, porters and mules resting under trees. The last scene shows the party carrying on along a path cut into a cliff towards plank roads attached to more distant rock faces under looming cliffs.

The 'primitive' blue-and-green landscape style of this painting has been identified with the royal painters of the early–mid-Tang period, Li Sixun or Li Zhaodao, and although they were dead before 756,

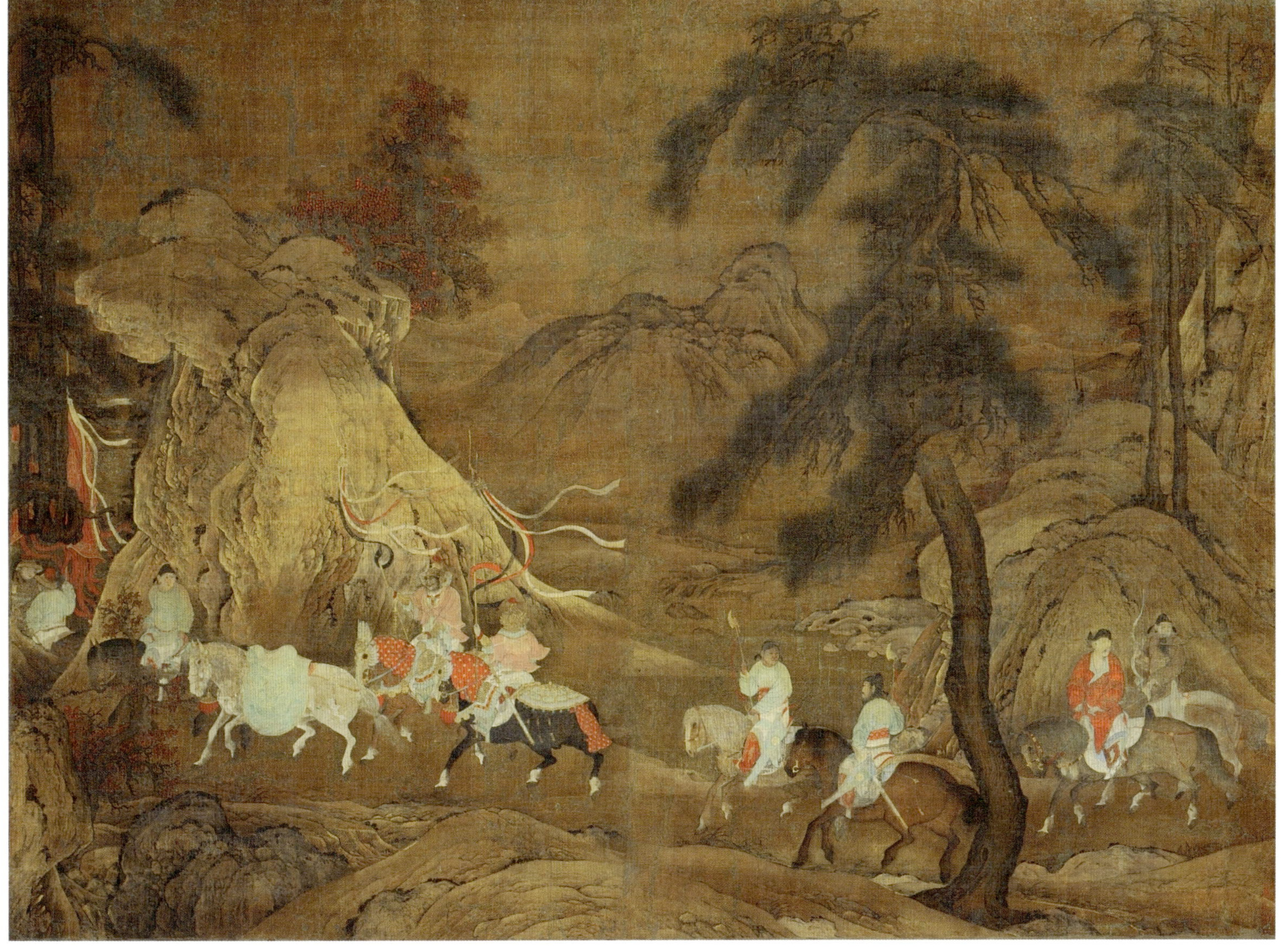

this landscape style remained current. These artists had many followers in the later Tang period and into the Song, and it is probably one of the latter who recreated this painting, reviving the Tang style. Modern scholars have suggested that this painting was probably inspired by Bai Juyi's ballad, believing that the half a century that had passed since the An Lushan Rebellion made it possible to use the theme without causing offence to the inner court.[20]

The New York painting is a little larger at 82.8 x 113.6 cm and has been identified as part of a narrative screen painting, now remounted in a hanging scroll.[21] It depicts a much closer-up view of a noble party under military escort travelling from right to left through rocky mountain scenery. Among some rather refined-looking pines are a few trees bearing red-hued autumnal leaves. The strongest clues to the subject of the scene depicted here are two linked features: the riderless white horse wearing a beautifully decorated saddle and the red-robed figure looking back out of the painting. As scholars have pointed out, this would seem to represent Emperor Minghuang turning to look back for his beloved consort after her execution, as he escapes through the mountains towards Shu. The fine, riderless animal would be Yang Guifei's mount. The painting may even illustrate specific parts of Bai Juyi's 'Song of Lasting Sorrow'.[22] This scene relates thematically to other paintings of Minghuang and Yang Guifei mounting horses. Typically, in those paintings, Minghuang is already mounted but turns with concern to see Yang mounting with great difficulty (see fig. 10). In one common interpretation these paintings show the couple preparing to leave the capital during the night, as An Lushan's rebel forces approach the city. The emperor's elaborate concern for Yang Guifei in these circumstances generates great pathos in the image.

The sophisticated landscape setting of the New

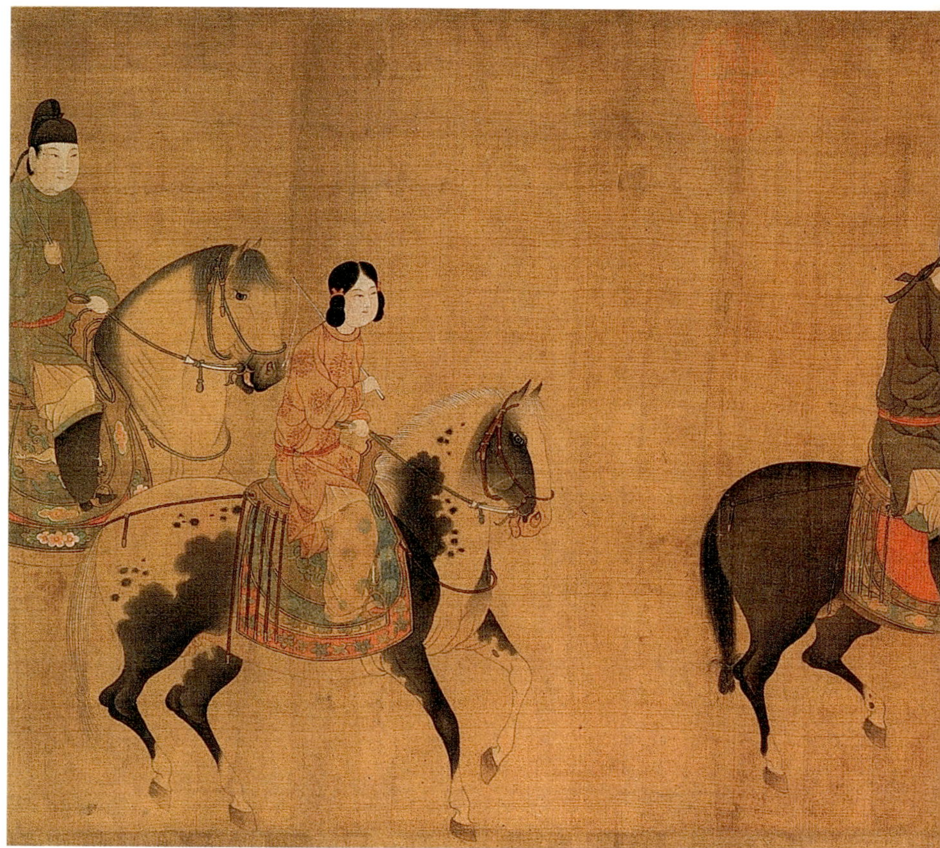

York painting and the somewhat academic treatment of the trees suggests that this painting originated at the early Southern Song (1127–1279) court, perhaps even in the reign of Emperor Gaozong (r. 1127–62), who, like Minghuang, had fled the capital during the national crisis of 1127 when the Jurchen Jin captured his father, Emperor Huizong (r. 1100–25). As a result of Gaozong's policy of national regeneration many narrative paintings with Confucian or didactic Chinese themes were created at Gaozong's court, and it is possible that this topic served as a pictorial trope for the national crisis culminating in the capture of most of the court by and the loss of half the Song empire to the Jurchen Jin dynasty (1115–1234) during the crisis of 1125–27. Its existence would stand as a stern warning against any kind of conduct that could lead to a recurrence of that disaster.

There are, in addition, a group of figure paintings that feature Yang Guifei and/or her sisters in the company of Emperor Minghuang, which appear to be Song, Jin and Yuan court paintings based on one or more originals by Minghuang's court painter Zhang Xuan (active 713–after 748). A handscroll after Zhang Xuan entitled *Spring Outing of Lady Guoguo* in the Liaoning Provincial Museum is now

Fig 5 Anon. (Song; attributed to Li Gonglin, after Zhang Xuan), *Evening Outing of Lady Guoguo (Liren xing tu)*. Handscroll; ink and colours on silk, 33.4 x 112.2 cm. National Palace Museum, Taipei.

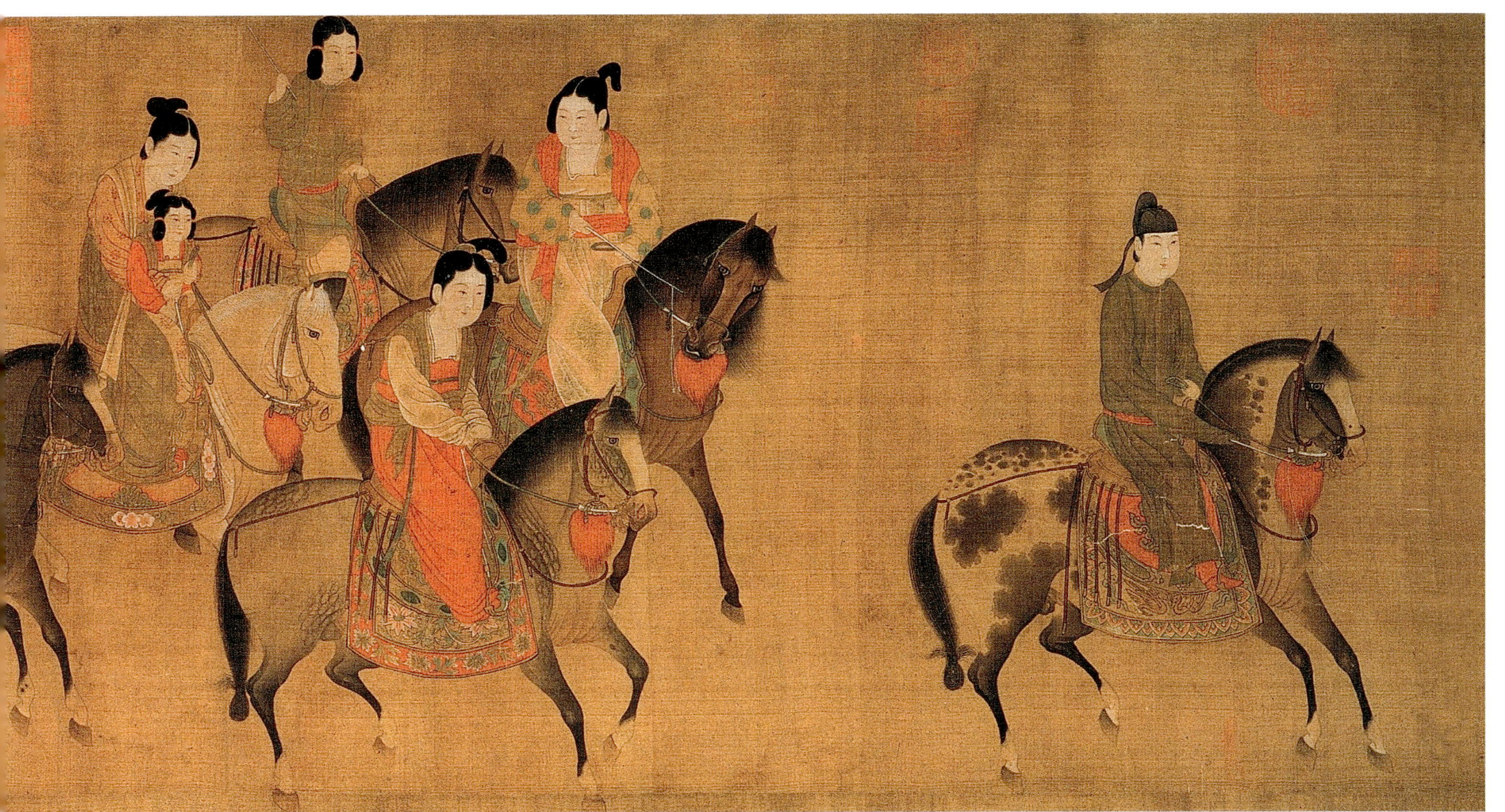

attributed to Song emperor Huizong and bears the inscription and seals of the Jin emperor Zhangzong (r. 1190–1208).[23] Another similar version, in the National Palace Museum in Taipei, entitled *The Ways of the [Court] Beauties (Liren xing tu)*, is better known in English as *Evening Outing of Lady Guoguo* (fig. 5). Unsigned, but said to be a copy by the scholar-painter Li Gonglin, it portrays a side-on view of three mounted palace women, one holding a girl in the saddle in front of her. They proceed from left to right, counter to the direction of viewing, in a kind of mini-narrative, attended by two serving women and escorted by three eunuchs. It may illustrate part of a poem entitled 'Liren xing' by Du Fu, about the superb entertainments put on by Minghuang for Yang Guifei and her sisters in the Tianbao reign period, or another by him about one sister, entitled 'Lady Guoguo':[24]

> *The Lady Guoguo enjoys imperial favours.*
> *At dawn she enters the Palace on horseback*
> *   [not dismounting].*
> *She scorns to defile her face with make-up*
> *   and powder;*
> *Her eyebrows only lightly brushed, she*
> *   appears before her lord.*

Lady Guoguo's disdain for cosmetics in poetry implies that she was unusually familiar and intimate with the emperor, but contrasts with the historical record. It has often been noted since at least the Song period that Yang Guifei and her sisters received 'a monthly stipend of 100,000 cash apiece for beautification alone'.[25] The use of cosmetics can be understood in terms of the history of paintings of court ladies and their code of moral–ethical conduct. In the scene of two ladies making themselves up in the *Admonitions* scroll attributed to Gu Kaizhi (fig. 6), the inscription reads, 'Men and women know how to adorn their faces, / But there is none who knows how to adorn his character. / Yet if the character be not adorned, / There is a danger that the rules of conduct may be transgressed …'[26]

There is considerable evidence that the cosmopolitan Tang capital was a place of changing tastes and of an acute awareness of fashion. The Yang sisters seem to have become national models of fashion, as evidenced from changes in the style of Tang paintings of court ladies over the eighth century in the archaeological record, including imperial tomb murals and other paintings. Predating them, from 706, is a mural featuring a painting of 'Ladies of the

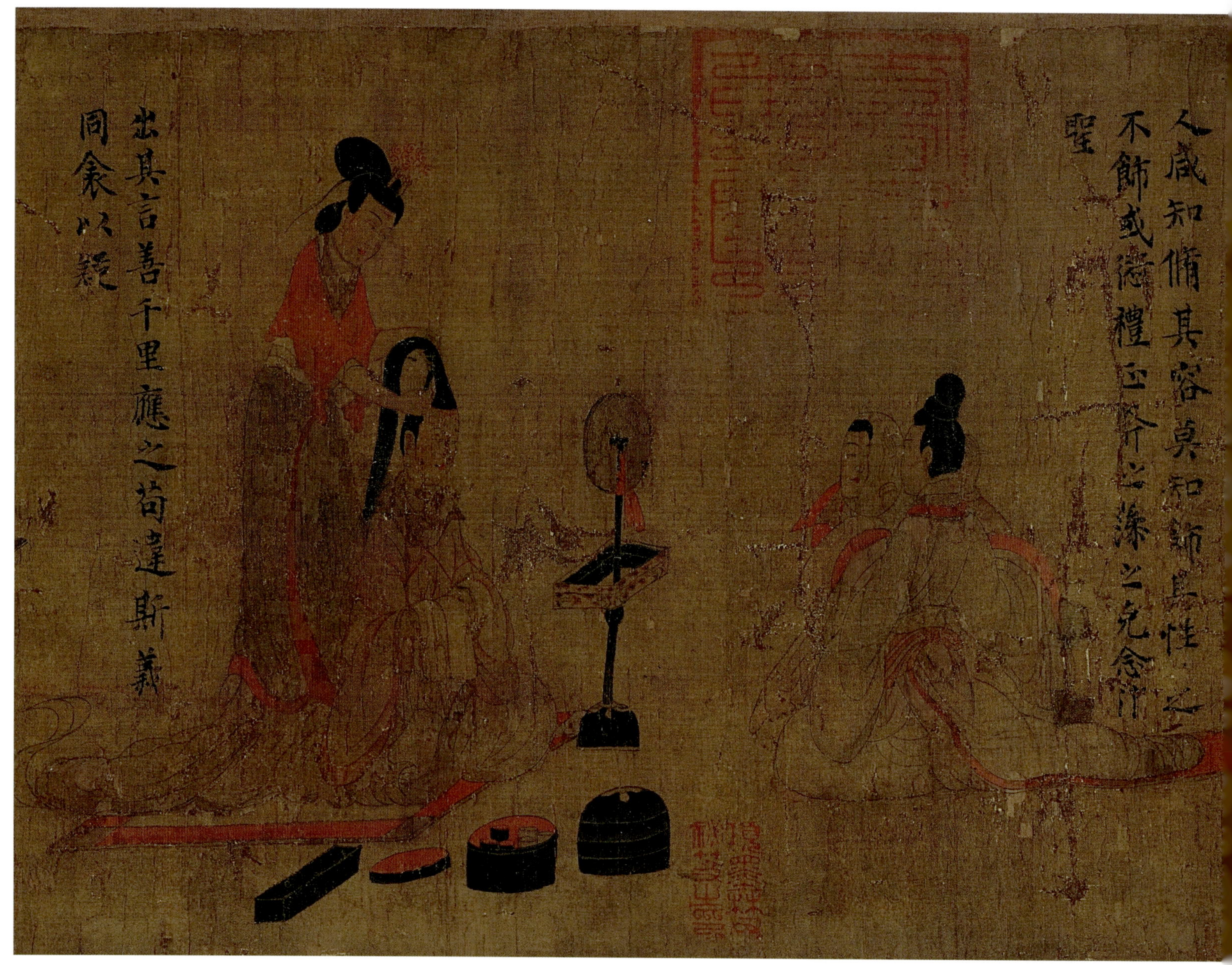

FIG 6 The 'toilette' scene, from *Admonitions of the Court Instructress* attributed to Gu Kaizhi (c.344–c.406; a 5th–6th century version after).

Court' in the tomb of Princess Yongtai in Qianxian, Shaanxi Province (fig. 7), close to the Tang capital at modern Xi'an. It shows the strong linear delineation used to render figures at this time. In terms of stylistic development, the sculptural bending of the hips and shoulders of the two central ladies, for instance, along with their close-fitting drapery, is here beginning to give them a heightened sensuous presence.

By the middle of the eighth century, however, the pictorial image of the court lady had become far more corpulent and more heavily made-up and rouged, as a kind of lush glamour came into vogue. Tradition has it that the widespread portrayal of plump ladies owed much to the physique of the emperor's favourite, Yang Guifei. Although this look did exist in early pictures of court ladies,[27] it does seem to have become the pervasive fashion at the very time when Yang Guifei was a national style icon and when figure painters like Zhang Xuan were active at court, during the Tianbao reign period (742–56). Images of these portly ladies have been found from Japan in the east (fig. 8) and Xinjiang in the west (fig. 9), suggesting that this was a vogue with appeal far beyond China.

Two mid-eighth-century paintings in Japan show that during the Nara period (710–94), when Chinese 'influence' was at its peak, Japanese artists quickly absorbed the new Tang styles. The screen of portly ladies under trees and a painting on hemp cloth of a portly Kichijōten, the deity of Love and Fertility, in Yakushiji Temple, Nara, were both once adorned with kingfisher feathers in imitation of the kind of

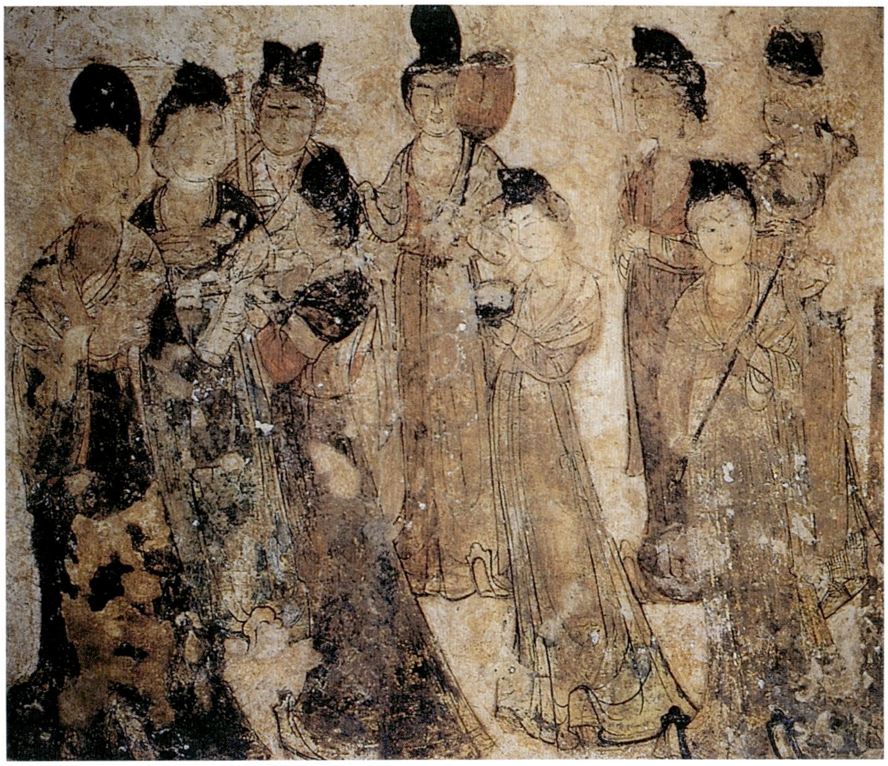

FIG 7 *Ladies of the Court*, dateable to 706. Detail of a mural from the tomb of Princess Yongtai in Qianxian, Shaanxi Province, 177 x 198 cm. Shaanxi Provincial Museum.

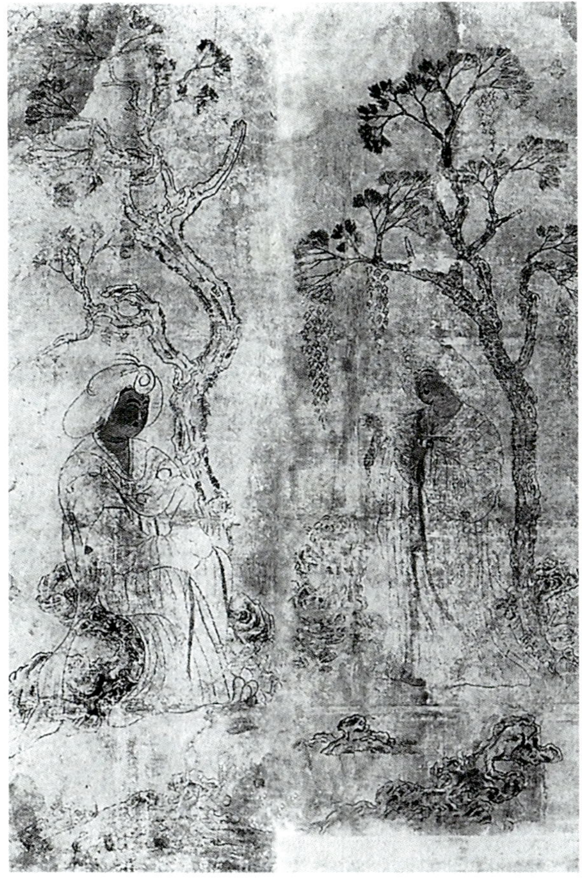

FIG 8 *Ladies Under Trees*, dateable to about 756. Screen painting; ink, colours and bird feathers on silk, 136 x 56 cm. Shōsōin Treasury, Nara, Japan.

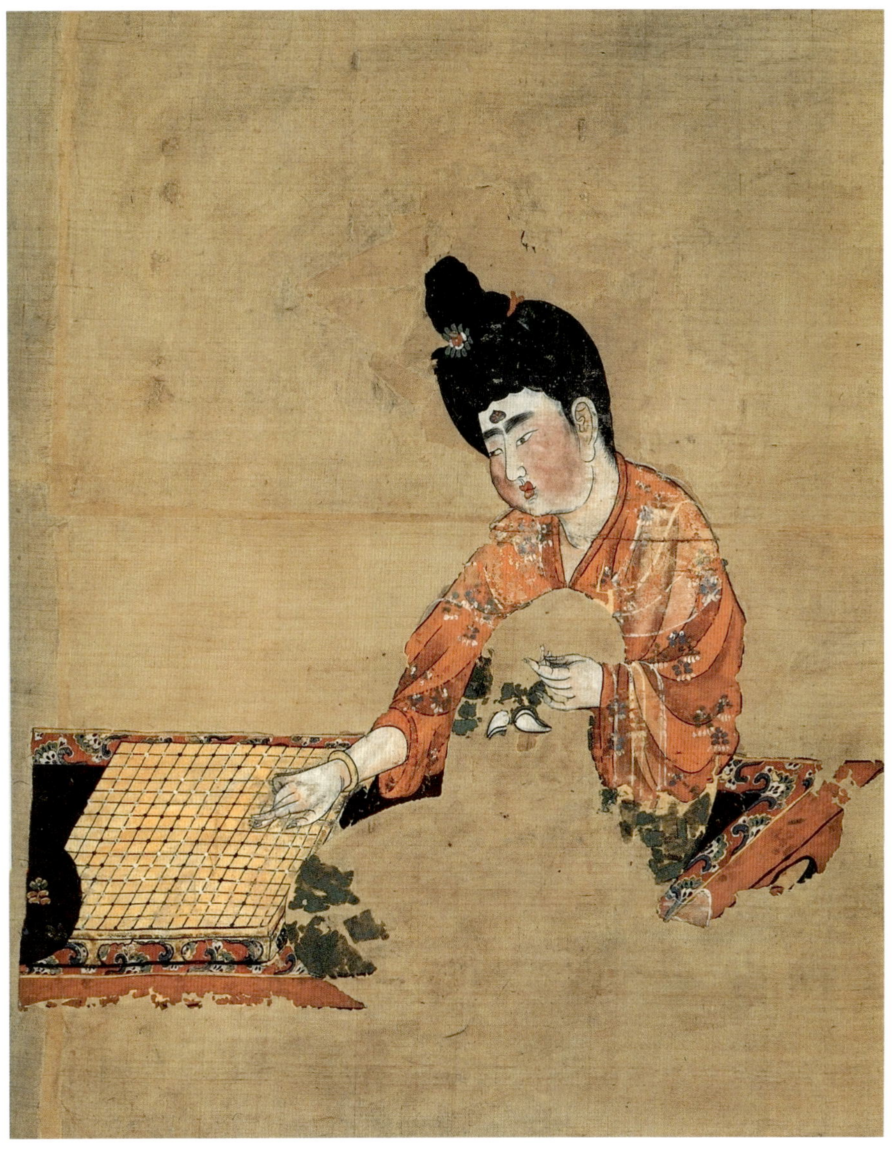

FIG 9 *Woman Playing Weiqi*. Fragment of a painted screen; ink and colours on silk, 63 cm high. From Astana Tomb 187, Turpan, Xinjiang Autonomous Region.

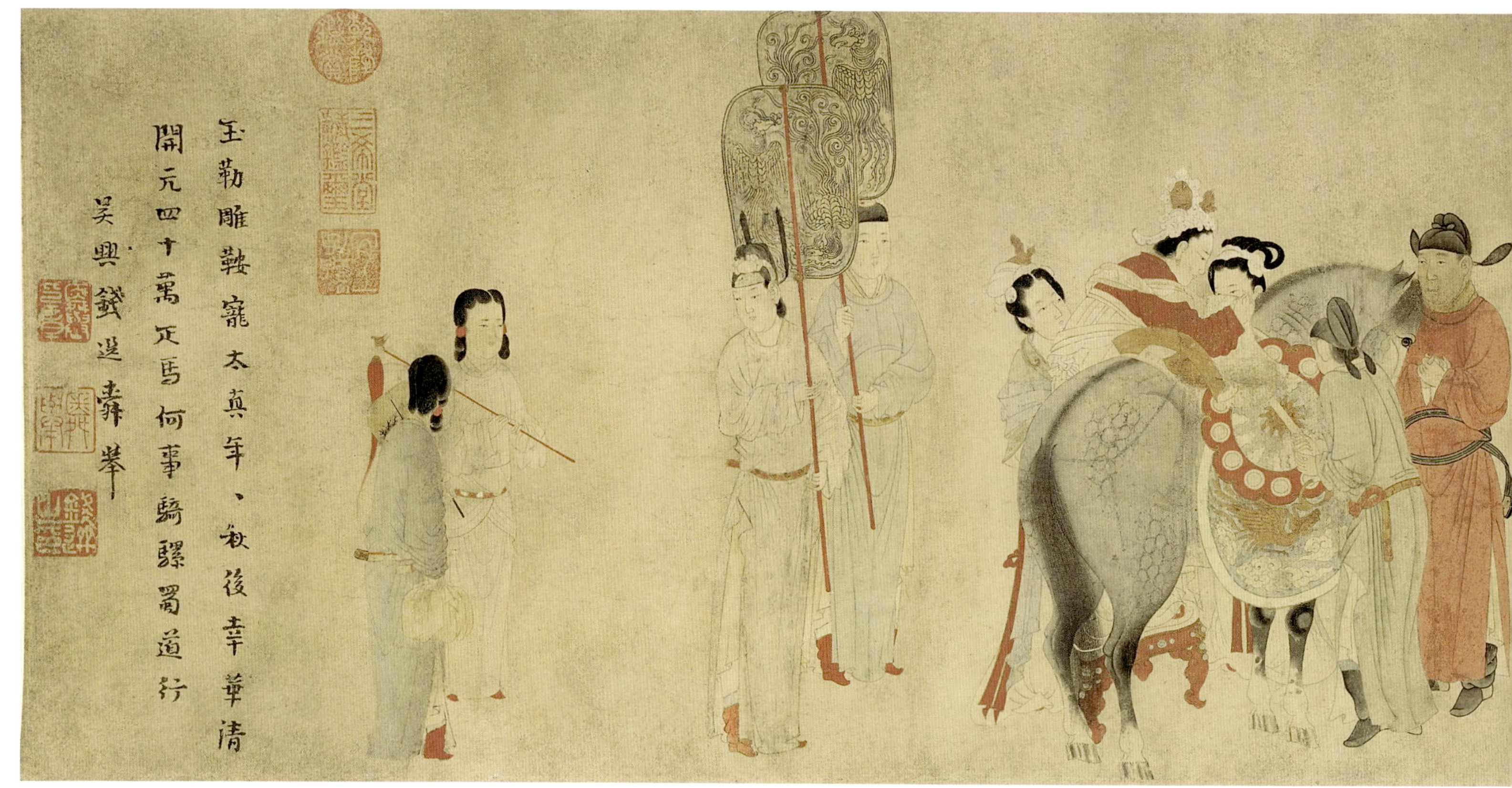

dress Yang Guifei had made popular when dancing. It is important to note how the distinctive physique of this time is portrayed in paintings not primarily through the representation of objectively large bodies, as one might expect a late-modern Western artist to do, but through qualities and traits of the body, and through activities.

Uninformed by the archaeological record, however, Kano Sansetsu's notion of mid-Tang figure paintings of Yang Guifei would have been shaped by canonical paintings, mainly of Song/Heian and later date, that had been handed down in collections, and by the living traditions, both elite and vernacular, of copying and reinventing past styles and subjects. Although such copies tended to generalise their sources, especially in the vernacular, they also deepened and enriched the tradition for contemporary audiences by making figures accessible – often by modernising the material culture or setting – as Li-chiang Lin argues when discussing the Ming artist Tang Yin's copy of the old master painting, *Night Revels of Han Xizai* (see p. 154). This effect is also discernible in the

ways the Minghuang–Yang Guifei story was embellished and retold in the intervening Song–Yuan period, often to suit a Confucian Chinese moral agenda.

Coming to the period of Mongol rule in China (thirteenth–fourteenth centuries), among the best-known painters of scenes of Minghuang and Yang Guifei was the celebrated late Song–early Yuan artist Qian Xuan (*c*.1235–1307). His handscroll *Yang Guifei Mounting a Horse* in the Freer Gallery, Washington, DC (fig. 10), is painted in an antiquarian vein that consciously refers to a Tang model such as Zhang Xuan, even while the topic can be seen to have served the artist's purpose as a Chinese loyalist to the defunct Song dynasty.[28] Visually, Song-dynasty paintings after Zhang Xuan (and others) present themselves as fairly straightforward pictorial copies or recensions of earlier works, albeit updated and modified in terms of brushwork and naturalism, but Qian Xuan's was painted at a time when artist's inscriptions, often of a poetic nature, were just beginning to occupy the pictorial space of a painting. *Yang Guifei Mounting a Horse* bears a poem-inscription by Qian Xuan reflecting on

FIG 10 Qian Xuan, *Yang Guifei Mounting a Horse*. Handscroll; ink and colours on paper, 29.5 x 117.0 cm. Freer Gallery of Art, Washington, DC. Purchase F1957.14.

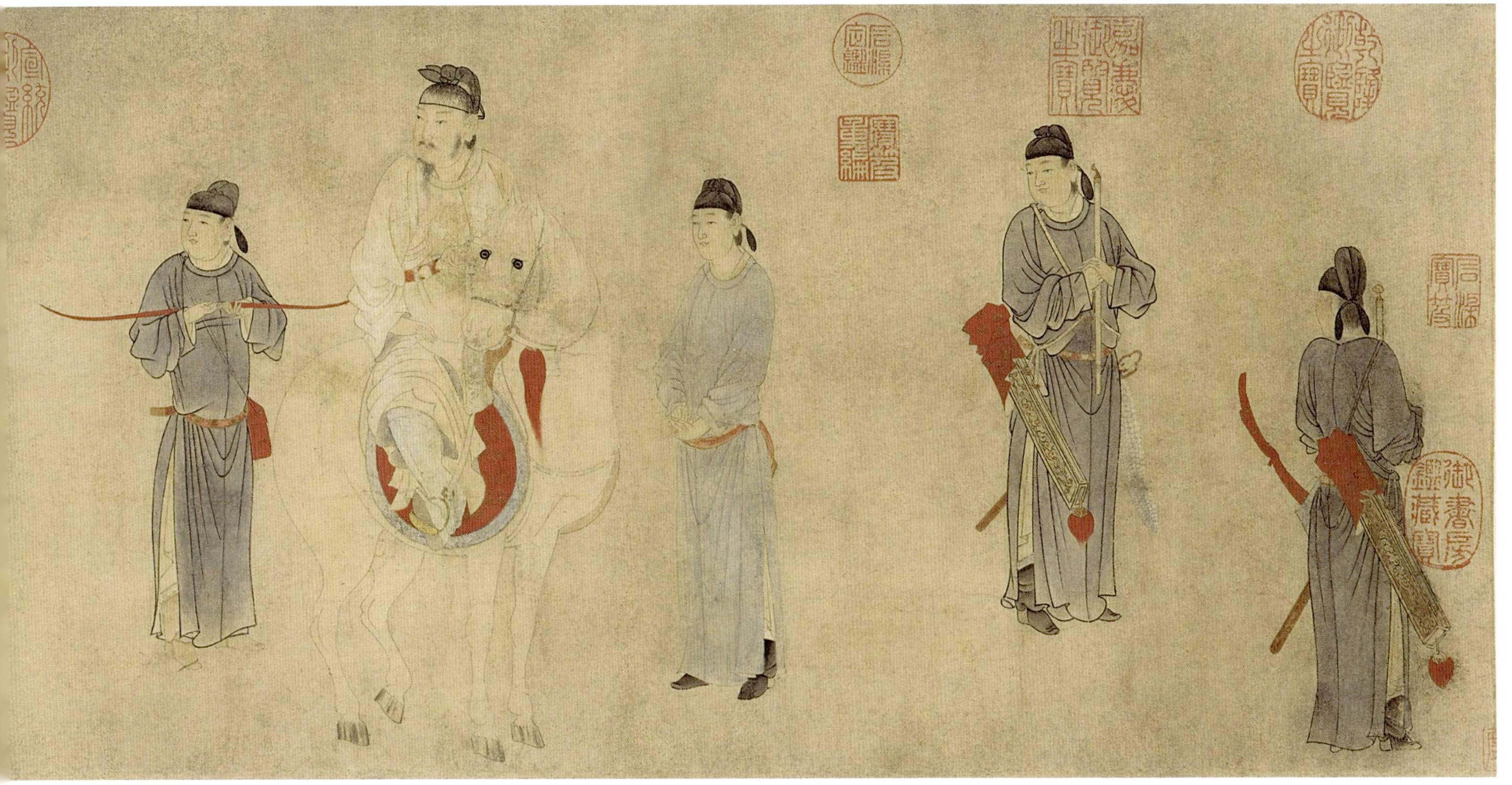

the Minghuang–Yang Guifei story, which is discussed below. Curiously, the *Chang hen ge* tale was not as comprehensively or widely illustrated as might be expected in later dynastic times (that is, second millennium AD) in China, perhaps because of the sensitivity of the subject at court.

As the illustrations in founding works of the 'court ladies' genre indicate, including the scenes of the *Admonitions* scroll dateable to the fifth or sixth century, Chinese painters had a predilection for capturing pivotal moments in human relationships. When the Minghuang–Yang Guifei story is illustrated in China it is often single apocryphal or didactic moments of the affair that are featured, being made to stand for the whole. The paintings of Yang Guifei awkwardly mounting a horse under Minghuang's doting gaze as they prepare to flee the palace is one example. Another is to be found in a scene of Yang Guifei dramatically cutting off a lock of her hair, which is depicted in a seventeenth-century handscroll of didactic subjects in the Freer Gallery, which is discussed below (see fig. 23).

The *Tale of Genji* is itself evidence that the subject was also painted in Heian Japan by court artist(s), but it was not a widely depicted subject before the late sixteenth century in Japan, as Matthew McKelway argues (see chapter four). The story has remained popular and highly recognisable in East Asia, notably in Chinese drama and fiction writing.[29] Since World War II a number of Chinese works have appeared under the title *Chang hen ge*, beginning with a film in Cantonese in black and white in 1952. Wang Anyi's celebrated 1996 novel of the same title, rendered into English as *Song of Everlasting Sorrow*, is a period drama that follows the life of a legendary Shanghai beauty from the 1940s to her murder in the 1980s. It was adapted for the stage in 2004 and the screen in 2005.[30] The focus of this book, however, is neither these books, dramas and films, nor the old Chinese and Japanese paintings, but rather the masterful *Chōgonka* painting in the Chester Beatty Library, executed in the early Edo period by Kano Sansetsu, head of the Kyoto Kano school from 1635 to his death in 1651.

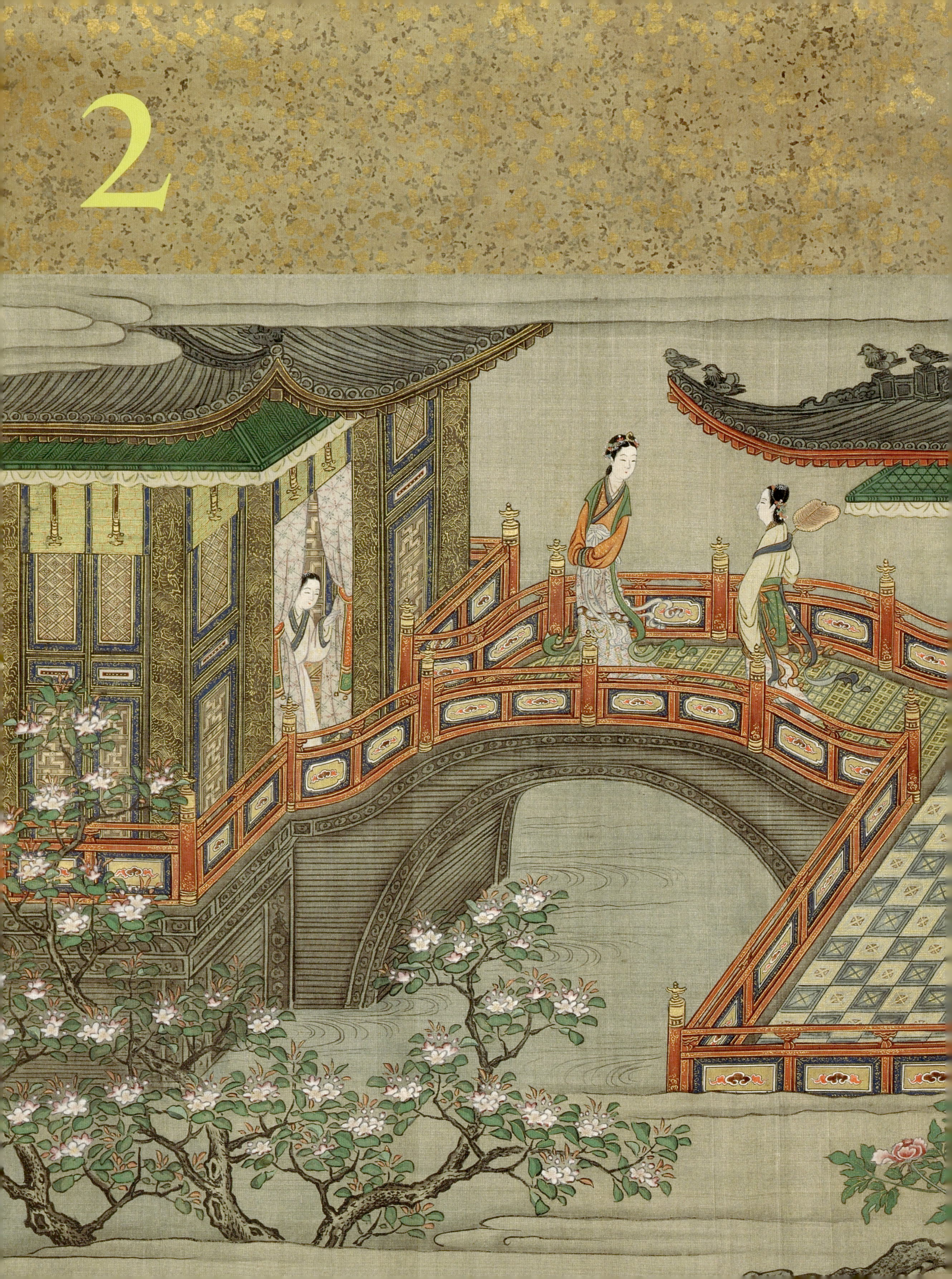
2

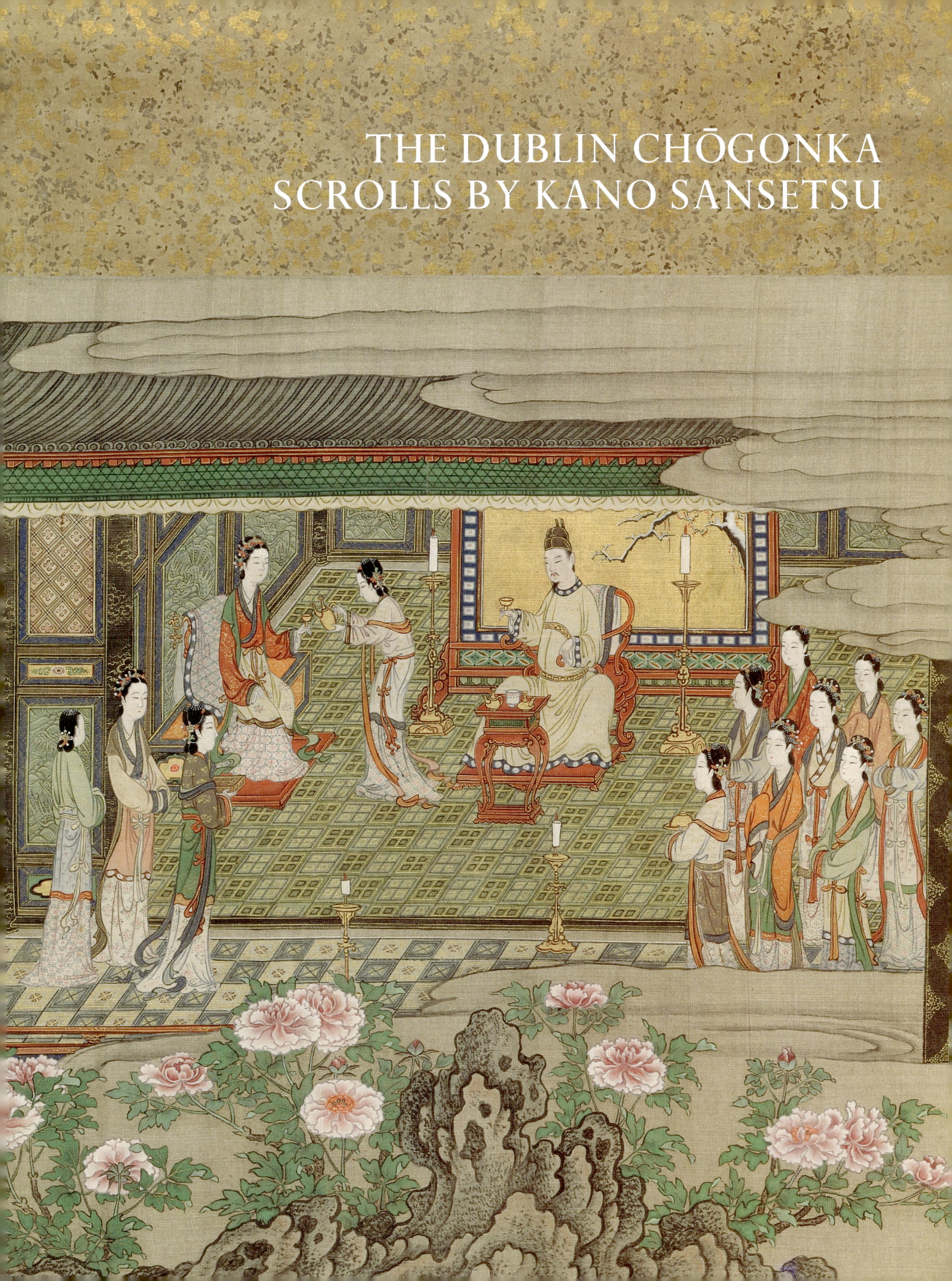
THE DUBLIN CHŌGONKA
SCROLLS BY KANO SANSETSU

THE DUBLIN *Chōgonka gakan* is a narrative painting closely based on Bai Juyi's (772–846) ballad 'Song of Lasting Sorrow' and, as such, gives visual form to poetry. Arguably, the painting is basically a translation of the poem more or less directly into visual imagery, yet in determining its historical position we also acknowledge a disparate tradition, as it were, of illustrating this story, or aspects of it. This is not to say that Sansetsu directly sourced his scenes, images and effects from his predecessors and contemporaries in China or Japan but for iconographic and technical purposes at least, he did incorporate devices and features from the wider world of East Asian visual art, and from narrative painting in particular. Sansetsu's connections with his forbears in the Kano school are the subject of considered discussion by Matthew McKelway in chapter four. Here, we consider mainly the formal plotting of the scrolls in relation to Chinese pictorial traditions, specifically the received type-forms for this genre and subject, and the narrative technique.

Overall, Sansetsu's painting has a stage-like quality. It appears to have some thirty-six scenes, eighteen on each of the two scrolls. Each scroll comprises six lengths of silk of roughly equal length (about 180 cm), while each length of silk presents a set, or 'act', of two or three painted scenes – recalling the format of scenes and acts in drama. In the first scroll the six 'acts' are:

- the discovery of Yang Guifei
- Minghuang and Yang Guifei's dalliance in the palace
- the rise of the Yang clan
- the neglect of state affairs and the foment of rebellion
- An Lushan's rebellion and the flight of the inner court
- the execution of Yang Guifei

Within and between these 'acts', the scenes are linked or divided using the signature visual tools of the Kano School: stylised clouds, powerful rock-forms, robust pines and other trees, and lavishly appointed buildings. The scenes are also plotted by various means such as the formal tipping and angling of the ground plane and the use of visual leitmotifs.

Broadly speaking, the stylistic features of the Dublin painting belong to the East Asian narrative tradition. In the treatment of figures, for instance, the social elite is by convention portrayed in a dignified manner and given mask-like faces. The labouring- and serving-class characters, including porters, grooms, soldiers and rebels are, by contrast, often rendered in burlesque caricature, as in traditional Japanese *emaki* (picture-scrolls) of the medieval period, and indeed in early Edo popular narrative scrolls and albums of the genre known as *Nara ehon* (Nara picture-books). The pictorial depiction of architecture, scenery, time and season is also conceived so as to suggest mood and to create atmosphere.

It is important to recognise that this is a strongly sympathetic portrayal of Tang-dynasty China. In one early depiction of Tang China in a Japanese handscroll the purpose was to show a Japanese visitor besting his Chinese hosts. This is also the case in a famous late twelfth-century illustration of the tale of the Japanese courtier Kibi's trials in China, *Minister Kibi's Trip to China (Kibi daijin nittō emaki)*, in the Museum of Fine Arts, Boston.[31] In that painting, Tang China is depicted as an outlandish, inhospitable place, whose people are disreputable. The Kibi painting is exceptional in this regard: other works, including various depictions of priests travelling to and from China, are rather exotic in tone. But in the case of the *Chōgonka* scrolls, what drives the narrative is epic and romantic rather than satirical or comic.

In part, formal elements connecting the scenes to China are crucial to the visual plotting. The plank-

Kano Sansetsu,'The fleeing court enters the mountains' (from **Flight through the mountains to Shu**), *Song of Lasting Sorrow*; scroll 2, the first length of silk.

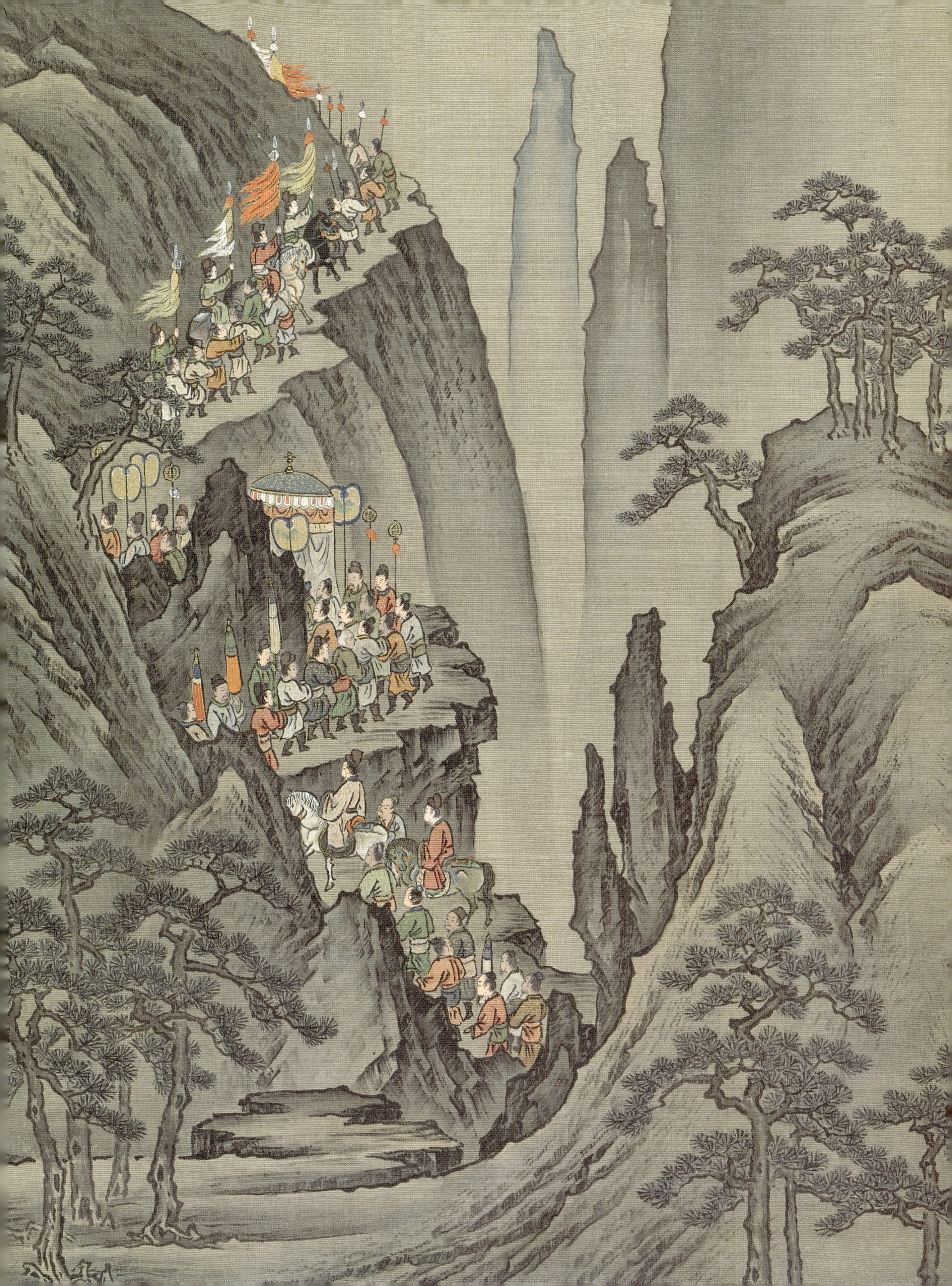

road route through the mountains from southern Shaanxi into Sichuan, for example, is an appropriate and specific image of the perils faced by Minghuang and his entourage as they escape the capital, and of the precariousness of human affairs. Elsewhere, intimate interiors conjure a sense of late-night passion, while towering, far-off palaces create an 'other-worldly' effect echoing the look of similarly themed paintings by mid-to-late Ming artists associated with the southern city of Suzhou, a cultural powerhouse. These include the professional Qiu Ying (1494–1552) and Wen Boren (1502–75), a nephew of the influential scholar-artist Wen Zhengming.[32]

There are no glaring indications in Sansetsu's early life of a future admiration for Chinese art. He joined the Kyoto branch of the Kano School under Sanraku and later married his daughter. On Sanraku's death in 1635 Sansetsu became master, a position he held until his own death in 1651. The Dublin painting dates to towards the end of that period: 1646–47. Despite his leadership role in the Kano School, Sansetsu's artistic vision has been described as eccentric, or else profoundly original.[33] He deeply admired Chinese painting, although he never visited China, and he was a scholar of painting: he compiled *History of Painting in this Realm* (*Honchō gashi*), completed by his son and pupil Kano Einō (1631–97) in 1693.[34]

Intellectually and as a painter, Sansetsu's interests chimed with those of the Kyoto patrons of the Kano School, as evidenced by his many paintings depicting Chinese subjects, such as his *West Lake* screens illustrating the Southern Song capital, Hangzhou (see fig. 62).[35] His signatures proudly display his regard for China, sometimes being written, as on the second Dublin *Chōgonka* scroll, in the clerical style developed in Han-dynasty (206 BC–AD 220) China (see fig. 83). This, even in seventeenth-century China, would have been construed as an antiquarian, scholarly

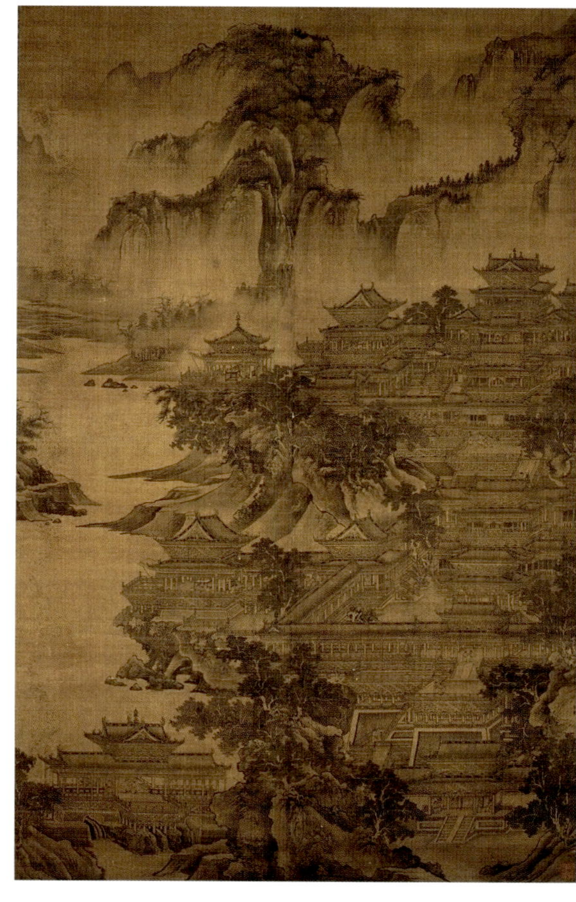

Fig 11 *Minghuang Avoiding the Summer Heat,* attributed to Li Rongjin (spurious seal of Guo Zhongshu) Hanging scroll; ink and colours on silk, 161.5 x 105.6 cm. Osaka Municipal Museum of Art.

mode of writing. Like his Edo contemporary and rival Kano Tan'yū (1602–74), who had an encyclopaedic knowledge of Chinese paintings in Japanese collections, Sansetsu admired Chinese paintings and had extensive access to the collections of temples and warlords.[36] These paintings had been transmitted to Japan since the High Tang, but perhaps only in significant numbers during the Yuan and early Ming periods. Sansetsu must have known from books, recensions and related images about canonical Chinese paintings like *Minghuang's Flight to Shu*, now in the National Palace Museum, Taipei.[37]

Much of the responsibility, as it were, for the transmission of Chinese painting subjects and styles to Japan lay with the Yuan masters who worked in Song and earlier styles, like supremely gifted early-

Yuan court painter Wang Zhenpeng (*c*.1280–1329) and his close followers, including Li Rongjin, whose art blurred the brittle stylistic distinctions between 'amateur' and 'professional' made by later Chinese critics. Li Rongjin seems to have specialised in hanging-scroll compositions, as detailed as they are large, of the opulent palaces of antiquity built among hoary mountains, in the mode of Guo Zhongshu (*c*.910–77), the leading Northern Song master of architectural or 'ruled line' painting (*jiehua*). A work in the Taipei Palace Museum bearing his seal is entitled *The Han Palace*.[38]

A strikingly similar painting in Osaka Municipal Museum of Art is entitled *Minghuang Avoiding the Summer Heat* (fig. 11), which bears a spurious seal of Guo Zhongshu and is probably by Li Rongjin.[39] It shows a vast and beautifully appointed palace standing majestically among cooling riverside mists deep in the mountains. These highlands are painted in the distinctive Li-Guo mode of the Northern Song landscape masters. Occupying half of the painting, the palace complex itself comprises numerous paved courtyards bounded by covered colonnades and interlinked by flights of steps, waterside pavilions and high-rise terraces, and is dotted with tiny figures. A generic scene, there is no reason why it should be seen to represent Minghuang avoiding the summer heat, but the attachment of the title to the painting clearly adds to the narrative interest of such a composition. How relevant were such images to the making of the *Chōgonka* painting in the form of a set of handscrolls? And what are the characteristics of the visual plotting of the narrative, be they Chinese, Japanese or a form of both? In the Dublin painting, what type-forms and stylistic sources from China can be identified, and what role might Sansetsu have assigned to them?

The point in asking these questions is not to suggest that *China* can resolve the puzzle of this painting for us but it should be borne in mind that despite its long history in Japan, the narrative is Chinese and Sansetsu deeply admired Chinese culture. We can assume that he wished to invest a degree of cultural authenticity into his painting by means of a judicious convergence with Chinese sources that were either known or becoming known in his circle of patronage. In a recent article on the Dublin *Chōgonka* painting the Japanese scholar Itakura Masaaki had proposed various Chinese painters and their works as sources, including Tang Yin and Qiu Ying (see above), and the eccentric landscapist Wu Bin (active 1568–1626)[40] – painters active in the century and a half to the mid-1640s, who were all representative of mid-to-late Ming literati painting culture.[41]

Much in vogue in early Edo Japan as contemporary sources about China were imported woodblock-print-illustrated books of literature and encyclopaedia, including *Extraordinary Views of the World [i.e. China] (Hainei qiguan)* of 1609, which catered to a growing market for tourist guides and travel literature, as well as *Pictorial Compendium of the Three Realms (Sancai tuhui)*, the encyclopaedia published in the same year. Both illustrate burgeoning tourist sites including the plank roads of southern Shaanxi (Minghuang's escape route), as well as the ranges of Mount Emei south of Chengdu in Sichuan (his place of refuge). It is worth noting that the socio-economic conditions for such publications across East Asia comprised a dramatically expanding literacy rate and new opportunities for social mobility; broadening global horizons, as new knowledge and knowledge systems were being introduced, by Jesuits, for example; and great leaps in print technology, which also contributed to the boom in the publishing industry. This may also have contributed to a Japanese nostalgia for old China, as portrayed in the *Chōgonka* scrolls.

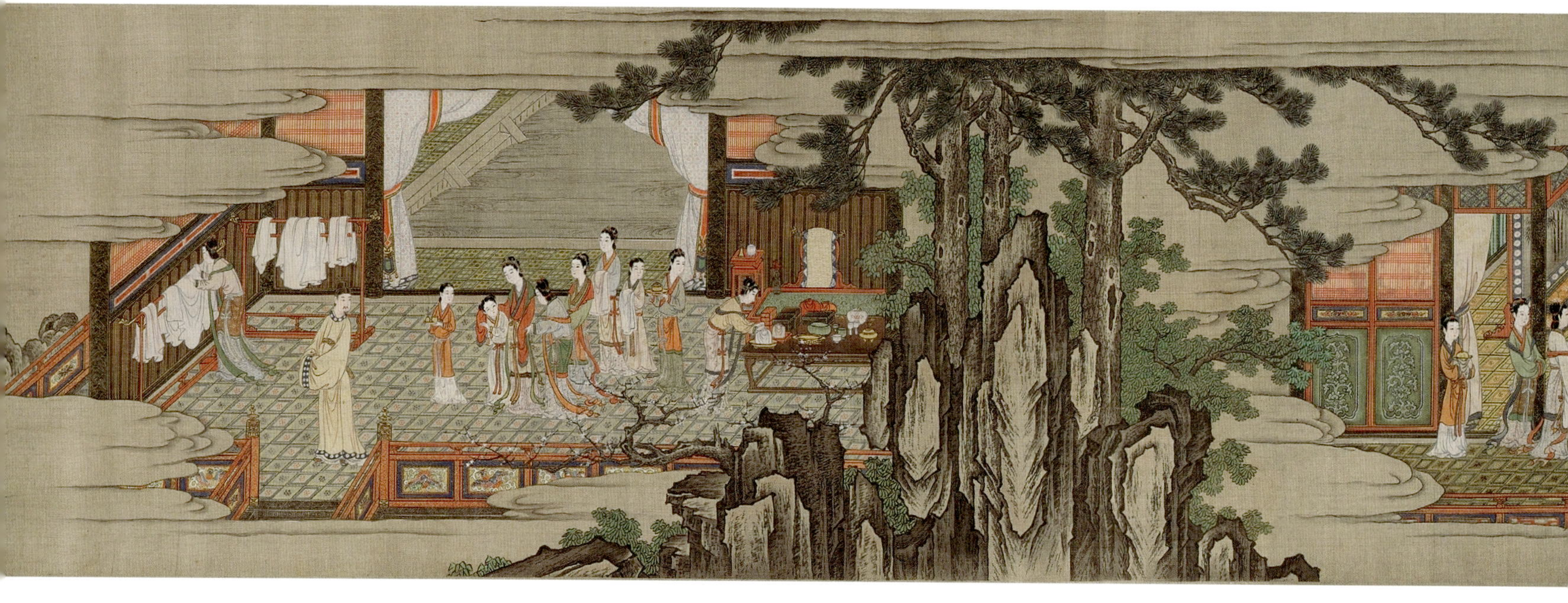

THE FIRST SCROLL

THE YANG LADY IS DISCOVERED (FIG. 12)

Han's sovereign prized the beauty of flesh,
  he longed for such as ruins domains;
for many years he ruled the Earth
  and sought for one in vain.[42]
A daughter there was of the house of Yang,
  just grown to maturity,
raised deep in the women's quarters
  where no man knew of her.

5 *When Heaven begets beauteous things,*
  it is loath to let them be wasted,
so one morning this maiden was chosen
  to be by the ruler's side.
When she turned around with smiling glance,
  she exuded every charm;
in the harem all who wore powder and paint
  of beauty then seemed barren.

In springtime's chill he let her bathe
  in Huaqing Palace's pools
10 *whose warm springs' glistening waters*
  washed flecks of dried lotions away.
Those in attendance helped her rise,
  in helplessness so charming –
this was the moment when first she enjoyed
  the flood of royal favour.

THE FIRST SCENE is a tiled courtyard of the Yang household. Although surrounded by a small but handsome stand of trees and one rather majestic overhanging pine on a rock, its buildings are simply appointed. To the right, speaking with her nurse, is the young Yang lady. She seems ready to emerge from the inner chamber, where she has been figuratively screened from the world by swathes of thickly draped curtains. To the left, her father and mother are seated to receive a visitor. From the emperor's envoy they hear the news that has set the household buzzing – that their beautiful daughter has been summoned to the imperial palace. The painting thus opens to a scene of one of Emperor Minghuang's scouts visiting the home of the Yang clan, where the young maiden who will become Yang Guifei is discovered. Intriguingly, Sansetsu's painting does not open as the ballad does, with an image of the restless emperor, but instead dramatises one of the significant elements of the romance: the maiden Yang's childhood in the bosom of a socially unexceptional family.

Plucked from this relative obscurity she is enrolled into the imperial harem where, as the following scene shows, she at once puts her rivals in the shade with her elegance and beauty. Between the scenes a flowering fruit tree points up the steps towards where the lady is seated. The simple surroundings of her childhood home are changed for the polychrome finery of Minghuang's 'back palace',

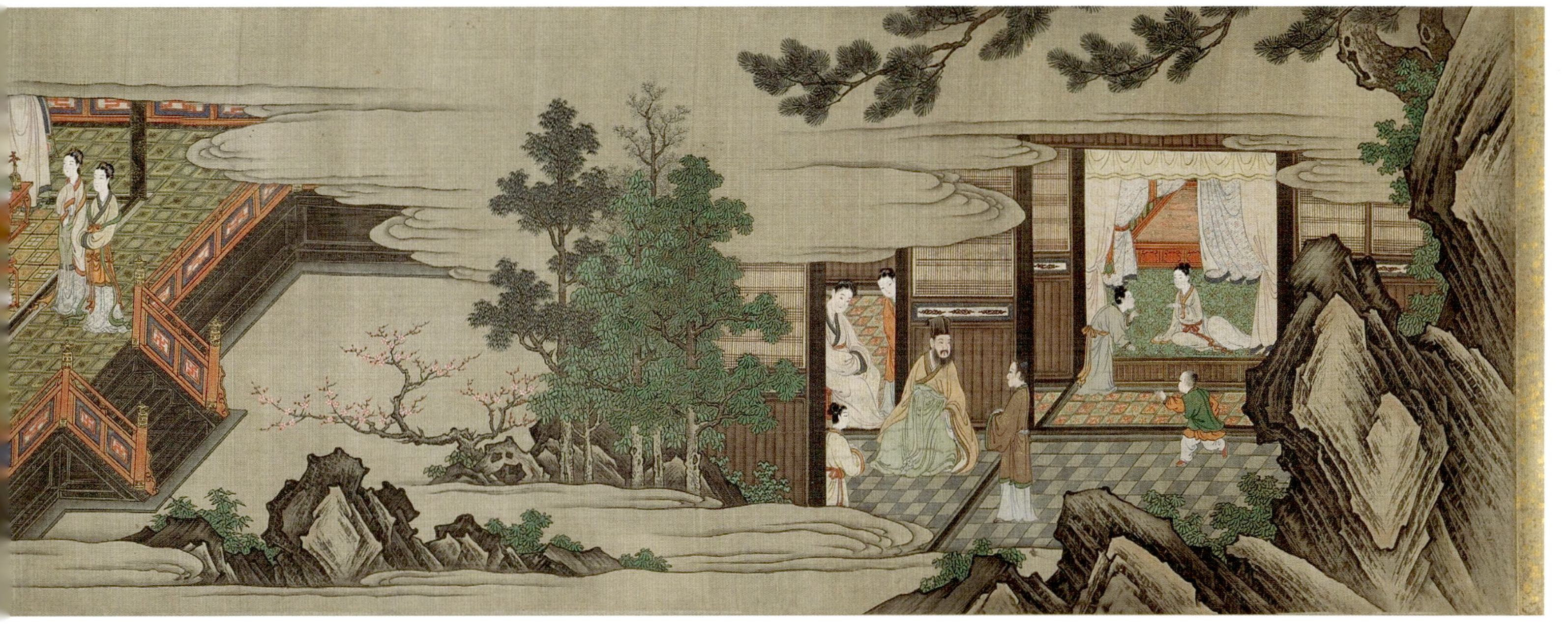

where his wives and concubines were quartered.

We should not underestimate the importance of the many lavish decorative surfaces as a technical and expressive feature of the pictorial narrative. Here, as throughout the painting, it is as much the opulently decorated detailing of the furnishings, architecture and plantings as any pictorial portrayals of Yang Guifei's figure that serve to enrich and deepen the mental impression of her physical beauty and allure.

Having exchanged her girlhood dresses for a fashionable floral headdress and swirling tassels to her robe, the Yang lady takes pride of place and sits on a long bench in front of a freestanding screen painted with a symbol of purity and nobility – ink bamboo.

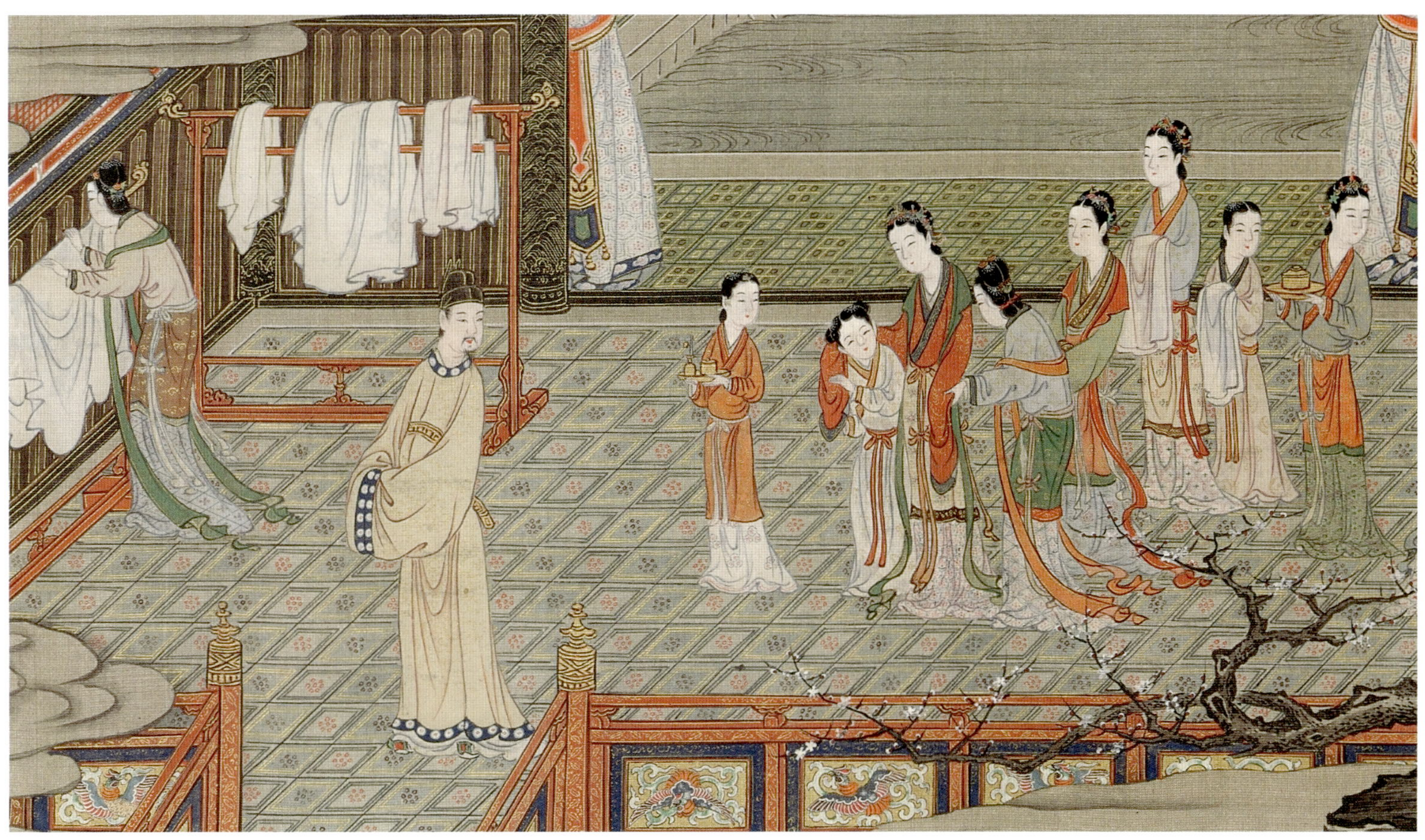

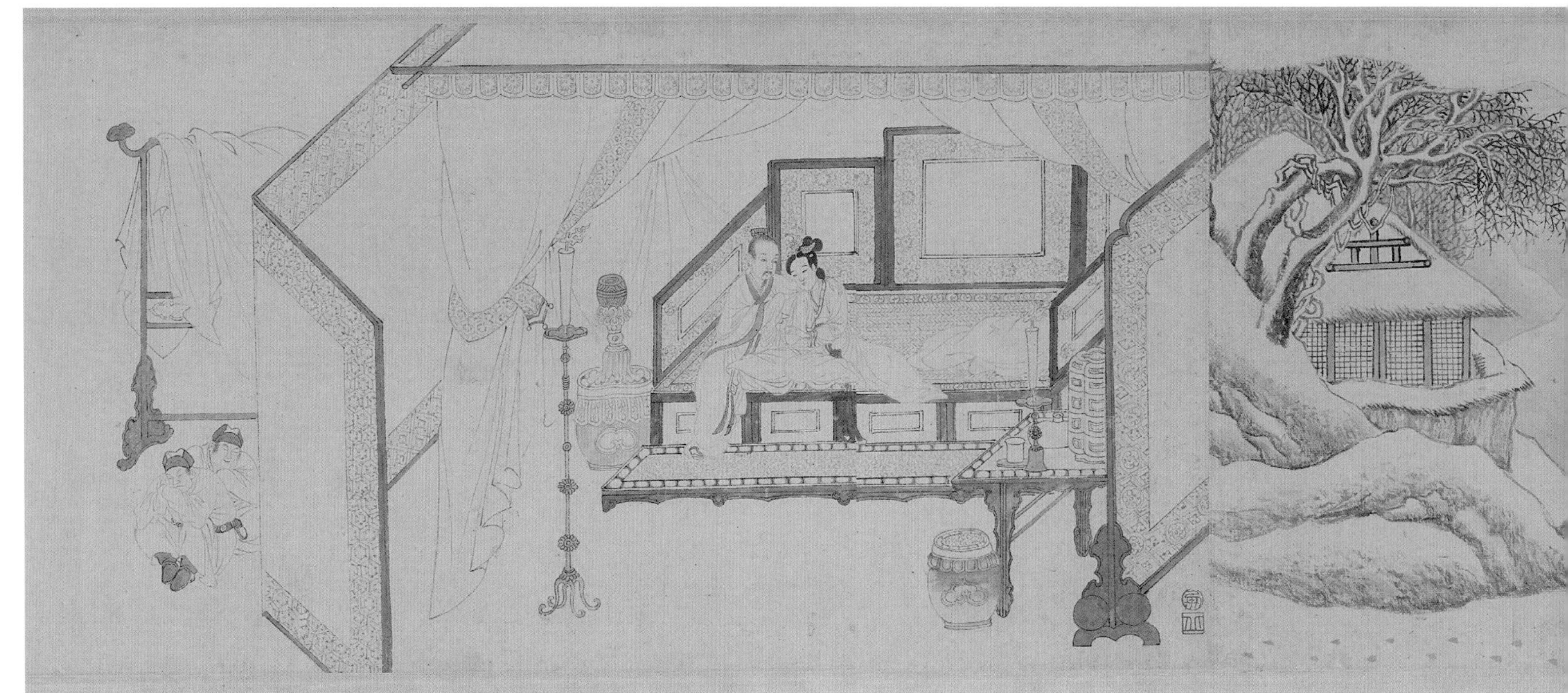

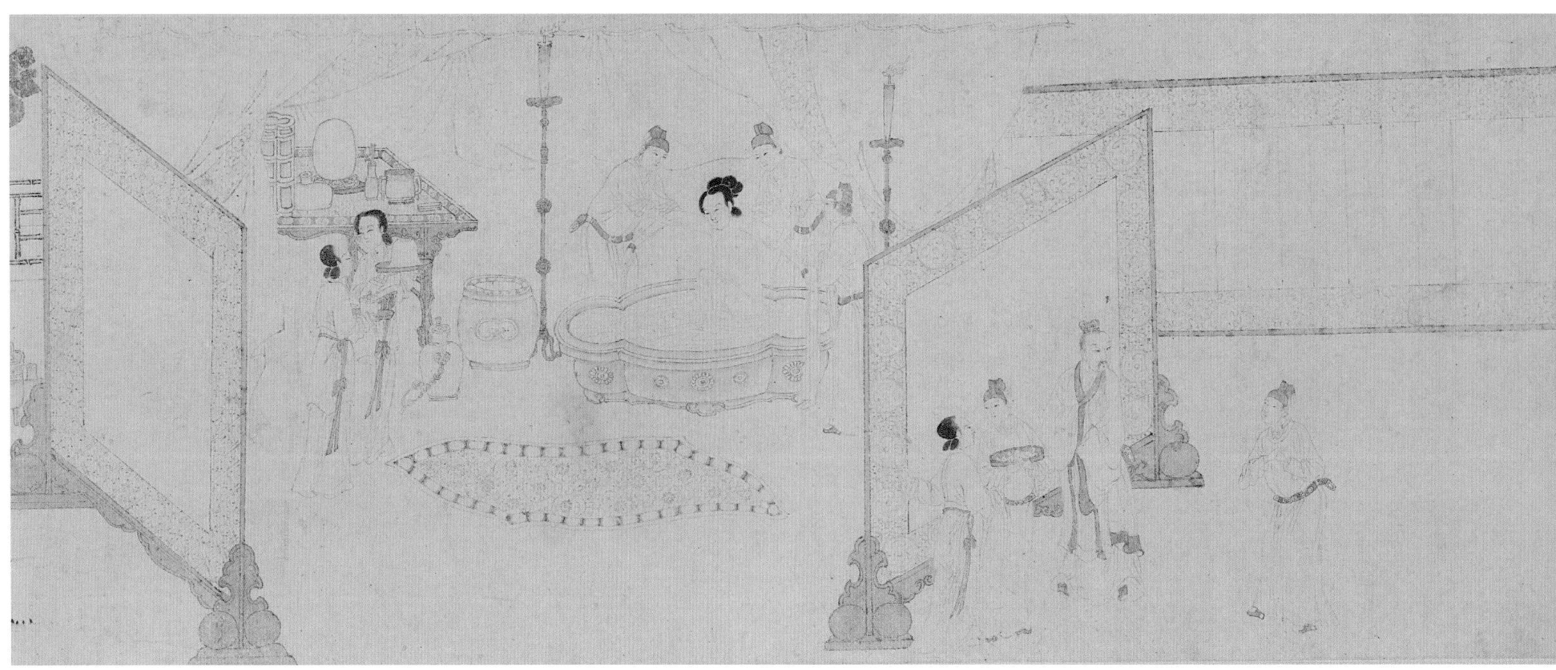

In a clever allusion, this style of ink bamboo painting – the bamboo clump in mist – recalls the work of one of China's best-known women artists, Guan Daosheng (d. 1319), the Duchess-of-State of Wei and wife of the Yuan statesman and artist, Zhao Mengfu (1254–1322). By implication, although anachronistically, the image serves to define this scene in the Tang imperial harem as a feminine space of the most rarefied and cultured kind. The figure of the Yang lady gestures, in what must be interpreted as a most gracious hand movement, towards two court ladies standing before her. Like the other two to the left, they appear to be gazing at her in admiration of her shining qualities. Each panel of the nearby railing is decorated with a multi-coloured phoenix, a symbol in dynastic China of the empress, and here, a portent of the Yang lady's heady rise to a position of supreme power in the Tang royal house.

In this version of the romance she does not attract the emperor's attention until some time later, when she is noticed by him one day stepping out of the hot spring at Huaqing (fig. 13), a spa that provided respite

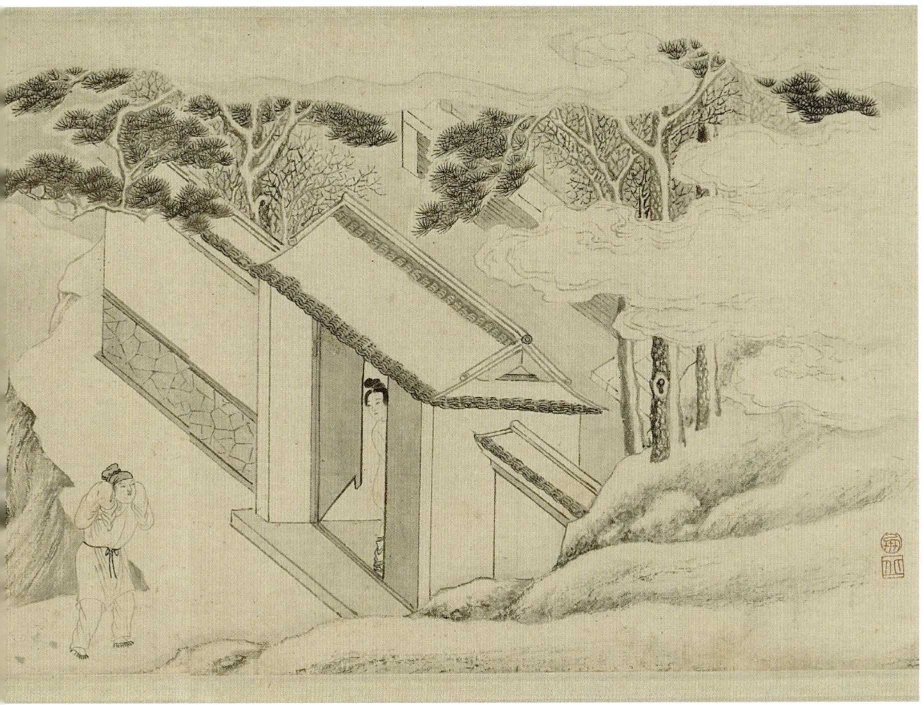

from the winter's chill at the imperial winter palace complex in the eastern suburbs of the capital. The wintry theme in the third scene is set by the flowering plum tree in the foreground, yet another powerful symbol of purity, long associated with lofty Chinese values of humanity, but also, appropriately, not without erotic connotations. The picture shows the Yang lady being supported at the elbow by maids, and in her helpless frailty she has literally turned the head of the emperor who stands a few feet away. For the sake of decorum, the emperor does not appear old and lustful, as the ballad might imply, but young and admiring; nor does the Yang lady step naked, or even wrapped in towels, from her steam bath, having been washed clean of her body lotions. Although the hot spring bubbles away naturalistically in the background, and a lady reaches to add another white towel to the jumble on the rails to the left, curiously, the Yang lady has already been fully dressed by her many admiring helpers. If the viewer's imagination is required to complete the scene visually, the essential concept – that Minghuang fell for her helpless demeanour – is conveyed by the body language and eye contact of the protagonists. To a Western eye accustomed to and conditioned by the tradition of the nude in art, this portrayal of Yang Guifei might seem prudish, but it is important to recognise that the human body was never represented in the objective

manner of European artists. Rather, the body in East Asian art should be recognised as defined by its own cultural sphere, in which clothing, setting, texture, body language and figural styling such as outline technique, for instance, all play significant roles in the creation of expression and meaning.

Kano Sansetsu's portrayal of Yang Guifei in the bath scene contrasts with a somewhat unusual depiction of a similar encounter in a scroll from late sixteenth-century China. The Han-dynasty empress Zhao Feiyan and her sister Bright Consort Zhao Hede (see chapter one) were subjects of a biographical narrative painting entitled *Spring Morning in the Han Palace* by You Qiu (1525–80) in the Shanghai Museum (fig. 14). Historically, the figure of Zhao Feiyan was understood as the idealised 'slim' beauty, in contrast to Yang Guifei's fuller figure. In You Qiu's scroll, which features a single nude depiction of each Zhao sister, Feiyan is portrayed half-hidden from the viewer by a door. As if to reaffirm the image of her as an idealised sex partner is the anachronism of her bound feet, which was a custom that was only introduced for Chinese women in the Song dynasty (960–1279). It is interesting to note, also, in the penultimate scene – of Zhao Hede at her bath (fig. 15) – that the emperor is an out-and-out voyeur. According to the accompanying text, when she discovers he is watching her she immediately covers herself and has the lights dimmed. The only way he can continue to spy on her on future nights is by bribing her servants to say nothing about his presence behind a screen.

In the opening biographical details, as indeed throughout, Bai Juyi's ballad is not historically accurate, nor, being a romance, was it intended as such. As noted above, the role of chronicler of the tale fell to Bai Juyi's friend Chen Hong. According to his 'Account', Minghuang spotted the Yang lady among the many court ladies of his own harem and his family's, whom he invited to bathe in the hot spring at Huaqing, and then charged his favourite eunuch Gao Lishi (683–762) with finding her:

> In those days every year in December the imperial entourage would journey to Huaqing Palace. The titled women, both from the inner palace and from without, would follow him like luminous shadows. And he would grant them baths in the warm waters there, in the very waves that had bathed the imperial sun. Holy fluids in a springlike breeze went rippling through those places. It was then that His Majesty's heart was smitten: for he had truly come upon the one woman, and all the fair flesh that surrounded him seemed to him like dirt. He summoned Gao Lishi to make a secret search for this woman in the palaces of the princes; and there, in the establishment of the Prince of Shou, he found the daughter of Yang Xuanyan. She had already become a mature woman.

Nevertheless, Kano Sansetsu conforms to and exploits this poetic licence to advantage. The Yang lady is said in the poem and shown in the painting, for instance, to be 'unknown'. It is true that she came from a relatively obscure clan, the Yang, but she was not removed from the bosom of her family by a talent scout on Minghuang's behalf. Chen Hong's 'Account' names her father as Yang Xuanyan. He was a man from Hongnong (Henan Province), who served as an official in Shu (Sichuan Province). Her own name was Yuhuan. Her parents both died when she was young and she was raised by an uncle, Yang Xuanjiao, who served as a military official in Henan. She was summoned to the palace in 732, but not to the emperor's harem. Rather, she was a wife of one of Minghuang's sons, Li Mao, who was the Prince of Shou.

After the deaths of his Empress Yuanxian and Consort Wuhui, who had both enjoyed the emperor's favour, none of the many daughters of good families in Minghuang's back palace caught his fancy. 'Fretful and displeased', as Chen Hong describes him, Minghuang took to gazing upon the women in his sons' entourages while they bathed in the hot springs at Huaqing. Minghuang became infatuated with Yang Yuhuan in the early 740s. The bathing scene in the *Chōgonka* makes sense as an illustration of Minghuang's first sight of her, or it might show another moment after Gao Lishi discovered her, which is recorded by Chen Hong:

> He ordered a special channel of the warm springs cut for her and commanded that it be offered to her gleaming fineness. When she came out of the water, her body seemed frail and her force spent, as if she could not even bear the weight of lace and gauze; yet she shed such radiance that it shone on all around her. His Majesty was most pleased.

In order to separate her formally from his son Li Mao, Minghuang had her take vows as a Daoist nun for two years and she took a new name, Taizhen (literally 'great true one'). Afterwards, she entered the emperor's harem and was bestowed the honorific title of 'Precious Consort' Yang in 745.[43]

In fact, Yang Guifei's clan was renowned for producing beauties, and the emperor was not attracted to her alone: he doted on her elder sisters as well and had them portrayed by his court artists. Part of the historical appeal of these portraits of the Yang sisters is that, because they predated that seismic moment for the Tang dynasty – An Lushan's rebellion – they

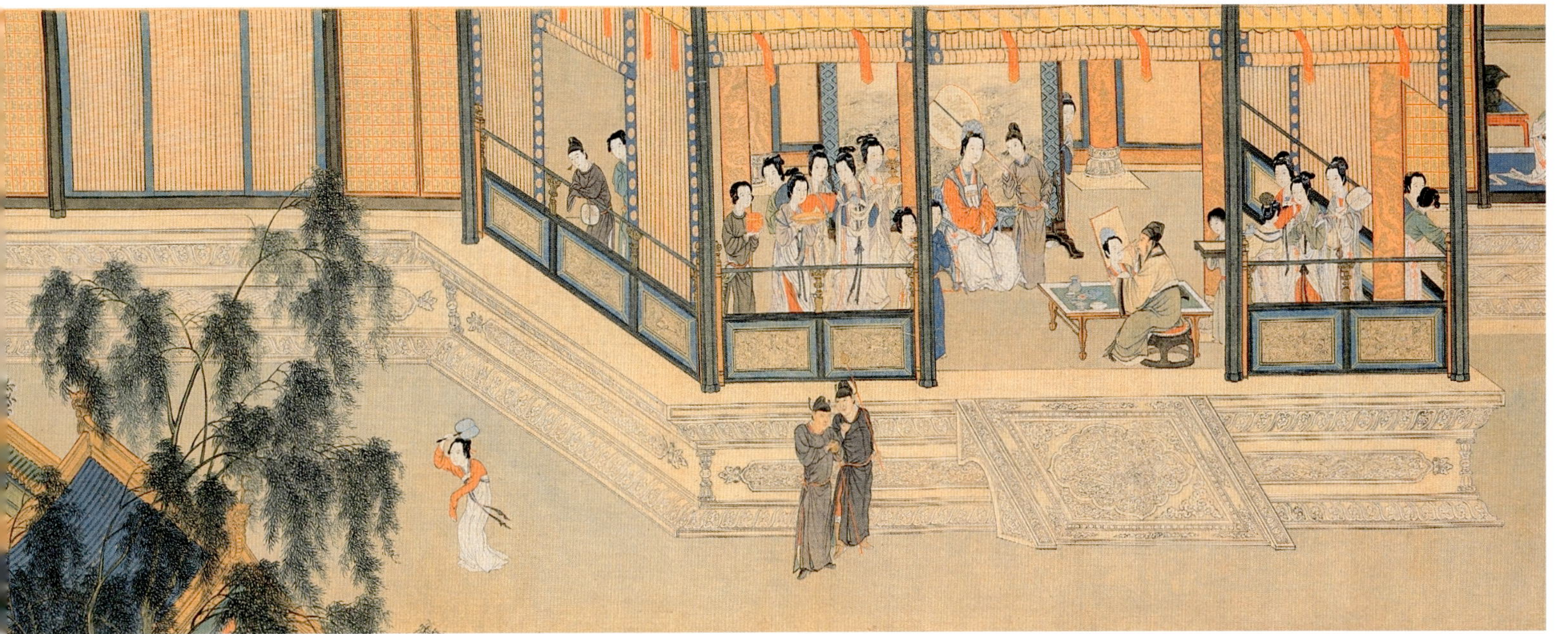

embodied, in the imaginination at least, a time of true dynastic greatness, before the loss of innocence. The ballad, however, concentrates entirely on Yang Guifei's relationship with Minghuang, and in an epic form not found in other historical anecdotes of their life together. Likewise, the Dublin *Chōgonka* was conceived as a full-blown narrative painting based on Bai Juyi's ballad, and rather than letting one or just a few pertinent scenes do duty for the entire story, Sansetsu elected to plot the tale in a series of many acts and scenes in a stage-like format. In part, this allowed for the use of more traditionally Japanese examples of visual suggestion, such as the lavish surface décor of drapery and furnishings, the manipulation of viewing angles on buildings, and the placement of symbolic plants and flowers close to events to suggest sentiment and mood or to otherwise convey ideas. These were devices that referred back to the early masterpieces of Japanese narrative art such as the *Tale of Genji* scrolls (see fig. 2), as already noted.

To keep his retelling relevant, however, and seemingly to update the iconography of opulence and beauty, Sansetsu seems to have referenced the art of more modern Chinese painters, among them Qiu Ying. As noted above, Qiu Ying is a possible formal source, particularly for the inner palace scenery, including the courtyards, colonnades and furnishings, but also for the figures of elegant palace ladies. Bai Juyi's ballad refers to the several thousand beauties of Minghuang's harem by reference to the 'Six Palaces', a

standard allusion to the palace lodgings of the court ladies during the Han dynasty. Pictorially, the 'Six Palaces' is precisely the topic of Qiu Ying's masterful handscroll *Spring Morning in the Han Palace* in Taipei (fig. 16). At first glance this handscroll appears to be a genre painting of mid-Ming beauties but the title also works as a kind of catch-all for vignettes of Han court ladies. Narrative elements in the painting include the scene of the beauties being painted, an allusion to the famous story of the righteous and beautiful Wang Zhaojun, who was one of the several thousand concubines of Han emperor Yuandi (r. 48–33 BC).[44]

Emperor Yuandi's successor on the Han throne was Chengdi, whose promotion of the willowy beauty Zhao Feiyan from dancing girl to empress was portrayed in You Qiu's *Spring Morning in the Han Palace*. Such stories provided precedents for Yang Guifei's dramatic rise that would have lain in the consciousness of viewers of the third scene of the *Chōgonka* scroll – that moment when, although literally thousands of women are available to him, Minghuang finds his head suddenly turned by his first glimpse of the Yang lady. Whereas Han emperors Yuandi and Chengdi went down in history as bad rulers who ultimately contributed to the usurpation of the dynasty by Wang Mang (the so-called interregnum period), through ballads like Bai Juyi's – which Kano Sansetsu stays true to – Minghuang's cultural image was preserved as that of an exemplary ruler who, late in life, got his wish for a woman who could topple kingdoms.

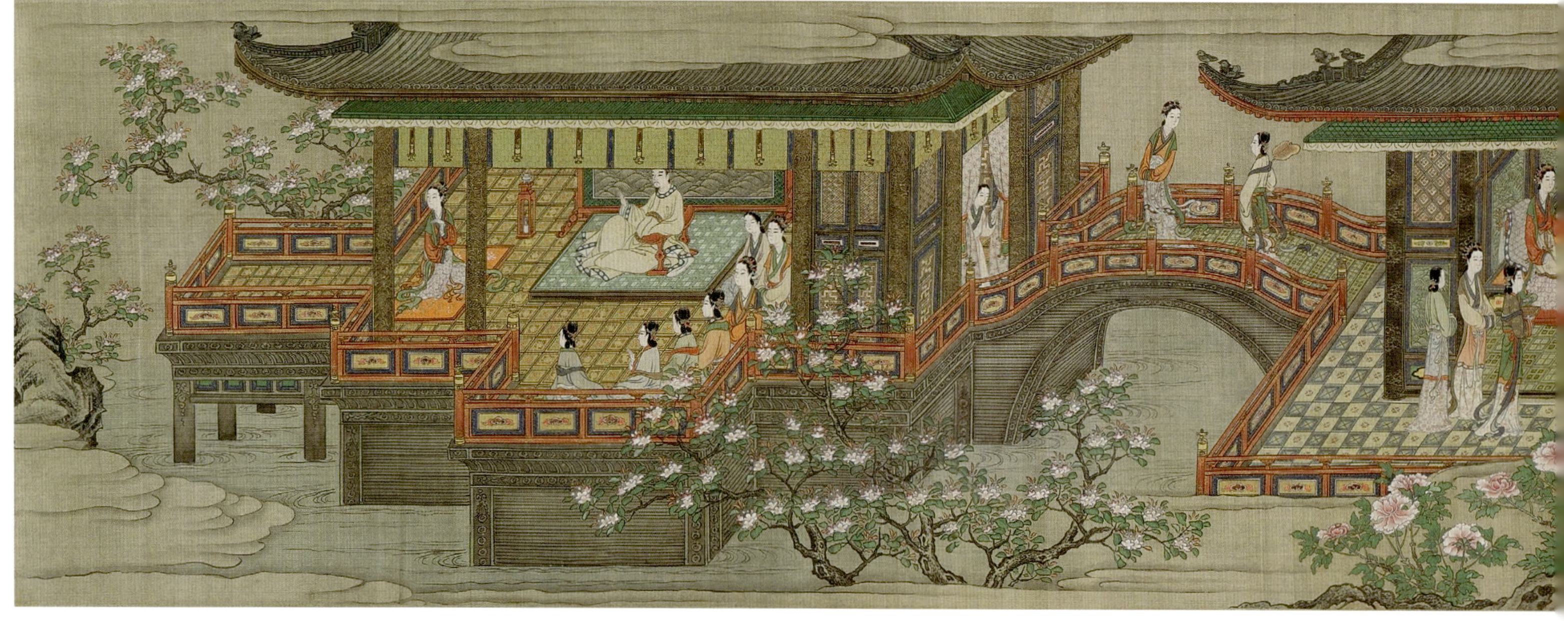

MINGHUANG'S DALLIANCE (FIG. 17)

Tresses like cloud, face like a flower,
 gold pins that swayed to her steps;
it was warm in the lotus-embroidered tents
 where they passed the nights of spring.
15 *And the nights of spring seemed all too short,*
 the sun would too soon rise,
from this point on our lord and king
 avoided daybreak court.

She waited his pleasure at banquets,
 with never a moment's peace,
their springs were spent in the outings of spring,
 he was sole lord of her nights.
In the harems there were beauties,
 three thousand there were in all,
20 *but the love that was due to three thousand*
 was spent on one body alone.
Her make-up completed in chambers of gold,
 she attended upon his nights,
when in marble mansions feasts were done,
 their drunkenness matched the spring.

IT IS AFTER MINGHUANG spies the Yang lady emerging, swaying, from the hot spring at Huaqing in the last scene that he first 'bestows his favour' on her, and these three pictures describe the unceasing nocturnal pleasures that they share thereafter in golden rooms and jade towers. In each case she is depicted in a position of favour to the emperor's right, while nearby plantings of shrubs and canopies of flowering trees in the height of bloom stand for her beauty. Even though others of his three thousand women stand by, she monopolises his attention, to the extent that he now skips the dawn audience during which the day-to-day matters of government business are conducted. Grave consequences are implied by this neglect of his duty as Son of Heaven in favour of sexual liaisons with Yang Guifei. In each of the three scenes the emperor's fixation with her is represented by a telling bodily action – his fixed gaze upon Yang Guifei while she is demurely engaged in one or another service on his behalf.

In the ballad, the poet repeatedly refers to spring, a euphemism by which the natural warming and vigorous growth of the season represent deepening sexual intimacy and climax. In fact, the repetition of the word 'spring' (*chun*) in the poem represents the couple's repeated sexual unions. The repeated references to spring also carry the tragic sense that the couple must make the most of this season, for later, after Yang Guifei's death, the emperor will live out the autumn and winter of his life alone.

FIG 17 Kano Sansetsu, Minghuang's dalliance, *Song of Lasting Sorrow*; scroll 1, the second length of silk.

FIG 18 'Minghuang and Yang Guifei in the nuptial bedchamber' (from Minghuang's dalliance), *Song of Lasting Sorrow*; (detail of fig. 17).

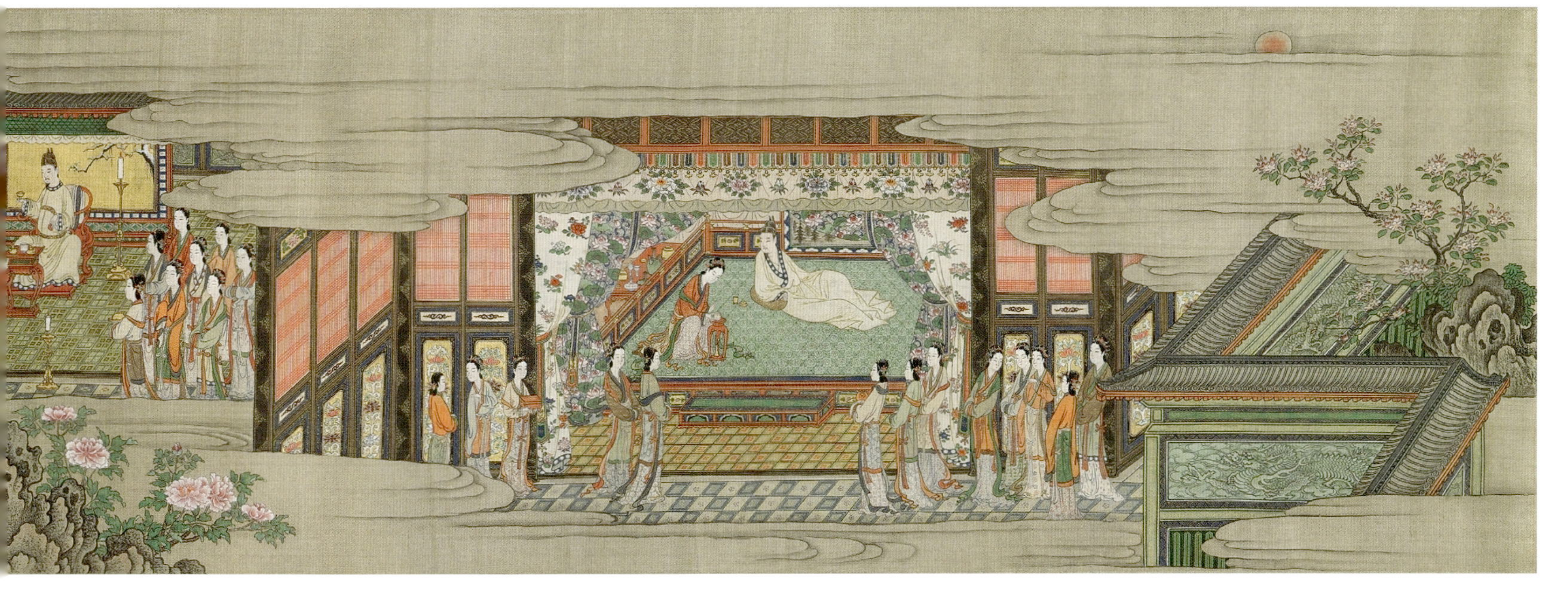

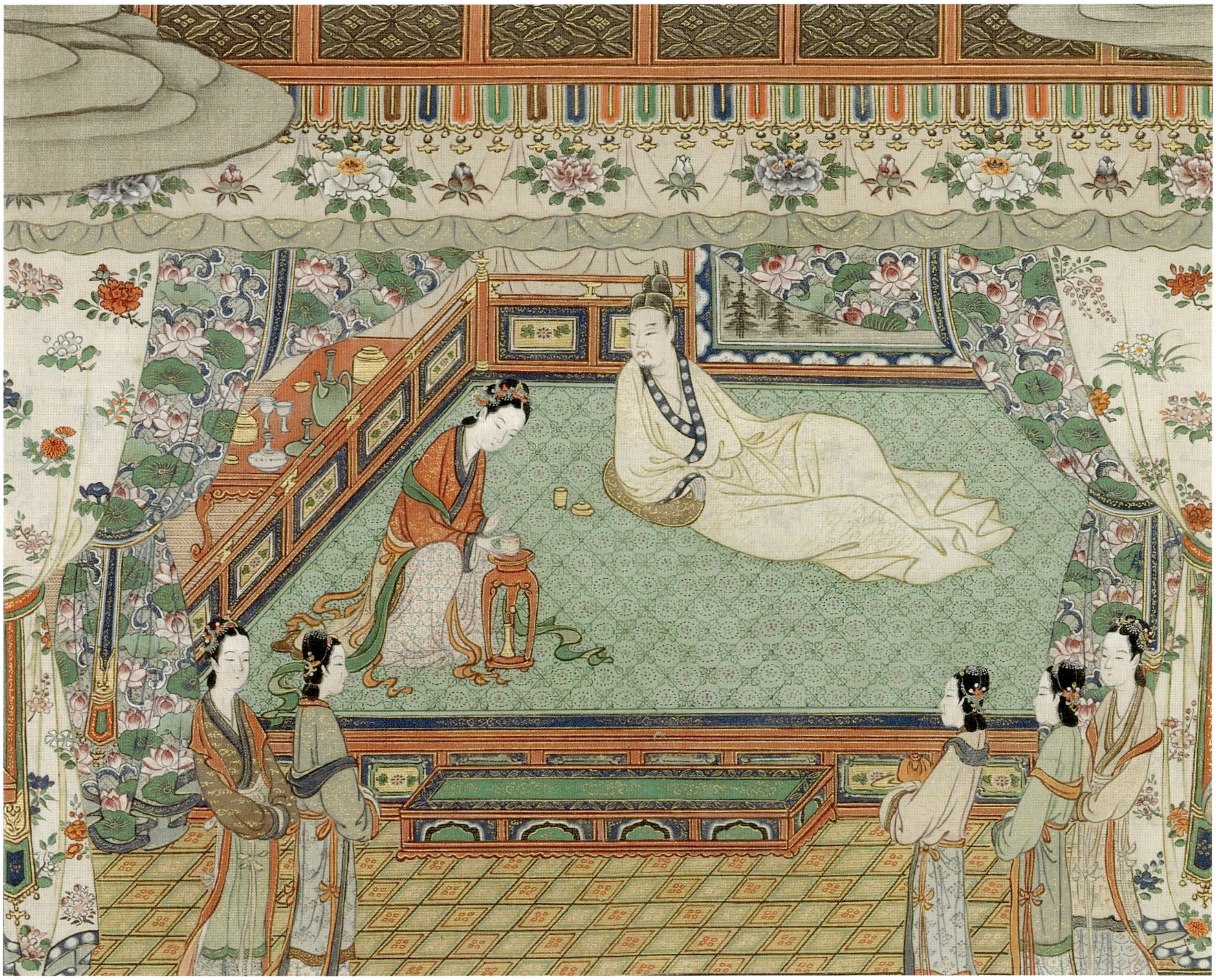

The first scene, one of the most remarkable of the entire painting, shows a strikingly rich depiction of the couple together, as Yang Guifei prepares a drink for the emperor on a tripod table stool in what appears to be her nuptial bedchamber (fig. 18). Lavish floral patterns of lotus and peony adorn the layers of curtains and fabrics of the room's furnishings. The thickness of the curtains conjures the atmosphere of intimacy between man and woman within this most private space, almost in spite of their having been tied back to allow the viewer a glimpse.

Behind Yang Guifei a low table is laid out with fine ceramic stem-cups, jars and a long-necked bottle-jar, all accurately reflecting a late-Ming notion of what might have sat on such a Tang table. In this heady atmosphere, Yang Guifei cuts the figure of a classic Chinese beauty. The tassels of her robe flutter and twist in an imaginary wind, betraying her inner emotional state, just as court ladies have been depicted in China since founding masters like Gu Kaizhi. The *Admonitions* scroll attributed to Gu Kaizhi features a scene of 'a lady reflecting on her duty' (fig. 19), in which the meditative woman's body, although relatively without form, takes on a sense of inner life via the energy of these tassels and the delicate linear qualities of the lines that describe them.

The *locus classicus* of the alluring female beauty in Chinese painting is perhaps the goddess of the Luo River, who appears in paintings attributed to Gu Kaizhi illustrating a prose-poem by Cao Zhi entitled 'Luoshen fu'. The poem is about a romantic but ultimately unsatisfactory encounter between the river goddess and the poem's author as he makes his way home after being dismissed from court.[45] The erotic nature of these paintings is matched by various Ming-dynasty woodblock images of the Minghuang–Yang Guifei affair, which are also erotically charged, as Li-chiang Lin describes in chapter five. In the *Chōgonka*

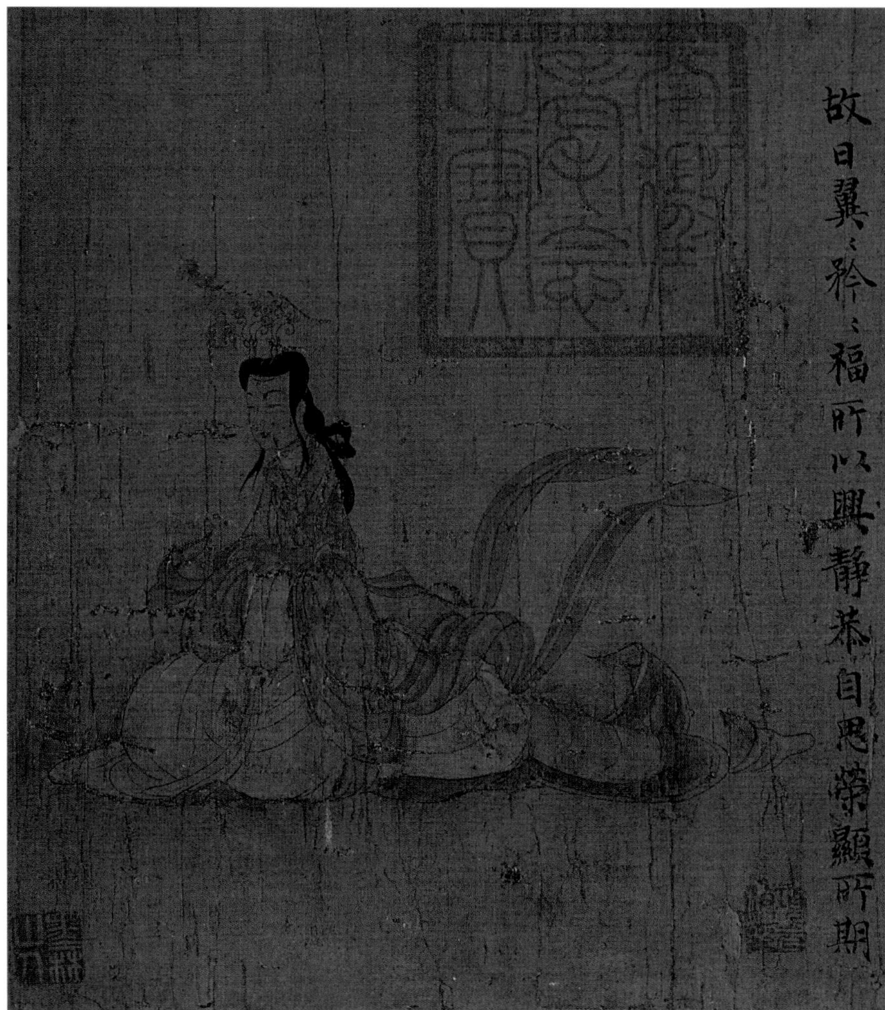

scrolls, however, the figures of Minghuang and Guifei lack the erotic charge that viewers of the *Nymph of the Luo River* paintings or the Ming woodblock publications might expect. Rather, it is the evocation of ambience, the cultural connotations of the fluttering drapery, the proximity of floral attributes and the recollection of literary images (like the goddess of the Luo River) that create a sense of Guifei's beauty.

The steadier ladies of the court are pictured looking in on the scene of Yang Guifei preparing drinks for the emperor from the terrace outside, just as the viewer must peer into the receding chamber in the middle of the scroll. As the emperor is drawn into a new life of

Fig 19 'Lady reflecting on her duty', *Admonitions of the Court Instructress* attributed to Gu Kaizhi (c.344–c.406; a 5th–6th century version after). Detail of a handscroll, now mounted as a panel; ink and colours on silk, 25 x 348.5 cm. © Trustees of the British Museum.

late-night revels, it is perhaps inevitable that he soon starts to absent himself from the dawn audience. It is an insightful image of his neglect of government, and one given added poignancy by the common knowledge that, historically, as An Lushan's rebel armies approached the capital in 756, courtiers turned up to the imperial dawn audience as usual to find that the emperor, Yang Guifei and their inner circle had fled in the night.

The second scene shows the couple drinking by candlelight in a large room with a wide roof overhanging the verandas.[46] The emperor is seated on a chair holding his cup of wine a little unsteadily as Yang Guifei, also seated, is served wine to his right. Their being seated on chairs is somewhat anachronistic, since chairs did not become common for sitting on in China until the Song dynasty, but it adds to the variety of these three scenes. This particular mini-narrative takes place on a carefully contrived stage, somewhat higher up in the picture plane than the nuptial bedchamber. Marking the back, behind the emperor, is a screen painted with a snow-covered flowering *prunus*, the first flower of the year and the symbol of the high-minded scholar. In the foreground is a clump of tree peony flowering among rocks. The lush peony in the height of its bloom symbolises not only Yang Guifei's beauty, but marks the time of late spring to early summer. The peony grows beside a specific type of rock from the vast Lake Tai, west of modern Shanghai. These prized rocks are immediately recognisable from their pitted and chiselled appearance, and they are believed to have been created over many years by the lapping waves of the lake. According to imperial lore, the Northern Song emperor, Huizong, lost his empire by commandeering official grain ships to transport these rocks to his capital, thereby weakening its military capability. Beside the peony, the rock may be read both as an iconic symbol of and perhaps an anachronistic warning to the emperor Minghuang. The peony

and the rock not only mirror the grouping of Yang Guifei and the emperor in the inner chamber opposite, but by its size and positioning, create the curious perspectival effect by which the viewer seems to be directly overlooking the scene beyond.

To the left of this scene is an intriguing depiction, over swirling waters, of a bridge on which are standing two ladies who seem to communicate through their expressions and deportment rather than through words. They are watched by a woman holding open the curtains on the far side. The tiles of the overhanging roof bear the figures of mandarin ducks, indicating that the emperor and Yang Guifei have become mates for life.

The bridge leads to the third scene, in which the emperor and Yang Guifei are seated on mats in a pillared island-pavilion. All the figures, including the ladies-in-waiting, gaze off to the viewer's left towards the flowering fruit tree (a pear?) that reaches up and out over the water, rounding off this 'act' of the narrative. The emperor is again seated in the centre, this time on a wide *tatami*-like mat and supported by a shaped armrest of the kind seen in ancient Chinese paintings of scholars. Again, a screen stands behind him, this one painted with billowing waves in the manner of Song court artists like Ma Yuan. He gestures with his left hand to Yang Guifei on his right. Also seated on a mat, she, for her part, turns to look at the flowering tree behind her, gesturing with her left hand.

In this final scene of the three (see fig. 75), there is a marked contrast between the dark colours of the blue-grey water, greyish clouds and roof tiles, along with the grey carved stone facing that underpins the pavilion – and the almost luminescent yellow tiled floor, gilded pillars, bright red balustrade and apple-green awning of the interior. In fact, this seems to be part of an interweaving narrative over the course of the three scenes, in a shift from day to night that is both literal and figurative. In these scenes, Minghuang and Yang Guifei's carousing lasts from daytime deep into the night, but the seasons and year seem also to be passing. Finally, the figure of Minghuang is shown as though consumed by the ever-growing brightness of his consort and unaware of how benighted he has become to the reality of the world beyond.

The bridge is a recurring and significant motif in the painting, although each time it appears (half a dozen times in all), it conveys a slightly different meaning. It appears once, here, in the first scroll, and at several junctures in the second. There are two bridges in the sequence describing the escape through the mountains. Then, back in the palace, in what may constitute a scene in its own right, there is a bridge strewn with autumn leaves that links two scenes of the emperor pictured alone, which vividly recalls the usage in the first scroll. Finally, two bridges appear at the end of the scroll, one U-shaped and the second arched – the first linking the palaces of heaven above the clouds, the second an enigmatic marker of the end of the scroll which symbolises the divide between Heaven and earth.

In the first scroll the bridge is visually quite prominent, although it is not mentioned in the ballad. It comes between the latter two of a suite of scenes portraying the late-night revelry of the protagonists in the context of a scroll where eye contact is used to represent a bond between individuals. The look exchanged by the two ladies that stand on the bridge may be significant, and there may be more to this transitional motif than a segue between early evening entertainment and night-time passion. It seems a strong enough feature to plant doubt in the viewer's mind about the wisdom of these actions, to the extent of being a kind of tragic warning of their consequence. Counting the scenes in the first scroll, there are seventeen fairly discrete 'scenes', so it is pos-sible this was intended to count as one in its own right, taking the total to eighteen.

A notable feature of these three scenes is that Yang Guifei is seated in each one, as if she were too frail to be active outside this domestic context. This physical quality is indeed suggested by Bai Juyi in his 'Song': it is her near-helpless exit from the hot springs at Huaqing that leads to her becoming 'a new recipient of the emperor's favour'. This moment was picked up on by Sansetsu, who faithfully portrays the emperor turning his head and gazing transfixed at the Yang lady for the first time; the steps from here to the consummation of their love he leaves to the imagination. This image of Yang Guifei chimes with the historical notion, observed above, that Yang Guifei provided a new model of female corporeal beauty in mid-eighth-century China. This was seen in a remarkable shift in the form of female figures in mid-Tang period paintings, as discussed above, but was also observable in the material culture of the time. Female tomb figurines, for instance, move from slender to plump in the middle of the eighth century. But the new types are not necessarily frail: polo-playing figurines remind us that elite women in the Tang were physically active and sporting. Sansetsu's painting does not portray Yang Guifei as especially plump, but does play up the appearance of feminine frailty in the hot spring scene. Later, to illustrate the ballad, it also shows her performing the athletic Whirl dance. It may seem contradictory to a modern eye that Yang Guifei could be both so frail and so vigorous, but this helps to highlight the significance for Sansetsu's audience of body-language and posture over corporeal physique.

Like her sisters, Yang Guifei must have been the subject of portraits by Minghuang's court painters. Although none survive, some of the Tang revivalist paintings of later Chinese artists open a window on what they may have looked like. Qian Xuan's *Yang*

Guifei Mounting a Horse in the Freer Gallery (see fig. 10), discussed above, may be based on a popular anecdote about Yang Guifei which relates that she was unable to mount a horse unassisted, an implication of how plump and frail she was but also of how desirable these qualities were in the eyes of the besotted emperor.[47] We will recognise how her physique is suggested by means of the action of her getting on a horse, rather than by any explicit description of her body.

Although Qian Xuan's painting is not intended as an illustration of Bai Juyi's text specifically, the image calls the whole story to mind, as the poem-inscription on the painting makes clear:

> Jade whips and carved saddles – how she was
>   doted on in the Taizhen Palace;
> Each year at the onset of winter, favoured at
>   the Huaqing hot springs.
> In the Kaiyuan, he commanded four hundred
>   thousand head of horses;
> How did he come to ride a mule when he
>   travelled the road to Shu?

Undoubtedly such a painting had a specific place within the socio-political context of Mongol rule in China[48] but it also drew upon Tang paintings known to Qian Xuan – perhaps works by Minghuang's court painters – as part of the creative practice.[49] Qian Xuan's painting is quite literal: he illustrates the first line of his own poem, showing Yang Guifei setting out from the palace with armed attendants. She is having difficulty getting into the 'carved saddle' on her dappled grey, while the servant girl behind holds her jade riding crop. Qian Xuan's painting makes use of the device of the emperor looking back towards Yang Guifei, a look echoed by his horse towards hers. As in the scene at the Huaqing hot spring, the focus of attention is Yang Guifei's beguiling frailty. In the Freer painting, she requires much assistance to mount her horse, amounting to a groom to hold the horse's head, two ladies and a stool on the near (left or mounting) side, and another groom pulling hard on the off-side stirrup to prevent the richly decorated saddle from slipping round under her weight. This anecdote alone must serve *pars pro totem* for the whole story of their affair.

When we consider Sansetsu's plotting of the *Chōgonka* narrative in sets of three or four consecutive scenes, it is apparent that this too has echoes of Tang genre painting. Through visual plotting, Tang paintings, as well as the Yuan reprises of them, unfold as narratives. In the case of *Yang Guifei Mounting a Horse*, the first two figures, as powerful as gate-posts, mark the head of a royal procession but also signal through their body language that there is some delay. The second group, which comprises the emperor and two servants (one who carries the fine imperial bow) confirms that whatever the delay is, it has captured the ruler's attention, and surely must be important. Then comes the reason for the delay: Yang Guifei's histrionic difficulty in carrying out such an everyday task as mounting a horse, which has placed such a demand on the imperial attention and has consequences. This is followed, finally, by some meaningful glances between the standard-bearers and servants.[50] In the end, Qian Xuan's painting does not depend on the poem for its understanding or reading, and the poem can be read independently, but their juxtaposition on the scroll adds a layer of complexity and depth that is both visual and literary – a new and original response to the question, voiced in the poem, of what led the emperor to mount a mule and escape across the mountains to Shu in 756. In a sense, Sansetsu's uninscribed painting takes this literary/visual play to another level, by challenging the Edo Japanese reader's knowledge of Bai Juyi's ballad.

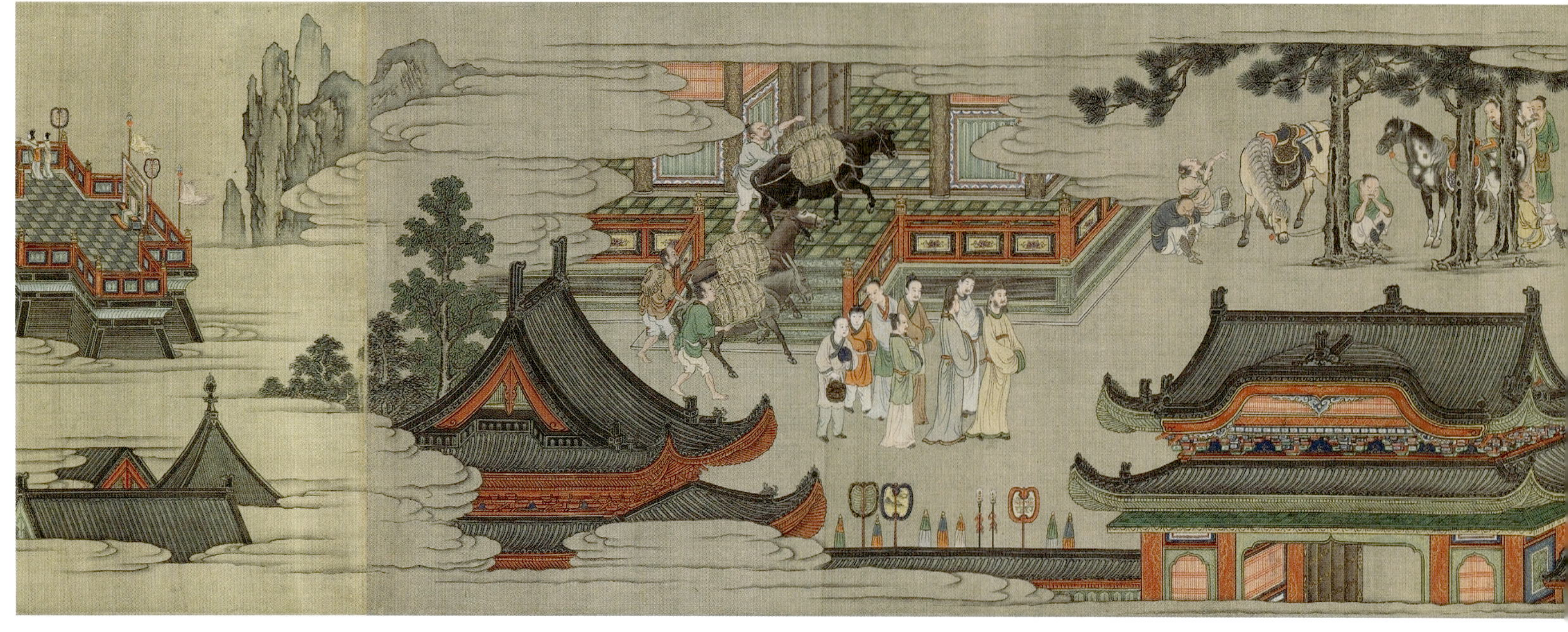

THE RISE OF THE YANG CLAN (FIG. 20)

Her sisters and her brothers all
*   were ennobled and granted great fiefs;*
a glory that any would envy
*   rose from her house.*
25 *This caused the hearts of parents*
*   all the world through*
to care no longer for having sons,
*   but to care to have a daughter.*

THIS SECTION OF THE SCROLL marks a complete change of scenery away from the imperial palace at the heart of the Tang capital. It describes the dramatic elevation of Yang Guifei's family members to positions of great power and authority through her influence on the emperor at court, and is based on just two couplets from Bai Juyi's ballad – amounting to a bold decision on Sansetsu's part. The generic events depicted here may be set in the Yang clan's ancestral home in Sichuan, or else, more likely, somewhere close to the seat of power in the capital, to indicate the clan's growing influence at court. The events take place over the decade between the consumation of Minghuang and Yang Guifei's love and the dalliance, and the tumultuous events of 755–56, which are described in the scenes that follow. One might argue that this passage is included merely to account for the passing of a number of years in the main plotline, but that would be to overlook the rich social detailing of these scenes – and the sense of injustice implied by it – that give an insight into An Lushan's motivation for rebellion.

In marked contrast with the previous suite of scenes, what we see here lacks the grandeur of the palace with its richly decorated interiors, established gardens and pavilions over water. Instead, here are all the signs of new wealth and status. In the opening scene the men of the house are seen standing about looking unsure of themselves as boxes and parcels of luxuries, carried in on poles by coolies, are counted.

FIG 20 Kano Sansetsu, The rise of the Yang clan, *Song of Lasting Sorrow*; scroll 1, the third length of silk.

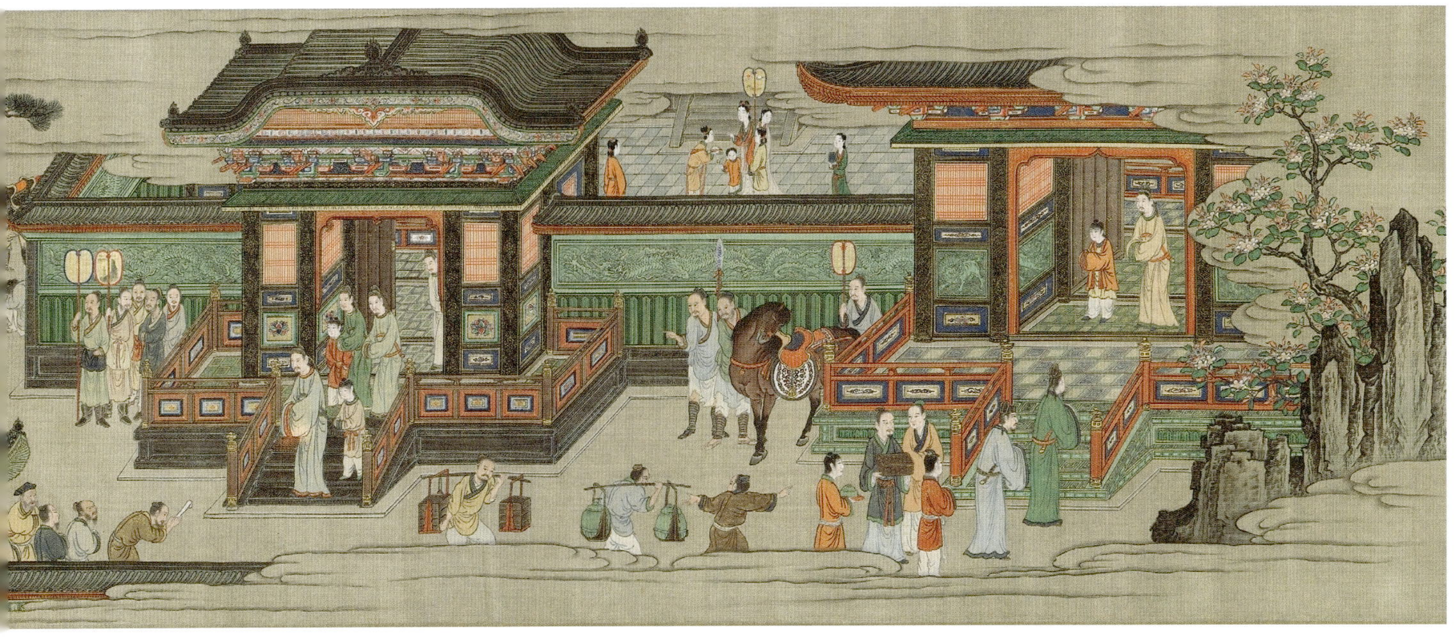

In a well-observed detail (fig. 21), the man standing awkwardly in the doorway to the right is tellingly caught between two impulses – bending his knees in a pose of supplication or submission, while at the same time holding out his joined hands in a gracious gesture. The latter seems to be a newly learned custom reflecting his rise in society, something unfamiliar enough to be mimicked by the little boy.

In the second scene, the men of the house receive a delegation. The leader, holding a jade tablet, bows in an obsequious posture towards the Yang host, now a man of consequence wishing to appear gracious (fig. 22). These men we now recognise as Yang Guifei's brothers – her elder brother Yang Guozhong, who goes on to become one of the most powerful men in the country, and her younger brother Qi.

By the third scene, the brothers are standing about with an air of self-importance, yet the implica-

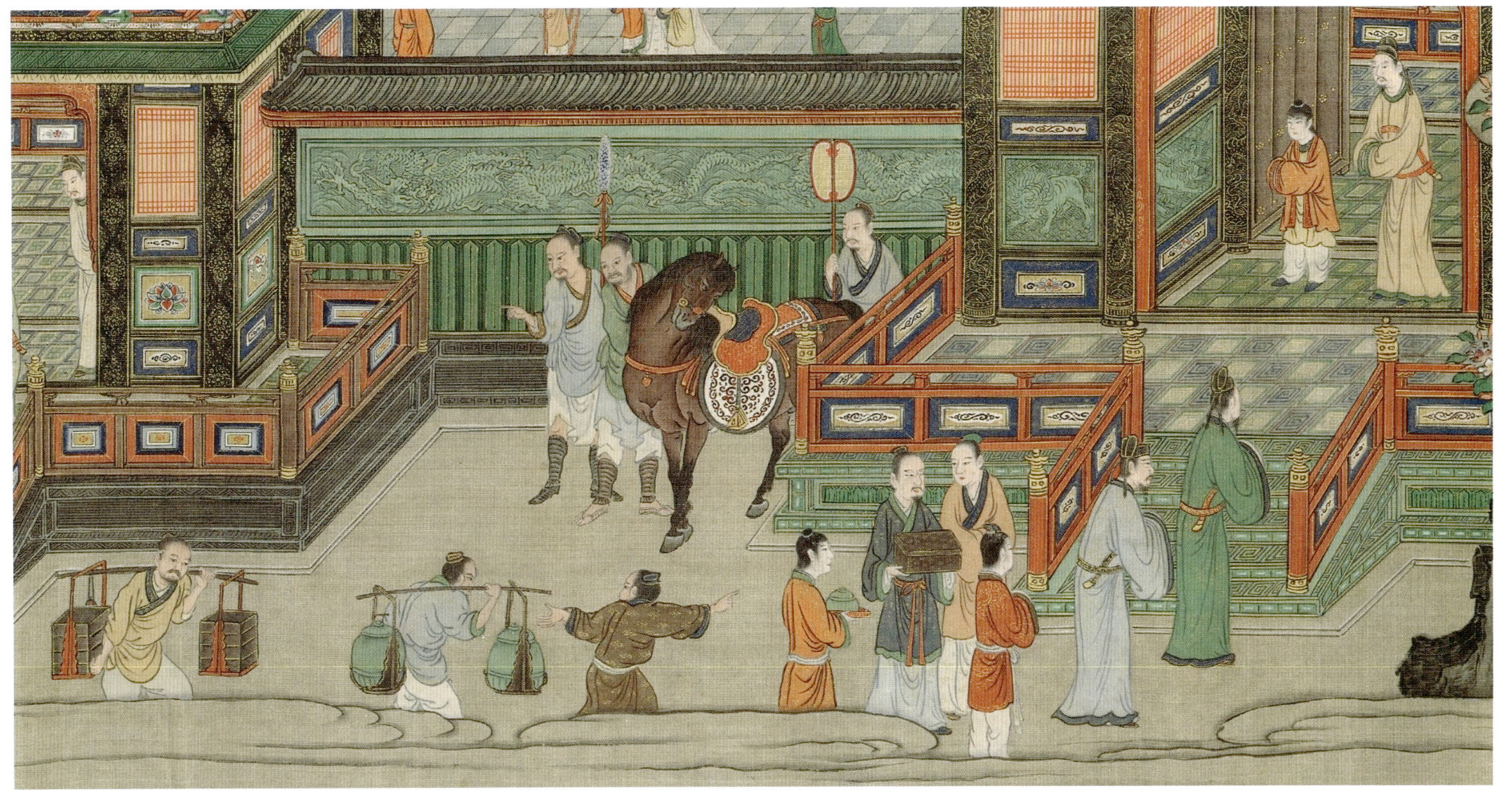

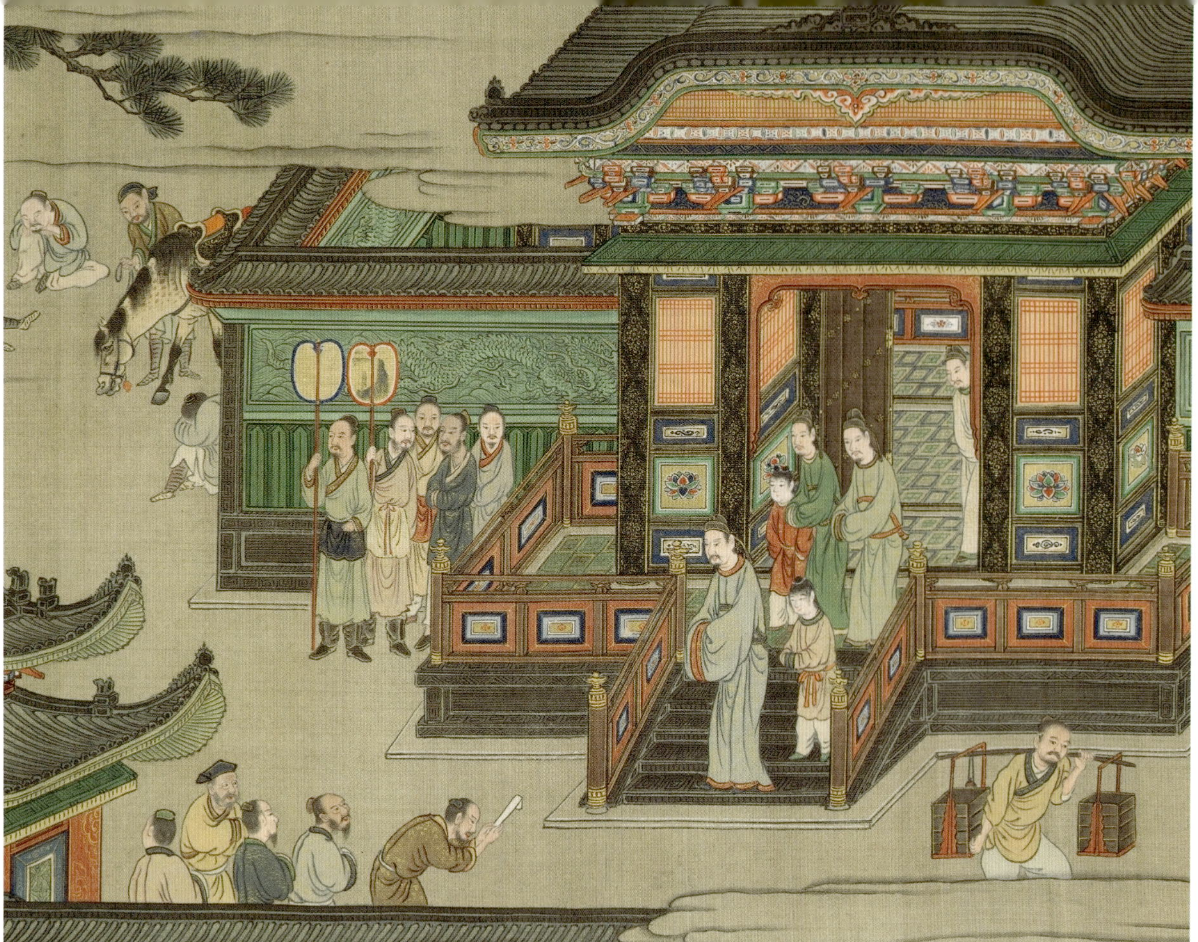

tions of vulgarity are still plain in the sight of heavily laden pack animals – an ox and two mules carrying gold, perhaps – being brought into the houses. Grooms and horses wait under the shade of trees to one side. Are they visibly idle for effect or is it that the stabling is not yet there for them in these upwardly mobile times? These impressions are all the more effective for the absence of any parents or elders here, in contrast with the austere yet dignified presence of the Yang household in the first scene.

Appropriately, there are few women about, since Yang Guifei and her sisters are all in the palace. The woman visible in the back courtyard of the first scene is a sister-in-law, perhaps While Yang Guifei was ranked 'Precious Consort', her older sisters received titles as Duchesses-of-State: Lady Guoguo (as described above), Lady Qinguo and Lady Hanguo.

This passage of the painting raises some interesting questions about the relationship between the text and how it is illustrated, and is revealing in terms of how Sansetsu went about turning poetic images into visual ones. Just as the ballad is composed of 120 lines arranged in couplets, so the painting has a structure of scenes within sets. And, overall, the painting upholds a balance between textual accuracy and strong visual effects. However, the ballad's content is not equally divided between the two scrolls: the first scroll illustrates the first twenty couplets only, while the second scroll contains the remaining forty. In part, this may be explained by the long dialogue between the Daoist and the spirit of Yang Guifei at the very end of the text. Yet there is also the fact that a painter needs to set the scene and build up visual tension by introducing images that he can repeat and exploit, such as the bridges.

This depiction of the rise of the Yang clan, although expanded from the two couplets of lines 23–26, conforms to the overall structure in showing three sequential scenes moving left to right within the unfolding drama. In the previous sequence of Minghuang's dalliance, the events could be read as occurring over the course of a night, and in light of the text, could also stand for repeated nights. Later, the climatic changes over three linked scenes suggest a passage of seasons and even years. These scenes of the enrichment and elevation of the Yang clan are both single and, by implication, repeated events over the years up to 755.

Sansetsu's reading of the tale is essentially of a romance between Minghuang and Yang Guifei, and he gives it centre stage so that all other events and actions take place in light of their relationship. His-

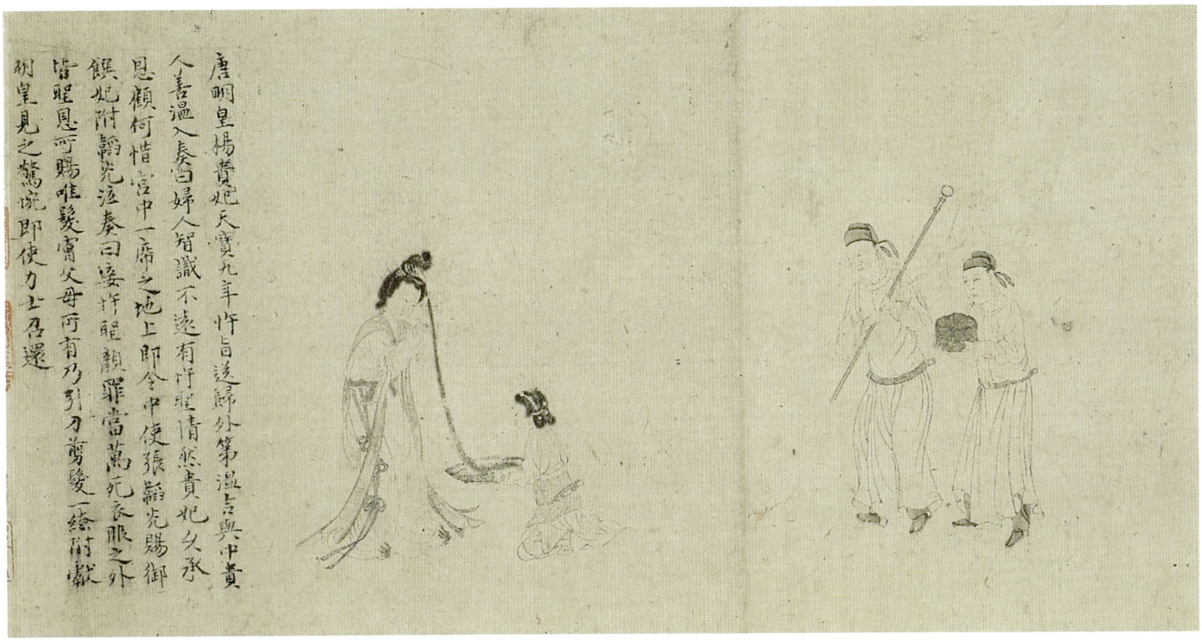

Fig 23 Anon. (17th century), 'Yang Guifei cutting off a lock of hair to send to Tang emperor Minghuang', *Illustrated Stories of Former Emperors and their Subjects (Qiandai junchen gushi tu)*. Detail of a handscroll; ink on paper. Freer Gallery of Art, Washington, DC. Gift of Eugene and Agnes E. Meyer, F 1970.37.

torically the Yangs rose to their positions of power through nepotism and patronage, but following Bai Juyi's lead, Sansetsu avoids directly casting aspersions on Yang Guifei's character. In light of the ballad, which describes the nationwide desire for daughters following her elevation, the depiction of the Yang household becomes a kind of model of good fortune.

Faithful to the ballad, this scroll naturally glosses over the tempestuous side of the lovers' relationship. In the Chinese tradition of portrayals of Yang Guifei and Minghuang, it is often lesser known or even tangential moments of their sexual relations that are featured. One of their more salient impasses from this period, for instance, became a painting subject in contemporary Ming China. A scene depicting 'Yang Guifei cutting off a lock of hair to send to Tang emperor Minghuang' appears in the seventeenth-century handscroll, *Illustrated Stories of Former Emperors and their Subjects (Qiandai junchen gushi tu*; fig. 23).[51] This illustrates a story from the year Tianbao 9 (750) in which Yang Guifei, having enraged the emperor and been banished from the palace, cuts off a lock of her hair to send to him – a gesture that prompts him to summon her back. In the painting, the lock is no trifle but appears to measure some yards, which would have had a significant impact on her 'look' and was viewed by the emperor as a serious act of contrition on her part. The combination of text and imagery, along with the scholar-style ink-outline technique of the painting, and indeed the selection of a pivotal moment to serve as the illustration of an entire story or anecdote, relates this narrative to the Chinese tradition of didactic illustrations about ladies in general (the *Female Classic of Filial Piety*, for instance) and court ladies in particular.

In literary history, if not in Bai Juyi's ballad, Yang Guifei is thus associated with one telling act of contrition. Her act of self-sacrifice is to shear off a lock of her hair, which regains her the emperor's favour. In art history, the connection between a lock of a consort's hair and the stability of the state underpinned one of the best-known scenes of the *Admonitions* scroll – the 'toilette' scene – which shows a court woman having her long hair brushed (see fig. 6). The accompanying text speaks of seeing beyond physical beauty and of 'correcting one's character as with an axe, embellishing it as with a chisel', words that Yang Guifei seems to have taken to heart in emperor Minghuang's eyes. In consequence, historically, his infatuation with her and her sisters continues, and Yang Guifei's influence becomes more pernicious and widespread, perhaps precipitating the rebellion of An Lushan in 755, which effectively broke the back of the dynasty. In Bai Juyi's ballad, this catastrophe is not blamed on Yang Guifei: its causes are not cited, and in addition, the emperor for his part is said to have wished for a woman capable of overturning a dynasty. Faithful to the ballad, Sansetsu's painting side-steps the issue of virtue–ethics to sustain the romantic focus.

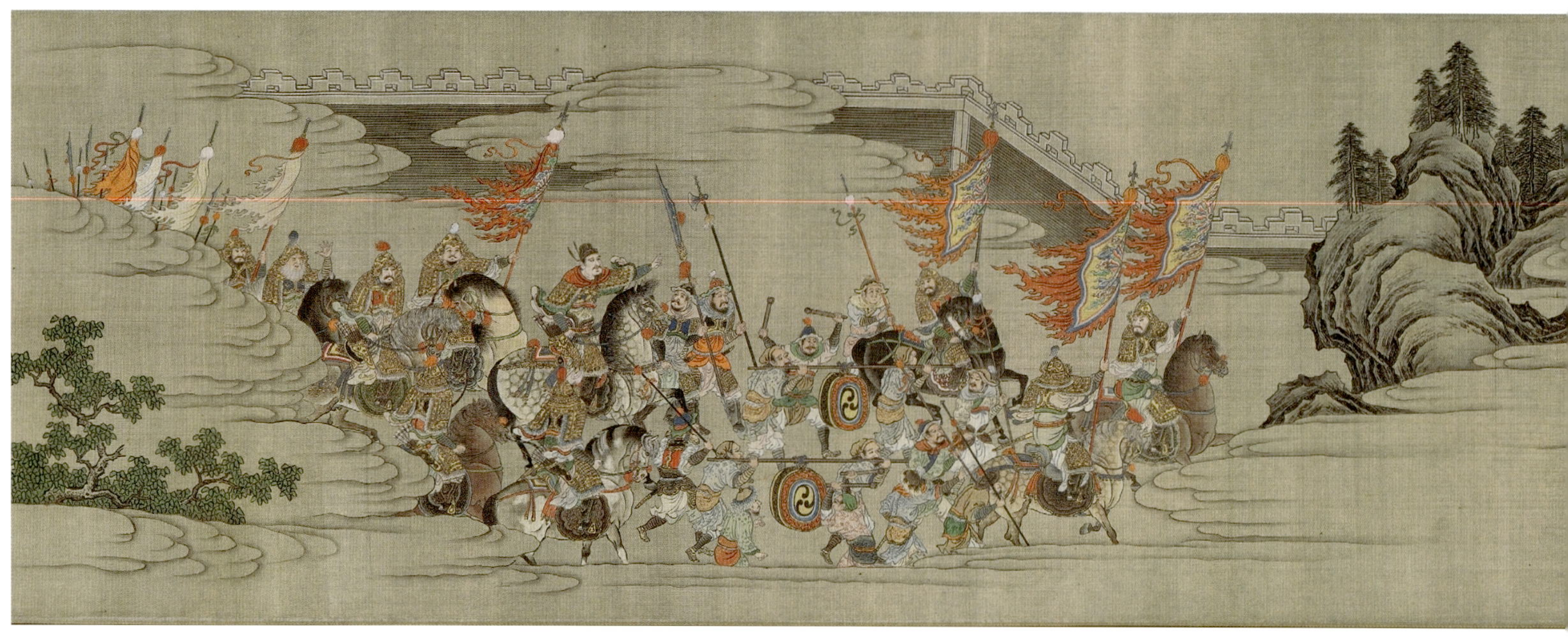

GENERAL AN LUSHAN REBELS (FIG. 24)

The high places of Mount Li's palace
rose up into blue clouds,
where the music of gods was whirled in winds
and everywhere was heard.

Songs so slow and stately dances,
notes sustained on flutes and harps,
30 *and all day long our lord and king*
could never look his fill.
Then kettledrums from Yuyang came
making the whole earth tremble
and shook apart those melodies,
'Coats of Feathers, Rainbow Skirts'.[52]

IN A KIND OF VISUAL CAESURA to this first scroll, and one that interprets the ballad quite literally, Sansetsu uses just two brilliantly contrasting scenes at this moment of the story. First, the ethereal heights of the complex of terraces and platforms built above the clouds on the peak of Mount Li are shown. This terrace, covered with gold, looks like it might have some important ritual function in the state calendar but on this occasion it is the scene of a music and dance performance by Yang Guifei. Seated before a panelled mountain landscape screen to the right, at the very top, is the emperor, who admires the turning form of Yang Guifei before him. As she dances, her tassels flutter and float about her. All around, on four sides, are musicians and court ladies. One level down, the eunuchs stand about, while ladies prepare delicacies in a screened-off area to the right. Sloping roofs of palace buildings and steep flights of steps are glimpsed here and there through the clouds below. There is no evidence of any lines of communication with the outside or 'real' world. Even the figures lowest down show no awareness of the advance of a rebellion.

The dance to the music of strings and flutes is about to be interrupted by the tremor of beating war-drums, in what proves to be the lovers' final moments of happiness together. The emperor is shown gazing unknowingly upon Yang Guifei for the last time on this terrace above the clouds, in a scene that will be

FIG 24 Kano Sansetsu, *General An Lushan rebels*, *Song of Lasting Sorrow*, scroll 1, the fourth length of silk.

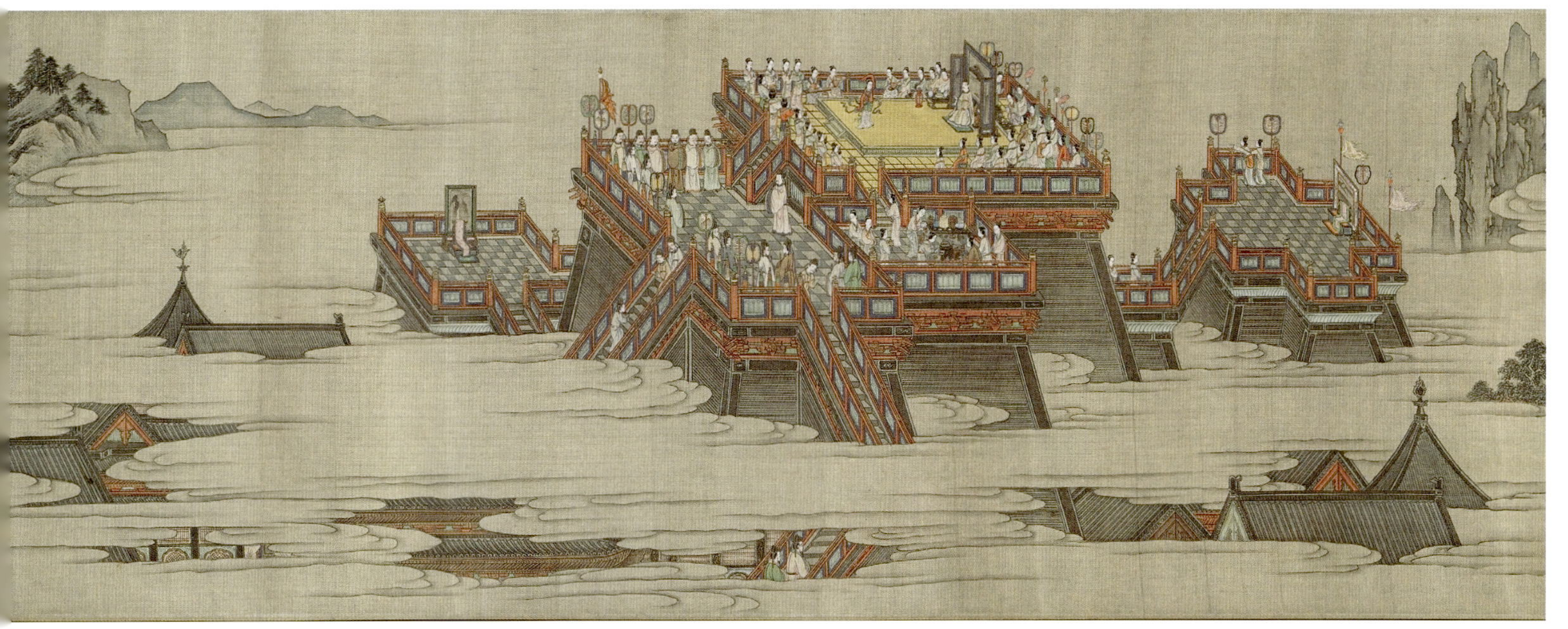

FIG 25 'An Lushan leads his rebel army to the walls of the capital' (from **General An Lushan rebels**), *Song of Lasting Sorrow*; (detail of fig. 24).

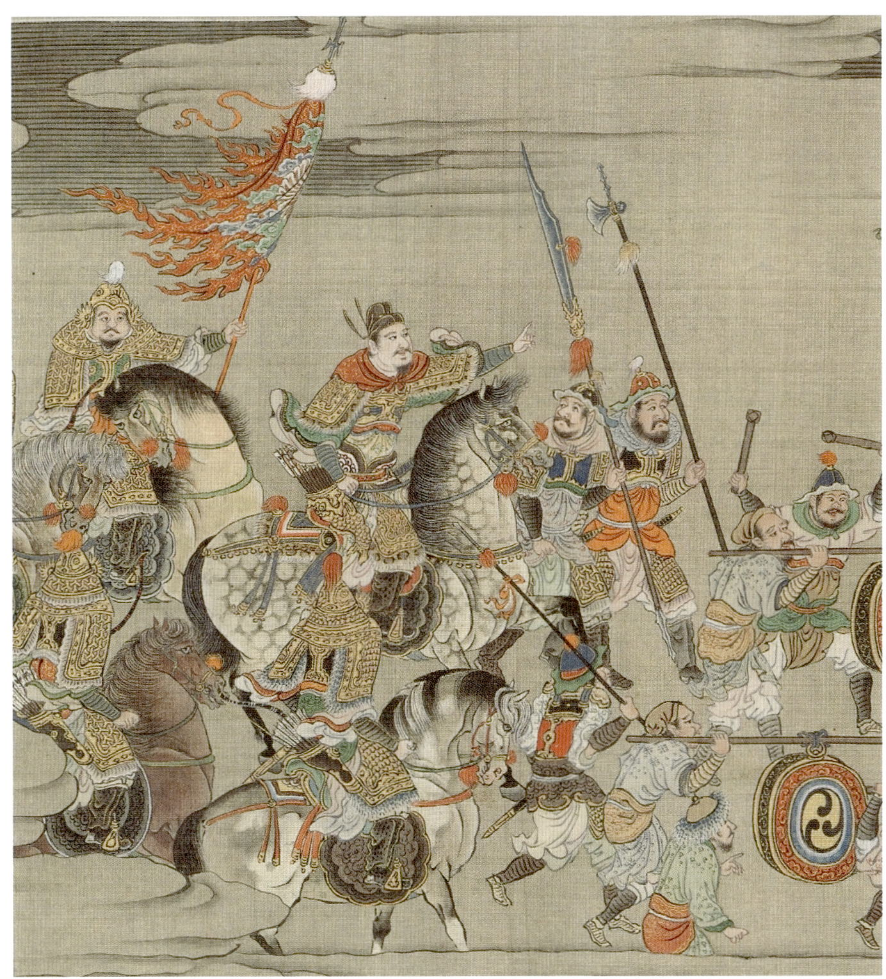

created again at the end of the scroll when the Daoist wizard visits the soul of Yang Guifei in the isles of the immortals.

This lofty view of the palace heights, with extensive terraces above clouds and roofs glimpsed below, drifts along until it is eventually bounded by the curving mountain chain. This view is in strong contrast with the other one in this pair of scenes – of the rebels. In front of the city walls, and very much at ground level, they cut awesome martial figures, especially in comparison with the tiny people up in the Li Palace. Wearing armour, and heavily armed, they march to the sound of bass drums or ride powerful chargers, while bright-orange-frilled banners stream out behind them in the wind. They move from left to right in the scroll, in awkward counter-movement to the right-to-left progress of the scroll, upsetting the visual harmony as well as the normal progress of time. They are led by the man mounted in the middle, An Lushan, a non-Chinese general and military governor, a protégé of Yang Guifei and favourite of Minghuang. An Lushan sits on a dappled grey (fig. 25). He has brought various generals with him, including one white-haired individual. Historically, having led his rebel army and taken the eastern capital, Luoyang, he marched on the Tang capital at Chang'an, and it is over Chang'an's walls that the beat of his drums poetically floods here. Although the ballad never makes clear why he marched on the capital, it was known that he harboured aspirations to be emperor and believed he could unite the country more successfully than Minghuang. Historically, he never succeeded: he was assassinated in 757.

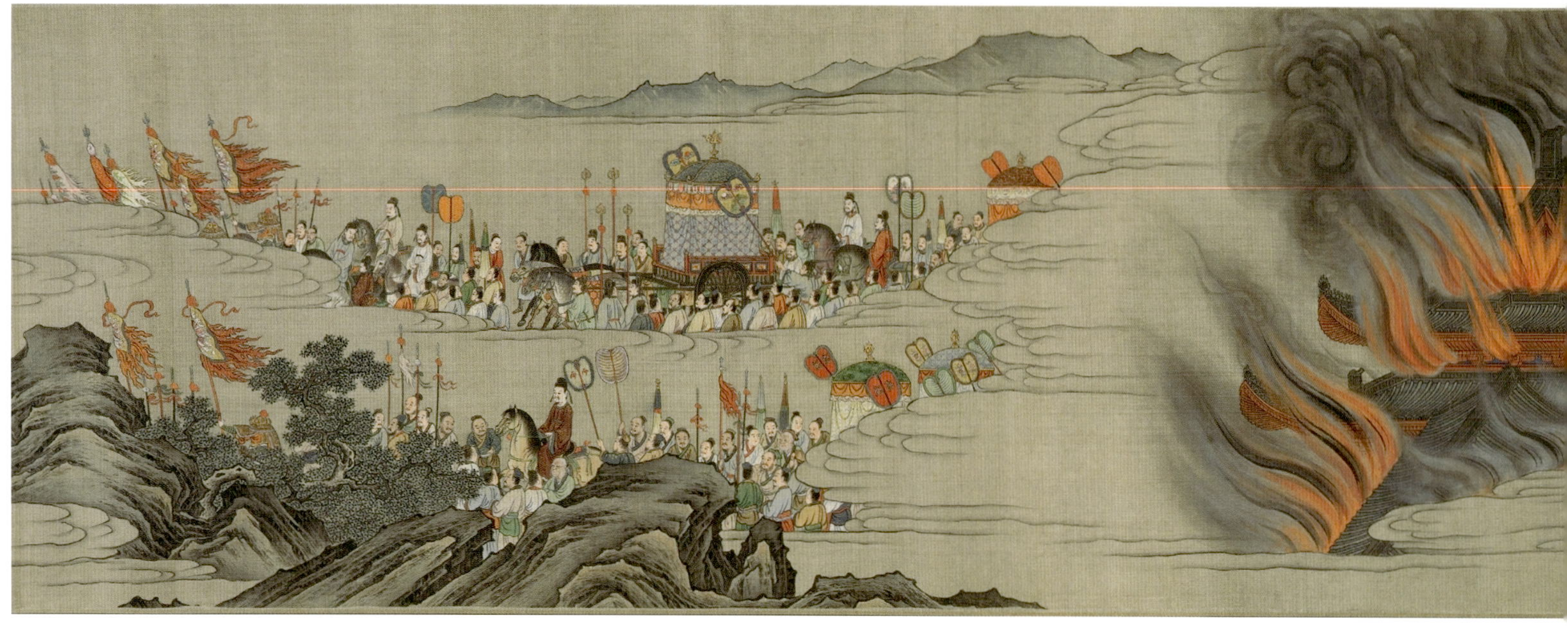

REBELS ENTER THE CAPITAL (FIG. 26)

From nine tiers of palace towers
  dust and smoke were rising:
a thousand coaches, ten thousand riders
  moving away southwest.

ECHOING THIS COUPLET with dramatic effect, the painting along this length of silk shows two more or less simultaneous scenes of action, either side of a stunning palace fire. First, to the right, in an abrupt reversal of direction from the previous scene, An Lushan's rebel soldiers charge through a gatehouse, which is cloaked in thick smoke, and into a palace precinct. As Chen Hong laconically writes: 'Tong Pass was left undefended, and the Kingfisher Paraphernalia of the imperial entourage had to set out southward.' The main palace building beyond the courtyard is already well ablaze, in the middle. On the blue tiled terrace, several looters, their faces contorted with gleeful menace, and one bearing away a precious zither on his shoulder, gaze up at the inferno. Tongues of smoking flame burst up from the eaves, while black and grey swirls of smoke snake up and leftward, morphing into thick clouds.

Emerging from a tiered bank of smoke wafting westwards, two columns of the emperor's inner circle are seen fleeing through the country, on into the scroll, to the west (fig. 27). In fact, the royal party has become separated, with the emperor's column, headed by the banners of the soldiers, passing close to the foreground rocks. To the rear, also headed by military banners, is Yang Guifei's procession. Her enclosed palanquin, identified by its phoenix finial and drawn by four horses, is surrounded by shuffling flag-bearing attendants, eunuchs and bodyguards.

FIG 26 Kano Sansetsu, Rebels enter the capital, *Song of Lasting Sorrow*; scroll 1, the fifth length of silk.

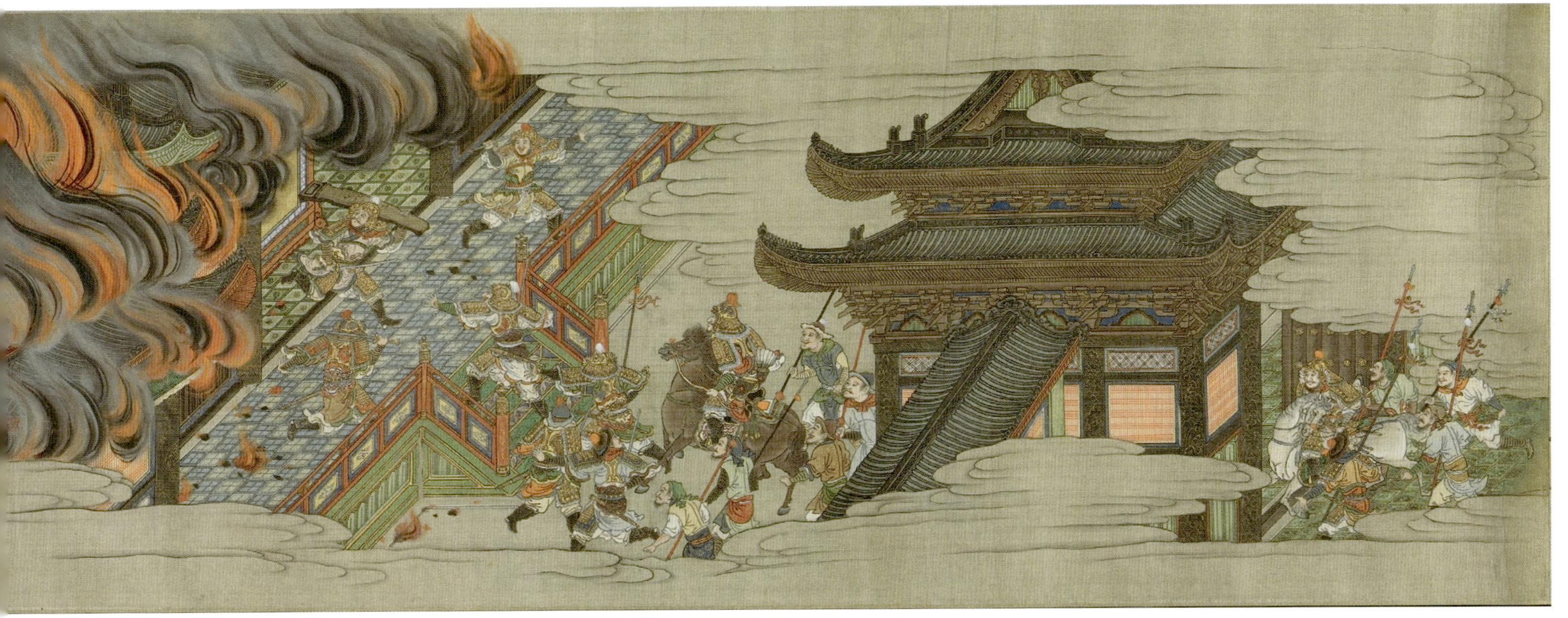

Some anxious glances are turned back towards the rising smoke over the capital, while the distant mountains in the far background are a forewarning of the terrain that lies ahead.

This is a brutally graphic picture of national disaster – rebels pour through a gate and torch and loot a palace building as the emperor and his inner retinue flee for their lives – and one that has a distinctively Japanese appeal. It is not that China's imperial palaces never suffered such fates, as any visitor to the Forbidden City, for instance, will know; rather that such scenes were rarely, if ever, depicted in Chinese painting, whereas in Japan there was a long tradition of it.

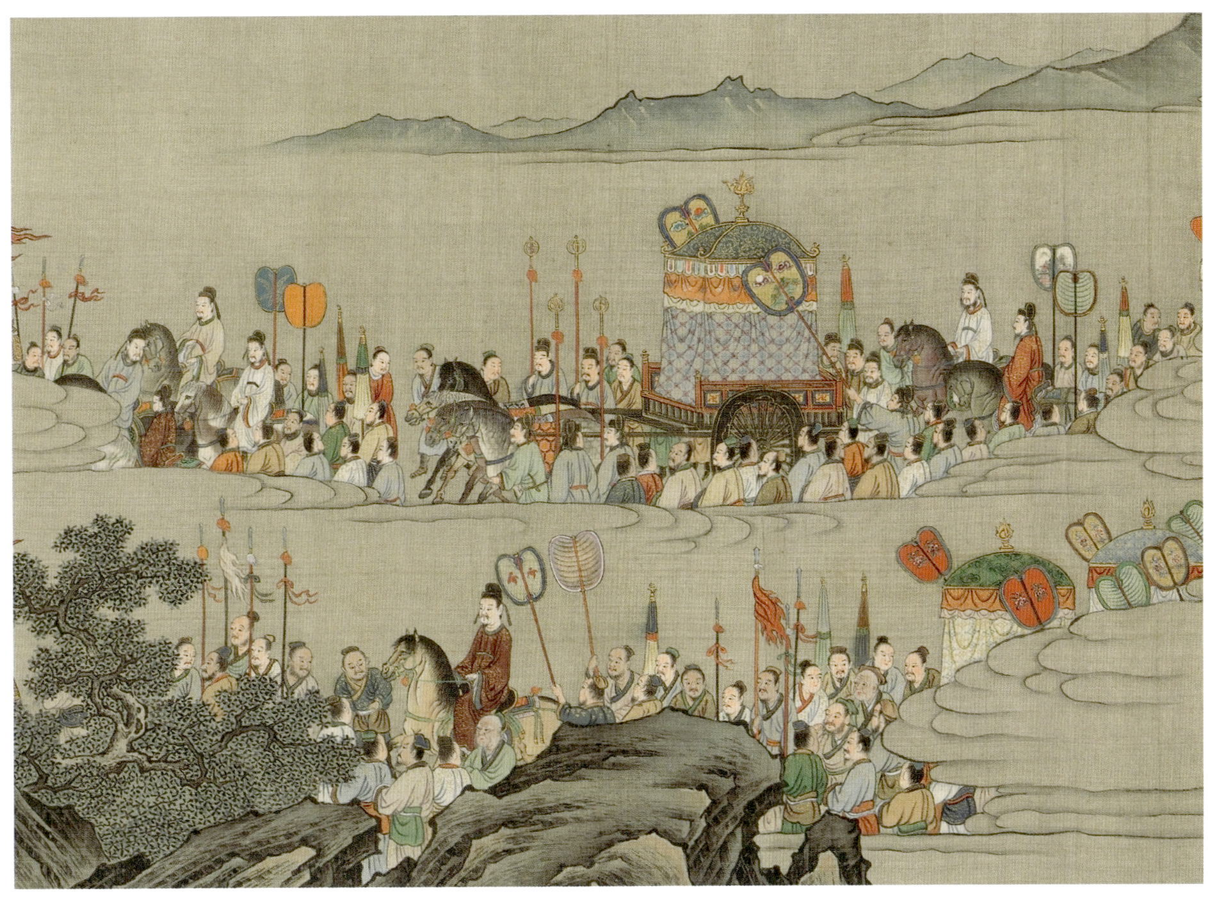

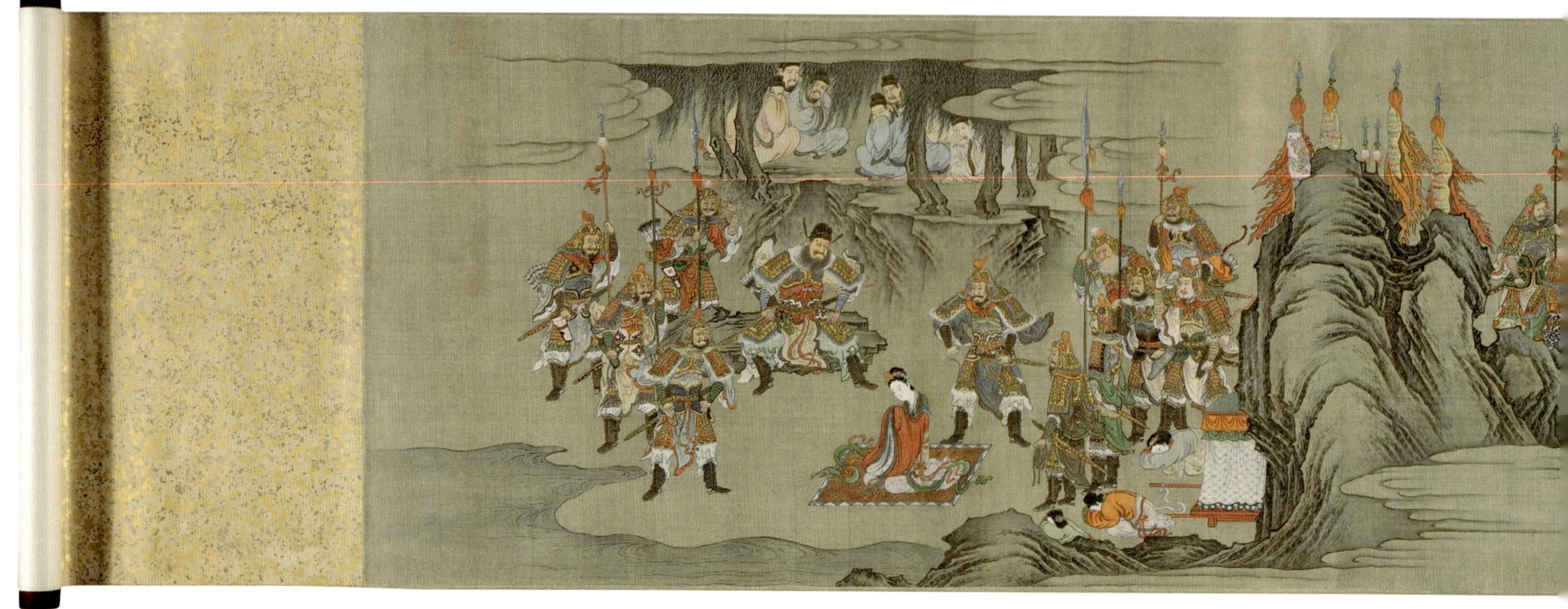

MUTINEERS DEMAND THE EXECUTION
OF YANG GUIFEI (FIG. 28)

35   *Swaying plumes of the royal banners were*
     moving ahead, then stopped
  west of the gates of the capital,
     just over a hundred miles.
  The six-fold army would not set forth,
     nothing could be done,
  and the fragile arch of her lovely brows
     there perished before the horses.

  Her flowered hairpins fell to earth,
     and no one picked them up,
40 *the kingfisher wing, the sparrow of gold,*
     the jade pick for the hair.

THE FAST PACE OF EVENTS continues through this set of scenes, the last of the first scroll. Framing the narrative are formations of clouds that spill forward from one scene to the next, willing on the action. Pictured among these clouds the characters appear cut off from one another and from reliable news of the unfolding events. The emperor's party becomes separated from Yang Guifei's, but each knows the rebels are in pursuit. Gaps in the clouds appear here and there to reveal decisive moments of the plot.

The setting of the first scene is the postal station at Mawei, some 50 km to the west of the capital on the canal running parallel but to the north of the Wei River. The emperor's entourage has been brought to a halt by the imperial bodyguard. Seated in the postal station, the emperor receives news from a eunuch (fig. 29). The tale does not diverge from historical fact so much as omit irrelevances, stating only that the army would not move on. The painting is consistent in its consideration of the train of events from the perspective of the two lovers. Historically, encountering another loyal body of imperial troops at Mawei, Minghuang's bodyguard discovered how Yang Guifei's powerful relatives, especially Yang Guozhong, had placed personal rivalries before the national interest during the early part of An Lushan's rebellion. In particular, they blamed them for the disastrous decision to engage the rebel army at the otherwise impregnable Tongguan Pass at the bend in

FIG 28 Kano Sansetsu, Mutineers demand the execution of Yang Guifei, *Song of Lasting Sorrow*; scroll 1, the sixth length of silk.

FIG 29 'The emperor is informed of the mutineers' demand for the life of Yang Guifei' (from **Mutineers demand the execution of Yang Guifei**), *Song of Lasting Sorrow*; (detail of fig. 28).

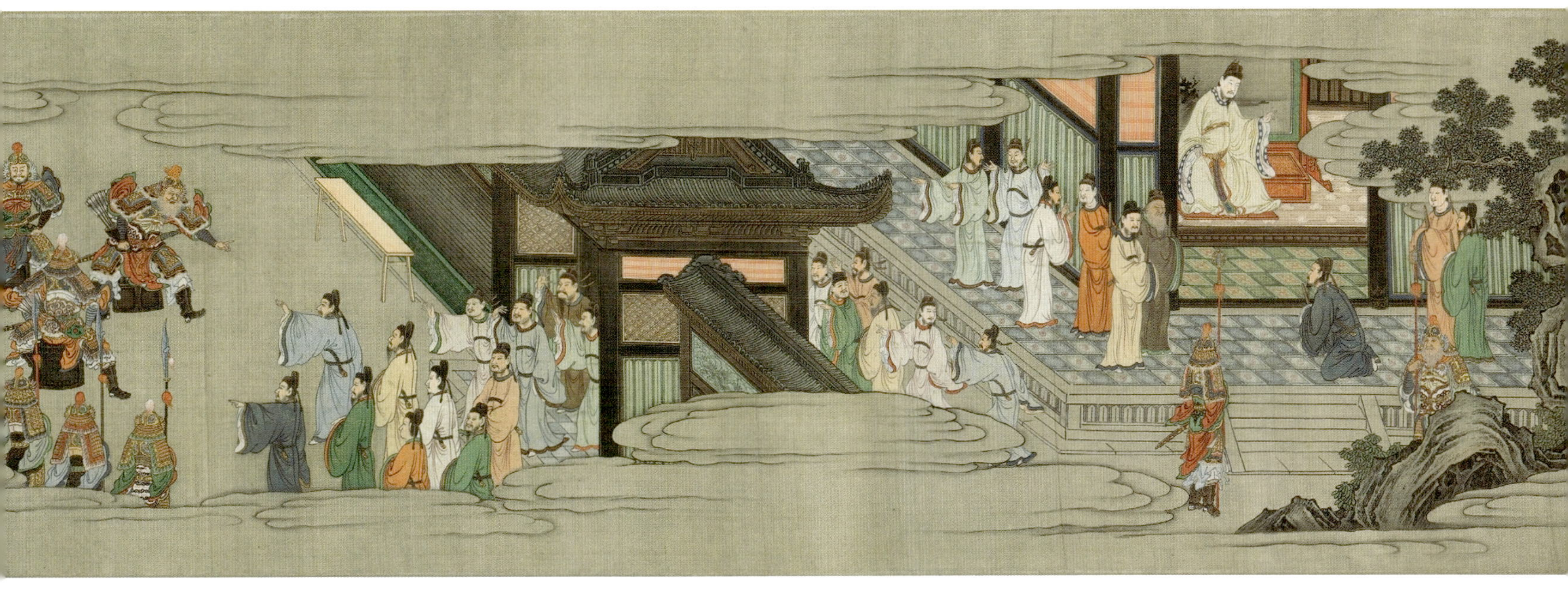

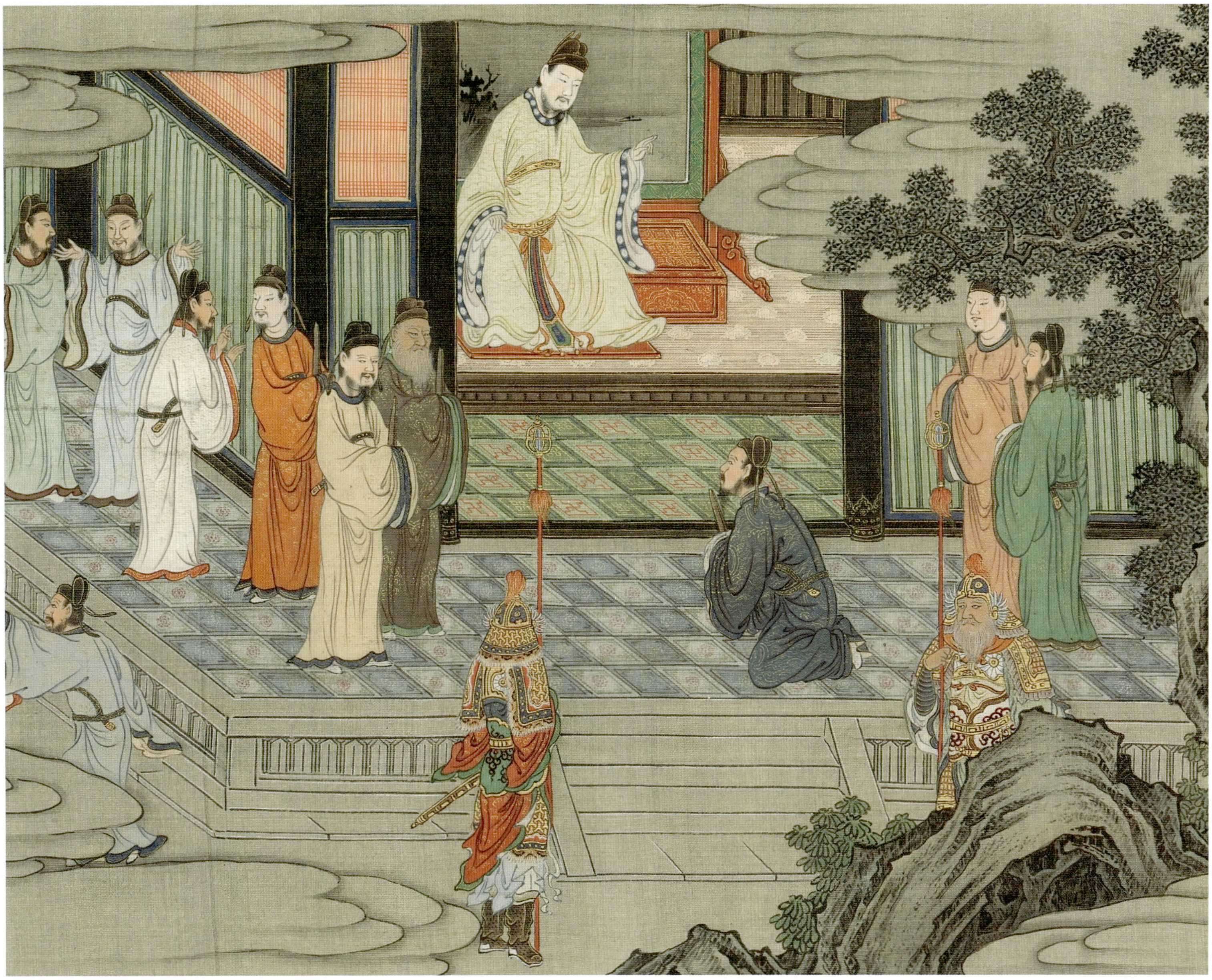

the Yellow River. The defeat of an imperial army on the seventh of the sixth month of 756 opened the rebels' way to advance west on the capital, which had in turn triggered the emperor's flight. Chen Hong's account of events reads as follows:

> After leaving Xianyang, their path came to Mawei Pavilion. There the Grand Army hesitated, holding their pikes in battle positions and refusing to go forward. Attendant officers, gentlemen of the court and underlings bowed down before His Majesty's horse and asked that this current Chao Cuo be executed to appease the world. [Yang Guozhong is referred to as Chao Cuo, a Western Han censor who advised the emperor Jing to reduce the territories of the imperial princes, which was the excuse for the Rebellion of the Seven Domains. Yang Guozhong is similarly being accused of having provoked An Lushan to rebellion.] Yang Guozong then received the yak-hair hat ribbons and the pan of water, by which a great officer of the court presents himself to the Emperor for punishment, and he died there by the edge of the road. Yet the will of those who were with the Emperor was still not satisfied. When His Majesty asked what the problem was, those who dared speak out asked that the Prized Consort also be sacrificed to allay the wrath of the world. His Majesty knew that it could not be avoided, and yet he could not bear to see her die, so he turned his sleeve to cover his face as the envoys dragged her off.

The emperor's informant in the first scene is probably his favourite eunuch, Gao Lishi, who had in fact warned the emperor against An Lushan and remonstrated with him about his devotion to Yang

Guifei. Perhaps he is telling the emperor of the fall of Chang'an to An Lushan (this happened on the seventeenth of the month), or of the further demands of the mutineers. Minghuang is portrayed as a fine figure of a man, dressed in yellow and seated in front of a painted screen depicting, perhaps ironically, a carefree fisherman in a detached ink landscape. To the left is a small courtyard; to the side of it, up against an outside wall, stands a plain table serving no obvious purpose other than to indicate how unexpected this imperial visit is to the local authorities. A flurry of nervous conversation and gesticulation by the attendants to the left indicates the source of the latest news through the gate: three awesome-looking but glum-faced military officers seated on stools (fig. 30). This we now recognise as the stand made by the imperial bodyguard against the Yang clique, and its demand for the life of Yang Guifei. For the sake of the dynasty, the emperor has no choice but to accede. Historically, he sent the eunuch Gao Lishi to take charge of the execution.

Beyond a tall rock topped by military flags and banners, the last scene in the painting depicts Yang Guifei's final moments by the canal. She is surrounded by heavily armed soldiers and a general who will witness the execution, and is already mourned to the right by her serving maids and by an assembly of eunuchs seated among the trees on the bank behind, who peer forward through a cloud window just as the viewer does opposite, from outside the scroll. Bai Juyi portrays Yang Gufei's death from the perspective of one who cannot bear to watch. Looking away, that person might only see the hairpins and ornaments, emblems of her position as Prized Consort, falling unheeded to the ground in the noisy struggle to hold her down. Chen Hong recorded that 'She struggled and threw herself back and forth in panic, but at last she came to death under the strangling cord.'

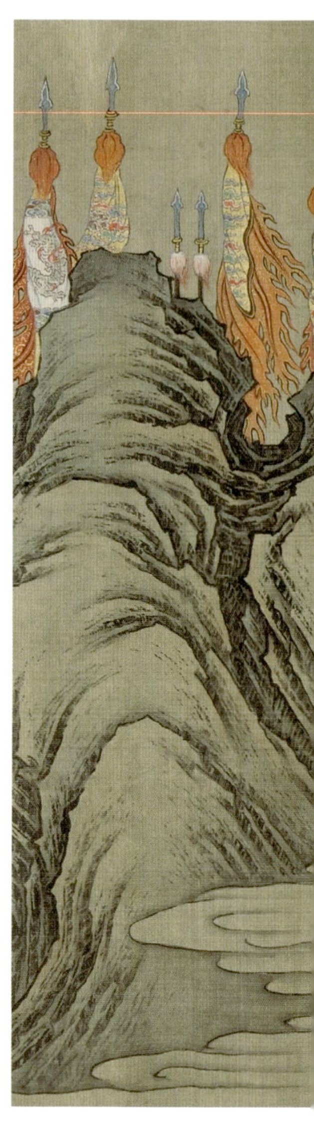

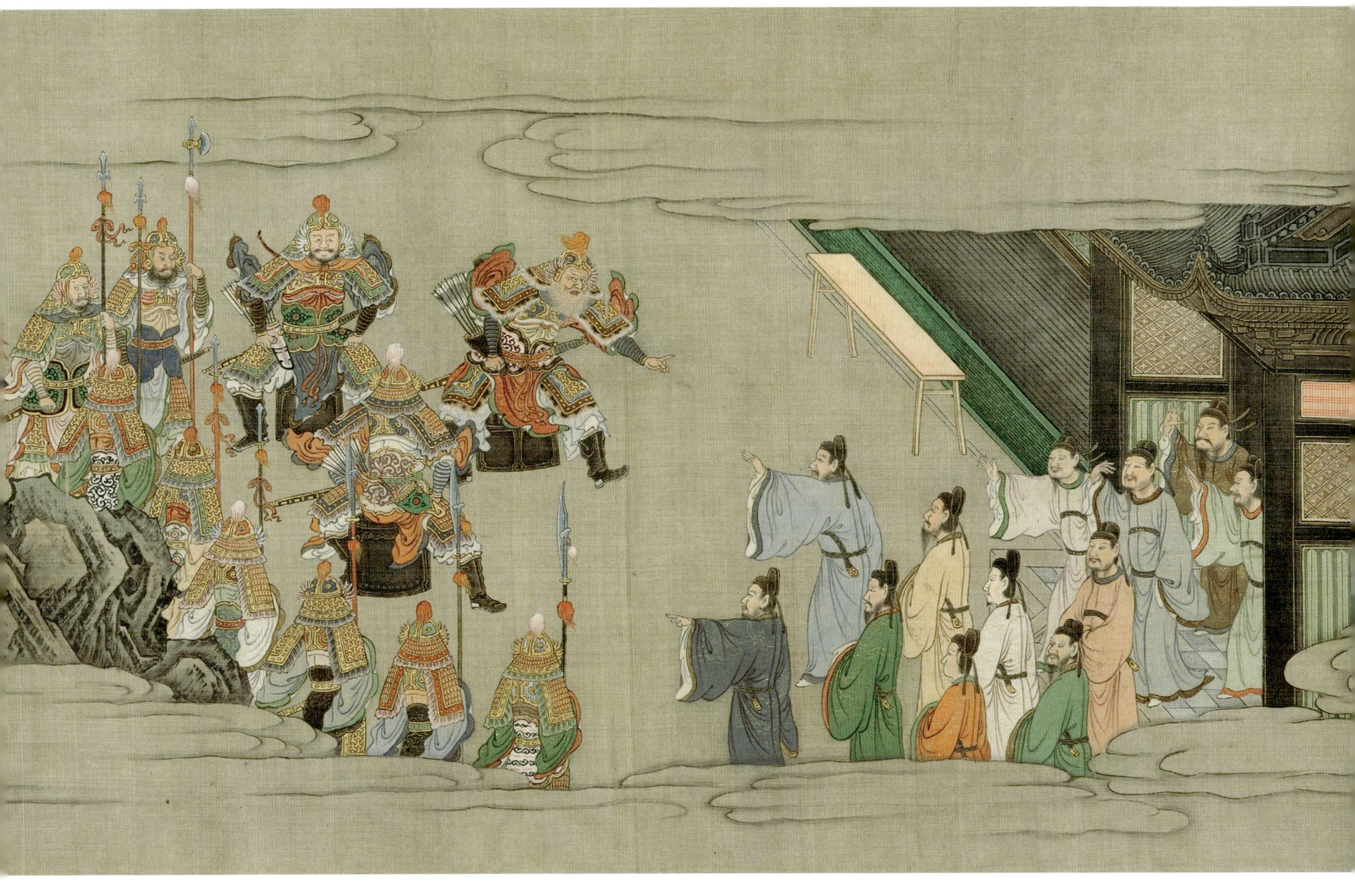

This final scene of the first scroll presents a rare but decisive deviation from the textual source. We may remember how, in the interests of visual propriety, the figure of Yang Guifei was fully clothed as she stepped out of the hot springs at Huaqing. Here, once again, the painting presents the moment of her death in an idealised way. She is seated on a square mat in the foreground, her head lowered and her neck bared. The dignity of her pose as she contemplates her fate emphasises the poetic sense of injustice, but also powerfully contradicts the original poetic image of this scene, in which, faced with death, she dramatically loses her composure. Bai Juyi describes her lovely eyebrows perishing 'before the horses' standing by the roadside, and her hair ornaments and jewellery flying as she struggles in vain. In the ballad, as in Chen Hong's 'Account', she does not

'die game', in the old parlance of public executions. Yet, in the painting, her outer appearance is a model of dignity: the swirling movements of her scarf in an imaginary wind are the only clues to the inner turmoil of her emotions. A soldier has planted his boot heavily on the edge of the mat, and holding the silken cord, he approaches uneasily to pass it around her neck. In a rather mawkish vignette, his companion holds another rope, which has not been needed to bind her. The dignified composure of Yang Guifei, which would not have been out of place for a samurai about to commit ritual suicide, reinforces the romantic interpretation of the event in this painting. It is left to her female attendants to throw themselves on the ground in tears. The bodyguards themselves appear grim-faced at the moment of carrying out their demand for her execution.

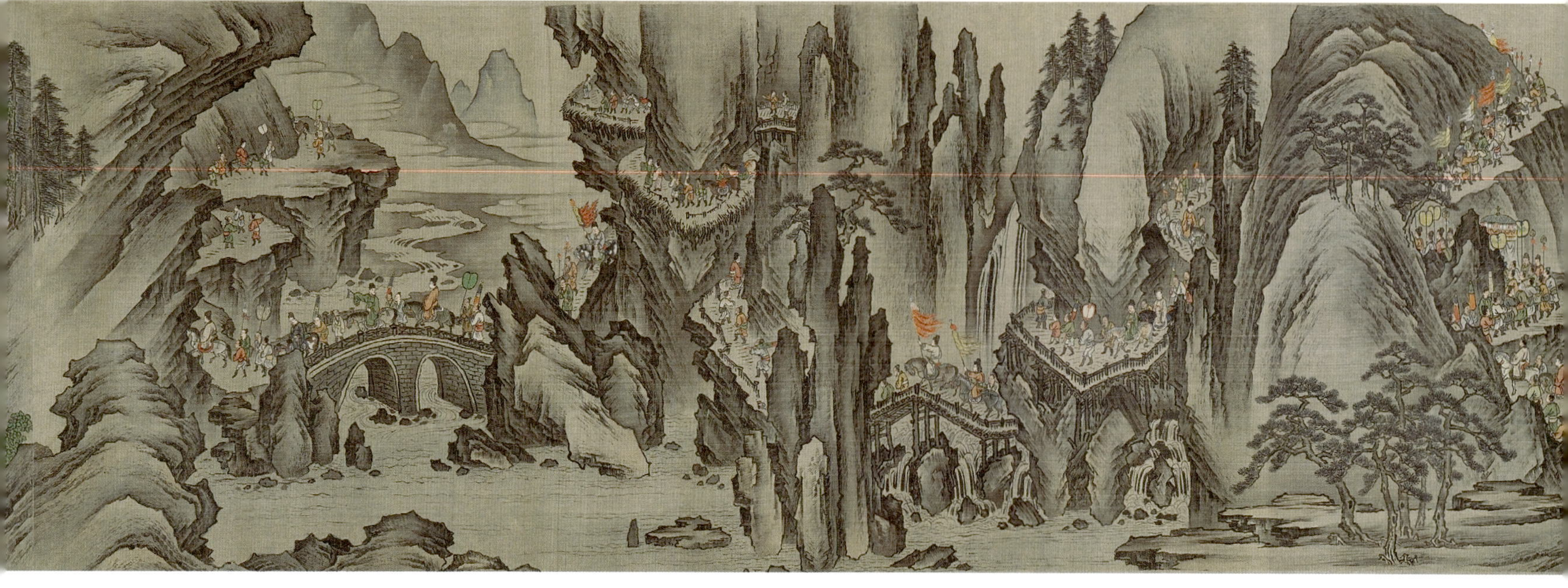

THE SECOND SCROLL

IF THE FIRST SCROLL traces the career of Yang Guifei, from her discovery in the Yang household as a young woman to her death at Mawei, the second scroll recounts the distraught Minghuang's solitary life after her death, and his desperate search for a way to communicate with her in the afterlife. Following the pattern of three grouped scenes per 'act', the second scroll of the painting describes the following events:

- the flight to Shu through the mountains
- Minghuang's eventual return to the capital
- his solitary mourning in the palace
- his engaging a Daoist wizard to find the soul of Yang Guifei
- the Daoist finding her abode in the isles of the immortals
- the Daoist's interview with her

As in the first scroll, the narrative is carefully paced so that the crucial moment, which occurs about two-thirds of the way through each scroll, is somewhat more drawn out visually. In each case, the fourth length of silk appears to contain two scenes rather than the usual three, with the 'extra' scene incorporated as a half scene, as it were, elsewhere.

Various devices are used to stop the format of the 'three-scene act' from becoming predictable. One example is that some scenes describing one piece of the action overlap or spill over into another. Another is the way that openings in clouds or buildings serve to frame figural scenes. In the second scroll, the third (Minghuang mourning) and sixth (the Daoist's interview with Yang Guifei) scene-sets are discrete and confined to one length of silk. Elsewhere, however, the pattern is broken up by the introduction of distinctive Kano School visual themes such as clouds or mountains. Events towards the end of the first scroll are glimpsed through openings in the rolling forms of clouds, an effect that reaches its climax in the opening passage of the second scroll, where two scenes are split across the silk. The next visual theme is landscape: a long passage of mountainous terrain follows. Later in the second scroll, the travels of the Daoist wizard in search of the soul of Yang Guifei spill over from the fourth silk onto the fifth, effectively linking the two.

These remarks presuppose one important factor about the mounting of the *Chōgonka* scrolls, namely the division of the painting into a pair of scrolls. It is likely that this was the format of the mounting in the late nineteenth century, when the painting was acquired by Louis Gonse. It was this mounting that deteriorated in condition over the course of the twentieth century, leaving the painting almost unrecognisable as a fine work by Kano Sansetsu. During the remounting in the early 1990s, the possibility was raised that the painting could, prior to this division into two scrolls, have been divided into three. We return to this absorbing question of the mounting format in the Coda that follows this chapter, in which another version of the painting is discussed.

FIG 31 'Kano Sansetsu (1590–1651), Flight through the mountains to Shu, *Song of Lasting Sorrow*, 1646–47. Scroll 2, the first length of silk; ink and colours on silk, 31.5 x 1070.0 cm. © Trustees of the Chester Beatty Library, Dublin.

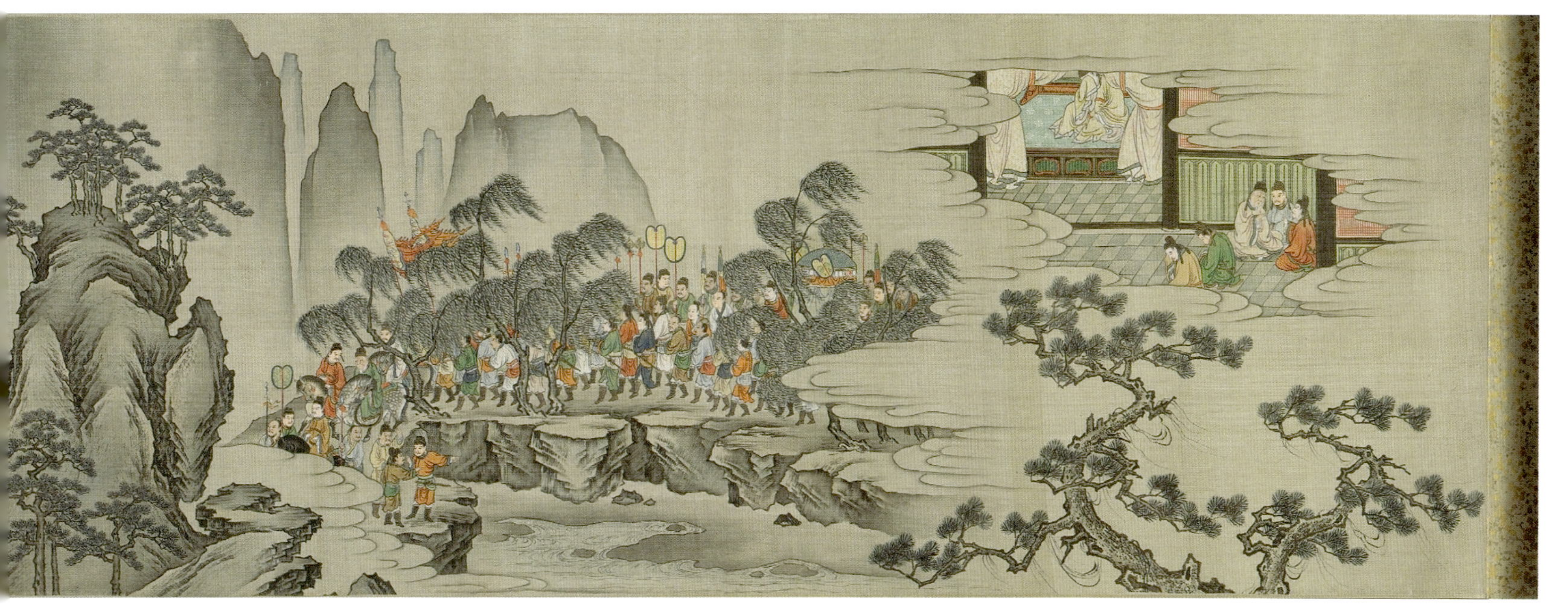

FLIGHT THROUGH THE MOUNTAINS
TO SHU (FIG. 31)

Our lord and ruler covered his face,
unable to protect her;
he looked around, and blood and tears
were flowing there together.

Brown dust spread in billows,
howling was the wind,
plank walkways wound into the clouds
as he climbed by Sword Tower Peak.

45 *And at the foot of Mount Emei*
travellers were few,
the royal banners shed no light,
the beams of sun were pale.

THE SECOND SCROLL BEGINS vividly with events in the aftermath of Yang Guifei's execution, firstly focusing intensely on Minghuang's personal reaction. Visually, the pictorial narrative in these opening scenes of the second scroll revolves around two pivotal representations of the place of Yang Guifei's death – Mawei. The scroll opens with the first of these, at or close to the moment of her execution. This is a split or double-scene effect, within the imaginary rectangular scene frame, made possible through the use of thick encircling clouds seen behind a windblown pine growing from below. Above the pine, a window opens in the stylised clouds to reveal the emperor, too prostrated by grief to look at the place of execution. He sits on a daybed in a building, his sleeve to his face in the conventional gesture of weeping, as a group of courtiers or eunuchs sit quietly outside his chamber, conferring or sobbing. The second 'half' of this scene, split by clouds, shows the imperial entourage, now moving again into a headwind, gazing upon the place of Yang Guifei's strangulation beside the canal at Mawei, as sheer peaks loom above. The figures look down, from among windblown willows, over the eroded banks of the canal into a kind of watery pit that opens up below them, in the lower left corner of the imaginary scene frame. The windy, cloudy atmosphere of this opening passage suggests that these two moments – the emperor appearing in the upper right, and Yang Guifei left buried in the lower left – are simultaneous. It is

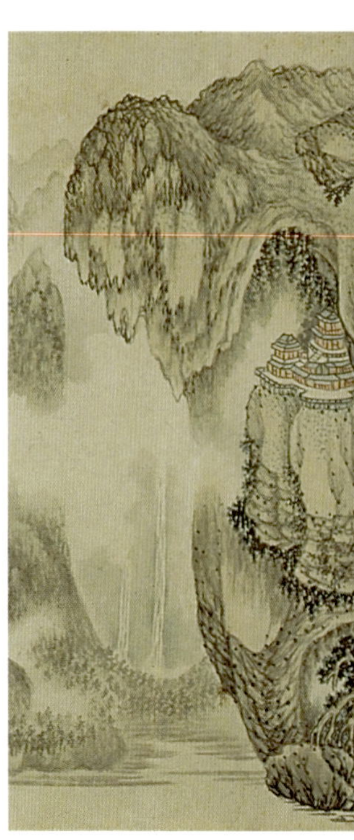

this watery pit that the party will revisit on its return to the capital several scenes later, although its depiction there (in Act 2, Scene 2) will be quite different.

Between these two views of Mawei is a sequence of three evocative scenes describing the emperor's flight over the Jian'ge mountain pass and the reestablishment of the court in exile under Mount Emei. The first two of these are painted on the first length of silk; the third opens the second length.

The hardship of the journey through the mountains is conveyed by two distinctive landscape passages. The first of these is open and rounded as the procession files up and down over the Jian'ge, or Sword Tower, Pass. First is an upward path cut into the side of a mountain. The imperial attendants and banner-bearers, seemingly accustomed only to a privileged palace life, cling to one another in single file. They round a mass of rock at the top and return, downward. Now, the same attendants appear strung out and exhausted, enclosed and oppressed by the looming cliffs. Gradually the path changes from one hewn into the rocky cliff-faces to one made of planks that cling to the sheer sides of the cliffs. The party crosses a mountain torrent and heads on among even more remote and crowded peaks.

The second distinctive landscape passage is centred on the double-arched stone bridge, and represents the group's arrival among the Emei Mountains, which symbolically stand for Shu or Sichuan. Here, the imperial party has come down from the plank roads to cross a broad rock-strewn stream that lines the floor of a clouded mountainous valley receding into the distance, and pass on along further flat outcrops of rock. Arching ominously above this bridge, darkening the scene, are looming mountaintops.

In the final mountainous scene to the left after the stone bridge, the court is shown assembled in ad hoc fashion among rustic, thatched-roofed buildings

settling into a period of exile, historically spent in Chengdu from the seventh month of 756 to the tenth month of 757. Although reduced to living under mere thatched roofs, some sense of dignity is imparted by the tall pines, nevertheless. The emperor sits alone. He is haunted by ominous sounds – but not by the dark tolling of a bell mentioned in Bai Juyi's original poem. He endures the screeching of apes (such as appear in other evocative poems), the animals that have made tourism to Sichuan's mountains and Mount Emei, in particular, what it is today. Alone with his thoughts, the emperor is unable to participate in state affairs, which his advisors conduct elsewhere. Perhaps they are now receiving the news which, historically, came some time after the emperor's arrival in Sichuan: that the Heir Apparent had usurped the throne (on the twelfth day of the seventh month of 756), a machination to which, as de facto 'retired emperor', Minghuang quietly acquiesced. Following this, and rounding off the episode of the flight to and exile in Shu, is shown the visit to Mawei on the way back to the capital a year later. Technically, the suite of scenes beginning with the court in exile is painted on the length of silk that follows this one, and so will be considered further in the next section, 'Return from Exile'.

The mountain regions through which Minghuang fled are well known not only for their topography but also because they are the topic of poetic evocations of their features and history. We mentioned earlier Li Bai's well-known poem entitled 'Hardships of the Road to Shu'. Although this was probably written before Minghuang's flight, it evokes the perilous journey along the plank roads, to the sound of howling apes, through the highlands of southern Shaanxi and down into Sichuan. To quibble, one might observe that in fact the plank roads lie between Baoji and the Jian'ge Pass, and not after the pass, as implied by the

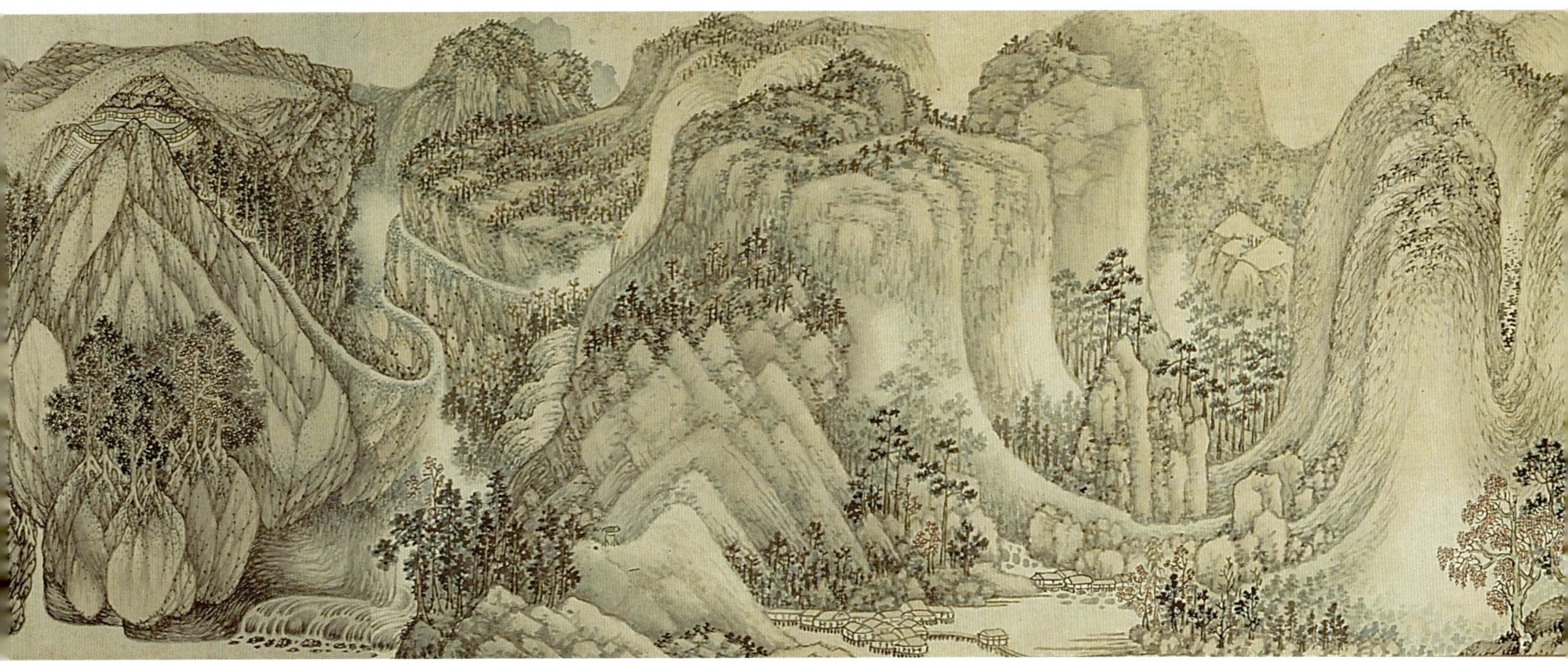

painting; and also, that Minghuang spent his exile in the provincial capital Chengdu, rather than the Emei Mountains, which lie well to the south of the city. However, Bai Juyi's decision to make the Emei Mountains the emperor's place of exile was an appropriate poetic gesture, and one that Sansetsu followed in his illustration. Arguably, depicting 'Minghuang in the mountains' had an established iconography that flourished in a whole subgenre of paintings with titles like *Minghuang Escaping the Heat*. That, and other titles like *Picking Melons*, have long been euphemisms for this tale, as we have noted, and Sansetsu would surely have been aware of this tradition of the Yuan-dynasty Li-Guo style through the many paintings in this style transmitted to Japan, and as evidenced from his West Lake screens and other paintings.

Given its popularity in both poetry and painting, this mountainous section of the *Chōgonka* painting has significant links to Chinese painting. The work of the late Ming painter Wu Bin, a master of 'weird' mountains, has been plausibly linked.[53] Any number of Wu Bin's paintings in attenuated formats, depicting attenuated forms, could be identified as references for the needle-pointed peaks and strangely shaped mountains found in the *Chōgonka* painting: *Steep Ravines and Flying Cascades* (National Palace Museum, Taipei) of before 1610; *Thousand Cliffs and Myriad Ravines* in the Palace Museum, Beijing;

Landscape of the Road to Shanyin in the Shanghai Museum (fig. 32), and so on. Most of these exemplify the late-Ming vogue for 'the strange' (*qi*), seen in both unusual landscape forms and in bizarre styles of calligraphy, and even in the antiquarian love of antiquities and obsessive collecting.

Among eminent Ming artists, Qiu Ying may be alone in having illustrated the *Chang hen ge* narrative in painting – in an attribution in the Shanghai Museum entitled *Jian'ge Pass*.[54] This hanging scroll, a probable excerpt from the narrative, depicts the view up a mountainous river valley under a leaden sky. Closest to the viewer at the bottom of the painting is a riderless horse, the symbol of the deceased Yang Guifei, being left behind by the last few courtiers. Further up in the painting, along the rising, receding valley, a column of fleeing courtiers lines the plank road as it winds its way up the sides of the steep cliffs before disappearing over the high peaks under the dark sky in the upper left corner. There is no evidence, however, that Sansetsu would have known about this work.

Even if Sansetsu had had such landscapes as these in front of him, he would still have had to digest their style and incorporate this type-form into his own pictorial narrative. How might he have done that? The mountain scenery contains its own mini-narrative centred upon the (recurring) motif of the stone bridge in

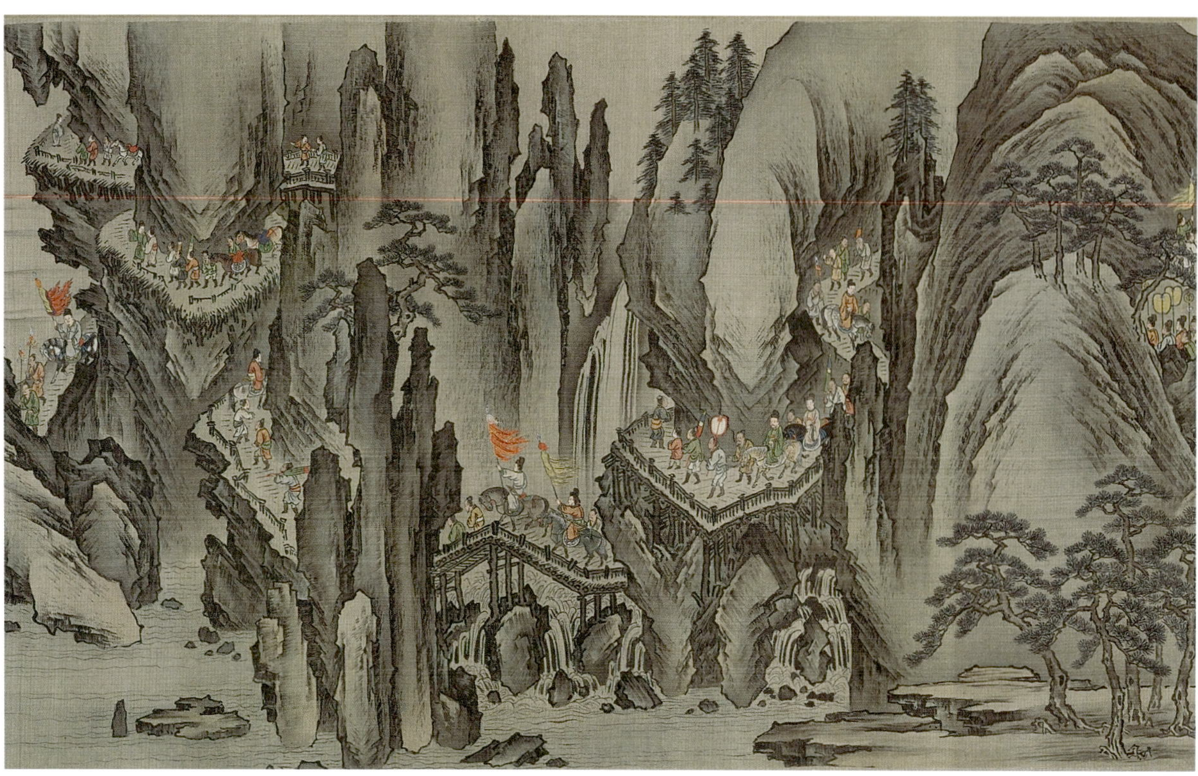

the centre, which lies in the cavernous depths of the
mountains hemmed in by overarching cliffs to each
side; the imperial party creep along under cliff faces,
enhancing the sense of darkness, oppression and fear
– illustrated in the couplet (lines 45–46):

> *And at the foot of Mount Emei*
> *travellers were few,*
> *the royal banners shed no light,*
> *the beams of sun were pale.*

The passage to the right, which illustrates the previous
couplet, is contrastive: the mountain scenery is open
and rounded as the imperial column first enters the
high peaks region of Sichuan via the Jian'ge pass (lines
43–44):

> *Brown dust spread in billows,*
> *howling was the wind,*
> *plank walkways wound into the clouds*
> *as he climbed by Sword Tower Peak.*

First, the column moves along the topsides of the slopes;
later, it creeps along the plank roads that are a major
tourist attraction of the region today (fig. 33). In the
Tang, the Jian'ge Pass actually gave its name to the region
beyond it to the southwest, Jiannan (South of Jian).

We may speak of the 'influence' of the strange
landscape style of Wu Bin – steep paths cut into softer
faces of cliffs and mountains; wooden structures pre-
cariously adhering to sheer rock where no path can
be cut; a wooden bridge spanning a mountain torrent
– but it was only given play within Sansetsu's grander
plan for this passage within the context of the full narrative picture-scrolls. And, the *Chōgonka* landscape
should also be judged in light of Sansetsu's own earlier
painting in this landscape mode, to which Matthew
McKelway refers in chapter four (see fig. 79).

It seems that on occasion Sansetsu employed
visual sources that were not yet widely known among
painters, including images from newly imported Chinese printed books.[55] Specifically, two late-Ming
printed books, *Hainei qiguan* and the encyclopaedia
Sancai tuhui, both contain pictures of the 'Plank
Roads to Sichuan' and of 'Mount Emei' (figs 34,
35).[56] Comparing them, it is evident from the lesser
pictorial legibility of the *Hainei qiguan* images that
they were either cribbed from those in the *Sancai
tuhui*, or were less well copied from a mutual source.
Curiously, the *Hainei qiguan* pictures make a greater
claim to cartographic accuracy by virtue of the place-
name captions that have been somewhat arbitrarily
added.

Looking more closely at the illustration, the

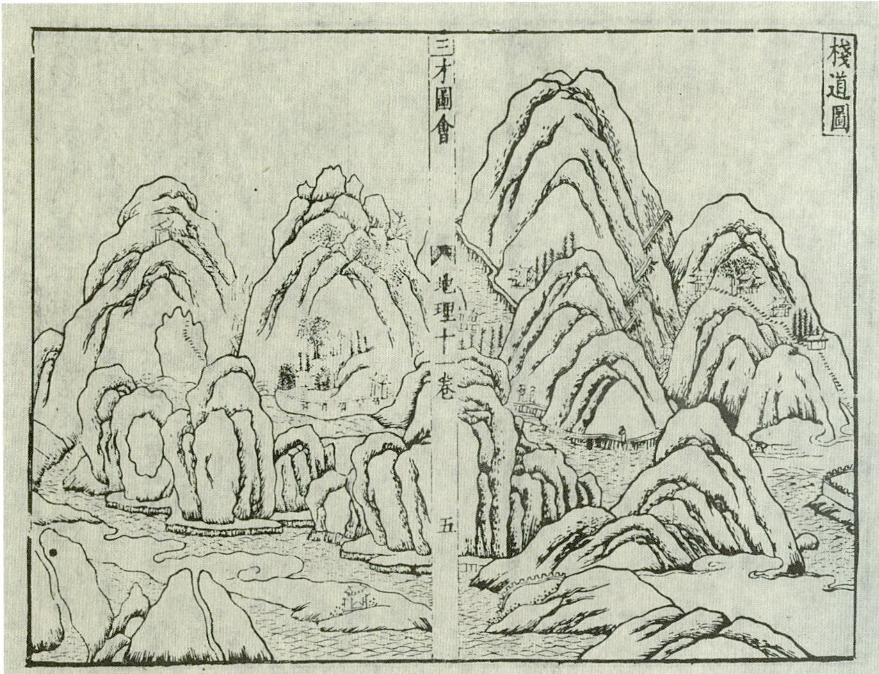

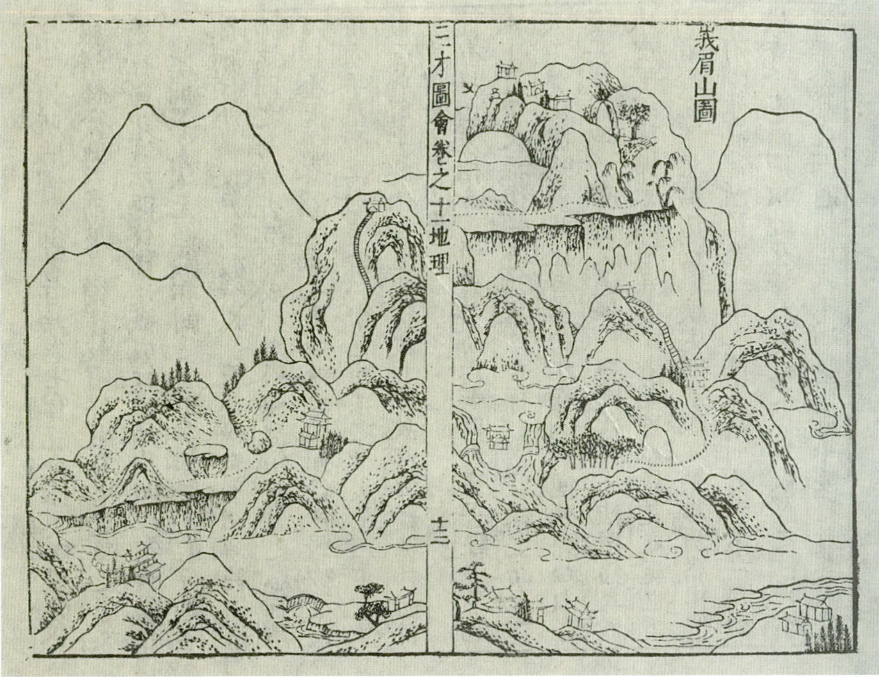

'Plank Roads to Sichuan', we see that geographically these roads lie southwest of Baoji (a city due west of Xi'an along the Wei River) and lead south through the precipitous terrain towards the mountain passes, of which the Jian'ge Pass is perhaps the best known, into the Sichuan basin. Said to have been built in the Qin dynasty (221–06 BC), these roads were once the only route from Xi'an down to Sichuan. The *Hainei qiguan* print is somewhat fanciful as a topographical picture, but effectively shows how the mountains loom above the main river arteries bounding the

region: the Wei to the north; the Jialing River to the west; and the Han River cutting from east to west through the middle.[57] Common currency, such a print of the 'Plank Roads to Sichuan' must have been of some interest to Sansetsu, if only as corroboration of the wooden cliff-face structures seen in paintings by artists like Wu Bin and Qiu Ying, or for a general iconography of 'snow-capped peaks' in the distance, and a river-below-mountain effect.

More than any of these images, however, it is the lines of Bai Juyi's poem itself that most influence the shaping of this mountain passage of the painting. In a quite literal interpretation of the lines quoted above, the painting shows the party proceeding from Jian'ge Pass along the plank roads and, immediately after, under the gloomy, enclosing cliffs of Mount Emei, as if these places were close in distance, rather than hundreds of miles apart: Sansetsu quite literally borrows Bai Juyi's poetic licence. It would seem from such a direct interpretation of the literature such as this that the plotting of the scroll vacillated from being fully illustrative of the text at the level of scenic detail, to being image-driven in terms of visual narration, through the use of repeated and decorative motifs and iconography. This textual conceit would no doubt have been appreciated by the more literary minded of Sansetsu's patrons, while pictorial references to Chinese paintings and pictures also lay within.

We may recall that this mountainous section of the scroll does not stand alone, but lies between two depictions of Mawei, the place of Yang Guifei's execution. Although the mountain passage represents a discrete section of the story, it also takes its place within the whole. Citing Ming paintings or woodblock prints as possible sources, therefore, does not give full satisfaction: these type-forms, or references to them, are deployed in the service of this much grander visual plot.

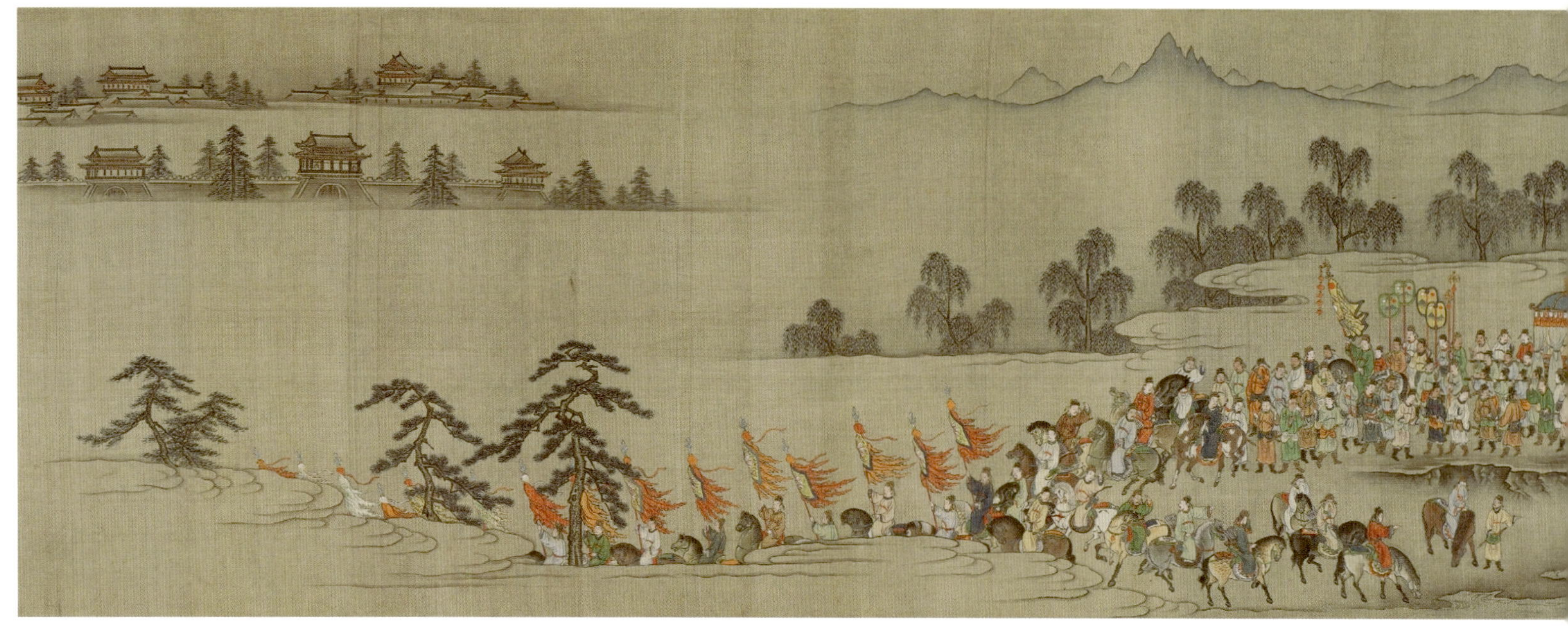

Shu's rivers' sapphire waters,
*   the green of hills in Shu –*
the state of His Royal Majesty's heart
*   every morning, every night.*
From an exile's palace he saw the moon,
*   hues that give heart pain;*
50 *in the rain of night he heard the bells,*
*   sounds that broke him within.*

Heaven revolved, the days spun round,
*   the dragon-carriage turned home,*
but reaching that spot he faltered
*   and could not leave it behind.*
Beneath the slopes of Mawei,
*   there in the mud and mire,*
he could not see where those features,
*   white as marble, died for naught.*

55 *Ruler and ministers looked at each other,*
*   all soaked their clothes with tears,*
then facing east toward the capital gates,
*   he let his horse take him home.*

IN THE FIRST SCENE, the emperor is shown seated in his makeshift court deep in the mountains. Under these thatched roofs among thin, spindly pines are various rooms, which might hold courtiers debating affairs of state as easily as children at play. In the lower rooms, the weapons of the imperial bodyguard stand on the floor along the interior walls. Clearly, the imperial party has recently arrived in this place, and there is no local armoury, nor has one yet been established. Under the moon, in an isolated upper story just below cloud level, the emperor is shown seated alone. He seems oblivious to the presence of two attendant women as he gazes blankly out through the lowered blind. An insight into his mood is suggested by the screen painting behind, which shows the mast-top of a small single-sail vessel being pressed along by a stiff breeze through dense, low-lying fog. Opposite his high window, pine trees cling improbably to the rocky pinnacles, which are home to mountain apes. According to the poem as transmitted in Japan, Minghuang is haunted not by the tolling bells of highland temples, but by the eerie night-time cries of the apes, under the cold moonlight. In the next-door room, maids prepare refreshments but the emperor has lost his appetite – a serving woman holds up her hand to delay the presentation of a plate. He seems also to have lost interest in restoring the government, having delegated all responsibility to his advisors. Lower down in this rustic precinct, the business of court goes on. Separate

FIG 36 Kano Sansetsu, Return to the capital, *Song of Lasting Sorrow*; scroll 2, the second length of silk.

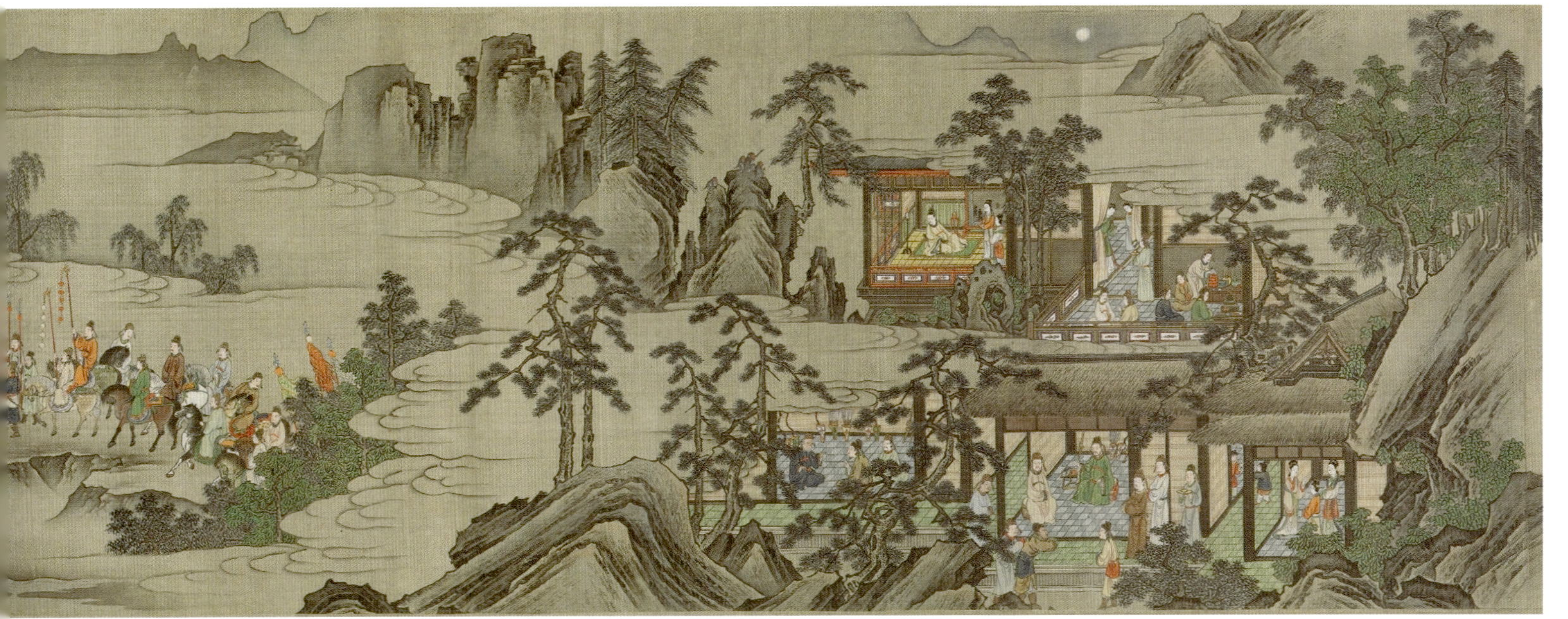

groups of men and women exchange the news; children play; and his Majesty's representative, seated, receives a lowly arrival, perhaps even the messenger bearing news of the succession.

A pair of tall pines standing on a triangular rocky bluff and silhouetted against clouds forms a natural division between this scene and the next – and marks a significant passage of time and space. Indeed, after these pines, a vast panorama opens out presenting the second and third scenes on the same length of silk, in which the emperor returns to the capital via Mawei in 757, once order had been restored to the empire. This scene is brought to a close where the length of silk ends, with a distant sketchy evocation of the capital in the upper left corner. The fortified tops of the city walls, the tree-tops and, beyond, the upper stories of further-off buildings represent the whole city.

In this panorama, what compels our attention is the dramatic rounded central scene with its overlapping concentric rings of mountains, clouds, trees and more clouds, all receding back into the pictorial space from the watery ditch in the immediate foreground. In the centre of this ringed tableau is Minghuang, now the retired emperor, and his colourful bannered escort, en route from Shu back to the capital, actually passing the place of Yang Guifei's execution by the road. Seated in the imperial palanquin, overcome by grief, he buries his face in his sleeves (fig. 37), as do many of the men in his escort, while others hold up their hands in gestures of grief and despair. The disconsolate mood of the courtiers is shared by the horses. The postures and facial expressions of the animals, especially those near the execution site, exhibit their own collective state of unease. This passage of the painting literally describes how Minghuang was unable to gaze upon the spot, as Bai Juyi describes it in the ballad.

The unusual spatial configuration of this particular scene was surely intended by Sansetsu to evoke one of the 'primitivist' landscape compositional types from early Chinese painting. This is the adoption of the 'space-cell', a framing device whereby a significant figure or place within a painting is placed inside an oval compositional frame. This device is found in early paintings but was also used periodically and self-consciously to evoke antiquity in the later literati tradition of Chinese painting.[58] The effect may also be recalled in scenes from derived copies of lost original paintings like the Tang painter-poet Wang Wei's iconic *Wangchuan Villa* scroll, where it appears repeatedly. The *Wangchuan Villa* composition was perhaps best known in China, from Song (960–1279) times on, via a copy made by Guo Zhongshu. This was recopied as a painting and also transmitted in the form of ink-rubbings made from a stone engraving (or engravings). An example of one such painting is the Yuan-dynasty *Wangchuan Villa*, dated 1342 and bearing the seal of Tang Di, in Kyoto National Museum (fig. 38).[59]

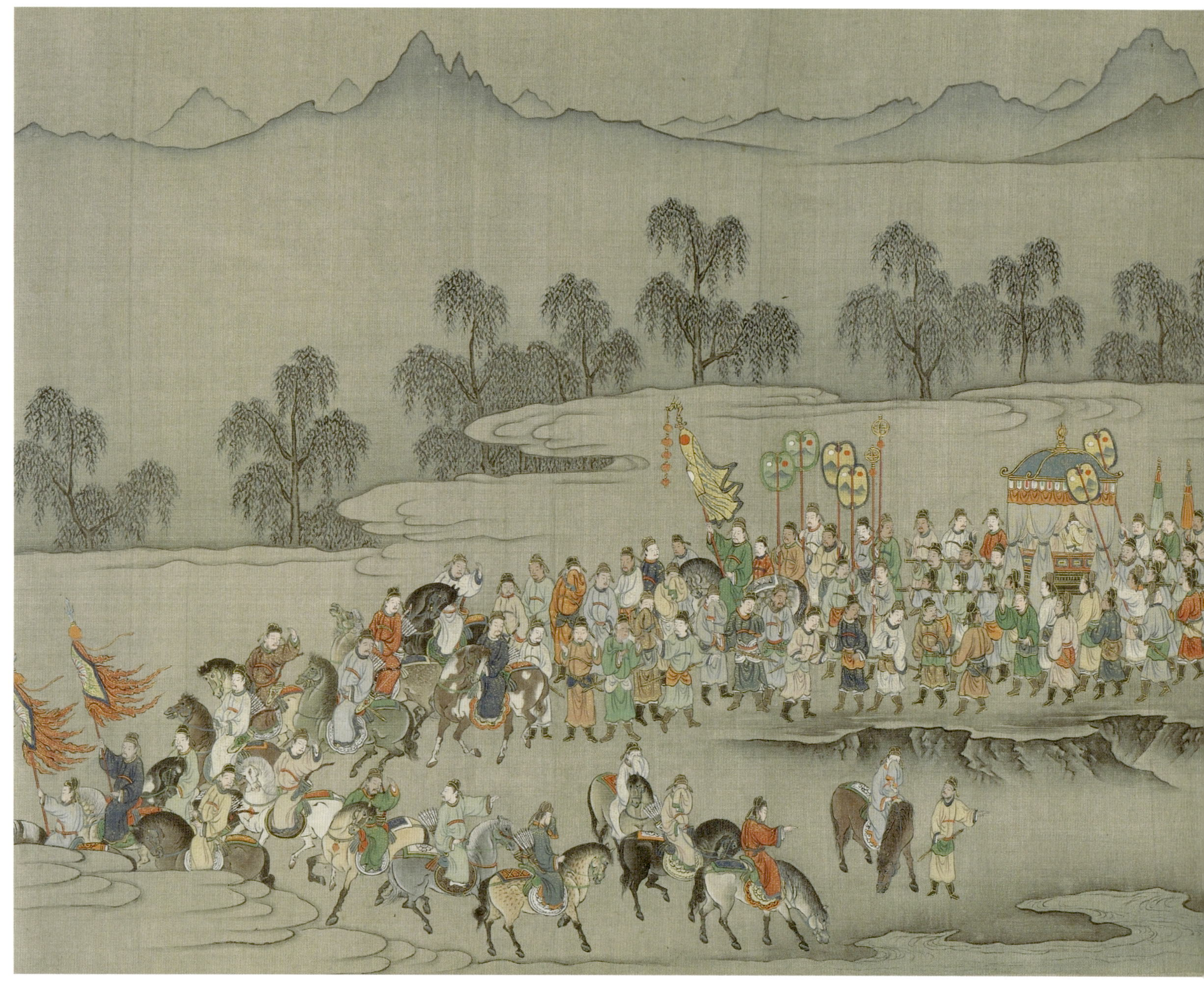

The use of the device in the Dublin scroll appears to have many facets, going beyond its potential simply to conjure up the mood of antiquity. Having a kind of stylised or stage-like quality, the circular shape around the emperor at Mawei also has a psychological intensity to it, since it embodies visually the idea of his separation from Yang Guifei in death and the consequent eternity of his suffering. This revolving visual and conceptual circle is only broken after a long pause, finally, by a spur – a train of half-seen, banner-bearing horsemen obscured by mist and trees – leading off to the left, towards the upper stories of the capital buildings in the distance. This is an illustration of line 56, to the effect that the emperor and his circle trusted their horses to take them home from here.

Standing back to view the painting, it is also possible to see how this archaistic, formalistic effect deliberately refocuses attention on the place of Yang Guifei's execution – how the place Mawei is used to potent dramatic and narrative effect. This is actually the third time the location is illustrated. It is first shown at the end of the first scroll, where Yang Guifei is about to be strangled. Then, the second scroll opens with the split scene, showing the emperor unable to pass by the spot 'until later', as the poem notes. Hence, in the diagonally divided scene to the right, he is shown by the use of a cloud window to be grieving elsewhere, as, in a visual eddy away from the onward movement of the column, one man points out to another the place where Yang Guifei's body has been thrown into the ditch. The

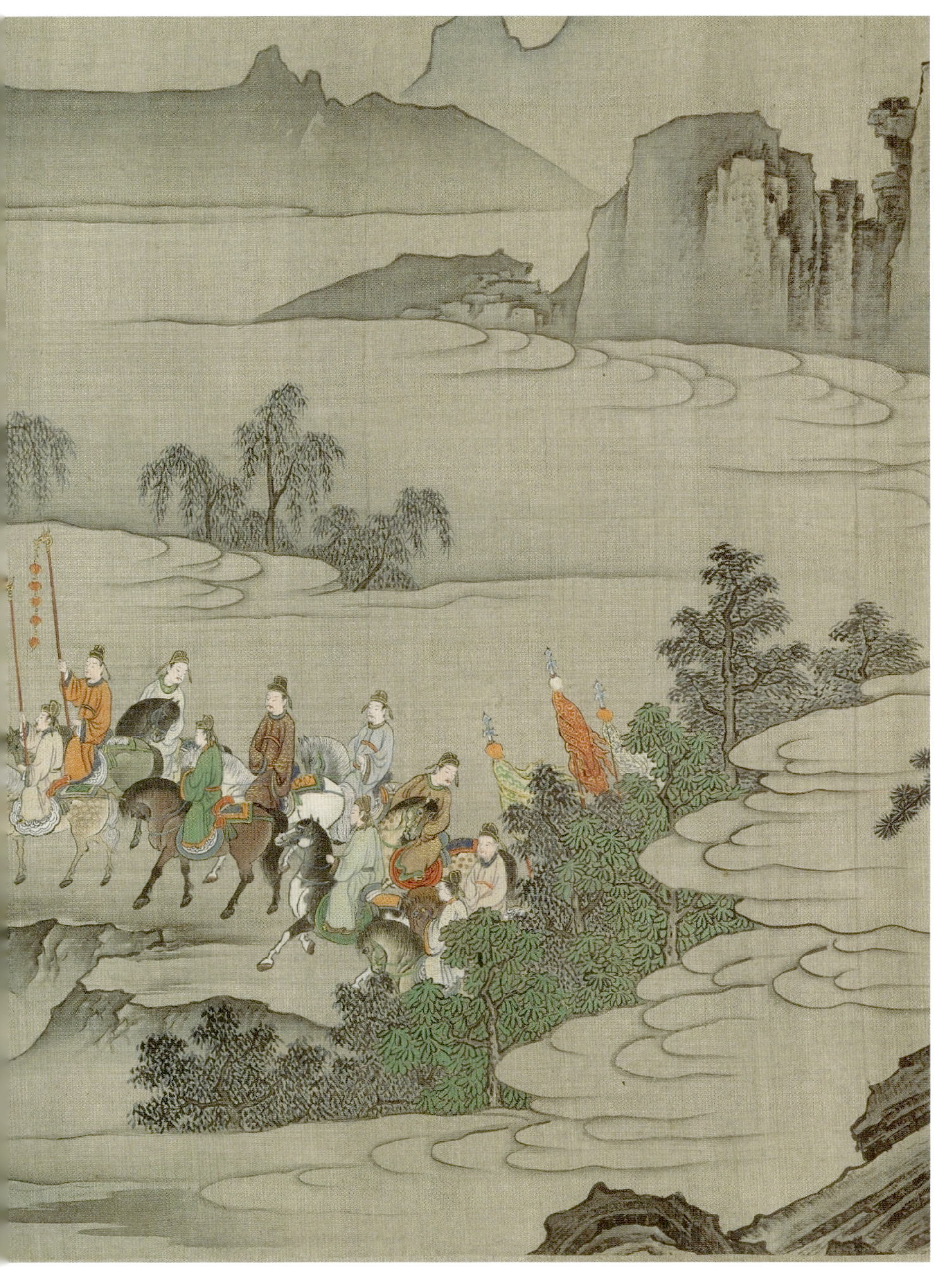

pine tree below does duty for the emperor; the tangled tendrils of creepers, like the outlines of his robe and nearby curtains, waver in the wind.

Finally, on the return journey to the capital, the imperial procession again passes Mawei. This deferred visit has been held back across almost two lengths of silk, as the plot and the scroll followed the dramatic side-show of the flight through the mountains to Shu. These two Mawei scenes flank or frame that whole passage of mountains. The composition of the first is diagonal, as if to show the emperor's alternatives – to visit it or not, in the midst of his flight. The second is circular, suggesting the emperor's enclosure or psychological encirclement by the event that has taken place on the site. The emotive power of the place, both on the emperor and the viewer, is brilliantly conveyed by these formal devices. In addition, the way that various figures in the scroll alternately turn away from or look and point towards the site tells of the conflicting emotions that seem to both attract and repulse the emperor – and we, the viewers – at the same time.

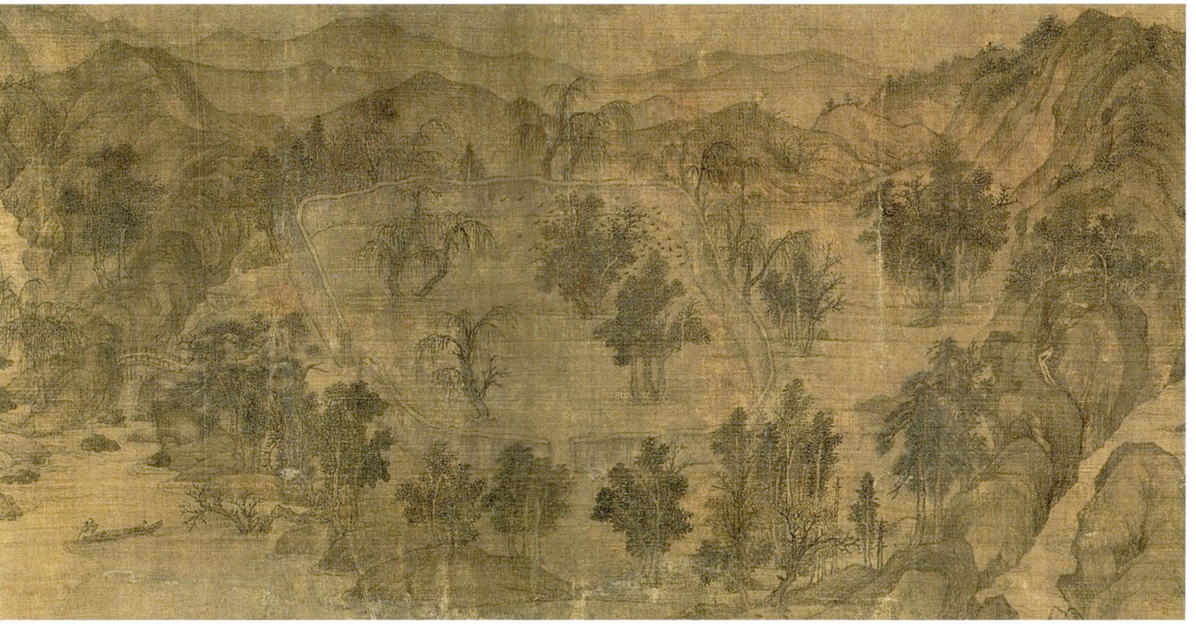

Fig 38 Tang Di (1296–1364), *Wangchuan Villa*. Detail of a handscroll; ink and light colour on silk, 34.8 x 509.1 cm. Kyoto National Museum.

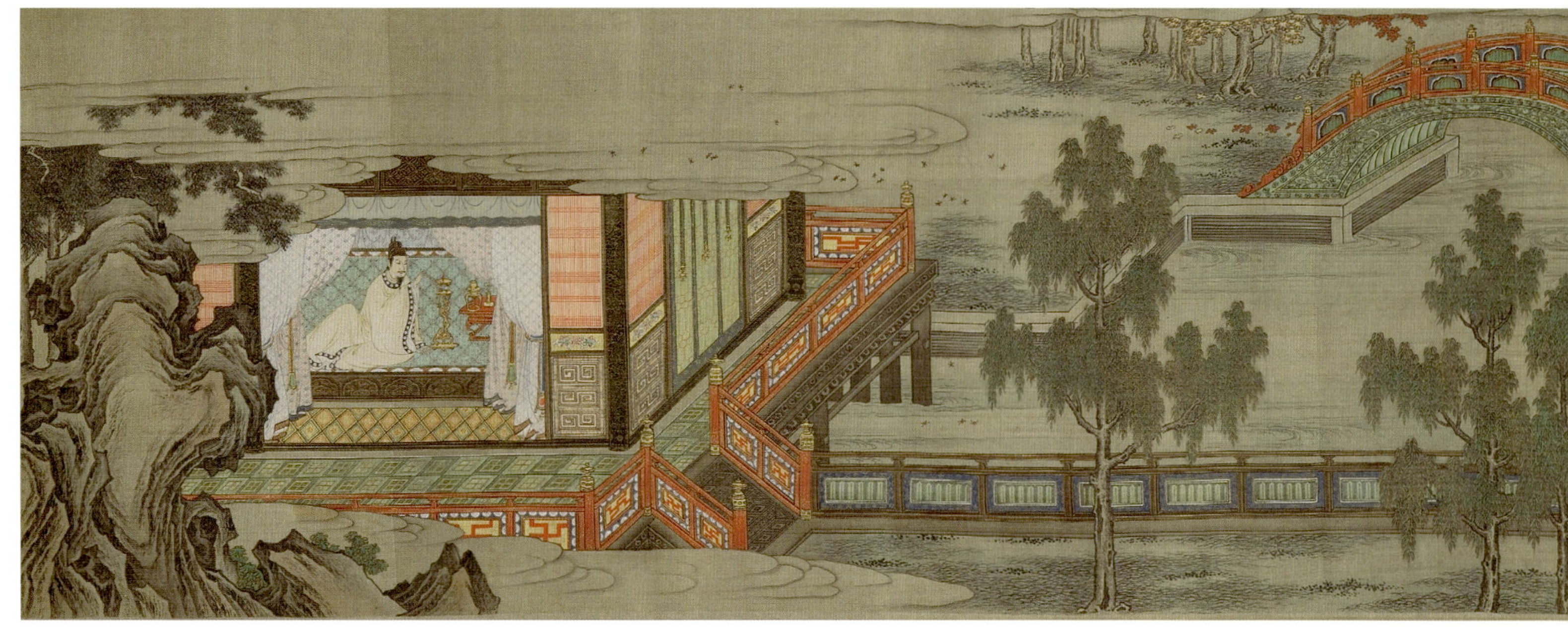

THE RETIRED EMPEROR MOURNS
YANG GUIFEI (FIG. 39)

When he was home, his pools and parks
 were all as they had been before,
there were lotuses in Taiye Pool and
 willows at Weiyang.

But the lotuses looked like her face,
 and the willows seemed like her brows,
60 before such scenes how could he stop
 his tears from streaming down? —
On days when plums and peaches
 opened in breeze of spring;
and in the season of autumn rain
 when beeches shed their leaves.

In the western palace and southern compound
 were many autumn plants
whose fallen leaves filled pavements,
 red, not swept away.
65 Performers of the Pear Garden,
 their hair newly touched with white;
eunuch attendants of pepper-walled harems,
 their blue-black brows showed age.

As glow-worms flew through twilight courts,
 he would sink into silent thought,
the wick of his lonely lamp burned low
 and still he could not sleep.
In the slow, slow beat of bells and drums
 his long nights would begin,
70 till the stream of stars was sparkling
 in skies approaching dawn.

The lovebird tiles were chill,
 heavy with flakes of frost,
the kingfisher quilts were cold
 without someone to share.

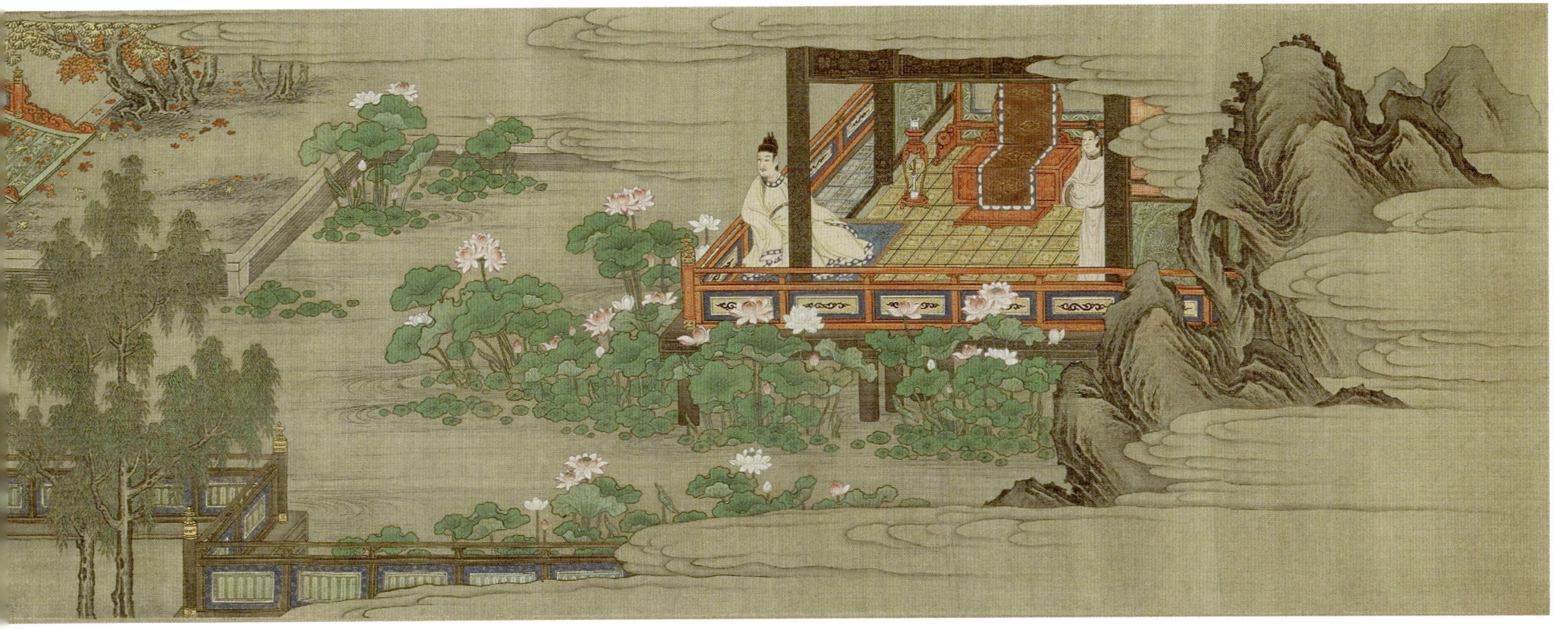

FIG 39 Kano Sansetsu, The retired emperor mourns Yang Guifei, *Song of Lasting Sorrow*; scroll 2, the third length of silk.

Overleaf:
FIG 40 The bridge scene (from **The retired emperor mourns Yang Guifei**), *Song of Lasting Sorrow*; (detail of fig. 39).

THESE THREE SCENES where the solitary emperor mourns his loss form a discrete core to the second scroll and present a compelling interplay between the poetic and pictorial qualities of time and space. That significant image – the bridge (fig. 40) – placed in the middle, acts like a kind of mirror between the two portraits of the mourning emperor to each side. The visual play on a mirror works alongside the theme of the inevitable progress of time, conveyed in this sequence by the changing of the seasons. The lotus in full bloom places the scene to the right in the blazing heat of late summer; the unswept autumn-hued leaves on the bridge show time moving on into the later part of the year; and finally, the sequestered and sleepless emperor tends his candle through a freezing winter night. This onward march of time towards winter reflects the retired emperor's darkening inner life over the course of the year just as the ballad does, but the effect of the mirrored portraits in the painting adds another dimension, by restarting the cycle over and over in an endless loop. In the winter scene, the holy Buddhist swastika symbol in the railing, which symbolises good fortune and well being, serves as a taunting reminder of his fate.

Centred on the bridge over Taiye's waters, the various movements of this ensemble of scenes seem conjoined like pieces in a jigsaw puzzle, while the diverse plants, groves and buildings stand for so many figures of the absent one, Yang Guifei. Lining the cen-

tral foreground is a stand of willows, images of feminine beauty and of Yang Guifei, indicating the frontage of the Weiyang Palace on the pond in the middle. Beyond, the leaves left lying on the steps mark the Western and Southern Palace precincts. To the left, the fireflies buzz in the night air outside the emperor's cloister. Like the mandarin drake that has lost his mate-for-life, Minghuang sits alone and sleepless inside, tending his guttering candle (fig. 41) The duck-and-drake roof tiles do not make their appearance here: they were illustrated previously on the roof of the palace during Minghuang's dalliance.

Opposite, the lakeside pavilion to the right overhangs Lake Taiye. This body of water is the visual key to this suite of scenes, linking left and right, foreground and background. Historically, its name alone would have been enough to recall imperial pleasure outings. It was the setting, for instance, for a dramatic incident in the love triangle between Han emperor Chengdi, his empress Zhao Feiyan and her sister Zhao Hede: while dancing, the empress was almost carried away into the sky – like a flying immortal – by strong winds.[60] Memories of such tales would have attached strong romantic associations to this place-name, reinforcing the emperor's sense of loss.

Minghuang's pavilion over Lake Taiye is decorated in sombre colours – browns and blues. The emperor's throne stands empty, and the picture-screen behind it bears no image, while his sitting mat has

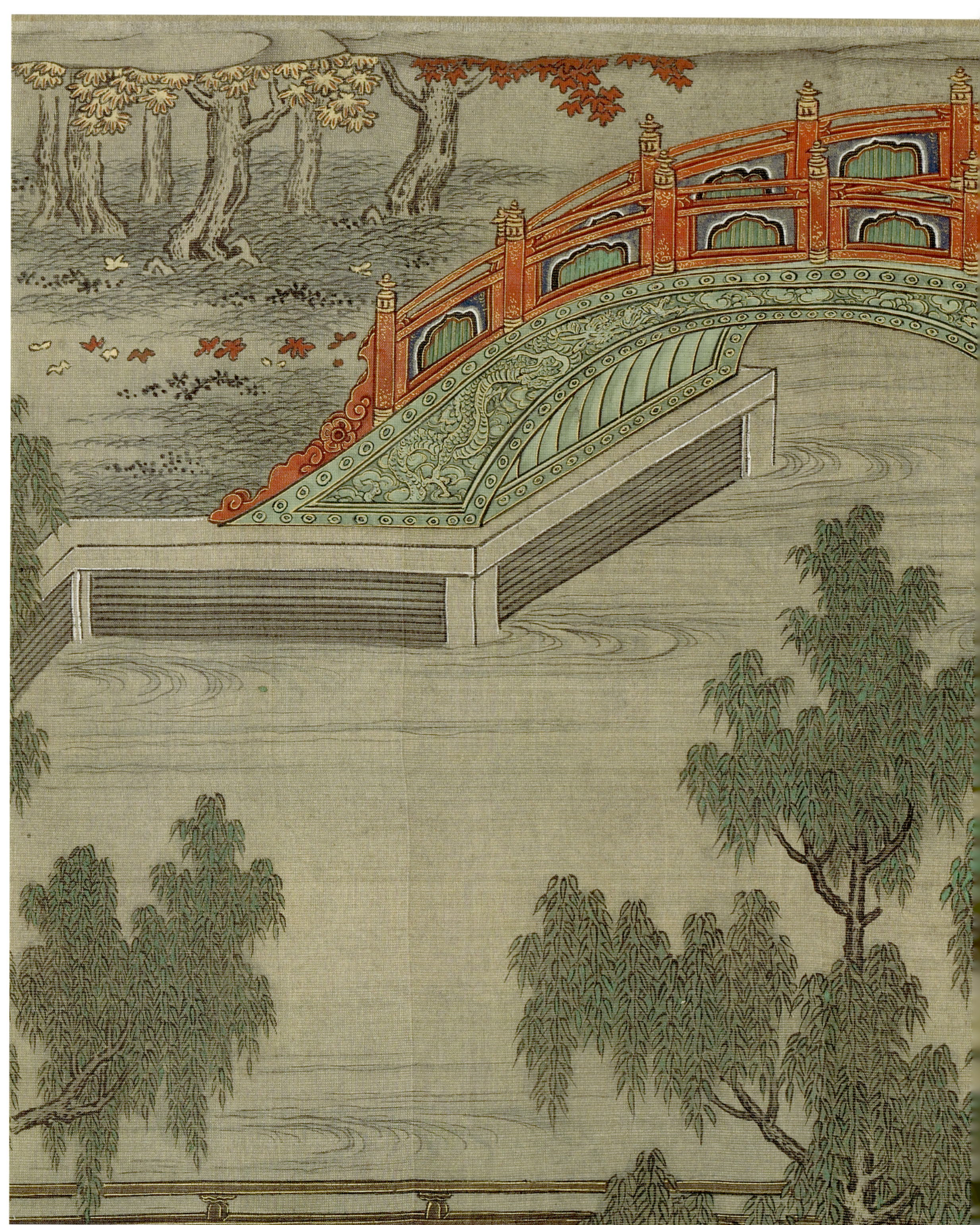

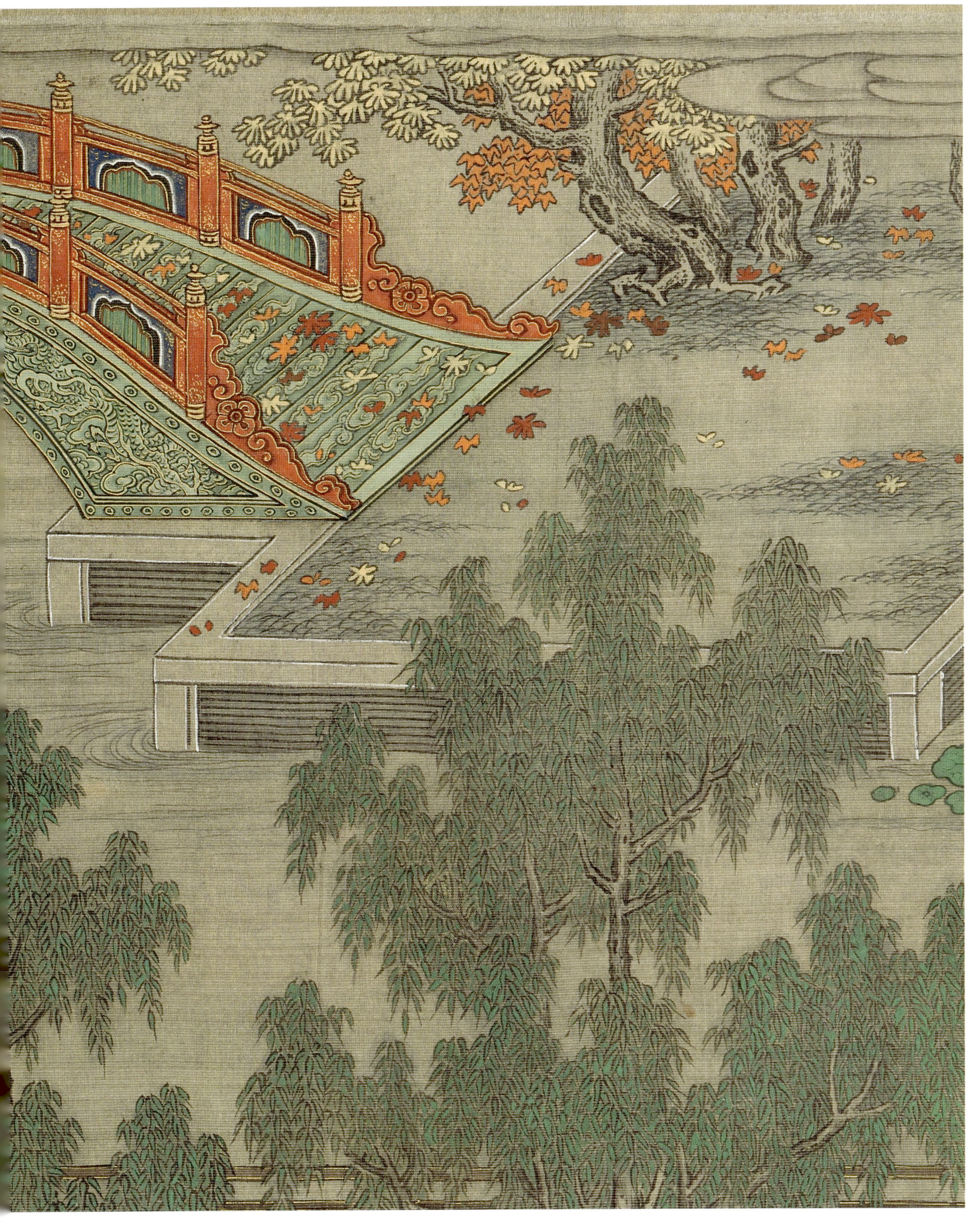

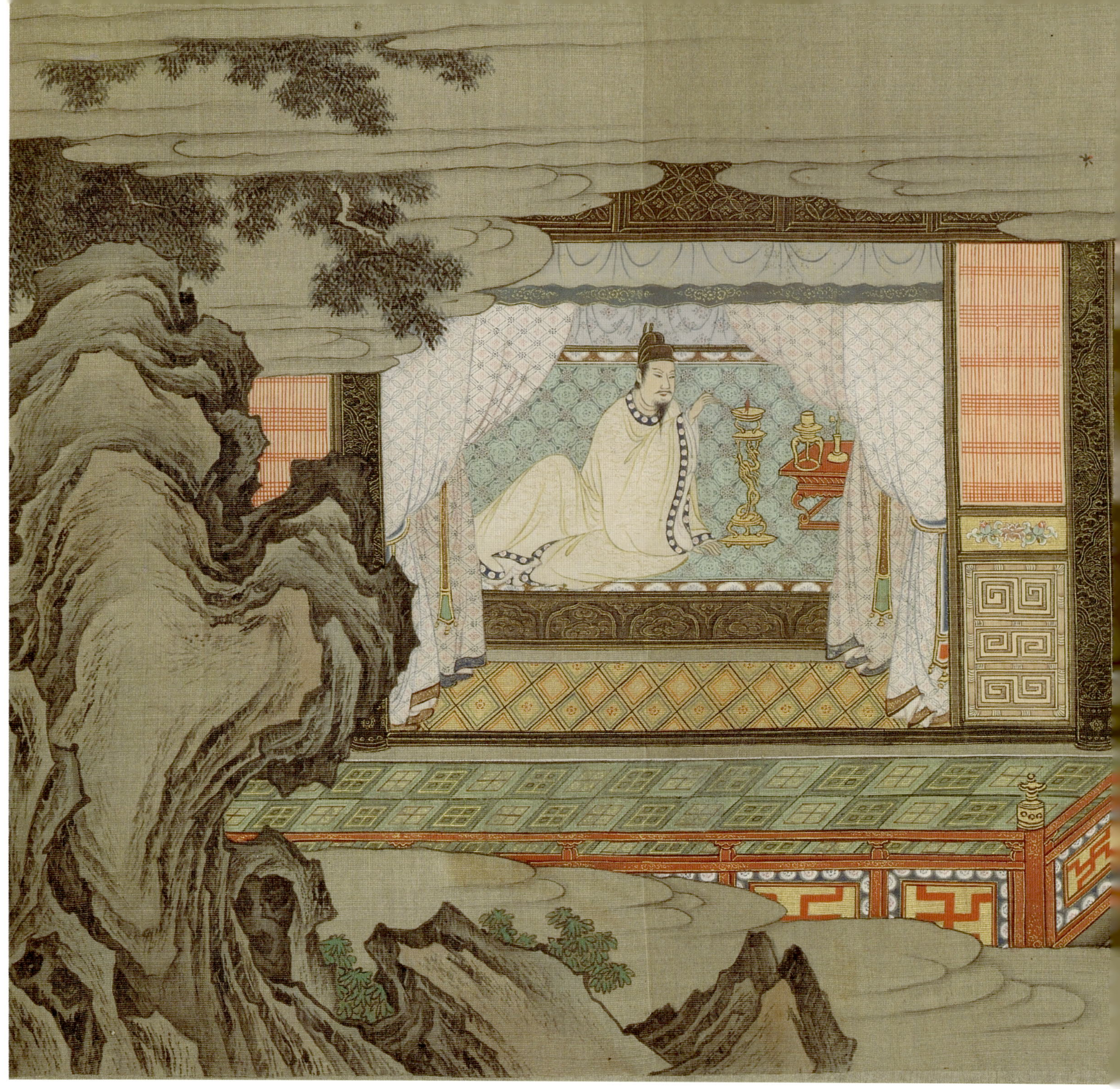

been moved next to the railing. From here, he looks out and down, wearing a muted expression of longing for his absent lover. Behind the figure of Minghuang, evoking his inner life, the small blue-and-white tripod vessel on top of the red-lacquer stand looks as if it is about to be swamped by the billowing waves painted on the screen behind it.

The pond is filled with blooms that were a classic symbol of Yang Guifei's beauty in Japan – lotus flowers. Here, we may imagine that the pairing of the lotus and nearby willow had powerful visual and emotive appeal, in part, through literary allusion. In the opening chapter of the *Tale of Genji*, the lotus and willow are the images used to evoke Yang Guifei's beauty. In a sense, the lack of any inscriptions from Bai Juyi's ballad on the *Chōgonka* painting challenges the viewer to recall and cite appropriate lines and match them to the scenes and their components as each is encountered – to hear the unseen bells and drums and cries of apes, as it were, and to scent the appropriate blooms.

At the same time, Sansetsu had available to him, through Chen Hong's companion 'Account', a vivid description of the scene:

FIG 41 'The emperor tending his candle on a winter night' (from The retired emperor mourns Yang Guifei), *Song of Lasting Sorrow*; (detail of fig. 39).

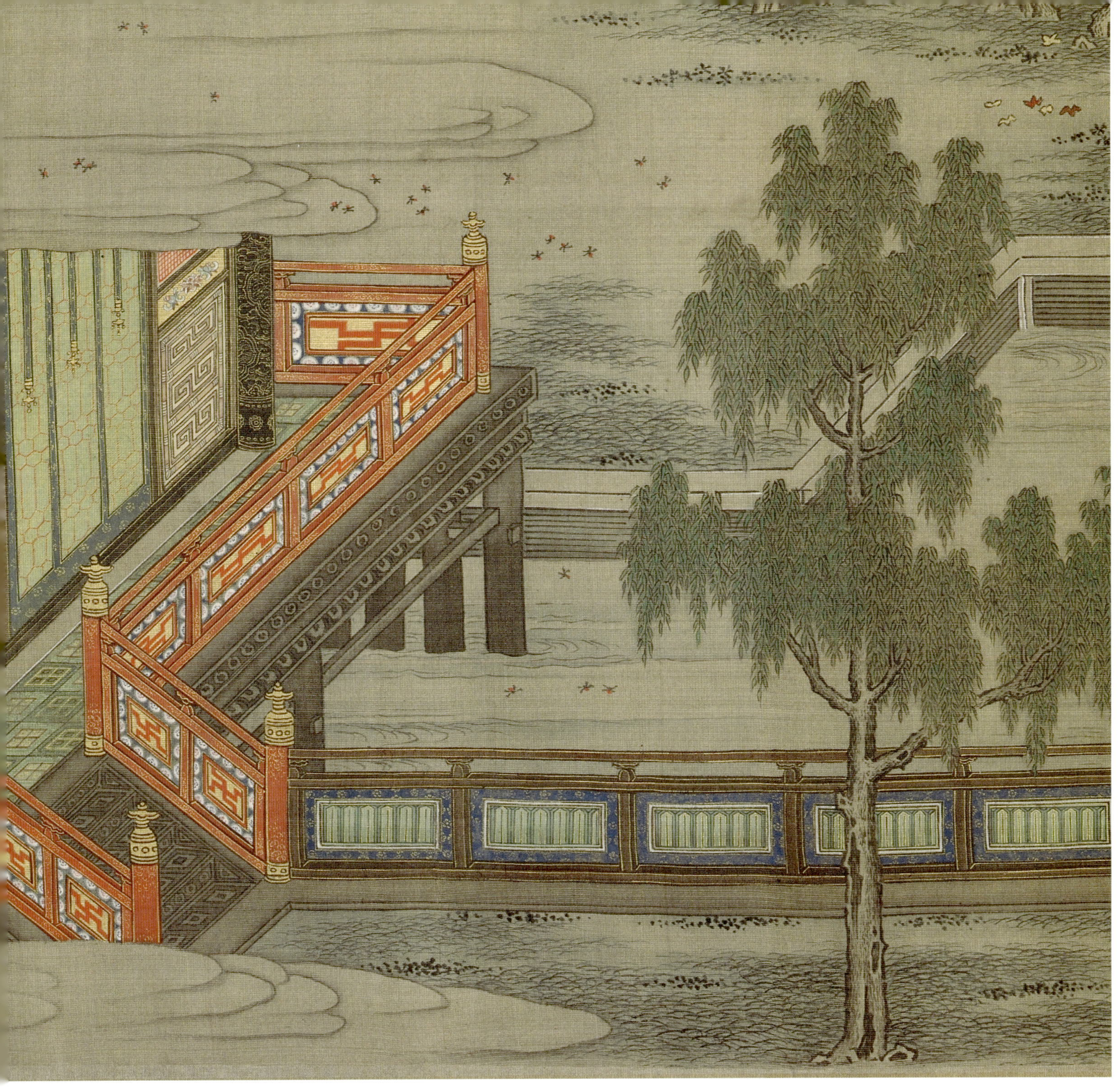

Xuanzong was honoured as His Former Majesty and given a separate establishment in the Southern Palace, then transferred to the western sector of the Imperial Compound. As time and events passed, all joy had gone from him and only sadness came. Every day of spring or night of winter, when the lotuses in the ponds opened in summer or when the palace ash trees shed their leaves in autumn, the performers of the Pear Garden Academy would produce notes on their jade flageolets; and if he heard one note of 'Coat of Feathers, Rainbow Skirts', His Majesty's face would lose its cheer, and all those around him would sob and sigh. For three years there was one thing on his mind, and his longing never subsided. His soul sought her out in dream, but she was so far away he could not reach her.

The section of the painting that follows begins to illustrate how this divide between the living and the dead might be bridged.

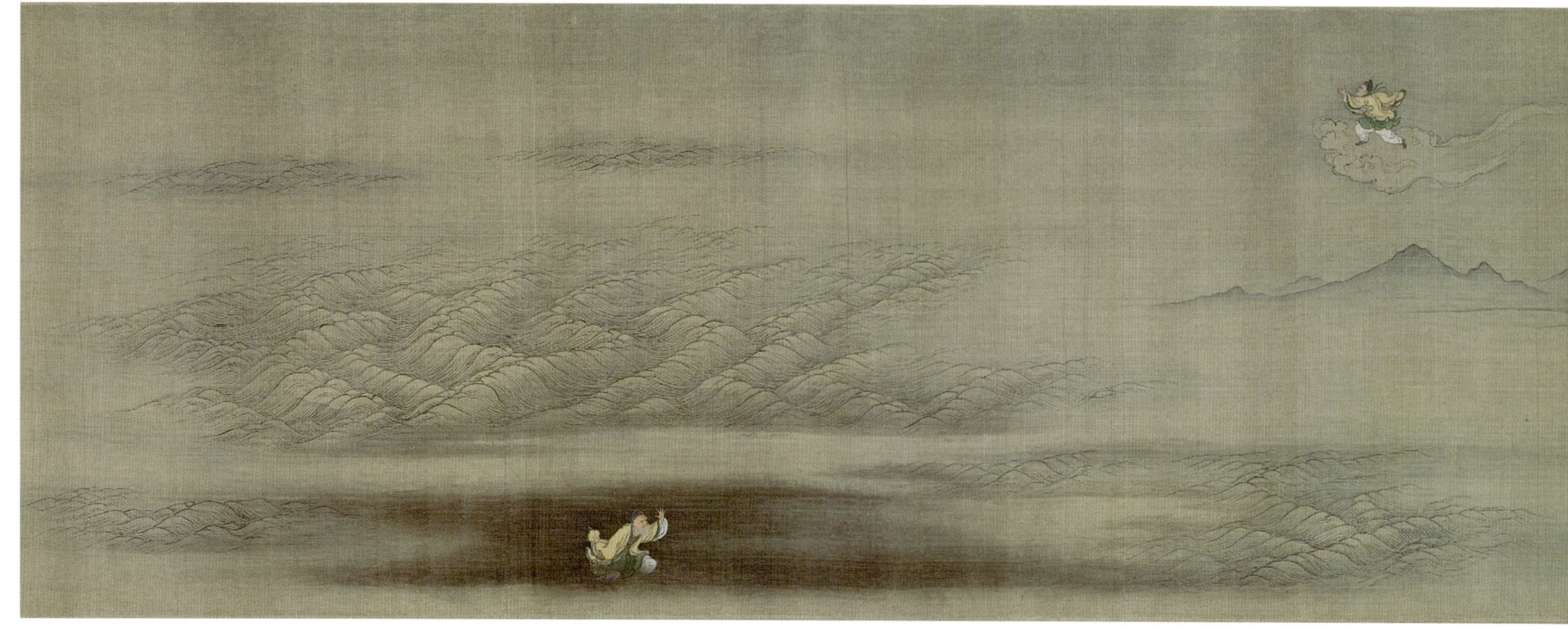

MINGHUANG ENGAGES
A DAOIST WIZARD (FIG. 42)

On forever, living and dead
*   were parted through the years,*
and never once did her wandering soul
*   find way into his dreams.*

75 *In Linqiong there was a wizard,*
*   guest in the gods' great citadel,*
*   who by the perfection of essence*
*   could bring the souls of the dead.*
*   He was touched by our ruler's*
*   restless, tossing love,*
*   and thus he gave the magician a task*
*   of making an earnest quest.*

*   He rode on vapours through the void,*
*   he sped like lightning along,*
80 *up into Heaven, down into Earth,*
*   seeking her everywhere.*
*   But from the sapphire star-web above*
*   to the yellow springs below,*
*   both were infinitely vast,*
*   in neither did he find her.*

A GIANT ROCK sprouting luxuriant trees and topped by clouds marks the opening of a new sequence of scenes. The emperor's reflections on the void between the living and the dead are immediately conjured up by these new surroundings: the mountaintop retreat looking down on pines and clouds is an appropriate venue for his interview with a Daoist wizard who travels in the heavens and under the earth, and who is able to communicate with spirits. Indeed, from here on, the scenery in the painting becomes gradually more ethereal. In this scene, Minghuang is again depicted as an imposing figure in a patterned imperial yellow robe. Behind him is a screen painted with an ink landscape, very much in the style of the Southern Song master Xia Gui, one that was most influential in Japan. In the screen painting, an appropriate and specific mood is conjured by the bucolic image of the moon reflected in water. To one side, on top of an outcrop of rock, is a four-poster pavilion, the iconic image of the Yuan master Ni Zan, as famed for his rustic style as his reclusion. In addition to this is a solitary pine, another symbol of the emperor and his state of mind. His sudden renewed interest in human affairs, for he is seen here coming out of mourning after several years to engage the Daoist in a search for the soul of Yang Guifei, is also suggested by the arrangement of cultural accoutrements on the table to one side: brushes, a scroll, a book and a collector's item or two.

FIG 42 Kano Sansetsu, Minghuang engages a Daoist wizard, *Song of Lasting Sorrow*; scroll 2, the fourth length of silk.

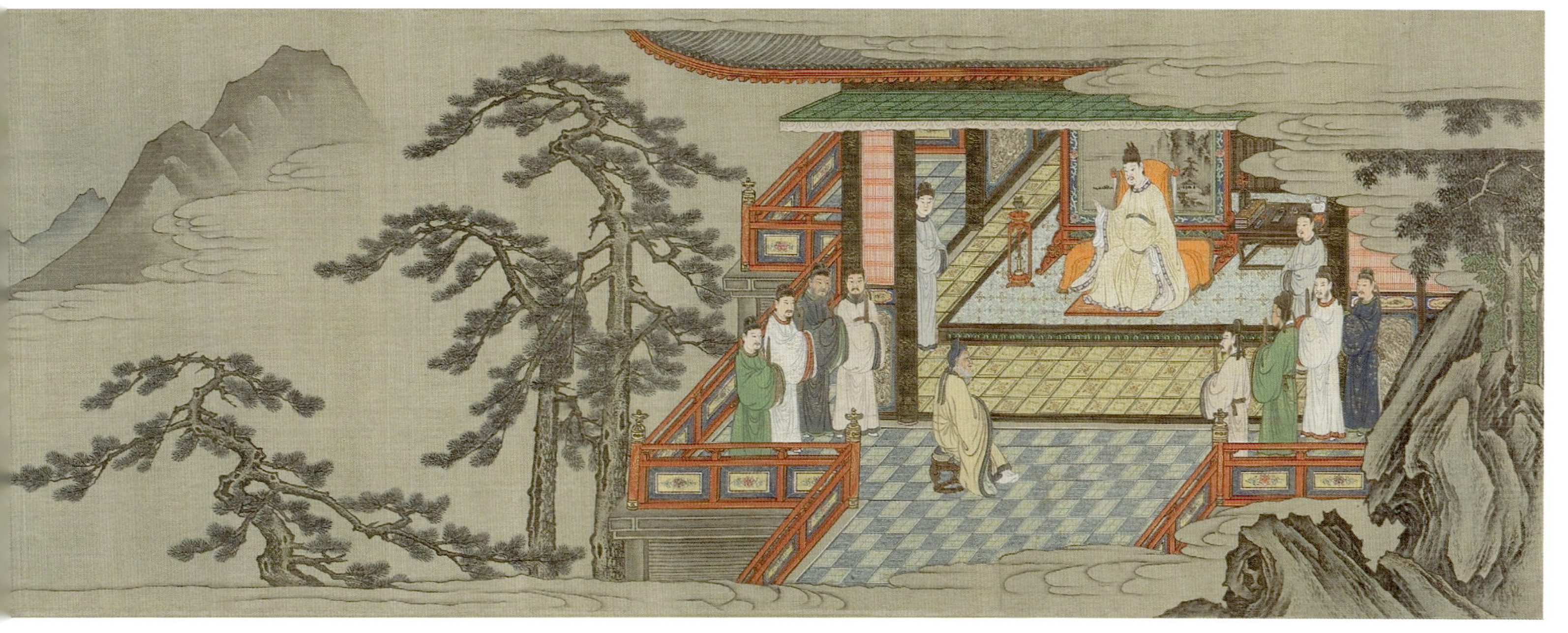

The following two scenes show the wizard riding a cloud, as the ballad describes, leftwards across the rosy sky and emerging, upwards and to the right, from his search of the black earth and the abyss (the Yellow Springs). Although, technically speaking, the length of silk ends at this point, the visual theme of the Daoist's search spills over into the first scene of the next silk. Hearing of a mountain of the immortals in the sea, where it is traditionally believed to have been, he sets out for that nebulous world, already appearing as little more than a speck speeding across the sky into the far distance. Together the three pictures of the Daoist travelling form a distinctive visual play, with dramatic shifts up and down, left and right and finally away, back into the scroll. All of this effectively marks that imaginary transition from the real world of Minghuang's sorrow to the ethereal world of the immortals.

FIG 43 Tang Yin, *Dreaming of Immortality in a Thatched Hut*. Handscroll; ink and colours on paper. Freer Gallery of Art, Washington, DC. Purchase, F1939.60

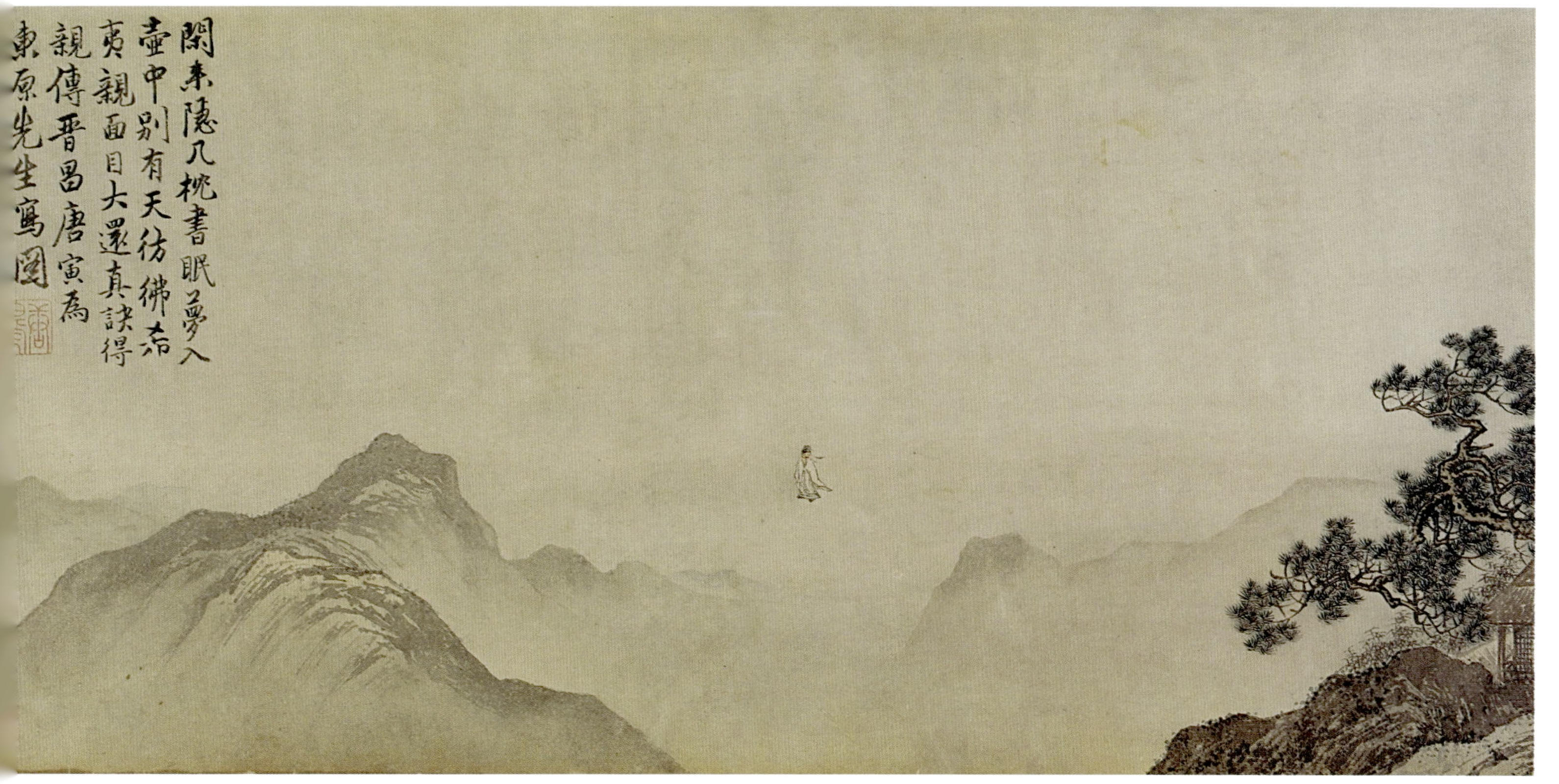

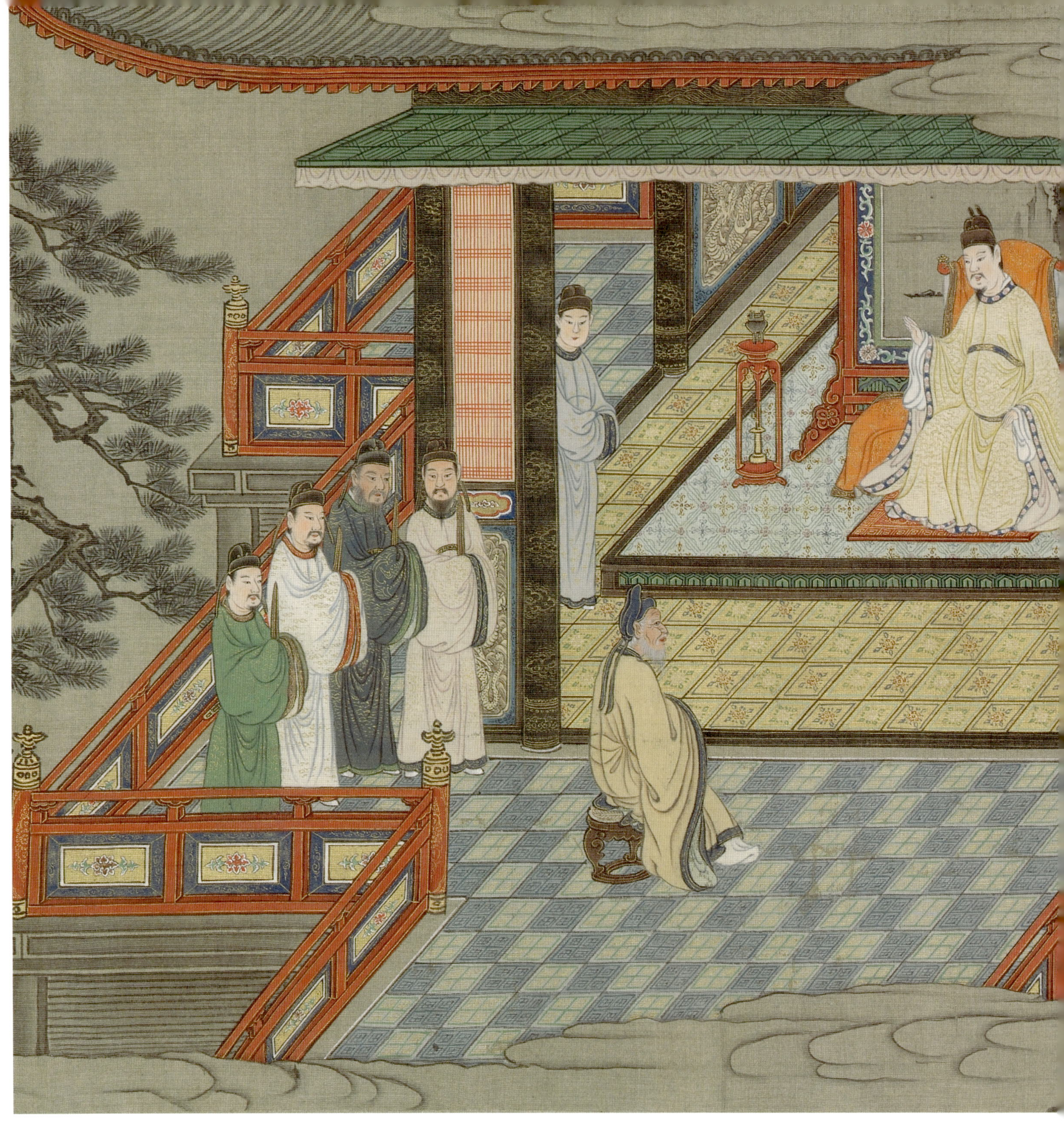

In part due to Sansetsu's repeated references to 'Chinese' motifs and devices, it is tempting to try to find precedents for such distinctive images as the flying wizard. As has been suggested by Masaaki Itakura, a similar figure of a flying Daoist appears in a well-known handscroll painting by the mid-Ming artist Tang Yin, *Dreaming of Immortality in a Thatched Hut* (fig. 43), though whether this painting would have been known to Sansetsu is uncertain.

Judging by some of the garden scenery in the Dublin *Chōgonka* painting, Sansetsu seems to have had some knowledge of this type of scenery in Tang Yin's oeuvre, along with that of Tang Yin's contemporary Qiu Ying. But we should keep in mind that both these artists were extensively faked by the makers of *Suzhou pian* (Suzhou forgeries) in later Ming China. To Sansetsu's credit, the visual interest of this passage is sustained on a par with the rest of the

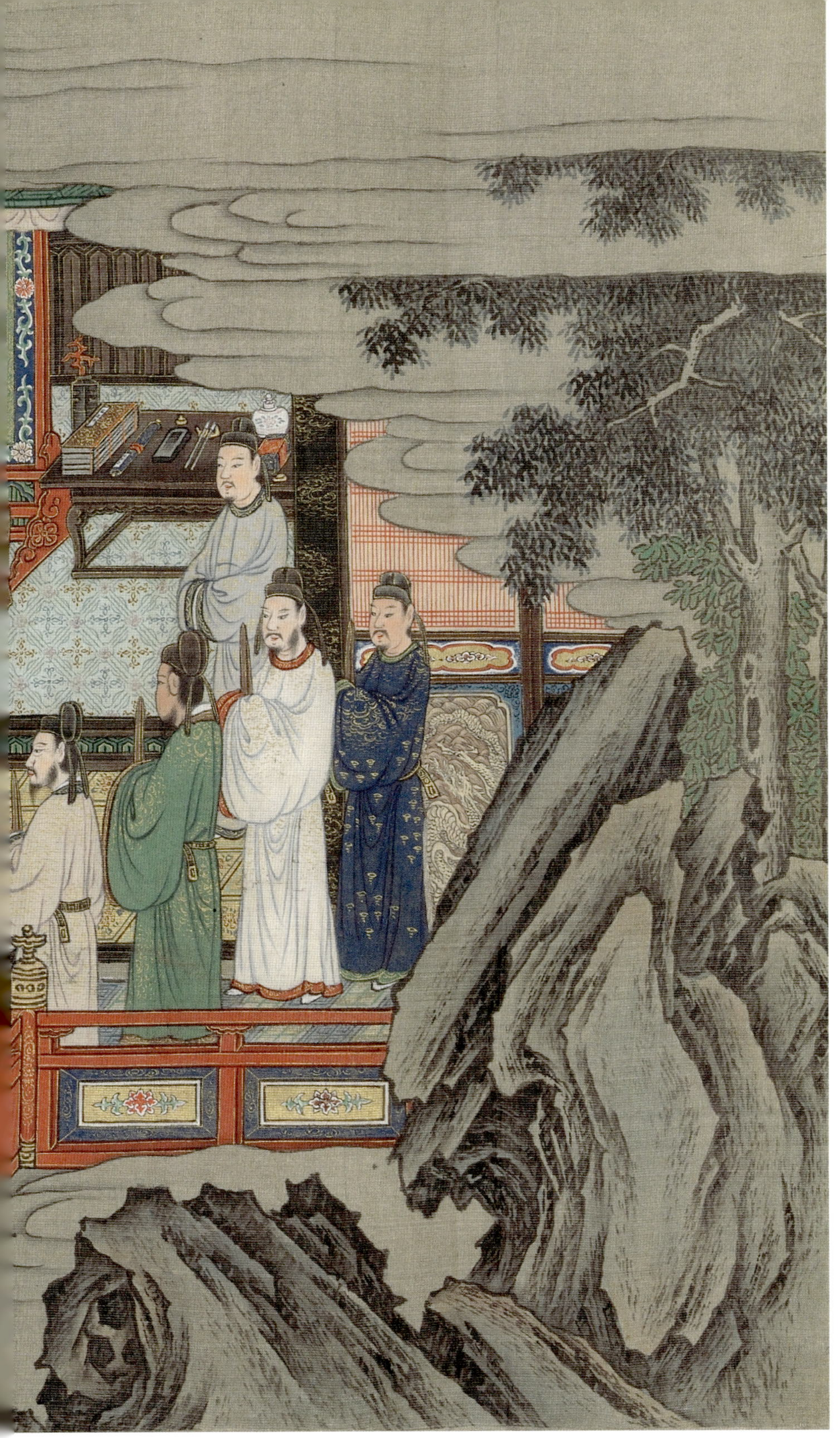

that a wizard came from Shu; and knowing that His Majesty was brooding so much on Yang the Prized Consort, he said that he possessed the skills of Li the Young Lord, the wizard who had summoned the soul of Lady Li for Emperor Wu of the Han. Xuanzong was very pleased, and ordered him to bring her spirit. The wizard then used all his skills to find her, but could not. He was also able to send his spirit on journeys by riding vapours; he went up into the precincts of Heaven and sank down into the vaults of the Earth looking for her; but he did not meet her. And then again he went to the margins and the encircling wastelands, high and low, to the easternmost extreme of Heaven and the Ocean, where he strode across Fanghu.

A notable comparison is made in this passage when the wizard presents his credentials to the emperor (fig. 44) by likening his skills to Li the Young Lord. Early in Chen Hong's 'Account', when Yang Guifei first appeared, he compared her 'sensuous allure' to that of Lady Li, the consort of Emperor Wu of the Han (r. 140–87 BC). Upon the death of Lady Li, the emperor wrote a *fu*-poem (ode or rhapsody) in her memory, entitled 'Ode on Lady Li' (*Li furen fu*).[61] He was for a long time inconsolable with grief, and no attempts by courtiers to distract him with entertainments succeeded. Eventually, in the year 121 BC, he summoned a wizard, the young Li (Li Shaoweng of Qi), who by practising his occult arts, was able to make Lady Li's image appear behind a curtain before the emperor's eyes. It is thought that Li used lights, shadows and illuminations, projected on curtains perhaps, or some other kind of stagecraft, to reproduce the figure of Lady Li, but in any event, the emperor is said to have honoured and rewarded him graciously.

painting, apparently undiminished by any knowledge of works like the *Suzhou pian*.

Chen Hong's account of this part of the narrative is insightful here. Speaking of Minghuang he writes:

For three years there was one thing on his mind, and his longing never subsided. His soul sought her out in dream, but she was so far away he could not reach her. It happened then

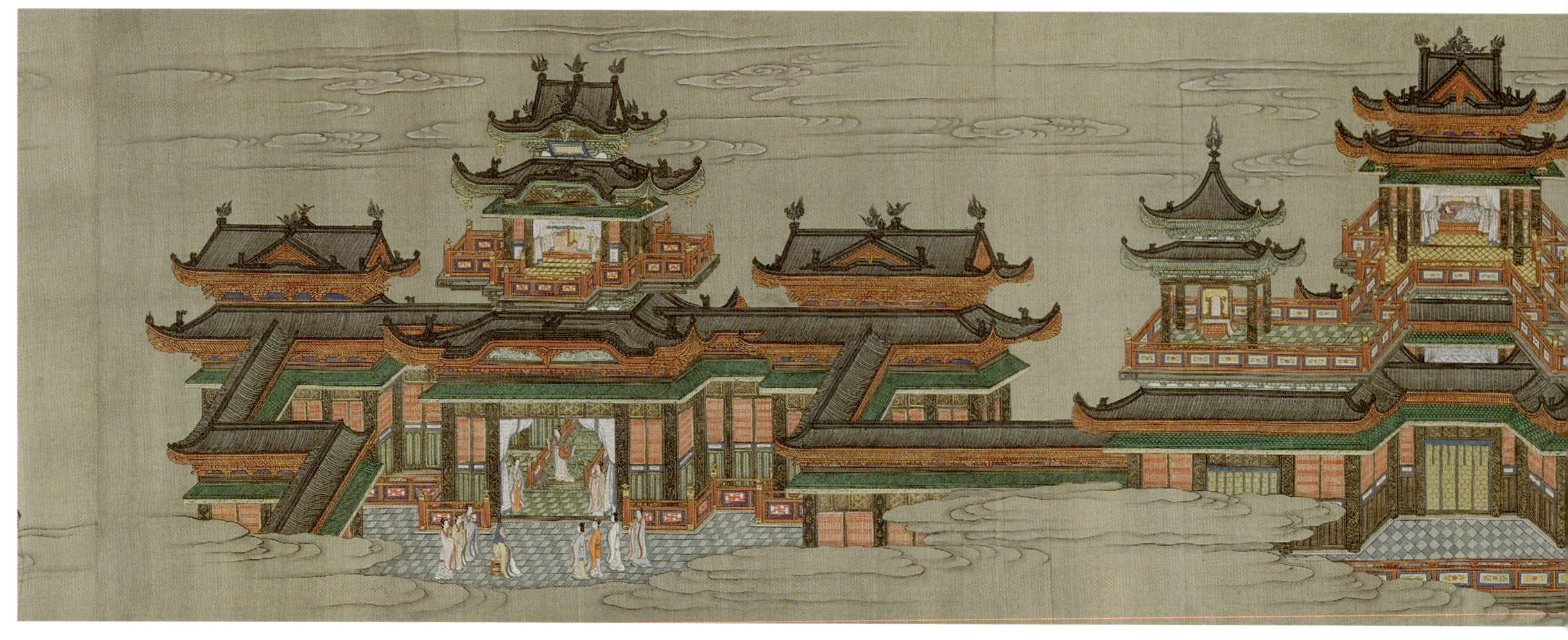

THE ISLES OF THE IMMORTALS (FIG. 45)

He came to learn that on the seas
  were mountains of the Undying,
those mountains lie in Emptiness
  remote and ethereal.

85 Sparkling grillwork of halls and towers
  where rainbow-clouds arose,
and in them the Undying were teeming,
  beings lovely and lissome.
Among there was a certain one
  who had the name Taizhen,
whose snowy flesh and flowerlike face
  seemed much like her he sought.

At the western cloister of golden tower
  he knocked at a door of jade,
90 and had the servant Little Jade
  take word to the Maid Shuangcheng.
When she heard the news of a messenger
  from the Son of Heaven of Han,
within the nine-flower hangings
  her dreaming soul woke with alarm.

She threw on robes, pushed pillow away,
  rose and paced about;
pearled dividers and silver screens
  opened down winding halls.
95 Her cloudlike tresses were half askew,
  she had freshly woken from sleep,
and her hat of flowers was not set straight
  as she came into the room.

Wind blew upon the goddess's sleeves,
  billowing as they rose,
and it still resembled her dancing
  'Coats of Feathers, Rainbow Skirts'.
Her marble features were sad and still,
  her tears were streaming down,
100 she was a branchful of blooming pear,
  bearing the rain of spring.

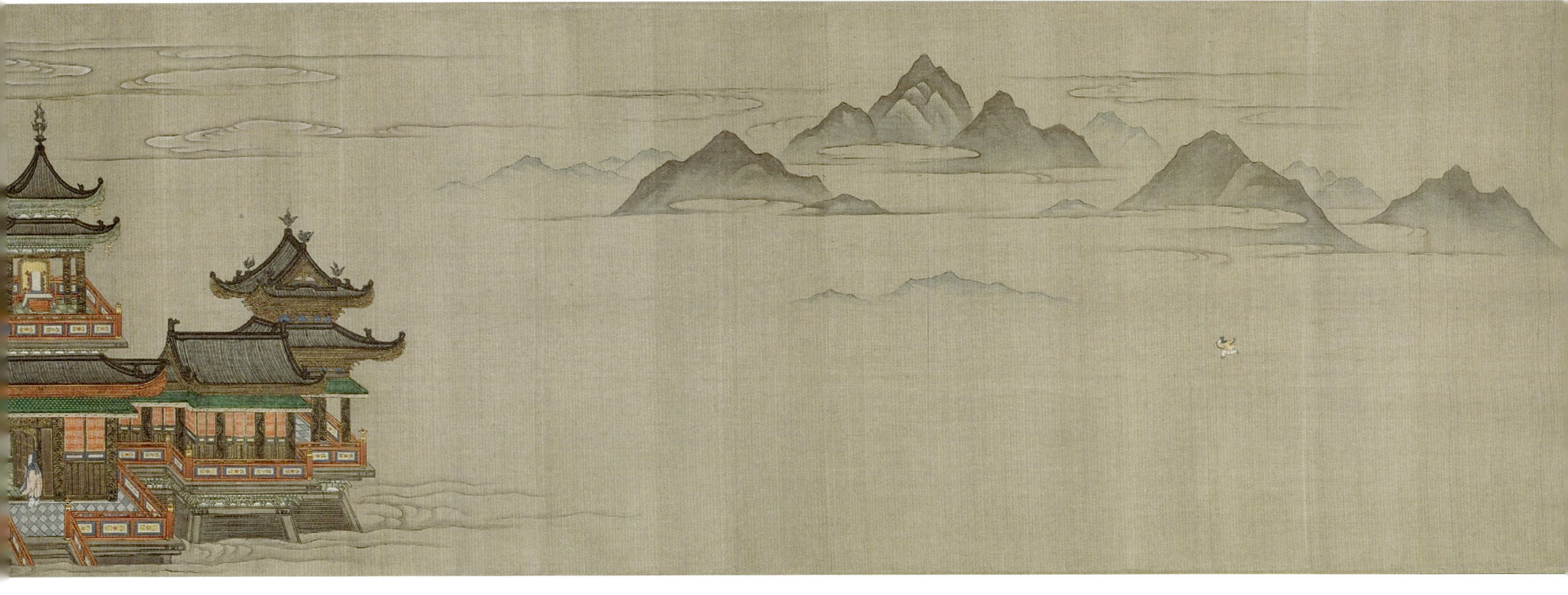

IN THE FIRST SCENE, the Daoist is a tiny speck flying over the waters and clouds towards the distant mountains: he has spied the isles of the immortals in the sea and travels there in search of the Jade Consort, the soul of Yang Guifei. Speckled sizing on the silk medium gives these mountains a subtle sparkling effect, suggesting their magical qualities.

Rather abruptly, in the second scene, he has arrived at his destination in the firmament and is seen knocking on a jade door at the western entrance of a vast and magnificent palace. Rosy clouds filling the skyline from here to the end of the scroll maintain the numinous atmosphere of the world of the immortals. The door is opened for the wizard by a jade woman. He enquires after the spirit of Yang Guifei, who is seen slumbering deep within the palace in a high tower with a double-tiered roof flanked by pavilions on a paved terrace.

The third view is again of the front of the extraordinary palace, but slightly from the right, in a more intimate view of an inner courtyard (fig. 46). Yang Guifei's bedchamber still sits at the top and is flanked by smaller towers, but these and many of the other rich architectural details have somehow changed their form, as if the entire palace of the immortals were a miraculous place in a constant state of transformation. In the foreground, the Daoist sits on a stool, in the same posture he held before Minghuang some scenes back. Before him, the figure of Yang Guifei arrives in haste, just as it is described in the ballad.

The narrative of this series of scenes is again made somewhat clearer in Chen Hong's 'Account':

He saw there the highest of the mountains of the Undying, with many mansions and towers; at the end of the western veranda there was a deepest doorway facing east; the gate was shut, and there was written, 'The Garden of Taizhen, Jade Consort'. The wizard pulled out a hatpin and rapped on the door, at which a young maiden with her hair done up in a double coil came out to answer the door. The wizard was so flustered he couldn't manage to get a word out, so the maiden went back in. In a moment another servant girl in a green dress came out and asked where he was from. The wizard then identified himself as an envoy of the Tang Son of Heaven and conveyed the command he had been given. The servant said, 'The Jade Consort has just gone to bed; please wait a while for her.' Thereupon he was swallowed up in a sea of clouds with the dawn sun breaking through them as down a tunnel to the heavens; then the jasper door closed again and all was still and without a sound.

The wizard held his breath and did not move his feet, waiting at the gate with folded hands. After a long time, the servant invited him to come in and said, 'The Jade Consort is

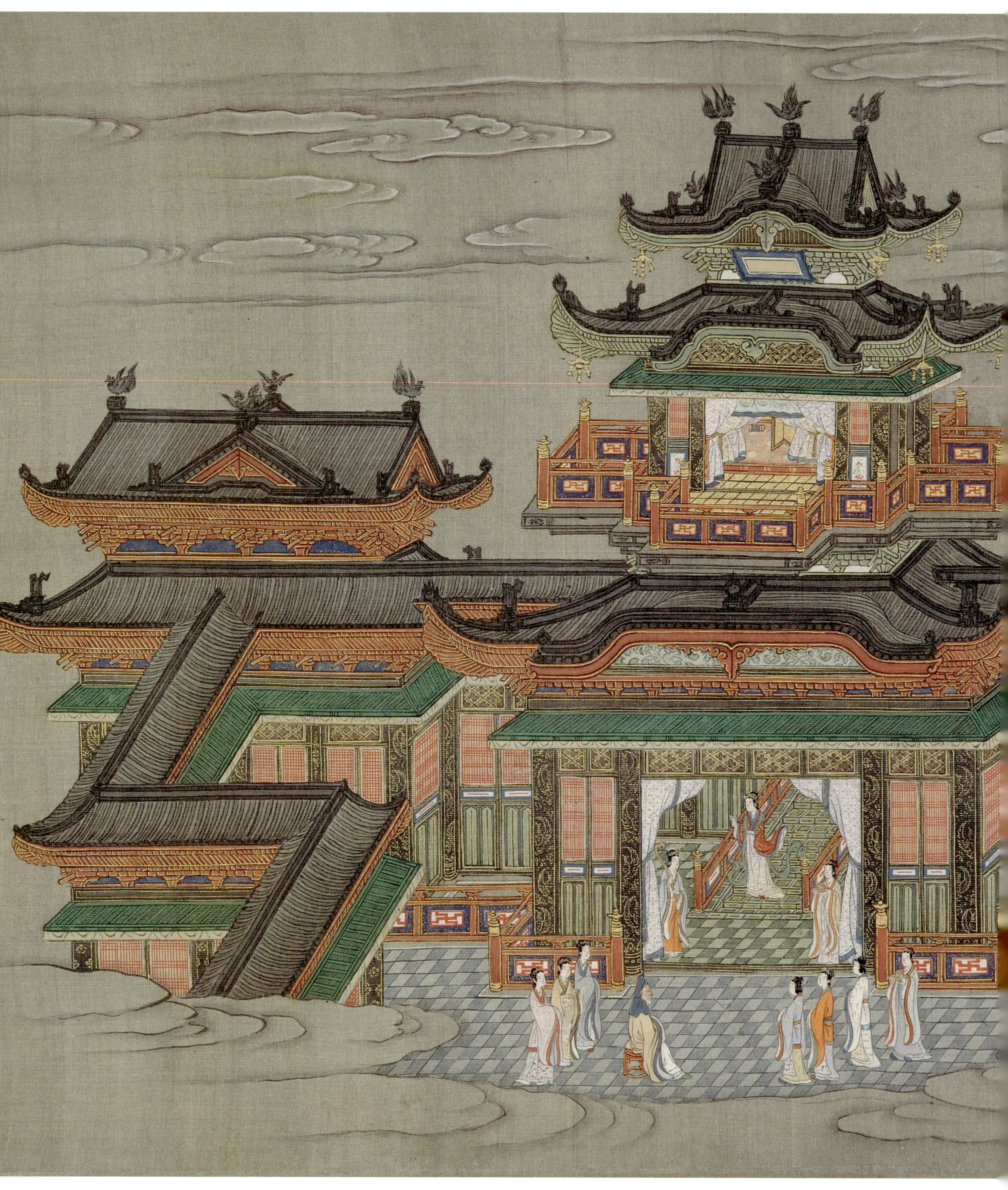

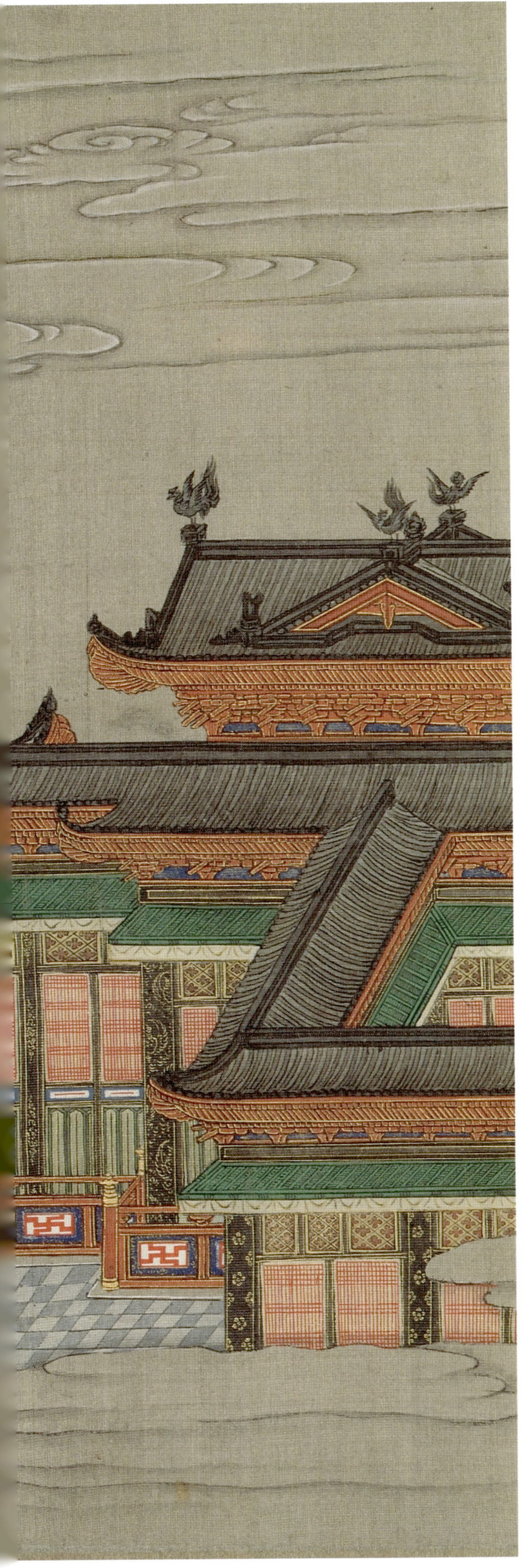

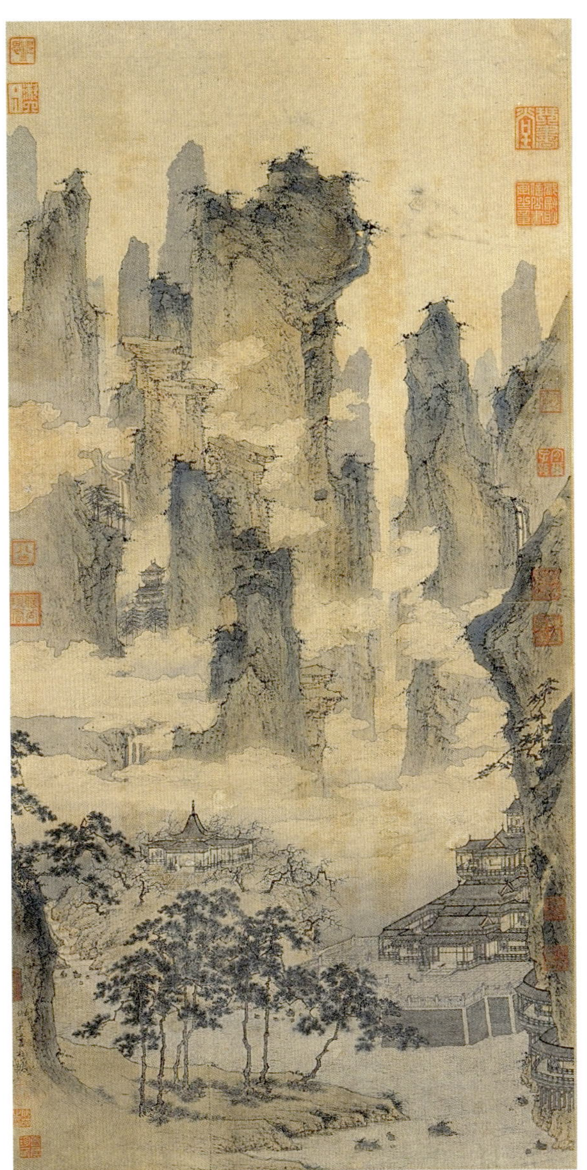

coming out.' Then he saw a person with a bonnet of golden lotuses, wearing lavender chiffon, with pendants of red jade hanging from her sash and phoenix slippers, and seven or eight persons in attendance on her.

Sansetsu was familiar with this kind of setting from any number of his other paintings of scenes of ancient China, but must also have learned something from one of the acknowledged Chinese masters of paintings of immortal palaces in the mountains, Qiu Ying. Qiu Ying's oeuvre is a plausible visual source for the ethereal palace exteriors and polychrome effects of the immortal realms. A fine example from that oeuvre is the small hanging scroll painting, *Pavilions in the Mountains of the Immortals*, dated 1550, in the National Palace Museum, Taipei (fig. 47).[62]

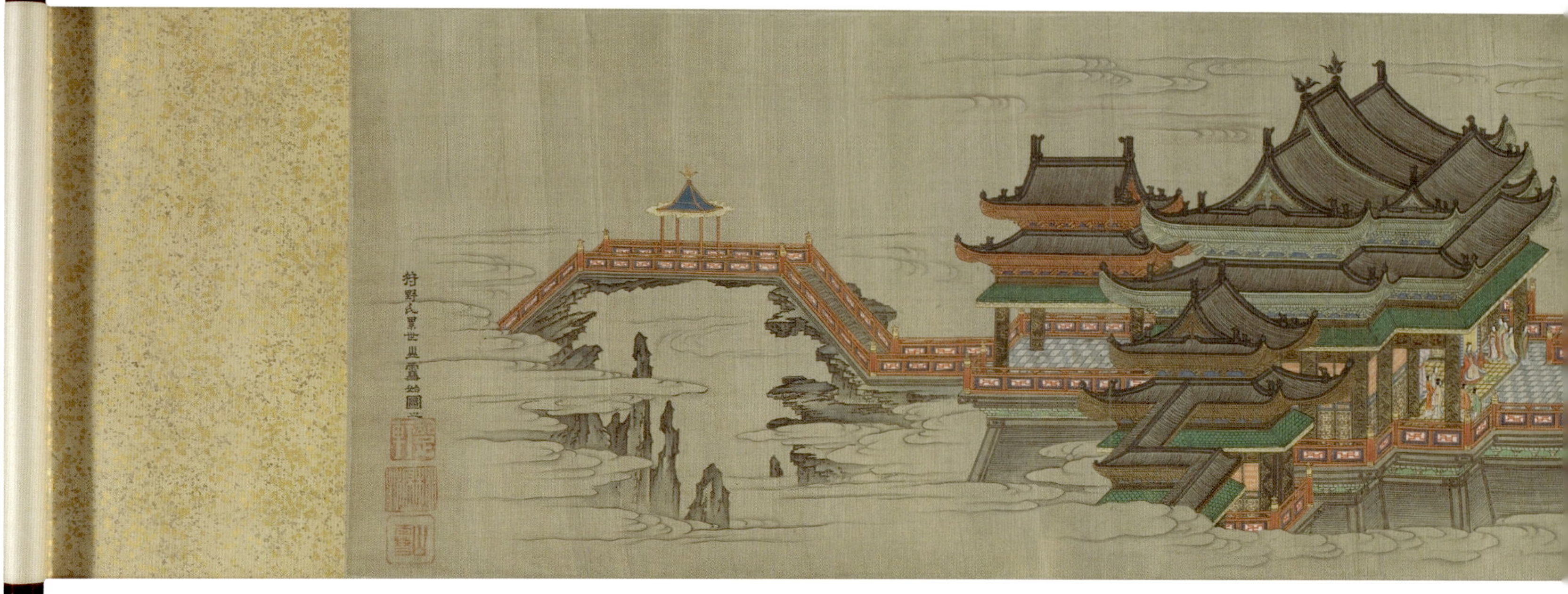

THE DAOIST'S INTERVIEW WITH THE SOUL OF YANG GUIFEI (FIG. 48)

Biting back feeling, she fixed her gaze,
  sent thanks to the ruler and lord:
once voice and visage are torn apart,
  vast emptiness lies between.
Broken forever, the love that was shared
  in the Court of Shining Light,
now days and the months pass but slowly
  in the Palace of Penglai.

105 When she turned her head to gaze back down
  to the realm of mortal men,
Chang'an she did not see,
  she saw only dust and fog.
She could only use things once shared
  to convey her depth of love —
an inlaid box and hairpin of gold
  he should carry back with him.

'Of the hairpin I will keep a leg,
  of the box I keep a panel;
110 the gold of the hairpin is sundered,
  the box's inlay divided.
If only your heart can be as firm
  as the inlay or the gold,
In Heaven or among mortal men
  we will someday meet again.'

Time came to go, and with passionate care,
  she sent a few more words,
and in those words there was a vow
  known to their hearts alone.
115 On the seventh day of the seventh month
  in the Palace of Lasting Life,
it was midnight, no one else was there,
  as they whispered privately:
if in Heaven, may we become
  those birds that fly on shared wing;
or on Earth, then may we become
  branches that twine together.
Heaven lasts, the Earth endures
  yet a time will come when they're gone,
120 yet this pain of ours will continue
  and never finally end.

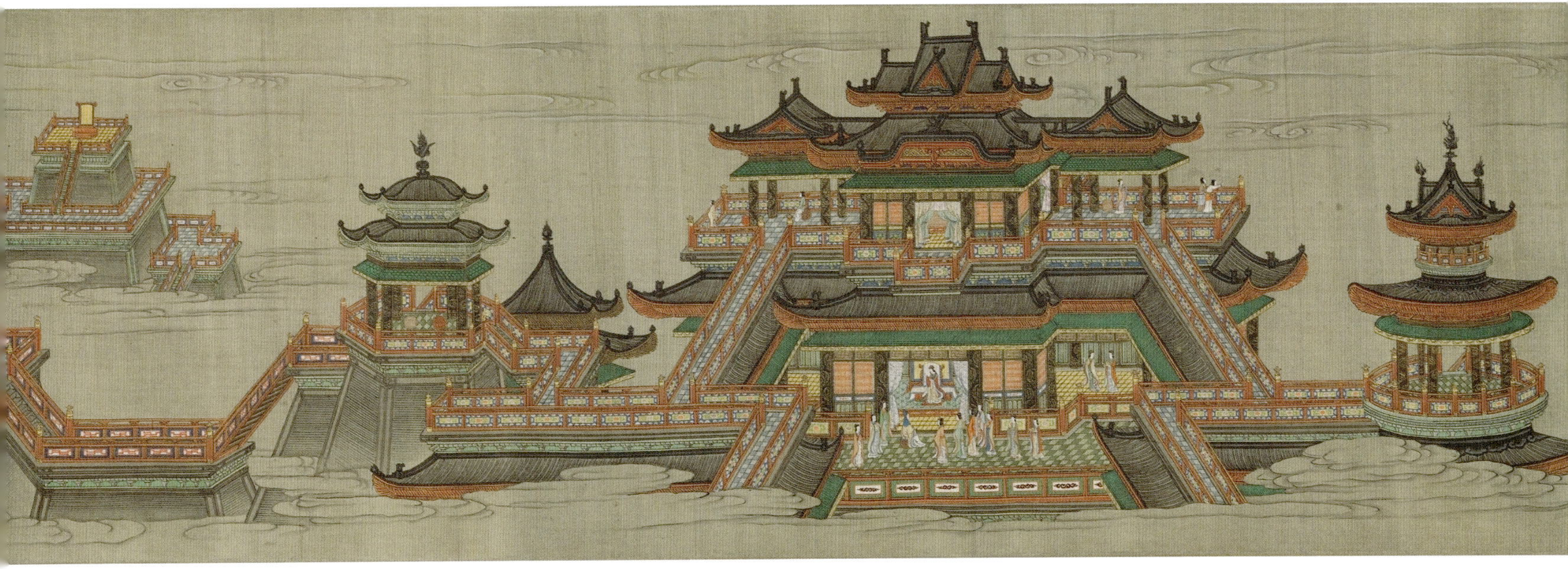

HERE IS THE FINAL PASSAGE of the painting, illustrating the last lines of the ballad describing the Daoist's interview with Yang Guifei. The ethereal, timeless and impenetrable qualities of Yang Guifei's heavenly abode are suggested by its height above rosy clouds, and the glimpsed, far-off quality of its opulent exteriors. In the first scene, the palace appears larger and even more magnificent than before – more tiered, more terraced and more populated with female immortals (fig. 49). In the central foreground the interview takes place. The soul of Yang Guifei stands in front of her chair and screen ensemble. She gesticulates with her arm as she contemplates her life on earth and imparts the words in the ballad to the wizard, who is seated on a low stool just outside her chamber on the veranda, surrounded by numerous attendants. Elsewhere on the high terraces of this ethereal building ladies stand or sit as they gaze out at the numinous, rainbow-coloured clouds. The earth cannot be seen from here. Chen Hong writes:

The wizard held his breath and did not move his feet, waiting at the gate with folded hands. After a long time, the servant invited him to come in and said, 'The Jade Consort is coming out.' Then he saw a person with a bonnet of golden lotuses, wearing lavender chiffon, with pendants of red jade hanging from her sash and phoenix slippers, and seven or eight

persons in attendance on her. She greeted the wizard and asked, 'Is the Emperor well?' Then she asked what had happened since the fourteenth year of the Tianbao Reign. When he finished speaking, she grew wistful and gestured to her servant to get a golden hairpin and inlaid box, each of which she broke in parts. She gave one part of each to the envoy, saying, 'Express my gratitude to the Emperor and present him with these objects as mementoes of our former love.'

The final passage of the painting features one last view of the interview in the palace of the immortals. Yang Guifei is seated surrounded by attendants as the Daoist turns to take his leave of her. He gestures back towards the earth and the emperor. He has promised to carry back to Minghuang her pledge of eternal love, as Chen Hong explains:

The wizard received her words and these objects of surety; he was ready to go, but one could see in his face that something was troubling him. The Jade Consort insisted that he tell her what was the matter. Then he knelt down before her and said, 'Please tell me something that happened back then, something of which no one else knew, so that I can offer to His Majesty as proof. Otherwise I am afraid

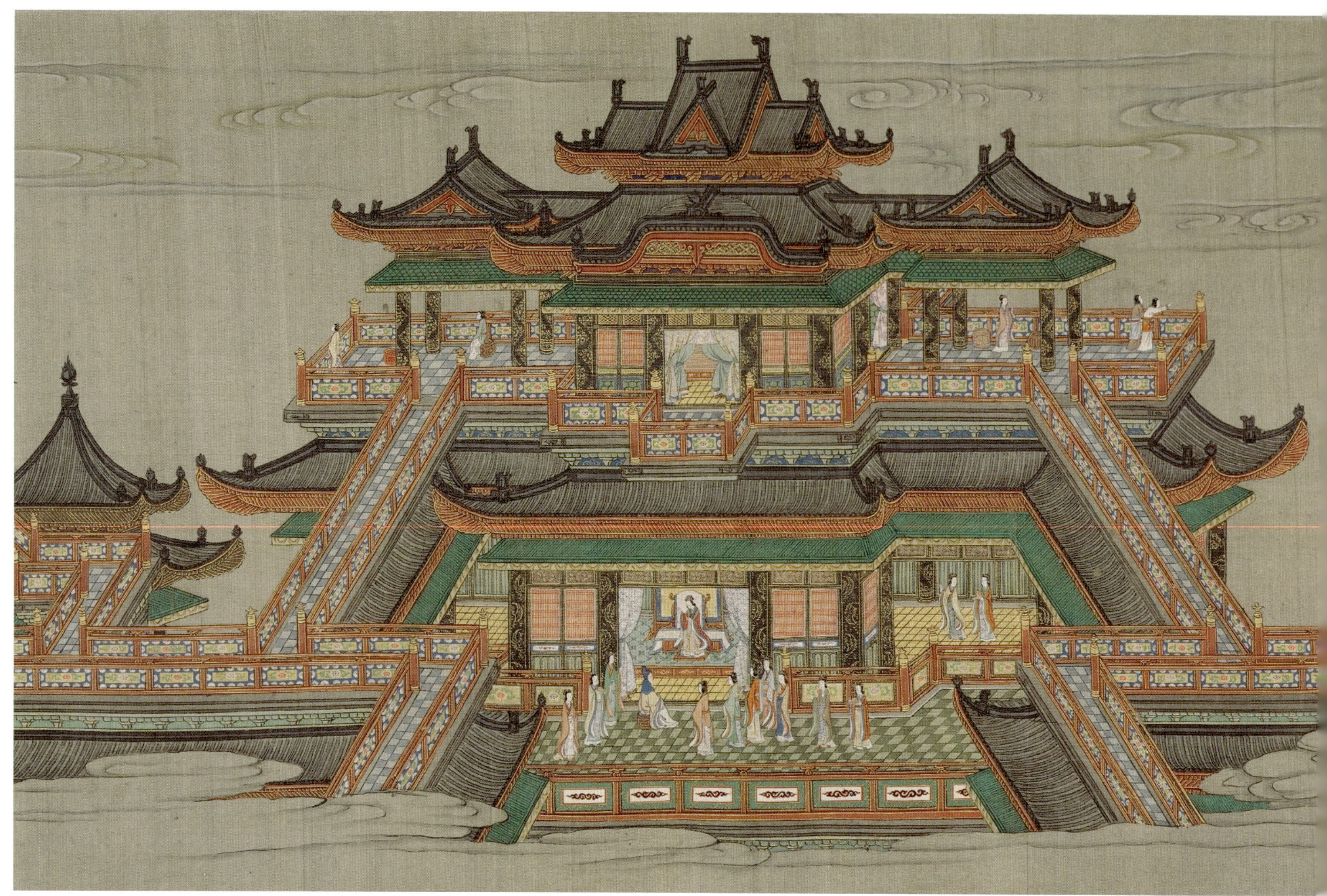

that with the inlaid box and the golden hairpin
I will be accused of the same kind of trickery
that Xin Yuanping practised on Emperor Wen
of the Han.' The Jade Consort drew back lost
in thought, as if there were something she were
recalling with fondness. Then very slowly she
said, 'Back in the tenth year of the Tianbao
Reign, I was attending on His Majesty, who
had gone to the palace on Mount Li to escape
the heat. It was autumn, in the seventh month,
the evening when the Oxherd and the Weaver
Star meet. It was the custom of the people of
Qin on that night to spread out embroidery
and brocade, to put out food and drink, to set
up flowers and melons, and to burn incense in
the yard – they call this 'begging for deftness'.
Those of the inner palace hold this custom in
particularly high regard. It was almost
midnight; and the guards and attendants in the
eastern and western cloisters had been

dismissed. I was waiting on His Majesty alone.
His Majesty stood there, leaning on his
shoulder, then looked up at the heavens and
was touched by the legend of the Oxherd and
the Weaver Star. We then made a secret vow to
one another, a wish that we could be husband
and wife in every lifetime. When we stopped
speaking, we held hands, and each of us was
sobbing. Only the Emperor knows of this.'

Then she said sadly, 'Because of this one
thought so much in my mind, I will be able to
live on here no longer. I will descend again to
the world below and our future destiny will
take shape. Whether in Heaven or in the
world of mortal men, it is certain that we will
meet again and form our bond of love as
before.' Then she said, 'His Former Majesty
will not be long in the world of men. I hope
that he will find some peace of mind and not
cause himself suffering.'

Fig 49 'The wizard and Yang
converse' (from **The Daoist's
interview with the soul of
Yang Guifei**), *Song of Lasting
Sorrow*; (detail of fig. 48).

The wizard's powers are such that he is not able to bring her back – only the tokens of her love. When she is selecting these, she recalls how, one evening when she was alone with Minghuang, he was moved by a particular romantic myth about two stars, Altair and Vega, known in Chinese folklore by the names of the Oxherd and Weaver Girl. In mythology, Vega is a hard-working silk weaver whose grandfather, the King of Heaven, rewards her industry by marrying her to the Oxherd, the star Altair on the other side of the Milky Way. Once married, they simply play together in the skies, to the neglect of their work, thus angering the King of Heaven. He banishes them, but allows them to meet on one night each year, the seventh night of the seventh moon, known as the 'night of sevens', and incidentally, East Asia's Valentine's Day.

In this final scene the enormous palace edifice is observed from the left, with a view across the multi-tiered sloping roofs and eaves. The swastika pattern on the railing (the same one that was seen when the emperor was alone in the palace), serves as a reminder of the eternity of their love and of everlasting sorrow. The device of a dipping, U-shaped walkway connects this last aspect with the previous view of the main palace building, an effect that is 'mirrored' behind the last palace building by the final, rather forlorn image of a humped bridge topped by a frail pavilion leading over rocky pinnacles into the clouds. This shift of angle is a classic formal device to counter and even reverse the leftward momentum of viewing a scroll, which uses visual signs to regulate and manage expectations. But it is perhaps only when one steps back to take in the entire final sequence of the scroll that the shifting perspective from which the palaces in the sky are seen becomes clear.

When the Daoist first arrives at the Western wing, the palace is seen from the front, with the central bay exaggeratedly splayed outwards towards the viewer, leading the eye back and up towards the figure of Yang Guifei, lying in the centre on the top-floor pavilion. Then, after a linking covered corridor, the palace, ever altering its form, is seen very slightly from the right. Next, following a gap, is an aspect that seems to combine these two views: it is seen both somewhat from the right and splayed. Finally, after crossing the dipping bridge and spying the platform above the clouds beyond in the distance, the viewer's position has 'swung' around and is almost side-on from the left, which has the effect of slowing and countering the visual momentum of viewing from right to left. This device of shifting the perspectives on palace buildings carries a certain authenticity from a similar one seen in the probable copies, or copies of copies, of mid-Tang paintings of palaces in landscapes.[63] The stairs, terraces and pavilions are seen sometimes laterally and sometimes frontally, in the manner of some Buddhist cave-temple murals of opulent palaces in paradise.[64]

The Daoist himself, like the viewer, here turns as if to fly back into the scroll – back towards the land of the living – while the bridge leads out of the end of the painting to an unknown place accessible by immortals only, recalling that unbridgeable gap between the living and the dead pondered on by Minghuang and acting as a poignant reminder of the lovers' infinite separation. Although the painting ends here, Chen Hong brought the story back to Tang China, to the final moment of Minghuang's life:

The envoy returned and presented this to His Former Majesty, and the Emperor's heart was shaken and much afflicted with grief. For days on end he could find no cheer. In the summer of that year, in the fourth month, His Majesty passed on.

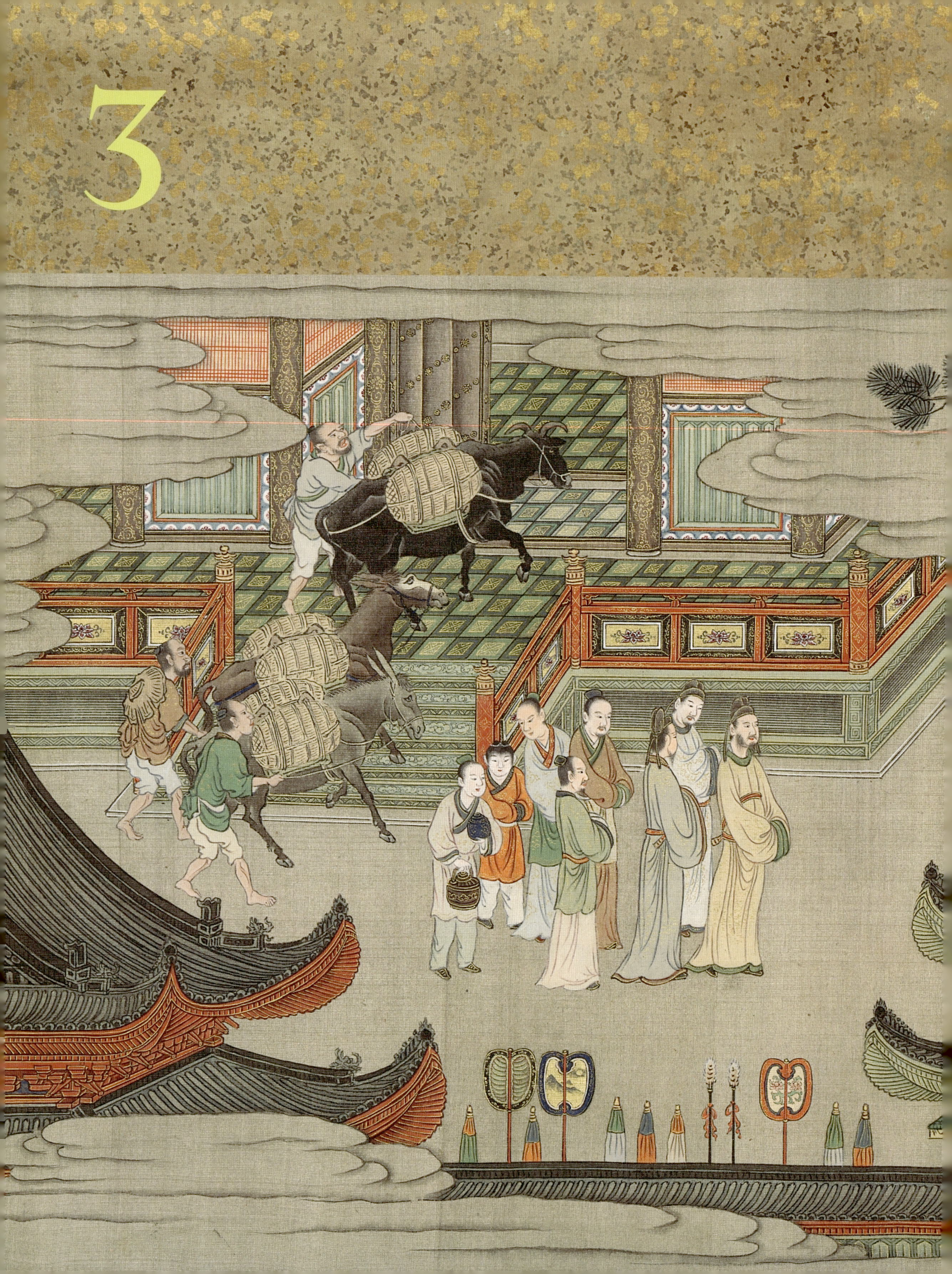
3

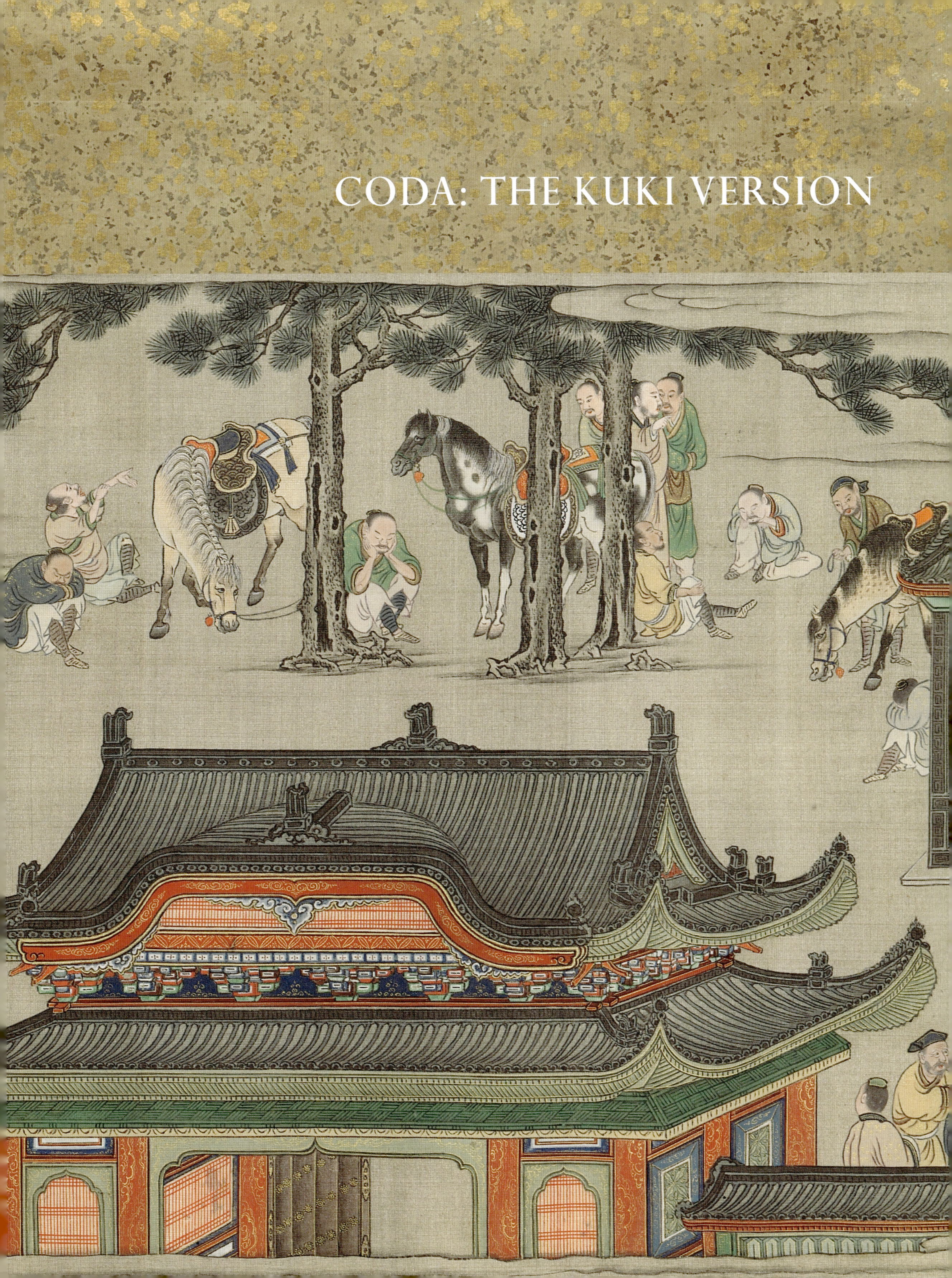

A S PREVIOUSLY DISCUSSED, the possibility exists that the Dublin *Chōgonka* scrolls might once have been mounted not as a pair of scrolls but as a set of three. This possibility was first raised during the remounting that took place in Tokyo in the early 1990s by Sakakibara Satoru.[65] Without textual records or documents to set the record straight, there is no way of knowing for sure whether the two-scroll format was the one first used when the painting had been completed (see p. 147). Without evidence to the contrary, we have assumed up to now that the two-scroll format was the original format, but what if the Dublin painting was once mounted as three scrolls, either under Sansetsu's supervision or later? What would it have looked like? Would this have been a plausible form, and if so, how would the tripartite division of the painting have changed the overall narrative interpretation?

In this coda to our close reading of the Dublin painting, consideration of these questions is the starting point for a short study of the other known version of the *Song of Lasting Sorrow* picture-scrolls, which was first published in the Japanese fine-art journal *Kokka* in 1893, and is now part of a private family collection in Japan. A comparison of the mountain scenery from the two versions shows how close they are (figs 50, 51). The present study of the three-scroll Kuki family version is based not on an examination of the actual scrolls, which are not currently accessible for research, but on a full set of black-and-white professional quality photographs in the Chester Beatty Library.[66] The three scrolls of the Kuki version divide the narrative up as follows:

SCROLL 1

- The discovery of Yang Guifei
- Minghuang and Yang Guifei's dalliance in the palace
- The rise of the Yang clan
- The neglect of state affairs and the foment of rebellion

SCROLL 2

- An Lushan's rebellion and the flight of the inner court
- The execution of Yang Guifei
- The flight to Shu through the mountains
- Minghuang's eventual return to the capital

SCROLL 3

- His solitary mourning in the palace
- His engaging a Daoist wizard to find Yang Guifei
- The Daoist's finding her abode in the isles of the immortals
- The Daoist's interview with her

In the reading of the Dublin painting in the last chapter, we saw how effective the two-scroll format was in narrative terms, in the way it highlights, first, six 'acts' describing Minghuang's life *with* Yang Guifei; and then six 'acts' illustrating his life *without* her. This emphasises the separateness of the worlds of the living and the dead, and heightens the sense of hopelessness and separation felt by the two lovers in the two pictorial halves of the romantic tragedy.

In the three-scroll scenario outlined above, the format of twelve 'acts' divided between two scrolls (six each), is reconfigured as four 'acts' over three scrolls. At this point, it should be acknowledged that this division into three scrolls also cogently structures another, distinctive version of the story. The first scroll introduces and develops the story of Minghuang's

Kano Sansetsu, 'Emperor Minghuang in exile' (from **Return to the capital**), *Song of Lasting Sorrow*; scroll 2, the second length of silk.

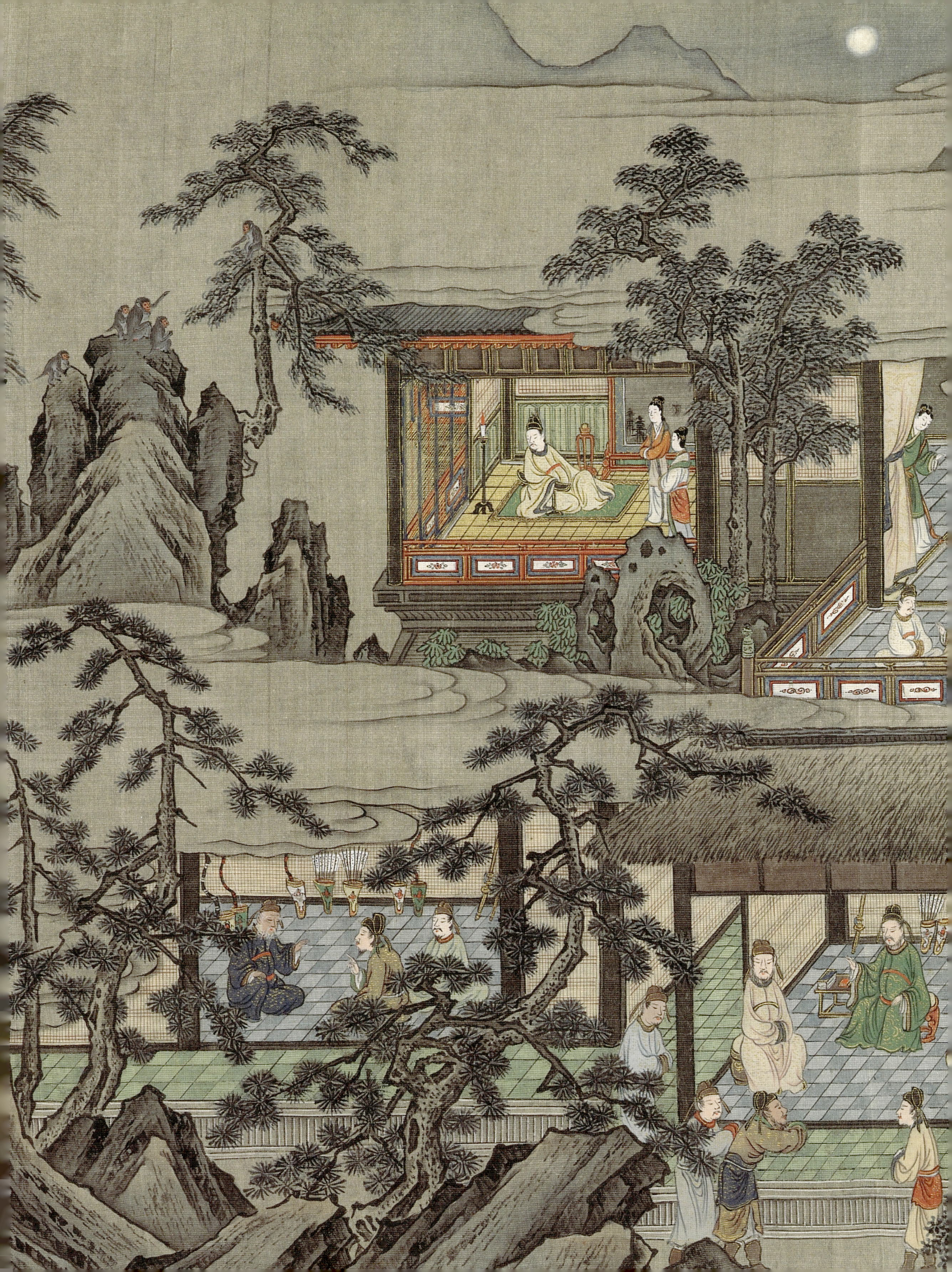

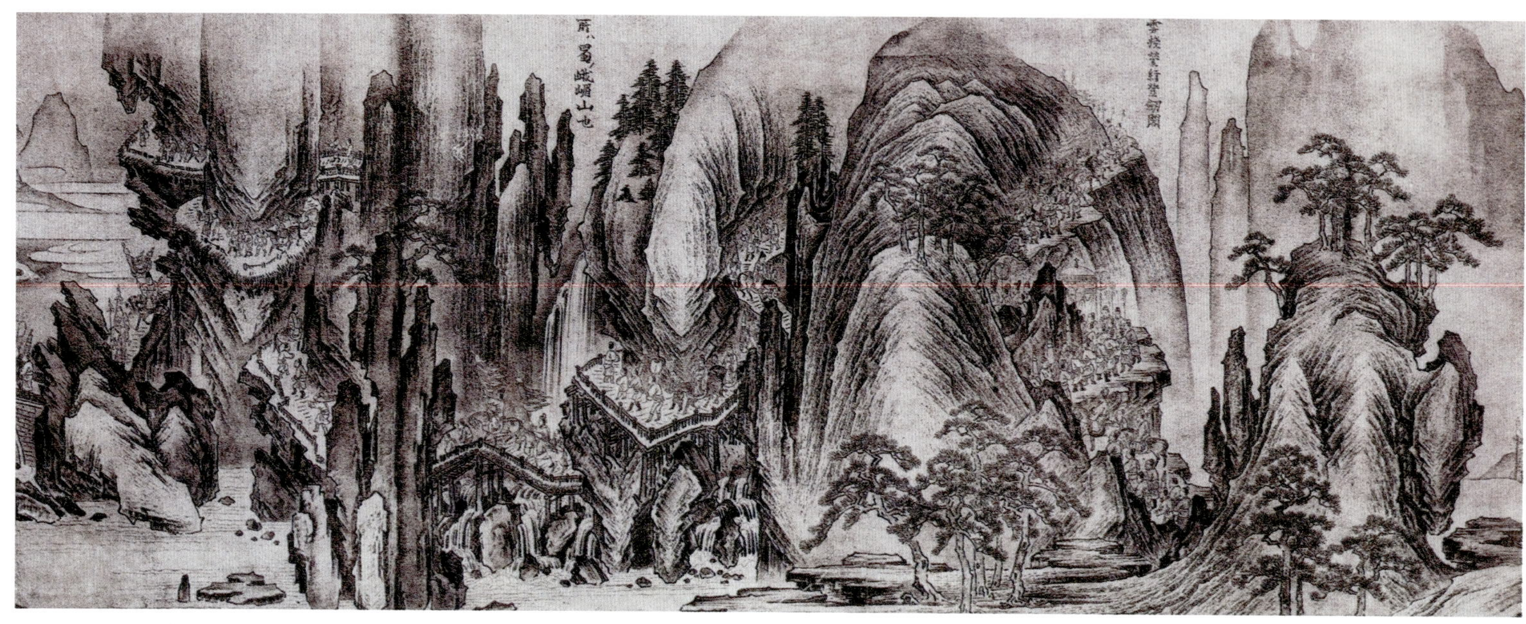

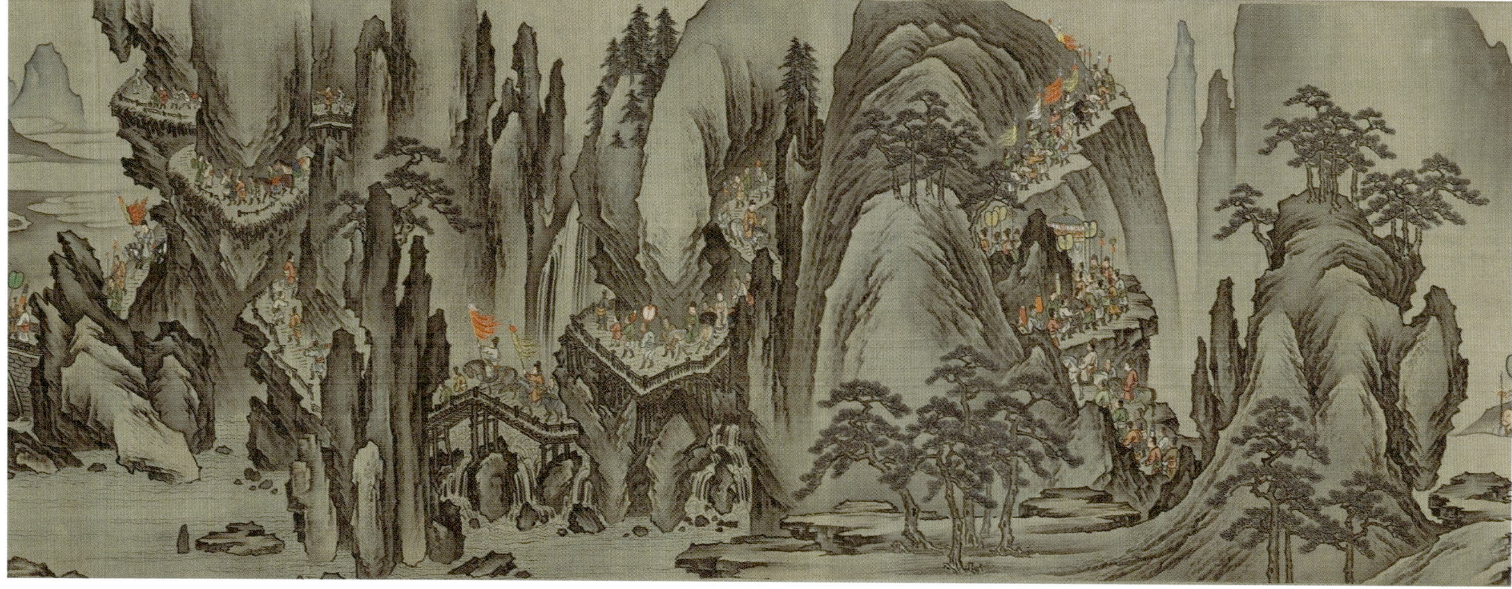

infatuation with Yang Guifei. The second treats the extended moment of crisis and violence, from the torching of the palace and Yang Guifei's execution, to the emperor's perilous flight to Shu and eventual return to the capital. The final scroll is altogether different in mood – contemplative and other-worldly – as it explores the emperor's life after Yang Guifei and the wizard's journey to the isles of the immortals.

What light can an examination of the pictorial structure and physical appearance of the Dublin painting throw on this three-scroll scenario? In a first of three Dublin scrolls, there are three joins of the 180 cm sections of silk and in each case, at each inter-act, there is pictorial continuity, such that dividing/linking clouds, walls, rocks or trees continue seamlessly across the silk divide. The first point at which the pictorial continuity

Fig 50 Scene depicting the escape through the mountains to Shu, from the Kuki version of *Song of Lasting Sorrow*. (After *Kokka* no. 44; 1893). Three handscrolls; ink and light colours on paper. Private collection, Japan. The caption to the right is line 44 of the ballad: 'Plank walkways wound into the clouds as he climbed by Sword Tower Peak.' The caption to the left reads, 'This place is Mount Emei in Shu.'

Fig 51 Scene depicting the escape through the mountains to Shu, from the Chester Beatty version of *Song of Lasting Sorrow*; scroll 2, the first length of silk.

is broken is at the end of this first scroll, between the initial appearance of An Lushan's rebels and the palace gate-house. Perhaps even more compelling is the way that the phalanx of rebels around An Lushan at the end of scroll 1 (in a three-scroll scenario) move from left to right, in what is a classic formal device for countering the right to left momentum of reading a handscroll *at its end*. A further consideration regarding the transition between a scroll 1 and scroll 2 is that there is some residual discolouration to the vertical strip of silk just to the left of the join between these two (that is, before the palace gate-house scene).

In scroll two of a three-scroll format, there is a similar arrangement. At first, the visual movement is strongly leftward, as suggested by the direction of the flames of the burning palace, the fleeing courtiers and also by the curved profiles of highlands. The shapes and profiles of rocks and trees after the bridge under Mount Emei reverse this visual momentum, which is finally brought to a halt by the eddying shape of the column around the site of Yang Guifei's execution. The first and third silk joins are, again as above, seamless. The second silk join is, of course, where the painting is currently divided. It is true that the scenery on either side of this join does not appear to flow, but this could be explained by the narrative, since at this point the emperor is said to have been unable to go near the spot where Yang Guifei was executed. If Sansetsu made this point by situating Yang Guifei's death by the water and the emperor's grief in different places, he also linked them visually using the 'cloud windows'. Eunuchs peer forward through a 'cloud window' down at Yang's execution; the same device above the pine in the next scene enables the viewer to peer in upon the emperor's grief.

When we come to a third of three scrolls there are no obvious pictorial discontinuities at any of the points where the silks join. Certainly, an original three-scroll

mounting for the Dublin set is plausible; it is even possible to go further and say that a three-scroll format is as likely to have been the original arrangement as a two-scroll one. As the other extant version of the *Chōgonka* by Kano Sansetsu in Japan, the Kuki version, is mounted in this three-scroll format, what is its relationship to the Dublin painting? Is it from Sansetsu's workshop, and if so, can it be identified as a preserved draft or a copy kept for reference in the studio? Or was it another copy made to order or for sale?

We know that Sansetsu entered the Kyoto Kano School workshop as a young man and worked his way up to become master of the studio in 1635, and we know that he was later succeeded by his son and disciple Einō (1631–97), indicating that there was a strong family ethos to this studio practice over the generations. Sansetsu's inscription on the Dublin *Chōgonka* painting indicates his pride in carrying the torch of his branch of the eminent Kano lineage. But beyond this, what can the style and execution of the painting tell us about his individual role as master of the Kano studio and about how he organised his various assistants, one of whom would be expected to carry the torch after his death?

Visual examination of the Dublin painting confirms that these scrolls were painted by a group of hands, including at least one that was clearly less accomplished than the others. Most of the painting is executed in a consistently professional manner, and it is really only in a few, apparently less important places that the quality of the finishing is diminished. There are examples, for instance, where the master and/or his senior assistants seem to have completed their work on a given area which then needed some filling in to be complete. Curiously, it is these areas that were deemed to be more peripheral in terms of the pictorial narrative that now shed the most light on the studio system.

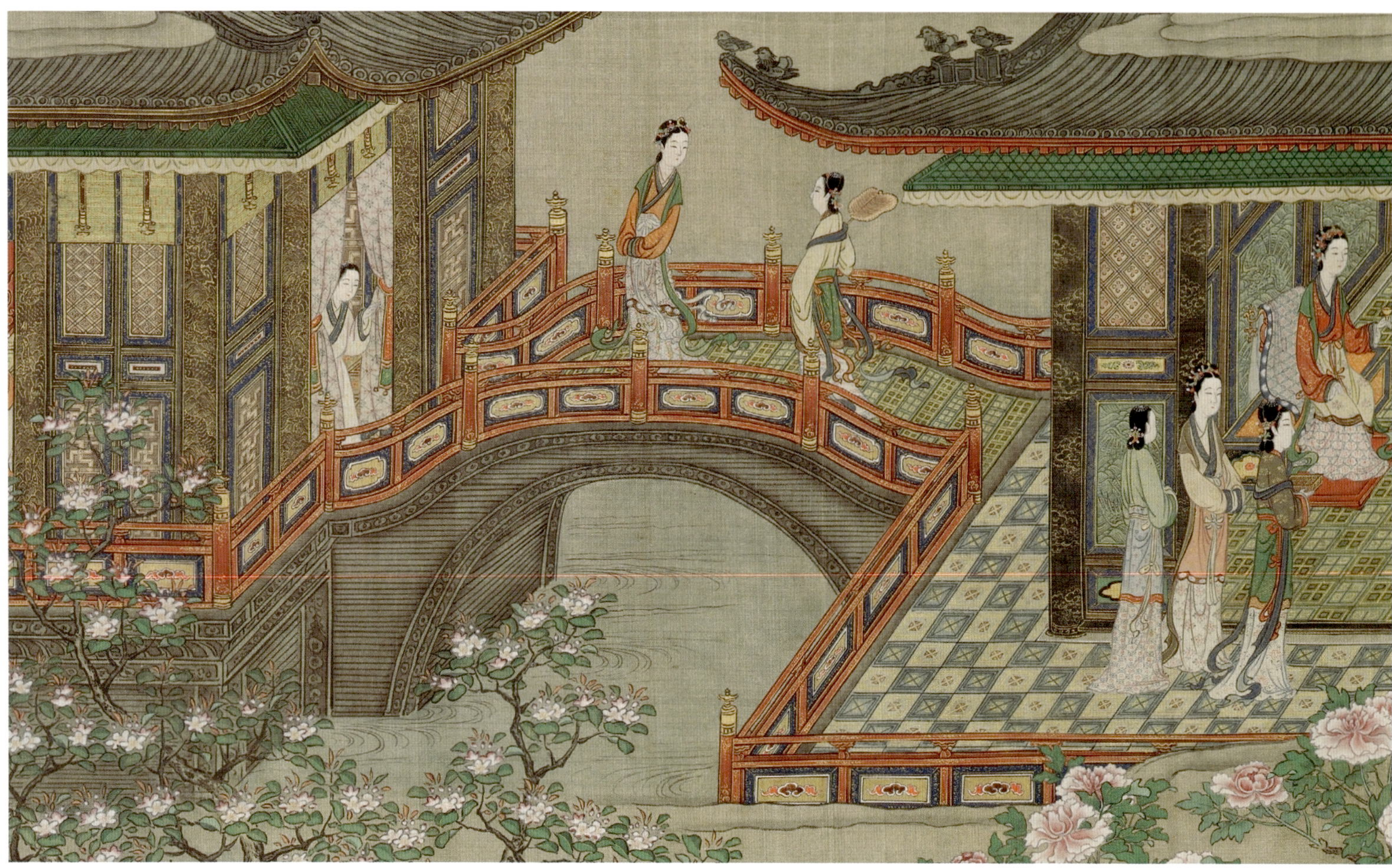

One example is the scene depicting a pavilion over water in the third scene of Minghuang's dalliance with Yang Guifei (figs 52, 53). The featured components of this building are its interior furnishings: they are highly decorative, comprising detailed patterns and motifs, and bright colours, and are all executed in a consistent, polished manner, possibly by two or more hands specialising, either generally or for the purpose of this scroll, in particular motifs, drapery effects or architectural features. Here, the contrast in finishing between the brightly lit decorative surfaces of the interior and the perfunctory grey-wash and line infilling of the stone facing below is stark. Judging by the standard of the hand assigned to fill it in, it would seem that the decorative facing of the base of this building was considered far less important.

The area below the left end of the bridge stands out as an area of visual confusion. The painting of the circle motif, for instance, is slap-dash, but the corner of the pavilion and the bridge is pictorial nonsense: the vertical cartouche containing a row of circles has been painted in the same plane as the bridge, yet the overhanging buttress above is part of

the pavilion. This part was done in a haphazard manner by someone with relatively little appreciation of the correct architectural details. In a sense, this did not matter: the weakest hand got the least important job – filling in repetitive details in grey ink.

Another example that throws light on the system by which the painting was completed can be found in the scenes depicting the rise of the Yang clan. Towards the end of this suite of scenes, between two buildings in the background, is a stand of three shade trees – strong pines with pock-marked trunks (see fig. 56). A quick glance shows that these ramrod straight pines were planted there at an early stage in the design process, in order to fill out the space between the two buildings to the left and right, and above the gatehouse roof below. The painting of the pine needle sprays above is somewhat flat, but the rendering of the trunks themselves suggests they were executed with the same attention to detail as the squared corners and walls.

What takes place among these pines in narrative terms is incidental – but at the same time technically fascinating. Behind the trees, two saddled horses

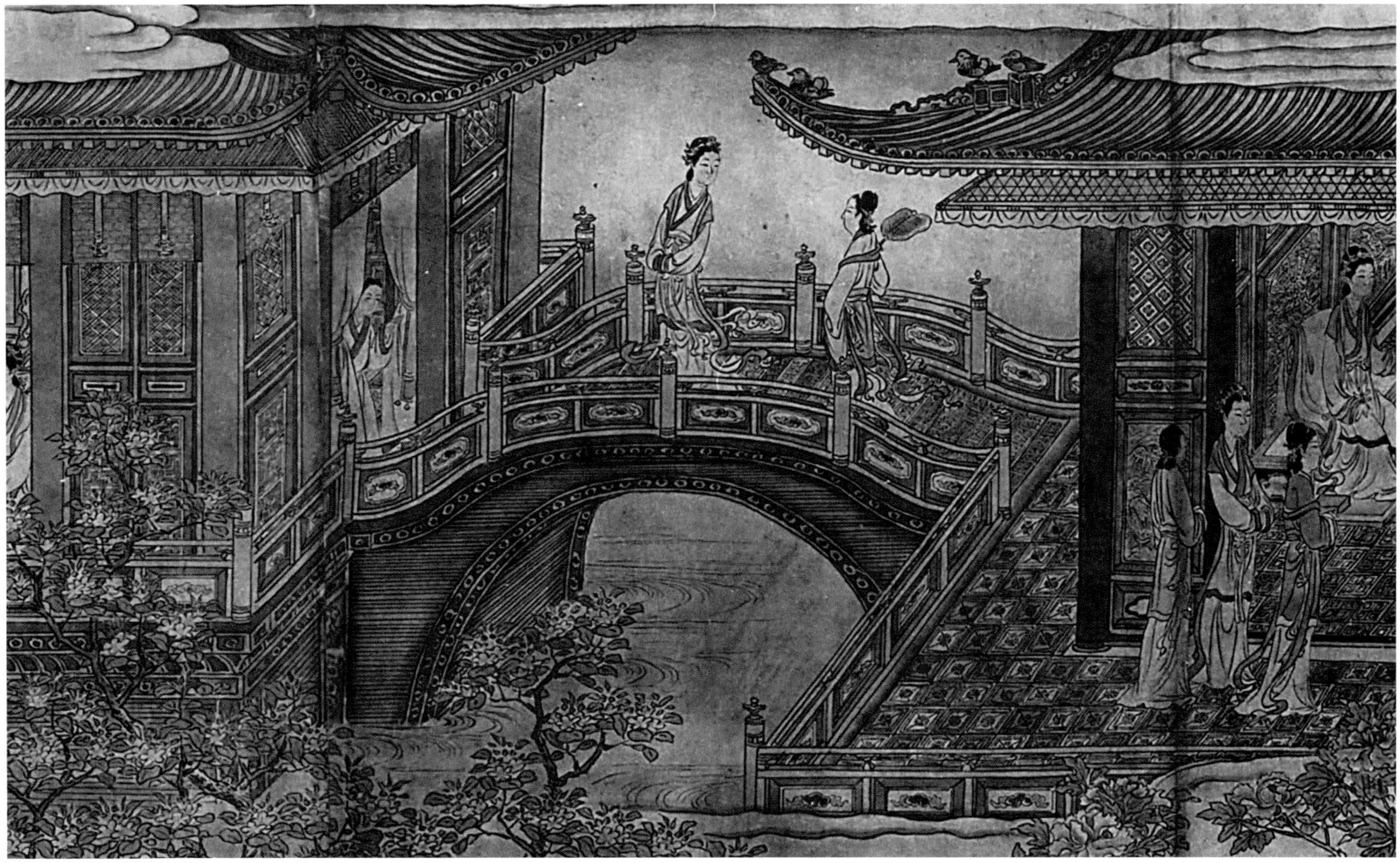

await their riders; seated on the ground leaning on buildings or tree trunks, the grooms mostly doze. The dun horse to the left is painted in a competent naturalistic manner, with its neck 'turning' back towards its reins. The dappled grey and black horse, however, is seen in a strange profile, divided into three parts by two of the pine trunks. The front-quarters of the horse look to have been executed in the same hand as painted the dun, but it would seem that the task of imparting a sense of organic unity to this figure as it passes behind two pine trunks was perhaps too challenging for the hand assigned to it. The tail section in particular seems to be at the wrong level and in another plane to the rest of the body.

The visual evidence of these weak links provides useful pointers as to how the painting was made in the studio hierarchy. At the top, the master was responsible for the overall layout and concept, and for the most significant pictorial details. Assistants at different levels filled in decorative details such as drapery and fabric patterns, ink washes and repeated motifs like tiles and panels. Finally, someone was responsible for filling in any minor areas that had not

been completed by painters higher up the studio ladder. It would be unfair to place too much emphasis on these few weak links in what is otherwise a powerful and imaginatively plotted pictorial narrative picture scroll, but they reveal much in terms of the skills and talents that would have been available in the studio.

One source that might offer an insight into the operations of Sansetsu's studio is Kano Einō's illustrated woodblock-printed book of the *Chōgonka* ballad, entitled *Chōgonka zushō* (literally, 'the *Chōgonka* illustrated in print') in five volumes published in the late 1670s (see figs 84, 85). Einō's book includes an annotated transcription of Bai Juyi's ballad in elegant cursive calligraphy interspersed with pictorial scenes. Most of these illustrations reprise the three-dozen scenes found in the Dublin version by his father, although there are a few extra that are not otherwise known. It is possible that in the final version Sansetsu omitted a few of the scenes he had drafted but in the end found he had no use for, and that these remained in the studio for reference or later use – such as in *Chōgonka zushō*. At the time, Sansetsu over-

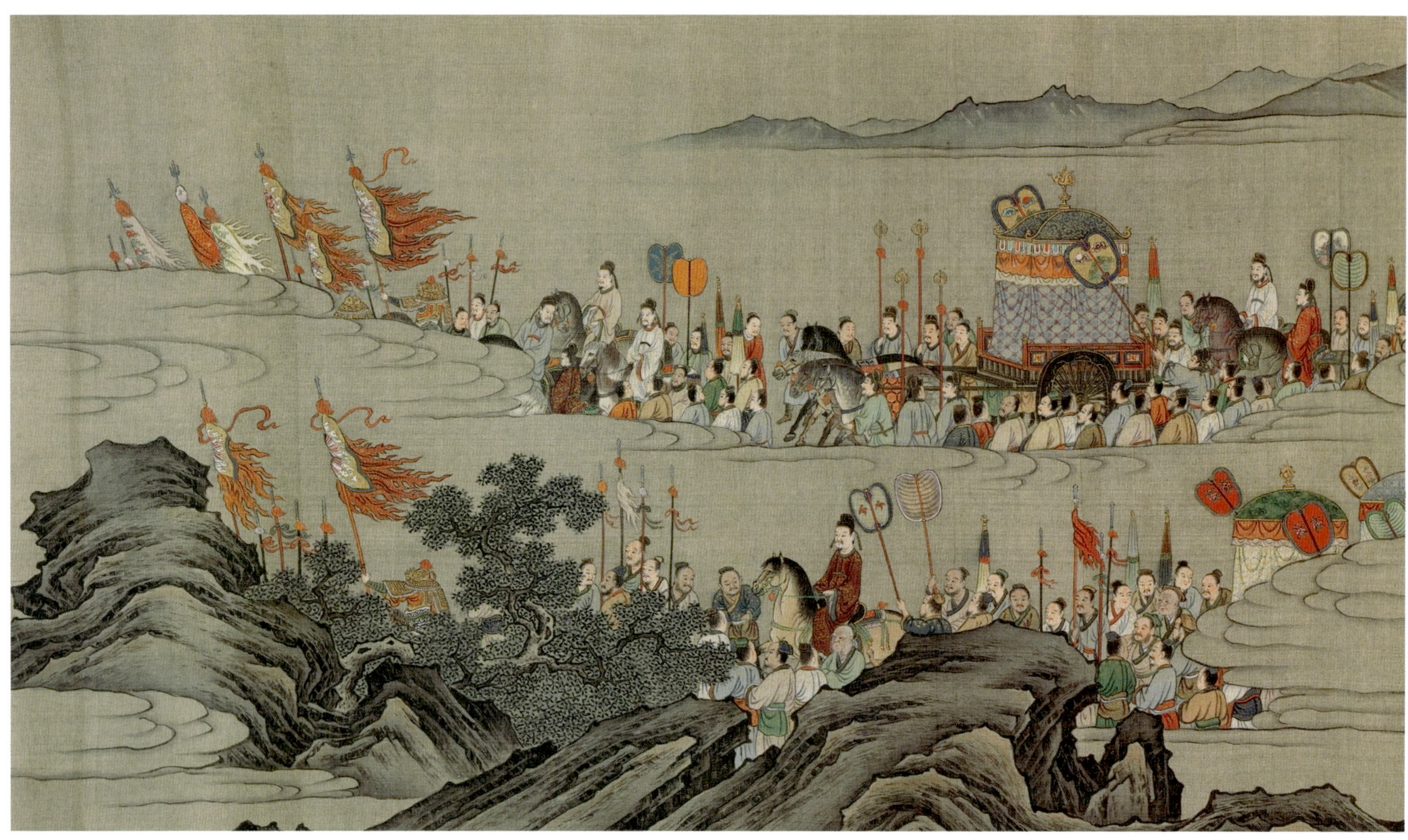

saw the making of the Dublin painting in the mid-1640s, Einō would have been about sixteen years old, and although he was presumably already engaged in his apprenticeship in the studio, any individual contributions are yet to be identified. Matthew McKelway discusses the *Chōgonka zushō* in chapter four.

Another source to refer to is the Kuki version of the *Chōgonka* scrolls. Its composition is virtually identical to the one in the Dublin *Chōgonka* scroll set, and it appears to have been made in Sansetsu's studio at the same time, about 1646–47. The painting in Dublin is of course undated; the Kuki version bears a dated inscription (of which more below). The Kuki version is undoubtedly very close to the Dublin one, although their exact connection is both an intriguing problem and a matter of speculation. There are a number of differences between the Dublin and Kuki versions, some of which have been noted. The Kuki version, mounted in three handscrolls, is painted on multiple sheets of paper almost as high as the scroll and about 25 cm wide (see table on p.102). Done in ink and light colours, at first glance, the Kuki *Chōgonka* resembles one of Sansetsu's preparatory drawings, such as those made for his screen compositions, but a closer look

shows it to be far more detailed. Still, its decorative detailing is far simpler than that of the Dublin painting, which was executed in bright mineral pigments on silk.

That the Kuki scrolls consist of multiple sheets of paper, only approximately 25 cm in width, strongly suggests that the work was conceived as a full-scale preparatory painting, or *gakō* (画稿), traditionally the penultimate stage in producing a finished work. The use of multiple small paper sheets was common practice in the creation of preparatory paintings on all formats.[67] Conversely, finished works of handscroll painting seldom employ such small sheets, being more typically produced on fewer sheets of greater length. A final, telling disparity between the Kuki and the Chester Beatty scrolls is their different approach to ornamental detail in architecture: the Kuki scrolls include much less than the Library scrolls, which leave no surfaces untouched by decorative flourishes.

The Kuki scrolls close with an inscription different from the signature and seals that appear at the end of the Dublin scrolls. The last Kuki scroll bears an inscription (see fig. 88) including a date in the first lunar month of the year Shōhō 3, corresponding to 1646; a note to say the painting was done in thirty-six scenes; and a

Fig 54 Scene depicting Minghuang's initial flight from the capital, from the Chester Beatty version of *Song of Lasting Sorrow*; scroll 1, the second length of silk.

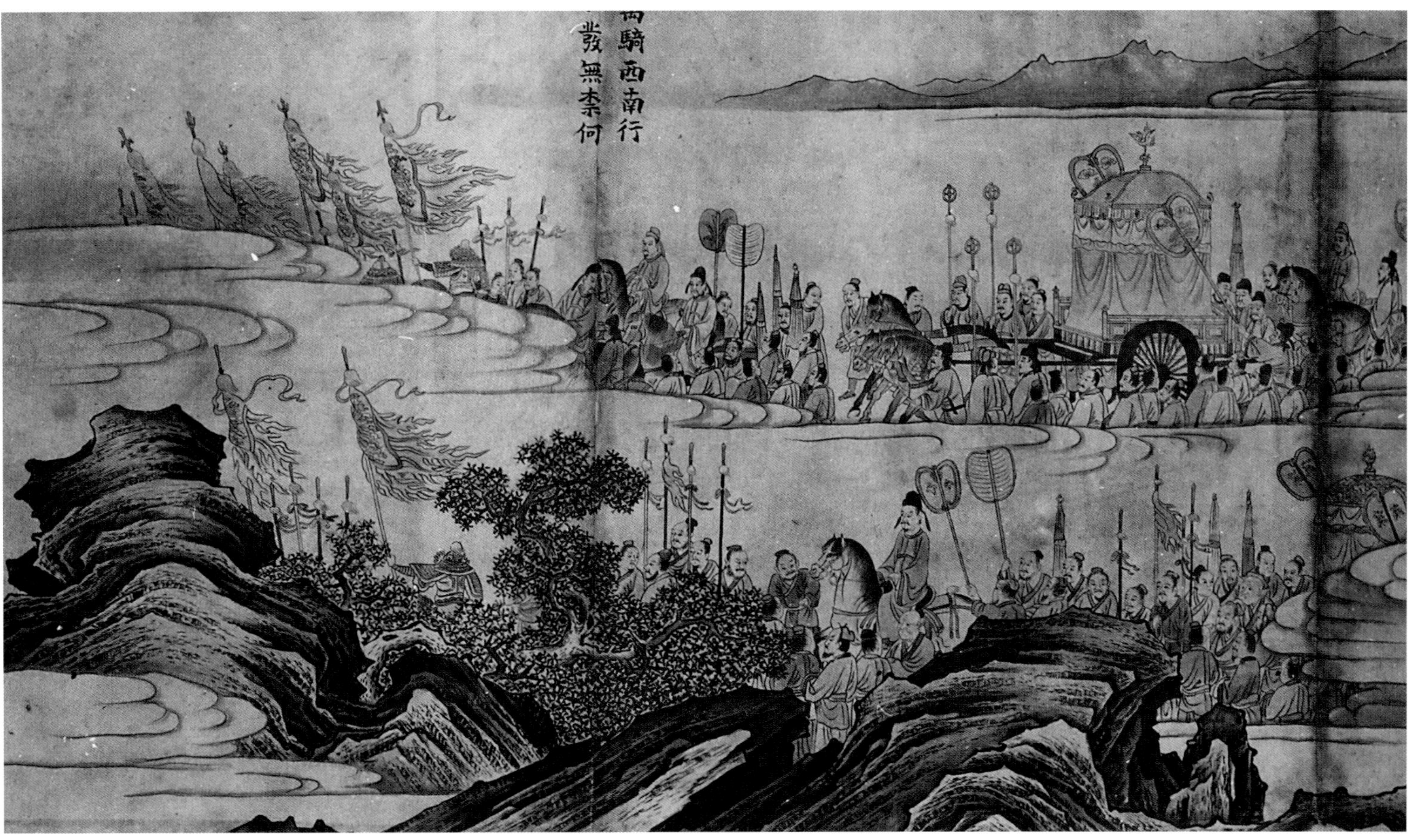

Fig 55 Scene depicting Minghuang's initial flight from the capital, from the Kuki version of *Song of Lasting Sorrow*.

signature reading *Kano Hokkyō*. *Hokkyō* (Bridge of the Dharma) was an honorific religious title of the highest recognition that Sansetsu received, as his teacher Sanraku had before him, in the seventh month of 1647 for the brilliant execution of an imperial commission – two scrolls at Tōfukuji that depict two of a set of thirty-three images of the bodhisattva Kannon (see p. 110).

Curiously, the words *Kano Hokkyō* appear to the right, and not on a line below the first part of the inscription, possibly because they were added later. The modern scholar Miyajima Shin'ichi believes the style of the Dublin scrolls to be 'similar to that of the Thirty-three Kannon scrolls and less orthodox than that of the [Kuki] scrolls'. Since the honorific title *Hokkyō* does not appear on the Dublin painting, he believes it to postdate the more 'orthodox' Kuki version. He thus dates the Dublin painting to 'between the first month of 1646 and the seventh month of the following year'.[68] Still unresolved, however, is the question of how the Kuki scrolls can be dated to the first month of 1646 when they also bear the title Sansetsu received in the seventh month of 1647. As noted above, it is possible the signature on the Kuki painting was added later, after the distinguished title

was bestowed on Sansetsu. This is plausible, for instance, whether the Kuki painting had remained in the studio or gone out to a patron.

In addition to a date and signature, the three scrolls of the Kuki painting carry inscriptions of selected passages from Bai Juyi's ballad, with occasional identifications of places, above or beside each of the thirty-six scenes. The Dublin painting, as already noted, does not include any of the text from the ballad, and calls entirely upon on the viewer's powers of poetic recollection for the identification of places and events. Is it possible that the Kuki version was a polished final draft for the Dublin version, which included the identifications of scenes and was executed on sheets of paper; or perhaps some other final form of the scroll intended to be kept as a record in the studio? It should be possible, through a close comparison of the two paintings, to establish the relationship between them and resolve these doubts. What follows is an attempt to raise questions and reach a tentative conclusion.

Two questions that might be considered together are why the Kuki version consists of three scrolls and the Dublin version, two; and why only the Kuki version features inscriptions. We explored above the structure and phrasing of the narrative in the *Chōgonka* scrolls, where the narrative was shown to have been developed, roughly, in twelve sets of three scenes, rather like acts and scenes of a play. In the Dublin version, each 'act' of three scenes takes place over one length of silk of approximately 180 cm. The implication was that this length of around 180 cm determined to a large extent the organisation of the whole narrative set. The table below shows how the action is presented in each of the two versions, and gives details per 'act' of the length of the silk (Dublin version) and the number of sheets of paper (Kuki version).

As the table indicates, the silks in the Dublin version are about 180 cm in length, which corresponds to seven sheets of paper in the Kuki version. The only exception is the piece of silk illustrating the rise of the Yang clan, which measures just 149.6 cm, corresponding to six sheets of paper. The right column of the table below indicates which lines of the ballad are inscribed. What the table cannot give are measure-ments of the Kuki scroll (these are not known), although with regard to its height, there is a certain amount of free space both at the top and at the bottom in comparison with the Dublin version.

Regarding the overall plotting of the narrative, both the two- and the three-scroll versions make good visual and narrative sense. The transmission of the Dublin version in a two-scroll format could suggest this was its original form. So significant an event as the death of Yang Guifei, which in Bai Juyi's ballad takes place just one third of the way through the sixty couplets of the text, for instance, occurs at the exact midway point of the Dublin version. She is about to be executed at the end of the first scroll, while at the beginning of the second, the emperor is pictured inconsolable with grief at the news of her death. As such, the cruel deed itself happens off-stage, as it were – between the scrolls – and the event acts as a searing visual caesura within the overall plotting over two long handscrolls.

At the same time, the pictorial divisions and tran-

CBL VERSION			ACTION	KUKI VERSION			
SCROLL (NO.)	'ACT'	SILK LENGTH (CM)		SCROLL	'ACT'	SHEETS (NO.)	LINES INSCRIBED
1	1	179.9	YANG GUIFEI IS DISCOVERED	1	1	7	3–4, 6, 10–11
1	2	181.1	MINGHUANG'S DALLIANCE	1	2	7	15, 18, 22
1	3	149.6	RISE OF THE YANG CLAN	1	3	6	23–24
1	4	180.5	GENERAL AN LUSHAN REBELS	1	4	7	27–30, 31–32
1	5	180.4	REBELS ENTER THE CAPITAL	2	1	7	34, 37
1	6	180.8 (1052.3)	EXECUTION OF YANG GUIFEI	2	2	7	'MAWEI', 38–39
2	1	178.8	FLIGHT TO SHU	2	3	7	42, 44, 'EMEI'
2	2	179.4	RETURN FROM EXILE	2	4	7	'SHU', 49–50, 51–55, 56
2	3	177.1	RETIRED EMPEROR MOURNS	3	1	7	57–60, 63–64, 67–68, 71
2	4	179.0	MINGHUANG ENGAGES WIZARD	3	2	7	73–75, 79–80
2	5	178.9	ISLES OF THE IMMORTALS	3	3	7	82–84, 85–89, 92, 95, 97–98
2	6	177.3 (1071.1)	DAOIST MEETS YANG GUIFEI	3	4	7	99, 108, 113–114, 115–120

sitions of the three-scroll Kuki version make equally good sense, with each scroll containing a sequence of four 'acts'. As such, the smooth flow of action is not interrupted from the end of one scroll to the beginning of another, as changes of scene take place in between. For example, the first scroll ends with an image of an innocuous bush after the rebels are shown advancing on the capital to the right; the second begins a new scene abruptly with the paved entrance to a gatehouse, through which the rebels pour on their way to torching the imperial palace further left.

What is remarkable about the Kuki scroll is that the seven sheets of paper per 'act' are themselves carefully orchestrated in relation to the painting. The sheets often cut through vertical structures such as tree trunks, pillars and walls, as well as the inter-act scenery where they would impinge least on the painting. At the same time, it also becomes noticeable how many features, such as pavilions or terraces are in fact centred within the sheets. If this was a preparatory version, the question arises of why the inscriptions of Bai Juyi's ballad were omitted from the 'final' Dublin version. It is possible that they were considered for inclusion in the 'draft' version but deemed unnecessary in the final one. This explanation has one further merit: it is not likely that a copy, if the Kuki version was a reference copy, would include inscriptions that did not exist in the original.

What can be said about qualitative differences in the execution of the two paintings? At even a cursory glance, it is clear that the Dublin version is more lavish. It is painted on silk, which takes decorative detail and infilling better, and it makes prominent use of bright colours and gold ink, featuring beautifully and painstakingly executed decorative patterns and motifs. It is possible that certain pictorial or decorative motifs, or types of work such as architectural or figure painting, could have been delegated to specialist assistants in the studio or workshop. The Kuki version, executed in light colours on paper, is accordingly far more *linear* in its overall style than the Dublin version; in other words, there is a more evident lack of restraint to the handling of ink in the freehand ink-outline technique used to render figures, landscape and plants, for instance. The decorative patterns are less pervasive and intense, and do not close in on these lines or tame their independent qualities as calligraphic traces, as in the Dublin version. Arguably, there is a single stylistic consistency within the Kuki version.

By reviewing the character of the paintings alone, it is very hard to determine for certain whether one version preceded the other, or whether they are both based on an earlier, separate draft. Generally speaking, the Kuki version is less finished than the Dublin one, so we would expect and duly find areas of decorative infilling and patterning left blank, for instance.

It may be possible to assess whether the Kuki scroll came first by examining the problem areas in the Dublin scrolls, identified above. In fact, it is quite often the case that a strange passage or transition in the Dublin painting can be explained by reference to the Kuki version. One example is in the scene of Minghuang's initial flight from the capital. At the head of the rear column, before it is engulfed in clouds, a mounted man turns his head to look back at the palanquin behind and his head awkwardly abuts the head of a horse immediately behind him (figs 54, 55). This appears in exactly the same way at the same point in the Kuki version. The 'error' in the 'final' version there may be explained by the way the two sheets of paper in the 'draft' were adjoined in the mounting: part of the painting at each edge has been lost, possibly because the painter slightly misjudged the transition, or because of a small overlap or cropping in the mounting process. An incidental point to note

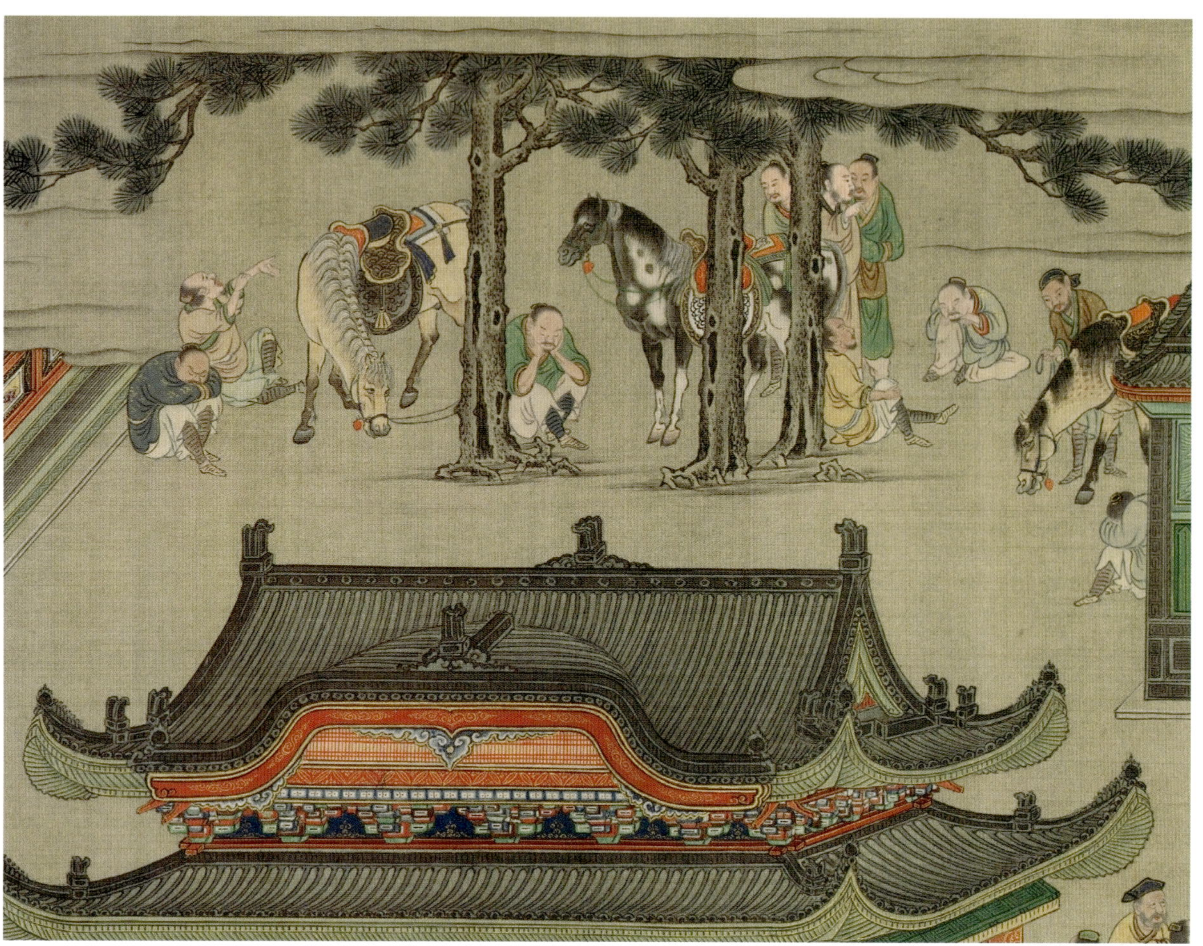

here is that the calligraphy above appears to overlap the two sheets, indicating that it was executed after the Kuki scrolls were mounted.

Earlier, we examined the discrepancy in the painting of the stone facing of the bridge in the suite of scenes depicting Minghuang's dalliance, where the left arch of the bridge meets the right end wall of the pavilion (see fig. 52). If the Kuki version is a model or draft (or if it reflects one), it might show the 'correct' drawing for this passage of architecture. It is worth noting that this exact point in the Kuki version is again where two sheets of paper meet – and where a small section of painting from the left edge of the right sheet is missing (see fig. 53). A missing passage in the Kuki version has a direct connection to an area of confusion in the Dublin version, indicating how closely the two paintings are related. The obvious conclusion is that the interpretation of this passage in the Dublin painting is an attempt to make sense of this confusing join in the Kuki scroll. Further research will determine if this is right.

Another problem area in the Dublin painting is the passage with the sleeping grooms, from one of the scenes depicting the rise of the Yang clan (figs 56, 57). In both paintings, the drawing in this section is confused and somewhat disconnected. Comparing the tack of the horse in each version (the one seen between the two trees to the right of the sleeping groom), in the Kuki version, the leathers used for the bridle, reins and martingale are all naturalistically painted in different widths, according to their purposes: the reins are thin, the bridle thicker, and the martingale thicker still. In the Dublin version, this level of detail is somewhat lost. A particularly noticeable difference is evident in the way the martingale relates to the horse's musculature. In the Kuki scroll, it is tight across his front quarters and digs into his muscles, creating a visible groove. In the Dublin scroll, this groove of muscle still appears in the animal's front quarters, but the thin martingale rides up above it – removing any naturalistic reason why the groove should be there. This might be explained by arguing that the rendering in the Dublin scroll is a typical 'error' or deviation of a copyist who did not pay sufficient attention to the naturalism of the model. However, in other respects throughout both scrolls,

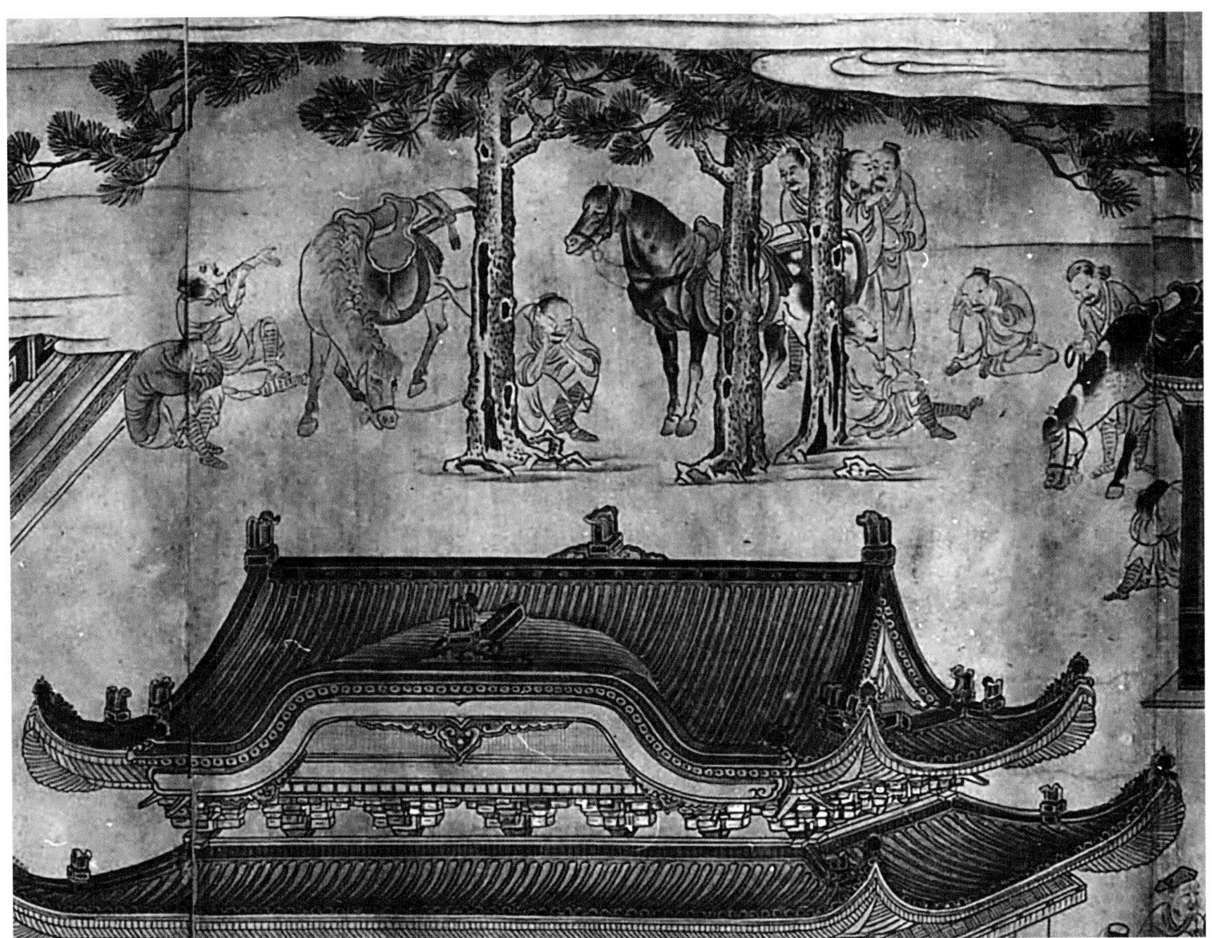

the attention to details like these is remarkable. Still, reinforcing the point that the Kuki version was a preparatory version, the Dublin one, in many other areas, seems to go its own way in executing to a high standard of 'finish' the areas and details that are only suggested by the Kuki scroll.

The scenes in which the tiny figure of the Daoist is shown flying to the isles of the immortals is a case in point. In the Kuki scroll, there are many horizontal bands of mist filling the middle portion of the scroll below the mountains where the figure flies. In the Dublin scroll, these bands do not feature. This would seem to rule out the Kuki scroll being a copy of the Dublin scroll, which in any case would be unlikely given the existence of the inscriptions on the Kuki version. It would be unlikely, in that scenario, that a copyist would go so far as to identify lines of the ballad and inscribe them on a copy where none appeared on the original. On balance, it seems fair to speculate that the Kuki version precedes the Dublin one and is, indeed, a preparatory version.

In conclusion, one might say that the Dublin version is richer and more 'finished', although it may also be described as somewhat less lyrical, and lacking the spontaneity and naturalness inherent in a more linear style. Nonetheless, it is evident that a firm executive hand underlay the conception and structure of the *Chōgonka* composition, which tallies with Sansetsu's insistence that he 'did it for first time'. At the same time, there are also interesting suggestions of delegation in the execution of the painting, as one would expect in a polished version on silk from a Kano School studio. The Kuki version may be more faithful to the design concept contained in the draft, in demonstrating which lines of the ballad were intended for emphasis, whereas the Dublin scroll, with its far more detailed decorative finish, shows us what the various talents within the studio system were capable of adding to a painting as it evolved from a draft to a finished product.

In the following chapter, Matthew McKelway examines closely the life and workshop practice of the Kano School, and Sansetsu in particular, adding to our understanding of the *Song of Lasting Sorrow* scrolls, their precedents in Japan and their posterity in woodblock-print form.

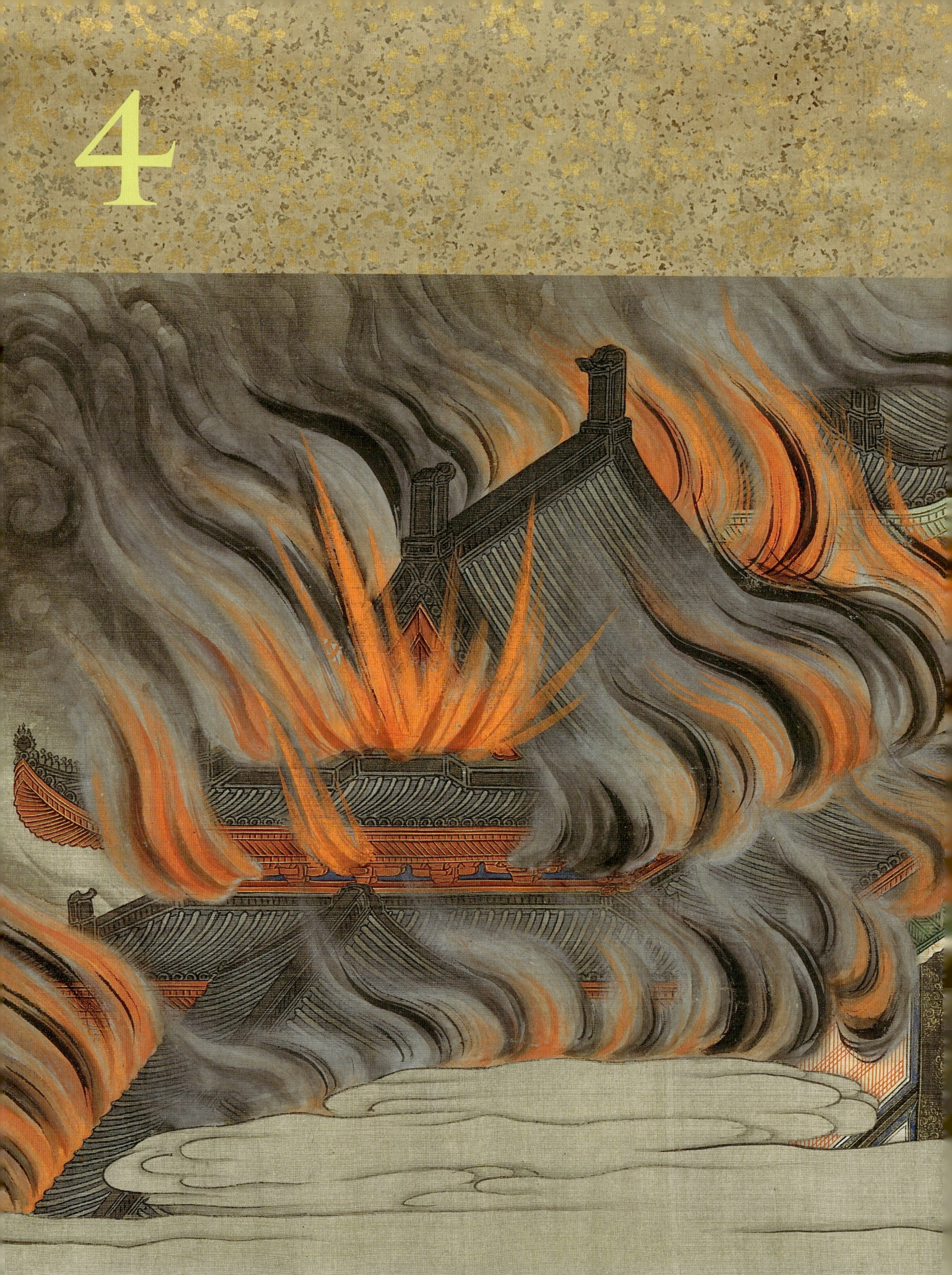
4

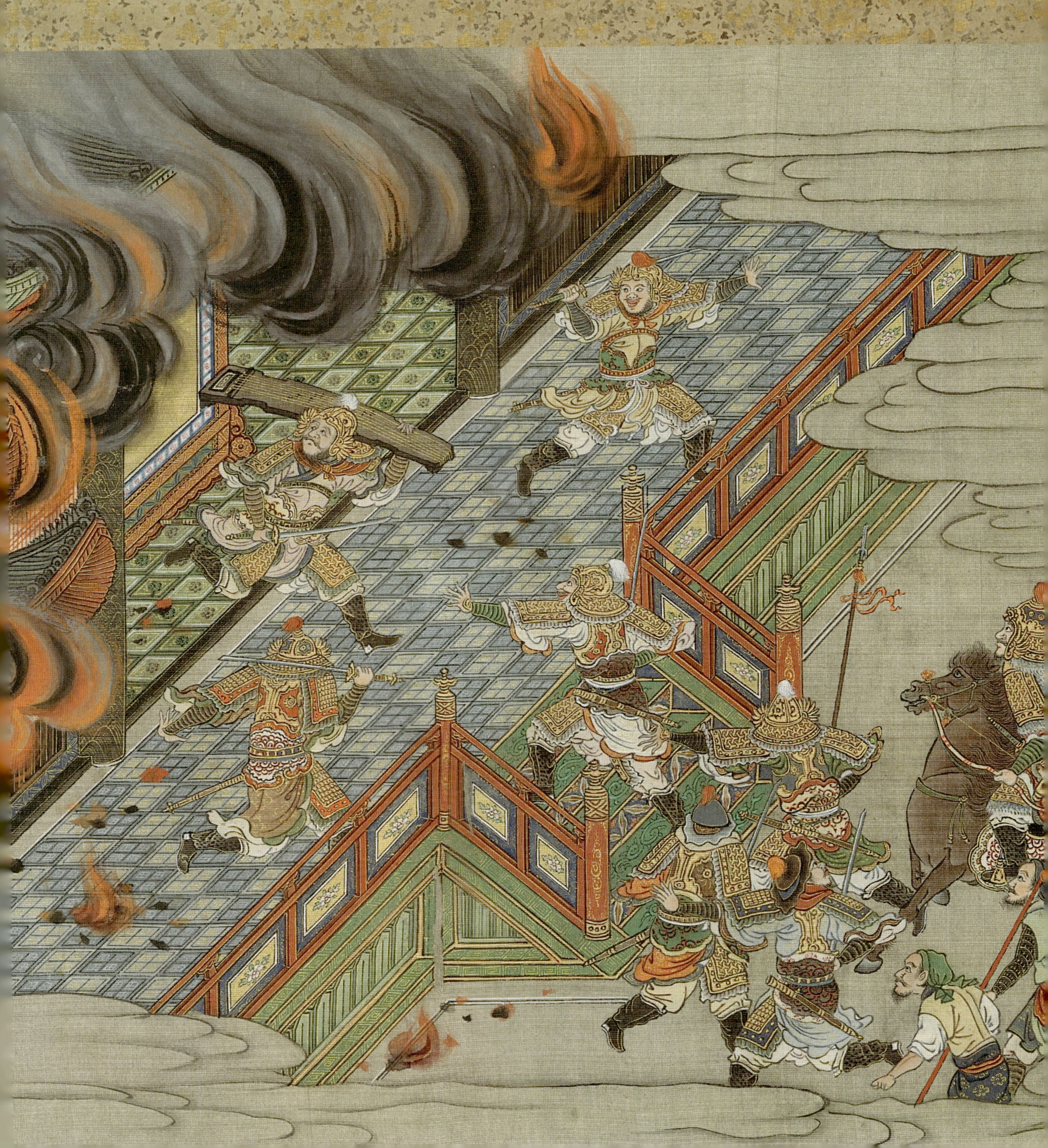

KANO SANSETSU AND KANO WORKSHOP PAINTINGS OF 'THE SONG OF LASTING SORROW'

JAPANESE ART OF THE early Edo period (1603–1868) has been characterised as reflecting an impulse to 'return to native traditions', or broadly defined in terms of a 'renaissance of classical culture' of the centuries before.[69] Woodblock-printed *Saga-bon* editions published and dispersed such Heian classics as the *Tales of Ise*, the calligrapher Hon'ami Kōetsu and painter Tawaraya Sōtatsu collaborated to produce scrolls of classical poetic anthologies, and masters of tea and garden design imbued *sukiya* architecture at Katsura and Shūgakuin with materials and forms that alluded to the court culture of the Heian period (794–1185): these would all indeed support the notion that decidedly nativist sensibilities infused the seventeenth century's developing tastes. One painter active in the century following national unification, however, produced works that spoke to an audience equally fascinated with China, interest in which deepened amidst official policies of diplomatic disengagement. Encouraged by members of a circle of intellectuals who promoted Neo-Confucian thought, this painter, Kano Sansetsu (1590–1651), evidently discovered in Chinese painting, literature, philosophy and mythology an inexhaustible source for artistic inspiration.

The Chester Beatty Library's *Chōgonka emaki* is a visual representation of an early ninth-century Chinese poem painted by a Japanese artist, Kano Sansetsu, almost a millennium later.[70] Despite these wide gaps in time and space, the *Chōgonka* scrolls remain the most complete known visual manifestation of Bai Juyi's (772–846) ballad, 'Song of Lasting Sorrow', and the painting that is most faithful to the Tang poet's text.[71] In two handscrolls that unroll to a total of nearly 22 metres (over 70 feet) Sansetsu vividly recounts the story of the tragic romance of the Tang-dynasty emperor Minghuang (Xuanzong; 685–762) and Yang Yuhuan, his 'precious consort'

(literally, 'Guifei'; 719–56). Uninterrupted by any text, Sansetsu's scrolls are a tour de force of continuous visual narrative, unravelling in a dazzling array of scenes set in palaces, gardens and landscapes. Sansetsu's work follows a long tradition in Japan, beginning as early as the ninth century, of depicting Bai Juyi's poem, but in important ways it departs from all previous representations of the ballad. In tandem with the other essays in this volume, which offer a close reading of the scrolls and an analysis of their iconographic sources, the essay that follows examines Kano Sansetsu's masterpiece in relation to other Japanese depictions of Bai Juyi's ballad, and investigates the factors in Sansetsu's artistic practice that inspired him to chart a completely new trajectory for what had become an age-old theme of painting.

KANO SANSETSU IN EDO-PERIOD TEXTS

Biographical information about Kano Sansetsu is scant. What is known can be culled from three kinds of sources: first, in documents written by his contemporaries that make reference to him; second, in the painting treatises that proliferated in the Edo period after the 1691 appearance of *History of Painting in this Realm* (*Honchō gashi*), which was authored by Sansetsu's son Kano Einō (1631–97) based on Sansetsu's drafts;[72] and third, from his few works that can be positively dated. Perhaps the most reliable document, which also happens to be the longest and earliest that describes the artist's life and background, is *Preface to the scroll painting relating the family of Kano Einō* (*Kano Einō kaden ga jiku jo*) by Hayashi Gahō (1618–88), a prominent Neo-Confucian scholar who succeeded his father Hayashi Razan (1583–1657) as director of the Confucian Academy in Edo. Included in the *Collected writings of Professor Gahō of the Hayashi Academy* (*Gahō-sensei ringakushi bunshū*), dated to 1669, Gahō's *Preface* is a biographical essay

Kano Sansetsu, 'The wizard requests an audience with Yang Guifei' (from Isles of the immortals), *Song of Lasting Sorrow*; scroll 2, the fifth length of silk.

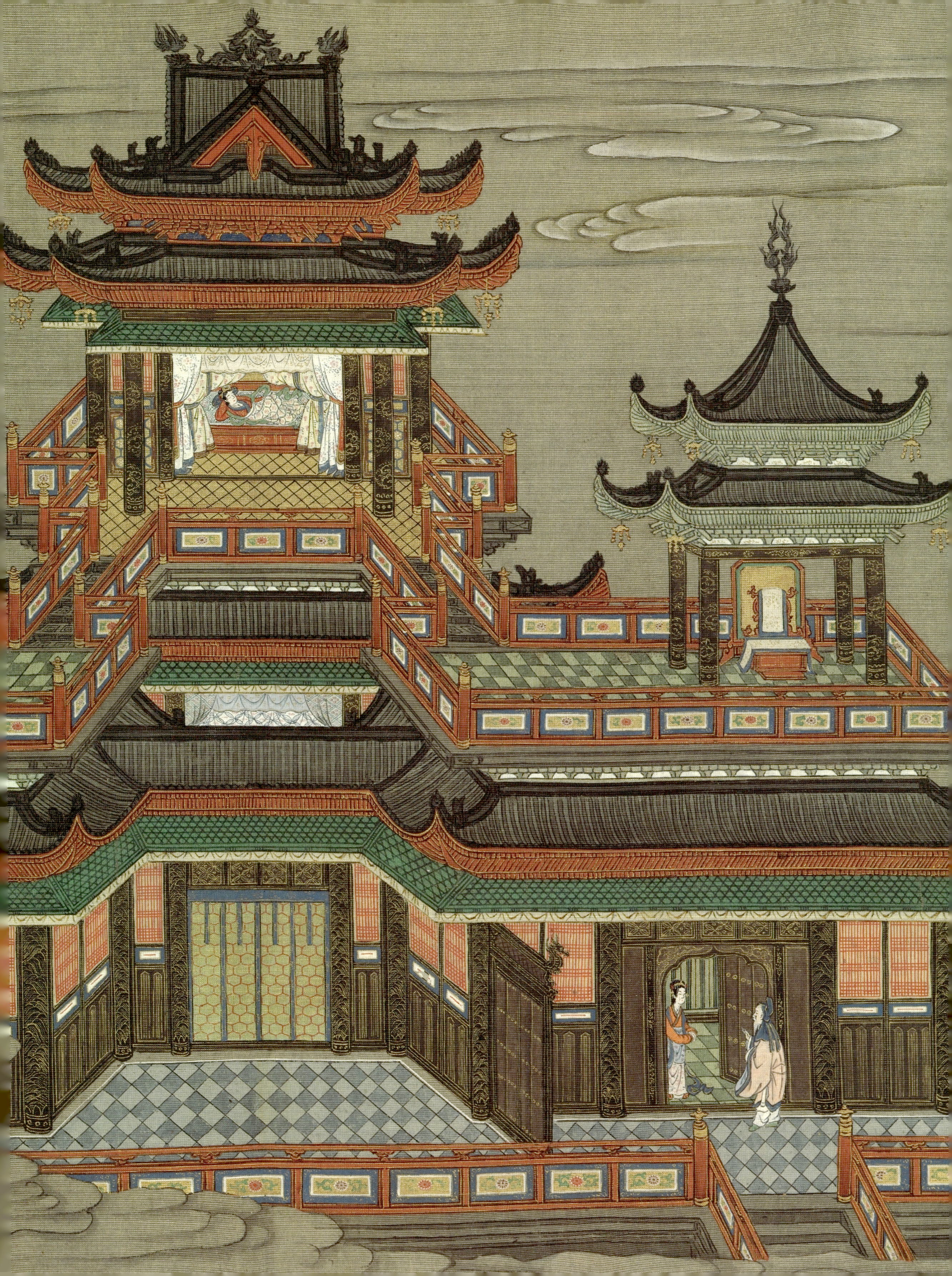

comprised of three sections devoted to Kano Sanraku (1559–1635), Sansetsu and Einō. The passage on Sansetsu relates the following outlines of his life: [73]

Sansetsu was of the Hata clan and of the Chiga family; his name as a youth was Hikozō; his father was called Dōgen, and his mother was of the Matsuura family. He was born in Hizen Province and for some reason moved to Naniwa [Osaka]. From the time he was a child Hikozō liked to paint, and although Dōgen discouraged this, he did not quit. Hikozō was only sixteen when his father died, and his uncle, a priest named so-and-so entrusted him to Sanraku, who made him his apprentice. He gradually progressed in the art of painting and Sanraku had him marry his eldest daughter; he then changed his name to Heishirō and received the Kano surname. When the aged Sanraku's designated successor died, he ordered Heishirō to succeed him in his family's art. He took the name Nuidonosuke and the artist's name (*gō*) Sansetsu. He produced paintings for the Imperial Palace, the Retired Emperor's Palace and Nijō Castle. Sansetsu was adept at writing, and often read such works as the *Xuanhe huapu* and *Tuhui baojian*, or studied the masterpieces of famous historical painters. He also studied the origins of the wondrous inks of our realm. He once met Kassho Dōen [Nawa Kassho] and came to prize Confucian learning and enquire about the classics. He then painted *Ten Views of West Lake* on fans and gave them to Dōen, who composed poems and a preface in appreciation, thus 'making indigo out of blue' [attesting to his accomplishment as a painter]. Master Fujiwara Seika also saw this painting

and composed a title and poem for this work, which described how he [Sansetsu] had grasped the process of transformation. The paintings of *Thirty-Three Kannons in Tōfukuji* are by Minchō, but two scrolls had been lost. Former Regent Kujō Sachiie [1586–1665] ordered Sansetsu to produce replacements for the lost scrolls and they were given to the temple. He was then promoted to the rank of *Hokkyō*. Sansetsu's character was such that he preferred solitude and disliked associating with vulgarity. He would immerse his heart only in painting and was adept at distinguishing fakes from authentic works of ancient painting. He took as his other artist's names Jasokuken, Tōgenshi and Shōhaku Sanjin. Sansetsu would often say that since the medieval period, those who painted ancient Chinese themes who would not look at original accounts but instead lose their way in popular explanations were not few. Thus one should investigate their accuracy and make a judgment, and correct the falsehoods. From things like not knowing to make Zhang Liang young but painting him with an adult's face in (depictions of) 'returning shoes at Xiapi'; to giving [Dong] Fangshuo a pair of attendants instead of one when he gazes at [Xi] Wangmu – using fresh ideas as the means to improve pictures of things; in every case he [Sansetsu] achieved this. Whether dragons in clouds, human figures, landscapes or birds and flowers, in each case he would study the traces and could master many of them. He also copied paintings of the 72 seasonal days and in his free time he wrote *Tokai hōkan meiroku* (*List of Names in the Tuhui baojian*), *Genji monogatari zu* (*Illustrated Tale of Genji*),

Huaji (*Digest of the Historical Record of Famous Painters*), *Buryō zakki* (*Miscellaneous notes on the peach-blossom spring*), *Gadan* (*Discourses on painting*), and so on. He thus planned to pass this to his descendants. On the twelfth day of the third month of Keian *kanoto-u* (1651), he died at age 62.

From this account, the following outlines of Sansetsu's life and career can be ascertained: like his father-in-law Sanraku, he came from outside the Kano clan, having been born to a family in Kyūshū; he went by the names Hikozō and Heishirō before taking the artist's name Sansetsu and the other *gō*, with which he signed and sealed his works; he achieved sufficient prominence as a painter leading the Kyoto Kano (*Kyō-gano*) workshop to gain the patronage of members of the court and Neo-Confucian intelligentsia; he was awarded the rank of *Hokkyō* (Bridge of the Dharma); he took a particular interest in the history of painting, especially Chinese, and strove for textual and iconographical accuracy in his own work; and he sought to pass on his knowledge through his own treatises and commentaries. Hayashi Gahō's account provides both anecdotal information about Sansetsu's life that we will see is corroborated by other sources, and also offers insights into his personality that can inform an analysis of his painting in general, and of the *Chōgonka* scrolls in particular.

Several other sources from Sansetsu's own lifetime substantiate and clarify the passage on the artist from Gahō's account quoted above. Both Fujiwara Seika (1561–1619), the founder of Neo-Confucianism in the early Tokugawa period, and Nawa Kassho (also Naba, 1595–1648), Seika's student (and Gahō's teacher), mention the fans that Sansetsu painted of China's famed West Lake in sections of their collected writings dated to 1519.[74] Seika writes that he 'com-posed a title for an album of fan paintings of West Lake painted by Kano Heishirō, in order to complete the poems by Dōen [Nawa Kassho]'. Kassho elaborates that 'I thanked Mr. Kano for the West Lake fan paintings with two poems and a preface; paintings by the generations of the Kano family have resounded throughout the realm. His artistic ideas are extremely refined, and do not flow with the currents of more common painting workshops. Among current artists, there are none who even know the names of such books as *Xuanhe huapu* and *Tuhui baojian*.'[75] Another passage in Kassho's collected writings dated to the sixth month, 1627, mentions thanking 'Kano Sansetsu for a fan painting of plum blossoms in snow and bam-boo in the wind' that when used would 'be cooling enough to let one forget how hot it actually is in the sixth month'.[76] Seika and Kassho's remarks indicate that Sansetsu already had contact with these learned men in 1619, when he was thirty; that engagement with Chinese painting treatises was part of the artist's practice from that relatively early point in his career; and that he was using the name Sansetsu by 1627. Any investigation of Sansetsu's work must therefore be predicated on the likelihood that it would be coloured in some way by the artist's historical fascination and desire for pictorial accuracy that Gahō and Kassho emphasise in their accounts.

Honchō gashi mentions Kano Sansetsu four times, but includes no biography – a choice that may represent the same deliberate authorial omission that excludes the work's stated author Kano Einō, who identifies himself in only a few passing references. The treatise underwent significant revision before it was published, chief among which was the provision of Hayashi Gahō's preface; the inclusion, at Gahō's suggestion, of a biographical entry on Kano Tan'yū (1602–74) and an expanded one on Sanraku based on Gahō's 1669 account; and changing the title from

Biographies of Painters of this Realm (*Honchō gaden*) to *History of Painting in this Realm* (*Honchō gashi*).[77] Nevertheless, Sansetsu's presence emerges from the lines of his son Einō's finished text. An especially telling passage appears in the first volume in the section, 'Painting Subjects' (*gadai*):

> Rivers and mountains of ten thousand *li*, waves and cliffs, or the Eight Views of Xiao Xiang, the Ten Views of West Lake, and the Ten Snows and Jinshan are all subjects of painting. Paintings on these subjects frequently appear today, but there are many who make mistakes in copying and learning from ancient paintings. For example, they depict sailboats on West Lake in Hangzhou because they don't realise how narrow the lake actually is. Or when they paint the 'Song of Lasting Sorrow' they don't realise that the *fuyō* in Taiye Pool are lotuses and depict them as tree peonies. My late father Master Tōgen lamented these ills and sought to correct many mistakes based on older paintings. Those who see these works should make these distinctions.

The 'Master Tōgen' (Master of the Peach Blossom Spring) refers to Sansetsu, following his use of the same *gō* in his paintings. As in Hayashi Gahō's *Preface*, this short list of painting subjects emphasises Sansetsu's annoyance with the mistakes painters commonly made, and identifies him as one who took pains to achieve pictorial correctness. The passage carries a subtle message: painters should follow Sansetsu's example and thus refer to Einō's art historical tome as one way to steer clear of iconographical mishaps. That the passage selectively mentions paintings of the 'Song of Lasting Sorrow' is significant, I think, because as we will see, Sansetsu's paintings of

the ballad would serve as a vehicle through which Einō could perpetuate the legitimacy of his father's approach to painting.

Sansetsu's other appearances in *Honchō gashi* are even briefer than the passage in 'Painting Subjects'. He shows up once, called Sansetsu, in reference to a painter-priest named Chōsen; again as 'Tōgenshi', quoted in a passage about Chinese paper; and finally in the Epilogue, where Einō relates the following:

> My predecessor [father] Master Tōgen recorded over a hundred skilled painters of our realm, prepared biographies of them, and had already completed a draft. However, he died before he could complete this effort. Ah, how tragic! I attempted to complete the editing in my free time from painting, but was unable to due to my lack of knowledge. Moreover, from the past there have not been accounts of painting in our realm that one could investigate. This made things even more difficult. At last I was able to assemble what I had seen and heard and continue my father's will.[78]

Einō thus credits his father with initiating a history of Japanese painting, and supports the image of Sansetsu as a learned, methodical painter-scholar. With references to Sansetsu coming at the beginning and in the Epilogue it becomes clear that although *Honchō gashi* includes no biographical account of him, the text, based on his drafts, is framed by and imbued with his presence.[79]

Kano Sansetsu's paintings colour and texture his contemporaries' accounts and anecdotes. Few of his works are dated, but when considered alongside biographical details, an impression emerges of an artist who had a career that spanned three decades, who commanded a broad range of painting subjects and

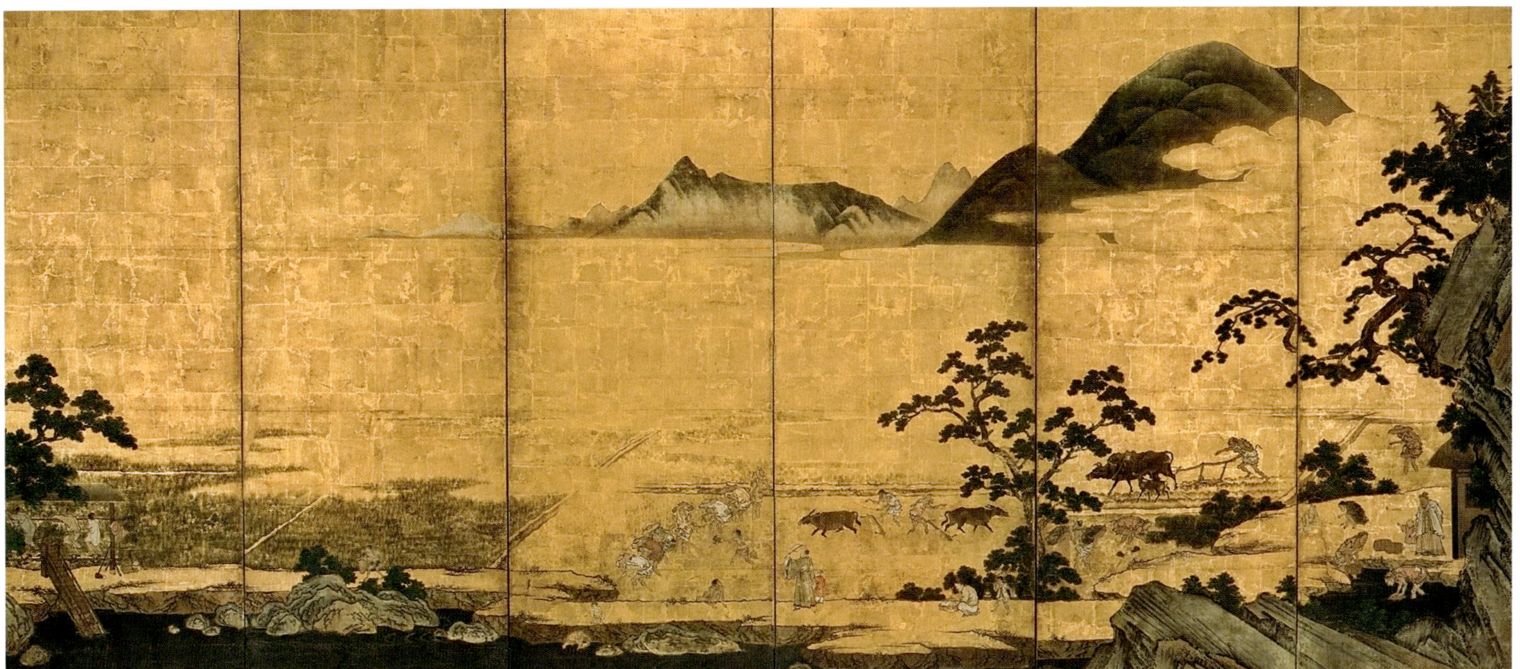

who presided over a large studio. The 1619 *Ten Views of West Lake* fans painted for Nawa Kassho are Sansetsu's earliest works recorded in documents. His earliest extant datable work is a section of the *Illustrated Legends of Taimadera* (*Taimadera engi*, *c*.1629–33), a series of handscrolls painted by a team of Kano painters that included Sanraku, his natural son Mitsutaka (Mitsunori), Kano Tan'yū and eight other painters.[80] The few works by Sansetsu that are dated include the following: twenty-one hanging scrolls depicting *Noted Confucians of Various Periods* painted for Hayashi Razan's Confucian Hall in Ueno in 1632; a votive painting (*ema*) of a horse bearing an inscription of Kan'ei 14 (1637) in Kiyomizudera; the two paintings of Kannon produced for Tōfukuji in 1647 that Hayashi Gahō mentions in *Kano Einō kaden ga jiku jo*; and *Dragon in Clouds*, painted on the ceiling of the Shariden of Sennyūji in 1647. Although they do not bear dates, other paintings on sliding panels, wooden doors and walls for three subtemples of Myōshinji monastery can be dated based on surviving documents or circumstantial evidence. Of these, Tenkyūin and Keishun'in, both built in 1631, are the earliest, and Tenshōin is a much later project from 1646.[81] Taken collectively, these works chart a thirty-year painting career filled with a wide variety of commissions for Buddhist temples, Confucian academics and court aristocrats.

The astonishing range of subject matter that Sansetsu painted supplies a compelling dimension to his biography that gives weight to Hayashi Gahō's and others' descriptions of an artist with probing scholarly interests. His extant oeuvre includes the naturalised repertoire of subjects expected from the Kano enterprise, such as screens of *Birds and Flowers*, *Dragon and Tiger*, *Agriculture in the Four Seasons* (fig. 58), and landscapes such as the *Eight Views of Xiao and Xiang*. True to *Honchō gashi*'s contention that the Kano mastered Japanese and Chinese subjects, Sansetsu also produced lyrical images of native scenery in screens of *Mount Fuji and Miho Pine Strand* (fig. 59), the shores of *Sumiyoshi*, *Suma* and *Akashi*, and the *Environs of Kyoto*.

His figural works, however, most clearly reveal the depth of his interest in Chinese subjects in their depictions of themes never or seldom before attempted in Japan. Sansetsu produced, for example, three different images of the *Poetic Gathering at the Orchid Pavilion*, one of which survives in a magnificent set of four eight-panel screens in the temple Zuishin'in (fig. 60).[82]

Although executed on medium-sized screens only slightly more than a metre in height, this work conveys monumentality and visual drama in its broad horizontal sweep of nearly ten metres. Its folded panels mimic the meandering course of the stream along which several dozen gentlemen compose poetry, while Wang Xizhi presides over the gathering from a heavily ornamented pavilion at the right edge.

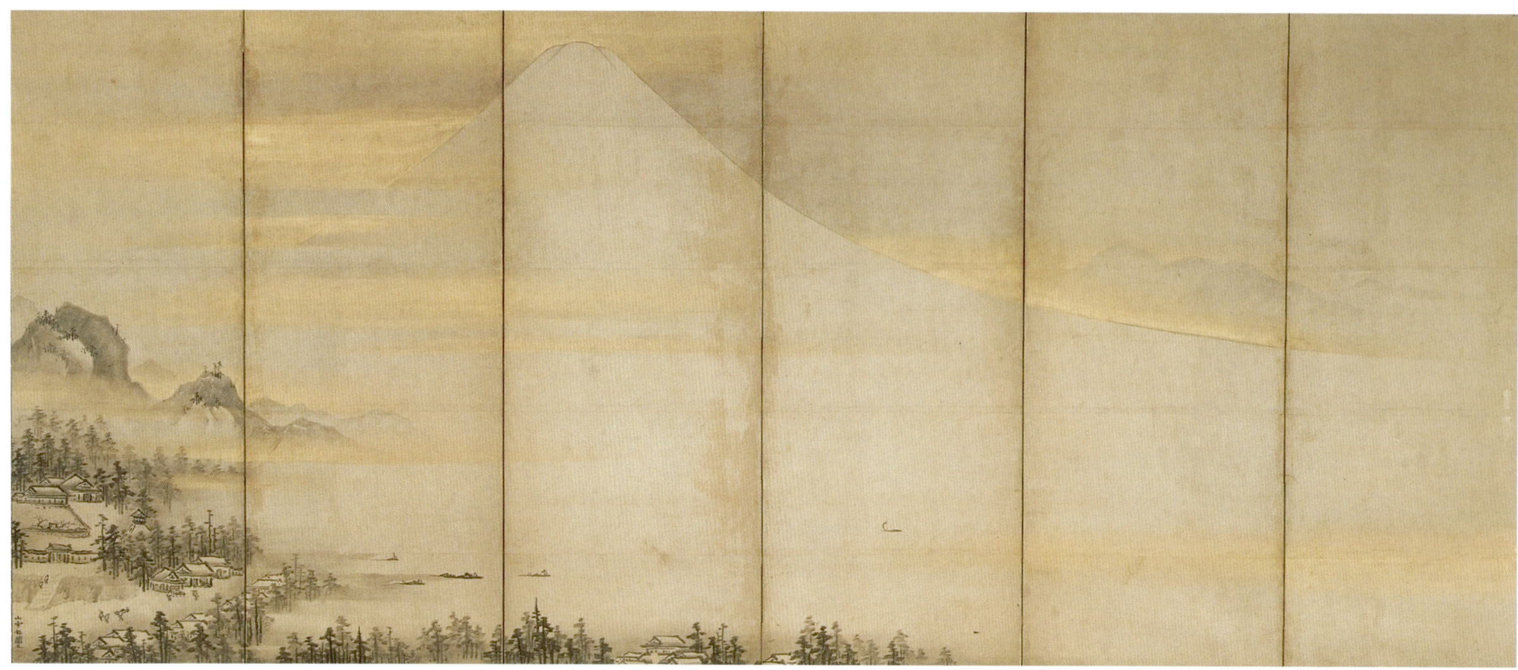

Other works, such as Sansetsu's numerous images of Chinese 'immortals' and legendary figures, attest to the artist's curiosity about newly imported Chinese illustrated books. His images of Daoist immortals, such as the *Taoist Immortals* (fig. 61) panels originally in Tenshōin draw on *Marvellous Traces of Immortals and Buddhas (Xian fo qi zong)* by Hong Zicheng (fl. 1596).

The *Noted Confucians of Various Periods* are closely based on *Yoktae kunsin tosang* (歴代君臣図像), itself based on Chinese sources and published in Korea in 1525, and available in a Japanese edition by the early seventeenth century.[83] Other works betray a deep engagement with Chinese poetry and prose literature. Sansetsu's screens of Hangzhou's West Lake present expansive images of two of the 'Ten Views' in a novel interpretation of what was by the painter's time a well-worn theme in the Kano repertoire (fig. 62).[84] The originality of Sansetsu's choice of subject matter and the unusual manner, often drawing on newly available sources of iconographic information for inspiration, with which he depicted them, must have struck contemporary viewers as utterly fresh and unexpected.[85] The visual novelty of Sansetsu's approach, the scope of his repertoire and the depth of his understanding of his subject matter together secured the success of the Kano studios in Kyoto. We will discover that his *Chōgonka* scrolls further confirm Sansetsu's contemporaries' anecdotes about his belief in the textual authority of Chinese classics.

FIG 59 (above and right): Kano Sansetsu, *Mount Fuji and Miho Pine Strand*. Pair of six-panel folding screens; ink and gold wash on paper. Each screen 153.5 x 360 cm. Shizuoka Prefectural Museum.

FIG 60 Kano Sansetsu, *Poetic Gathering at the Orchid Pavilion*. Four eight-panel folding screens; ink, colours and gold on paper. Each screen 107.5 x 237.6 cm. Zuishin'in, Kyoto. Left screen.

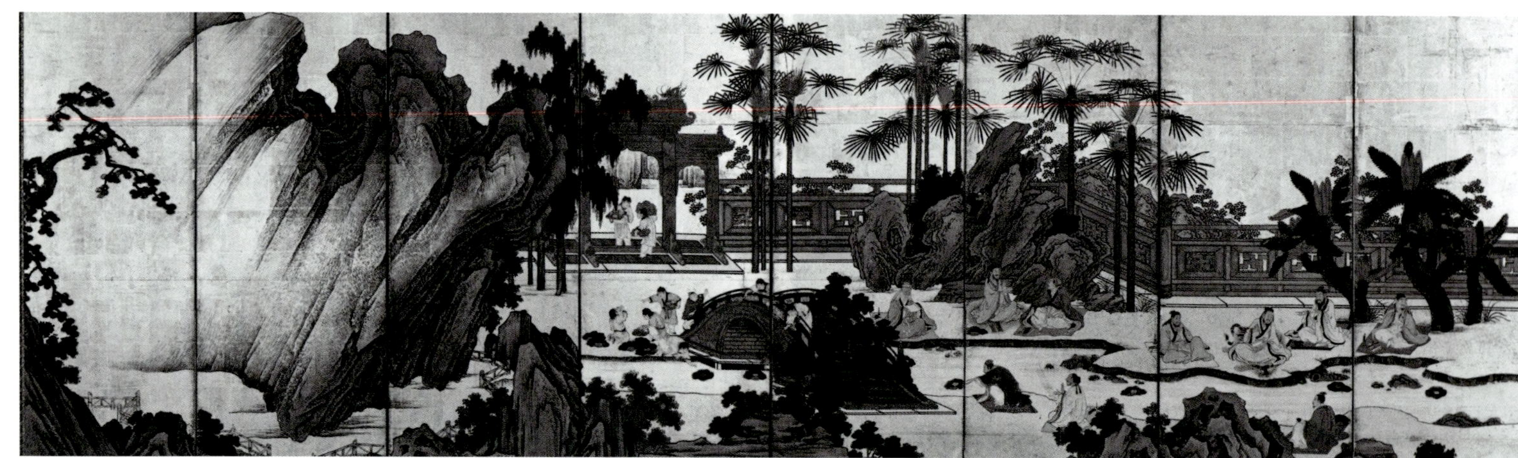

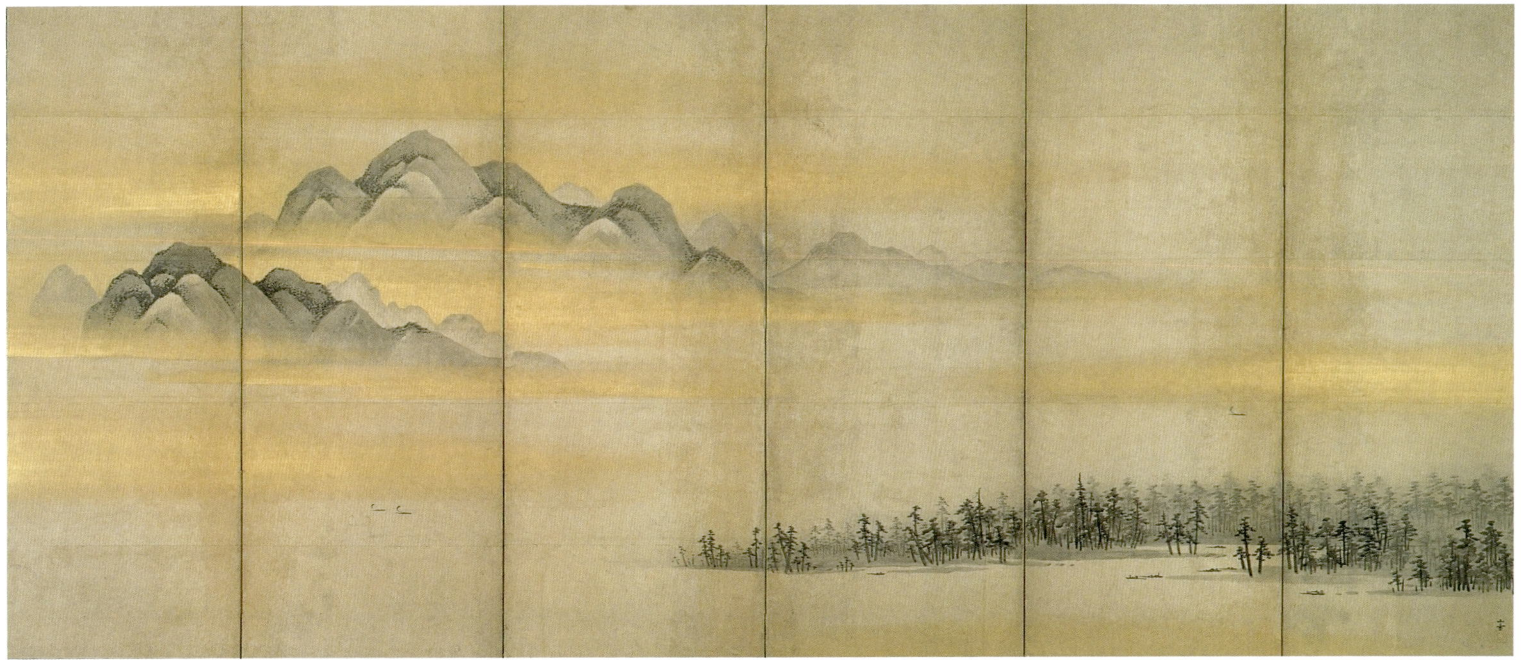

The 'Song of Lasting Sorrow' in Japanese Painting

Bai Juyi's 'Song of Lasting Sorrow' is a theme that falls well within the range of subjects in which Sansetsu excelled as a painter. Unlike many of the artist's other works, however, visual representations of the Tang poem already had a long history in Japan. In a postscript to his own collected works, *Boshi wenji*, compiled in 845, Bai Juyi mentions his awareness of the fame his verse had attained in Korea and Japan during his own lifetime.[86] The earliest paintings in Japan that depicted scenes related to Emperor Minghuang may even have been produced during his reign, decades before Bai Juyi set the emperor's tragic romance to verse. *Kokka chinpō chō*, an inventory of treasures given to Tōdaiji in 756 and preserved in the Shōsōin, includes screen paintings on Tang palace themes among the twenty it lists.[87] One, *Six-panel screen of viewing a musical performance before the Qinzheng Pavilion of the Great Tang* (*Daitō kinseirō zen kangaku zu byōbu rokusen*), has been conjectured to have depicted Minghuang enjoying music with his court, while another, *Six-panel screen of a palace in the ancient style of Great Tang* (*Daitō koyō kyūden zu byōbu rokusen*), was clearly also an image of imperial palaces in Chang'an or Luoyang.[88] A well-known passage from the first chapter of the *Tale of Genji*, written in the early eleventh century, specifically mentions 'The Song of Lasting Sorrow' and paintings of its story of the ill-fated romance between the

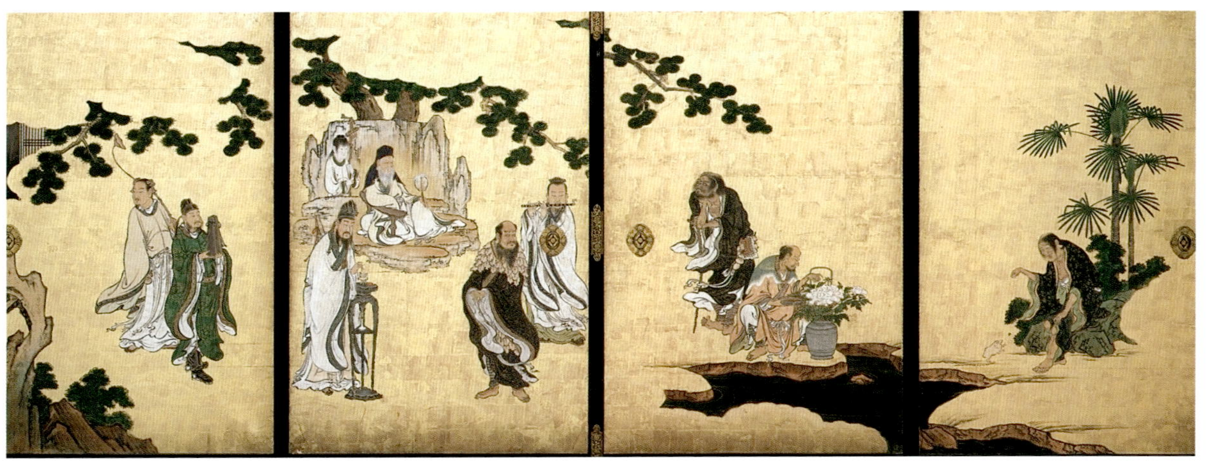

Fig 61 Kano Sansetsu, *Taoist Immortals*, Edo period, *c*.1647. Four sliding door panels; ink, colours and gold on paper. Each panel 166.37 x 115.57 cm. Minneapolis Institute of Arts, The Putnam Dana McMillan Fund (63.37.1-4).

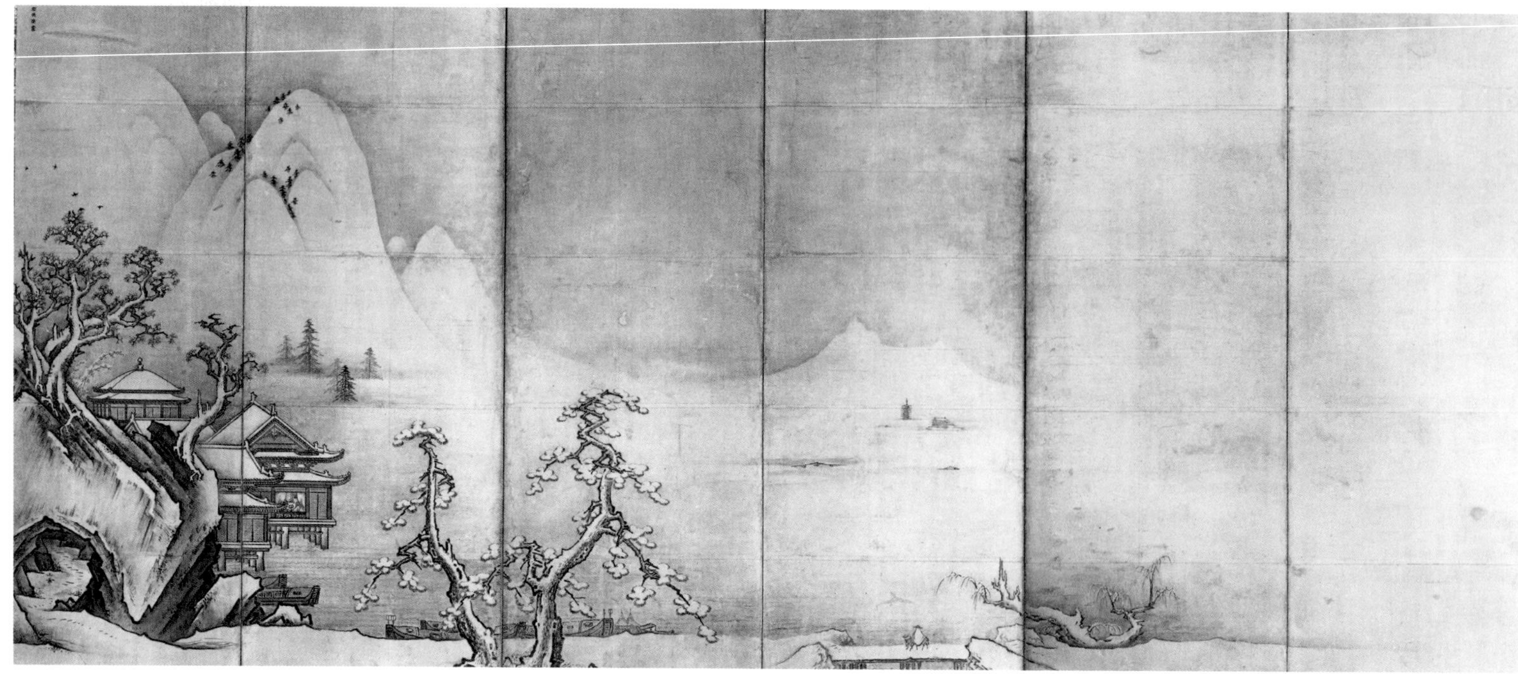

emperor Minghuang and his beautiful consort, Yang Guifei: 'Of late, he had taken to looking day and night at a group of pictures representing scenes from 'The Song of Lasting Sorrow' – paintings commissioned by Retired Emperor Uda, who had also commanded Ise and Tsurayuki to compose verses to go with them.'[89] This passage, describing the Kiritsubo emperor mourning the death of Genji's mother, refers to images on folding screens prepared for Emperor Uda (867–931). Murasaki Shikibu, author of the *Tale*, clearly knew of Emperor Uda's screens, which are also mentioned in the *Ise-shū*, or collected poems of Lady Ise (*c*.872–*c*.938), who composed ten verses on the painting. Although the screen is now lost, Ise's poems describe pictures of a mourning Minghuang and scenes of paradise that come from the 'Song of Lasting Sorrow'.[90] A poem on Minghuang, for example, evokes a scene from the screens and could also easily describe a section in Sansetsu's *Chōgonka* scrolls (fig. 63).

Kaerite | kimi omooyuru | hachisu ba ni |
    namida no tama to | okiite zo miru
Ever since my return | ceaselessly I think of you
    | while looking at the lotus leaves |
the jewel-like dew on them | must be my
    teardrops [91]

Lady Ise's language evokes a scene in which Minghuang, returned from exile in Shu, gazes out at lotus blossoms in Taiye pool, his mind obsessed with the memory of his lost beloved. In the other five poems, Ise ponders the thoughts of Yang Guifei, living in a timeless limbo in the realm of immortals. As in the poems on Minghuang, Lady Ise assumes the voice of her subject:

Ki ni mo oizu | hane mo narabezu | nani shika
    mo | namiji hedatete | kimi o kikuran
Though we pledged to be, | neither interlocked
    trees | nor one-winged birds, we are. |
Beyond the waves, | how can I still hear from you?

Like the other poems of the series, Ise's verses allude to poetic and visual elements (the lovers' pledge, birds of one wing, waves that separate the world of the living from the world of immortals) that Sansetsu's scrolls would recapitulate centuries later. The Heian poet's language shows knowledge of Bai Juyi's poem but also betrays a visual exposition on a screen painting that vividly captured the poem. Even if the abovementioned Shōsōin screens did not specifically depict Emperor Minghuang's court, it is clear from the existence of 'palace screens' and Emperor Uda's screens that by the early Heian period there existed in Japan a fertile visual and poetic consciousness for the production of images related to the 'Song of Lasting Sorrow'.

The late Heian and early medieval period saw

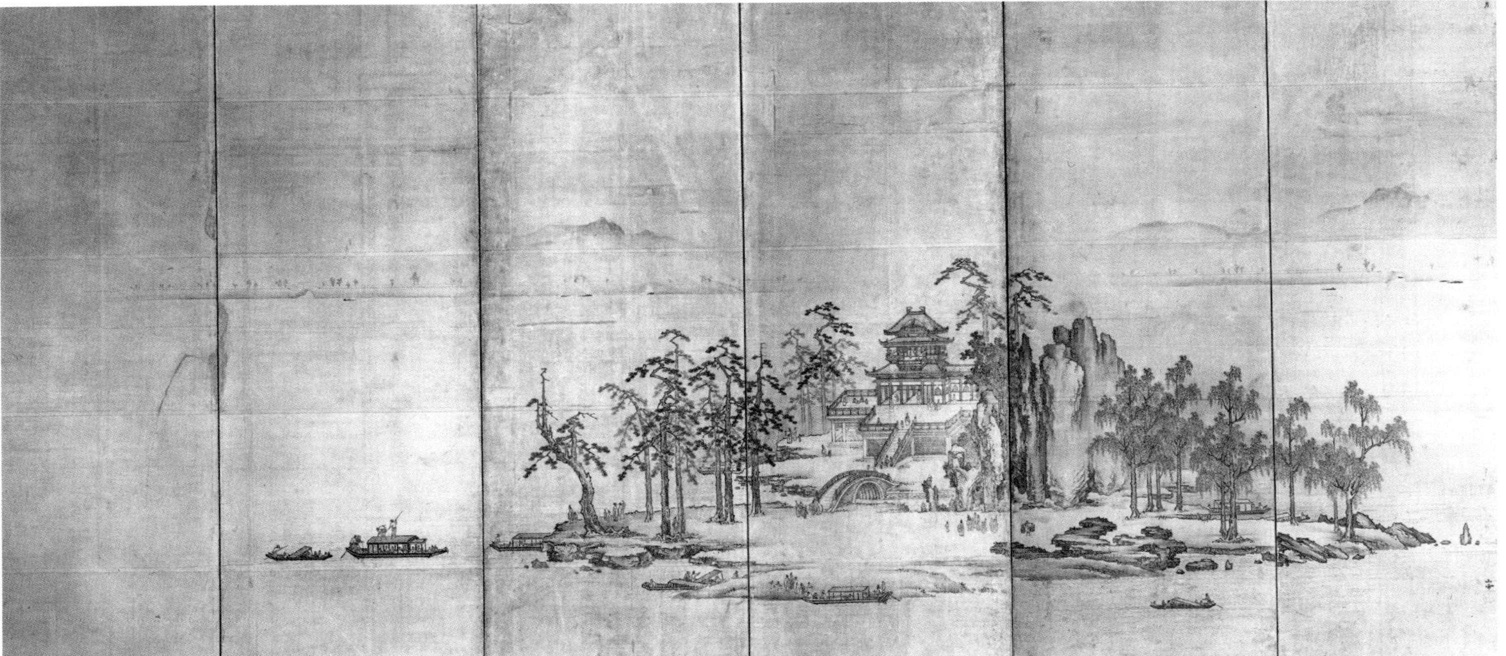

continued interest in painted renderings of the 'Song of Lasting Sorrow'. *Gyokuyō*, the diary of Kujō Kanezane (1149–1207), for example, mentions in 1191 the existence of a 'Chōgonka no e' painted by Fujiwara Michinori (Shinzei, 1106–59), a central figure in the Heiji Disturbance of 1159.[92] This lost work (destroyed by fire in 1270), according to Kanezane's diary, was understood as a political warning to the cloistered Emperor GoShirakawa (1127–92) against supporting the treacherous upstart Fujiwara Nobuyori (1130–59).[93] According to the *Tale of the Heiji Disturbance* (*Heiji monogatari*) also, '…Shinzei, in a burst of audacity, drew a picture showing the olden times when An Lushan of the Tang was arrogant, and making it into three scrolls, presented it to the Retired Emperor, but the Emperor still was not convinced and [continued to] favour [Nobuyori] more than others'.[94] Shinzei's three-scroll image may have persuaded GoShirakawa, but evidently not his son, Emperor Sanjō; nor did it save Shinzei himself, whose death forms a central part of the Heiji story. More than the tragic romance that the Kiritsubo emperor dwells on then, the *Song of Lasting Sorrow* found additional use as a mirror of imperial behavior and as a tool for remonstrance. The painted poem's political function, however, would fade from images produced in succeeding centuries.

The earliest extant images of Minghuang and Yang Guifei in Japan are fan paintings produced in workshops active in Kyoto in the fifteenth to sixteenth century. Today, mounted in albums and on folding screens for preservation, these images demonstrate the continued reception of Bai Juyi's ballad in Japanese visual production, and show how the original plot as told in the poem developed in medieval Japan. One of the keys to the continuing popularity of Bai Juyi's work was that, like most celebrated works of literature, particularly literature in Chinese, the 'Song of Lasting Sorrow' was known and appreciated in easily readable digests written in Japanese. As Masako Nakagawa Graham has shown, works of classical and medieval Japanese literature such as the *Konjaku monogatari-shū*, *Kara monogatari*, *Hōbutsu-shū*, *Taiheiki* and *Yōkihi monogatari* richly embroidered Bai Juyi's ballad, in effect creating accessible alternate texts that presented points of view often different from the Tang poet's original work.[95] The many alternate, derivative texts are beyond the focus of this essay, but some shared characteristics that elucidate how Bai Juyi's ballad would be re-imagined in painting should be mentioned. First, the original poem, with its rhythmic organisation of seven-character stanzas, was reworked as a prose exposition – a *monogatari* – that would be read or recited aloud. Second, the retellings of the 'Song of Lasting Sorrow' gradually developed a range of subplots and episodes that were not part of the original poem. Third, as a matrix of stories related to the original plot of a love story with a sad ending, the subplots could be easily

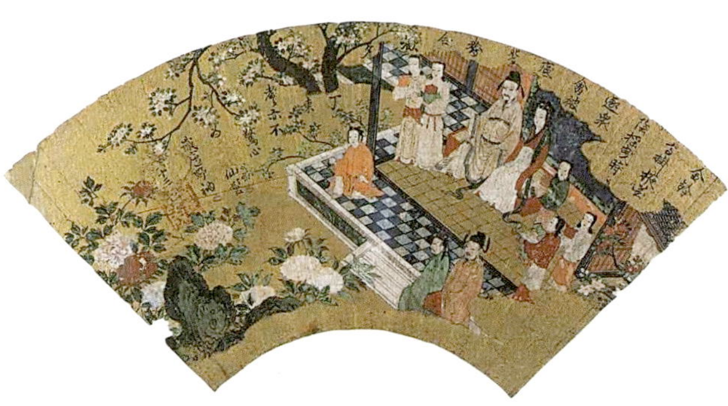

isolated and re-contextualised in visual form without the risk of forgetting the original story. Technically speaking, therefore, prior to Kano Sansetsu's work most representations of the 'Song of Lasting Sorrow' in Japan actually refer to a whole range of images that may be more accurately termed 'Legends of Minghuang and Yang Guifei'.

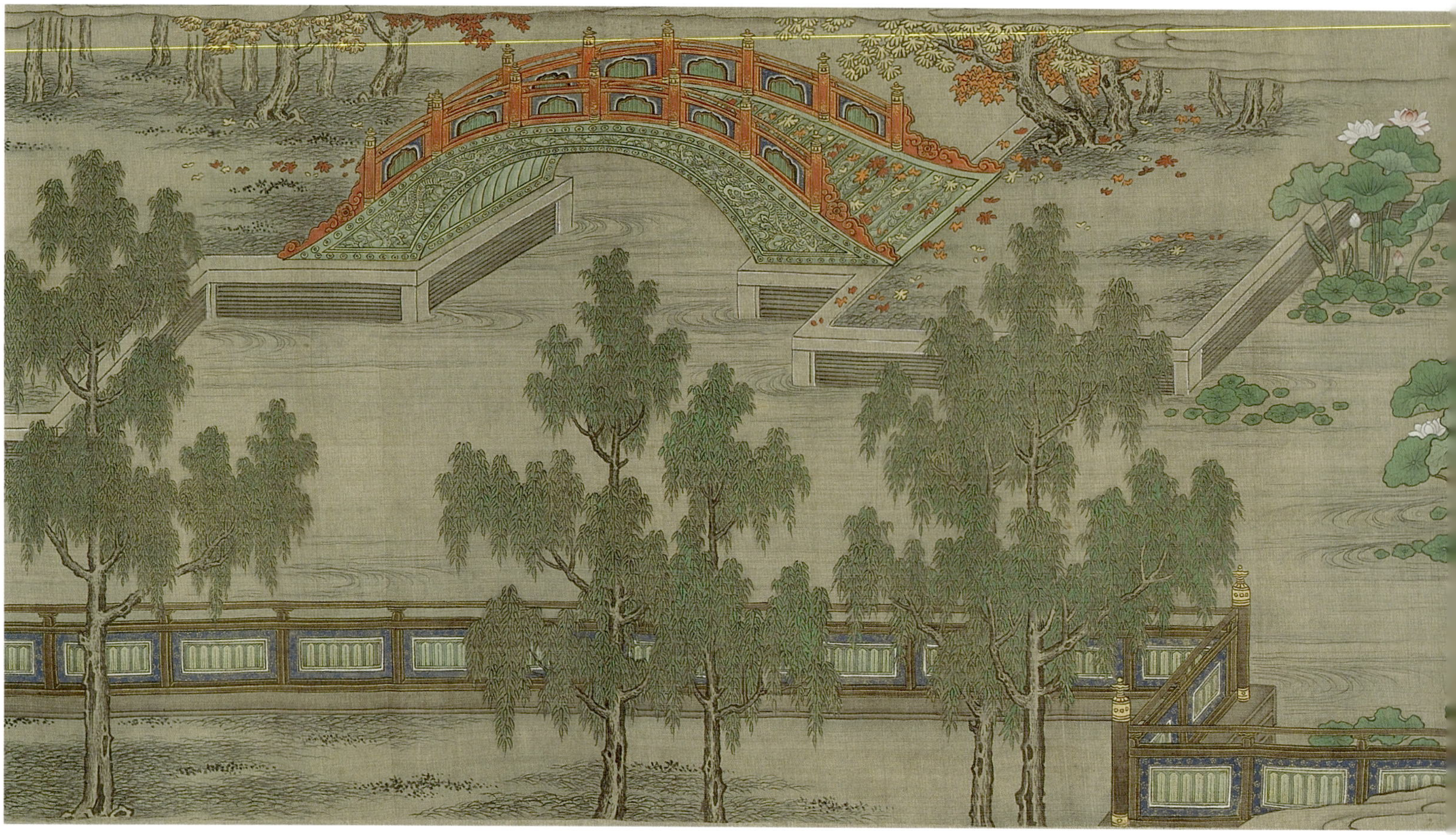

Another source of Minghuang–Yang Guifei stories was *Forgotten matters of the Kaiyuan-Tianbao eras* (*Kaiyuan tianbao yishi*) by the Five Dynasties writer Wang Renyu (880–956).[96] This series of anecdotes not incorporated in official histories includes some that would be selected for representation in painting in Japan. *Kaiyuan tianbao yishi* was published in a Japanese edition in 1639, but extant volumes in Japan indicate that Chinese editions had reached the archipelago in the fifteenth century, if not earlier.[97] The inspiration for several poems on Minghuang and Yang Guifei by Su Shi (1037–1101), *Kaiyuan tianbao yishi* may have originally been brought to Japan by Gozan Zen priests, as Takemura Yasuyuki has speculated.[98]

Exactly when these alternate texts began to have an impact on painting is unclear; the earliest visual evidence can be found on late medieval folding fan paintings. Two large groups of folding fan paintings produced between the late fifteenth and early sixteenth century provide the most substantial range of images that illustrate the phenomenon of an expanded Minghuang–Yang Guifei story. The first of these, a set of sixty fans now in the Nara National Museum, includes two based on Minghuang–Yang Guifei legends.[99] One, *Xuanzong and the Golden Bell*, depicts the sovereign and his consort sitting in an open structure overlooking a garden (fig. 64). Kneeling on the checkerboard-tiled veranda, a palace attendant pulls a red cord attached to enormous peonies to scare away birds that would damage the garden. *Kaiyuan tianbao yishi* provides the source for this image in a section with the heading, 'Golden Bells

FIG 64 Anon. (inscription by Setsurei Eikin. Muromachi period, 1509), *Xuanzong and the Golden Bell*. From an album of fan paintings; ink, colours and gold on paper, 47.6 x 19.3 cm. Nara National Museum.

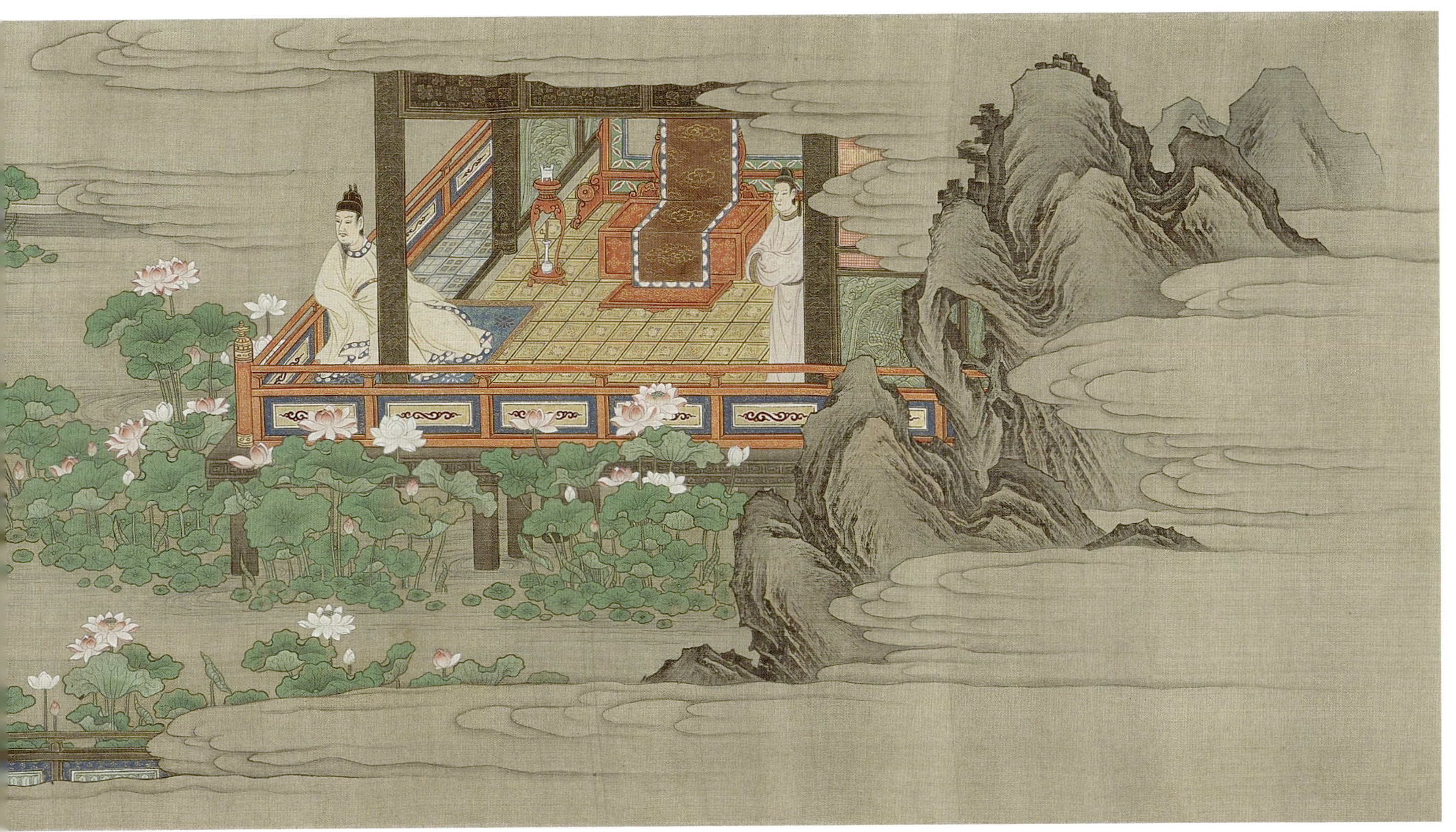

on Flowers', although it is Minghuang's brother Ning-wang who is identified in the episode. At some point Ningwang was replaced by Minghuang in the story. According to *Kaiyuan tianbao yishi*:

> In the early years of the Tianbao era, Ningwang was being waited upon daily. He enjoyed song and music, radiating a stately elegance none of the feudal lords could match. In spring, strings would be made from cords of red silk, on which golden bells were densely hung and tied to flowering twigs in the garden. Whenever crows and magpies flocked to the blossoming trees, [Ningwang], out of fondness for the flowers, would order his official [in charge of the] garden to pull the cord with the bells to startle them. This became a widely emulated practice in the palace.[100]

A second image, stylistically similar to the example above, depicts Minghuang and Yang Guifei seated in a garden under spreading roses and surrounded by attendants. The subject of the second fan is less clear than the first, but it evidently derives from the same range of episodes that drew from and elaborated upon the lines of Bai Juyi's ballad devoted to describing the couple's 'feasting in jade towers and succumbing to wine', although nowhere in the poem do we encounter bird-startling bells or rose gardens.[101] Setsurei Eikin (d. 1537), a Zen priest from Kenninji active in the early sixteenth century, inscribed the first fan, *Xuanzong and the Golden Bell*, with a Chinese poem. Although Eikin's date of birth is unknown, the presence of his colophon securely dates the fans to sometime in the late fifteenth or early sixteenth century.

Fans in the second group number among the 240 folding fans mounted on eight six-panel folding screens belonging to the Nanzenji monastery. The Nanzenji fans present a virtual catalogue of late medieval painting, comprising works on native and Chinese themes in polychrome with gold leaf, ink monochrome, and in ink and light colours.[102] Nine images depict six different Minghuang and Yang Guifei vignettes: three of the *Elegant Battle*; two of *Xuanzong and the Butterfly*; and one each of *Playing Go with the Lady of Guo*, *Xuanzong and Yang Guifei in the Carriage*, *Xuanzong and the Golden Bell*, and

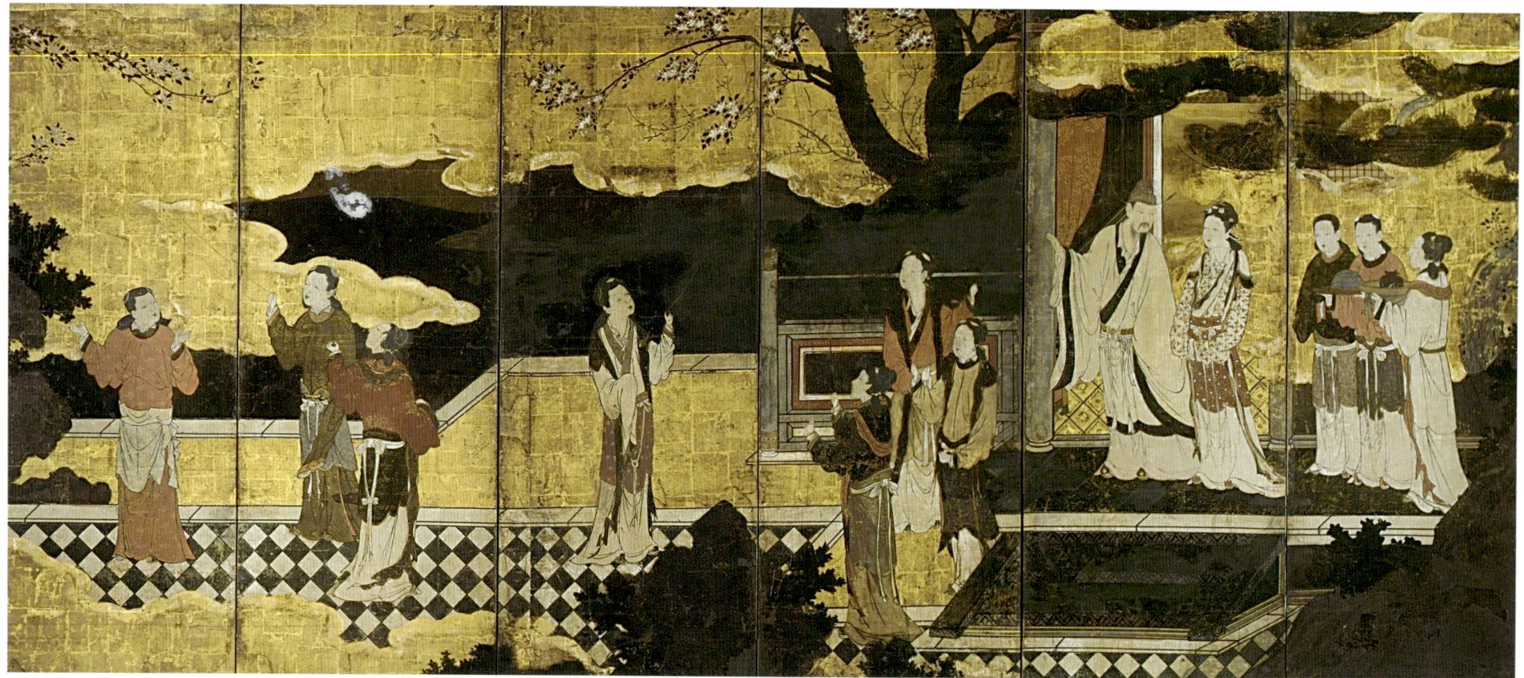

Flute Duet. One fan of *Xuanzong and the Butterfly*, another story originating in *Kaiyuan tianbao yishi*, also bears a poem by Setsurei Eikin like the *Golden Bell* painting mentioned above, and evidently came from the same original set.[103] All of these pictures share an emphasis on the emperor and his concubine's romance and their carefree, pleasurable lives. *Flute Duet*, which shows the besotted pair playing a single flute, and *Xuanzong and Yang Guifei in the Carriage* both highlight the couple's inseparability, and do so without a hint of the problems that Yang Guifei's special favours will eventually bring about. Like the fans from the Nara National Museum set, none of the Nanzenji fans represent Bai Juyi's poem per se, but rather depict the paramours in their exotic world, oblivious to impending upheavals and eternal regret.

SCREEN PAINTINGS OF MINGHUANG AND YANG GUIFEI

Paintings produced by Kano workshop artists offer clear evidence for the continued popularity of Minghuang–Yang Guifei pictures around the turn of the seventeenth century. These works, many of which are executed on folding screens, should be understood within the cultural contexts of the years surrounding Toyotomi Hideyoshi's invasions of Korea, the introduction of moveable type to Japan and renewed interest in Chinese printed books such as the *Illustrated Arguments in the Mirror of the Emperors* (*Teikan zusetsu*), which was reprinted in Japan in 1606 by order of Hideyoshi's son, Toyotomi Hideyori (1593–1615).[104] Although *Chōgonka* images had a long history in Japan by the Momoyama period (1573–1615), the reframing of Minghuang–Yang Guifei stories in the brilliant panels of gilded screens rejuvenated the theme with a new opulence.[105] Although no extant works on folding screens are firmly dated, prior to his forced suicide, Sen no Rikyū (1522–91) bequeathed a pair of gilded screens depicting Yang Guifei to the abbot of Daitokuji, Kokei Sōchin (1532–97), according to a surviving letter from the tea master's hand.[106] The existence of Rikyū's screens in 1591 indicates that such works were being produced in the last decades of the sixteenth century and were treasured works of the elite. As the following examples will show, Kano workshop painters in particular appear to have played a key role in producing these works as they incorporated Minghuang and Yang Guifei-related themes into their vast pictorial repertoire.

Two screen paintings, both originally paired with now lost partners, in the Freer Gallery and the Museum of Fine Arts, Boston, illustrate the Kano workshop's expansion of *Chōgonka*-derived subject matter into screen paintings in the Momoyama period. The Freer screen, *The Chinese Emperor Minghuang and his Concubine Yang Guifei, with Attendants on a Terrace*, depicts the 'Golden Bell' episode depicted on the fan discussed above (fig. 65).

FIG 65 *The Chinese Emperor Minghuang and his Concubine Yang Guifei, with Attendants on a Terrace*, attributed to Kano Eitoku, Momoyama period, late 16th century. Six-panel folding screen; ink, colour and gold on paper, 156.7 x 360.6 cm. Freer Gallery of Art, Washington, DC. F1900.10.

Standing in an open pavilion, Minghuang gestures to Yang Guifei to gaze out at palace ladies who pull strings attached to the boughs of blossoming trees. In this work the artist, traditionally identified as Kano Eitoku, presents the figures along a stage-like space in the foreground, and frames them with large rocks, trees and a backdrop of gold clouds. Birds flying above, at the top edge of the second panel from left, remind us of the story, one of many in which the emperor entertains his mistress.

The screen in the Museum of Fine Arts, *Emperor Xuanzong Bringing Forth the Drum to Cause the Flowers to Bloom*, illustrates another episode of imperial debauchery (fig. 66). This story, originally based on the Tang-dynasty author Nan Zhuo's *Deerskin Drum Record (Jiegulu)*, relates an episode in which the music-loving emperor, after seeing willows and apricot trees blooming in the second lunar month, composes a piece, 'Enjoying the Light of Spring', which he performs with court musicians in his garden.[107] According to the story, when the emperor played his drum, all the flowers in the garden suddenly burst into bloom. In the Museum of Fine Arts screen, Yang Guifei appears on the raised platform with the emperor, who beats a drum to the accompaniment of musicians at lower right. Flowering trees rise against the gold clouds, which highlight the imperial couple. Like the Freer screen, *Emperor Xuanzong Bringing Forth the Drum to Cause the Flowers to Bloom* portrays a single episode, with figures arranged in a line across all six panels of the screen. Both works grant their viewers glimpses of imperial gardens in Minghuang's palace, a distant setting that could only be imagined.

The Freer and Boston screens are only two of the numerous Momoyama-period screen paintings that depict stories about Minghuang and Yang Guifei. A more thorough accounting of all of these works will have to await further study,[108] but I think it would demonstrate that these images constituted yet another genre of painting in the Kano repertoire, like their numerous images depicting cityscapes, westerners in Japan, Tartars hunting and scenes of agriculture, to

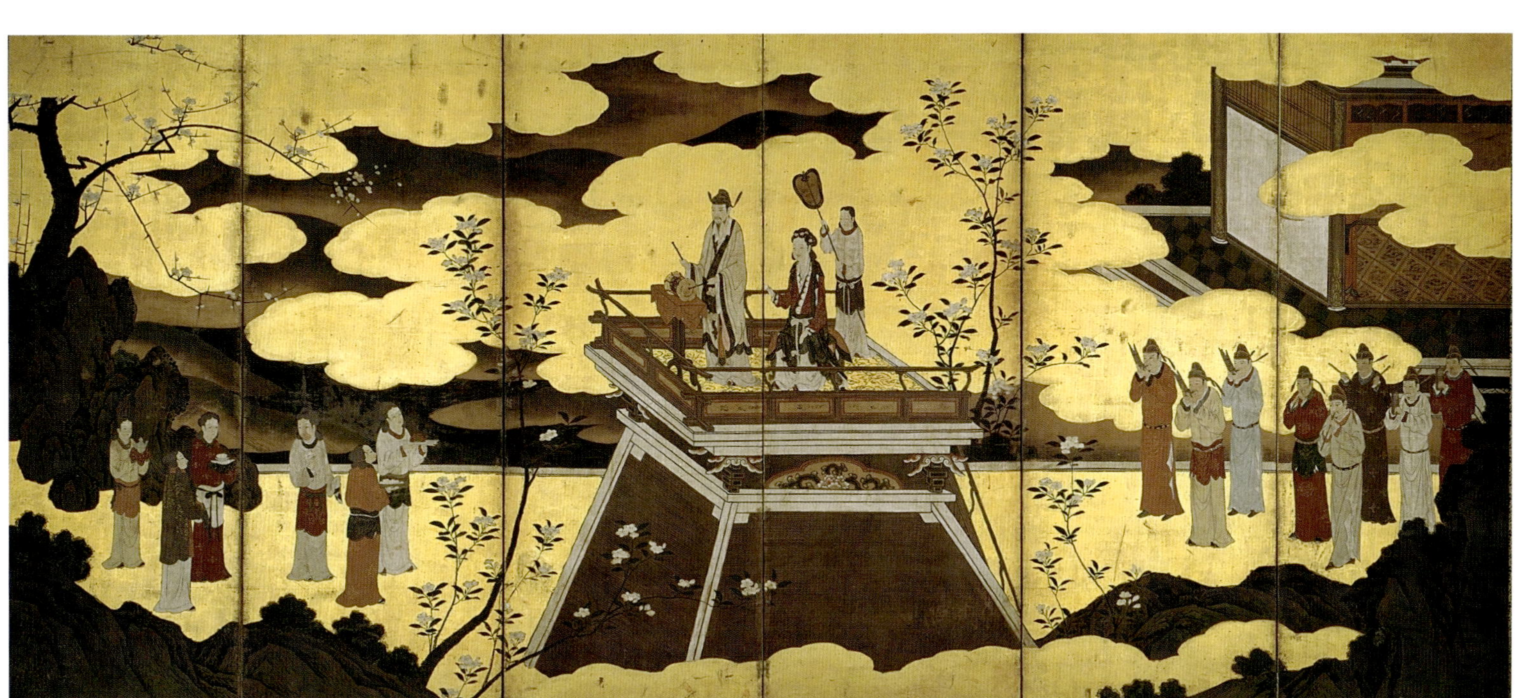

name only a few.[109] These works reflect an early modern visual consciousness or range of imagery related only tangentially to Bai Juyi's ballad. Screen paintings representing Minghuang and Yang Guifei provided viewers with pictures that celebrated a faraway romance and shielded them from the historical realities of Minghuang's double loss of empire and beloved.

Depictions of Minghuang and Yang Guifei may have taken on added significance in the political context of the ascendancy and collapse of Toyotomi rule in the late sixteenth and early seventeenth century. During his rule Toyotomi Hideyoshi expressed his passion for continental culture and his desire to equal or surpass the imagined wonders of China in concrete ways, through for example, outfitting his castle at Osaka with a golden tearoom, or more catastrophically, with his attempts to invade Ming China via Korea in the Bunroku and Keichō campaigns of 1592–98. *Taikō ki*, Oze Hoan's account of Hideyoshi's life, includes in its description of the cherry-blossom viewing at Daigo in 1598 a report of Hideyoshi's having cords attached to the cherry trees, in the manner of 'golden bell' pictures like the Freer screen. Although Hoan makes no direct reference to Minghuang and Yang Guifei in the passage, his description establishes a clear connection:

Looking out over the eastern valley, one could
see a red cord fastened firmly to a long rope
that connected to bells hung hither and
thither, for the purpose of scaring off birds
that flocked in the blossoms. Truly, this calls to
mind Kensai's[110] opening verse to 'Gokarei'
['bells to protect the flowers']—
No more birds—Hang the flower-bells
  from the tempest
Tori hanashi | arashi ni tsuke yo |
  hana no suzu.[111]

In the midst of Hideyoshi's day of revelry with his immediate family and hundreds of retainers, in which no expenses were spared to outfit the festivities with tea houses, prized tea vessels, works of calligraphy, folding screens and other accoutrements, the re-enactment of a well-known story about Minghuang may have signified Hideyoshi's general tendency for self-aggrandisement through the equation of his flower-viewing event with Minghuang's. As if to make the association even clearer, Hoan alludes to the 'Elegant Battle, in which flowered armies of Tang Xuanzong's rear palace disported', in his description of the descent to drunken antics at the end of the Daigo outing.[112] These references show that the Minghuang–Yang Guifei stories that had become painting subjects occupied the visual consciousness of Hideyoshi and his entourage, so that we find them acting out scenes from some of the very paintings that adorned their Momoyama domiciles.

An example of just such a painting depicting the Emperor Minghuang that was probably produced for Hideyoshi is the painting of *Xuanzong Unearthing the Jade* still *in situ* in the Gyokuza (literally, 'jade throne') room in the Shoin of Yoshimizu Shrine, formerly the Yoshimizuin temple in Yoshino (fig. 67).[113] The painting, a set of large murals in the ornamental alcove (*tokonoma*) and adjacent walls, depicts another episode from *Kaiyuan tianbao yishi*, in which the emperor orders his attendants to excavate a spot in his garden emitting a mysterious light, upon which they discover a precious jade with the characters 'Peace and Tranquility under Heaven' inscribed in seal script. The painting, executed in bright pigments and gold leaf, depicts several figures standing in a palace garden of cycads, palmettos, other exotic plants and decorative Lake Tai rocks at right, and another group excavating the jade at left. The compositional arrangement of a building at right, with large figures in the foreground

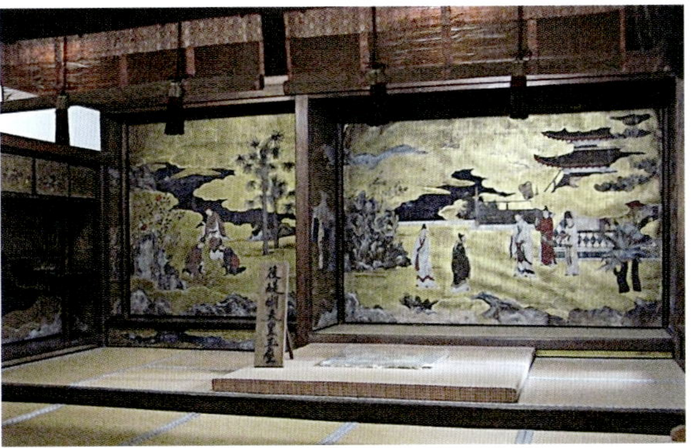

FIG 67 *Xuanzong Unearthing the Jade*, Momoyama period, late 16th century. *Tokonoma* (alcove) painting; ink, colours and gold on paper. Gyokuza, Shoin of Yoshimizu Shrine, Nara Pref. Shoin of Yoshimizu Shrine, Nara Pref.

bordered by rocks, and the paved border of an indigo pond in the background, echoes that of *The Chinese Emperor Minghuang and his Concubine Yang Guifei, with Attendants on a Terrace*, and other works by Kano painters.[114] The Shoin of Yoshimizuin is thought to be the lodging (*ryokan*) prepared for Hideyoshi described in *Taikō ki*'s account of the Yoshino Cherry Blossom Excursion of 1594.[115] The placement of this painting in the *tokonoma* and adjacent alcove would have provided a dignified and auspicious backdrop for Hideyoshi during his spring outing.

By the early seventeenth century Minghuang–Yang Guifei pictures occupied a sufficiently significant part of the repertoire of painters in the Kano and other workshops for their various subplots to merit inclusion in the earliest treatise of painting subjects. The various subplots we encounter in late Muromachi- and Momoyama-period depictions of Minghuang and Yang Guifei are catalogued in *Kōsoshū* (*Collection of Paintings*), one of the earliest Japanese painting treatises, written by Kano Ikkei (1599–1662) in 1623. Ikkei's treatise, an exhaustive accounting of Chinese figure-painting themes, includes over two dozen titles of works related to Minghuang and Yang Guifei. Divided between two sections, 'Emperors' and 'Beauties', respectively, these titles reflect the focus in early modern screen paintings on incidents tangentially related to the *Chōgonka* text. We encounter titles and

descriptions of images depicting Yang Guifei emerging from her bath, playing a flute with Minghuang, watching the 'Elegant Battle' of court ladies armed with flowers, watching the flowers bloom to the beat of Minghuang's drum, listening to Minghuang's 'Golden Bell' in the garden, and dancing for the sovereign.[116] Brief descriptions that follow the titles provide indications as to content. For example, on *Picture of Gold Bells on the Flowers* (*Kajō kinrei zu*) the author relates: 'Also called Bells to Protect the Flowers; An image of Guifei and Minghuang looking at the flowers to which bells were attached because of the birds when the flowers were in full bloom.' The *Picture of the Elegant Battle* (*Furyūjin zu*) is described as 'Minghuang and Guifei, when slightly drunk, divided over 100 palace ladies into two garrisons and enjoyed watching them do battle with blossoming branches around Taiye Pool.'[117] More descriptive is the entry for *Minghuang Playing Go with the Lady of Guo* (*Meikō Hōkoku iki zu*): 'Minghuang plays *Go* with the Lady of Guo; when Guifei sees that Minghuang is about to lose, she releases a puppy she has been holding on the *Go* board, scattering the playing pieces; Lady Guo is Guifei's older sister.'[118] Only the last image listed in the Yang Guifei section, *Minghuang Watching the Dance* (*Meikō setsubu zu*) bears a clear, narrative relationship to the 'Song of Lasting Sorrow': 'At the moment Guifei dances the Song of the Rainbow Robe to Xuanzong's accompaniment on the *shō*, Lushan arrives from Yuyang to stage his rebellion, causing Xuanzong and Guifei to flee in a carriage for the province of Shu, but along the route at the field of Mawei Yang Guifei is executed.'[119] As much a guide to the subjects of painting as a manual designed to provide correct details of pictorial content, *Kōsoshū* sheds light on the process by which these themes were codified: the entries listed in Kano Ikkei's treatise closely match extant images

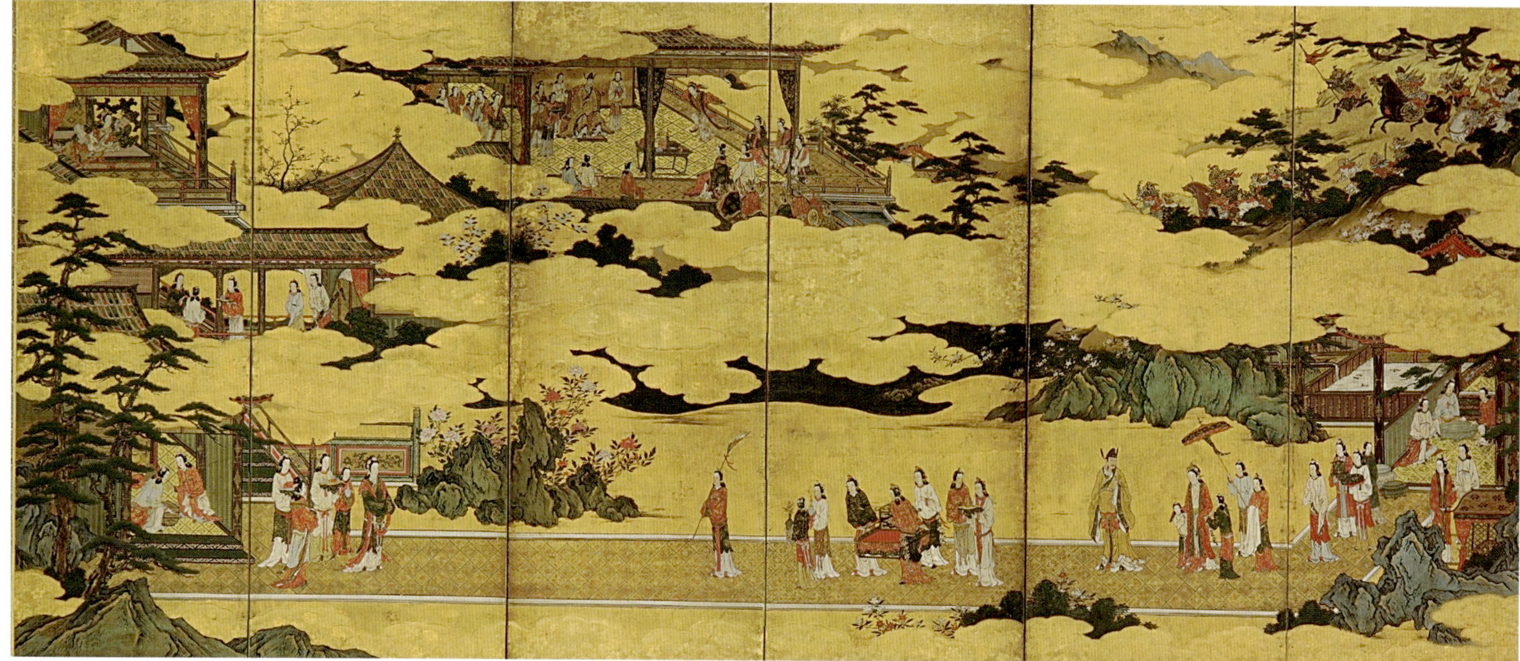

on folding fans and screen paintings of Minghuang and Yang Guifei, and reflect the overwhelmingly felicitous mood of these pictures. Nevertheless, as the final title and description indicate, images that exposed the dramatic narrative moments of An Lushan's insurrection and Yang Guifei's death were not unheard of. Before turning to Kano Sansetsu's *Chōgonka* handscrolls, we will briefly examine two screen paintings of the story that may have foregrounded Sansetsu's work. These screen paintings, unlike most other Momoyama-period images of Minghuang and Yang Guifei that represent auxiliary legends to Bai Juyi's ballad, are relevant to Sansetsu's work as visual representations of the 'Song of Lasting Sorrow' itself.

KANO MITSUNOBU'S
'THE SONG OF LASTING SORROW' SCREENS

The most magnificent and complete depiction of the 'Song of Lasting Sorrow' created before Kano Sansetsu's handscrolls is the pair of screens, *Scenes from the Life of the Minghuang Emperor and Yang Guifei*, unsigned but attributed to Kano Mitsunobu (1565–1608) (fig. 68).[120] This work is sumptuously executed in ink, polychrome and gold leaf. Multi-layered clouds with raised edges and interior floral patterns, built up with gesso-like shell paste (*gofun*) and gilded over, divide the overall composition into seven spatial cells in which the artist places discrete

episodes from Bai Juyi's poem. Jagged-edged rocks, pine trees and buildings further demarcate these spaces and lead us in clockwise motion through the action portrayed in both screens. Staging the narrative in a series of ornate sets of glazed tiled pavilions, gold foil and landscape elements that glisten with gold highlights, Mitsunobu creates a visually dense, overpowering image of the story.

The Freer screens' innovative composition tightly links the two screens of the pair. Rather than organising passages of the story in evenly scaled spatial cells, as is often the case with screens of the *Tale of Genji*, Mitsunobu instead sets off two or three scenes in an upper register against a larger scene in the lower register of each screen, inviting the viewer to proceed clockwise in both screens. An overriding concern with maintaining spatial logic may have determined this peculiar layout, for architectural elements anchor portions of the foregrounds and corners of both halves of the pair. As a result, with the aid of the gold clouds we can perceive both screens as describing palpable, believable spaces in which disparate temporal moments can occur, as in the case of stage-sets in theatre. Another result is that the composition modulates our movement through the story, skipping quickly over episodes in the upper register and moving more slowly through those in the foreground. The screens' particular narrative rhythm moulds our experience of

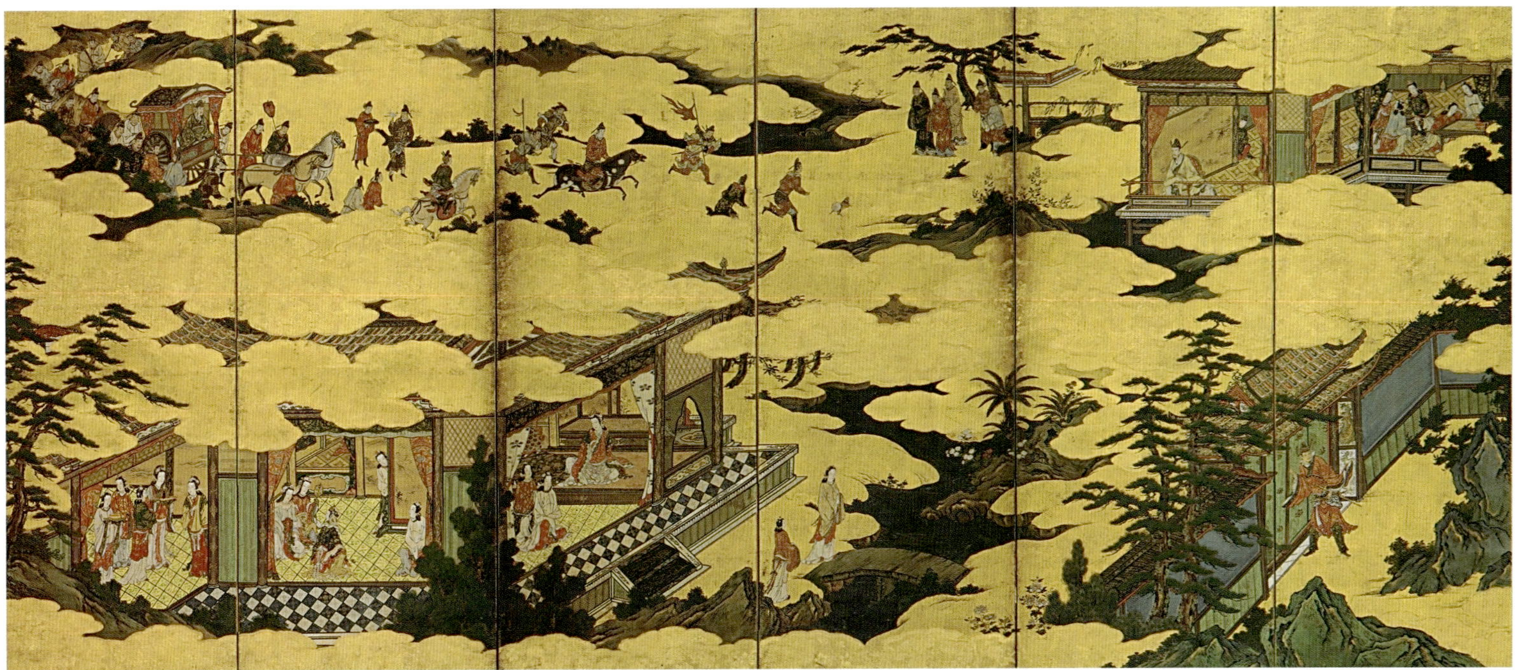

the story overall, so that we are left to concentrate on broad spaces of lavish palatial splendour.

The left screen begins in the foreground, with a long procession of figures moving along a tiled walkway from right to left. A bath at the right edge identifies the setting as the pool at Huaqing, where Minghuang first glimpses Yang Guifei; we see the two in the second panel, with Yang Guifei 'proffered by maidens, bearing her fragile form'. Various other palace ladies await the couple at far left at the base of a pavilion framed by peonies and pine trees. Continuing in the upper left corner of the left screen, the story finds Minghuang and Yang Guifei deeply in love, lying together on a bed, gazing out at polychrome glaze-tiled pavilions. At first glance, this scene appears to fall early in the lovers' story, before the following scene, where a more spacious structure emerges from behind layered

clouds to display the spectacle of Yang Guifei dancing to the 'Song of the Rainbow Robe and Coat of Feathers' in the cloud-piercing Li Palace. But the artist inserts two key details in the first scene – a slender tree and a bird flying above a gold cloud – that reveal a sophisticated understanding of the poem coursing through the gilded panels. In the final verse of Bai Juyi's poem, Taizhen (the spirit of Yang Guifei) sends the bereaved Minghuang a message, recalling how:

> *On the seventh day of the seventh month*
> *in the Palace of Lasting Life,*
> *it was midnight, no one else was there,*
> *as they whispered privately:*
> *if in Heaven, may we become*
> *those birds that fly on shared wing;*
> *or on Earth, then may we become*
> *branches that twine together.* [121]

Close inspection shows the bird to be a curious creature, of one body and two heads, in what is evidently the artist's visual interpretation of 'those birds that fly on shared wing' (fig. 69). The tree towards which the bird flies seems deliberately placed with its two branches crisscrossing each other as they reach upwards. The scenes in the upper register of these leftmost panels thus fall chronologically in the correct part of the composition as a whole, but should be

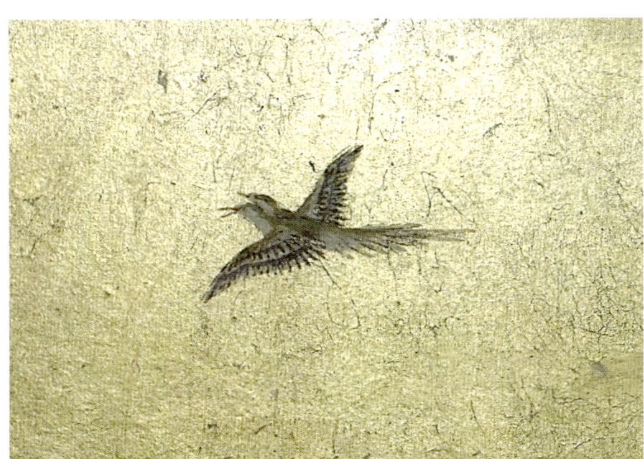

Fig 69 Kano Mitsunobu, *Scenes from the Life of the Minghuang Emperor and Yang Guifei*; (detail of fig. 68).

understood as a flashback – part of the lengthy conversation Yang Guifei has with Minghuang's wizard at the end of the poem.[122]

The 'drums of war' soon interrupt as An Lushan, on horseback in the upper right corner, gallops towards the capital to stage his revolt.

The action continues in the upper left corner of the right screen, where Minghuang rides in a carriage along a curving path. Evidently following Yang Guifei's execution at Mawei, Minghuang appears here making his journey into exile in Shu alone.[123] In the second panel from right, he reappears, mourning in solitude in a pavilion overlooking a pond. Branches of a willow tree to his left place the scene after his return to Chang'an and recall the following passage from Bai Juyi's 'Song':

> *When he was home, his pools and parks*
> *were all as they had been before,*
> *there were lotuses in Taiye Pool,*
> *and willows at Weiyang.*
> *But the lotuses looked like her face,*
> *and the willows seemed like her brows,*
> *before such scenes how could he stop*
> *his tears from streaming down?–*[124]

The emperor gazes longingly towards a palace in the left foreground. Isolated from the rest of the composition by clouds, the pond and other landscape motifs, this palace is recognisable as the abode of Taizhen (Grand Verity), the spirit of Yang Guifei, who resides in the realm of immortals. The Daoist wizard whom Minghuang has sent searching for her knocks at the gate at lower right; Taizhen sits regally on a raised platform and is attended by numerous court ladies, bringing the story to a close.

Mitsunobu's lavish screens supply a bare visual outline of the 'Song of Lasting Sorrow', touching on key moments, whose inclusion suggests an underlying assumption that viewers were familiar with the story. The flashback to the couple's midnight vows in the left screen supports such a reading of the screens, for only the viewer well-versed in the poem and its intricate visual imagery would easily understand the compositional accommodations that place the scene in that position. The artist does not supplement the screens with superfluous episodes like those we have encountered in other works, and instead fixes our focus on a visual exposition of Bai Juyi's text. The spatial adjustments and choices the folding screen format presented to the artist, however, result in key absences within the visual narrative: the climactic scene of Yang Guifei's execution is omitted, literally falling between the screens, and the renowned passage describing Minghuang's arduous journey to Shu – a theme common in Chinese painting – is drastically abbreviated to an image of Minghuang in a carriage. While the emperor's grief does come through in the right screen, the Freer screens may be best interpreted as a work that celebrates the glory of the story rather than its tragic conclusion.

Another screen – a recent discovery exhibited as *Chōgonka zu byōbu* (screen of 'Song of Lasting Sorrow') in the Suntory Museum in 2000 – allows us to draw additional interpretive conclusions about the Freer screens (fig. 70). Also produced in the early seventeenth century by an artist in Mitsunobu's circle, the single screen repeats many of the episodes in the Freer screens, but also incorporates significant alterations.[125] The anonymous artist devotes the foreground once again to a procession from the pool at Huaqing, with Yang Guifei supported by attendants and a cast of characters in poses nearly identical to those in the Freer screens. The scene in which the emperor and his concubine gaze out of a pavilion also resembles that of the Freer screens, although it reappears in the screen's upper right corner, in a mirror

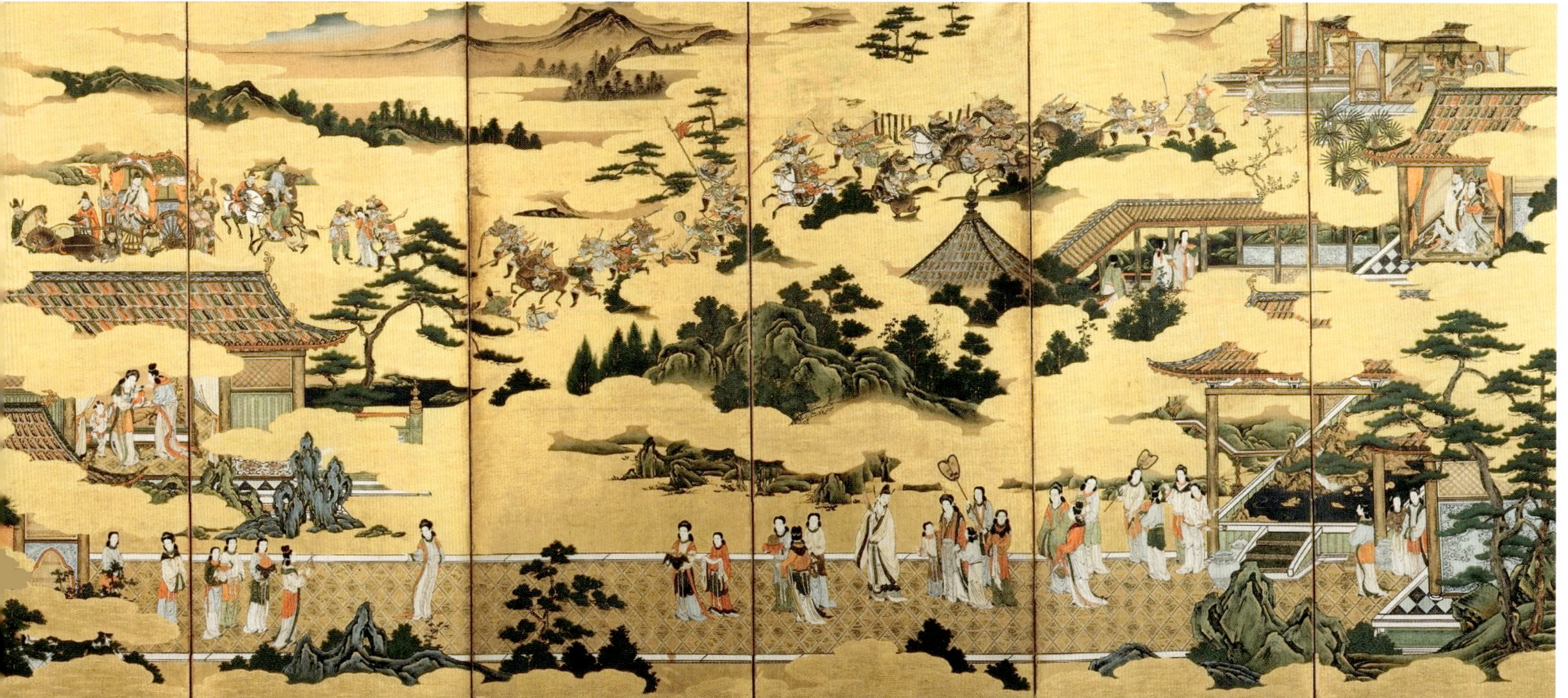

image of Mitsunobu's composition, and the two-headed bird is absent. An Lushan's rebellion again spills into the screen from the upper right corner, racing across the upper register as in the Freer screens. In the second panel, however, the artist of the *Chōgonka* screen adds an episode markedly absent from the Freer screens: three soldiers strangle Yang Guifei as the hapless emperor and mounted courtiers who flee before her look back in horror. The motivations for the inclusion of this violent moment are unclear, although they might be understood to endow the screen with greater narrative clarity; perhaps the screens were produced for a patron less familiar with the story. While I do not think that such works as the Freer screens and the present work were designed for a singular didactic purpose, the presence at several points within the gold clouds of cartouches in raised *gofun* (ground shell paste) labelling people or places suggests that this *Chōgonka* screen was conceived with visual and narrative aids in mind. In every way as visually impressive as Mitsunobu's screens, the *Chōgonka* screen nevertheless makes explicit the reason for Minghuang's lasting sorrow by incorporating the murder at Mawei. It is impossible to know why such a compositional choice was made, but a similar change in tone will factor into Kano Sansetsu's conception for his own handscrolls of the *Song*.[126]

KANO SANSETSU AND THE *SONG OF LASTING SORROW*

In the scrolls now in the Chester Beatty Library, Kano Sansetsu created the ultimate depiction of the 'Song of Lasting Sorrow', a painting that followed centuries of attempts at capturing the meaning and tenor of Bai Juyi's poem, sometimes from the work itself, but more often through reference to other versions of the story. In contrast to the larger system of images depicting Minghuang–Yang Guifei legends, stories that take us away from *Chōgonka*, Sansetsu's scrolls offer a corrective version that restores the word to the image, although paradoxically without the inclusion of any written text.

As Shane McCausland's essay has shown, the Chester Beatty scrolls are not Sansetsu's only representation of the 'Song of Lasting Sorrow'. In addition to the scrolls in the Kuki collection, which appear to be a preparatory work or final draft for the Chester Beatty scrolls, Sansetsu produced at least one screen painting on the theme of Minghuang and Yang Guifei. This *Screen Painting of Minghuang and Yang Guifei*, probably the remaining half of a pair, depicts Yang Guifei dancing to the musical accompaniment of five court ladies while Minghuang, seated on a leopard skin-covered dais, prepares to join in with his own flute (fig. 71).[127] Sansetsu arrays the tableau of figures across

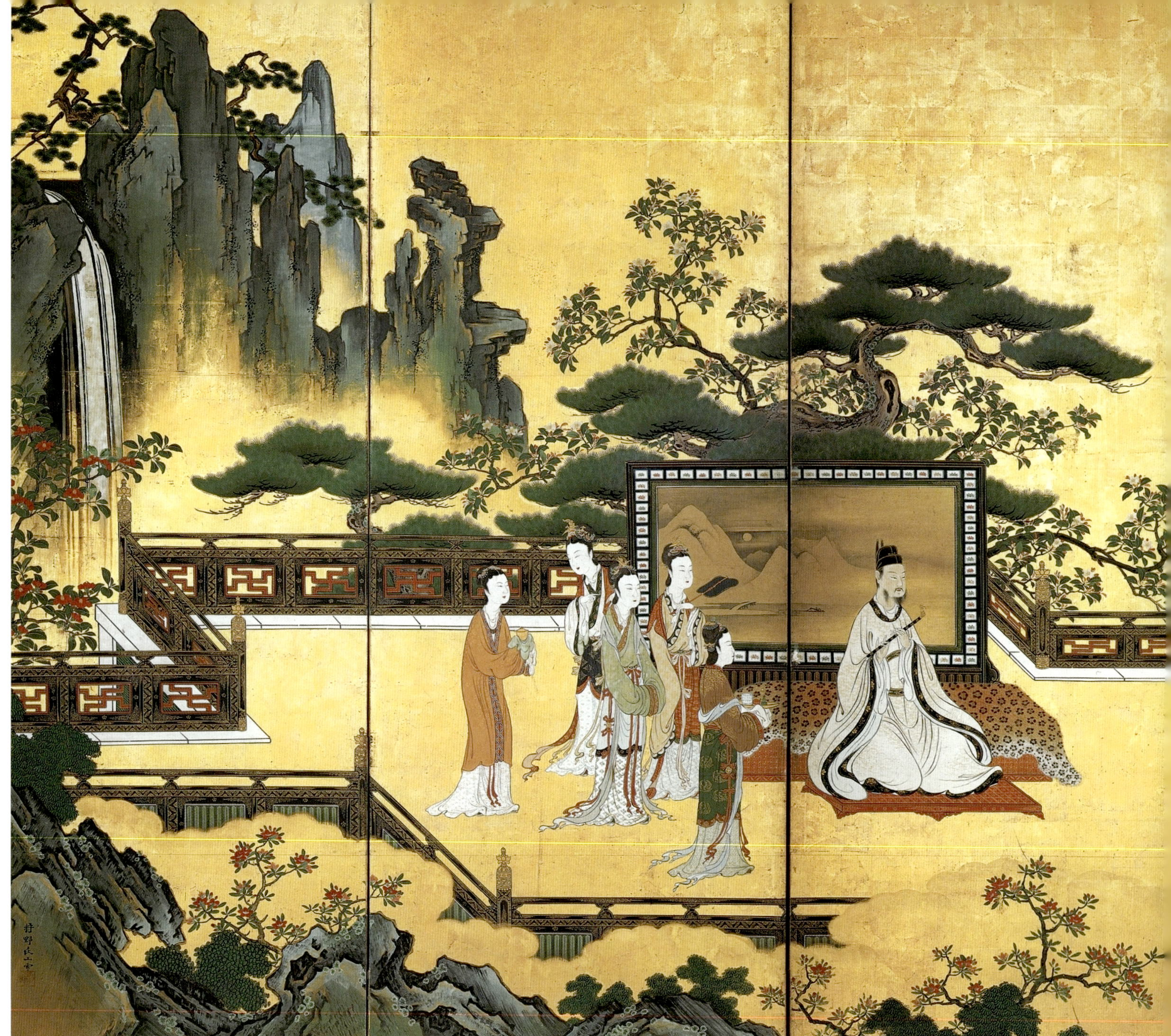

a broad terrace behind which mountains rise on the left and an azure pool spreads out to the right. The upper half of the painting is sheathed in gold leaf, which simultaneously acts as a backdrop and lends the composition a sense of limitless space. Hemp palms, azaleas, pines, camellias, a blossoming apricot tree and sharply sculpted rocks frame the scene and enliven the formal geometry of the lacquered balustrades that surround the terrace.

The screen depicts the revels at Li Palace, where Yang Guifei dances in the Freer screens by Kano Mitsunobu. Sansetsu renders the same scene in one of the most dramatic passages of the Chester Beatty scrolls with a complex system of cloud-piercing terraces, on the highest of which Yang Guifei performs her dance in a pose that mirrors that of Sansetsu's screen (fig. 72).

In the scroll version, Sansetsu supplies a full orchestra and a larger group of attendants, but otherwise the two works bear the marks of the same artist: Minghuang sits before a similar free-standing screen of a monochrome ink landscape in both works, both terraces appear paved in gold, and the nearby mountaintops and clouds convey the terraces' sheer altitude. While other artists might have contented themselves with repeating a compositional template from one format to another, Sansetsu alters it by reversing the positions of emperor and concubine, and shifting the sovereign ninety degrees.

Minghuang and Yang Guifei follows Bai Juyi's text in its depiction of a specific scene from the

FIG 71 Kano Sansetsu, *Minghuang and Yang Guifei*, Edo period, 17th century. Six-panel screen; ink, colour and gold on paper, 155.2 x 361.4 cm. Yamanaka Seikadō, Tokyo.

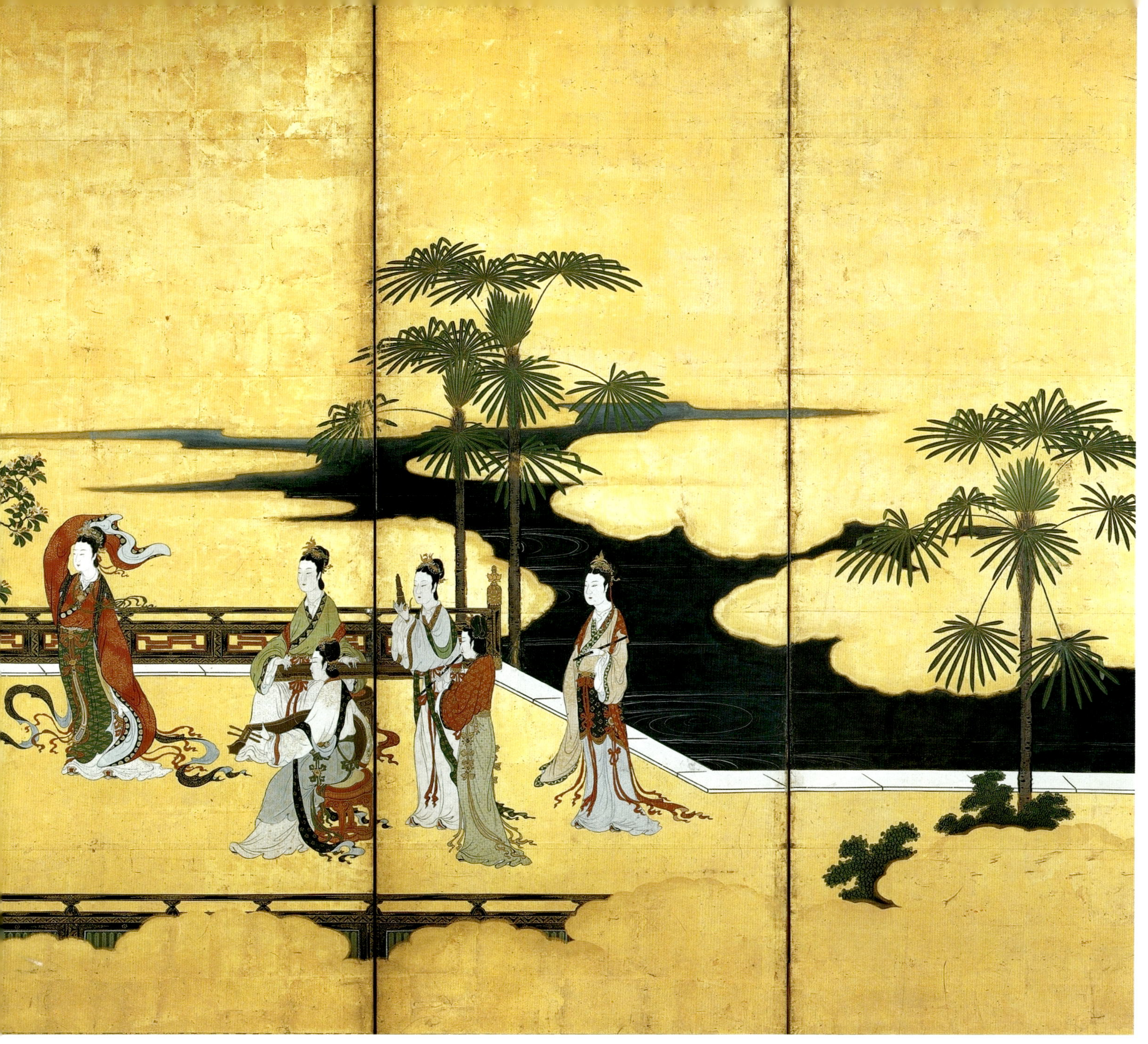

poem, but comes out of the same conceptual mould as the Momoyama-period screen paintings depicting miscellaneous episodes about the emperor and his concubine examined above. Compositionally, *Minghuang and Yang Guifei* follows the *mise-en-scène* formula of *The Chinese Emperor Minghuang and his Concubine Yang Guifei, with Attendants on a Terrace* in the Freer Gallery. The artists of both works spread figures across a flat foreground bordered by rectangular paving stones that define a wall overlooking a garden or pond beyond. Rocks and trees anchoring one corner of the picture, along with gold clouds that border the painting's lower edge, serve as repoussoirs in both screens, enhancing the illusion of space, but also providing viewers with something beyond which

they can behold the story. Gold foil covers much of the surface of both works, further highlighting the action. In *Minghuang and Yang Guifei* Kano Sansetsu thus produces an image that follows an older representational formula, and in essence recreates a Momoyama-period approach to visualising a *Chōgonka*- inspired theme.

The *Chōgonka* scrolls in the Chester Beatty Library could not be visually or conceptually more distant from the screen paintings of Minghuang and Yang Guifei by Sansetsu and other Kano painters. In every way the scrolls manifest the artist's technical dexterity and versatility, but also his efforts to produce a work through which viewers could more authentically experience Bai Juyi's poem. Five of the work's basic formal attributes announce Sansetsu's intentions to approximate a work of Chinese painting, specifically. First, Sansetsu must have deemed the handscroll format a more effective medium for his retelling of the entire text than the panels of folding screens, which might have fragmented or abbreviated the narrative. Second, the use of silk, more widely used in handscrolls in China than in Japan, represents a costly departure from paper, the more common medium for handscrolls in Japan. Third, as recent conservation work on the scrolls has revealed, Sansetsu applied extensive pigments on the *back* of the scrolls, thus employing verso-painting techniques more commonly associated with Buddhist images in China and Japan.[128] Fourth, the absence of any text other than the artist's signature marks a clear distinction from Japanese narrative handscrolls, in which

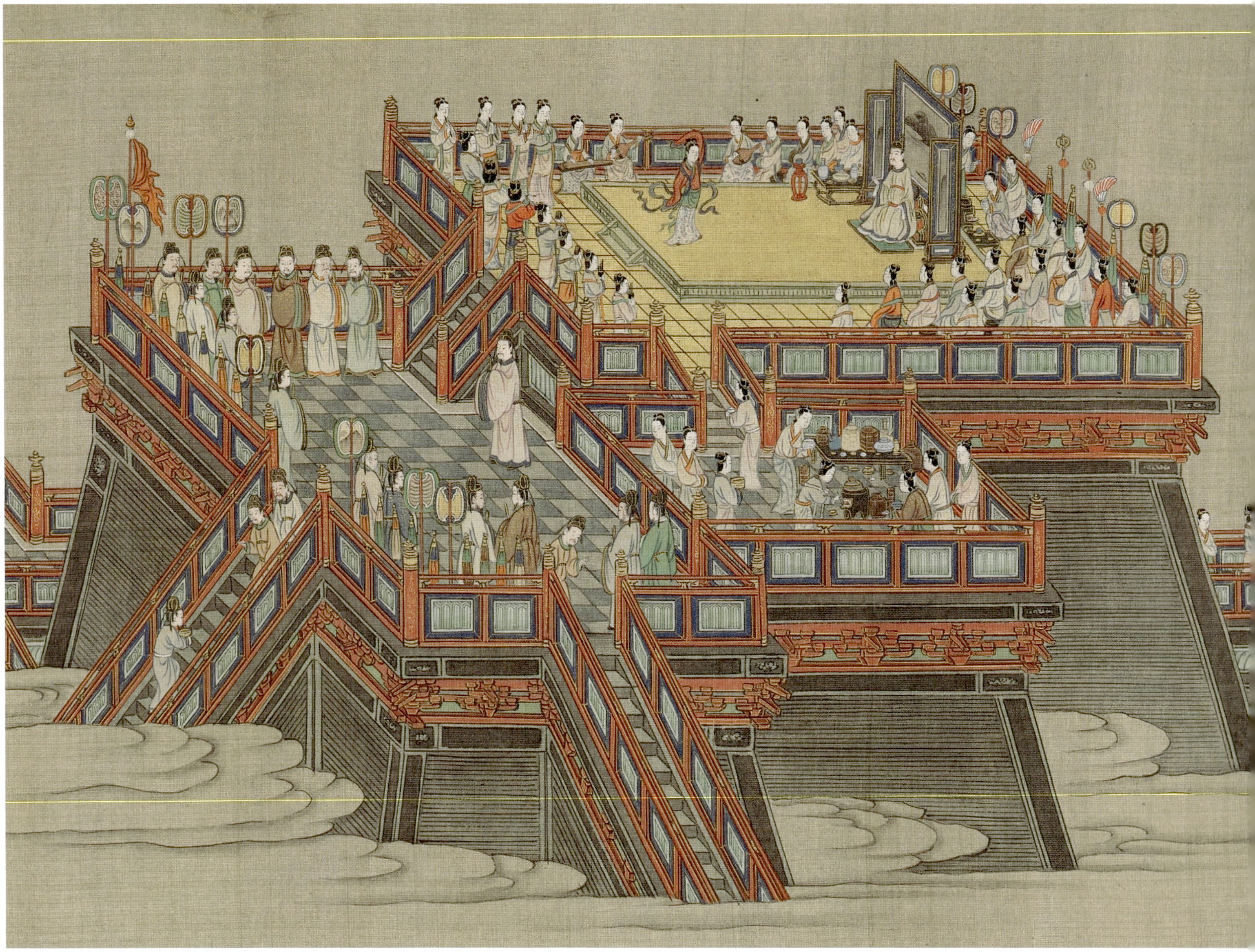

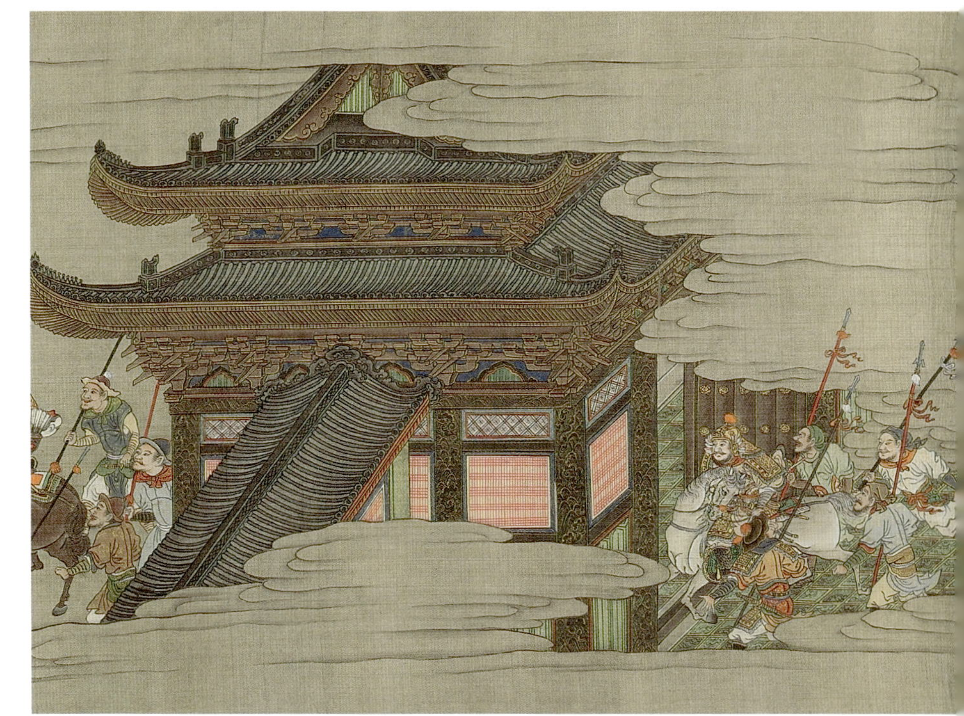

Fig 72 Kano Sansetsu, 'Revels at the Palace of Li' (from **General An Lushan rebels**), *Song of Lasting Sorrow*; scroll 1, the fourth length of silk.

Fig 73 Kano Sansetsu, 'General An Lushan enters the Capital' (from **Rebels enter the capital**), *Song of Lasting Sorrow*; scroll 1, the fourth and fifth lengths of silk.

texts are arranged either separately in sections alternating with painted scenes, or inscribed directly into the painting. Sansetsu's execution of a continuous image, which he knits together with trees, rocks and passages of mist and clouds, appears to reveal his understanding that Chinese painted narratives operated according to visual conventions different from indigenous ones. Finally, the artist's use of a primarily ink monochrome palette for landscape elements contrasted with bright pigments for figures and buildings follows established norms in continental or Chinese-inspired painting. When considered together with the scrolls' overall composition, these formal elements highlight the virtuosity and invention with which Sansetsu created his work and visually manipulated Bai Juyi's text for maximum emotional effect.

Today the *Chōgonka emaki* consists of two handscrolls, but there is ample reason to believe that the work was originally divided into three scrolls, as is the case with the Kuki *Chōgonka* scrolls.[129] As Shane

McCausland has shown, the Chester Beatty scrolls were formed by joining together twelve separate rolls of silk, each measuring approximately 180 cm, six to a scroll, into the two scrolls in which they are currently mounted.[130] Close examination of the seams between sections of silk reveals that they sometimes differ in terms of wear and colouration, as is especially clear between sections four and five of the first scroll, and between sections two and three of the second. Additionally, the presence of representational techniques particular both to Japanese narrative scrolls and Kano Sansetsu's oeuvre supports the three-scroll hypothesis.

For example, at the end of section four, which the painter frames and punctuates with a leafy tree, An Lushan and his men gallop towards the Palace of Li, where we have just left the terraces where Yang Guifei dances for her sovereign (fig. 73). The Sogdian general and his men thus move into the scroll from the left, emerging from behind clouds that still conceal

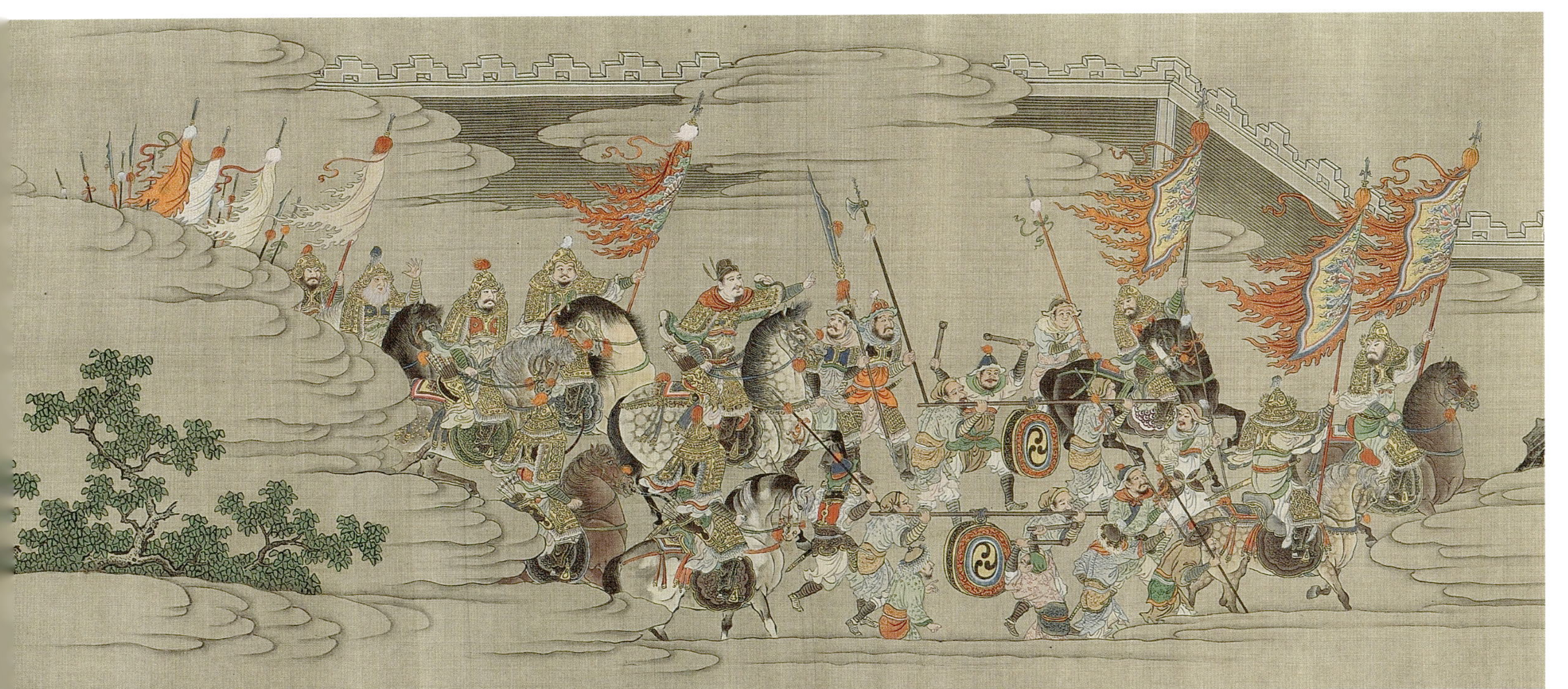

several pennants and spear-bearers. This rightward movement, which runs opposite the handscroll's natural narrative flow from right to left, has precedents in such classic works of narrative handscrolls as the late twelfth-century *Illustrated Legends of Mount Shigi*, where the technique is employed to depict a flashback in the Engi Emperor's dream of a chakra-rolling sword deity.[131] In Sansetsu's work, however, the device of bringing An Lushan into the scroll from the left appears rather to serve as a means of signalling the end of the first scroll. The next scene, where rebel soldiers rush through gates to sack the palace, abruptly reverses the action, proceeding from right to left. This sudden reversal is awkward in the scroll's present format, but when reconsidered as the beginning of the second scroll, it comes across as a dramatic start to steadily mounting action.

The seam between sections two and three of the second scroll (or collectively, sections eight and nine) reveals a different kind of disjuncture, here both compositional and narrative. Borne in a palanquin, a weeping Minghuang passes by Mawei, while his procession snakes into mist below the ramparts of the capital, Chang'an. Blue-tinged peaks to the citadel's right, bands of mist below its walls and the dramatic reduction in the turrets' scale all reinforce the sense of distance to the figures' destination (fig. 74). Sansetsu employs similar techniques of extreme reduction in scale to emphasise spatial depth in other works, such as his screen paintings of West Lake (see fig. 62). Here, he uses the physical setting to mark a pause in the narrative, before the setting changes in the next passage to the gardens of Minghuang's former palace. In the scrolls' current state, the shift from distant city to palace interior appears rushed and defies the handscroll format's peculiar spatial logic. When viewed as the commencement of the third scroll, however, we can see the mist and rocks that open to reveal the depressed

former emperor at Taiye Pool as the physical statement of a shift in the narrative's setting (see fig. 63).

Thus divided into three scrolls, in lengths of 691.1 cm, 719.4 cm and 712.2 cm, respectively, of four sections each, how does the narrative unfurl? The first scroll begins with the discovery of the Yang daughter in her father's household. Appropriate to the commencement of the story, Sansetsu frames the scene – and introduces the entire image – with a massive boulder and pine tree that reaches beyond the picture's upper edge (see fig. 12). Proceeding scenes, interspersed with more rocks and trees to provide transitions between the changing settings, trace Yang Guifei's arrival at court, which, once reached, unrolls uninterrupted in scenes of her days with Minghuang in a series of lavishly appointed palace structures accented by flowering plants and ornamental garden

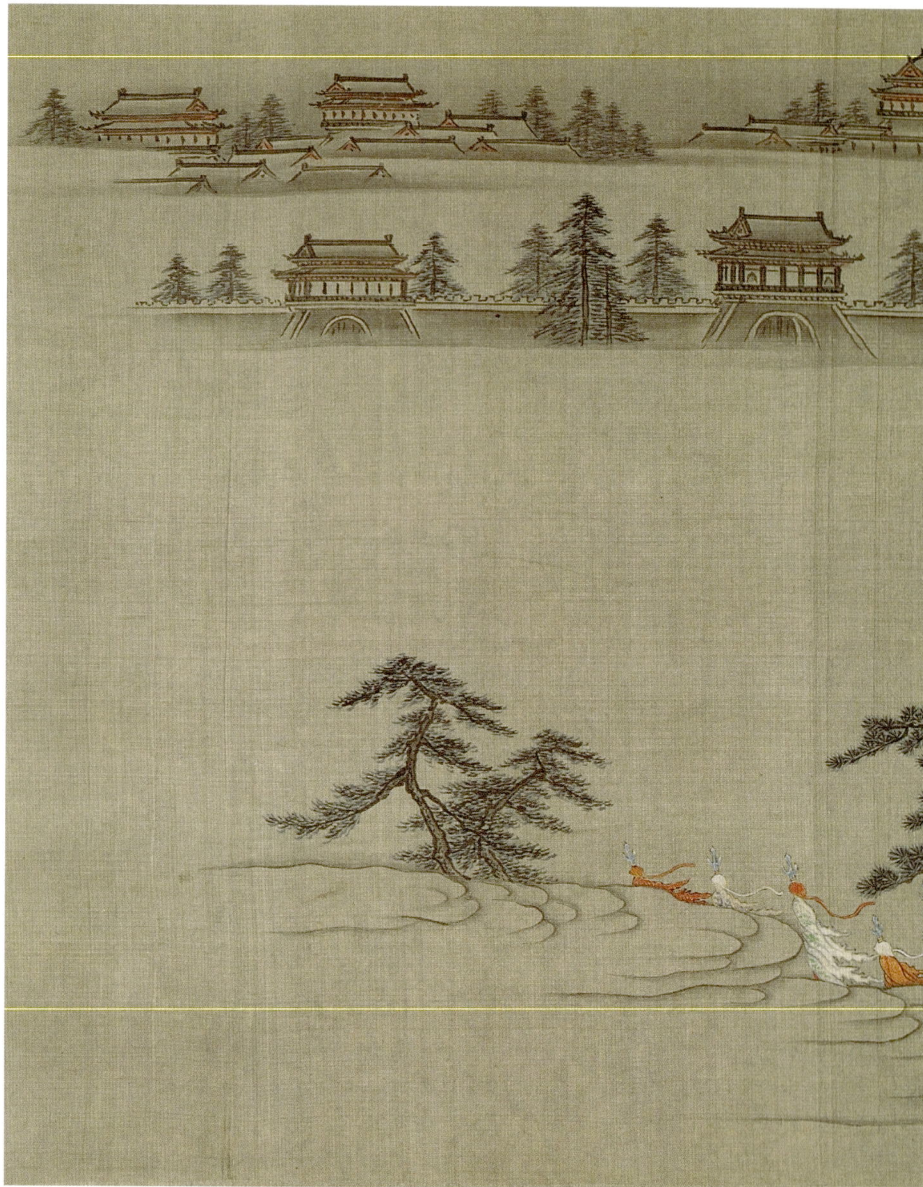

Fig 74 Kano Sansetsu, 'Minghuang's entourage approaches the distant ramparts of Chang'an' (from **Return to the capital**), *Song of Lasting Sorrow*; scroll 2, the second length of silk.

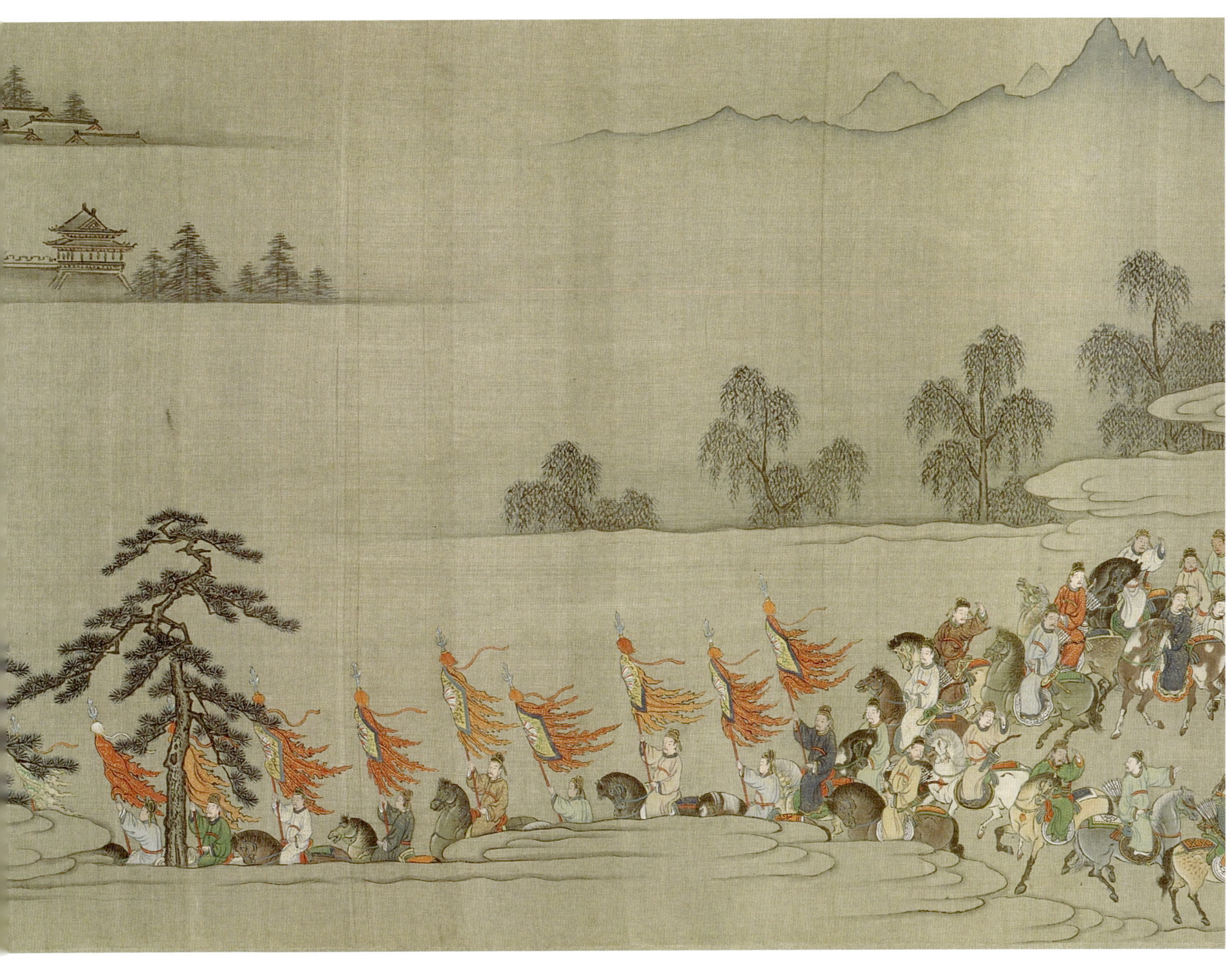

Overleaf:
Fig 75 Kano Sansetsu, 'Minghuang forswears the duties of the morning' (from **Minghuang's** dalliance), *Song of Lasting Sorrow*; scroll 1, the second length of silk.

rocks. Sansetsu offers the viewer visual cues to the ballad's text in deceptively incidental details in these passages, such as the lotus motifs on curtains that frame a scene of Yang Guifei and the emperor, who 'forswore the duties of the morning', or mandarin duck-shaped roof tiles in the next scene (fig. 75). These images are remarkable for their intoxicating array of palace furnishings: vessels of celadon and gold, lacquered columns with cloud and dragon motifs, paintings-within-paintings on screens of landscapes, trees and waves, terraces paved with gilded tiles. After passages chronicling the Yang family's rise to glory and the revelries in the Li Palace, the first scroll is brought to a close by the rightward thrust of An Lushan and his troops. In tableaux that begin with languorously paced images of indulgence, the first scroll chronicles Yang Guifei's social and physical rise, literally to the dizzying heights of the Li Palace, and ends with the arrival of An Lushan, yet unnamed in the poem, but signalled by the ominously rumbling 'drums of Yuyang'.

The second scroll is all action and rising drama. It begins with the catastrophe of An Lushan's coup d'état, the violence and chaos rendered with the looted palace set to flame (see fig. 26). The emotional punch that such a depiction of a conflagration would have carried for the viewer in fire-prone Kyoto cannot be overestimated; Sansetsu must have understood the means to portray such a calamity from familiarity with depictions in other handscrolls, though it is unclear whether he ever saw the most famous of such images, the *Ban Dainagon ekotoba* scrolls and the *Burning of the Sanjō Palace* scroll of the *Heiji monogatari emaki*.

Still, the similarities between Sansetsu's palace

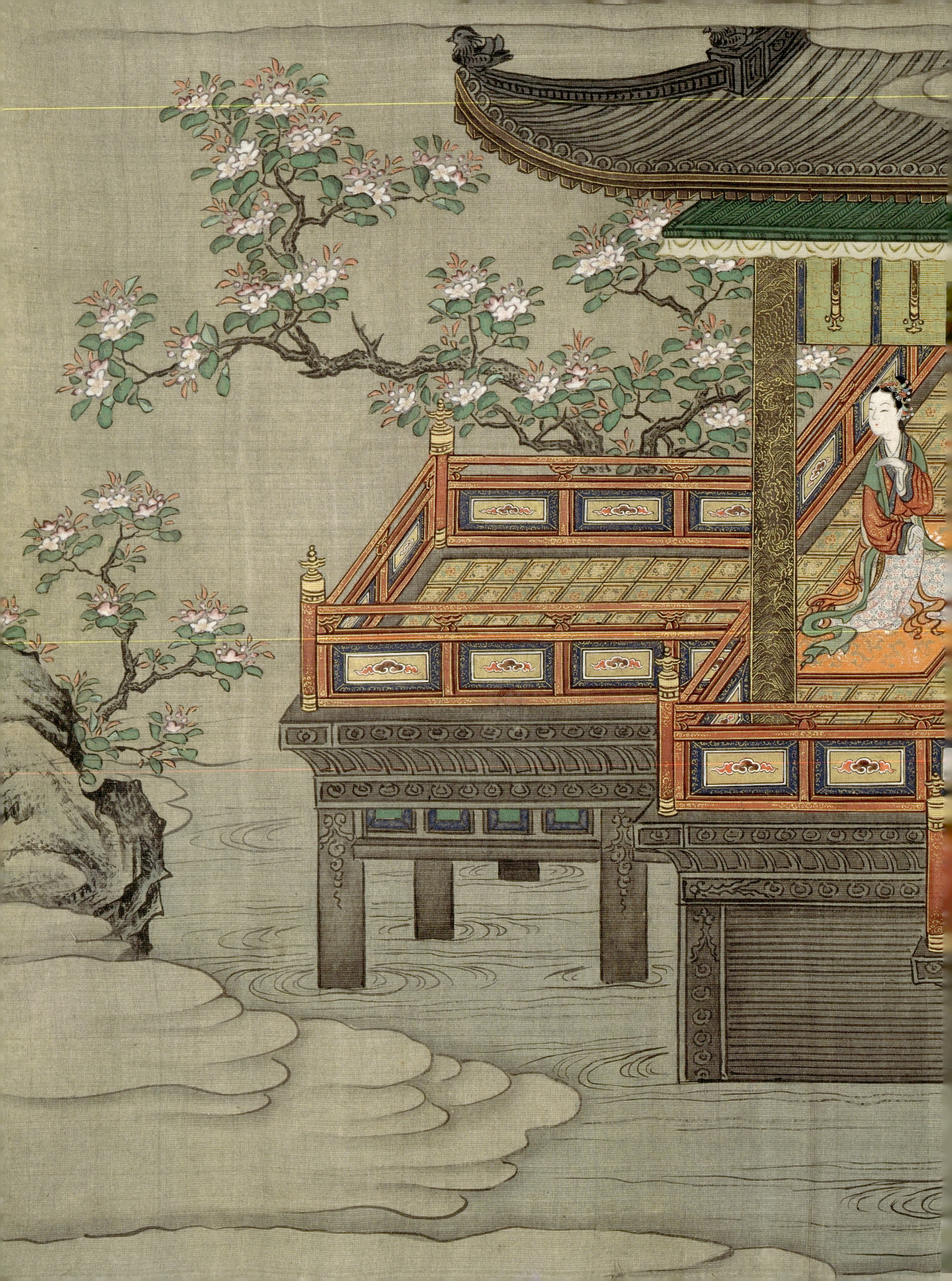

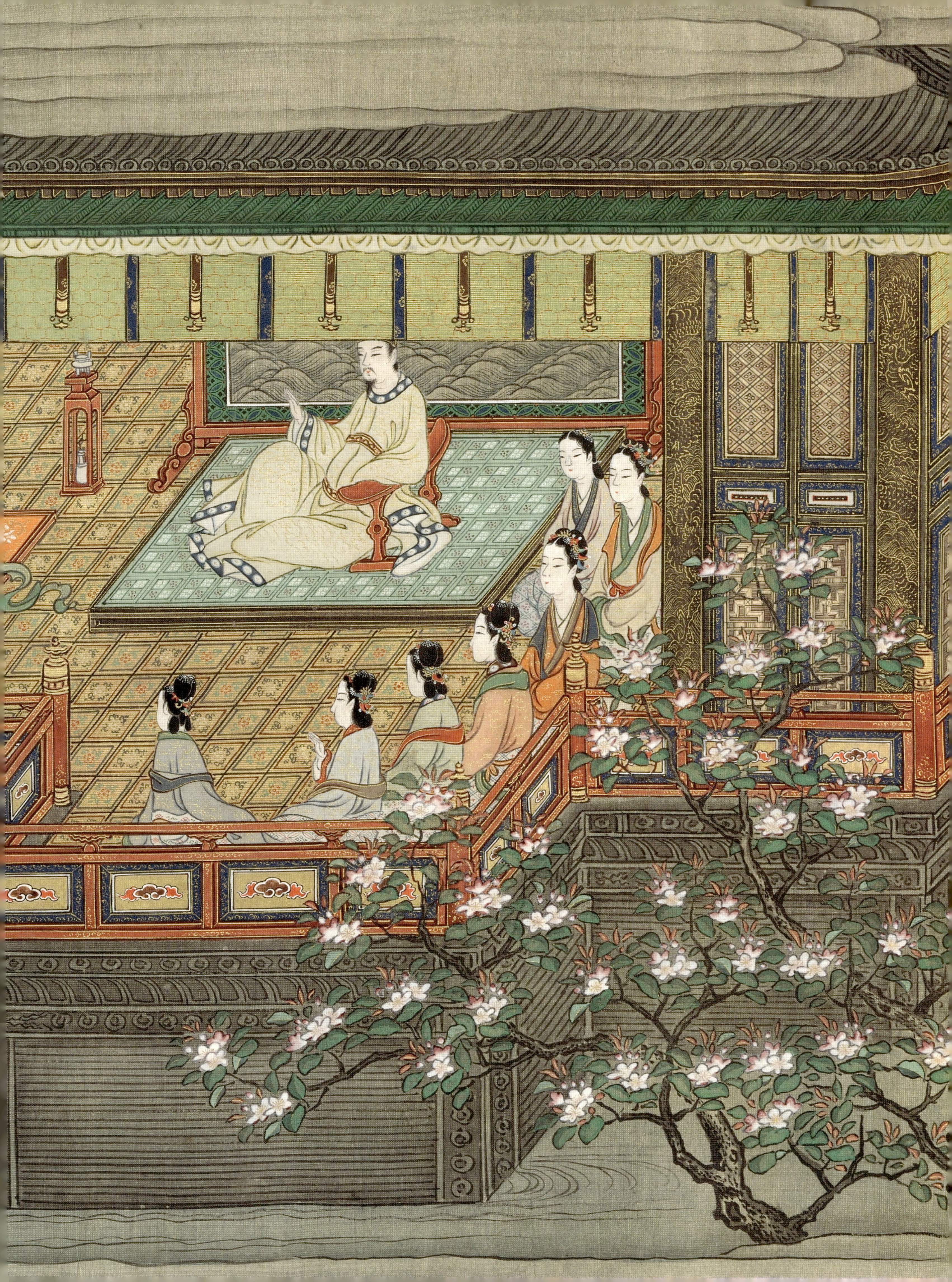

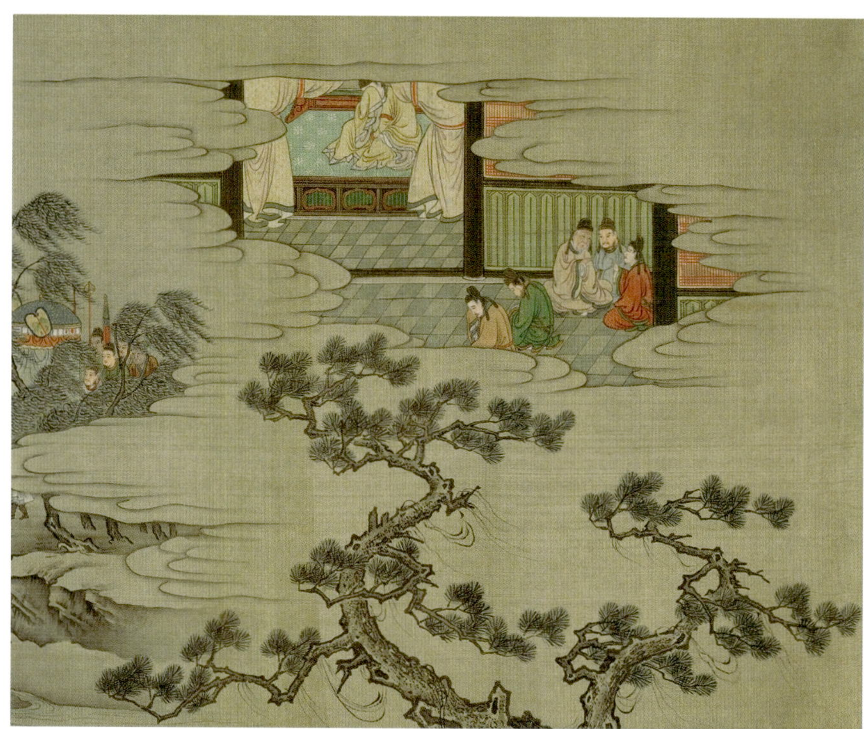

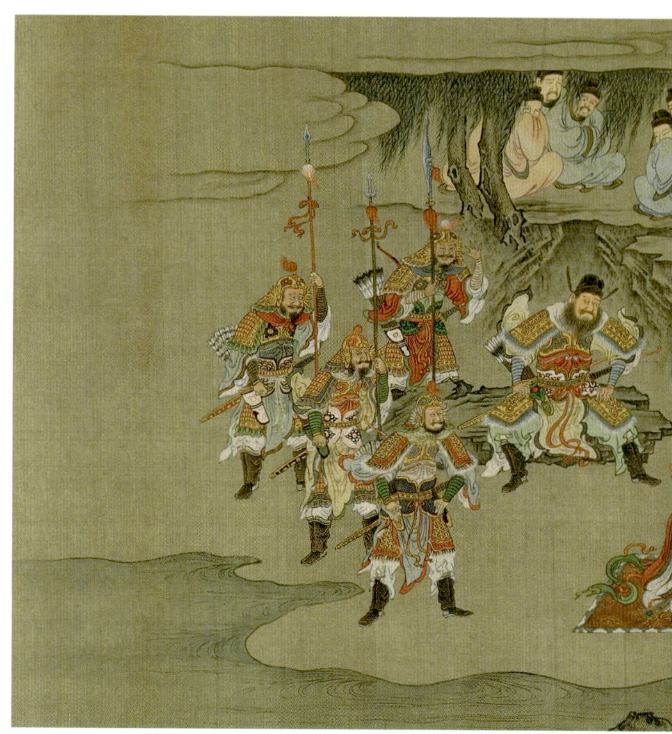

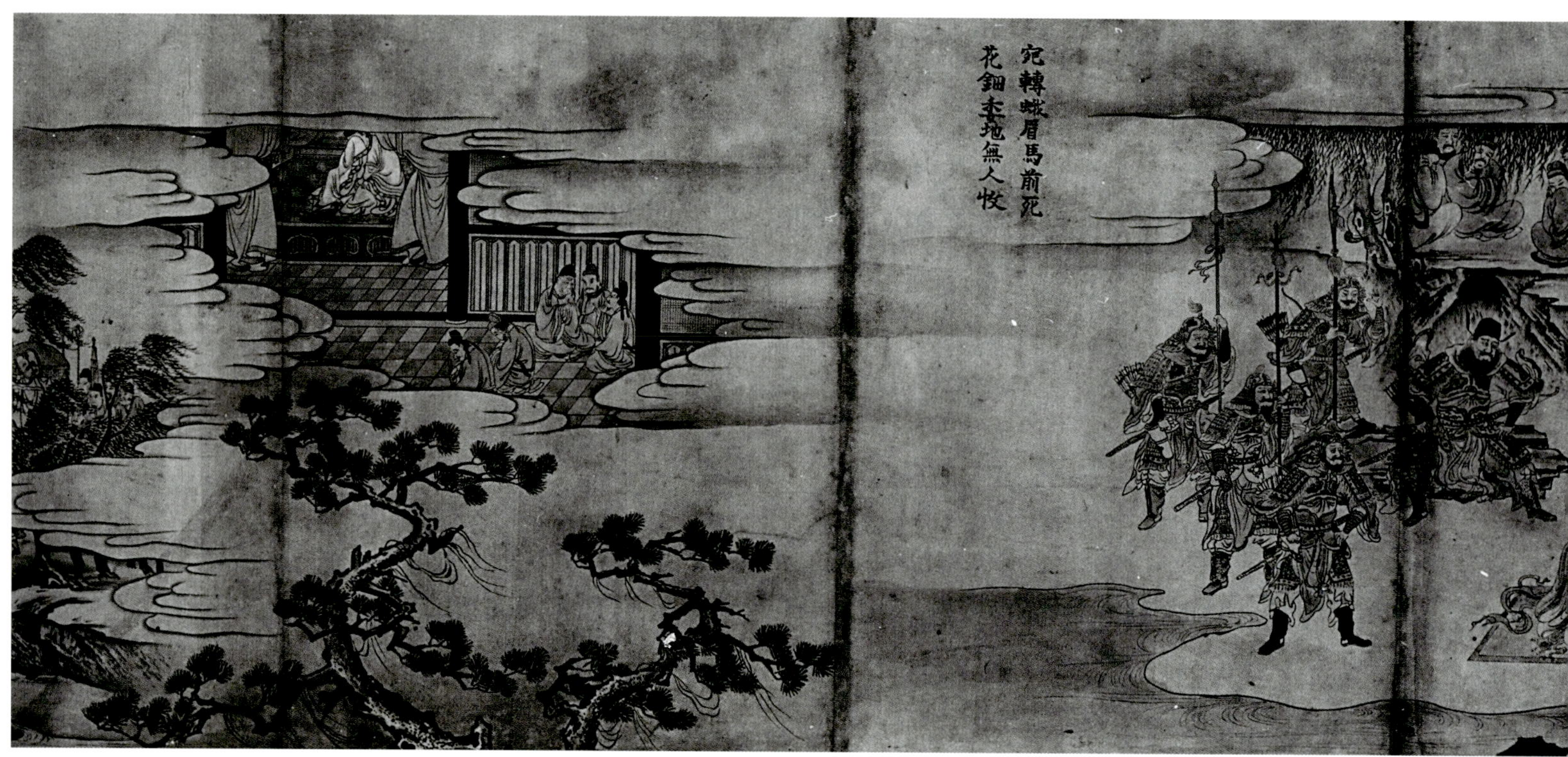

exploding with fire and the fires in these earlier works are unmistakable. We should also note that Sansetsu goes beyond the requisites of the text in his depiction, for the text mentions only that 'by the nine-layered walls and watchtowers, dust and smoke arose', implying but not describing a full-blown inferno.[132] Out of the purple smoke emerge Minghuang and Yang Guifei, hidden in an imperial carriage, and their retinue. In the scenes that follow we find the emperor and his courtiers learning of the six legions' refusal to proceed further, and then the moment of Yang Guifei's execution at Mawei (fig. 76). In the scene that immediately follows, mist breaks behind a wind-tossed pine to reveal the grieving Minghuang. Although in their present state the *Chōgonka* scrolls divide between the first and second scrolls at this point, Bai Juyi's text would argue against this division in Sansetsu's painting:

Her flowered hairpins fell to earth,
and no one picked them up,
the kingfisher wing, the sparrow of gold,
the jade pick for the hair.
Our lord and ruler covered his face,
unable to protect her;
he looked around, and blood and tears
were flowing there together.

Minghuang's reaction is immediate; he cannot bear to watch the execution, but when he uncovers his eyes, he sees the spot where his mistress has just died. A detail of the same section in the Kuki scrolls shows how this transitional passage was probably handled originally. Although the Mawei scene shifts quickly to the windblown pine and distraught emperor, shading in the dividing mists crosses the paper seam dividing the two scenes, making for a smoother transition (fig. 77). While this evidence alone does not prove that the Chester Beatty scrolls were not initially mounted as two scrolls, the compositional and narrative flow in this passage of the Kuki scrolls supports the logic behind a three-scroll format. The poem then quickly shifts settings to the mountains of Shu:

Brown dust spread in billows,
howling was the wind,
plank walkways wound into the clouds
as he climbed by Sword Tower Peak.
And at the foot of Mount Emei
travellers were few,
the royal banners shed no light,
the beams of sun were pale.

Ever faithful to the text and tone of the ballad, Sansetsu parts the mist again and winds Minghuang's entourage around Mawei, where an attendant points out where Yang Guifei was strangled. The painter next shifts to the scrolls' most dramatic passage, taking us deep into the undulating and precipitous mountains of Shu (fig. 78). Although the 'journey into Shu' episode of the poem comprises only a few lines, Sansetsu draws them out to maximum visual and emotional effect, deploying his mastery of monochrome ink landscape painting to evoke a fantastic wilderness of sharply contoured peaks, deep chasms and the infamously vertiginous plank road to Shu. Rising and falling in wave-like forms of overlapping planes accented with repeated texture strokes, these surreal mountains evoke the dream-like state of Minghuang's exile. A prolific painter of landscapes, Sansetsu orchestrates in the scene of the emperor's journey a complex array of peaks, bridges, valleys, mesa-like outcroppings and distant views to maximise the sensation of actual space and the remoteness of this region.

Sansetsu produced another landscape, titled *Pangu Valley* (*Bankoku zu*) on a box inscription by Sansetsu's descendent Kano Eigaku (1790–1867), that bears a close relationship to the 'road to Shu' passage in the Chester Beatty scrolls (fig. 79). As Hayashi Susumu has noted in his thorough study of *Pangu Valley*, though now mounted as a hanging scroll, it was originally a short handscroll that Sansetsu painted late in his career for his friend Nawa Kassho.[133] As a picture based on a preface by the Tang-dynasty poet Han Yu that represents an idealised vision of paradise of immortals, *Pangu Valley*, as Hayashi argues, may be understood as a kind of literati painting, presaging the works of such painters as Ike Taiga (1723–76) and Yosa Buson (1716–83). With so many visual similarities to the Dublin scrolls – sharply contoured, vertical peaks, snaking rivers, waterfalls, winding plank roads – we might detect an element of artistic pride in Sansetsu's repeat performances of these virtuosic landscapes, and perhaps find the notion of Shu as a dreamscape underscored by its resonances with the paradisiacal vistas of Pangu.

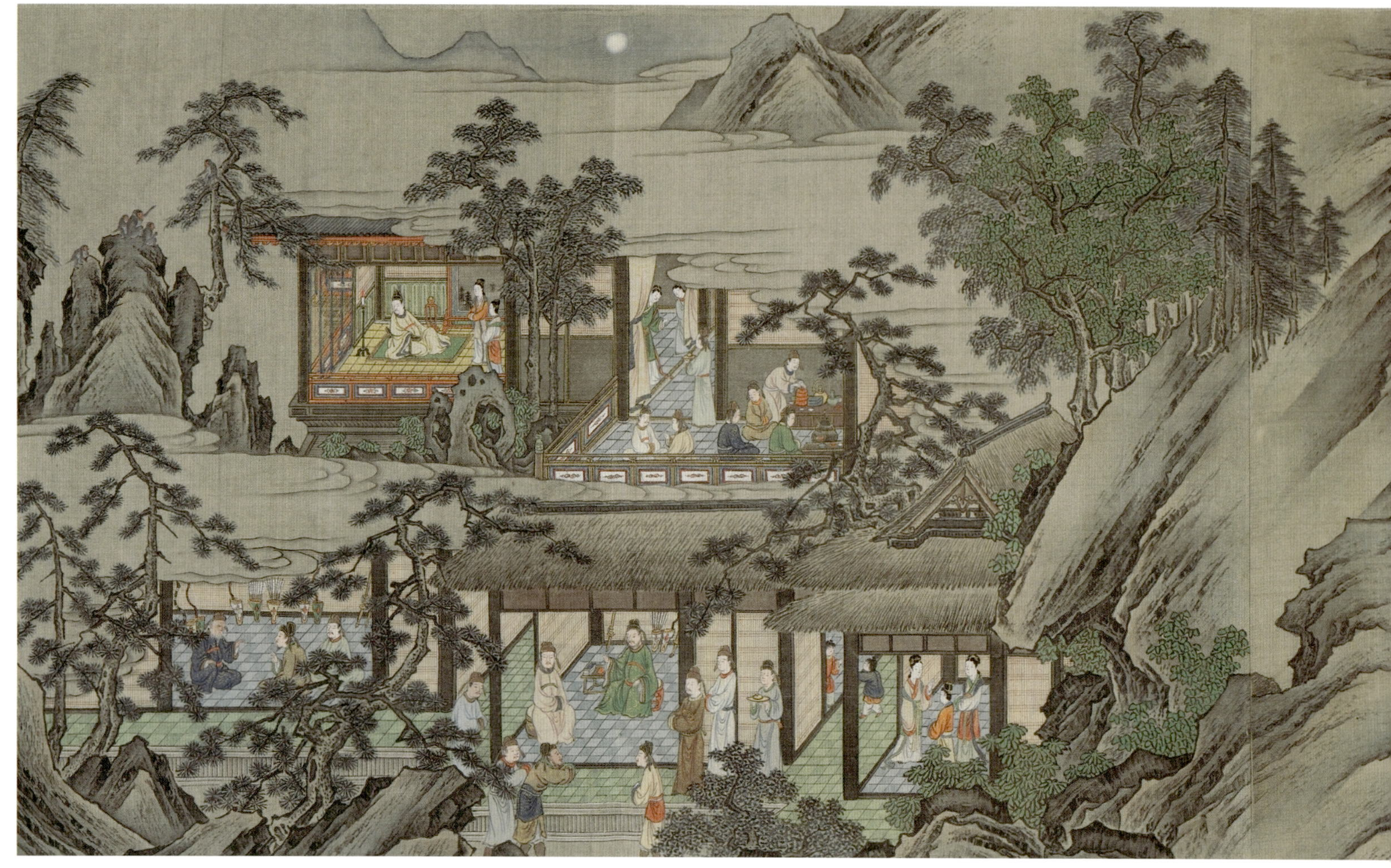

The ominous landscape continues into night, where we find Minghuang sorrowing 'from dawn to dusk' in his palace-in-exile – a group of buildings, including some with rustic thatched roofs, tucked into a narrow, moonlit valley whose impenetrability Sansetsu emphasises by surrounding it with pines, firs and jagged rocks. Sansetsu's inclusion of a troop of monkeys in the trees outside Minghuang's chambers again reveals the artist's attention to the specific language of the verse: standard versions of Bai Juyi's text describe 'bells, sounds that broke within him', but Sansetsu refers to the variant of the text more common in Japan,

> From the exile's palace he saw the moon
>   whose colours pained his heart,
> In the night rain he heard the monkeys,
>   whose cries cut through his gut.[134]

More pines, rocks and mist intercede, after which Minghuang and his court return to Chang'an against a backdrop of mountains that slowly recede into the

distance, bringing a putative second scroll to a close. The second scroll begins violently, with the sack of Chang'an, and builds to an initial narrative climactic moment with the death of Yang Guifei, whose figure kneels in the foreground, appearing larger than in any other scene in the scrolls. But Sansetsu then inserts the scrolls' visual climax with the long landscape of Minghuang's journey into exile, which appropriately falls in the centre of what would have been the second, central scroll. Before proceeding to the psychologically focused third scroll, the painter calms his image with the placid, open spaces of Minghuang's return to the capital as the retired emperor. By paying heed to the ways in which the artist paces the invisible lines of Bai Juyi's poem, we can thus confirm how the scrolls reveal a dramatic structure that affects our perception of the ballad.

What would have been the third scroll opens with a scene familiar from Kano Mitsunobu's screens, *Scenes from the Life of the Minghuang Emperor and Yang Guifei*, where Minghuang gazes longingly towards Taiye Pool. Sansetsu's rendering of this scene

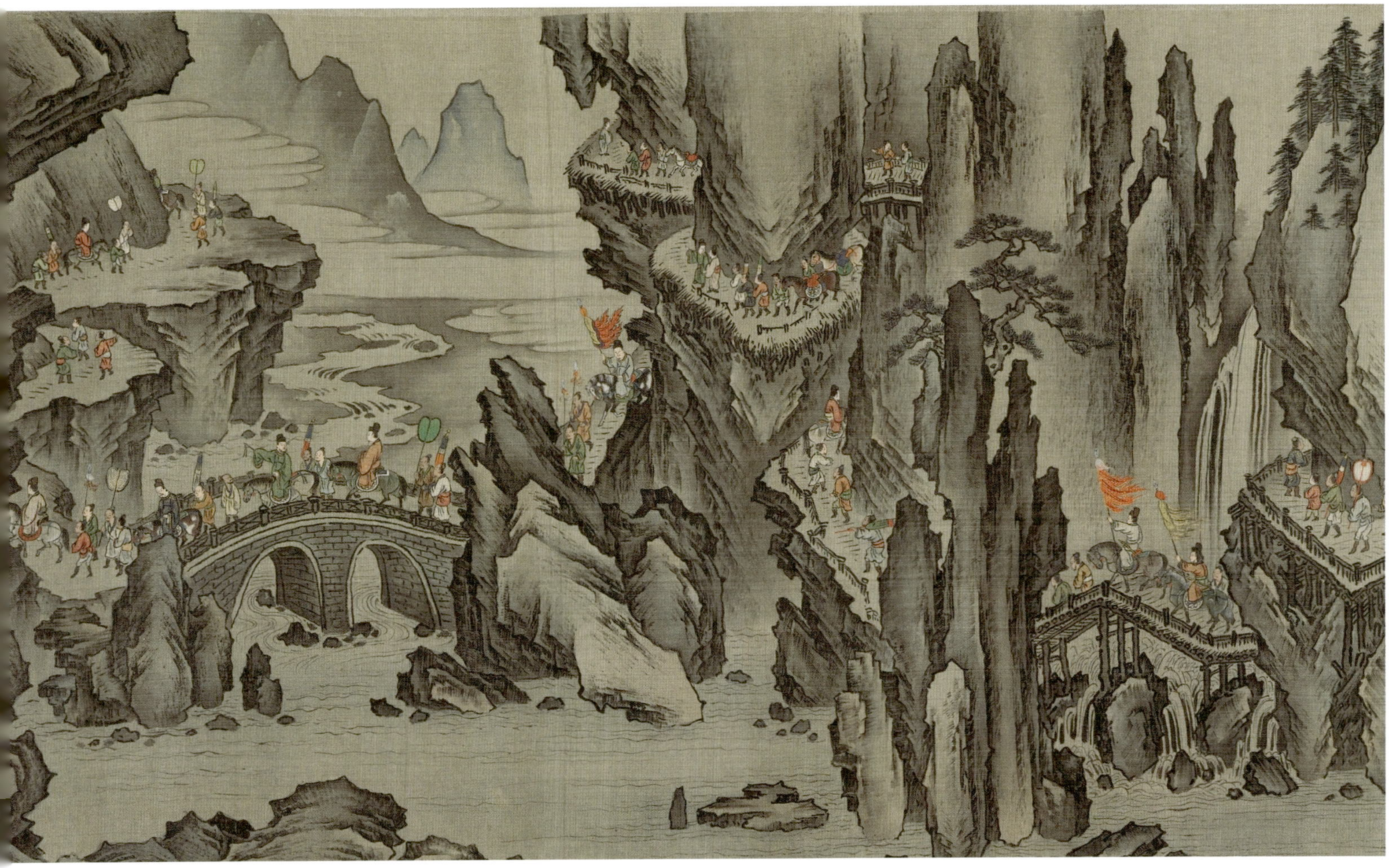

Fig 79 Kano Sansetsu, *Pangu Valley*. Hanging scroll; ink on paper, 31.5 x 122.8 cm. Yūgensai Museum.

quotes the emperor's pose from the screens, but adds a profusion of blossoming lotuses (see fig. 63). These flowers' presence confirms both the corresponding verse of the ballad and also the meticulous attention to iconographical accuracy that Kano Einō ascribed to his father: '…Or when they paint the 'Song of Lasting Sorrow', they don't realise that the *fuyō* in Lake Taiye are lotuses and depict them as tree peonies…' Beyond the lotuses a stand of willows takes us to another image of an insomniac Minghuang enduring

the long night. In Sansetsu's depiction of these palace scenes around Taiye Pool, he renders the metaphorical references to Yang Guifei (lotuses and willows) and enriches his picture with the scattered autumn leaves, overgrown grasses and fireflies with which Bai Juyi intensifies the depressing autumn mood of the emperor's return. Even the 'duck and drake tiles' are depicted in the scroll, though Sansetsu places them early in the scroll (in section 2) in visual reiteration of the lovers' bonds. The astute viewer, well-versed in

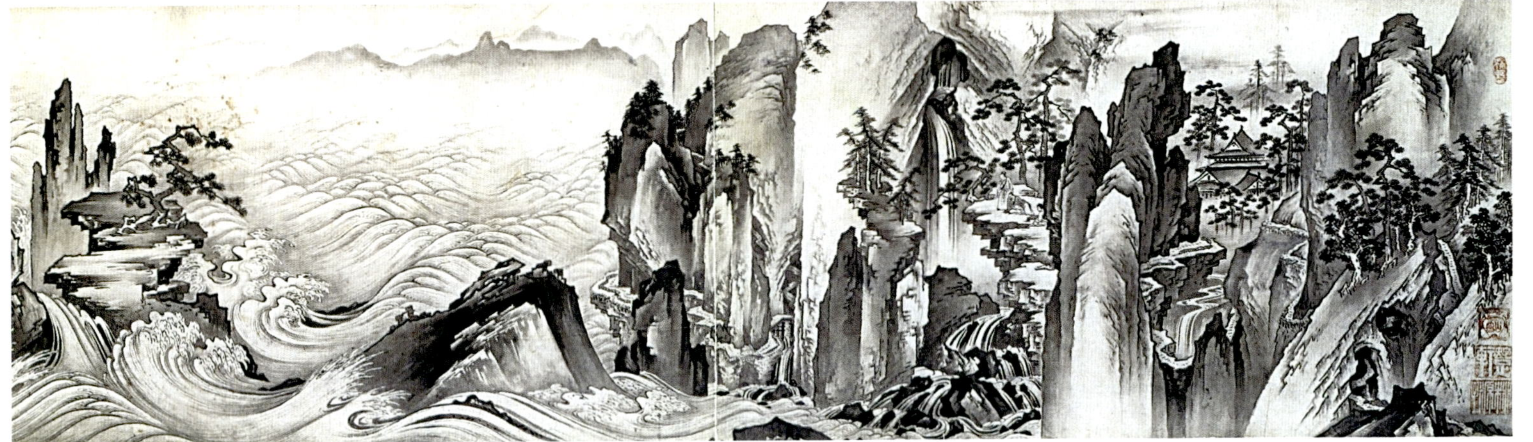

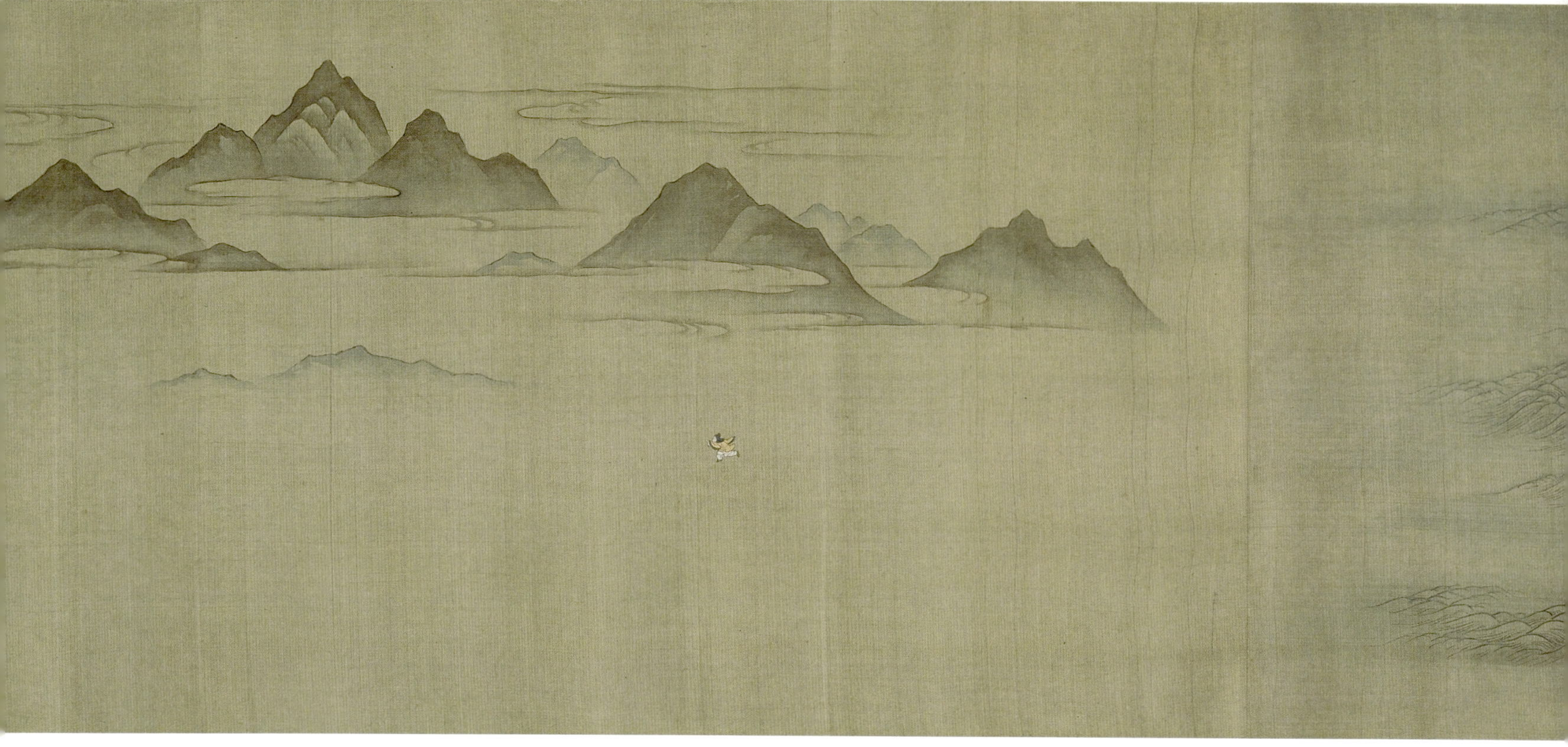

the ballad, would have made the visual connection early on and then remembered the sculpted tiles while viewing these later scenes, where they are absent. Once again we find Sansetsu's painting close to the text while at the same time finding room for modulation.

The end of the ballad provides Sansetsu with the greatest freedom for invention in the final two sections of the *Chōgonka* scrolls. Replete with fanciful imagery, the poem's representation of the wizard's journey to find Yang Guifei's spirit in the land of the immortals presented the painter with particular challenges beyond those posed by the requisites of portraying the concrete, if exotic, environments of palace interiors and Chinese mountains. Commencing with a close-up view of the emperor consulting with the wizard, the scroll opens into its most arresting passage, the seemingly endless expanse of a seascape and distant mountains through which the wizard journeys (fig. 80). Sansetsu manipulates our perceptions of space as we unroll the scroll towards its conclusion by showing the wizard three times – hurtling on a cloud into the sky, submerged beneath the surface of the sea and finally as a tiny figure riding the wind into the distance. By changing the wizard's size and shifting his pictorial position in each appearance, Sansetsu enhances the illusion of spatial depth in the narrow

confines of the horizontal format of the handscroll, and shows us how far the wizard has had to travel.

Wispy clouds in ink monochrome transform into clouds etched in purple and gold before which float the magical palaces of Taizhen in the final sections of the scroll. In a tour de force of ruled-line architectural representation, Sansetsu conjures impossibly elaborate pavilions where Yang Guifei's spirit resides. These structures, heavily ornamented with sculpted finials, lacquered columns and gilded brackets reappear four times, marking four distinct moments in the wizard's encounter with Taizhen. But instead of repeating the same structure four times, Sansetsu alters its shape and colour, and rotates it slightly with each reappearance. A technique familiar also from the narrative scrolls of Sansetsu's contemporary, Iwasa Matabei (1578–1650), the constantly changing architectural setting amplifies the sensation of fantasy in the scroll's final passages.[135] Beyond the scene where the wizard takes his leave of Taizhen floats a multi-terraced pavilion like the one at the Li Palace in the first scroll; like the 'drake tiles' these terraces that climb to an emphatically empty golden throne echo those earlier scenes at the Li Palace and provide a visual reference for Taizhen's nostalgic recollection of vows exchanged on the seventh day of the seventh month (fig. 81).

Fig 80 Kano Sansetsu, 'The wizard's quest' (from Minghuang engages a Daoist wizard), *Song of Lasting Sorrow*; scroll 2, the fourth length of silk.

Fig 81 Kano Sansetsu, 'The wizard takes leave' (from The Daoist's interview with the soul of Yang Guifei), *Song of Lasting Sorrow*; scroll 2, the sixth length of silk.

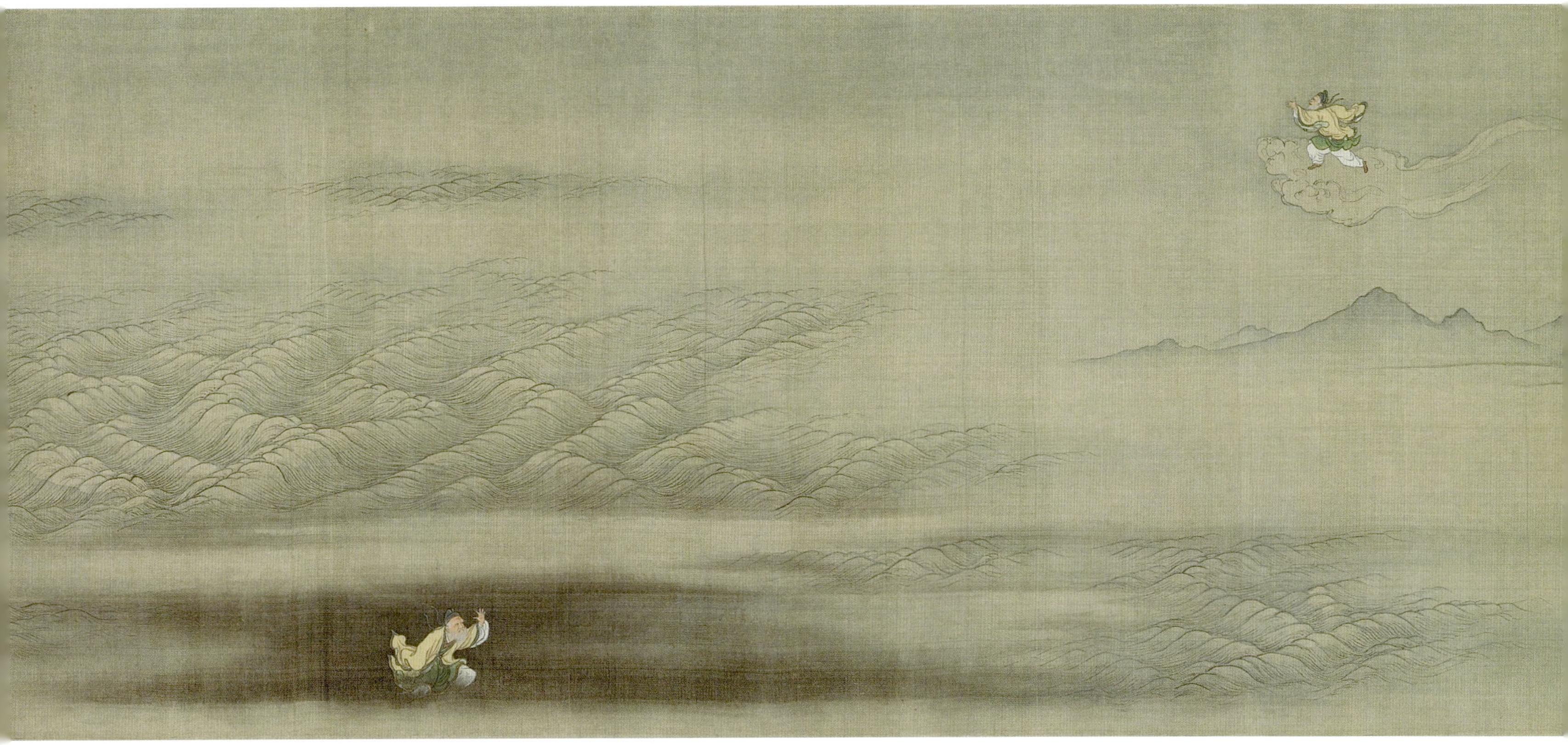

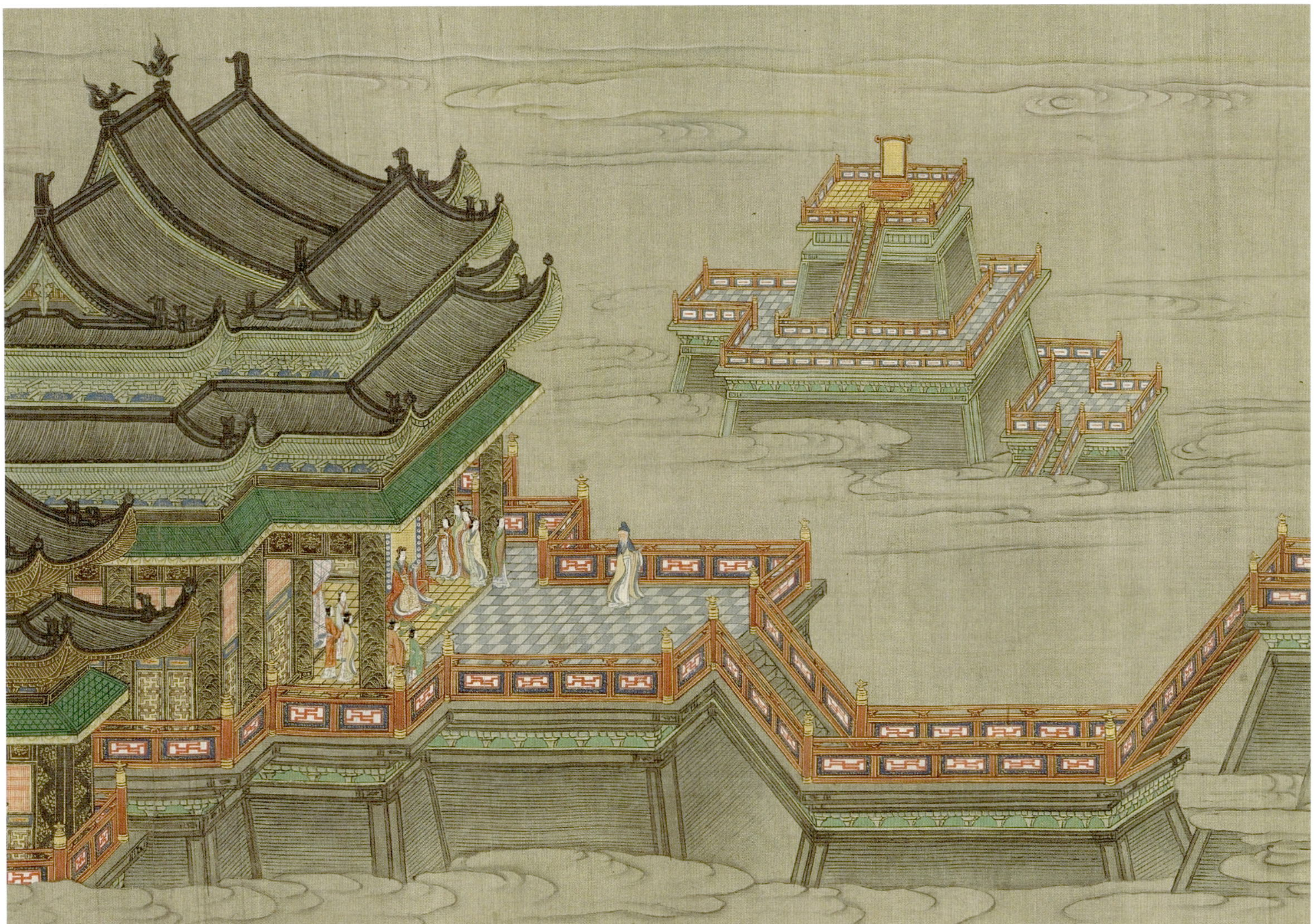

KANO SANSETSU AND KANO WORKSHOP PAINTINGS OF 'THE SONG OF LASTING SORROW'

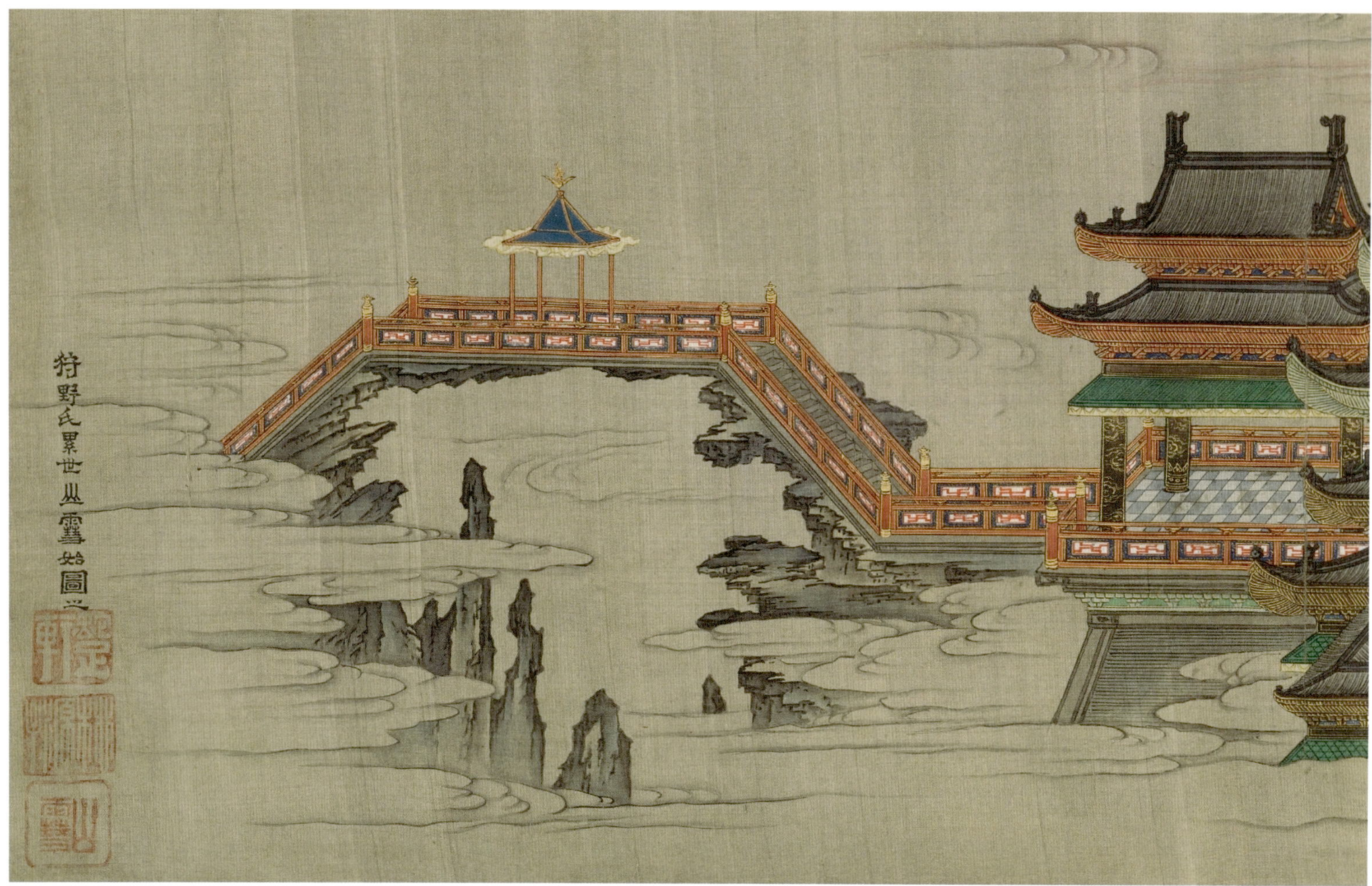

At the end of the scroll, a floating bridge – perhaps an allusion to the 'floating bridge of dreams' in the *Tale of Genji* – leads us to the artist's signature (fig. 82):

This, painted for the first time by Sansetsu, of all the generations of the Kano clan.
Kano-shi ruisei Sansetsu hajimete kore zusu.

Three seals follow the signature. Read 'Jasokuken', 'Tōgenshi' and 'Sansetsu', they bespeak the artist's Sinophilia and artistic identity (fig. 83). 'Jasokuken' (蛇足軒 'Legged Snake Studio') alludes to a story from the *Intrigues of the Warring States* (*Zhan guo ce*) about a servant who paints with such speed that he has the leisure to add legs to his image of a snake; 'Tōgenshi' (桃源子 'Master of the Peach Blossom Spring') refers to Tao Yuanming (365/372–427), the Eastern-Jin-dynasty poet of the peach blossom spring story; 'Sansetsu' (山雪 'Mountain Snows') takes the first characters of the names of the painter's actual and imagined mentors, Sanraku and Sesshū (Tōyō, 1420–1506). In

its length and content, the combined signature and seals are unique among known works by Sansetsu. He uses the same signature, 'Kano-shi ruisei Sansetsu hajimete kore zusu', but not the seals, on only one other work, a handscroll, *Chinese Sages in the Shishinden* (*Shishinden kenjō zu kan*), painted in ink and colours on silk, like the Chester Beatty scrolls.[136] 'Kano-shi ruisei Sansetsu' appears on two other works, the triptych *Descent of Sakyamuni, Dragon and Tiger*; and *White-robed Kannon*, a painting on silk in the collection of Tenshōin, the temple for which Sansetsu produced the *Assembled Immortals* panels. The phrase 'hajimete kore zusu' ('this, painted for the first time') appears on one other work, Sansetsu's screens, *Mount Fuji and Miho Pine Strand*, in the Shizuoka Prefectural Museum.[137] That the signature asserts the artist's originality and correctness in depictions of Mount Fuji has been persuasively argued; in the case of the *Chōgonka* scrolls, when viewed against the broader corpus of paintings on Bai Juyi's ballad, the signature takes on added weight.[138] Meticulously brushed in clerical script, use of which itself constitutes a consciously archaicising

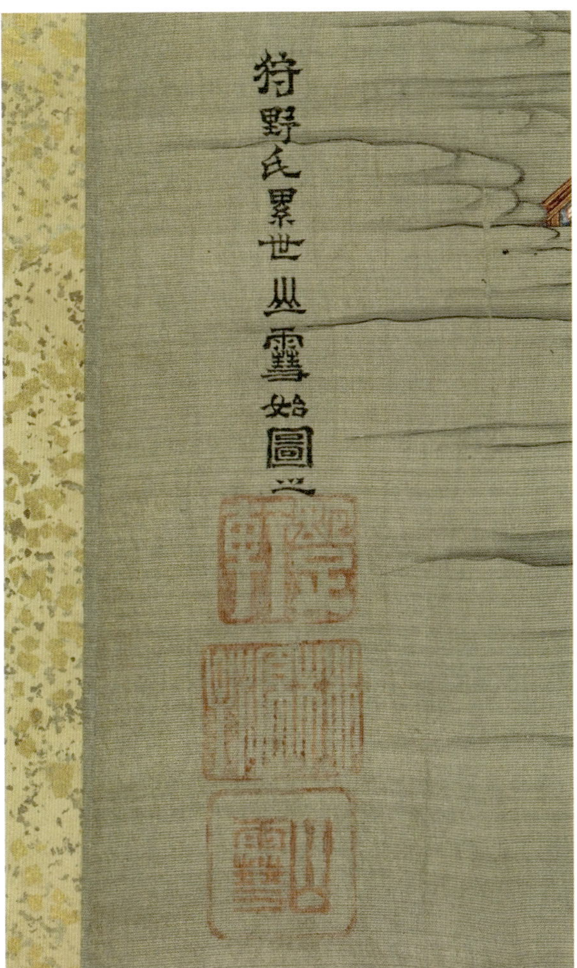

Fig 83 The three seals and artist's signature at the end of *Song of Lasting Sorrow*; (detail of fig. 82).

gesture in which the characters of Sansetsu's name accrue multiple strokes, Sansetsu's signature states definitively that of all the painters of the Kano clan, including his dozens of cousins in Edo, he is the first to paint a complete and accurate picture of the 'Song of Lasting Sorrow'.[139]

The originality Sansetsu claims for his painting is complicated by the question of which sources he consulted in order to complete the handscrolls in the Chester Beatty Library. Hayashi Gahō's account in *Kano Einō kaden ga jiku jo* first noted Sansetsu's study of ancient works of Chinese and Japanese painters, and current research on the artist's work has confirmed his propensity to mine other sources for his own paintings.[140] In the case of the *Chōgonka* scrolls, Sakakibara Satoru has called attention to similarities between passages in *Genjō Sanzō e*, the twelve-scroll pictorial account by Takashina Takakane (active early fourteenth century) of the Tang-dynasty monk Xuanzang's journey to India, raising the possibility that Sansetsu consulted these treasured scrolls.[141] A work that describes in vivid detail the exotic settings through which Xuanzang travelled, *Genjō Sanzō e* seems an apposite object of study for Sansetsu, particularly in light of the artist's connection to the Kujō family, members of whom had served as abbots of Daijōin, the princely sub-temple of Kōfukuji, and the handscrolls' former owner.[142] The Kujō were among Sansetsu's later patrons, as we will see below. But beyond such hints of exposure to earlier works, more precise identification of exterior sources of inspiration for the *Chōgonka* scrolls remains elusive.[143]

CHŌGONKA ZUSHŌ AND THE AFTERLIFE OF SANSETSU'S MASTERPIECE

Part of the question of Sansetsu's creative process can be answered by examining *Chōgonka zushō*, a manual for reading and painting the 'Song of Lasting Sorrow', produced by Kano Einō in 1677.[144] *Chōgonka zushō* is organised into five books, with a preface about Bai Juyi's ballad at the beginning of the first and a Japanese text of the ballad followed by a postscript at the end of the fifth book. The contents between these frames consist of line-by-line explications, primarily in easily readable *kana* script, of Bai Juyi's verses, each of which is rendered with readings of characters and indications of word order according to Japanese grammar, interspersed with twenty-four monochrome illustrations. Descriptive in content, the explanations appear to have been partly intended as a guide for painters, who could use the illustrations as a guide. The glosses of each line of the poem, combined with the illustrations, could alternatively have functioned as a tool for maximising the reader's comprehension of each verse of the poem, much in the same way annotated editions of Shakespeare's plays are read today. For example, the familiar line, *'there were lotuses in Taiye Pool, and willows at Weiyang'* receives the following commentary:

Taiye is the name of a pond. Gorgeous *fuyō* had been planted in this pond. *Fuyō* signifies lotuses. Weiyang means Weiyang Palace and is the name of a palace. Willows were planted in front of this Weiyang Palace.

The passage, which echoes Einō's description of his father's concerns about iconographical accuracy, clears the confusion Japanese readers may have had about Bai Juyi's use of the term *fuyō*, which could also signify a type of hibiscus, for lotus blossoms. Two pages after this passage, an illustration depicts Minghuang looking out over a lotus-filled pond, providing yet further clarification (fig. 84).

The linear image is closely based on the same scene in Sansetsu's *Chōgonka* scrolls (see fig. 63); while Einō has made slight modifications, the figure of Minghuang and the lotuses appear in the same configuration, and such minor details as the swirling ripples and designs on the railing of the veranda betray a copyist's hand. Comparison of other images from the *Chōgonka zushō* with the *Chōgonka emaki* shows that with few exceptions Einō based the illustrations on his father's scrolls. Images of Taizhen's palace in the final book of *Chōgonka zushō* drastically abbreviate Sansetsu's complex architectural renderings, but even here printed images excerpt vignettes of the deceased Yang Guifei's encounter with Minghuang's wizard (fig. 85).

The final section of *Chōgonka zushō*, an epilogue, informs the reader about its conception and the underlying motivations behind the work:

These images were based on those by my father, who gathered old works and supplemented them with new ones. I painted supplements to those parts that were lacking, but I do not know who produced the

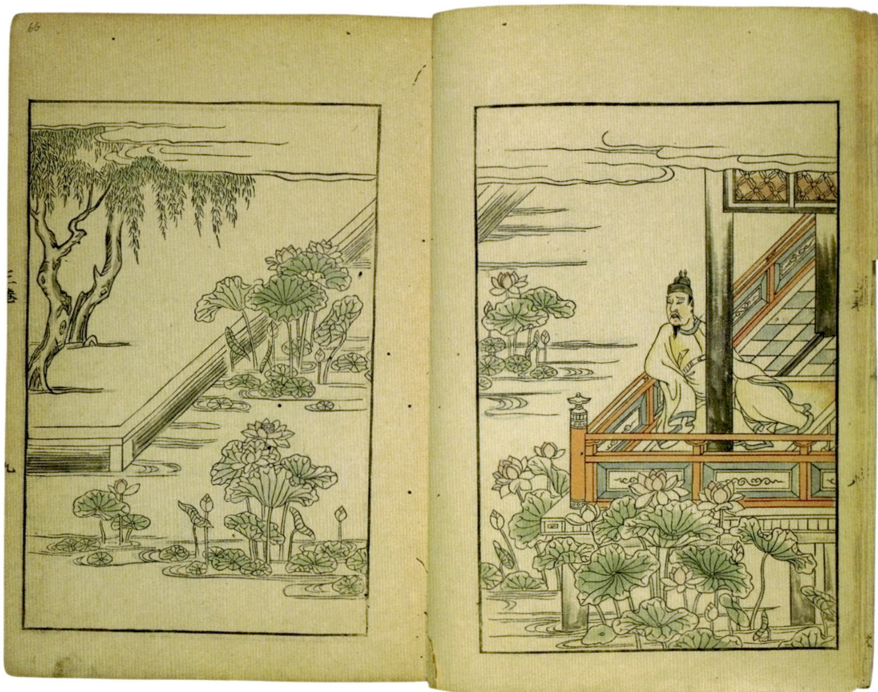

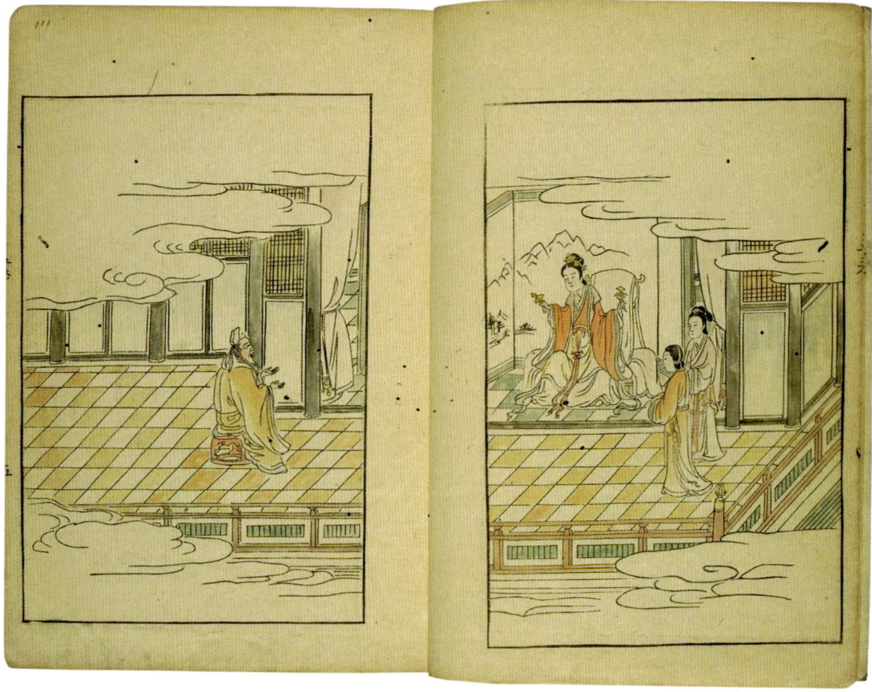

commentaries of the poem. This was for a long time kept in our house. There were once of course paintings from Tang [China] of the *Chōgonka*, but none of them have been handed down. In our realm, according to the text of the *Tale of Genji* there were paintings of the *Chōgonka* that Teijinoin (Emperor Uda) had painted, as well as folding screens and sliding panels depicting Xuanzong and Guifei, but they were not so spectacular and in fact have many mistakes. For example, some do

FIG 84 Kano Einō, *Chōgonka zushō*, 1677. Book 3, pages 8 (verso) and 9 (recto). The British Library.

FIG 85 Kano Einō, *Chōgonka zushō*, 1677. Book 5, pages 4 (verso) and 5 (recto). The British Library.

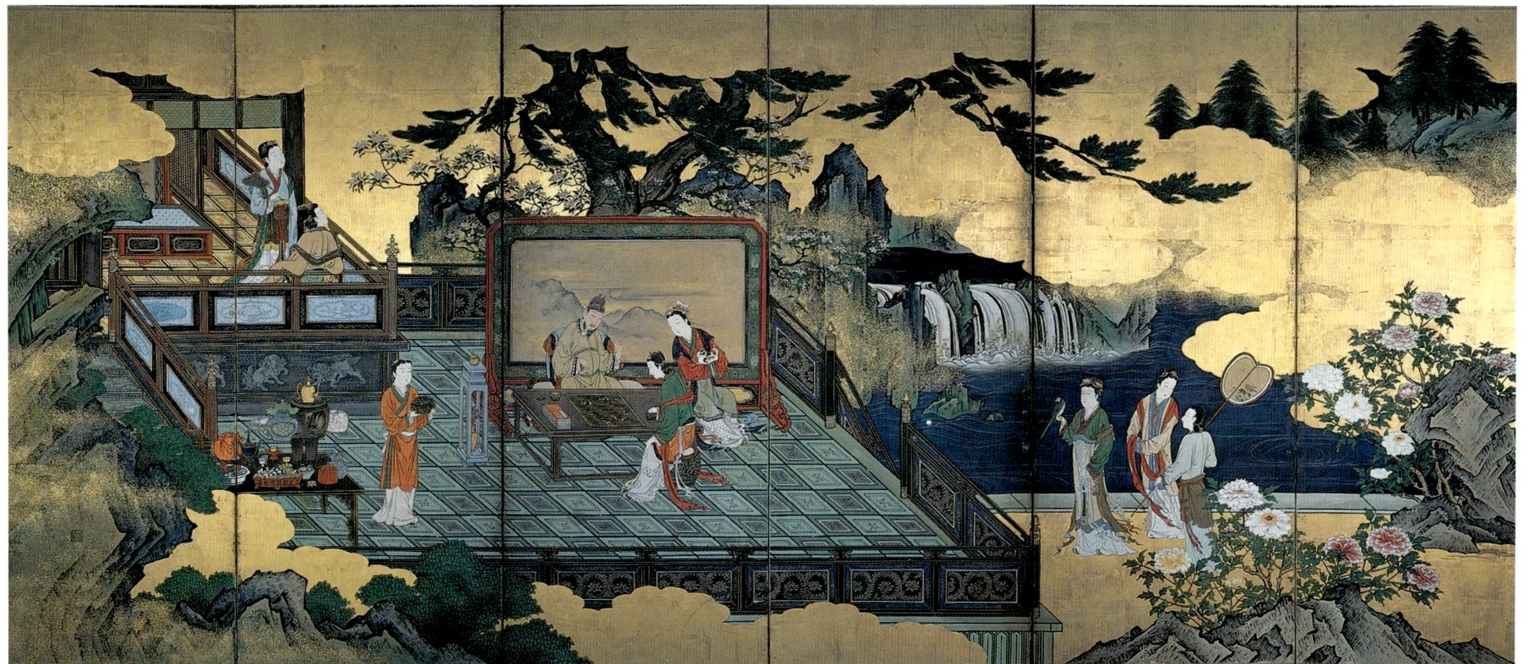

not know that the '*fuyō*' of Taiye Pool are lotuses and depict them as tree peonies. There are too many other slight mistakes to mention. My father regretted these things and poured his heart into only those places that could be corrected. However, these were kept secretly in our house so people did not know. If it were not his sincere intention, there would surely be many people who thought that he was wasting his time trying to understand even such trifling matters. I leave this to those who, even though they do not regret not knowing the essence of the text, could look back at the *shō* [digest], enjoy the pictures, forget the long days of spring and place this by their pillows when they pass the long nights of autumn. The so-called Japanese text is said to be by Shōyōin Sanetaka [Sanjōnishi Sanetaka] but it doesn't sound quite plausible. [...]

> Empō 5 [1677] eighth month fifteenth day
> Epilogue by Saikō Ekitei Shujin [Kano Einō, 1631–97]

In providing an account of *Chōgonka zushō*, Kano Einō's epilogue reveals several things about his primary source – Sansetsu's *Chōgonka* scrolls. First, the scrolls were the product of Sansetsu's study of old paintings, but were augmented with his own 'new' images. Second, the *Chōgonka* scrolls appear to have

been the fruits of long years of study and preparation, through the course of which the painter attempted to identify and expunge the infelicities of older works. Third, since Einō's images printed in 1677 are based on his father's, it would appear that the younger artist retained in his possession the drafts for Sansetsu's scrolls, if not the actual work, for over two decades after the latter artist's death in 1651. Fourth, and perhaps less apparent, an impression of Sansetsu as an artist who closely guarded his work, and who may have been misunderstood by others, emerges from his son's brief account. It is striking that Einō's comments confirm – without parroting – much of what Hayashi Gahō writes in his *Kano Einō kaden ga jiku jo*.

Beyond its possible uses as a manual for reading and painting the 'Song of Lasting Sorrow', *Chōgonka zushō* functions on an abstract level as a work that aims to codify what Kano Sansetsu had accomplished in painting: if the silk handscrolls were destined for the private experience of an individual patron, the printed guide to the ballad could transmit and lend weight to its vision through its exposure to the broader audience of readers who acquired it. We could address the question of whether *Chōgonka zushō* ultimately had much of an impact in either its concrete or abstract functions in two ways: first, in terms of its impact on how Bai Juyi's ballad was subsequently visualised, and second, specifically in the degree to which Kano Sansetsu's vision was perpetuated. These questions merit a more

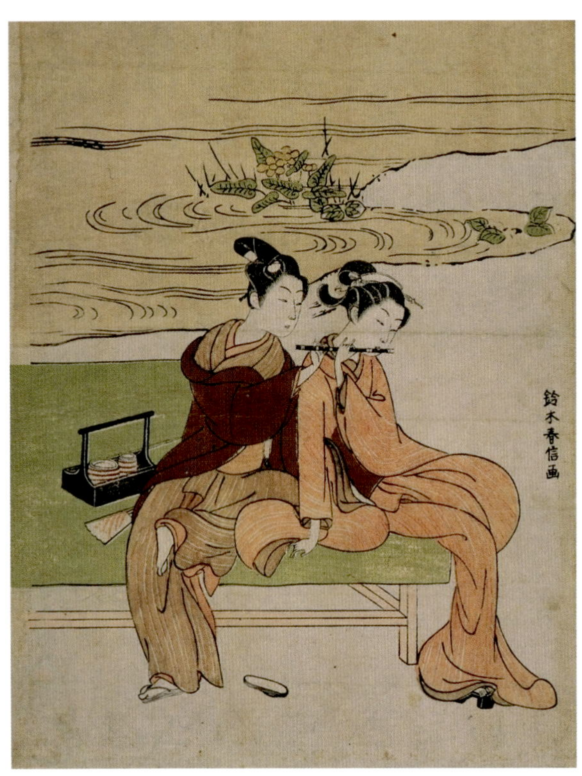

screen, particularly in its architectonic rocks, brilliant colours and abundant gold, closely matches that of Sansetsu's screen, *Minghuang and Yang Guifei*, and some details of the *Chōgonka* scrolls, the son's work departs from the purposes that his *Chōgonka zushō* apparently espoused and returns us to the light drama of apocryphal episodes.

The very medium – the woodblock print – in which *Chōgonka zushō* was produced may in the end have ensured the failure of its project to secure the veracity of Kano Sansetsu's vision. In the decades after *Chōgonka zushō* was printed, artists in eighteenth-century Kyoto and Edo would shift the focus of images of Yang Guifei and Minghuang to single depictions of the concubine as an exotic Chinese 'beauty', or in parodying, *mitate* images that superimposed idealised visions of contemporary Japanese courtesans onto familiar episodes, such as the lovers' famous *Flute Duet* in a woodblock print of two young lovers by Suzuki Harunobu (1724–70) (fig. 87).[146]

The overall thematic change that these images manifest signals a general shift in viewer interest from the romantic or tragic aspects of Bai Juyi's ballad to the erotic vision of Yang Guifei as one of the top beauties of all time. While Momoyama images on screen paintings, even if they drew on subplots unrelated to the ballad, may yet have borne a synecdochical relationship to Bai Juyi's poem, Edo-period representations of Yang Guifei steadily distance themselves from the Chinese text. In works of *ukiyo-e*, such as Utagawa Toyokuni's *Three Beauties* (*San bijin*), we encounter Yang Guifei grouped together with other beauties, stripped of literary context, and reduced to an ideal against which the greatest courtesans of the day could be compared.

If Kano Einō produced *Chōgonka zushō* in order to promote his father's vision of Bai Juyi's ballad to a wider audience, for what contexts did Sansetsu orig-

thorough analysis than the present essay allows, but they can be addressed through a broad assessment of the directions in which *Chōgonka* imagery would develop in the mid-to-late Edo period.[145]

A single folding screen by Kano Einō, *Minghuang Playing Go with the Lady of Guo*, reprises a theme listed in *Kōsoshū*, Kano Ikkei's compendium of Chinese painting subjects (fig. 86). This work depicts Minghuang playing a game of Go with one of Yang Guifei's sisters, the Lady of Guo, on a terrace of celadon-glazed tiles overlooking a pool bordered by enormous peonies and fir trees. The painting's languorous mood belies the tension of the Go players, whose eyes are fixed on the board. As Ikkei explains in *Kōsoshū*, the Lady of Guo is about to make a winning move that will be thwarted by her sister, who releases the puppy she holds onto the board, thus ruining her sister's victory and protecting her beloved Minghuang's pride. Although the style of Einō's

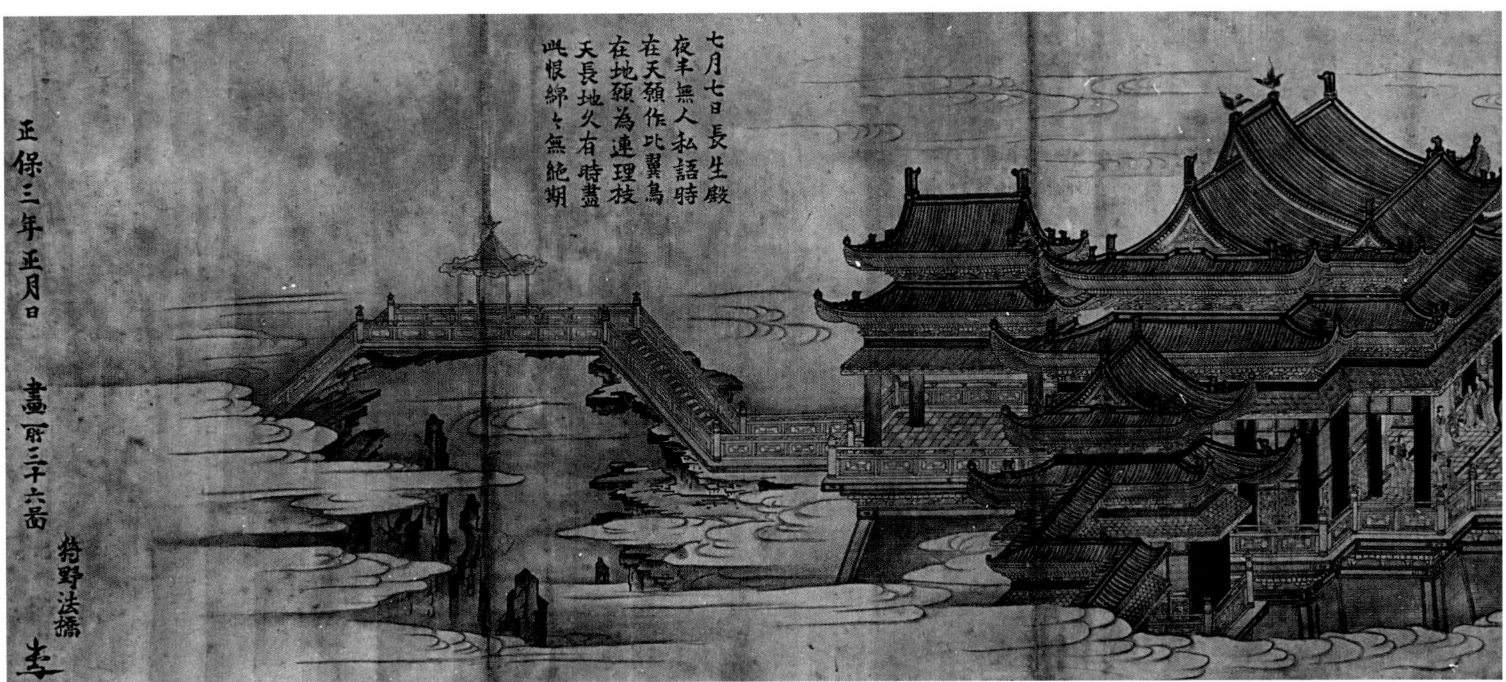

FIG 88 Kano Sansetsu, Kuki version of *Song of Lasting Sorrow*. Three handscrolls; ink and light colours on paper. Private collection, Japan. Detail, scroll 3.

inally design his scrolls to be seen? The provenance of the *Chōgonka* scrolls before their acquisition by Chester Beatty, in the mid-1920s, unfortunately, is unknown, beyond the fact that they once belonged to Louis Gonse.[147] A note in *Compendium of considerations of old paintings, revised and expanded* (*Teisei zōho kōko gafu*) by Kurokawa Mayori (1824–1906) describes 'Two handscrolls of *Chōgonka e*; painted by Kano Sanraku; on silk with bright pigments; an incomparable work, in the collection of a merchant in Owari.'[148] Kurokawa's note has been taken at face value as a reference to a lost work by Sansetsu's father, Sanraku, and understood as a probable source for Sansetsu's scrolls. But the two-scroll format and silk medium, along with the fact that until the postwar period Sanraku and Sansetsu's works were often confused to the point that they were viewed almost interchangeably, should raise the question of whether the scrolls Kurokawa mentions were not indeed Sansetsu's, the very works kept today in Dublin. If this were the case, however, we would still have little more than a vague idea of the scrolls' location and possession by a merchant in the nineteenth century.

Our final task in examining the *Chōgonka* scrolls is to consider the nature of their reception in late seventeenth-century Kyoto, the milieu in which Sansetsu produced his work. Beyond the style of the *Chōgonka emaki*, which reveals little of the influence of Sanraku that Tsuji and others have identified in the Tenkyūin room paintings, two sources shed light on the possibility that the scrolls were among Sansetsu's last works. First, we can return to Einō's epilogue to *Chōgonka zushō*, which indicates that Sansetsu expended much effort in researching and 'gathering old works' (*furuki o atsume*) to complete the scrolls. Second, the Kuki scrolls end with an inscription different from the signature on the Chester Beatty scrolls. The inscription at the end of the Kuki scrolls includes, in addition to Sansetsu's name, a date and an honorary title: 'Shōhō 3, a day in the first month; thirty-six scenes for the Painting Bureau; Kano Hokkyō Sansetsu' (*Shōhō sannen shōgatsubi edokoro sanjūroku zu Kano Hokkyō Sansetsu*) (fig. 88). However, the fact that the date, which corresponds to 1646, precedes by one year Sansetsu's attainment of the honorary title *Hokkyō* (Bridge of the Dharma) in Shōhō 4 after he completed the two paintings of the Bodhisattva Kannon for Tōfukuji cited in Hayashi Gahō's account above, has raised doubts about the inscription's authenticity. Although Sakakibara and Miyajima have noted the discrepancy between the Kuki scrolls' inscription and the date of the *Hokkyō* award, does the problematic date alone discount the inscription?

As Miyajima Shin'ichi has noted, the placement of 'Kano Hokkyō' to the right of the Kuki scrolls' colophon suggests that Sansetsu added his surname and title after his conferral of the *Hokkyō* honour, so that the original inscription would have included the date and note on the thirty-six scenes, followed simply by 'Sansetsu', the two-character signature that appears on most of the artist's other works.[149] The calligraphic style of the Kuki scrolls' final inscription also appears to match Kano Sansetsu's own. The boxy, sharp-edged standard script of the characters from the Shōhō date through 'Kano Hokkyō' resembles those in the poetic and descriptive annotations throughout the Kuki scrolls, as well as inscriptions that appear on other works, such as his *West Lake* screens or a painting of the Chinese transcendent Ma Shihuang in a private Japanese collection.[150] Additionally, the cursive 'Sansetsu' signature at the end of the Kuki inscription, while different from the artist's more formal calligraphy, closely matches his signature on a letter that survives in the temple Jishōji.[151] The authenticity of the Kuki scrolls' calligraphy, then, leads to the conclusion that Sansetsu completed the scrolls in 1646 and added the phrase 'Kano Hokkyō' soon after. If the Kuki scrolls were, as I believe, a final preparatory painting for the scrolls in the Chester Beatty Library, it would follow that the latter work, which does not bear the *Hokkyō* title, was executed around 1646, before Sansetsu's promotion.

The Kuki scrolls' colophon may yield still other clues. The inscription 'thirty-six scenes for the Painting Bureau' suggests the possibility of a commission for a member of the court aristocracy, since 'painting bureau' (*edokoro*) in the late medieval and early modern period referred to painting studios that the imperial court officially supported.[152] The inscription appears to indicate that the Kuki scrolls were somehow connected to these court-based studios. Why would the author of the Kuki scrolls' inscription – either Sansetsu or someone else – have taken the trouble to note the painting bureau?

While Kano Sansetsu's distant relatives in Edo, led by Kano Tan'yū, produced paintings for the shogunate, its vassals, the major Buddhist temples it sponsored, and for its castles and mausolea, Sansetsu and his father Sanraku had to pursue different arenas of patronage in Kyoto. In recent years, scholars have begun to reconstruct the networks for which the Kyoto Kano produced their works, and in the case of Sansetsu, particularly in his later career, it has become clear that the court aristocracy provided a major source of support. As several scholars have shown, Sanraku and Sansetsu both enjoyed the patronage of the Kujō, one of five top-ranked families (*gosekke*) descended from the Fujiwara, whose scions occupied the positions of chancellor (*sesshō*) and regent (*kanpaku*) for centuries.[153] Sanraku produced room paintings depicting the 'Battle of the Carts' scene from the 'Heartvine' (*Aoi*) chapter of the *Tale of Genji* for the Kujō in the early seventeenth century, and Kujō Sachiie's diary, the now lost *Gonikki bibō*, mentions in a 1655 entry that 'Kano Sanraku, Sansetsu, and Einō, these three generations frequented our house.'[154]

As Hayashi Gahō notes in his biographical sketch of Sansetsu, it was the former Regent Kujō Sachiie who commissioned the painter to provide two replacements for the lost images of Kannon by the mid-Muromachi painter Kichizan Minchō (1352–1431) for Tōfukuji, the Kujō's tutelary temple, and that promotion to the *Hokkyō* rank soon followed.[155] Kujō efforts to promote Sansetsu are further evident in a document from the painter's own hand. The document, *Memo of gifts from the Painter Hokkyō* (*Eshi Hokkyō onreimotsu oboe*), one of the Kyoto-Kano documents preserved in the Suzuka family archive, lists works that Sansetsu and his studio prepared in gratitude for bestowal of the *Hokkyō* title.[156] The list mentions an unnamed member of the Kujō house (probably Sachiie) as agent (*shissō*) for the commission and production of several screen paintings for the imperial palace. A date of Shōhō 4 (1647), seventh month, second day is given for the imperial commission (*chokkyo*) followed by another, eighth month twenty-fifth day, for attendance and formal presentation of the four pairs of screens at the imperial court. For the imperial palace (*kinchū*) were prepared the screens, *Mount Fuji, Seikenji, Mount Ashitaka and Miho Pine Strand*; for the Retired Emperor's palace (*hon'in*), *Landscapes of the Four Seasons*; for the New Retired Emperor's palace (*shin'in*), *Birds and Flowers of the Four Seasons*; and the Retired Empress's palace (*nyoin*), *Suma, Akashi and Wakaura*. Each pair of screens, according to the document's final notes, was executed in light colours, and measured five *shaku*, five *sun* (approximately 167 cm) in height. This large commission of screen paintings demonstrates the close links to court circles that Sansetsu had achieved through his work for the Kujō.[157] Although no further documentation connects the *Chōgonka* scrolls to Sansetsu's patrons at court, the 'painting bureau' reference at the end of the Kuki scrolls would appear to reflect a link, and possibly a court-based commission, again, probably in association with the Kujō.

Several other works by Sansetsu indicate the possible extent of Kujō patronage. They include: (1) room paintings for Daitsūji, a monastery in Nagahama belonging to the Ōtani branch of the True Pure Land Buddhist sect based at Higashi Honganji; members of the Kujō family served as abbots of both Daitsūji (Jūkō) and Higashi Honganji (Kōjū, 1602–58) around Sansetsu's lifetime; (2) depictions of the *Orchid Pavilion Gathering* on sliding panels for Higashi Honganji (no longer extant) and two pairs of eight-panel screens for Zuishin'in (see fig. 60), a temple where Kujō Sachiie's brother Zōkō (active late sixteenth–seventeenth century) and son Eigon served as abbots; and (3) a dragon painting

(dated eighth month, Shōho 4) on the ceiling of the Shariden of Sennyūji, a monastery with close links to the imperial court since the medieval period. Of the works, now lost, that entered the modern era in the collection of the Kujō family, the handscroll, *Chinese Sages and Philosophers*, is worth noting for its thematic resonance with Sansetsu's *Chōgonka* scrolls.[158] The *Orchid Pavilion Gathering* paintings, the *Chinese Sages and Philosophers*, and scrolls of the *Song of Lasting Sorrow* all share an interest in the Chinese classics, and may reveal a shared taste between Kujō Sachiie, who was Sansetsu's almost exact contemporary, and the painter for images based on classical Chinese themes.

The Chester Beatty Library's *Chōgonka* scrolls synthesise Kano Sansetsu's identity as an artist with a predilection for learned, correct depictions of continental themes, and demonstrate the enduring position such images occupied in Japanese visual culture into the early Edo period. Unlike works that Sansetsu produced in the circles of Neo-Confucian intellectuals who supported his work, however, the *Chōgonka* scrolls build upon a long tradition in Japan of visualising Bai Juyi's ballad and popular legends that had grown around the story of Minghuang and Yang Guifei. While Sansetsu's scrolls emphasise the ballad's psychological and romantic themes rather than its larger political and historical lessons, his work betrays an unwavering commitment to representing Bai Juyi's text true to its intensely visual language. Although the poem and tales would continue to inspire paintings in ways that did not reflect the preferences Sansetsu and his son Einō espoused in their images, treatise and the digest, *Chōgonka zushō*, Sansetsu's masterpiece survives as a testament to his art and as an important trace of the Sinophilia shared among the court aristocracy in early modern Japan.

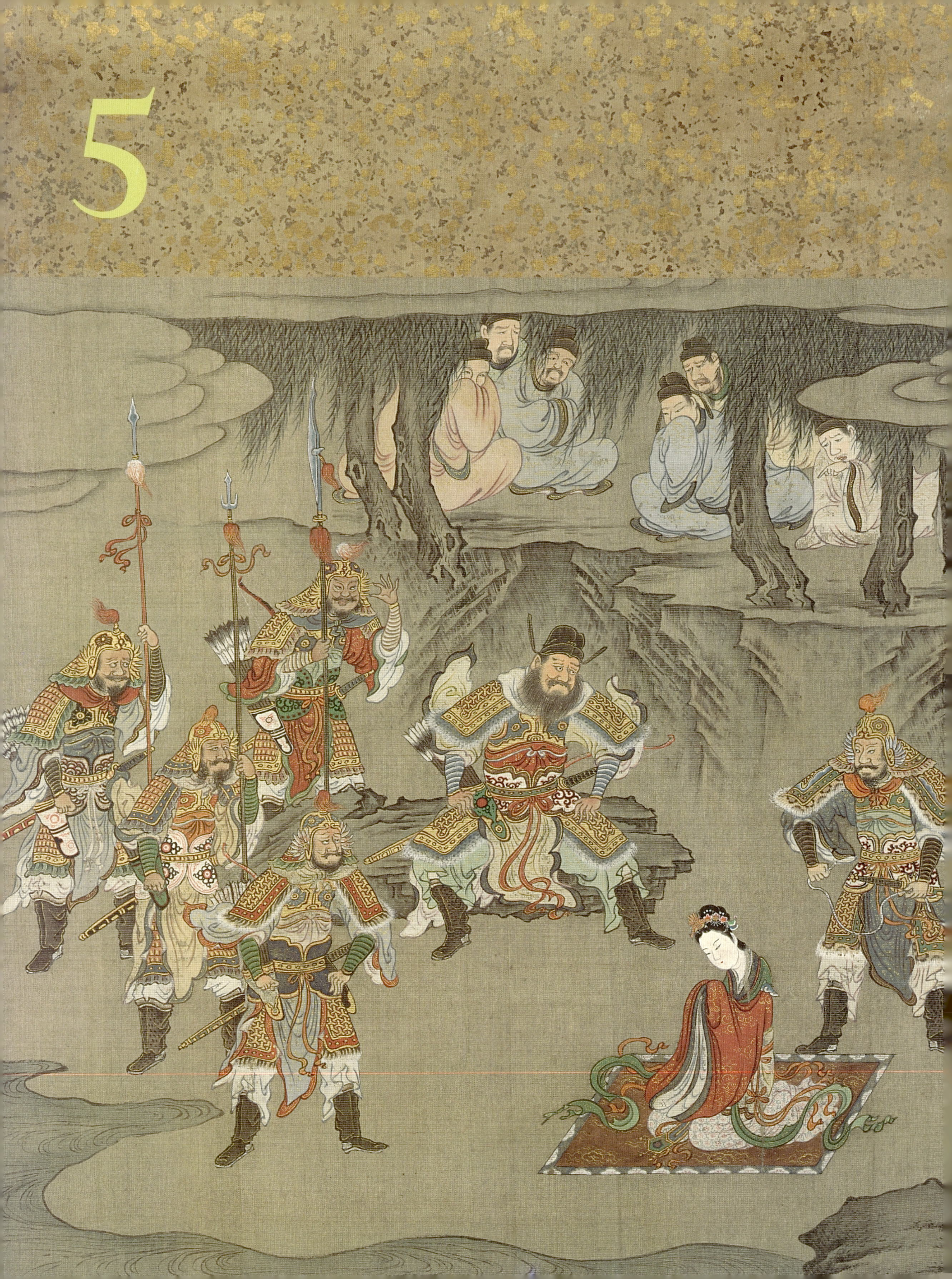
5

MING PAINTINGS AND PRINTS: POSSIBLE SOURCES FOR KANO SANSETSU'S CHŌGONKA SCROLLS

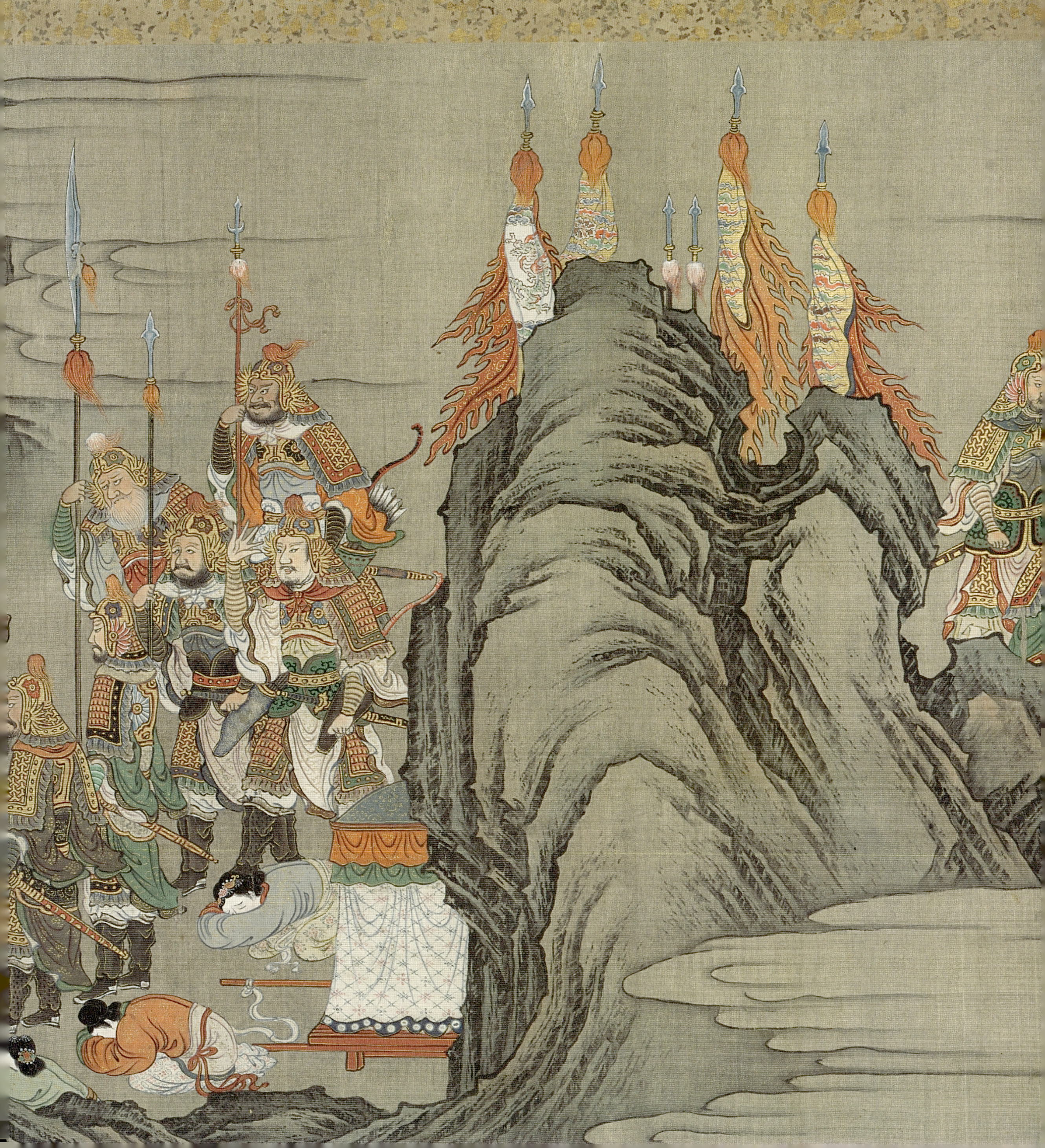

KANO SANSETSU (1590–1651) claimed that he created the *Song of Lasting Sorrow* painting *(Chōgonka gakan)* himself, instead of following models from the past. Many anonymous Chinese paintings that take as their subjects in some way the story of Minghuang (685–762) and Yang Guifei (719–56) did exist, and could have served as his inspiration,[159] but it seems that Sansetsu's *Chōgonka* painting was like no other of the time. Most notably, no other painting of this period was a full and complete illustration of the 'Song of Lasting Sorrow' poem, not even in China. Paintings depicting legends about Minghuang and Yang Guifei had been created throughout Chinese history, but most of them illustrated just one or two episodes from these stories. Nor is any ancient Chinese painting illustrating the entire poem recorded or extant today.[160] Even though illustrating the *Chōgonka* had a long tradition in Japan since the Heian period, Sansetsu was still proud to claim that he had created a new version himself.[161]

How, then, did Sansetsu come to conceive the whole structure of this extensive painting? Researchers have observed that he was friends with the learned scholars of his day. Thus, he may have had help on the correct interpretation of the poem as he designed the scroll.[162] However, even if he did understand the ballad more subtly than other painters, it remained no easy task to translate that narrative into a visual work of art.

In Sansetsu's Japan of the early seventeenth-century, great quantities of paintings as well as books were being imported from China. The images preserved by the pre-eminent Kano Tan'yū (1602–74) in *Small Sketches by Tan'yū (Tan'yū shukuzu)* clearly show that many Chinese paintings and printed materials were at the Japanese artist's disposal. That *Small Sketches by Tan'yū* includes images from Chinese printed books[163] suggests that, in the eyes of Tan'yū

and later Kano School painters, these printed images were as important as paintings.[164]

The Chinese illustrated book, *Illustrated Arguments in the Mirror of the Emperors (Dijian tushuo; Teikan zusetsu)* is perhaps the best-known example of a book whose images were later widely used by Japanese artists. This title was originally created as an imperial textbook to educate the young Ming emperor Wanli (r. 1573–1620). It appeared in Japan at least as early as 1606, and went on to inspire and generate many Japanese mural paintings as well as reprints.[165] Numerous other books provide evidence that ample resources from China circulated in the Japanese art market.[166] Not only were many books imported into Japan, some of them were newly published when they got sold to Japan.[167]

So, what kinds of Chinese visual sources might Sansetsu have drawn on in the creation of the *Chōgonka* scrolls? The following essay examines paintings and, in particular, prints from Ming China, that Sansetsu might have taken advantage of in the creation of his masterpiece, especially focusing on the figure representations.

SOURCES IN MING PAINTINGS OF THE IMPERIAL PALACE AND DECADENT LIFESTYLES

Among the possible resources at Sansetsu's disposal in early seventeenth-century Japan, imported Ming paintings, especially those from the southern cities of Suzhou and Hangzhou, stand out. Professor Itakura has pointed out paintings like Tang Yin's *Dreaming of Immortality in a Thatched Hut (Mengxian caotang tu;* see fig. 43) and Qiu Ying's *Jiucheng Palace (Jiuchenggong tu)* as possible sources.[168] He also observes that the many forgeries from late-Ming Suzhou recorded in Tan'yū's *Small Sketches* are evidence that such paintings circulated in seventeenth-century Japan. Moreover, they could have provided

Kano Sansetsu, 'The wizard and Yang converse' (from **The Daoist's interview with the soul of Yang Guifei**), *Song of Lasting Sorrow,* scroll 2, the sixth length of silk.

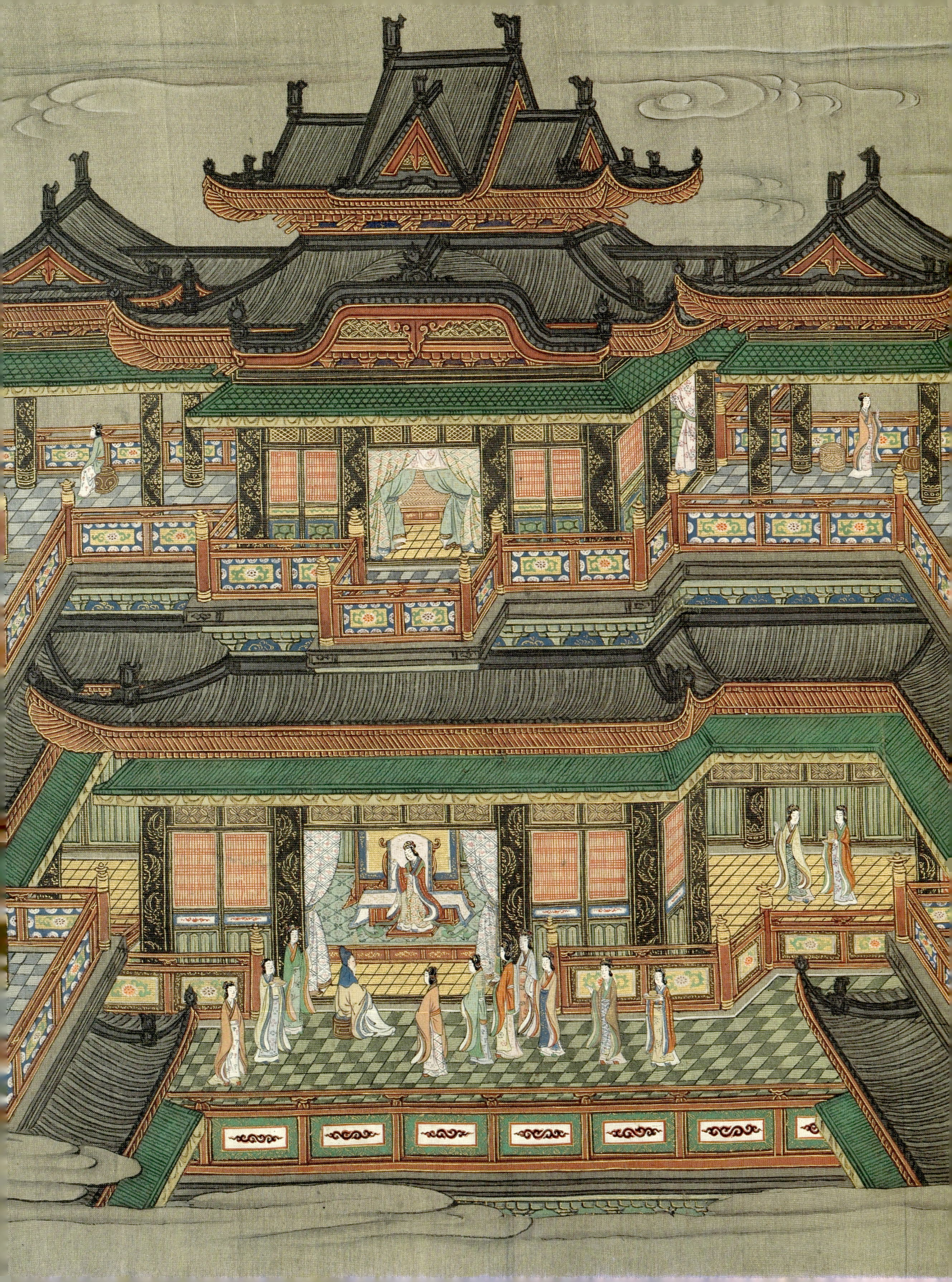

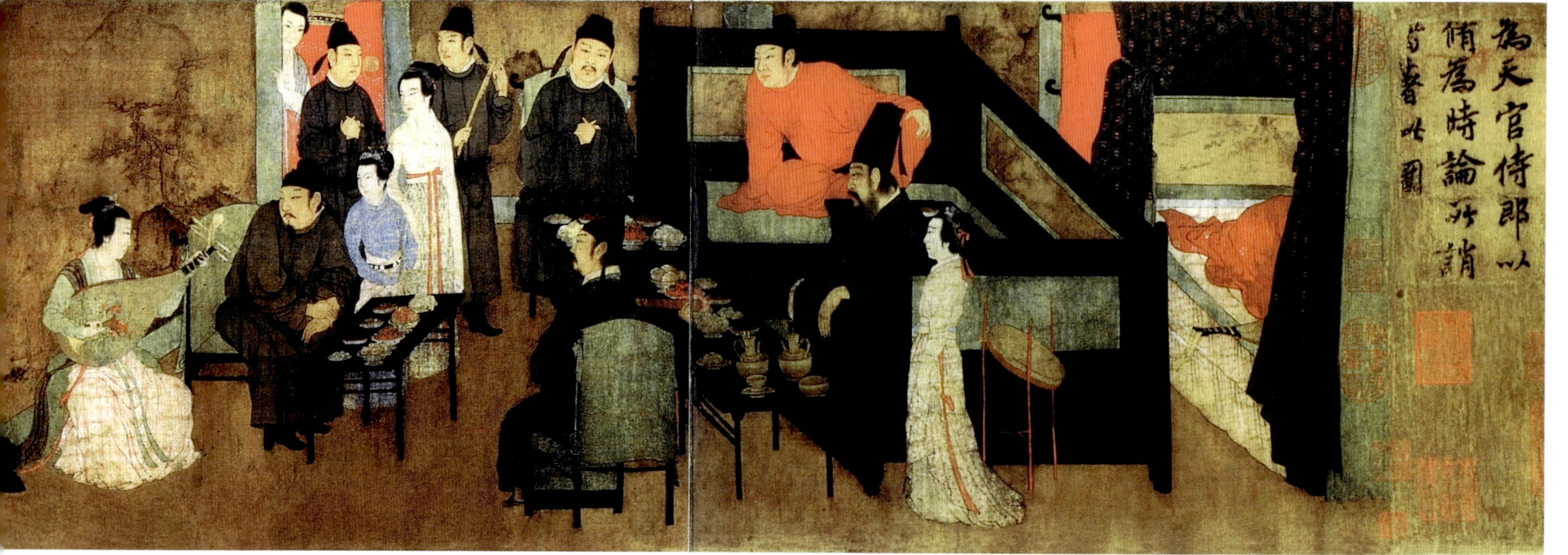

為天官侍郎
偹為待論所
韶
寫此圖

FIG 89 Gu Hongzhong (10th century), *Night Revels of Han Xizai (Han Xizai yeyantu)*. Detail of a handscroll; ink and colours on silk, 28.7 x 333.5 cm. Palace Museum, Beijing.

Sansetsu with motifs and type-forms for the depiction of palace structures.[169] Judging from the great sum of late Ming forgeries extant today, it is hard to imagine that Sansetsu would not somehow have made use of them. The spurious signatures of Chinese old masters on these paintings were placed there to bewilder Ming collectors,[170] but these same works were no doubt also being imported into the Japanese art market from China in great numbers. Japanese painters like Kano Tan'yū were eager to record these paintings to employ later for creative inspiration.

Sansetsu might have learned from these paintings not simply about motifs, but also about floral and ornate fabric patterns and gaudy colour schemes, as well as the meticulous detailing of imperial lifestyles. Perhaps the most famous decadent lifestyle to capture the Chinese artist's imagination is depicted in the famous handscroll, *Night Revels of Han Xizai (Han Xizai yeyantu)*, about the hedonism of a courtier. One Ming version of the scroll painting attributed to Tang Yin, now housed in Chongqing Municipal Museum in Sichuan, illustrates the highly extravagant lifestyle that could be enjoyed by wealthy people in the Ming. The so-called Tang Yin version adopts the basic compositional scheme of the famous early version by Gu Hongzhong (tenth century; fig. 89), but it also deliberately fills the whole scroll with excessive and conspicuous Ming material culture (fig. 90). Flowery – or even gaudily patterned – fabrics cover much of the furniture, with further precious objects added to celebrate the opulent lifestyle. Even though this painting illustrates a story that took place in tenth-century China, the affluence connoted by the material culture in it was that enjoyed by the rich and famous in the Ming dynasty.[171] The pronounced materialism seen in this kind of painting may have inspired Sansetsu, for a similar ambiance exudes from his *Chōgonka* painting.

SOURCES IN MING WOODBLOCK PRINTS

As noted above, in Kano Tan'yū's *Small Sketches* there are images of Ming woodblock prints recorded alongside the paintings, and it is these that probably carry more significance than the paintings when attempting to analyse and locate the sources of Sansetsu's inspiration.[172] When Sansetsu's son Kano Einō (1631–97) recorded that his father collected images from ancient paintings to create his *Chōgonka* work (see p. 144),[173] it is likely that these images did not include just paintings. The sheer quantity of Chinese woodblock-printed books that had been imported into Japan during the sixteenth and seventeenth centuries, as well as the quality of the illustrations in them by Chinese artisans and artists, undoubtedly provided remarkable resources for Japanese artists.[174]

Furthermore, by comparing Sansetsu's *Chōgonka* painting with prints illustrating Minghuang and Guifei legends, we may arrive at a keener understanding of Sansetsu's creation. In the section that follows, Ming woodblock-printed images that directly illustrate the Minghuang and Guifei legends will be compared with the figure presentations in Sansetsu's *Chōgonka* painting. In addition, other

CHINESE ROMANCE FROM A JAPANESE BRUSH

154

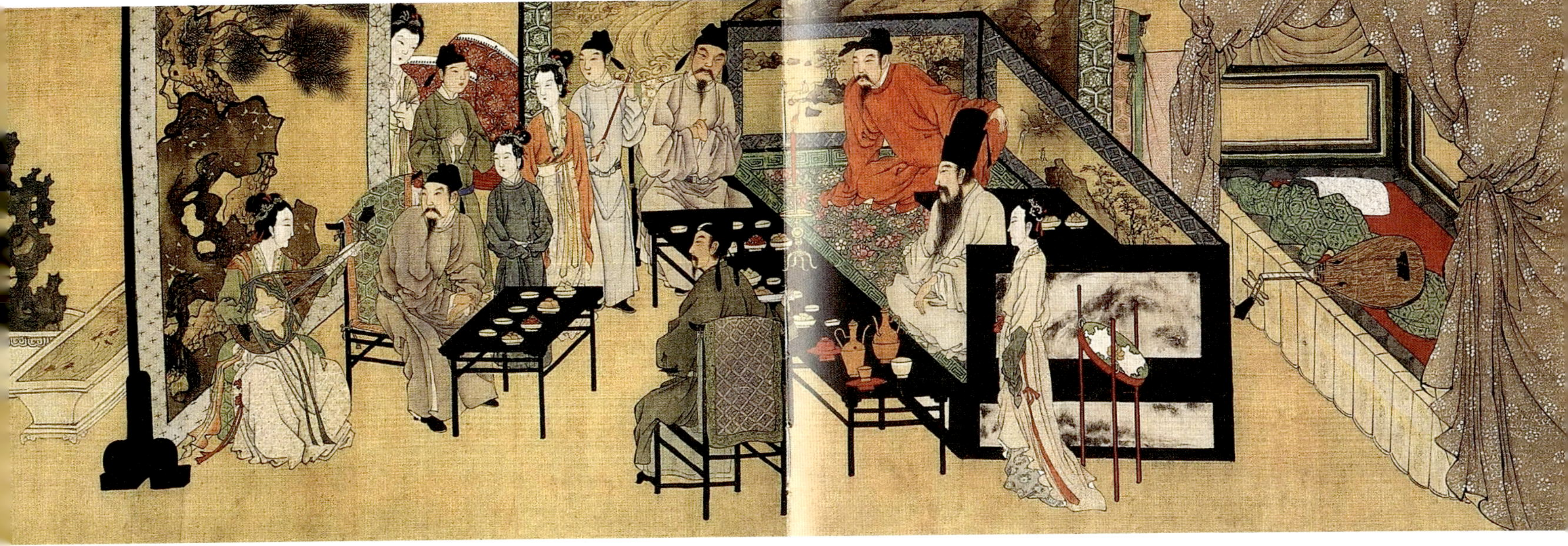

illustrations not directly related to Minghuang and Guifei legends will also be examined, since Sansetsu may also have been inspired by these.

IMAGES OF YANG GUIFEI LEGENDS IN CHINESE ILLUSTRATED BOOKS

In Ming woodblock prints, illustrations of the Minghuang and Guifei stories can be found in drama books as well as in novels. One Yuan drama entitled, *Tang Minghuang [Listening to] the Rain Falling on Chinese Parasols on an Autumn Night* (*Tang Minghuang Qiuye Wutongyu*; hereafter *Wutongyu*), even inspired three different versions of illustrations. Written by the famous Chinese playwright Bai Pu (1226–*c*.1306), this Yuan play retold the love story of Minghuang and Yang Guifei and became a very popular drama from the time of its creation. From the mid-Ming period, when the publishing industry was thriving, this work was selected for and illustrated in anthologies of Yuan drama, such as *Selected Yuan Dramas* (*Yuanqu xuan*) published in 1615–16, *Ancient Dramas* (*Gu zaju*) published in 1619, and *Newly-Carved Ancient and Modern Famous Dramas – Anthology of Libation to the River* (*Xinjuan gujin mingju Leijiang ji*; hereafter *Leijiang ji*), published in 1633.[175]

Like most Yuan dramas, *Wutongyu* comprises four acts. There are two illustrations in the *Leijiang ji* anthology (figs 91, 92), while *Gu zaju* and *Yuanqu xuan* have four each (figs 93–96 and 97–100, respectively). In comparing them, it is clear that the *Leijiang ji* prints (figs 91, 92) may be based on the *Gu zaju*

ones (figs 93, 94). The very similar compositions found in both versions show their affiliations. Even though one of the episodes in the *Leijiang ji* (fig. 92) is actually about Yang Guifei being offered lychees (her favourite fruit) that have been brought a thousand miles for her, the artist composed a dancing scene. In the *Yuanqu xuan* edition, however, a picture of the same title depicts Minghuang and Guifei enjoying the day, as a soldier rushes in with the lychees (fig. 98). The *Gu zaju* and *Leijiang ji* illustrations were both carved in minute detail (note especially the flowery patterns on the costumes and carpets), exemplifying the trend towards extravagant expressionism in the late Ming period.

In fact, the playwright Bai Pu conceived the last scene as a rather regretful episode in which Minghuang dreams about Yang Guifei, but wakes up to a gloomy world without his beloved. The lingering mournful tone was what Bai Pu meant to create in this drama. The illustrations in the *Leijiang ji* (fig. 91) and *Gu zaju* (fig. 93) depict this ephemeral dream as a happy reunion between the couple. Only the *Yuanqu xuan* edition pointedly describes a remorseful Minghuang standing in the night, after a swift sweet dream, facing a neglected garden covered with falling leaves and listening to the rain falling on the parasols (fig. 97).

In one way, the *Yuanqu xuan* illustrations are more subdued in their depiction, and more faithful to the original text. The other two versions, published later, show happier scenes. The brief happiness of the

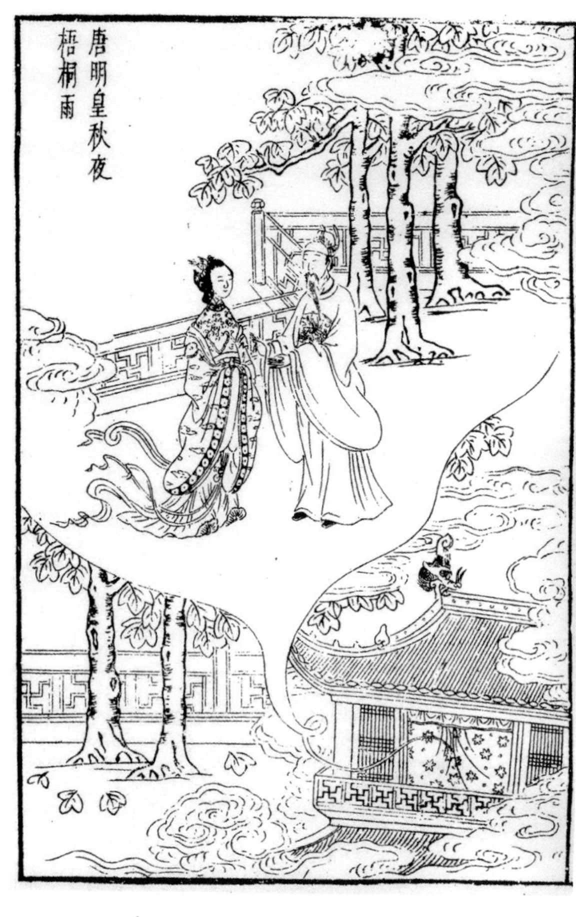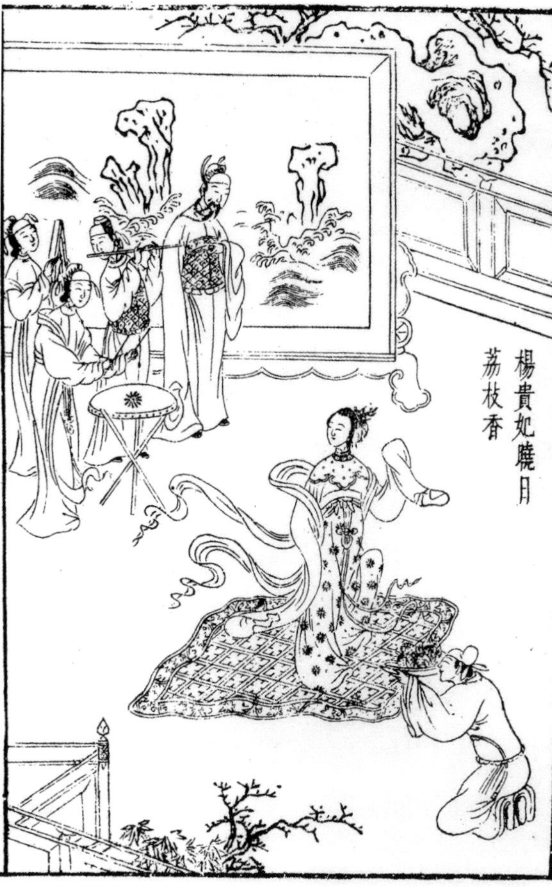

FIG 91 'Minghuang dreams of Yang Guifei', *Wutongyu* (*Leijiang ji* anthology), 1633. Woodblock-printed book.

FIG 92 'Yang Guifei is presented with lychees', *Wutongyu* (*Leijiang ji* anthology), 1633. Woodblock-printed book.

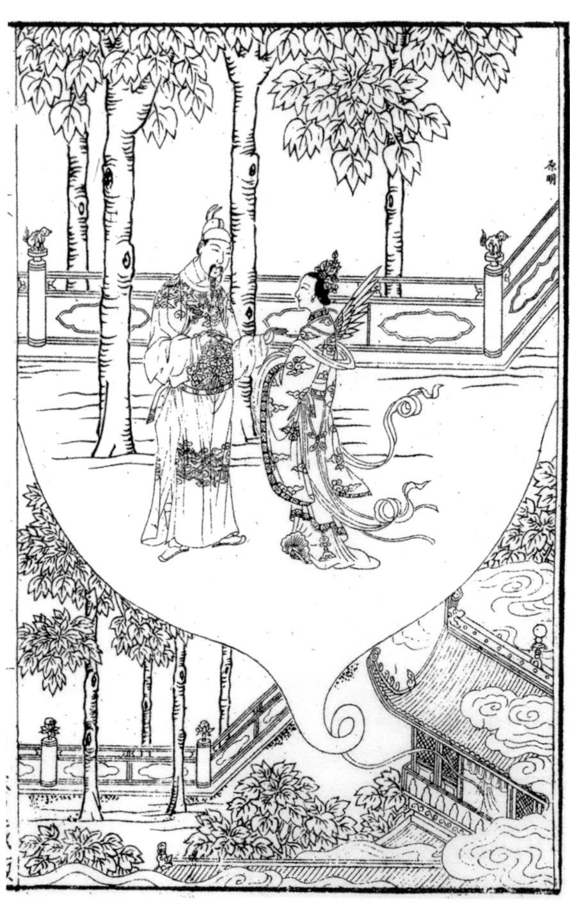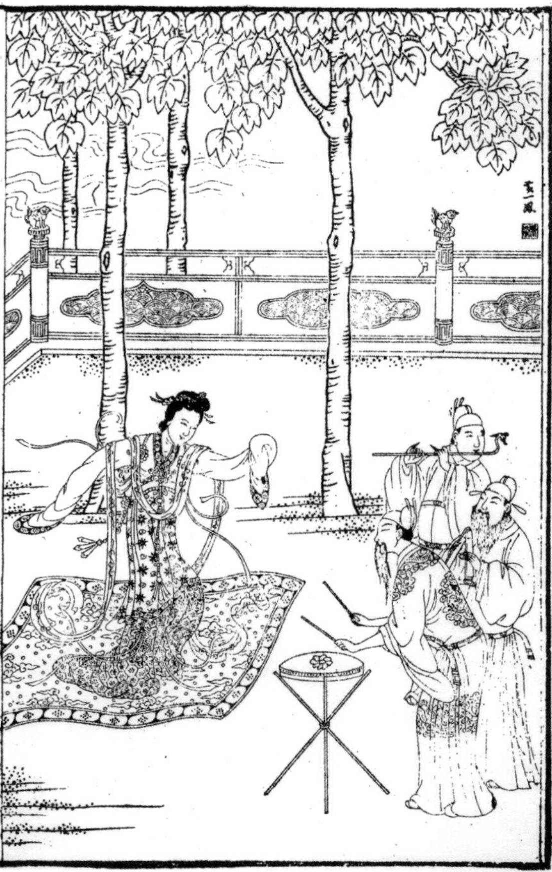

FIG 93 'Minghuang dreams of Yang Guifei', *Wutongyu* (*Gu zaju* anthology), 1619. Woodblock-printed book.

FIG 94 'Yang Guifei's dancing scene', *Wutongyu* (*Gu zaju* anthology), 1619. Woodblock-printed book.

FIGS 95, 96 Illustrations from the drama *Wutongyu* (*Gu zaju* anthology), 1619. Woodblock-printed book.

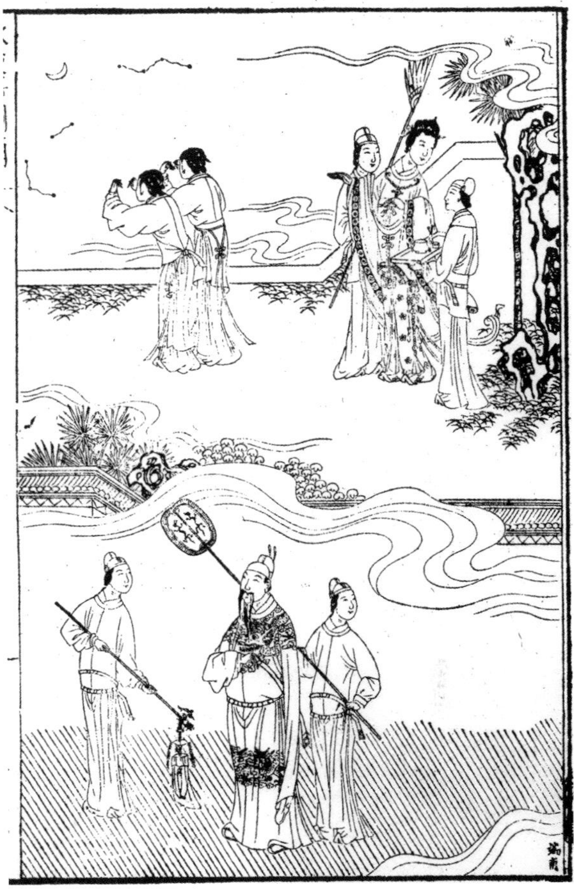

FIG 97 'Listening to the rain falling on the parasols', *Wutongyu* (*Yuanqu xuan* anthology), 1615–16. Woodblock-printed book.

FIG 98 'Yang Guifei is presented with lychees', *Wutongyu* (*Yuanqu xuan* anthology), 1615–16. Woodblock-printed book.

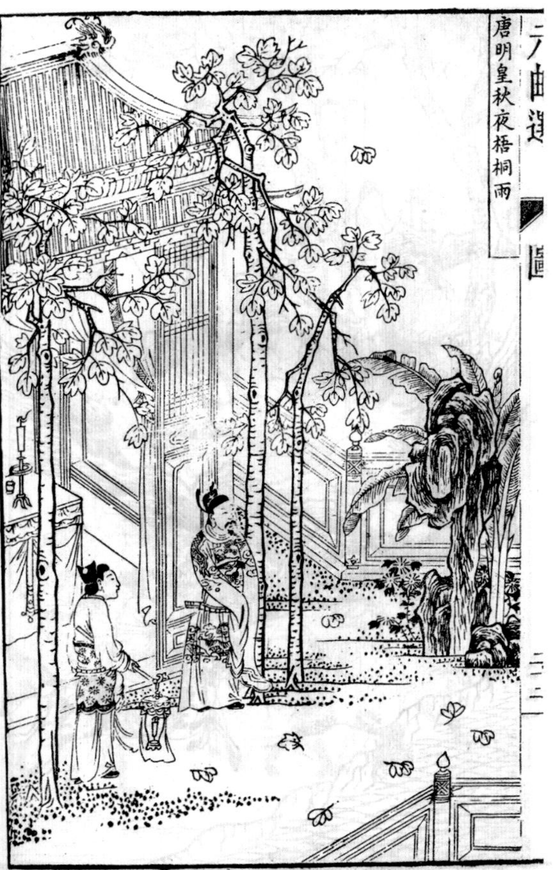

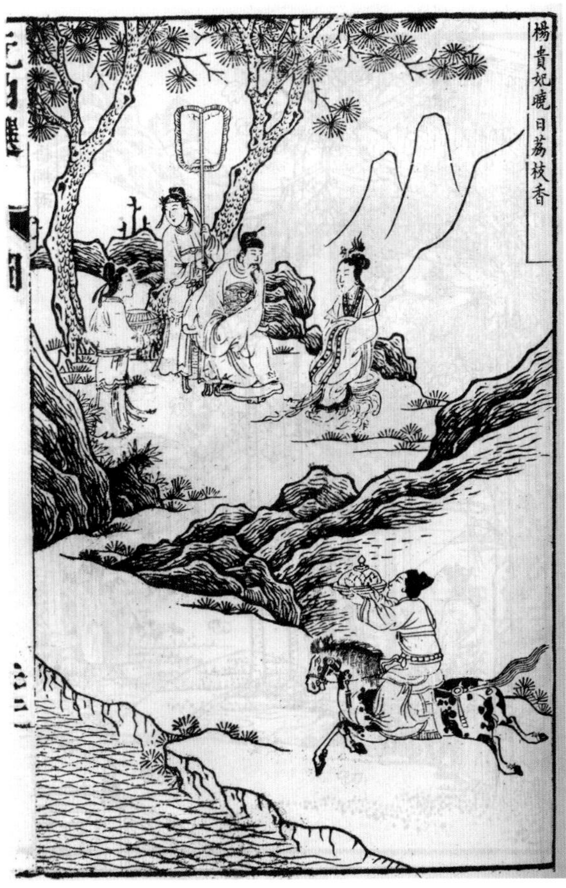

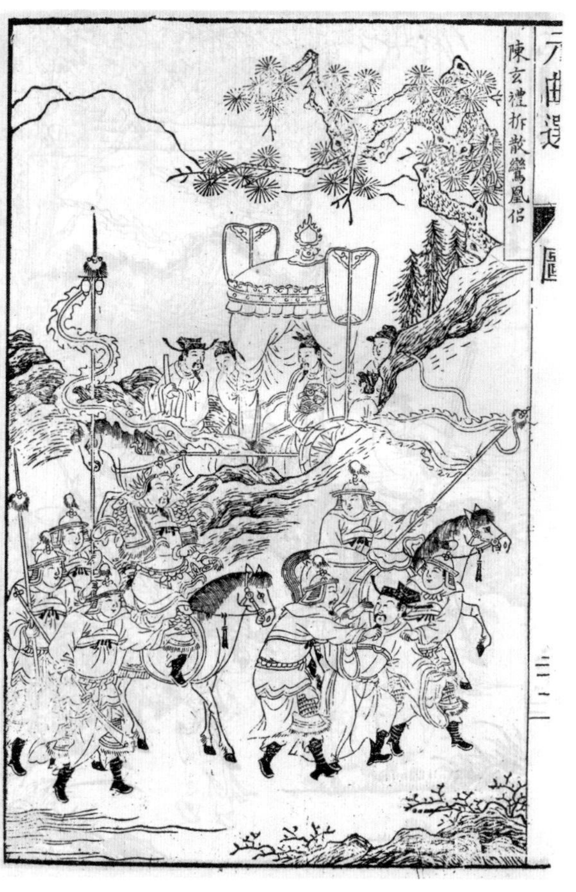

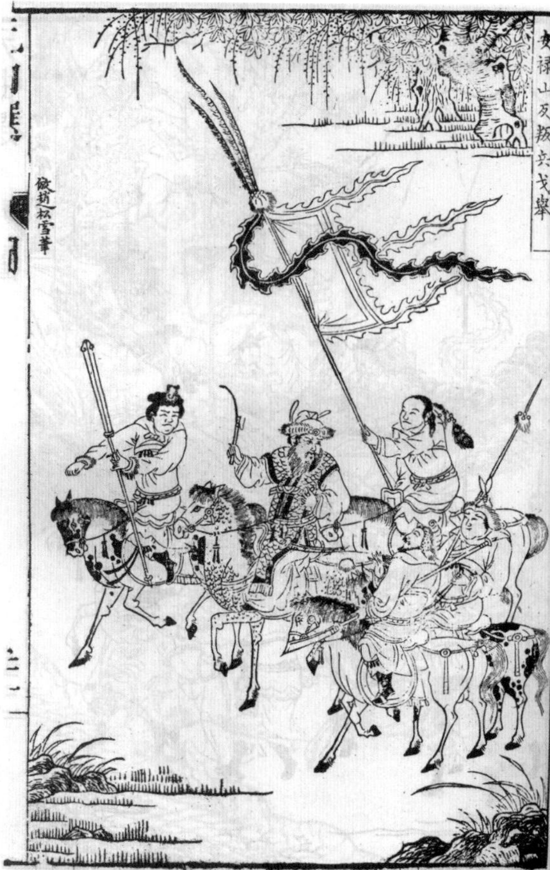

Fig 99 'Minghuang and the inner court escape', *Wutongyu* (*Yuanqu xuan* anthology), 1615–16. Woodblock-printed book.

Fig 100 'An Lushan rebels', *Wutongyu* (*Yuanqu xuan* anthology), 1615–16. Woodblock-printed book.

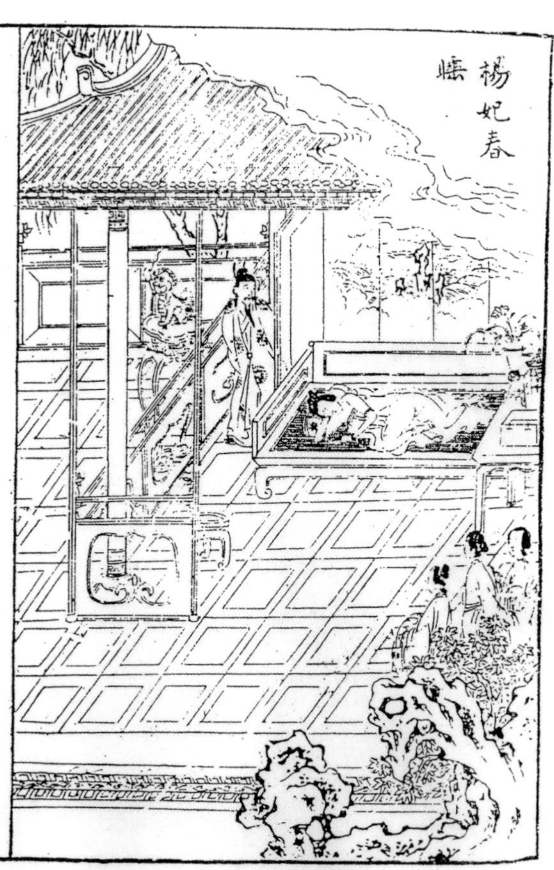

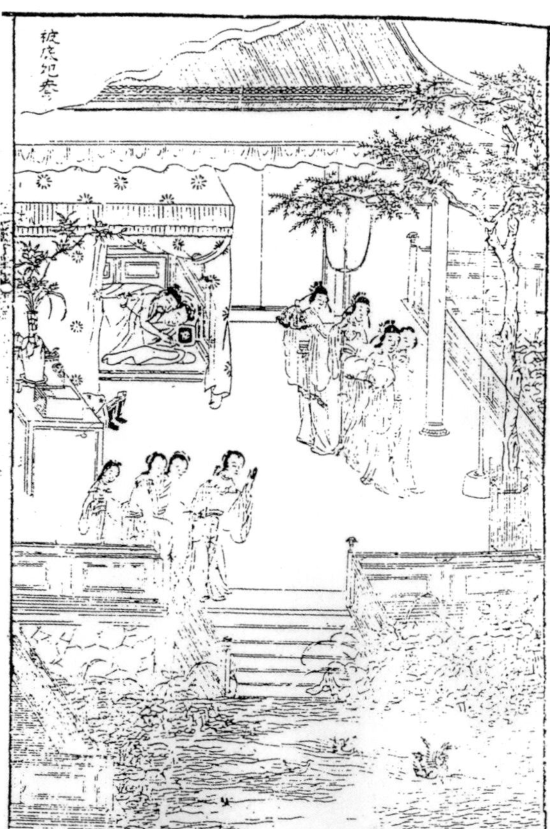

Fig 101 'Consort Yang sleeping seductively' (*Yangfei chunshui*), *Complete History of Yang Guifei* (*Tang Guifei Yang Taizhen quanshi*). Woodblock-printed book.

Fig 102 'Coupling under the comforter' (*Beidi yuanyang*), *Complete History of Yang Guifei* (*Tang Guifei Yang Taizhen quanshi*). Woodblock-printed book.

dream scene was meant, through contrast, to high-light the bitter reality that Minghuang was going to endure for the rest of his life, but this is turned into a seemingly happy-ending reunion. It seems that as time went by, the tragic mood of the *Wutongyu* was increasingly neglected, as late-Ming readers and pub-lishers leaned towards a happier conclusion to the story.

Not only were Yuan dramas republished with new Ming illustrations, some Ming dramas also adapted stories about Minghuang and Guifei.[176] One of the more famous ones was *Tale of the Startled Geese (Jinghong ji)*.[177] Another, less well-known drama is *Spring Outing of the Emperor and Consort (Difei chunyu)*.[178] The former has thirty-nine acts and the latter just one. The *Jinghong ji* focuses on the complicated love triangle between Minghuang, Guifei and her supposed love-rival Meifei (Plum Consort),[179] while the *Difei chunyu* relates a single episode in which Minghuang and Guifei enjoy a wonderful spring outing. A love rivalry and a pleas-ure outing are the new focal points, rather than any kind of portrait of the mournful, retired monarch. The illustrations in these dramas are not of the same standard as those in the *Wutongyu,* indicating that these two books were probably more affordable, which in turn sheds some light on the reading prefer-ences of a broad public.

Fiction was another popular literary form wherein the Yang Guifei legends were elaborated or reinterpreted. At least one work of fiction, *Complete History of Yang Guifei (Tang Guifei Yang Taizhen quanshi* or just *Yang Taizhen quanshi*), was written and illustrated during the Ming dynasty.[180] The name Taizhen in this title is the Daoist name Yang Guifei took when she became a nun – an arrangement that enabled her first marriage to be annulled in prepara-tion for her union with Minghuang. Judging by its

illustrations, this book was an adaptation of various anecdotes from other documents and books. Some of the illustrations are shockingly graphic and erotic. In one picture, 'Consort Yang sleeping seductively' (*Yangfei chunshui*; fig. 101), Yang Guifei is shown still sleeping at noon, having been exhausted by the previ-ous night's sensual pleasure with the emperor. After holding court, the emperor comes to visit Guifei, only to find her lying asleep in bed covered by a very thin layer of gauze, through which the contours of her voluptuous body can be seen.

Another illustration from the same book, 'Cou-pling under the Comforter' (*Beidi yuanyang*; fig. 102) depicts Minghuang and Guifei making love. The cou-ple are shown lying in bed one day, as some palace ladies marvel at a beautiful pair of mandarin ducks (*yuanyang*) swimming by. Minghuang boasts that the beauty of the pair of ducks cannot compare with that of him and his beloved. The drapery is partly drawn back to enable the viewer to spy Minghuang on top of Guifei, smiling, as they embrace one another with bare arms. Even though there are only a few such erotically charged pictures, it is not difficult to imag-ine that Minghuang and Guifei legends would have served as a luscious topic for pornographic publica-tions. This book, with its scandalous text and a few seductive illustrations, was obviously targeted at such a readership.

When we consider the illustrations in *Wutongyu* and *Yang Taizhen quanshi,* it seems clear that there was a gradual shift of focus from following the text to concentrating on the erotic elements of the story. In *Wutongyu,* the dancing and dream reunion scenes are the primary focus, whereas in *Yang Taizhen quan-shi* it is the explicit lovemaking scene. The Minghuang and Guifei legends provided material for artists to portray sensual pleasures, something with which late Ming people were very familiar.

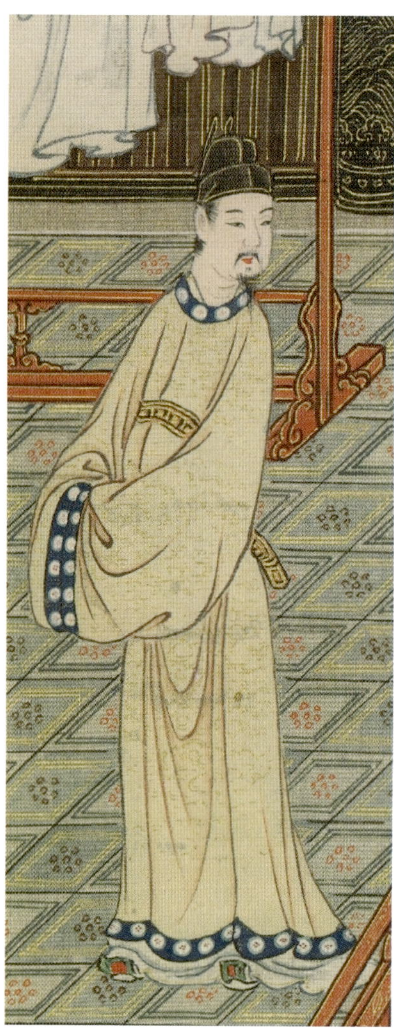

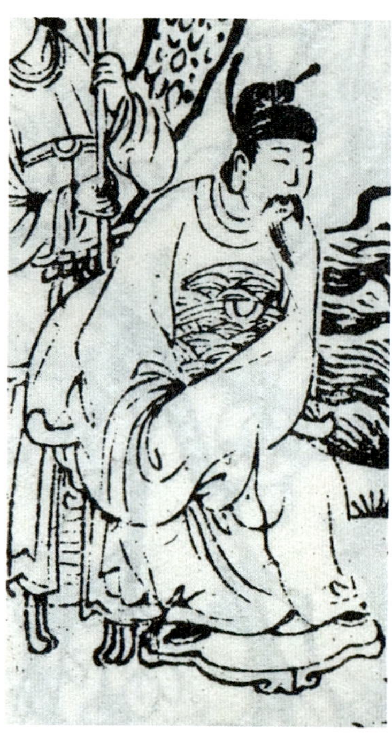

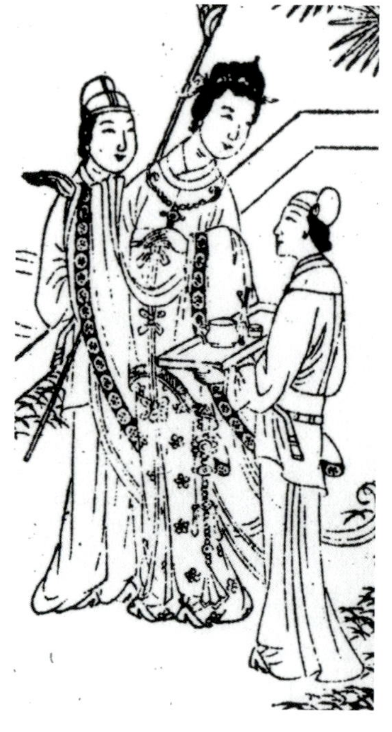

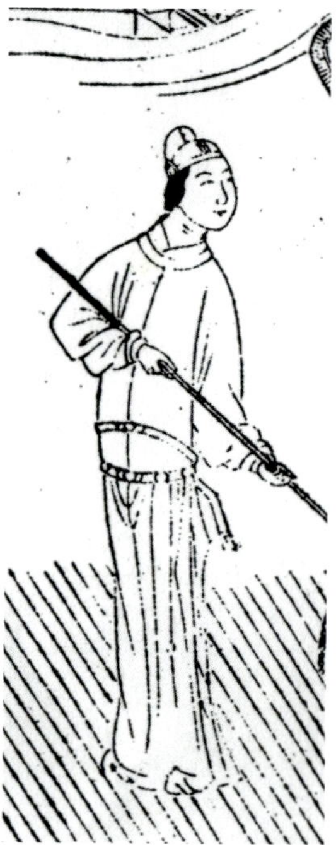

SIMILAR IMAGES IN LATE MING PAINTINGS AND BOOK ILLUSTRATIONS

Even though Sansetsu's *Chōgonka* painting contains no direct compositional resemblance to these pictures in *Wutongyu* and *Yang Taizhen quanshi*, the figure types and poses do reveal a connection. One example is the *Chōgonka* scene in which Guifei has just finished taking her bath in the Huaqing Pool. Too weak to stand on her own, she is supported by female attendants as Minghuang watches and waits for her. His hands folded and concealed by long, wide sleeves, Minghuang's torso is slightly twisted as he turns to his left to look at his beautiful concubine (fig. 103). The angled pose and folded sleeves quite closely resemble those of the figure of Minghuang in *Wutongyu* (*Yuanqu xuan* anthology; fig. 104), even if he is seated in this illustration. Figures with twisting torsos and attenuated neck-lines feature in a number of late-Ming woodblock prints, including some in the *Wutongyu* (*Gu zaju* anthology; figs 105, 106).

If Sansetsu was not directly inspired by these illus-trations, he may have been by other late-Ming wood-block prints, since this kind of elongated figure with its distinctive curvy torso was a popular way to render figures. Yang Guifei is depicted in this way in the danc-ing scene of Sansetsu's scroll, where her floating sleeve held up high and the quivery ribbons of her robe accentuate the curvaceous and slender shape of her body (fig. 107). In fact, the standard figure of a Tang beauty such as Yang Guifei was far more substantial than is portrayed here.[181] This slender body-type is more akin to certain female types seen in late-Ming woodblock prints. A scene in a Yuan drama in *Newly-Carved Ancient and Modern Famous Dramas – Anthology of the Willow Branches* (*Xinjuan gujin mingju Liuzhi ji*) shows several courtesans dancing (fig. 108).[182] The poses, and the trembling and flying sleeves and ribbons are quite similar in both pictures, particularly with regard to the stress put on the rhythm of the drawing outlines. Actually, dancing girls were a most popular theme in late-Ming prints, and Sansetsu would have had little trouble locating one in an

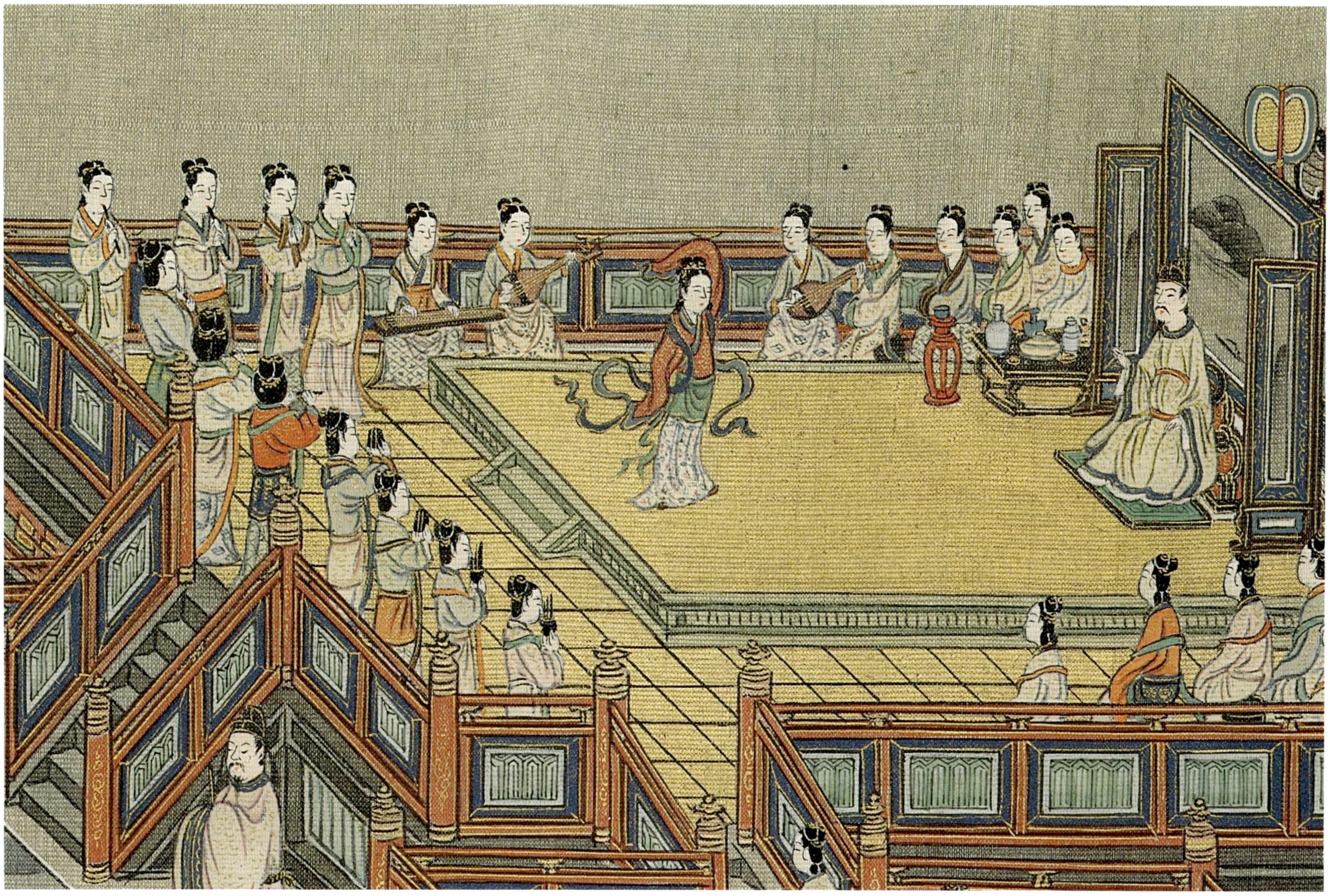

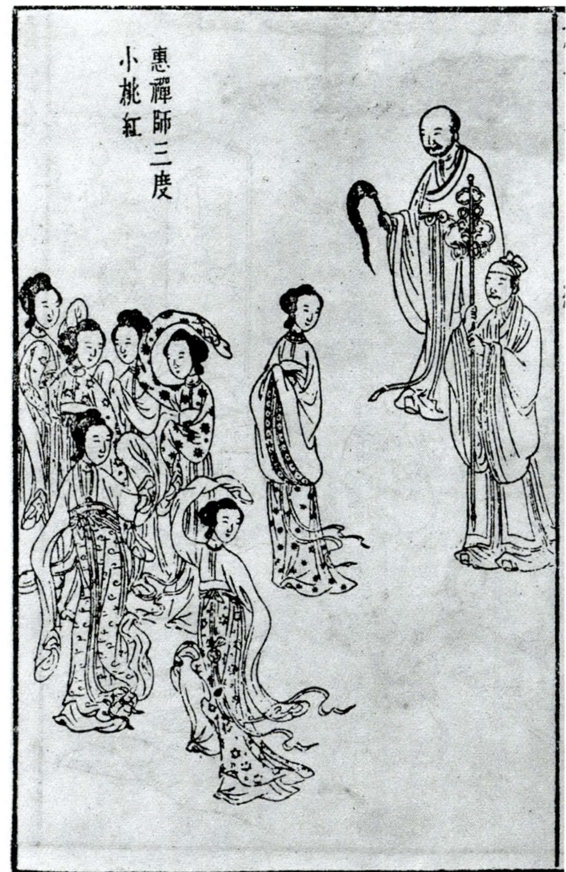

FIG 107 Kano Sansetsu,
'Yang Guifei dances before
Minghuang' (from **General
An Lushan rebels**), *Song of
Lasting Sorrow*; scroll 1,
the fourth length of silk.

FIG 108 A dancing scene
from the drama anthology
Liuzhi ji, 1633.

imported Chinese book as a model for his painting.

Nonetheless, as has been noted, the so-called *Suzhou pian* forgeries would have provided Sansetsu with numerous meticulously executed details of the prosperous material life that late-Ming people enjoyed.[183] Figures in these kinds of paintings were usually rendered in Qiu Ying or Tang Yin style, so it is likely enough that Sansetsu would have depicted his figures in those styles. When we compare four main figures in Sansetsu's *Chōgonka* painting (fig. 109) with Qiu Ying (fig. 110) and Tang Yin (fig. 111) paintings and a late-Ming print (fig. 112), it is clear they all share certain characteristics, including the poses, and the slender, round-shouldered body types.

Indeed, the interest in showy, floating ribbons and on curvy figural contours makes Sansetsu's figures appear closer to those in the late-Ming prints. Identical figure types and comparable compositions in the *Chōgonka* painting (fig. 113), and one such illustration (fig. 114) from the *Anthology of Poetry in Wu Region (Wusao ji)*, further strengthen the argument

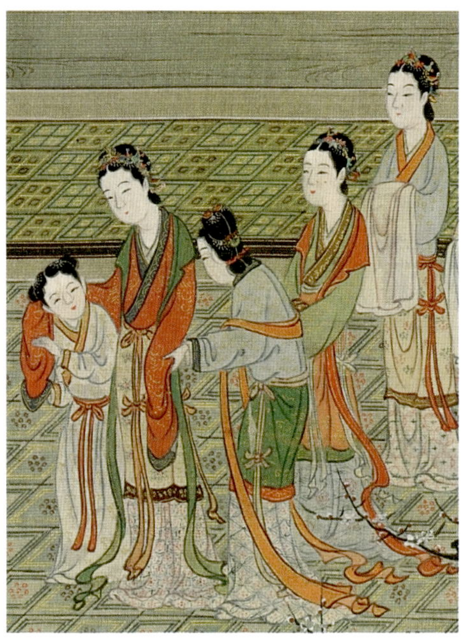 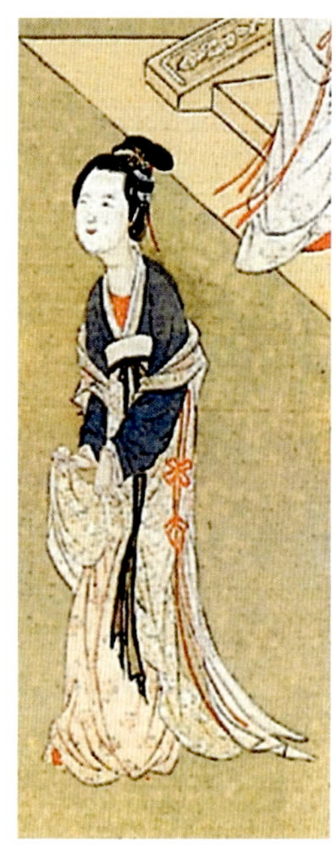 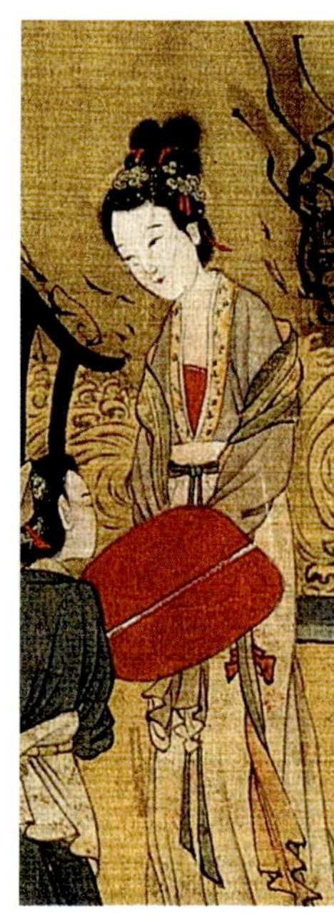 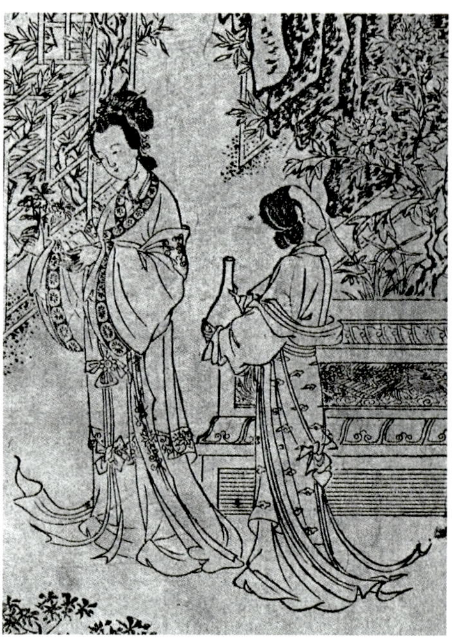

that Sansetsu employed late-Ming woodblock prints as his inspiration in creating his unique painting. The portrayal of the rebel generals (fig. 115) is also quite similar to that seen in the illustrations of the *Wutongyu* drama (*Yuanqu xuan* anthology; fig. 116).

Small Sketches by Tan'yū, introduced above, includes copies of woodblock-printed illustrations to the late-Ming popular drama, *Story of the Western Wing (Xixiang ji)*,[184] which is further evidence of the availability in the seventeenth century of these printed images. Such woodblock-printed illustrations, whether originally made for drama anthologies or for entertaining fiction, provided ample Chinese figure-types for Japanese painters to choose from. That these printed images were recorded alongside Chinese paintings also clearly shows the attitude of later Kano painters towards those materials, namely that they were treasured as much as paintings.

This short chapter has briefly examined possible sources – chiefly among paintings and prints – that Sansetsu may have drawn on as he began to compose his *Chōgonka* painting. Ming paintings, especially those made in Suzhou then imported into Japan, seem to be likely sources for the depiction of the magnificent palace scenes, and the rich descriptions of

material culture and decadent lifestyles. As well as these, Ming woodblock prints presented another valuable repertoire for the creation of the figure-types in the *Chōgonka* painting. Considering that other Kano painters extensively copied Ming woodblock-printed book illustrations, such as *Illustrated Arguments in the Mirror of the Emperors (Teikan zu)*, it is probable that Sansetsu also made use of Chinese woodblock prints in the creation of his paintings.

The Minghuang–Yang Guifei stories in Ming woodblock prints and paintings are variously depicted – as elegant-but-sad or else emphasising earthly pleasures – but Kano Sansetsu, in spite of the rich materialism of his depiction, defined a singularly purer representation of Minghuang and Guifei, following the literary tradition. Minghuang's sorrow, in the middle, and Guifei's solitude, at the end, are clearly and unambiguously conveyed, echoing the original Chinese literary tradition and thus turning Bai Juyi's 'Song of Lasting Sorrow' into a romantic narrative painting in a grand style. This was a result achieved, probably, with the help of his literati friends and with the tremendous visual resources at his disposal at that time – something worthy of further investigation.

Above left to right:
Fig 109 Kano Sansetsu, detail of 'Yang Guifei emerges from the hot spring at Huaqing', (from **The Yang lady is discovered**), *Song of Lasting Sorrow*; scroll 1, the first length of silk.

Fig 110 Qiu Ying, a court lady in *Spring Morning in the Han Palace*. Detail of a handscroll; ink and colours on silk, 30.6 x 574.1 cm. National Palace Museum, Taipei.

Fig 111 A courtesan in *Night Revels of Han Xizai (Han Xizai yeyantu)*, attributed to Tang Yin. Detail of a handscroll; ink and colours on silk, 30.8 x 547.8 cm. Chongqing Municipal Museum, Sichuan Province.

Fig 112 A courtesan from a print in *Wusao ji*, 1637. Woodblock-printed book.

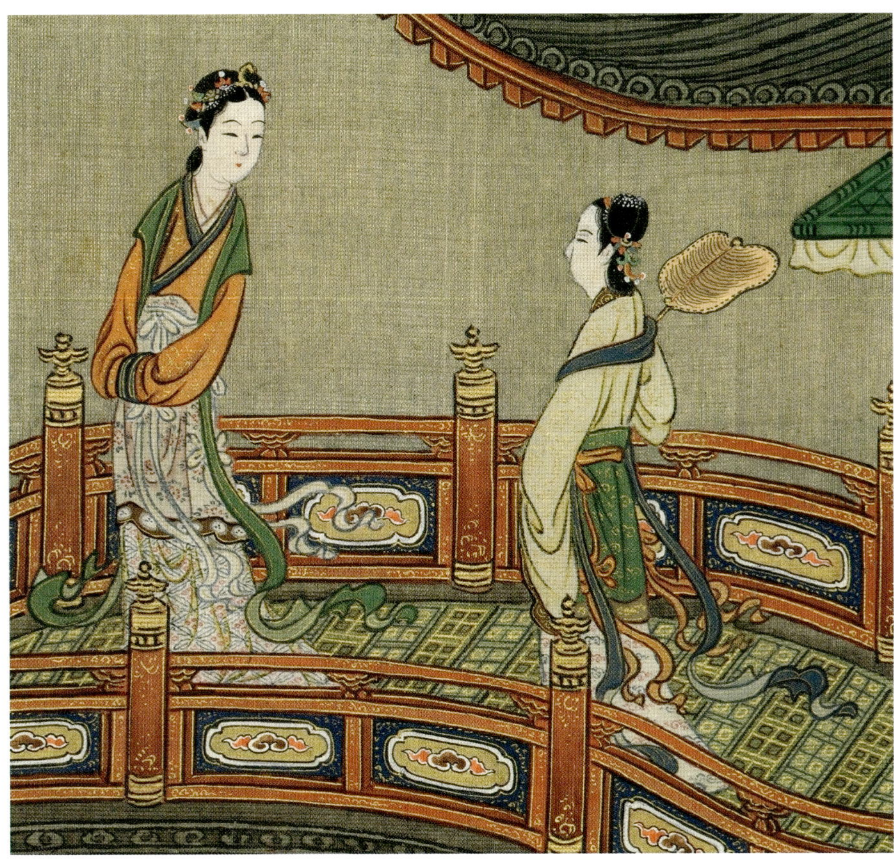

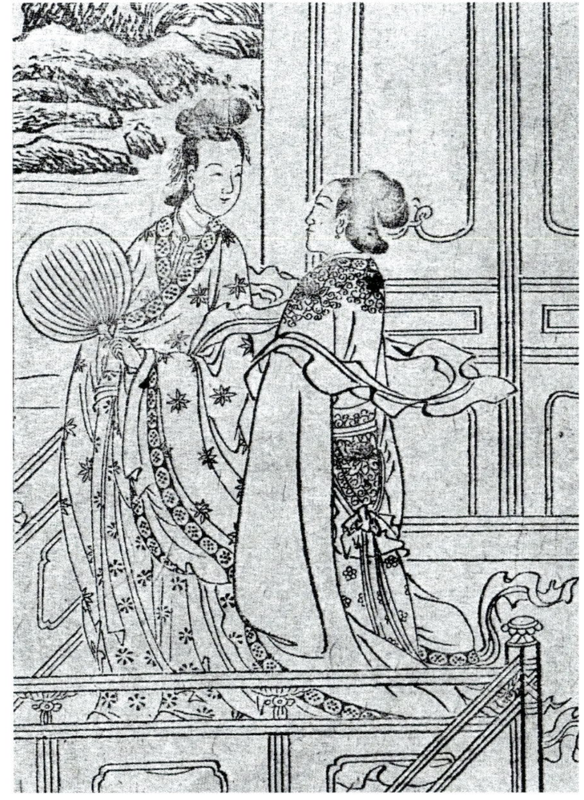

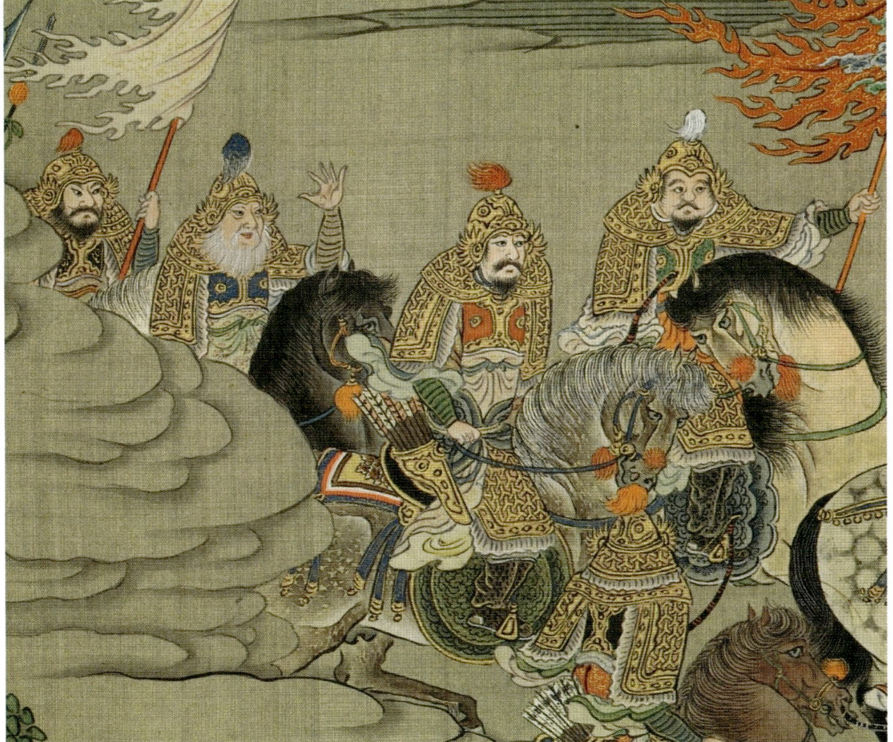

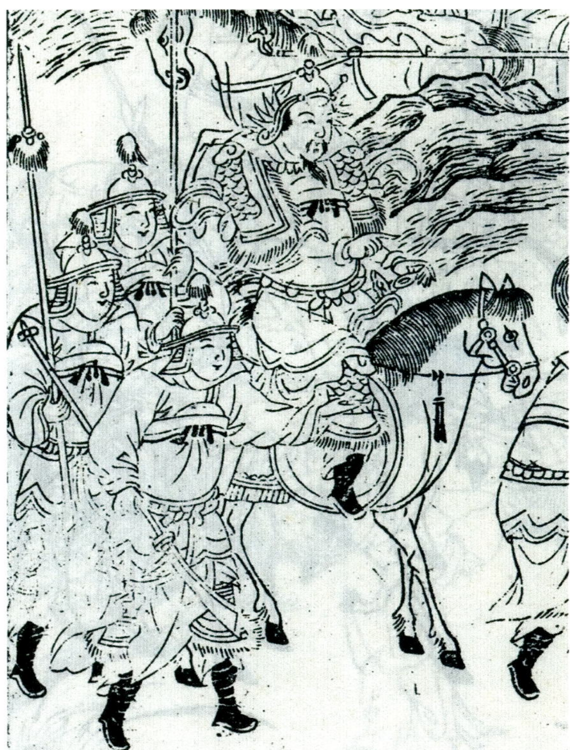

Top left:
Fig 113 Kano Sansetsu, female attendants on a bridge (from **Minghuang's dalliance**), *Song of Lasting Sorrow*; scroll 1, the second length of silk.

Top right:
Fig 114 Detail of courtesans from a print in *Wusao ji*, 1637. Woodblock-printed book.

Bottom leftt:
Fig 115 Kano Sansetsu, rebel generals (from **General An Lushan rebels**), *Song of Lasting Sorrow*; scroll 1, the fourth length of silk.

Bottom right:
Fig 116 Tang generals in *Wutongyu* (*Yuanqu xuan* anthology).

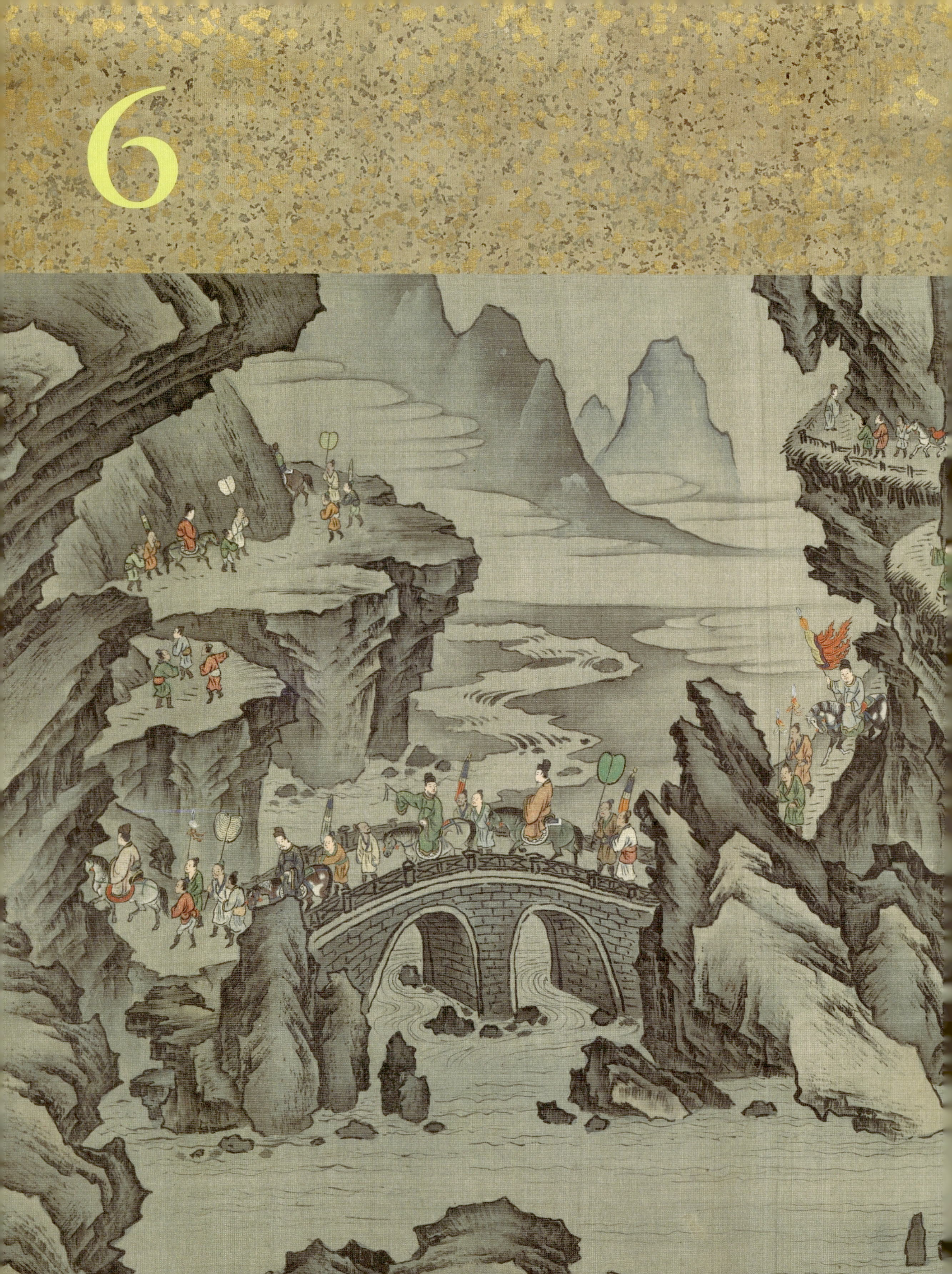

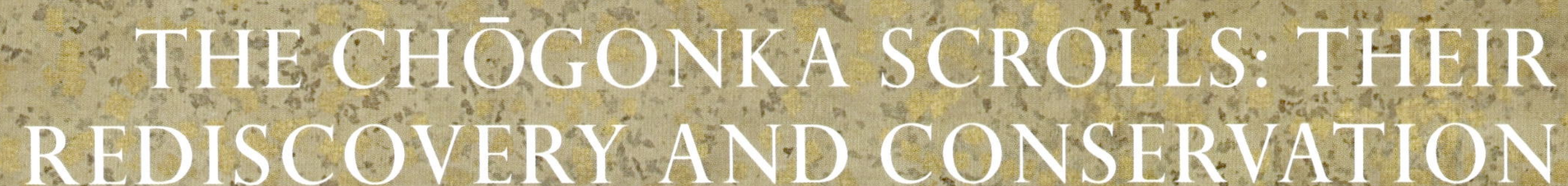

THE CHŌGONKA SCROLLS: THEIR REDISCOVERY AND CONSERVATION

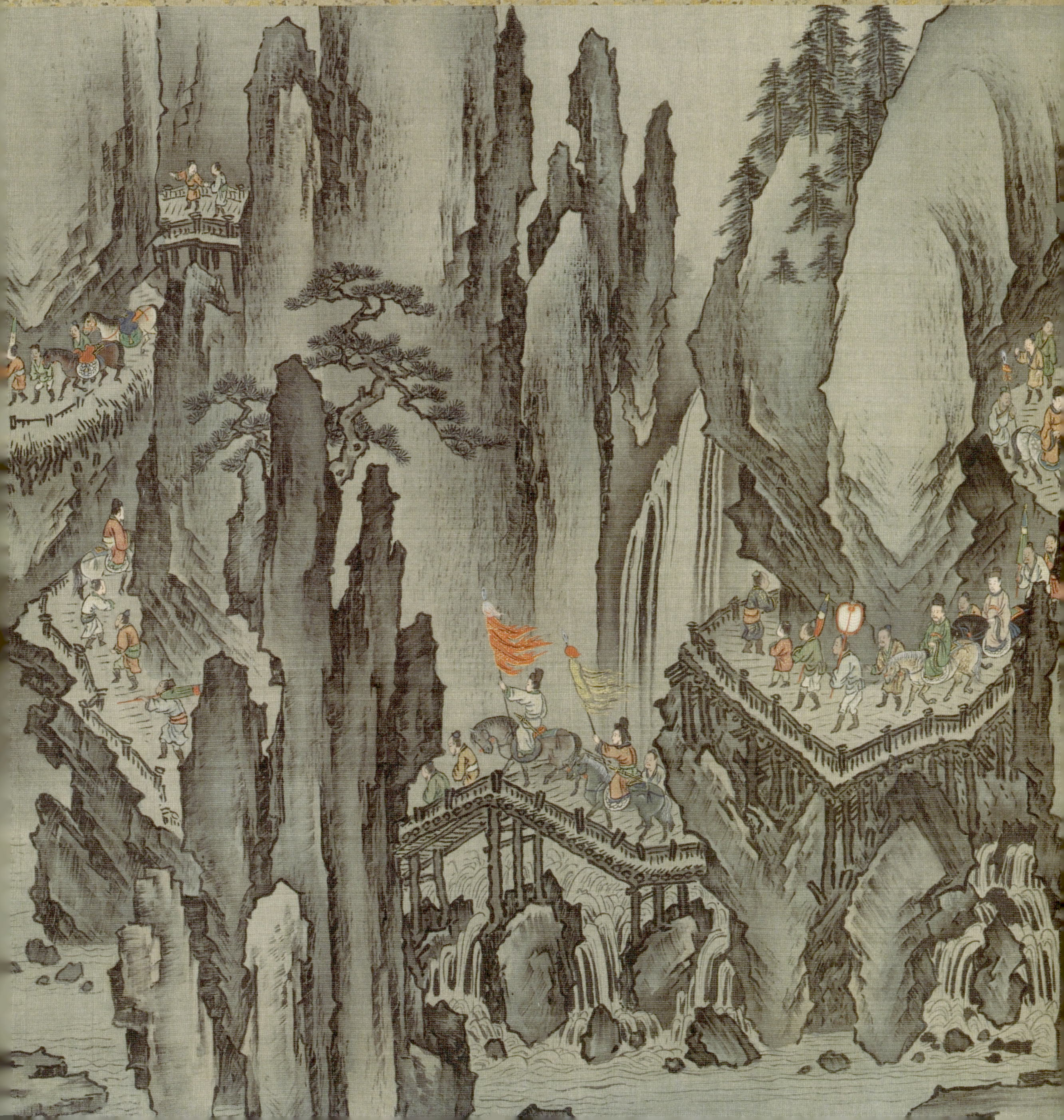

THERE ARE FEW RECORDS concerning Chester Beatty's (1875–1968) early acquisition of Japanese art. It is known that the collection of decorative arts (*netsuke*, *inro* and *tsuba*) was made in his early days in New York through the oriental art dealer Yamanaka Shokai. And it is well documented that the famous collection of Japanese woodblock prints was formed for him in the 1950s by the eminent English scholar Jack Hillier (1912–95). However, for some time the beautiful painted scrolls and albums in the Chester Beatty collection were mistakenly understood to be acquisitions of Beatty's later years.[185]

Prior to the August 1978 symposium on *Nara ehon* at the Library, I was researching the Beatty archives, but almost despaired of ever finding anything of relevance. Late one winter evening, I found an old and timeworn brown file in a long-abandoned box in the Library. That file contained the notes of Chester Beatty's visit to Japan in spring 1917, including the details of his visits to antique dealers in Kyoto, Nara, Osaka and Yokohama, together with details of his purchases as well as application forms for shipment to New York. From these archives it was possible to confirm that during his stay in Japan Chester Beatty purchased many *Nara ehon* and other painted albums and scrolls of the late Muromachi and Edo periods. The old file also included a photograph of a dinner party hosted by Yamanaka Sadaichi of Yamanaka Shokai in Osaka, in honour of Chester Beatty and his family (fig. 117).

In the same file I found a few letters and telegrams from Mr Yataro Okita of Nara, who acted as an interpreter and assistant to Beatty. In his letter of April 1918, I noticed that Beatty had purchased one of the *One Million Pagodas and Dharani Prayers* (*Hyakumantō dhāranī*), dated 768. After several months of searching, I discovered it among the Chinese collections, together with several Japanese Buddhist

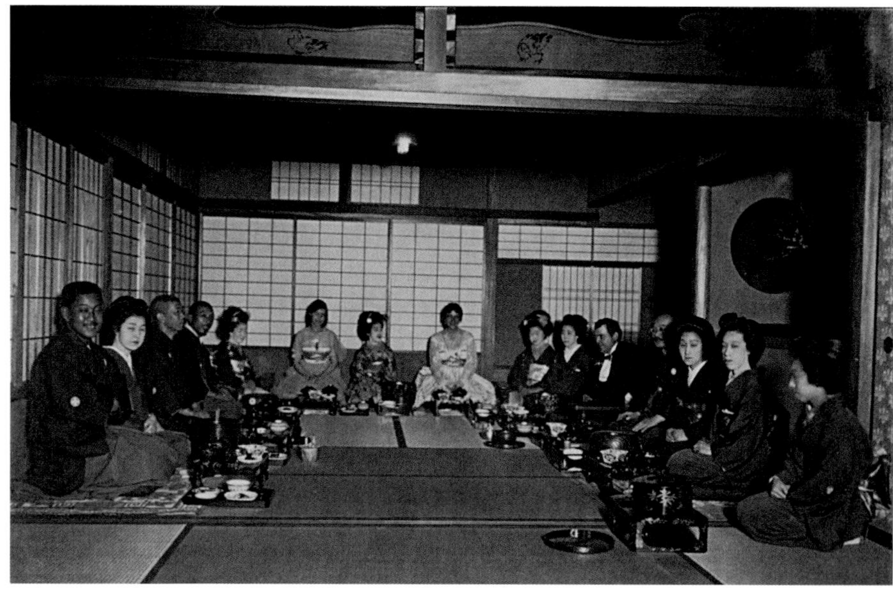

manuscripts. In the Chinese collection I also found a paulownia-wood box, the label of which announced it contained two scrolls of the *Chōgonka gakan*. Assisted by the then Far Eastern curator Jan Chapman, I opened the box with no little excitement: 'Chōgonka' was the well-known Chinese legend of Yang Guifei (719–56), which had greatly influenced Heian-period literature in Japan.

The scrolls consist of some thirty-six scenes that are minutely painted in full colour on silk, with touches of gold and silver. Unfortunately, no text accompanies the poem, but the epic story can be traced from these detailed paintings. The signature of Kano Sansetsu (1590–1651) at the end of the second scroll left me puzzling as to why this item was stored in the Chinese collection. The authenticity of the signature seemed uncertain, so I started to study the style of Kano School paintings. With the help of some Japanese specialists, I came to the conclusion that these two scrolls should belong in the Japanese and not the Chinese collection. The typical style of the Kano School is readily observed in the paintings, in particular in the rugged grandeur of the mountains

FIG 117 Photograph of a dinner party hosted by Yamanaka Sadaichi of Yamanaka Shokai in Osaka, in honour of Chester Beatty and his family, 1918.

FIGS 118, 119 Detail from *Mutineers demand the execution of Yang Guifei*, before restoration (fig. 118 top), showing detached silk and staining; and after restoration (fig. 119 bottom). *Song of Lasting Sorrow*; scroll 1, the sixth length of silk.

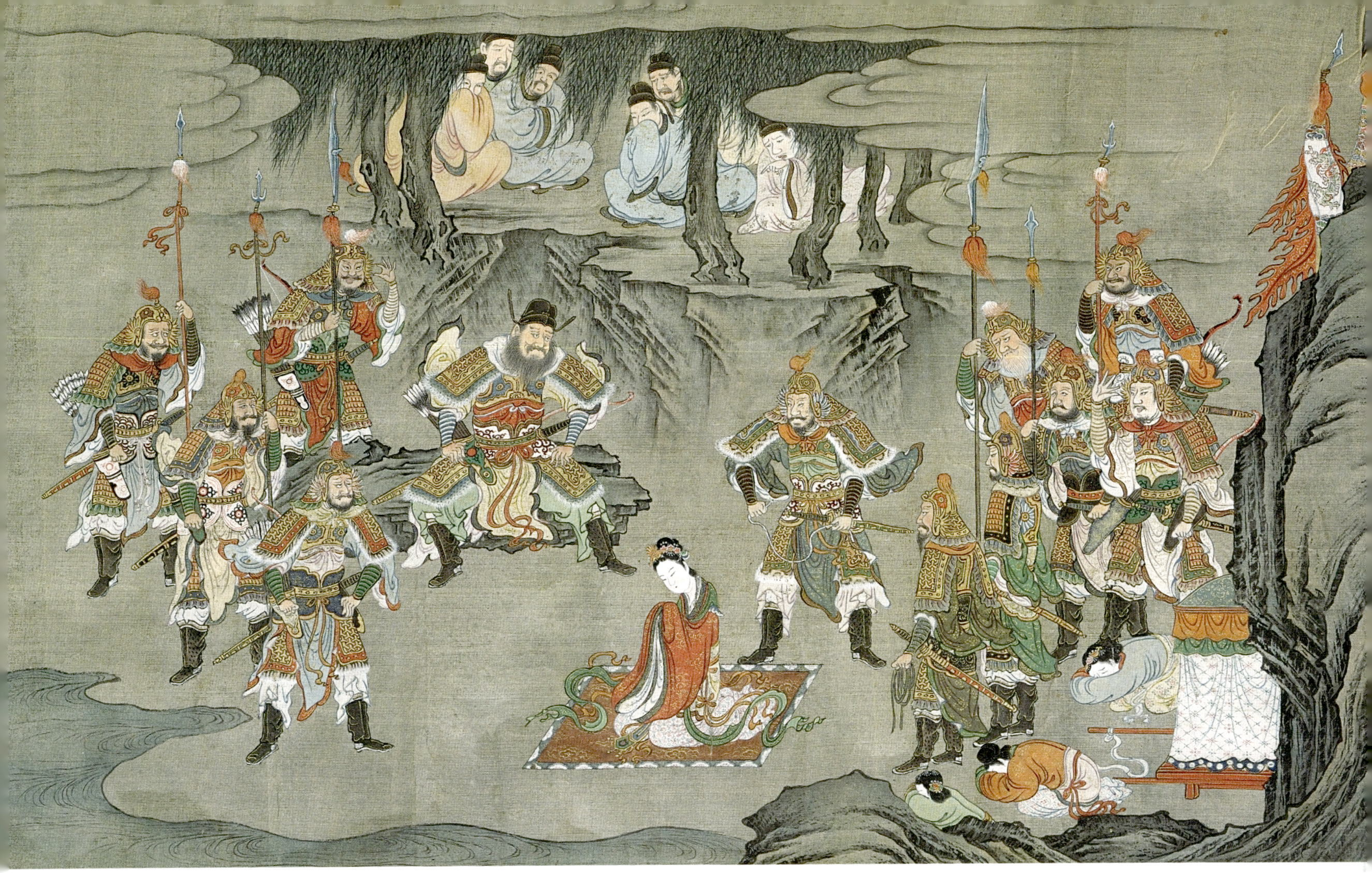

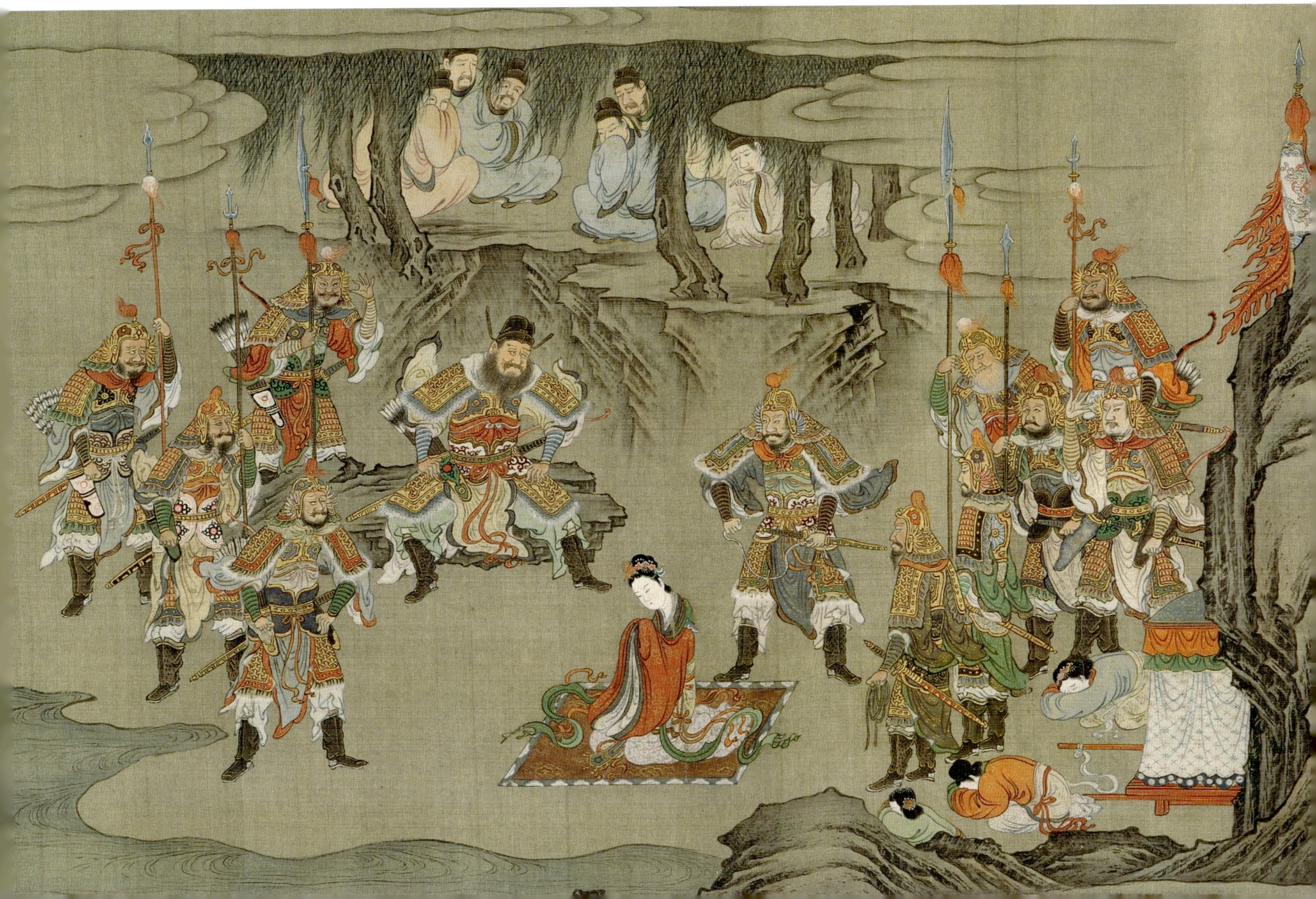

and in the aged trees. Although the paintings lacked some strength and vitality, I was convinced that they were Japanese and so transferred the item to the Japanese collection. Some years later, Professor Wakisaka, who came to the Library to see these scrolls, suggested that the lack of strength in the paintings was due to the delicacy of the silk material and their miniature scale.

Prior to the 1978 *Nara ehon* symposium in Dublin, I made a rough list of the painted scrolls and albums in the Japanese collection for the participants. In it I included the *Chōgonka* scrolls. The participants studied the *Nara ehon* collection thoroughly, but the *Chōgonka* scrolls did not arouse much interest.

A few days after the symposium ended, a Japanese scholar visited the Library without an appointment. He knew that there had been a symposium, yet insisted on seeing materials that had not been studied by the symposium delegates. I wondered why this scholar requested to see manuscripts that were not *Nara ehon*. After consulting the Director, I obtained permission for access for two days only. After glancing at the list of the Japanese collection, he asked me to get out the *Chōgonka* scrolls and several Buddhist manuscripts. The scholar was delighted to find the *Chōgonka* scrolls, for which he had apparently been searching for many years – in Japan as well as in China. In fact, he was a well-known professor of Chinese literature called Kawaguchi Hisao, from the University of Kanazawa. I clearly remember his joy and excitement. He then asked if he could extend his stay at the Library for several more days. During this time he studied and photographed the scrolls thoroughly. Later, in 1982, his book *Chōgonka emaki* was published by Taishukan Shoten in Tokyo, and included all his 'research' photographs.

Meanwhile, after the 1978 symposium, one of the participants, Mr S. Sorimachi, volunteered pri-

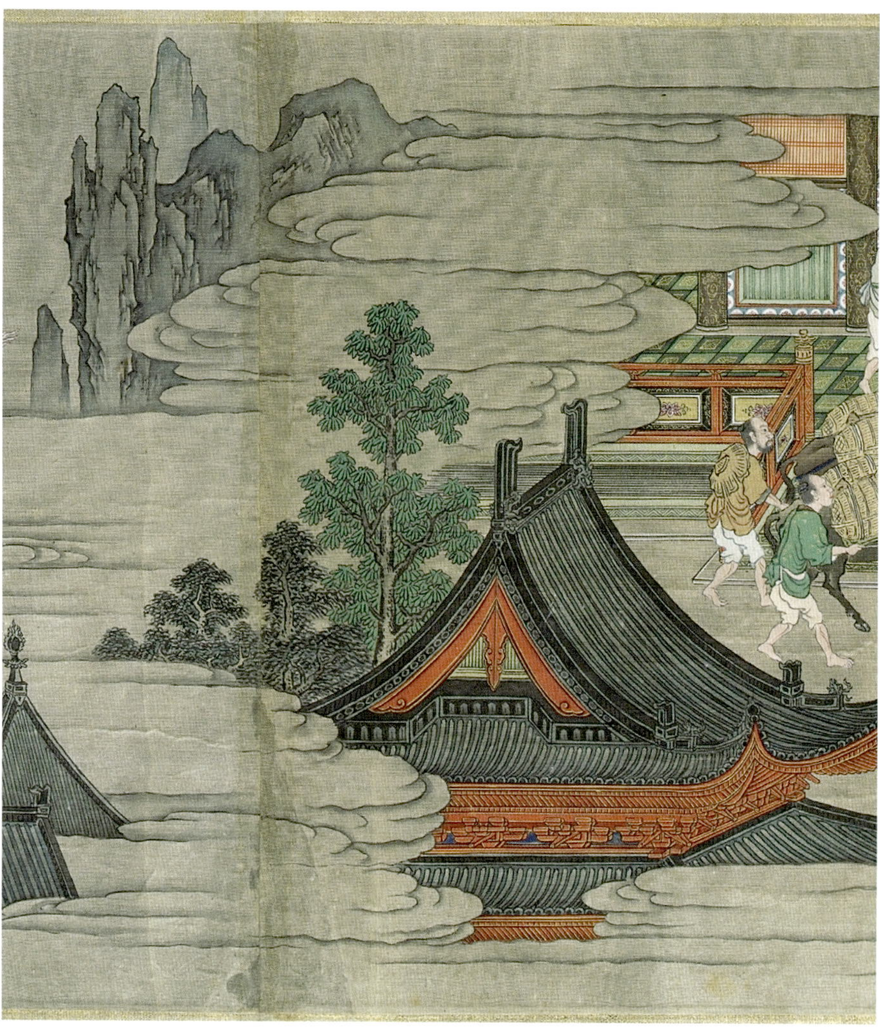

vately to compile the first catalogue of the Library's Japanese manuscripts, which would be entitled *Japanese Illustrated Books and Manuscripts*. Mr Sorimachi returned to Dublin in the spring of the following year (1979) and spent two weeks carrying out his research carefully and patiently. Mr Sorimachi's catalogue was, without question, a major contribution to research on the Japanese collection. In fact, this catalogue was completed and distributed to participants at the *Nara ehon* research meetings held in Tokyo and Kyoto in 1979. During his stay at the Library and after his return to Tokyo, I worked with Mr Sorimachi on the whole series of catalogue entries. I gained valuable experience from that work, even though from time to time I was rather puzzled and confused by his comments and explanations. In particular, his comments on the *Chōgonka gakan*, which had been thoroughly studied by Professor Kawaguchi, disturbed me: 'These scrolls are copies of an original … They were probably copied from one of the many fine copies of original Chinese scrolls … They were grandly done –

FIGS 120, 121 Detail from *The rise of the Yang clan* before restoration (fig. 120 above), showing staining at the join of two silk sections; and after restoration (fig. 121 right), *Song of Lasting Sorrow*, scroll 1, the third length of silk.

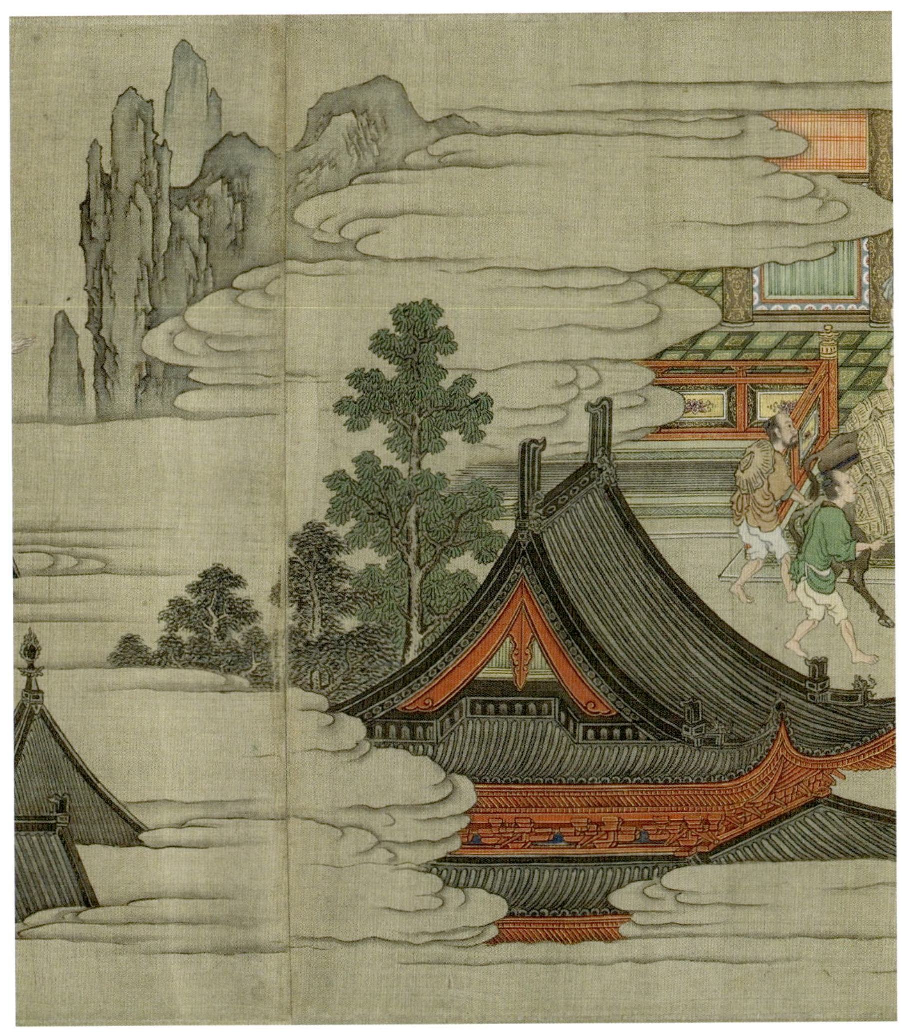

in excellent quality – but the signature and seals of the artist were apparently added later.' The views expressed by Mr Sorimachi gave me much food for thought and stimulated me to engage in further research; I never gave up investigating the issue.

Many specialists on the Kano School, including Professors Sakakibara and Wakisaka and a few other scholars, helped me greatly in this pursuit. After long discussions with them, we came to the conclusion that these scrolls were likely to be the only existing picture-scrolls on this subject, although there must have been some original paintings that Kano Sansetsu had copied. The only other painting of this story had featured in an early issue of the Japanese fine-art journal, *Kokka* (no. 44), in 1893. That painting, however, had been executed on paper rather than on silk, and in ink and light colours. Up until 1988 when they resurfaced, it was not known whether these scrolls, which had been in the collection of the Kuki family of the city of Kobe, were still in existence. Professor Wakisaka confirmed that compositionally they were very

similar to the Chester Beatty version, but the quality of the painting was greatly inferior.

Convinced of these opinions and thus of the value and rarity of the Library's scrolls, I then became rather concerned about the condition they were in. The state of the scrolls was so poor that rolling and unrolling them was very difficult without causing further damage. The condition of the scrolls was assessed by the specialist Japanese conservator Mr Handa, of Tokyo National Museum, who undertook work at the Chester Beatty Library on conservation projects sponsored by The Japan Foundation. Mr Handa made the following observations: As would be expected with paintings of this age, the scrolls had been previously restored, and the later re-lining was causing damage. Many parts of the silk supports had separated from the lining papers and become creased. A number of these creases had split, and pieces of the silk support had fallen off. The silk support had become especially wrinkled where it had delaminated from the lining papers at the tightly rolled ends of the scrolls (figs 118, 119). These wrinkles and split seams between sections of the paintings had been temporarily repaired at one time or another with thick paste, which had caused staining (figs 120, 121). In some areas, the pigments applied to the back of the silk supports had transferred to the surface of the delaminated lining papers. The structure of the silk was misaligned, causing distortion of the painting, and there were many small unsightly stains and flyspots. The gold-leaf border along the top and bottom of the paintings was stiffer than the main support and gave rise to numerous small length-wise creases (figs 122, 123).

On Mr Handa's recommendation, the Library was chosen to be included in a project for the restoration of Japanese art in European and American Collections. This new project for international cooperation was established by the Japanese Agency for

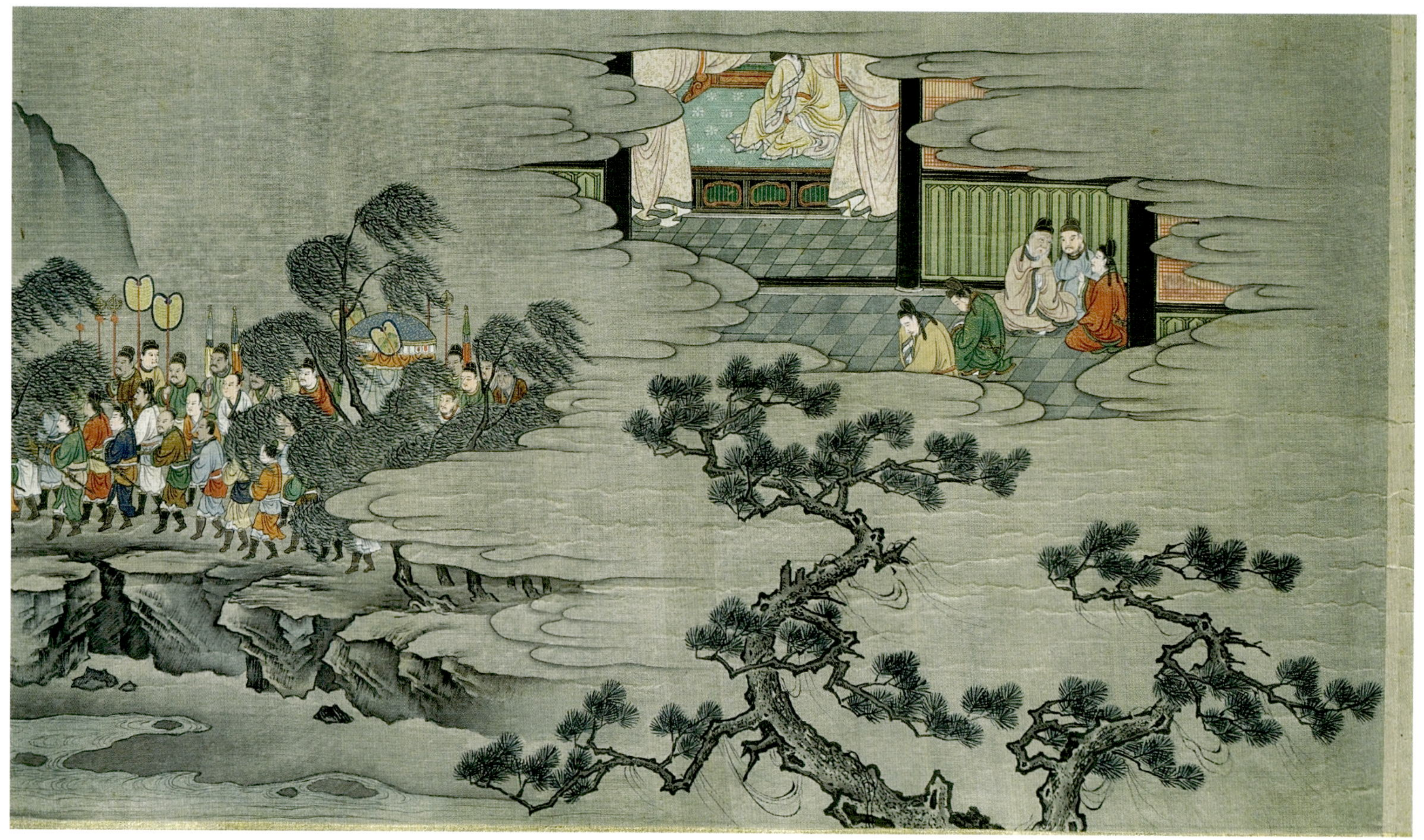

Cultural Affairs, the Tokyo National Research Institute of Cultural Properties, the Tokyo University of Fine Arts and Music, and the Art Research Foundation. Thus, in the spring of 1994, the *Chōgonka* scrolls were brought for restoration to Japan, where they were treated at the Handa Studio in Tokyo National Museum. The head of this project was Professor Hirayama, who had visited the Library a few years before the project began with several art specialists and had examined the *Chōgonka* scrolls. The checking and documentation of the scrolls' condition took place at Tokyo National Museum, during a meeting attended by many art specialists and several people from restoration studios. I was able to attend the meeting since I was in Tokyo at that time.

The conservation treatment was carried out in the following stages using traditional materials:[186] The flaking and lifting pigments were consolidated from the front with a 3% solution of *sanzenbon nikawa* (a mixture of animal glues) applied with a fine brush.

Since the paintings had already delaminated in many areas, the lining papers could be easily removed after only a light application of water to the back. Pigments that had transferred to the detached lining were re-adhered in their original locations using a 6% solution of animal-skin glue. In areas where the pigments on the back of the silk supports were still adhered to the lining papers, sections of the papers were left in place and reduced in thickness. A dilute solution of animal-skin glue was applied to these pigments from the front of the paintings. The remaining lining papers were removed, fibre-by-fibre, from the back of the silk.

The paintings were then placed face-up on top of a layer of blotting paper spread over a suction table. Room temperature water was applied to the front of the paintings and the discolouration was drawn into the blotting paper using suction. The overall soiling and staining was considerably reduced by this procedure.

The first new lining paper chosen was thin *mino* paper coloured with a mixture of *yasha* dye (natural

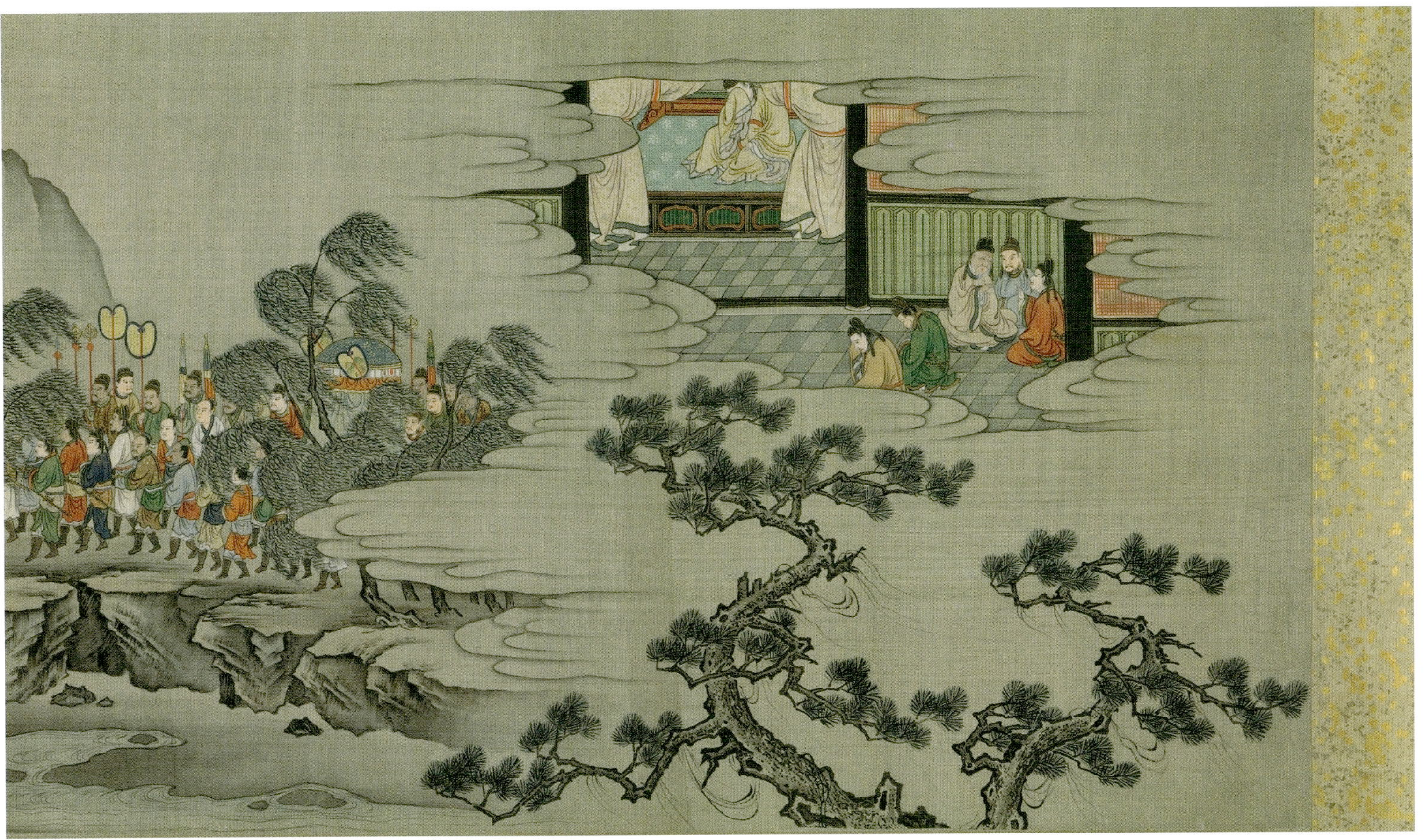

brown dye) and *sumi* (ink). Great care was taken when selecting a suitable colour for this first lining paper, as it would be visible from the front of the painting and greatly influence the final appearance. The seams of the new lining papers were positioned in inconspicuous places so as not to be distracting. The distorted silk weave was realigned where possible. A temporary facing paper was then applied to strengthen the paintings, so that silk infilling of lost areas could be done; repairs were shaped to fit the area of loss exactly, using artificially aged silk, which was applied to the front with paste and then toned. A subsidiary lining was applied to strengthen and improve flexibility, and paper reinforcement strips were then attached to the back of the paintings.

Fabric borders decorated with gold leaf had previously been added to the edges of the scroll, however these had caused damage to the original so were not replaced; instead narrow paper strips *(fukurin)* were pasted over the top and bottom edges of the supports to protect the silk. The final smooth-textured paper backing was then applied to facilitate repeated rolling and unrolling. The temporary protective lining was then removed from the front, endpapers were replaced and a new cloth cover attached. The new format and fabric for the outer covers of the hand scrolls were selected following consultation with experts involved in the project. The previous title labels were reused, since the seals of Chester Beatty and the previous owner (Louis Gonse) were on them. Paulownia-wood roller clamps *(futomaki soejiku)* were fitted over the lower roller rods *(jiku)* to increase their circumference, reducing the risk of damage due to tight rolling of the painting. The scrolls are stored in a new paulownia-wood box. The sensitive and skilful conservation of these important scrolls has made it possible for them to be enjoyed by thousands of visitors since their return to the Chester Beatty Library in 1995; and ensured the preservation of the paintings for many generations to come.

APPENDIX

Han's sovereign prized the beauty of flesh,
*   he longed for such as ruins domains;*
for many years he ruled the Earth
*   and sought for one in vain.*
A daughter there was of the house of Yang,
*   just grown to maturity,*
raised deep in the women's quarters
*   where no man knew of her.*
5 *When Heaven begets beauteous things,*
*   it is loath to let them be wasted,*
so one morning this maiden was chosen
*   to be by the ruler's side.*
When she turned around with smiling glance,
*   she exuded every charm;*
in the harem all who wore powder and paint
*   of beauty then seemed barren.*

In springtime's chill he let her bathe
*   in Huaqing Palace's pools*
10 *whose warm springs' glistening waters*
*   washed flecks of dried lotions away.*
Those in attendance helped her rise,
*   in helplessness so charming –*
this was the moment when first she enjoyed
*   the flood of royal favour.*

Tresses like cloud, face like a flower,
*   gold pins that swayed to her steps;*
it was warm in the lotus-embroidered tents
*   where they passed the nights of spring.*
15 *And the nights of spring seemed all too short,*
*   the sun would too soon rise,*
from this point on our lord and king
*   avoided daybreak court.*

She waited his pleasure at banquets,
*   with never a moment's peace,*
their springs were spent in the outings of spring,
*   he was sole lord of her nights.*
In the harems there were beauties,
*   three thousand there were in all,*
20 *but the love that was due to three thousand*
*   was spent on one body alone.*
Her make-up completed in chambers of gold,
*   she attended upon his nights,*
when in marble mansions feasts were done,
*   their drunkenness matched the spring.*

Her sisters and her brothers all
*   were ennobled and granted great fiefs;*
a glory that any would envy
*   rose from her house.*
25 *This caused the hearts of parents*
*   all the world through*
to care no longer for having sons,
*   but to care to have a daughter.*

The high places of Mount Li's palace
*   rose up into blue clouds,*
where the music of gods was whirled in winds
*   and everywhere was heard.*

Songs so slow and stately dances,
*   notes sustained on flutes and harps,*
30 *and all day long our lord and king*
*   could never look his fill.*
Then kettledrums from Yuyang came
*   making the whole earth tremble*
and shook apart those melodies,
*   'Coats of Feathers, Rainbow Skirts'.* [188]

From nine tiers of palace towers
   dust and smoke were rising:
a thousand coaches, ten thousand riders
   moving away southwest.

35   *Swaying plumes of the royal banners*
   were moving ahead, then stopped
west of the gates of the capital,
   just over a hundred miles.

The six-fold army would not set forth,
   nothing could be done,
and the fragile arch of her lovely brows
   there perished before the horses.

Her flowered hairpins fell to earth,
   and no one picked them up,
40   *the kingfisher wing, the sparrow of gold,*
   the jade pick for the hair.
Our lord and ruler covered his face,
   unable to protect her;
he looked around, and blood and tears
   were flowing there together.

Brown dust spread in billows,
   howling was the wind,
plank walkways wound into the clouds
   as he climbed by Sword Tower Peak.
45   *And at the foot of Mount Emei*
   travellers were few,
the royal banners shed no light,
   the beams of sun were pale.

Shu's rivers' sapphire waters,
   the green of hills in Shu –
the state of His Royal Majesty's heart
   every morning, every night.
From an exile's palace he saw the moon,
   hues that give heart pain;
50   *in the rain of night he heard the bells,*
   sounds that broke him within.

Heaven revolved, the days spun round,
   the dragon-carriage turned home,
but reaching that spot he faltered
   and could not leave it behind.
Beneath the slopes of Mawei,
   there in the mud and mire,
he could not see where those features,
   white as marble, died for naught.

55   *Ruler and ministers looked at each other,*
   all soaked their clothes with tears,
then facing east toward the capital gates,
   he let his horse take him home.

When he was home, his pools and parks
   were all as they had been before,
there were lotuses in Taiye Pool and
   willows at Weiyang.

But the lotuses looked like her face,
   and the willows seemed like her brows,
60   *before such scenes how could he stop*
   his tears from streaming down? –
On days when plums and peaches
   opened in breeze of spring;
and in the season of autumn rain
   when beeches shed their leaves.

In the western palace and southern compound
 were many autumn plants
whose fallen leaves filled pavements,
 red, not swept away.
65 Performers of the Pear Garden,
 their hair newly touched with white;
eunuch attendants of pepper-walled harems,
 their blue-black brows showed age.

As glow-worms flew through twilight courts,
 he would sink into silent thought,
the wick of his lonely lamp burned low
 and still he could not sleep.
In the slow, slow beat of bells and drums
 his long nights would begin,
70 till the stream of stars was sparkling
 in skies approaching dawn.

The lovebird tiles were chill,
 heavy with flakes of frost,
the kingfisher quilts were cold
 without someone to share.
On forever, living and dead
 were parted through the years,
and never once did her wandering soul
 find way into his dreams.

75 In Linqiong there was a wizard,
 guest in the gods' great citadel,
who by the perfection of essence
 could bring the souls of the dead.
He was touched by our ruler's
 restless, tossing love,
and thus he gave the magician a task
 of making an earnest quest.

He rode on vapours through the void,
 he sped like lightning along,
80 up into Heaven, down into Earth,
 seeking her everywhere.
But from the sapphire star-web above
 to the yellow springs below,
both were infinitely vast,
 in neither did he find her.

He came to learn that on the seas
 were mountains of the Undying,
those mountains lie in Emptiness
 remote and ethereal.

85 Sparkling grillwork of halls and towers
 where rainbow-clouds arose,
and in them the Undying were teeming,
 beings lovely and lissome.
Among there was a certain one
 who had the name Taizhen,
whose snowy flesh and flowerlike face seemed
 much like her he sought.

At the western cloister of golden tower
 he knocked at a door of jade,
90 and had the servant Little Jade
 take word to the Maid Shuangcheng.
When she heard the news of a messenger
 from the Son of Heaven of Han,
within the nine-flower hangings
 her dreaming soul woke with alarm.

She threw on robes, pushed pillow away,
   rose and paced about;
pearled dividers and silver screens
   opened down winding halls.
95 *Her cloudlike tresses were half askew,*
   she had freshly woken from sleep,
and her hat of flowers was not set straight
   as she came into the room.

Wind blew upon the goddess's sleeves,
   billowing as they rose,
and it still resembled her dancing
   'Coats of Feathers, Rainbow Skirts'.
Her marble features were sad and still,
   her tears were streaming down,
100 *she was a branchful of blooming pear,*
   bearing the rain of spring.

Biting back feeling, she fixed her gaze,
   sent thanks to the ruler and lord:
once voice and visage are torn apart,
   vast emptiness lies between.
Broken forever, the love that was shared
   in the Court of Shining Light,
now days and the months pass but slowly
   in the Palace of Penglai.

105 *When she turned her head to gaze back down*
   to the realm of mortal men,
Chang'an she did not see,
   she saw only dust and fog.
She could only use things once shared
   to convey her depth of love –
an inlaid box and hairpin of gold
   he should carry back with him.

'Of the hairpin I will keep a leg,
   of the box I keep a panel;
110 *the gold of the hairpin is sundered,*
   the box's inlay divided.
If only your heart can be as firm
   as the inlay or the gold,
in Heaven or among mortal men
   we will someday meet again.'

Time came to go, and with passionate care,
   she sent a few more words,
and in those words there was a vow
   known to their hearts alone.
115 *On the seventh day of the seventh month*
   in the Palace of Lasting Life,
it was midnight, no one else was there,
   as they whispered privately:
if in Heaven, may we become
   those birds that fly on shared wing;
or on Earth, then may we become
   branches that twine together.
Heaven lasts, the Earth endures
   yet a time will come when they're gone,
120 *yet this pain of ours will continue*
   and never finally end.

CHEN HONG (EARLY NINTH CENTURY),
'AN ACCOUNT TO GO WITH THE "SONG OF LASTING SORROW"' [189]

DURING THE KAIYUAN REIGN, the omens of the Stair Stars showed a world at peace, and there were no problems throughout the land within the four circling seas. Xuanzong, having been long on the throne, grew weary of having to dine late and dress while it was still dark for the dawn audience; and he began to turn over all questions of government, both large and small, to the Assistant Director of the Right, Li Linfu, while the Emperor himself tended either to stay deep in the palace or go out to banquets, finding his pleasure in all the sensual delights of ear and eye. Previously the Empress Yuanxian and the Consort Wuhui had both enjoyed His Majesty's favour, but each in turn had departed the world; and even though there were in the palace over a thousand daughters of good families, none of them really caught his fancy. His Majesty was fretful and displeased.

In those days every year in December the imperial entourage would journey to Huaqing Palace. The titled women, both from the inner palace and from without, would follow him like luminous shadows. And he would grant them baths in the warm waters there, in the very waves that had bathed the imperial sun. Holy fluids in a springlike breeze went rippling through those places. It was then that His Majesty's heart was smitten: for he had truly come upon the one woman, and all the fair flesh that surrounded him seemed to him like dirt. He summoned Gao Lishi to make a secret search for this woman in the palaces of the princes; and there, in the establishment of the Prince of Shou, he found the daughter of Yang Xuanyan. She had already become a mature woman. Her hair and tresses were glossy and well arranged; neither slender nor plump, she was exactly of the middle measure; and there was a sensuous allure in her every motion, just like Lady Li of Emperor Wu of the Han. He ordered a special channel of the warm springs cut for her and commanded that it be offered to her gleaming fineness. When she came out of the water, her body seemed frail and her force spent, as if she could not even bear the weight of lace and gauze; yet she shed such radiance that it shone on all around her. His Majesty was most pleased. On the day he had her brought to meet him, he ordered the melody 'Coats of Feathers, Rainbow Skirts' played to precede her. And on the eve when their love was consummated, he gave her, as proofs of his love, a golden hairpin and an inlaid box. He also commanded that she wear golden earrings and a hairpick that swayed to her pace. The following year he had her officially listed as Guifei, Prized Consort, entitled to half the provision as an empress. From this point on she assumed a seductively coy manner and spoke wittily, suiting herself to His Majesty's wishes by thousands of fetching ways. And His Majesty came to dote on her ever more deeply.

At this time the Emperor made a tour of his nine domains and offered the gold-sealed tablets in ceremonies on the Five Sacred Peaks. On Mount Li during snowy nights and in Shangyang Palace on spring mornings she would ride in the same palanquin as the Emperor and spend the night in the same apartments; she was the main figure of feasts and had his bedchamber all to herself when he retired. There were three Great Ladies, nine Royal Spouses, twenty-seven Brides of the Age, eighty-one Imperial Wives, Handmaidens of the Rear Palace, Women Performers of the Music Bureau – and on none of these was the Son of Heaven the least inclined to look. And from that time on, no one from the Six Palaces was ever again brought forward to the royal bed. This was not only because of her sensual allure and great physical charms, but also because she was clever and smart, artful at flattery and making herself agreeable, anticipating His Majesty's wishes – so much so that it cannot be described. Her father, her uncle and her brothers were all given high honorary offices and were raised to ranks of Nobility Equal to the Royal House. Her sisters were enfeoffed as Ladies of Domains. Their wealth matched that of the royal house; and their carriages, clothes and mansions were on a par with the Emperor's aunt, Princess Taichang. Yet in power and the benefits of imperial favour, they surpassed her. They went in and out of the royal palace unquestioned, and the senior officers of the capital would turn their eyes away from them. There were doggerel rhymes in those days that went:

> If you have a girl, don't feel sad;
> if you have a boy, don't feel glad.

and:

> The boy won't be a noble,
>   but the daughter may be queen;
> so look on your daughters now
>   as the glory of the clan.

To such a degree they were envied by people.

At the end of the Tianbao Reign, her uncle Yang Guozhong stole the position of Chancellor and abused the power he held. When An Lushan led his troops in an attack on the imperial palace, he used punishing Yang Guozhong as his pretext. Tong Pass was left undefended, and the Kingfisher Paraphernalia of the imperial entourage had to set out southward. After leaving Xianyang, their path came to Mawei Pavilion. There the Grand Army hesitated, holding their pikes in battle positions and refusing to go forward. Attendant officers, gentlemen of the court and underlings bowed down before His Majesty's horse and asked that this current Chao Cuo be executed to appease the world. [Yang Guozhong is referred to as Chao Cuo, a Western Han censor who advised the emperor Jing to reduce the territories of the imperial princes, which was the excuse for the

Rebellion of the Seven Domains. Yang Guozhong is similarly being accused of having provoked An Lushan to rebellion.] Yang Guozong then received the yak-hair hat ribbons and the pan of water, by which a great officer of the court presents himself to the Emperor for punishment, and he died there by the edge of the road. Yet the will of those who were with the Emperor was still not satisfied. When His Majesty asked what the problem was, those who dared speak out asked that the Prized Consort also be sacrificed to allay the wrath of the world. His Majesty knew that it could not be avoided, and yet he could not bear to see her die, so he turned his sleeve to cover his face as the envoys dragged her off. She struggled and threw herself back and forth in panic, but at last she came to death under the strangling cord.

Afterward, Xuanzong came to Chengdu on his Imperial Tour, and Suzong accepted the succession at Lingwu. In the following year the Monster himself [An Lushan] forfeited his head, and the imperial carriage returned to the capital. Xuanzong was honoured as His Former Majesty and given a separate establishment in the Southern Palace, then transferred to the western sector of the Imperial Compound. As time and events passed, all joy had gone from him and only sadness came. Every day of spring or night of winter, when the lotuses in the ponds opened in summer or when the palace ash trees shed their leaves in autumn, the performers of the Pear Garden Academy would produce notes on their jade flageolets; and if he heard one note of 'Coat of Feathers, Rainbow Skirts', His Majesty's face would lose its cheer, and all those around him would sob and sigh. For three years there was one thing on his mind, and his longing never subsided. His soul sought her out in dream, but she was so far away he could not reach her.

It happened then that a wizard came from Shu; and knowing that His Majesty was brooding so much on Yang the Prized Consort, he said that he possessed the skills of Li the Young Lord, the wizard who had summoned the soul of Lady Li for Emperor Wu of the Han. Xuanzong was very pleased, and ordered him to bring her spirit. The wizard then used all his skills to find her, but could not. He was also able to send his spirit on journeys by riding vapours; he went up into the precincts of Heaven and sank down into the vaults of the Earth looking for her; but he did not meet her. And then again he went to the margins and the encircling wastelands, high and low, to the easternmost extreme of Heaven and the Ocean, where he strode across Fanghu.

He saw there the highest of the mountains of the Undying, with many mansions and towers; at the end of the western veranda there was a deepest doorway facing east; the gate was shut, and there was written, 'The Garden of Taizhen, Jade Consort'. The wizard pulled out a hatpin and rapped on the door, at which a young maiden with her hair done up in a double coil came out to answer the door. The wizard was so flustered he couldn't manage to get a word out, so the maiden went back in. In a moment another servant girl in a green dress came out and asked where he was from. The wizard then identified himself as an envoy of the Tang Son of Heaven and conveyed the command he had been given. The servant said, 'The Jade Consort has just gone to bed; please wait a while for her.' Thereupon he was swallowed up in a sea of clouds with the dawn sun breaking through them as down a tunnel to the heavens; then the jasper door closed again and all was still and without a sound.

The wizard held his breath and did not move his feet, waiting at the gate with folded hands. After a long time, the servant invited him to come in and said, 'The Jade Consort is coming out.' Then he saw a person with a bonnet of golden lotuses, wearing lavender chiffon, with pendants of red jade hanging from her sash and phoenix slippers, and seven or eight persons in attendance on her. She greeted the wizard and asked, 'Is the Emperor well?' Then she asked what had happened since the fourteenth year of the Tianbao Reign. When he finished speaking, she grew wistful and gestured to her servant to get a golden hairpin and inlaid box, each of which she broke in parts. She gave one part of each to the envoy, saying, 'Express my gratitude to the Emperor and present him with these objects as mementoes of our former love.'

The wizard received her words and these objects of surety; he was ready to go, but one could see in his face that something was troubling him. The Jade Consort insisted that he tell her what was the matter. Then he knelt down before her and said, 'Please tell me something that happened back then, something of which no one else knew, so that I can offer to His Majesty as proof. Otherwise I am afraid that with the inlaid box and the golden hairpin I will be accused of the same kind of trickery that Xin Yuanping practised on Emperor Wen of the Han.' The Jade Consort drew back lost in thought, as if there were something she were recalling with fondness. Then very slowly she said, 'Back in the tenth year of the Tianbao Reign, I was attending on His Majesty, who had gone to the palace on Mount Li to escape the heat. It was autumn, in the seventh month, the evening when the Oxherd and the Weaver Star meet. It was the custom of the people of Qin on that night to spread out embroidery and brocade, to put out food and drink, to set up flowers and melons, and to burn incense in the yard – they call this 'begging for deftness'. Those of the inner palace hold this custom in particularly high regard. It was almost midnight; and the guards and attendants in the eastern and western cloisters had been dismissed. I was waiting on His Majesty alone. His Majesty stood there, leaning on his shoulder, then looked up at the heavens and was touched by the legend of the Oxherd and the Weaver Star. We then made a secret vow to one another, a wish that we could be husband and wife in every lifetime. When we stopped speaking, we held hands, and each of us was sobbing. Only the Emperor knows of this.'

Then she said sadly, 'Because of this one thought so much in my mind, I will be able to live on here no longer. I will descend again to the world below and our future destiny will take shape. Whether in Heaven or in the world of mortal men, it is certain that we will meet again and form our bond of love as before.' Then she said, 'His Former Majesty will not be long in the world of men. I hope that he will find some peace of mind and not cause himself suffering.'

The envoy returned and presented this to His Former Majesty, and the Emperor's heart was shaken and much afflicted with grief. For days on end he could find no cheer. In the summer of that year, in the fourth month, His Majesty passed on.

In winter of the first year of the Yuanhe Reign, the twelfth month (February 807), Bai Juyi of Taiyuan left his position as Diarist in the Imperial Library to be sheriff of Chou County. I, Chen Hong, and Wang Zhifu of Langya had our homes in this town; and on our days off we would go together visiting sites of the Undying and Buddhist Temples. Our discussion touched on this story, and we were all moved to sighs. Zhifu lifted his winecup to Bai Juyi and said, 'Unless such an event finds an extraordinary talent who can adorn it with colours, even something so rare will fade away with time and no longer be known in the world. Bai Juyi is deeply familiar with poetry and has strong sentiments. Why doesn't he write a song on the topic.' At this Bai Juyi made the 'Song of Lasting Sorrow'. It is my supposition that he was not only moved by the event, but he also wanted to offer warning about such creatures that can so enthral a man, to block the phases by which troubles come, and to leave this for the future. When the song was finished, he had me write a prose account for it. Of those things not known to the general public, I, not being a survivor of the Kaiyuan, have no way to know. For those things known to the general public, the *Annals of the Reign of Xuanzong* are extant. This is merely an account for the 'Song of Lasting Sorrow'.

NOTES

GENERAL NOTES:

The reader is directed to the Bibliography for sources for which full citations do not appear in the Notes.

In the Notes and Bibliography sections, titles of works are given first in the original language, followed by the English translation. In the main section of the book, the English translation is given first.

Translations of Japanese texts in chapter four are by the author, Matthew P. McKelway, unless otherwise indicated.

1   Kate Robinson, 'An Edo Masterwork Restored. The Chogonka Scrolls in The Chester Beatty Library, Dublin', p. 77.

2   See Miyajima Shin'ichi, 'Chōgonka zukan'.

3   Sorimachi Shigeo, *Nihon eiribon oyobi ehon mokuroku* (Japanese Illustrated Books and Manuscripts in the Chester Beatty Library, Dublin, Ireland).

4   Mrs Ushioda worked as a volunteer in the 1970s.

5   Kamitaka Tokuharu et al. (eds), *Kano Sansetsu ga Chōgonka gakan* (The *Song of Lasting Sorrow* picture-scrolls by Kano Sansetsu).

6   This ballad and others, e.g. 'Song of the Lute', (see Burton Watson [trans. and ed.], *Columbia Book of Chinese Poetry: From Early Times to the Thirteenth Century* [New York: Columbia University Press, 1984]) are sometimes taken as evidence of Bai Juyi's sympathetic attitude towards women.

7   For the 'official' biography of Zhao Feiyan, see Ban Gu, *Han shu* (History of the Former Han Dynasty), 12 vols (Beijing: Zhonghua, 1975), vol. 12, *juan* 97b, pp. 3988–99.

8   Biographies of Yang Guifei in *Jiu Tang shu* (Old History of the Tang Dynasty), vol. 7, *juan* 51, pp. 2178–81 and *Xin Tang shu*, (New History of the Tang Dynasty), vol. 11, *juan* 76, pp. 3493–96; and of Emperor Minghuang in *Jiu Tang shu*, vol. 1, *juan* 7, pp. 165–238 and *Xin Tang shu*, vol. 1, *juan* 5, pp. 121–54.

9   This and the succeeding translations of Tang poems are from Stephen Owen (ed. and trans.), 'Interlude: Xuanzong and Yang the Prized Consort', in *An Anthology of Chinese Literature*: *Beginnings to 1911*, pp. 441–57. The Romanisation has been standardised. For the text of 'Lament by the River' (Ai jiang tou) see *Quan Tang shi* (Complete Collection of Tang Poetry), pp. 2509–10.

10 See, for example, Ling Xuan (Han dynasty), *Zhao Feiyan wai zhuan*, 1 vol.; Ming Wanli (1573–1620), woodblock edition published by Cheng Rong, series *Han Wei congshu*; also You Qiu's handscroll, *Spring Morning in the Han Palace*, in the Shanghai Museum, discussed by Wang Huanli, 'Hangong chunxiao tujuan', in *Shimao fengqing – Zhongguo*

gudai renwu hua (Hong Kong: Wen Wei Publishing, 2008), p. 39.

11 'Long chi' in *Quan Tang shi*, p. 6195; translation by Owen, *An Anthology of Chinese Literature*, pp. 452–53.

12 Translation by Owen, *An Anthology of Chinese Literature*, pp. 441–58.

13 For the full text and citation, see Appendix; translation by Owen, *An Anthology of Chinese Literature*, p. 452. The English title of Bai Juyi's ballad, *Chang hen ge*, has been modified ('sorrow' for 'pain').

14 See Arthur Waley, *The Life and Times of Po Chü-i*. See also the translation by Owen, *An Anthology of Chinese Literature*.

15 Murasaki Shikibu, *The Tale of Genji* (trans. Edward Seidensticker).

16 Paintings with 'picking melons' in the title are recorded, for instance, in the late-Song/early-Yuan connoisseur Zhou Mi's catalogue, *Yunyan guoyan lu*, of about 1298, for which see, Ankeney Weitz, *Zhou Mi's Record of Clouds and Mist Passing Before One's Eyes: an annotated translation* (Leiden; Boston: Brill, 2002).

17 After quoting Ye Mengde's (1077–1148) description of 'a copy after Li Sixun's painting, *Minghuang's Journey to Shu*' in *Bishu luhua*, in which Ye Mengde remarks upon the euphemism of 'picking melons', Max Loehr (1903–88) has argued that 'Minghuang picking melons' is a separate theme; see Max Loehr, *The Great Painters of China*, p. 66.

18 See Li Lin-ts'an, 'A Study of the Masterpiece "T'ang Ming-huang's Journey to Shu"', *Ars Orientalis* 4 (1961), pp. 315–21; *Daguan: Bei Song shuhua tezhan*, exh. cat. (Taipei: National Palace Museum, 2006), no. 22. Yang Xin has dated this painting to the Yuan dynasty; see 'Hu Tinghui zuopin yu "Minghuang xing Shu tu" de shidai tantao', *Wenwu* 1999.10, pp. 94–100.

19 For the Metropolitan painting, see Wen C. Fong, *Beyond Representation: Chinese Painting and Calligraphy, 8th–14th Century* (New York: Metropolitan Museum of Art, 1992), pl. 3. Another scene of figures in a mountain landscape in the University Museum, Philadephia, entitled *Minghuang's Journey to Shu* and formerly attributed to Li Zhaodao, is illustrated by Alexander Soper in 'A ninth-century landscape painting in the Japanese Imperial Palace and some Chinese parallels', *Artibus Asiae*, vol. 29, no. 4 (1968), pp. 335–50, fig. 2.

20 See Loehr, *Great Painters*, p. 69, referring to Waley, *The Life and Times of Po Chü-i*, p. 45; see also Wu Hung, 'The Origins of Chinese Painting', in Richard Barnhart et al., *Three Thousand Years of Chinese Painting*, n. 81.

21 Fong, *Beyond Representation* (as n. 19), p. 26ff.

22 Ibid.; see also Li Lin-ts'an, 'A Study of the

Masterpiece "T'ang Ming-huang's Journey to Shu"' (as n. 18).

23 This is illustrated and discussed in Barnhart et al., *Three Thousand Years of Chinese Painting*, pl. 72.

24 Discussed and translated in Loehr, *Great Painters*, p. 45ff and p. 65; Lady Guoguo is discussed on p. 47. For the texts, see *Quan Tang shi*, p. 1703 ('Liren xing') and p. 2580 ('Guoguo furen'). For another translation of 'Liren xing', by Elling Eide, see Victor Mair (ed.), *The Columbia Anthology of Traditional Chinese Literature* (New York: Columbia University Press, 1996), pp. 300–02.

25 Guo Ruoxu, *Tuhua jianwen zhi*; see Alexander Soper (trans. and annot.), *Kuo Jo-hsü's Experiences in Painting (T'u-hua chien-wen Chih), An Eleventh Century History of Chinese Painting Together with the Chinese Text in Facsimile* (American Council of Learned Societies, 1951), p. 193, fn. 630; also quoted in Loehr, *Great Painters*, p. 48.

26 Tr. after Arthur Waley; see Shane McCausland (ed.), *Gu Kaizhi and the Admonitions Scroll* (London: British Museum Press, 2003), pp. 15–17.

27 Wu Hung, in Barnhart et al., *Three Thousand Years of Chinese Painting*, p. 75.

28 A probable Southern Song (early 13th century) fan painting mounted as an album leaf in the Museum of Fine Arts, Boston, entitled *Yang Guifei Mounting a Horse* (MFA 12.896), also depicts this scene. For a study of the subject, see Elizabeth Owen, 'Love Lost: Qian Xuan (*c*.1235–1307) and Images of Emperor Minghuang and Yang Guifei'.

29 Examples of dramas are the *zaju* (variety play) entitled *Wutong you* (Rain on the Wutong Tree) by Bai Pu (1227–1306) and Hong Sheng's (1605–1704) *Changsheng dian* (Palace of Lasting Life).

30 The 1952 film was directed by Wui Ng and produced in Hong Kong; the 2005 title was directed by Stanley Kwan and produced by the Shanghai Film Studio.

31 MFA 32.131; illustrated in Hideo Okudaira, *Narrative Picture Scrolls*, fig. 41.

32 A late Ming (16th–17th century) handscroll illustration of the flight to Shu scenery, traditionally attributed to Qiu Ying, is in the Freer Gallery, Washington, DC (F1993.4). See: http://www.asia.si. edu/collections/singleObject.cfm?ObjectId=48858.

33 Tsuji Nobuo was the first art historian to group Sansetsu together with a group of so-called 'eccentric' painters. See Tsuji Nobuo, *Kisō no keifu* (The Lineage of Eccentrics), and for discussions in English, see Matthew McKelway, 'Autumn Moon and Lingering Snow: Kano Sansetsu's West Lake Screens', p. 44.

34 Kano Einō (comp.), *Honchō gashi* (History of Painting in this Realm), in Kasai Masaaki (ed.) et al., *Yakuchū honchō gashi* (History of Painting in this

35 Realm, Annotated).

35 See McKelway, 'Autumn Moon and Lingering Snow', pp. 33–80.

36 The topic of Yukio Lippit, 'The Birth of Japanese Painting History: Kano Artists, Authors, and Authenticators of the Seventeenth Century', PhD diss., Princeton University, 2003.

37 Loehr identified this as an early illustration of Bai Juyi's ballad; see *Great Painters*, p. 69.

38 Illustrated in *Gugong shuhua tulu* (Taipei: National Palace Museum, 1990), vol. 4, p. 157 (Cheng 223.48, Guhua yi 02.09.00260).

39 Itakura Masaaki, *Gen jidai no kaiga: Mongoru sekai teikoku no isseiki* (Painting of the Yuan Period: the Century of the Mongol World Empire), exh. cat. (Tokyo: Yamato Bunkakan, 1998), no. 13. The links between this painting and the Taipei one are discussed here by Itakura.

40 Itakura Masaaki, 'Kano Sansetsu ga egaita *Chōgonka zu*: itan kara koten e' (Kano Sansetsu's Painting of the *Chōgonka*: From Nonconformity to Classicism).

41 The movement of painted images of all qualities across Eurasia at this early modern date is not in doubt. Related works of an ephemeral kind have survived even in Europe: anonymous Chinese workshop paintings like the 16th-century one in ink and colours on silk entitled *Palace Scene with Female Orchestra*, in Schloss Ambras in Innsbruck, (illustrated in Craig Clunas, *Pictures and Visuality in Early Modern China*, pl. 34). It is compositionally crude but brightly coloured with reds and greens, and intriguing as a workshop reflection of this 'period style'.

42 *Chang hen ge* text in *Quan Tang shi*, p. 3435; translation by Owen, *An Anthology of Chinese Literature*, pp. 442–47.

43 For a modern historical account see Denis Twitchett and John K. Fairbank (general eds), *The Cambridge History of China,* vol. 3*,* Sui and T'ang China; part 1 (Cambridge: Cambridge University Press, 1979) pp. 589–906.

44 The subject of another narrative painting by You Qiu in the Shanghai Museum. The emperor engaged the portraitist Mao Yanshou to create a portfolio of his women's portraits. When the beautiful Lady Zhaojun refused to bribe the artist, he made her look ugly. Believing the likeness to be true, the emperor, who had never laid eyes on her, chose her to be given away to a visiting barbarian chieftain in 33 BC. When she came out to be presented, the emperor realised what had happened and had the painter executed.

45 The extant copies of early *Luoshen* paintings were mostly done in the Northern Song period, but one version in the British Museum – of disputed but possibly 15th-century date – suggests this subject was also painted in to the Ming. This group of

46 Kawaguchi Hisao, in *Chōgonka emaki* (The *Song of Lasting Sorrow* picture-scroll), p. 18, cites a line of Li Bai's poetry describing this candle-lit spring night scene as a nostalgic allusion to the time of Wei emperor Wendi (r. 535–51).

47 Illustrated and discussed in James Cahill, *Hills Beyond a River: Chinese painting of the Yüan Dynasty, 1279–1368* (New York; Tokyo: Weatherhill, 1976).

48 See Owen, 'Love Lost'.

49 In this respect, Qian Xuan was not unlike some of his younger contemporaries – scholar-painters like Ren Renfa (1254–1327) and the widely accomplished Zhao Mengfu (1254–1322) – who were reviving Tang styles based on the extant Tang works circulating among collectors by court artists like Han Gan. Qian Xuan probably knew or knew of a painting of this subject by Minghuang's court painter Han Gan, for such works are recorded in inventories like *Yunyan guoyan lu* by his contemporary, the connoisseur and doyen of the late Song–early Yuan collecting world, Zhou Mi. For this text, see Weitz, *Zhou Mi's Record of Clouds and Mist* (as n. 16).

50 For a similarly plotted Tang-style handscroll, see Ren Renfa's *Three Horses and Four Grooms* (Cleveland Museum of Art, 1960.181) at: http://www.clemusart. com/explore/ artist.asp?artistLetter=R&recNo=54

51 Discussed in Julia K. Murray, 'What is "Chinese narrative illustration"?', *The Art Bulletin*, vol. 80, no. 4 (December 1998), p. 608.

52 A famous musical suite and dance associated with Yang Guifei.

53 Itakura, *Gen jidai no kaiga* (as n. 39).

54 See *Zhongguo gudai shuhua tumu*, series, (Beijing: Wenwu chubanshe, 1986), vol. 3: Hu 1–829.

55 See McKelway, 'Autumn Moon and Lingering Snow', p. 36, citing Hayashi Susumu, 'Kano Sansetsu no *Bankoku zu* ni tsuite' (On Kano Sansetsu's *Pangu Valley* Hanging Scroll).

56 *Hainei qiguan* (Extraordinary Views of the World [i.e. China]), *juan* 8, p. 552ff; *Sancai tuhui* (Pictorial Compendium of the Three Realms), *dili juan* 11, p. 5a–b ('Plank Road') and p. 13a–b ('Mount Emei'), vol. 1, p. 367 and p. 371 respectively.

57 The illustration may roughly be taken as a view looking west. In the *Hainei qiguan* version, Baoji is identified by caption at the bottom right; above it is the Dasan Pass (about 30 km to the southwest), and above that is Fengling, probably the peak above the county town of Feng County, about 50 km southwest of the Dasan Pass. Baocheng (called Liangzhou in the Tang), which lies some 150 km to the south of Baoji on the Han River, is named to the left of Baoji at the bottom. The Jiangling River is

named in the bottom left corner. The pass to the south at Qipan, roughly 150 km south-south-west of Baocheng, is named in the top left corner.

58 E.g., by Zhao Mengfu in his *Mind Landscape of Xie Youyu* (Princeton University Art Museum), an imaginary recreation of a Six Dynasties portrait-in-a-landscape by Gu Kaizhi. The portrait subject is depicted seated on a deliberately tipped-up ground plane within a kind of oval cave entrance in a rocky blue-green hill. For a study of this painting, see Shane McCausland, '"Like the gossamer threads of spring silkworms" – Gu Kaizhi in the Yuan Renaissance', in McCausland (ed.), *Gu Kaizhi and the Admonitions Scroll* (as n. 26).

59 For the full painting, see Itakura, *Gen jidai no kaiga* (as n. 39), cat. no. 6. For an engraving dated 1617 and measuring 30 x 487.5 cm, in the Department of Art and Archaeology, Princeton University, see Fong, *Beyond Representation* (as n. 19), fig. 27.

60 See Ling Xuan, *Zhao Feiyan wai zhuan* (as n. 10). Illustrating this scene in the Shanghai Museum scroll, *Spring Morning in the Han Palace*, You Qiu showed the emperor and his new favourite Hede on the imperial barge.

61 For 'Ode on Lady Li', see Ban Gu, *Han Shu* (as n. 7), *juan* 97a, pp. 3953–54; Burton Watson (trans.), *Courtier and Commoner in Ancient China: Selections from the History of the Former Han* (New York: Columbia University Press, 1974), pp. 249–51.

62 Illustrated and discussed by Wen C. Fong and James C.Y. Watt, *Possessing the Past: Treasures from the National Palace Museum, Taipei* (New York: Metropolitan Museum of Art, 1996), pl. 204.

63 An example is the hanging scroll in Taipei attributed to Li Zhaodao, entitled *Winding River (Qujiang tu)*, which depicts a massive palace complex over an artificial lake to the southeast of the Tang capital. Illustrated in *Gugong shuhua tulu* (as n. 38)*,* vol. 1, p. 17.

64 For examples, see the mid-8th-century mural illustrations of the *Amitayurdhyana Sutra* in Cave 172 at Dunhuang, Gansu Province (in Barnhart et al., *Three Thousand Years of Chinese Painting*; fig. 66a & b).

65 Sakakibara Satoru, 'Chōgonka e no koto' (The matter of the *Song of Lasting Sorrow* painting).

66 Obtained with the assistance of colleagues in Japan through Kobe City Museum, and placed in the Library by former curator, Mrs Yoshiko Ushioda.

67 See for example, *Ishiyamadera engi emaki kōhon (*Preparatory Paintings for the Illustrated Legends of Ishiyamadera), 1805, by Tani Bunchō, in the collection of the Tokyo National Museum. http://webarchives.tnm.jp/archives/img/43372.

68 Miyajima, 'Chōgonka zukan', nos 33–34.

69 See, for example, Felice Fischer, *The Arts of

Hon'ami Kōetsu: Japanese Renaissance Master (Philadelphia: Philadelphia Museum of Art, 2000), p. 13. More recently, the notion of a 'classical revival' has come under scrutiny. See Elizabeth Lillehoj et al., *Critical Perspectives on Classicism in Japanese Painting, 1600–1700* (Honolulu: University of Hawai'i Press, 2004).

70 Prior to this volume, the Chester Beatty Library's *Chōgonka* scrolls have been fully reproduced in various publications, including: (1) Kobayashi Tadashi (ed.), *Hizō Nihon bijutsu taikan* (Japanese Art: The Great European Collections); (2) The Chester Beatty Library (ed.), *The Chogonka Scroll: A Japanese Masterpiece of the Seventeenth Century*; CD-ROM for Macintosh or Windows; one disk (Dublin: The Trustees of the Chester Beatty Library, 1997); and (3) Kamitaka et al. (eds), *Kano Sansetsu ga Chōgonka gakan*.

71 Unless otherwise indicated, quotations of translations of the 'Song of Lasting Sorrow' follow those in Owen, *An Anthology of Chinese Literature*, pp. 442–47, and Kamitaka et al. (eds), *Kano Sansetsu ga Chōgonka gakan*.

72 The treatise entitled *Honchō gashi* was published in 1693 but first appeared under the title *Honchō gaden* (Biographies of Painters of this Realm) in 1691. For a detailed analysis of the process by which the treatise was completed and published, see Kasai Masaaki (ed.), 'Kaidai', in Kasai, *Yakuchū honchō gashi*, pp. 511–17. For analyses of *Honchō gashi* in English, see Quitman Eugene Phillips, 'Honchō gashi and the Kano Myth', *Archives of Asian Art* 47 (1994), pp. 46–58; and Lippit, 'The Birth of Japanese Painting History' (as n. 36), especially ch. 5.

73 The phrasing of this translation is based on the punctuated *kanbun* version that appears in Kasai, *Yakuchū honchō gashi*, pp. 363–65.

74 *Seika bunshū* (Seika's Collected Writings) and *Kassho ikō* (Kassho's Manuscripts): both are quoted in Yamato Bunkakan (ed.), *Kano Sansetsu: Senkyō e no sasoi* (Kano Sansetsu: Invitation to the Realm of Immortality), p. 102.

75 Ibid.

76 Ibid.

77 For a concise account of the process by which the changes in the text occurred, see Kasai, *Yakuchū honchō gashi*, pp. 511–17, and Lippit, 'The Birth of Japanese Painting History' (as n. 36), pp. 500–15.

78 See Kasai, *Yakuchū honchō gashi*, pp. 392, 434 and 451–52.

79 The lengthy account given for Kano Sanraku, which appears at the end of the section devoted to schools of painters, might also be understood as a legitimising gesture that underscores the primacy of the Kyoto-Kano.

80 Painters of each scroll are listed with indications of which sections they painted at the end of each of the

three scrolls that comprise the *Taimadera engi*. 'Kano Nuidonosuke Fujiwara Sansetsu' is credited with the fifth section of the first scroll. See Nara Kokuritsu Hakubutsukan (ed.), *Shaji engi e* (Illustrated Legends of Temples and Shrines) (Tokyo: Kadokawa Shoten, 1975), p. 122.

81 The Tenkyūin room paintings have been the subject of numerous studies regarding their authorship, with scholarly opinion divided between those who consider the mural paintings and sliding panel paintings in the principal rooms to be the work of Sansetsu alone, and those who consider them to be the work of both Sansetsu and Sanraku (together with studio assistants). I subscribe to the theory, first proposed by Doi Tsugiyoshi in 1935, that Sansetsu was the primary artist of the project. See Doi Tsugiyoshi, 'Tenkyūin shōhekiga no hissha mondai' (Problems of Authorship of the Tenkyūin Room Paintings), *Tōyō bijutsu* (Arts of East Asia) 21 (1935), pp. 11–44. See also Yamane Yūzō et al., 'Tenkyūin shōhekiga no kenkyū' (Study of the Tenkyūin Room Paintings), *Kokka* 839 (1962), pp. 51–97. For a succinct overview of the scholarship on the Tenkyūin paintings, see Sakakibara Satoru, 'Tenkyūin shōhekiga kenkyū shōshi' (Short History of Studies of the Tenkyūin Room Paintings), *Kobijutsu* 98 (1991), pp. 44–47. The Tenshōin panels are now divided between the Metropolitan Museum of Art (*Old Plum*) and the Minneapolis Institute of Art (*Immortals*).

82 The other two images were sliding panels produced for Higashi Honganji and the Kōun'an subtemple of Kenninji. The former is preserved in a preparatory sketch illustrated in Doi Tsugiyoshi, *Kano Sanraku/Sansetsu*, p. 138, fig. 38.

83 See Sugihara Takuya, 'Kano Sansetsu hitsu Rekisei taijuzō ni tsuite' (Kano Sansetsu's Paintings of Noted Confucians of Various Periods), *Bijutsushi kenkyū* (The Study of the History of Art) 30 (1992), pp. 83–104. See also Kitano Yoshie, 'Sansetsu to shōrai hanpon' (Sansetsu and Imported Copybooks), in Machida Shiritsu Kokusai Hanga Bijutsukan (ed.), *Chūgoku shōkei: Nihon bijutsu no himitsu o sagure* (Longing for China: Searching for Secrets to Japanese Art), (Machida, 2007), p. 77.

84 See McKelway, 'Autumn Moon and Lingering Snow', pp. 33–80.

85 Tsuji Nobuo found in Sansetsu's more mannered images – especially the distorted forms of his *Old Plum* fusuma panels now in the Metropolitan Museum of Art – compelling reasons to place him at the beginning of his now classic 'lineage of eccentrics', an approach to comprehending Edo period painting through a loose grouping of painters notable for their penchant for unorthodox, bizarre styles or imagery. See Tsuji, *Kisō no keifu*, ch. 2, esp. pp. 58–59.

86 Masako Nakagawa Graham, *The Yang Kuei-fei Legend in Japanese Literature*, pp. 65, 70, n. 1.

87 Kōno Motoaki, 'Katarai: Genji monogatari to Chōgonka' (Conversations: The *Tale of Genji* and the *Song of Lasting Sorrow*), in Santorii Bijutsukan, *Deai to katarai: Koji jinbutsu ga to monogatari e* (Encounters and Conversations: The Painted Worlds of Legendary and Fabled People) (Tokyo: Suntory Museum, 2000), p. 6.

88 The *Kokka chinpō chō* catalogues the over 600 objects formerly belonging to Emperor Shōmu that Empress Kōmyō dedicated to Tōdaiji on the twenty-first day of the sixth month, 756.

89 Helen Craig McCullough, *Genji and Heike: Selections from The Tale of Genji and the Tale of the Heike* (Stanford: Stanford University Press, 1994), p. 32.

90 For the texts and translations of each of these poems, see Graham, *The Yang Kuei-fei Legend in Japanese Literature*, pp. 74–76.

91 Translation from Graham, *The Yang Kuei-fei Legend in Japanese Literature*, p. 75.

92 See Graham, *The Yang Kuei-fei Legend in Japanese Literature*, pp. 76–77, and Yoshida Yūji, 'Chōgonka fusuma-e ichi isaku: "Meikō setsubu zu" ni yosete' (A Sliding-Panel Painting of the *Song of Lasting Sorrow*: 'Minghuang Preparing to Dance'), pp. 17–18.

93 Ibid.

94 The *Heiji Monogatari*, quoted from Edwin Reischauer and Joseph Yamagiwa, *Translations from Early Japanese Literature* (Cambridge: Harvard University Press, 1951), p. 403.

95 For a full discussion of these texts and their formation of variant versions of the Xuanzong–Yang Guifei story, see Graham, *The Yang Kuei-fei Legend in Japanese Literature*, ch. 5–6.

96 Takeda Tsuneo, 'Gensō kōtei e' (Paintings of Emperor Hsüan Tsung), p. 16. See also Kawai Masatomo (ed.), *Kerun Tōyō Bijutsukan* (Cologne Museum of East Asian Art), *Hizō Nihon bijutsu taikan*, vol. 8 (Tokyo: Kōdansha, 1992), pp. 228–30. For the complete text of *Kaiyuan tianbao yishi*, see *Kaiyuan tianbao yishi*, in Congshu jicheng chubian (ed.), *Minghang zalu*, (Beijing: Zhonghua Shuju, 1985), pp. 1–30.

97 See Takemura Yasuyuki, '"Kaigen tenpō iji" no denrai ni tsuite: Nihon denzon no Ō Jinyū jijo o megutte' (On the text of 'Kai yuan tian bao yi shi': concerning the preface by Wang Renyu introduced to Japan), *Bungaku kenkyū* (Studies in Literature) 102 (2005), p. 54, p. 63, n. 2.

98 Takemura, '"Kaigen tenpō iji"', p. 54.

99 The fans are often referred to collectively as the 'Sasama fans' after their former owner, Sasama Kiyoshi. According to Narazaki Muneshige, the sixty images, mounted in an accordion album, may

originally have been mounted on a pair of folding screens. See Narazaki Muneshige, 'Sasama-ke zō senmen gajō' (The Album of Fan Paintings in the Sasama Collection), *Kokka* 845 (1962): pp. 339–81.

100 I am grateful to Chun-Yi Tsai, doctoral candidate at Columbia University, for her assistance in translating this passage.

101 Quote based on translation in Kamitaka et al. (eds), *Kano Sansetsu ga Chōgonka gakan*, p. 4.

102 Like the fans in the Nara National Museum group, many of the Nanzenji fans have inscriptions by Zen priests active in the late Muromachi period. According to Takeda Tsuneo, the fans can be dated to between 1533 and 1621, the earliest and latest death-dates of the priests. See Takeda Tsuneo, 'Nanzenji-zō senmen harimaze byōbu ni tsuite' (Studies of the Fan-Pasted Folding Screens in the Possession of the Nanzenji Temple), *Kokka* 872 (1964): pp. 9–61. The story of Xuanzong and the butterfly in *Kaiyuan tianbao yishi* relates that one spring, a butterfly the emperor released to fly about his gathered maidens landed on Yang Guifei, marking her as the one to whom he would bestow his special favour. See *Kaiyuan tianbao yishi* (as n. 96), p. 3.

103 See Takeda, 'Nanzenji-zō senmen harimaze byōbu ni tsuite' (as n. 102), p. 21, fig. 37.

104 Sakakibara Satoru, '"Teikanzu" shōkai', in Machida Shiritsu Kokusai Hanga Bijutsukan, *Kinsei Nihon kaiga to gafu, edehon ten: Meiga o unda hanga* (Early Modern Japanese Painting, Painting Manuals and Copybooks: Printed Images that Produced Masterpieces) (Tōkyō-to Machida-shi: Machida Shiritsu Kokusai Hanga Bijutsukan, 1990), p. 128.

105 Although the following discussion focuses on folding screen images of Yang Guifei and Minghuang, it should be noted that paintings on other formats, such as folding fans and handscrolls, continued to be produced in the late 16th–early 17th century. For example, the Tokyo National Museum exhibited a single handscroll entitled *Handscroll of the Song of Lasting Sorrow* (*Chōgonka emaki*) in 'Emaki', an exhibition of narrative scrolls held in 1974. Based on the photographs reproduced in the exhibition catalogue, the work appears to illustrate episodes, such as Yang Guifei bathing, and of An Lushan, that were not part of Bai Juyi's ballad. See Tokyo Kokuritsu Hakubutsukan, *Tokubetsuten: Emaki* (Special Exhibition: Illustrated Scrolls) (Tokyo National Museum, 1974), cat. 16.

106 The letter is undated but mentions the writer's own impending death, and can thus be dated to 1591. See Kuwata Tadachika, *Teihon Sen no Rikyū no shokan* (Standard Edition of Sen no Rikyū's Letters) (Tōkyō: Tōkyōdō Shuppan, 1971), pp. 603–06. See also Takeda, 'Gensō kōtei e', p. 17.

107 Kano Hiroyuki, *Jidai byōbu shūei, kaisetsu hen*

(Masterpieces of Folding Screens, Explanatory Notes) (Kyoto: Shikōsha, 2003), p. 18.

108 Ikeda Mariko names twenty different single and paired screens of Xuanzong–Yang Guifei themes in her 2003 study, but her list, based on previously published works, represents only part of what must have been an enormous corpus of works. Screens in the Musée Guimet, for example, are not included, nor are the works published in the final volume of *Nihon byōbu e shūsei*, Takeda Tsuneo, et al., *Bekkan: byōbu e taikan* (Supplementum: Survey of Screen Paintings); *Nihon byōbu-e shūsei* (Compendium of Japanese Screen Paintings) (Tokyo: Kōdansha, 1981). See Ikeda Mariko, 'Nihon ni okeru Gensō Yōkihi zu: Kinsei shoki no gadai to zuyō' (Images of Xuanzong and Yang Guifei in Japan: Painting Subjects and Compositions in the Early Modern Period), *Bijutsushi kenkyū* 41 (2003), p. 44.

109 *Nihon byōbu-e shūsei*, the most thorough compendium of screen painting genres, reproduces three examples depicting *The Elegant Battle* (MOA Museum), *Golden Bell* and *Flute Duet* (Fugen'in temple) and *Emperor Xuanzong Bringing Forth the Drum to Cause the Flowers to Bloom* (private collection). See Toda Teisuke et al. (eds), *Jinbutsu ga: Kanga kei jinbutsu* (Figure Paintings: Chinese-style Figures), *Nihon byōbu-e shūsei*, vol. 4 (Tokyo: Kōdansha, 1980), pp. 72–73.

110 Inawashiro Kensai (1452–1510), *renga* poet.

111 Oze Hoan, *Taikō ki; Shin Nihon koten bungaku taikei* (New Compendium of Classical Japanese Literature) 60 (Tokyo: Iwanami Shoten, 1996), p. 482.

113 Takeda, 'Gensō kōtei e', p. 19.

114 Takeda judges the brushwork of the Yoshimizu Shrine panels to reflect the work of an artist 'in the circle' of Kano Mitsunobu. See Takeda, 'Gensō kōtei e', p. 19.

115 Nara-ken Kyōiku Iinkai, *Jūyō bunkazai Yoshimizu Jinja shoin shūri kōji hōkoku sho* (Report on the Conservation of the Yoshimizu Shrine Shoin, Important Cultural Property) (Nara-ken Kyōiku Iinkai, 1972), p. 24, cited in Takeda, 'Gensō kōtei e', p. 19.

116 See Sakazaki Shizuka, *Nihon garon taikei* (Compendium of Treatises on Japanese Painting), vol. 2 (Tokyo: Meicho Fukyūkai, 1980), pp. 90–91, 134–135.

117 Ibid., p. 135.

118 Ibid.

119 Ibid.

120 The Freer screens were first published by Doi Tsugiyoshi in 1965, and Suzuki Hiroyuki followed with a more extensive analysis in 1980. See Doi Tsugiyoshi, 'Amerika de mita shōhei ga' (Mural Paintings I Saw in America), MIZUE 729 (Nov., 1965), and Suzuki Hiroyuki, 'Kinsei shoki ni okeru

"Chōgonka e": Furia Bijutsukan bon "Meikō Yōkihi zu byōbu" o chūshin ni shite' (Early Modern Paintings of the *Song of Lasting Sorrow*: The 'Screens of Minghuang and Yang Guifei' in the Freer Gallery), in Toda Teisuke et al. (eds), *Jinbutsu ga: Kanga kei jinbutsu; Nihon byōbu-e shūsei*, vol. 4 (Tokyo: Kōdansha, 1980), pp. 152–58.

121 Translation by Owen, *An Anthology of Chinese Literature*, p. 447.

122 Suzuki, 'Kinsei shoki ni okeru "Chōgonka e"', pp. 152–53.

123 According to Suzuki Hiroyuki, the procession could also represent Minghuang's return from exile to Chang'an in 757. See Suzuki, 'Kinsei shoki ni okeru "Chōgonka e"', p. 153.

124 Adapted from Owen, *An Anthology of Chinese Literature*, pp. 444–45.

125 Now in the collection of the Tokyo National Museum, the screen was published in Santorii Bijutsukan, *Deai to katarai: Koji jinbutsu ga to monogatari e*, exh. cat. (Suntory Museum, 2000), cat. 44, p. 118.

126 Other works produced in the early 17th century also depicted An Lushan's rebellion, as Yoshida Yūji has shown in an article on a pair of six-panel screens, formerly mounted as sliding panels, in the temple Enjōji in Sakai. This work depicts An Lushan and his troops attacking a palace, from which Minghuang and Yang Guifei depart in a carriage. See Yoshida, 'Chōgonka fusuma-e ichi isaku' (as n. 92), pp. 15–22.

127 Titled *Meikō Yōkihi zu byōbu* (*Screen Painting of Minghuang and Yang Guifei*), this work was first exhibited at the Kyoto National Museum in 2001. The artist signed the screen 'Kano shi Sansetsu', and stamped it with his 'Sansetsu' seal in the lower left, indicating that it was the left screen of a pair. In the catalogue entry on the screen, Kano Hiroyuki speculates that it takes the theme 'Meikō setsubu zu' from *Kōsoshū*, and that the other half would have depicted An Lushan's attack, as indicated in *Kōsoshū*'s synopsis of the theme. See Kyoto Kokuritsu Hakubutsukan (ed.), *Hyūman imeeji: wareware wa ningen o dono yō ni hyōgen shite kita no ka* (Special Exhibition: Human Images) (Kyoto National Museum), pp. 66–67, 284.

128 Conservators at the Handa Kyūseidō studio based in the Tokyo National Museum discovered applications of pigments on the backs of the silk sections of the scrolls during conservation work in 1993. See Hirayama Ikuo et al., *Zaigai Nihon Bijutsu no shūfuku: kaiga* (Restoration of Japanese Art in European and American Collections: Painting) (Tokyo: Chūō Kōronsha, 1995), pp. 294–99. For photos of the verso painting, see Asahi Shinbun Nichiyōban (ed.), *Meiga Nihonshi* (Japanese History in Masterpieces), 1 (Tokyo: Asahi

Shinbunsha, 2000), pp. 32–35.

129 First proposed by Sakakibara Satoru; see Kobayashi (ed.), *Hizō Nihon bijutsu taikan*, p. 257.

130 See McCausland in present volume, p. 36.

131 Yoshiaki Shimizu, 'The *Shigisan-engi* Scrolls, *c.*1175', *Studies in the History of Art* XVI (1985), pp. 120–21.

132 From the translation of 'The Song of Lasting Regret' in Mair (ed.), *The Columbia Anthology of Traditional Chinese Literature* (as n. 24), p. 481.

133 See Hayashi Susumu, *Nihon kinsei kaiga no zuzō gaku: Shukō to shin'i* (Iconography of Early Modern Japanese Painting: Ideas and Meanings) (Tokyo: Yagi Shoten, 2000), pp. 82–83.

134 My translation. The replacement of 'bells' with 'monkeys' appears to have occurred early in Japan. *Wakan rōeishū* (*c.*1018) includes the line, replacing 'bell' with 'monkey'.

135 In Iwasa Matabei's *Jōruri* scrolls, the luxuriant interior of Princess Jōruri's palace changes subtly with each scene of her encounter with the hero, Ushiwaka. See Tsuji Nobuo et al., *Emaki Jōruri: Tsuyama-han Matsudaira-ke denrai* (The *Jōruri* Scrolls from the Matsudaira Collection in Tsuyama Domain) (Iwasa Matabei Kōbō), (Kyoto: Kyōto Shoin, 1977), pl. 38–47.

136 The whereabouts of this work are unknown, but Doi Tsugiyoshi, who saw them in an unnamed private collection in Kyoto, reproduces a detail showing two of the Chinese sages. See Doi, *Kano Sanraku/Sansetsu*, pp. 108–09, fig. 18.

137 Yamashita Yoshiya, 'Kano Sansetsu hitsu "Fuji Miho matsubara zu byōbu": zuyō no genryū to kakushinsei ni tsuite' (Kano Sansetsu's *Screens of Mount Fuji and Miho Pine Strand*: The Origins and Originality of Their Composition), *Shizuoka kenritsu bijutsukan kiyō* (Shizuoka Prefectural Museum Journal) 2 (1984): pp. 6–23.

138 Yukio Lippit makes a case for this assertion in a broader analysis of Kano Tan'yū's many paintings of Mount Fuji. See Lippit, 'The Birth of Japanese Painting History' (as n. 36), pp. 158–63.

139 A similar hand revealing a penchant for clerical script can be detected in inscriptions that appear on the scrolls in the Kuki collection, and also on Sansetsu's *West Lake* screens, particularly in the character for 'snow'. See McKelway, 'Autumn Moon and Lingering Snow', p. 54, fig. 3b.

140 On specific evidence for Sansetsu's use of Chinese paintings as sources for his own work, see the following: Hayashi, 'Kano Sansetsu no *Bankoku zu* ni tsuite', pp. 7–37, esp. pp. 25–34; Kitano, 'Sansetsu to shōrai hanpon' (as n. 83); Sugihara, 'Kano Sansetsu hitsu Rekisei taijuzō ni tsuite' (also as n. 83); and in the present volume, Lin, Li-chiang, 'Ming Paintings and Prints: Possible Sources for Kano Sansetsu's *Chōgonka* Scrolls'.

141 Sakakibara, 'Chōgonka e no koto', pp. 276–77.

142 Today, the three scrolls of *Genjō Sanzō e* are in the collection of the Fujita Museum, Osaka, but *Kanmon gyoki*, the diary of Prince Fushimi Sadafusa (1372–1456), explicitly states that in the early 15th century the scrolls were in the possession of the Daijōin temple. The close links between aristocrats in Kyoto like Sadafusa and the Nara-based abbots of Daijōin appear to have occasioned viewings of the *Genjō Sanzō* scrolls in the capital, for the diaries of abbots of the Daijōin, *Daijōin jisha zōji ki*, and of the courtier Sanjōnishi Sanetaka (1455–1537), *Sanetaka kō ki*, recount loans and viewings several times in the 15th and early 16th century. See Komatsu Shigemi (ed.), *Genjō Sanzō e ge* vol. 3, *Zoku Nihon no emaki* vol. 6 (Tokyo: Chūō Kōronsha, 1990), pp. 129–33.

143 Itakura Masaaki has noted the similarities between three Chinese handscroll paintings and Sansetsu's scrolls: Wu Bin, *Road through Mountain Shadows* (1608, Shanghai Museum); Tang Yin (1470–1523), *Dreaming of Immortality in a Thatched Hut* (undated, Freer Gallery of Art); and Qiu Ying (1494–1552), *Jiucheng Palace* (undated, Osaka Municipal Museum). See Itakura, 'Kano Sansetsu ga egaita *Chōgonka zu*', pp. 11–12.

144 Wakisaka Atsushi, 'Chōgonka emaki kō' (A Consideration of the *Chōgonka* Scrolls), pp. 11–17.

145 Beyond the scope of the present study are several anonymous scroll paintings and painted books depicting the 'Song of Lasting Sorrow' that are grouped within the general rubric of *Nara ehon* (Nara picture-books). Although like the Kuki scrolls – and perhaps the Chester Beatty scrolls in their original form – some *Nara ehon* versions are also comprised of three scrolls, their compositions are markedly different from Sansetsu's images and alternate with passages of text. Examples in Osaka Ohtani University and the Kuyō Bunko are based on *Yōkihi monogatari* (Tale of Yang Guifei), an illustrated book in three volumes printed *c.*1658–72, and are thus later in date than the works under consideration in this book. The Osaka Ohtani University scrolls are accessible in detail on the following website: http://www2.osaka-ohtani.ac.jp /chougonka/index.html. For reproductions of two other similar scrolls, see Nakano Kōichi (ed.), *Nara ehon emaki shū 9: Chōgonka, Buke hanjō, Fujibukuro no sōshi*.

146 For a discussion of depictions of 'Chinese Beauties' by painters active in late 18th-century Kyoto, see Timothy Clark, 'Japanese Paintings of Chinese Beauties in the Late Edo Period', in Miyeko Murase (ed.), *The Arts of Japan: An International Symposium* (New York: Metropolitan Museum of Art, 2000), pp. 221–251.

147 McCausland, in present volume, p. 8.

148 See Wakisaka, 'Chōgonka emaki kō', pp. 14–15.

149 See Hirayama Ikuo et al., *Zaigai Nihon Bijutsu no shūfuku: kaiga* (as n. 128), pp. 216, 218. A survey of Sansetsu's works reproduced in the Yamato Bunkakan's catalogue of its exhibition, *Kano Sansetsu: Senkyō e no sasoi*, reveals no single habit for the artist's signatures, but among the works that are signed, most are signed simply 'Sansetsu', with one or more seals. The signature on the Kuki scrolls does not appear to be inconsistent with these patterns of usage.

150 See Yamato Bunkakan (ed.), *Kano Sansetsu: Senkyō e no sasoi*, cat. no. 31, p. 72.

151 Yamato Bunkakan (ed.), *Kano Sansetsu: Senkyō e no sasoi*, cat. no. 43, p. 93.

152 For discussions of the Painting Bureau, see John Rosenfield, 'Japanese Studio Practice: The Tosa Family and the Imperial Painting Office in the Seventeenth Century'; Peter Lukehart (ed.), *The Artist's Workshop* (Washington, DC, 1993), pp. 79–101; and Kamei Wakana, '"Edokoro azukari Tosa Mitsunobu" no saikentō' (A Reconsideration of Tosa Mitsunobu, Director of the Painting Bureau), part 2 of Chino Kaori et al., 'Haabaado Daigaku Bijutsukan zō "Genji monogatari gajō" o meguru shomondai' (The Tale of Genji Album in the Harvard University Art Museum), *Kokka* 1222 (1997), pp. 15–18.

153 See Kawamoto Keiko, 'Kujō ke denrai no kuruma arasoi zu o megutte' (Battle of the Carriages, a Screen Painting Once Owned by the Kujō Family), in Yamane Yūzō-sensei koki kinenkai (ed.), *Nihon kaiga shi no kenkyū* (Studies in the History of Japanese Painting) (Kyoto: Yoshikawa Kōbunkan, 1989), pp. 291–94.

154 Kawamoto, 'Kujō ke denrai no kuruma arasoi zu o megutte', p. 292.

155 A note of authentication, dated to Kanbun 3 (1663), third month, twelfth day, by Kano Einō, that accompanies the two paintings of Kannon by Sansetsu corroborates Gahō's account. Einō's note, which corresponds in date to the 13th anniversary of Sansetsu's death, states that it was former Regent Kujō Sachiie who commissioned the Kannon paintings. See Doi Tsugiyoshi, *Sanraku to Sansetsu* (Sanraku and Sansetsu); *Nihon no bijutsu* 172 (September 1980), p. 37, fig. 32.

156 Reproduced in Yamato Bunkakan (ed.), *Kano Sansetsu: Senkyō e no sasoi*, p. 99.

157 Igarashi Kōichi, '17 seiki: Kyō-gano to Edo Kano', *Kano-ke eshi no tayō na shigoto* (Various Tasks of Painters in the House of Kano), Musashino Bijutsu Daigaku Bijutsu Shiryō Toshokan, Musashino Bijutsu Daigaku, October 21, 2006.

158 From the collection of Marquis Kujō (Kujō kōshaku ke), *Chinese Sages and Philosophers* was auctioned in Tokyo in July 1922, and *Hotei*, a hanging scroll in

the collection of Kujō Michihide (1895–1961), was published in *Kokka* in 1934. See Yamato Bunkakan (ed.), *Kano Sansetsu: Senkyō e no sasoi*, p. 106.

159 For records of these paintings, see Hu Fengdan, *Mawei zhi* (Gazetteer of Mawei) (Nanking: Jiangsu guji chubanshe, 1990), ch. 4.

160 For Chinese paintings illustrating Minghuang and Yang Guifei stories, see Owen, 'Love Lost'. To date, no continuous multi-scene narrative paintings about Minghuang and Guifei have been identified.

161 Itakura, 'Kano Sansetsu ga egaita *Chōgonka zu*', pp. 6–7. My thanks go to Professor Itakura for sending me this insightful article, which inspired my research.

162 Itakura, 'Kano Sansetsu ga egaita *Chōgonka zu*', p. 8.

163 For example, the images from *Hainei qiguan* were among those recorded in Tan'yū's *Small Sketches*; see Itakura Masaaki, 'Tan'yū *shukuzu* kara mita Higashi Ajia kaigashi – shōshō hakkei o rei ni' (East Asian Painting History seen from the *Small Sketches* by Tan'yū – Taking the 'Eight Views of Xiao-Xiang' as an Example), pp. 111–38.

164 See studies by Ōba Osamu that document the import of books into Japan during the Ming period; especially *Kanseki yunyū no bunkashi: Shōtoku Taishi kara Yoshimune e* (The cultural history of imported Chinese books in the Edo period: from Prince Shōtoku to Yoshimune) (Tokyo: Kenbun, 1997).

165 For a summary of Japanese scholarship on *Teikan zusetsu*, see Machida Shiritsu Kokusai Hanga Bijutsukan, *Kinsei Nihon kaiga to gafu, edehon ten: Meiga o unda hanga* (as n. 104); see also Lin, Li-chiang, 'The Creation and Transformation of Ancient Rulership in the Ming Dynasty (1368–1644) – A look at the *Dijian tushuo* (Illustrated Arguments in the Mirror of the Emperors)'.

166 Itakura, 'Tan'yū *shukuzu* kara mita Higashi Ajia kaigashi', p. 115.

167 Ōba, *Kanseki yunyū no bunkashi: Shōtoku Taishi kara Yoshimune e* (as n. 164), pp. 100–01.

168 For a reproduction of the *Mengxian caotang* painting, see Anne De Coursey Clapp, *The Painting of T'ang Yin* (Chicago & London: The University of Chicago press, 1991), pl. 6; as for the *Jiucheng Palace* painting, there is one copy housed in the Osaka Municipal Museum of Art.

169 Itakura, 'Kano Sansetsu ga egaita *Chōgonka zu*', pp. 10–11.

170 On famous forged paintings in the Ming period, see Yang Renkai, *Zhongguo shuhua jianding xuegao* (Preliminary studies on the authenticity of Chinese calligraphy and paintings) (Shenyang: Liaohai, 2000), pp. 217–23.

171 Decadent lifestyles of the late Ming are recorded in many documents, and have been widely researched. To name a few, see Lin Liyue: 'Shibian yu zhixu – Mingdai shehui fengshang xiangguan yanjiu pingshu' (Social Transformation and Continuity – Evaluating research on Ming society and style), *Mingdai yanjiu tongxu*, no. 4 (2001.12), pp. 9–19; Wu Renshu, *Pin wei she hua: wan Ming de xiaofei shehui yu shidafu* (Taipei: Zhongyang yanjiuyuan, Lianjing, 2007).

172 Itakura, 'Tan'yū *shukuzu* kara mita Higashi Ajia kaigashi', pp. 111–38.

173 Kano Einō, *Chōgonka zushō*, for which see Itakura, Kano Sansetsu ga egaita *Chōgonka zu*, pp. 7–8.

174 See Ōba Osamu, *Edo jidai ni okeru Tōsen mochiwatashisho no kinkyū* (Studies on Chinese books imported into Japan in the Edo period) (Suita-shi: Kansai Daigaku Tōzai Gakujustsu Kenkyūjo, 1981 [1967]). Wang Yong et al., *Zhong-Ri shuji zhi lu yanjiu* (Research on the traffic of books between China and Japan) (Beijing: Beijing tushuguan chubanshe, 2003).

175 The *Yuanqu xuan* was compiled by Zang Maoxun (1550–1620) and published by Bogutang; *Gu zaju* was compiled by Wang Jide (?–1623) and published by Guquzhai; and *Leijiang ji* was compiled by Meng Chengshun (?–1684). For further details, see Zeng Yongyi, *Zhongguo gudian xiju de renshi yu xinshan* (Understanding and Appreciation of Chinese Classical Drama) (Taipei: Zhengzhong, 1991), pp. 5–7.

176 This essay does not consider dramas or works of fiction in which Minghuang and Guifei are not the protagonists, such as the drama *Caihao ji* (Tale of the Colourful Brush), which tells the story of the poet Li Bai (701–62) in Minghuang's time.

177 The poet Cao Zhi (192–232) coined the term *jinghong* (startled goose) to depict the willowy figure and graceful movement of the nymph of the Luo river in his 'Nymph of the Luo River Ode' (Luoshen fu). On the authorship of *Jinghong ji*, see Kang Baocheng (annot.), *Jinghong ji Yanmei ji* (Tale of the Startled Geese, Tale of the Salty Plum), pp. 1–6.

178 The *Difei chunyu* is included in *Gu mingjia zaju* (Poetic Dramas by Old Masters), edition by Chen Yujiao (1544–1611), with a postscript dated no later than 1589. The author of the *Difei chunyu* was Cheng Shilian (fl. 2nd half of the 16th century). Wang Daokun also composed a drama relating to the Minghuang and Guifei story, entitled *Tang Minghuang qixi Changshengdian* (Tang Minghuang at the Palace of Long-Life on the 'Night of Sevens'), which is not extant.

179 Although Meifei is cited in many sources as Yang Guifei's rival in love, her existence is still questioned. The earliest references date to the Song dynasty, but she is not mentioned in the official histories, *Jiu Tang shu* and *Xin Tang shu*. For further research on Meifei, see Takemura Nariyuki, *Yōkihi Bungakushi kenkyū* (Tokyo: Genbun, 2003), pp. 208–11 and 329–55.

180 This novel was written by Xihu Meidaoren (Plum Daoist of West Lake). The National Library in Beijing has one incomplete copy. For a modern reproduction, see Jin Peilin and Zhou Xinhua (eds), *Guben xiaoshuo banhua tulu* (Catalogue of Ancient Editions of Print Illustrations), vol. 2, pp. 614–25.

181 A 'slender' Yang Guifei contradicts most people's image of her. This issue is not explored further here, but the transformation of images of Yang Guifei in Japan, as well as in China, merits further research.

182 *Liuzhi ji* is part one of *Xinjuan gujin mingju*, compiled by Meng Chengshun. *Leijiang ji*, discussed above (see n. 175), is part two.

183 Itakura Masaaki observes that the figure types in Sansetsu's *Song of Lasting Sorrow*, as well as in other scrolls attributed to him, are quite similar to those in Ming painting; see 'Kano Sansetsu ga egaita *Chōgonka zu*', pp. 10–11. For forgeries in late Ming China, see Yang Chenbin, 'Tan Mingdai shuhua zuowei' (On the making of forgeries in Ming China), in Yang Renkai (ed.), *Zhongguo gujin shuhua zhenwei tujian*, (Shenyang: Liaoning huabao, 1996); Ellen J. Laing, 'Suzhou Pian and Other Dubious Paintings in the Received Oeuvre of Qiu Ying', *Artibus Asiae*, vol. 59, no. 3/4 (2000), pp. 265–95.

184 For illustrations, see *Tan'yū shukuzu*, vol. 2 (Kyoto: Dōhōsha, 1980–81), pp. 31–32, 191. For the *Xixiang ji* prints, see Ma Meng-ching, 'Fragmentation and Framing of the Text: Visuality and Narrativity in Late-Ming Illustrations to *The Story of the Western Wing*', PhD diss., Standford University, 2006.

185 See Yoshiko Ushioda, 'Sir Chester Beatty and his Japanese Collection', pp. 235–41.

186 The detailed description of the conservation treatment of the scrolls is taken directly from notes in Hirayama Ikuo et al., *Zaigai Nihon Bijutsu no shūfuku: kaiga* (as n. 128), pp. 295–99. Additional details are from the research notes of Yoshiko Ushioda, taken when she was a curator at the Library, and the notes she made while studying in Mr Handa's restoration studio at Tokyo National Museum.

187 *Chang hen ge* text in *Quan Tang shi*, p. 3435; translation by Owen, *An Anthology of Chinese Literature*, pp. 442–47.

188 A famous musical suite and dance associated with Yang Guifei.

189 *Chang hen ge zhuan* text in *Quan Tang shi*, pp. 4816–19; translation by Owen, *An Anthology of Chinese Literature*, pp. 448–52.

SELECT BIBLIOGRAPHY

CHINESE

Hainei qiguan: Yang Erzeng, *Hainei qiguan* (Extraordinary Views of the World [i.e. China]), 1609, reprint. Series, *Zhongguo gudai banhua congkan erbian*, vol. 8. Shanghai: Shanghai guji chubanshe, 1994.

Jin Peilin and Zhou Xinhua (eds), *Guben xiaoshuo banhua tulu* (Catalogue of Ancient Editions of Print Illustrations). Beijing: Xianchuang shuju, 2006.

Jiu Tang shu: Liu Xu, *Jiu Tang shu* (Old History of the Tang Dynasty); 16 vols. Beijing: Zhonghua, 1975.

Kang Baocheng (annot.), *Jinghong ji Yanmei ji* (Tale of the Startled Geese, Tale of the Salty Plum). In *Ming Qing chuanqi xuankan* (Anthology of poetic dramas of the Ming and Qing dynasties). Beijing: Zhonghua, 2004.

Li Lin-ts'an, *Minghuang xing Shu tu* de yanjiu (Research on the painting of *Minghuang's Flight to Shu*). In *Zhongguo minghua* yanjiu (Research on famous Chinese paintings), vol. 1. Taipei: Yiwen yinshuguan, 1973.

Quan Tang shi: Peng Dingqiu et al. (comps), *Quan Tang shi* (Complete Collection of Tang Poetry). Beijing: Zhonghua shuju, 1960.

Sancai tuhui: Wang Qi and Wang Siyi (comps), *Sancai tuhui* (Pictorial Compendium of the Three Realms), 1609; reprint of Wanli edition in Shanghai Library. Shanghai: Shanghai guji chubanshe, 1988.

Xin Tang shu: Ouyang Xiu and Song Qi, *Xin Tang shu* (New History of the Tang Dynasty), 20 vols. Beijing: Zhonghua shuju, 1975.

JAPANESE

Chesutaa Biitii Raiburarii emaki ehon kaidai mokuroku (Descriptive catalogue of picture-scrolls and picture-books in the Chester Beatty Library). Tokyo: Bensei Shuppan, 2002.

Doi Tsugiyoshi, *Kano Sanraku/Sansetsu*. Series, *Nihon bijutsu kaiga zenshū*, vol. 12, Shūeisha, 1981.

Hayashi Susumu, 'Kano Sansetsu no *Bankoku zu* ni tsuite' (On Kano Sansetsu's *Pangu Valley* Hanging Scroll). *Yamato Bunka* 82, 1989, pp. 7–37.

Itakura Masaaki, '*Tan'yū shukuzu* kara mita Higashi Ajia kaigashi – shōshō hakkei o rei ni' (East Asian Painting History seen from the *Small Sketches by Tan'yū* – Taking the 'Eight Views of Xiao-Xiang' as an Example). In Satō Yasuhiro (ed.), *Kōza Nihon bijutsushi* (Discourses on the history of Japanese art), vol. 3, *Zuzō no imi* (Meanings of images). Tokyo: Tokyo Daigaku Shuppankai, 2005, pp. 111–38.

Itakura Masaaki, 'Kano Sansetsu ga egaita *Chōgonka zu* – itan kara koten e' (Kano Sansetsu's painting of the *Chōgonka:* From Nonconformity to Classicism). University Press, 404 (June 2006), pp. 6–12.

Kamitaka Tokuharu et al. (eds), *Kano Sansetsu ga Chōgonka gakan* (The *Song of Lasting Sorrow* picture-scrolls by Kano Sansetsu). The Chester Beatty Library, Shohan, Yomigaeru emaki, ehon 2. Tokyo: Bensei Shuppan, 2006.

Kano Einō, *Chōgonka zushō*, 1677. British Library: Or.74.cc.7, volumes 1–5.

Kano Einō (comp.), *Honchō gashi* (History of Painting in this Realm), 1693. In Kasai Masaaki (ed.) et al., *Yakuchū honchō gashi* (History of Painting in this Realm, Annotated). Tokyo: Dōhōsha, 1985.

Kawaguchi Hisao, *Chōgonka emaki* (The *Song of Lasting Sorrow* picture-scrolls). Tokyo: Taishūkan Shoten, 1982.

Kitano Yoshie, 'Kano Sansetsu hitsu Saiko zu byōbu' (The West Lake screens painted by Kano Sansetsu). *Kokka* no. 1227, 1998, pp. 29–31.

Kobayashi Tadashi (ed.), *Hizō Nihon bijutsu taikan* (Japanese Art: The Great European Collections), vol. 5. The Chester Beatty Library. Tokyo: Kōdansha, 1993.

Miyajima Shin'ichi, 'Chōgonka zukan'. In Hirayama Ikuo et al., *Zaigai Nihon bijutsu no shūfuku* (Restoration of Japanese art in European and American Collections). Tokyo: Chūō Kōronsha, 1995.

Nakano Kōichi (ed.), *Nara ehon emaki shū 9: Chōgonka, Buke hanjō, Fujibukuro no sōshi* (Collection of *Nara ehon* picture-scrolls: *Song of Lasting Sorrow*, Buke hanjō, The Tale of Fujibukuro). Tokyo: Waseda Daigaku Shuppanbu, 1998.

Sakakibara Satoru, 'Chōgonka e no koto' (The matter of the *Song of Lasting Sorrow* painting). In *Chesutaa Biitii Raiburarii*. Series, *Hizō Nihon Bijutsu Taikan*, vol. 5. Tokyo: Kodansha, 1993, pp. 276–80.

Sorimachi Shigeo, *Japanese Illustrated Books and Manuscripts in the Chester Beatty Library, Dublin, Ireland* (*Nihon eiribon oyobi ehon mokuroku*). Tokyo: The Kōbunsō, 1979, no. 87.

Takeda Tsuneo, 'Gensō kōtei e' (Paintings of Emperor Hsüan Tsung). *Kokka* no. 1049 (1982), pp. 13–25.

Tsuji Nobuo, *Kisō no keifu* (The Lineage of Eccentrics). Tokyo: Bijutsu Shuppansha, 1970.

Wakisaka Atsushi, 'Chōgonka emaki kō' (A Consideration of the *Chōgonka* Scrolls). *Nihon bijutsu kōgei* 621 (June, 1990), pp. 11–17.

Yamato Bunkakan (ed.), *Kano Sansetsu: Senkyō e no sasoi* (Kano Sansetsu: Invitation to the Realm of Immortality). Exh. cat., Yamato Bunkakan, 1986.

Yoshida Yūji, 'Chōgonka fusuma-e ichi isaku: "Meikō setsubu zu" ni yosete' (A Sliding-panel Painting of the *Song of Lasting Sorrow*: 'Minghuang Preparing to Dance'). *Nihon bijutsu kōgei* (Japanese Fine and Applied Arts) (June 1979), pp. 15–22.

WESTERN LANGUAGES

Barnhart, Richard M. et al, *Three Thousand Years of Chinese Painting*. New Haven: Yale University Press; Beijing: Foreign Languages Press, 1997.

Clunas, Craig, *Pictures and Visuality in Early Modern China*. London: Reaktion, 1997.

Graham, Masako Nakagawa, *The Yang Kuei-fei Legend in Japanese Literature*. New York: The Edwin Mellen Press, 1998.

Lin, Li-chiang, 'The Creation and Transformation of Ancient Rulership in the Ming Dynasty (1368–1644): A look at the *Dijian tushuo* (Illustrated Arguments in the Mirror of the Emperors)'. In Dieter Kuhn & Helga Stahl (eds), *Perceptions of Antiquity in Chinese Civilization*. Heidelberg: Edition Forum, 2008, pp. 321–59.

Loehr, Max, *The Great Painters of China*. New York: Harper and Row, 1980.

McKelway, Matthew, 'Autumn Moon and Lingering Snow: Kano Sansetsu's West Lake Screens'. *Artibus Asiae*, vol. 62, no. 1 (2002), pp. 33–80.

McKelway, Matthew, *Capitalscapes: Folding Screens and the Political Imagination in Late Medieval Kyoto*. Honolulu: University of Hawai'i Press, 2006.

Mair, Victor H. (ed.), *The Columbia History of Chinese Literature*. New York: Columbia Univ. Press, 2001. Esp. ch. 54, 'The Reception of Chinese Literature in Japan', pp. 1086–87.

Murasaki Shikibu (trans. Royall Tyler), *The Tale of Genji*. New York: Viking, 2001.

Murasaki Shikibu (trans. Edward Seidensticker), *The Tale of Genji*. New York: Vintage Books, 1990.

Okudaira, Hideo, *Narrative Picture Scrolls*. Series, *Arts of Japan 5*. New York & Tokyo: Weatherhill/Shibundo, 1973.

Owen, Elizabeth M., 'Love Lost: Qian Xuan (*c.*1235–1307) and Images of Emperor Minghuang and Yang Guifei'. PhD diss., Yale University; Ann Arbor: UMI, 2005.

Owen, Stephen (ed. and trans.), 'Interlude: Xuanzong and Yang the Prized Consort'. In *An Anthology of Chinese Literature: Beginnings to 1911*. New York: Norton, 1996, pp. 441–57.

Pulleyblank, Edwin G., *The Background of the Rebellion of An Lushan*. London: Oxford University Press, 1955.

Robinson, Kate, 'An Edo Masterwork Restored. The Chōgonka Scrolls in The Chester Beatty Library, Dublin'. *Irish Arts Review*, vol. 16 (Yearbook 2000), pp. 73–80.

Stone, Charles R., *The Fountainhead of Chinese Erotica: the Lord of Perfect Satisfaction (Ruyijun zhuan)*. Honolulu: University of Hawai'i Press, 2003.

Ushioda, Yoshiko, 'Sir Chester Beatty and his Japanese Collection'. *Japan Forum*, vol. 2, no. 2 (November 1990), pp. 235–41.

Ushioda, Yoshiko, *Tales of Japan: Three Centuries of Japanese Painting from the Chester Beatty Library, Dublin*. Alexandria, VA: Art Services International, 1992.

Waley, Arthur, *The Life and Times of Po Chü-i*. London: Allen and Unwin, 1948.

INDEX

NOTE: Page numbers in italic refer to the captions for the illustrations.

A

'An Account to Go with the "Song of Lasting Sorrow"' (Chen Hong) 17, 20, 63
complete text 176–79
quoted 24, 43–44, 62, 78–79, 83, 85–87, 89–90, 91
Admonitions of the Court Instructress (attrib. to Gu Kaizhi)
'Lady Ban declining to ride in the imperial palanquin' 22, *23*
'Lady reflecting on her duty' 48, *48*
The 'toilette' scene 29, *30*, 55
Agriculture in the Four Seasons (Kano Sansetsu) 113, *113*
An Lushan Rebellion 8, 20, 56–59
Anthology of Poetry in Wu Region see *Wusao ji*

B

Bai Juyi 25
Chang hen ge see *Chang hen ge* ('Song of Lasting Sorrow')
'The Girl Who Danced the Whirl' 23–24
Bai Pu, *Wutongyu (Tang Minghuang Qiuye Wutongyu (Tang Minghuang [Listening to] the Rain…))* 155, *156–58*, 159, 160, *160–61*, 162, *163*
Ban Dainagon ekotoba scrolls 133
Ban *Jieyu* (Consort Ban) 22
Bankoku zu (Pangu Valley) (Kano Sansetsu) 137, *139*
Beatty, A. Chester, acquisition of *Chōgonka* scrolls 166
beauty, female
models of 30, 48, 50, 146, 160–61, *161*, *162*
symbols of 78
books see drama; travel literature; woodblock-print-illustrated books; *names of individual writers and titles of works*
Bridge of the Dharma see *Hokkyo*
bridge motif 50, 67–68, 75, 142

C

Cao Zhi, *'Luoshen fu'* 48
Chang hen ge, works under this title 33
Chang hen ge ('Song of Lasting Sorrow') (Bai Juyi) 8, 20, 24
complete text 172–75

historical accuracy of 43–44
inscriptions of, on Kuki scroll 101, 102
Japanese admiration and representations of 25, 115
Japanese text of, in *Chōgonka zushō* 143–45
quoted 51, 68, 125, 126, 137, 138
Sansetsu's interpretation of 16–17, 36, 149, 152, 162
see also Bai Juyi
Chapman, Jan 166
Chen Hong see 'Account to Go with the "Song of Lasting Sorrow"'
Chengdi, Han Emperor 20, 22, 45, 75
The Chinese Emperor Minghuang and his Concubine Yang Guifei, with Attendants on a Terrace (attrib. to Kano Eitoku) 16, 120–21, *120*, 123
Chinese painting
of figures 32, 36, 43, 160–61
ink bamboo painting 41–42
Japanese interest in 25, 26–30, 36, 38–39
landscape styles 27–28, 67, 68, 71–72
Sansetsu's knowledge of 36, 38, 82, 110, 112, 113–14, 154, 161
'transmission' of, to Japan 30, 38–39, 67, 68, 152–63
see also woodblock-print-illustrated books
Chinese Sages in the Shishinden (Kano Sansetsu) see *Shishinden kenjo zu kan*
Chōgonka emaki (Kawaguchi Hisao) 168
Chōgonka gakan, in Japanese painting 115–20
Chōgonka gakan (Dublin scrolls) 8, 14, 36–39, 45, 108, 127, 129–33
artist's signature, seals and authenticity 8, 14, 100, 130, 142–43, *143*, 147–48, 166, 169
comparison with *Chōgonka zushō* 144–46
comparison with late-Ming prints 161–62
Ming artworks as sources for 152–63
provenance and dating 8, 147–49, 166–68
repair and conservation 14, *166*, *168*, 169–71, *170*
rolled scrolls, showing outer covers 9

scroll 1: *10–11*, 40–63, 132–33, *137*
see also General An Lushan rebels; Minghuang's dalliance; Mutineers demand the execution of Yang Guifei; Rebels enter the capital; rise of the Yang clan; Yang lady is discovered
scroll 2: *12–13*, 64–91, 133–37, *137*
see also Daoist's interview with the soul of Yang Guifei; Flight through the mountains to Shu; isles of the immortals; Minghuang engages a Daoist wizard; retired emperor mourns Yang Guifei; Return to the capital
a three-scroll format 64, 94–99, 131–32
comparison with Kuki version 100–105, 137, 169
see also Kano Sansetsu
Chōgonka gakan (Kuki version) 94, 97, *97*, 99
comparison with Dublin scrolls 100–105, 137, 169
inscription and date 147, 148
Chōgonka zu byōbu (screen of 'Song of Lasting Sorrow') (Kano School) 126–27, *127*
Chōgonka zushō (Kano Einō) 99–100, 143–46, *144*, 147, 149, 154
Collection of Paintings (Kano Ikkei) see *Kōsoshū*
Compendium of considerations … (Kurokawa Mayori) see *Teisei zōho kōko gafu*
Complete History of Yang Guifei see *Tang Guifei Yang Taizhen quanshi*
court ladies 22, 29–32, *30*, *31*, 42, 45
courtesans (*Wusao ji*) 161–62, *162*, *163*

D

The Daoist's interview with the soul of Yang Guifei (Dublin scroll 2) 88–91, *89*
final scene 142, *142*
'The wizard takes leave' 140, *140*
'The wizard and Yang converse' 89, *90*, 152
Deerskin Drum Record see *Jiegulu*
'Dragon Pool' (Li Shangyin) 22–23
drama
Late Ming 162

Yuan 155–59, *156–58*, 160, *161*
Dreaming of Immortality in a Thatched Hut (Tang Yin) *81*, 82, 152
Du Fu
'Lady Guoguo' 29
'Lament by the River' 22

E

Emperor Xuanzong Bringing Forth the Drum to Cause the Flowers to Bloom (formerly attrib. to Kano Sanraku) 121, *121*
Emperor Xuanzong's Flight to Shu see *Minghuang xing Shu tu*
eroticism, in depictions of Minghuang and Yang Guifei legends 48, *158*, 159
escape through the mountains to Shu see Flight through the mountains to Shu
Evening Outing of Lady Guoguo (attrib. to Li Gonglin, after Zhang Xuan) see *Liren xing tu*
Extraordinary Views of the World see *Hainei qiguan*

F

fan paintings, of Minghuang and Yang Guifei 117, 118–20
fiction, Yuan *158*, 159
Flight through the mountains to Shu (Dublin scroll 2) 64, 65–69, 97
detail, before restoration 169, *170*
'Exile to Shu' 137, *138*
'The fleeing court enters the mountains' 36
'Travelling along the plank road' 17, 68, *68*
Flight through the mountains to Shu (Kuki version) 97
Flute Duet (Suzuki Harunobu) 146, *146*
forgeries (*Suzhou pian*) 82, 152, 154, 161
Forgotten matters of the Kaiyuan-Tianbao eras (Wang Renyu) see *Kaiyuan tianbao yishi*
Fujiwara Michinori (Shinzei) 117
Fujiwara Seika 111

G

gakō (preparatory painting) 100
Gao Lishi 62

Gaozong, Emperor 28
General An Lushan rebels (Dublin
scroll 1) *10*, 13, *56–57, 56*
'An Lushan leads his rebel army to
the walls of the capital' *57, 57*
rebel generals 162, *163*
'Revels at the Palace of Li' 128, *131*
'Yang Guifei dances before
Minghuang' *20*, 160, *161*
Genji Monogatari (*The Tale of Genji*)
(Murasaki Shikibu) 25–26, 33, 78,
115–16, 142, 144
Genji Monogatari (*The Tale of Genji*)
scroll, 'The Law' *25, 25*, 45
Genjō Sanzō e (Takashina Takakane)
143
'The Girl Who Danced the Whirl'
(Bai Juyi) 23–24
'The Girl Who Danced the Whirl'
(Yuan Zhen) 23
Gonikkibibō (Kujō Sachiie) 148, 149
Gonse, Louis 8, 64, 147
GoShirakawa, Emperor 117
Gu Hongzhong, *Han Xizai yeyantu*
(*Night Revels of Han Xizai*) 154, *154*
Gu Kaizhi *see Admonitions of the
Court Instructress*
Gu zaju anthology *see Wutongyu*
(*Gu zaju* anthology)
Guan Daosheng 42
Guo Zhongshu, *The Han Palace* 39
Gyokuyō (Kujō Kanezane) 117

H

Hainei qiguan (*Extraordinary Views of
the World*) (Yang Erzeng) 39, 68, 69
Hakurakuten *see* Bai Juyi; *Chang hen
ge* ('Song of Lasting Sorrow')
The Han Palace (Guo Zhongshu) 39
Han Xizai yeyantu (*Night Revels of
Han Xizai*) (Gu Hongzhong) 154,
154
Han Xizai yeyantu (*Night Revels of
Han Xizai*) (attrib. to Tang Yin) 32,
154, *155*, 161, *162*
Han Yu 137
Handa, Mr/Handa Studio 169, 170
'Hardships of the Road to Shu' (Li Bai)
22
Hayashi Gahō, *Kano Einō kaden ga
jiku jo* (*Preface to the scroll painting
relating the family of Kano Einō*)
108–11, 143, 145, 148

Heiji monogatari (*Tale of the Heiji
Disturbance*) 117, 133
Hirayama Iku 8, 170
History of Painting in this Realm
(Kano Einō) *see Honchō gashi*
Hokkyō (Bridge of the Dharma),
Sansetsu awarded title 101, 110,
111, 147–48
Honchō gashi (*History of Painting in
this Realm*) (Kano Einō) 38, 108,
111–12, 139
Hong Zicheng, *Xian fo qi zong*
(*Marvellous Traces of Immortals and
Buddhas*) 114
Huizong, Emperor, *Spring Outing of
Lady Guoguo* 28–29

I

*Illustrated Arguments in the Mirror of
the Emperors* see *Teikan zusetsu*
illustrated books *see* woodblock-print-
illustrated books
*Illustrated Stories of Former Emperors
and their Subjects* see *Qiandai
junchen gushi tu*
ink bamboo painting 42
Ise-shū (collected poems of Lady Ise)
116
The isles of the immortals (Dublin
scroll 2) 84–87, *85*
'The spirit of Yang Guifei rises to
meet the wizard' 85, *87*
'The wizard requests an audience
with Yang Guifei' *108*
Iwasa Matabei 140

J

Japanese painting
'influence' of China on 30, 38–39,
67, 68, 152–63
studio practice 97–100
traditional motifs 45
Jiegulu (*Deerskin Drum Record*)
(Nan Zhuo) 121
Jiuchenggong tu (*Jiucheng Palace*)
(Qiu Ying) 152

K

Kaiyuan tianbao yishi (*Forgotten
matters of the Kaiyuan-Tianbao eras*)
(Wang Renyu) 118–19, 120, 122
Kano Eigaku 137
Kano Einō 97

Chōgonka zushō 99–100, 143–46,
144, 147, 149, 154
Honchō gashi (*History of Painting in
this Realm*) 38, 108, 111–12, 139
*Minghuang Playing Go with the Lady
of Guo* 145, 146
Kano Einō kaden ga jiku jo (*Preface to
the scroll painting relating the family
of Kano Einō*) (Hayashi Gahō)
108–11, 143, 145, 148
Kano Eitoku (attrib. to), *The Chinese
Emperor Minghuang and his
Concubine Yang Guifei, with
Attendants on a Terrace* 16, 120–21,
120, 123
Kano Ikkei, *Kōsoshū* (*Collection of
Paintings*) 123–24, 146
Kano Mitsunobu, *Scenes from the Life
of the Minghuang Emperor and Yang
Guifei* 16, 124–27, *124*, *125*
Kano Sanraku 16, 38, 101, 110, 111,
147, 148
Kano Sanraku (formerly attrib. to),
*Emperor Xuanzong Bringing Forth
the Drum to Cause the Flowers to
Bloom* 121, *121*
Kano Sansetsu 14, 36, 38, 45, 101
biographical accounts of 108–12,
145, 148
datable work 113–14, 147–48
Hokkyō title awarded 101, 110, 111,
147–48
knowledge of Chinese painting 36,
38, 82, 110, 112, 113–14, 130–31,
154, 161
Kujō patronage of in Kyoto 148–49
work by
Agriculture in the Four Seasons 113,
113
Bankoku zu (*Pangu Valley*) 137,
139
Chōgonka gakan (Dublin scrolls)
see *Chōgonka gakan* (Dublin
scrolls)
Chōgonka gakan (Kuki version)
97
Kannon scrolls 101, 110, 147, 148
Minghuang and Yang Guifei
127–29, *128*, 146
Mount Fuji and Miho Pine Strand
113, *114*
*Poetic Gathering at the Orchid
Pavilion* 113, *114*

Shishinden kenjo zu kan (*Chinese
Sages in the Shishinden*) 142, 149
Taoist Immortals 114, *115*
Ten Views of West Lake (fan
paintings) 110, 111, 113
Views of West Lake 38, 114, *116*,
132
see also *Chōgonka gakan*, the Dublin
scrolls
Kano School
Chōgonka zu byōbu (screen of 'Song
of Lasting Sorrow') 126–27, *127*
and workshops 8, 16, 97, 120, 123,
148–49, 166–68
see also Kano Sanraku; Kano
Sansetsu
Kano Tan'yū 38, 111, 113, 148
Tan'yu shukuzu (*Small Sketches by
Tan'yu*) 152, 154, 162
Kawaguchi Hisao, *Chōgonka emaki*
168
Kibi daijin nittō emaki (*Minister Kibi's
Trip to China*) 36
Kichizan Minchō, *Thirty-Three
Kannons in Tofukuji* 110, 148
Kokka (fine-art journal) 94, 169
Kōsoshū (*Collection of Paintings*)
(Kano Ikkei) 123–24, 146
Kujō family 148–49
Kujō Kanezane, *Gyokuyō* 117
Kujō Sachiie, *Gonikkibibō* 148, 149
Kuki version see *Chōgonka gakan*
(Kuki version)
Kurokawa Mayori, *Teisei zōho kōko
gafu* (*Compendium of considerations
…*) 147

L

Ladies of the Court (*c.* 706) 30, *31*
Ladies Under Trees (*c.* 756) 30, *31*
'Lady Guoguo' (Du Fu) 29
'Lament by the River' (Du Fu) 22
Landscape of the Road to Shanyin
(Wu Bin) 67, *67*
landscape painting
Chinese 67, 71
in *Chōgonka gakan* 67–69
early-mid Tang 26–29
'The Law', from *Genji Monogatari
emaki* (*The Tale of Genji*) scroll 25,
25, 45
Leijiang ji anthology see *Wutongyu*
(*Leijiang ji* anthology)

Li Bai, 'Hardships of the Road to Shu' 22

'Li furen fu' ('Ode on lady Li') (Emperor Wu) 83

Li Gonglin (attrib. to, after Zhang Xuan), *Liren xing tu* (*Evening Outing of Lady Guoguo*) 28, 29

Li Rongjin 39

Li Rongjin (attrib. to), *Minghuang Avoiding the Summer Heat* 38, 39

Li Shangyin, 'Dragon Pool' 22–23

Li Shaoweng (Li the Young Lord) 83

Li Sixun 26, 27

Li Zhaodao 26, 27

Li-chiang Lin 32

Liren xing tu (*Evening Outing of Lady Guoguo*) (attrib. to Li Gonglin, after Zhang Xuan) 28, 29

literature *see* drama; travel literature; woodblock-print-illustrated books; *names of individual writers and titles of works*

Liuzhi ji anthology (1633), a dancing scene 160, *161*

'Luoshen fu' (Cao Zhi) 48

M

Marvellous Traces of Immortals and Buddhas see Xian fo qi zong

Ming paintings, as visual sources for *Chōgonka gakan* 152–63

Minghuang (Xuanzong), Emperor *see* Yang Guifei and Minghuang stories

Minghuang and Yang Guifei (Kano Sansetsu) 127–29, *128*, 146

Minghuang Avoiding the Summer Heat (attrib. to Li Rongjin) 38, 39

Minghuang engages a Daoist wizard (Dublin scroll 2) 80–83, *80*

'Minghuang commands the wizard to search for Yang's spirit' *82*, 83

'The wizard's quest' 140, *140*

Minghuang Playing Go with the Lady of Guo (Kano Einō) 145, 146

Minghuang xing Shu tu (*Emperor Xuanzong's Flight to Shu*) (Metropolitan Museum version) 27, 28

Minghuang's dalliance (Dublin scroll 1) *10*, 46–51, *46*

female attendants on a bridge 98, *98*, 104, 161, *163*

'Minghuang forswears the duties of the morning' 133, *133*

'Minghuang and Yang Guifei in the nuptial bedchamber' *47*

Minghuang's dalliance (Kuki version), bridge scene 98, *99*, 104

Minghuang's Flight to Shu (Tapei version) 17, 26–27, *26*, 38

Minghuang's Journey to Shu (early Tang) 26–27

Minister Kibi's Trip to China see Kibi daijin nittō emaki

'Mount Emei', from *Sancai tuhui* 68, *69*

Mount Fuji and Miho Pine Strand (Kano Sansetsu) 113, *114*

Murasaki Shikibu, *Genji Monogatari* (*The Tale of Genji*) 25–26, 33, 78, 115–16, 142, 144

Mutineers demand the execution of Yang Guifei (Dublin scroll 1) *10*, 60–63, *63*, 136, *137*

'A confrontation between civil and military officers' 62, *63*

detail, before restoration 8, 166, 169

'The emperor is informed of the mutineers demand for the life of Yang Guifei' 60, *61*

N

Nan Zhuo, *Jiegulu* (*Deerskin Drum Record*) 121

Nanzenji monastery fan paintings 119–20

Nara ehon (Nara picture-books) 36, 166, 168

Nawa Kassho 111, 137

Ni Zan 80

Night Revels of Han Xizai see Han Xizai yeyantu

Noted Confucians of Various Periods see Yoktae kunsin tosang

O

'Ode on lady Li' *see 'Li furen fu'*

Oze Hoan, *Taiko ki* 122

P

painting(s) *see* Chinese painting; fan paintings; Japanese painting; screen paintings

Pangu Valley (Kano Sansetsu) *see Bankoku zu*

patronage, in Kyoto 148–49

Pavilions in the Mountains of the Immortals (Qiu Ying) 87, *87*

Pictorial Compendium of the Three Realms see Sancai tuhui

'Plank Roads to Sichuan', from *Sancai tuhui* 68–69, *69*

Poetic Gathering at the Orchid Pavilion (Kano Sansetsu) 113, *114*

Pollard, Clare 14

Preface to the scroll painting relating the family of Kano Einō see Kanō Einō kaden ga jiku jo

prints *see* woodblock-print-illustrated books

provenance, of Dublin *Chōgonka gakan* 8, 147–49, 166–68

Q

qi ('the strange') 67, 68

Qian Xuan, *Yang Guifei Mounting a Horse* 28, 32–33, *32*, 50–51

Qiandai junchen gushi tu (*Illustrated Stories of Former Emperors and their Subjects*) 'Yang Guifei cutting off a lock of hair to send to Tang emperor Minghuang' 33, 55, *55*

Qiu Ying 38, 45, 67

Jiuchenggong tu (*Jiucheng Palace*) 152

Pavilions in the Mountains of the Immortals 87, *87*

Spring Morning in the Han Palace (details) 45, *45*, 161, *162*

R

Rebels enter the capital (Dublin scroll 1) *11*, 58–59, *58*

'General An Lushan enters the Capital' 131–32, *131*

'The inner court flees the capital' 58–59, *59*, 133–36

Minghuang's initial flight *100*, 103

Rebels enter the capital (Kuki version), Minghuang's initial flight *101*, 103

The retired emperor mourns Yang Guifei (Dublin scroll 2) 74–79, *75*, *118*, 132, 138–39, 144

'The bridge scene' 75, *75*

'The emperor tending his candle on a winter night' 75, *78*

Return to the capital (Dublin scroll 2) *12*, 70–73, *73*

'Minghuang's entourage approaches the distant ramparts of Chang'an' 132, *132*

'The imperial party revisits Mawei' 71, *72*

Return to the capital (scroll 2, Kuki version), 'Emperor Minghuang in exile' 94

The rise of the Yang clan (Dublin scroll 1) *11*, 52–55, *52*

detail, before restoration 168, *169*

resting horses and grooms 98–99, 104, *104*

'Yang Guifei's family receive further riches' 53, *54*

'Yang Guifei's family receive riches and honours' 53, *53*

The rise of the Yang clan (Kuki version), resting horses and grooms 105, *105*

'ruled line' painting 39

S

Sancai tuhui (*Pictorial Compendium of the Three Realms*) (comp. by Wang Qi and Wang Siyi) 39

'Mount Emei' 68, 69

'Plank Roads to Sichuan' 68–69, 69

Sansetsu *see Chōgonka gakan*, the Dublin scrolls; Kano Sansetsu

Scenes from the Life of the Minghuang Emperor and Yang Guifei (Kano Mitsunobu) 16, 124–27, *124*, *125*

screen paintings, of Minghuang and Yang Guifei 120–24

by Kano Mitsunobu 124–27, *124*, *125*

by Kano Sansetsu 127–29, *128*

Sen no Rikyū 120

Setsurei Eikin 119, 120

Sheng Tang (High Tang) 25

Shishinden kenjo zu kan (*Chinese Sages in the Shishinden*) (Kano Sansetsu) 142, 149

Small Sketches by Tan'yu (Kano Tan'yū) *see Tan'yu shukuzu*

'Song of Eternal Remorse' (Waley) 25

Song of Lasting Sorrow see 'Account to Go with the "Song of Lasting Sorrow"'; *Chōgonka gakan*; Yang Guifei and Minghuang stories

'Song of Lasting Sorrow' (Bai Juyi) *see Chang hen ge*

'space-cell' device 71–72, 124
Spring Morning in the Han Palace (details) (Qiu Ying) 45, *45*, 161, *162*
Spring Morning in the Han Palace (details) (You Qiu) 43, *43*, 45, *162*
Spring Outing of Lady Guoguo (Emperor Huizong) 28–29
Suzhou pian (forgeries) 82, 152, 154, 161
Suzuki Harunobu, *Flute Duet* 146, *146*
symbols
  bridge motif 50, 67–68, 75, 142
  of female beauty 78
  phoenix, as empress's symbol 42

T

Taikō ki (Oze Hoan) 122
Taizhen, Lady (pseudonym for Yang Guifei) 23, 44
Takashina Takakane, *Genjō Sanzō e* 143
The Tale of Genji see *Genji Monogatari*
Tale of the Heiji Disturbance see *Heiji monogatari*
Tang Di, *Wangchuan Villa* 71, *73*
Tang dynasty
  art and culture 25, 26–30
  Sansetu's depictions of 36
Tang Guifei Yang Taizhen quanshi (*Complete History of Yang Guifei*)
  Beidi yuanyang ('Coupling under the comforter') *158*, 159
  Yangfei chunshui ('Consort Yang sleeping seductively') *158*, 159
Tang Minghuang Qiuye Wutongyu (*Tang Minghuang [Listening to] the Rain…*) (Bai Pu) see *Wutongyu*
Tang Yin, *Dreaming of Immortality in a Thatched Hut* 81, 82, 152
Tang Yin (attrib. to)
  Han Xizai yeyantu (*Night Revels of Han Xizai*) 32, 154, *155*
  a courtesan 161, *162*
Tan'yu shukuzu (*Small Sketches by Tan'yu*) (Kano Tan'yū) 152, 154, 162
Taoist Immortals (Kano Sansetsu) 114, *115*
Teikan zusetsu (*Illustrated Arguments in the Mirror of the Emperors*) 120, 152, 162
Teisei zōho kōko gafu (*Compendium of considerations …*) (Kurokawa Mayori) 147

Ten Views of West Lake (Kano Sansetsu) 110, *111*, 113
Thirty-Three Kannons in Tofukuji (Kichizan Minchō) 110, 148
Toyotomi Hideyoshi 120, 122–23
travel literature 39, 143

U

Uda, Emperor of Japan 26, 116, 144

V

Views of West Lake (Kano Sansetsu) 38, 114, *116*, 132

W

Wakisaka, Professor 168, 169
Waley, Arthur, 'Song of Eternal Remorse' 25
Wang Anyi 33
Wang Qi see *Sancai tuhui*
Wang Renyu, *Kaiyuan tianbao yishi* (*Forgotten matters of the Kaiyuan-Tianbao eras*) 118–19, 120, 122
Wang Siyi see *Sancai tuhui*
Wang Wei, *Wangchuan Villa* scroll 71
Wang Zhenpeng 39
Wangchuan Villa scroll (Wang Wei) 71
Wangchuan Villa (Tang Di) 71, *73*
Wen Boren 38
Woman Playing Weiqi (Astana Tomb 187) 30, *31*
women
  artists 42
  court ladies 22, 29–32, *30*, *31*, 42, 45
  models of female beauty 30, 48, 50, 146, 160–61, *161*, *162*
  symbols of female beauty 78
woodblock-print-illustrated books 39, 108, 114, 120
  Chōgonka zushō (Kano Einō) 99–100, 143–46, *144*
  Late Ming 68, 160–62, *160*, *161*, *162–63*
  Ming 39, 152, 154–59, *156–58*
Wu Bin 39
  Landscape of the Road to Shanyin 67, *67*
Wu, Han Emperor, *'Li furen fu'* ('Ode on lady Li') 83
Wusao ji (*Anthology of Poetry in Wu Region*), courtesans 161–62, *162*, *163*

Wutongyu (*Tang Minghuang Qiuye Wutongyu* (*Tang Minghuang [Listening to] the Rain…*)) (Bai Pu) 155, *156–58*, 159, 160, *160–61*, 162, *163*
Wutongyu (*Gu zaju* anthology)
  illustrations from the drama 155, *157*
  'Minghuang dreams of Yang Guifei' 155, *156*
  'Yang Guifei with her attendants' 155, 160, *160*
  'Yang Guifei's dancing scene' 155, *156*
Wutongyu (*Leijiang ji* anthology)
  'Minghuang dreams of Yang Guifei' 156, *156*
  'Yang Guifei is presented with lychees' 155, *156*
Wutongyu (*Yuanqu xuan* anthology)
  'An Lushan rebels' 155, *158*
  'Listening to the rain falling on the parasols' 155, *157*
  'Minghuang and the inner court escape' 155, *158*
  'Minghuang sitting in a garden with Guifei' 160, *160*
  Tang generals 162, *163*
  'Yang Guifei is presented with lychees' 155, *157*

X

Xian fo qi zong (*Marvellous Traces of Immortals and Buddhas*) (Hong Zicheng) 114
Xuanzong (Minghuang), Emperor see Yang Guifei and Minghuang stories
Xuanzong and the Golden Bell (Anon, inscription by Setsurei Eiken) 118–19, *118*
Xuanzong Unearthing the Jade (Momoyama period) 122–23, *123*

Y

Yamanaka Shokai 166
Yang clan 44, 52–55
Yang Erzeng, *Hainei qiguan* (*Extraordinary Views of the World*) 39, 68, 69
'Yang Guifei cutting off a lock of hair to send to Tang emperor Minghuang', from *Qiandai junchen gushi tu* (*Illustrated Stories of Former Emperors and their Subjects*) 33, 55, *55*

Yang Guifei and Minghuang stories
  Edo-period representations of Yang Guifei 146, *146*
  images in Chinese art and literature 20–33, 155–59, *156–57*, 159
  Japanese screen paintings of 120–29, *124*, *125*, *128*
Yang Guifei Mounting a Horse (Qian Xuan) 28, 32–33, *32*, 50–51
The Yang lady is discovered (Dublin scroll 1) 11, 40–45, *40*, 132
  'The emperor turns to gaze at his beautiful concubine' 160, *160*
  'The emperor watches Yang emerge from the hot spring at Huaqing' *41*, 42–43
  'The Yang lady arrives at the palace' *14*
  'Yang Guifei emerges from the hot spring at Huaqing' 161, *162*
Yataro Okita 166
Yoktae kunsin tosang (*Noted Confucians of Various Periods*) 114
Yoshiko Ushioda 14
You Qiu, *Spring Morning in the Han Palace* (details) 43, *43*, 45, *162*
Yuan Zhen, 'The Girl Who Danced the Whirl' 23
Yuandi, Han Emperor 45
Yuanqu xuan anthology see *Wutongyu* (*Yuanqu xuan* anthology)

Z

Zeami 25
Zhang Hua 22
Zhang Xuan, paintings after 28–29, *28*, 32
Zhao Feiyan, Han empress 20, 22, 43, *43*, 45, 75
Zhao Hede 22, 43, *43*, 75

ACKNOWLEDGEMENTS

At the Chester Beatty Library, thanks are especially due to Philip
Roe, who coordinated the picture research, as well as to Sinéad
Ward, Frances Narkiewicz, Rie Mishima and Laura Muldowney.
The *Chōgonka* scrolls were photographed by Denis Mortell.

We would like to acknowledge the assistance of the following
people who helped in the preparation of the book in various
ways, from reading the text and offering comments at the
manuscript stage, to helping obtain photographs, to editing
expertise and general encouragement: Itakura Masaaki, Yukio
Lippit, Melanie Trede, Melissa McCormick, Matthew Welch,
James Ulak, Hamish Todd, Maya Hara, Kobayashi Tadashi,
Yamashita Yoshiya, Mori Mitsuyo, Fukushi Yuya, Sakaguchi
Satoko, Yamaguchi Katsura, Yamanaka Takeo, Amemiya
Mutsuko, Helga Fleishman, Emily Sano, Clara Pyo, Cory
Grace, DeAnn Dankowski, Chun-Yi Tsai and Sandra Pisano.